FLAXYARD ENVIRONMENTAL DEVELOPMENT COMPANY LIMITED
Hazelbury Manor, Near Box, Wiltshire SN14 9HX   Tel: 0225 810715   Telex: 44616

'As Chairman of a property development and construction group, I give my full support to the Conservation and Development Programme for the UK. Initiatives that aim to make conservation an integral part of future development are to be encouraged and welcomed.'

Ian Pollard
Chairman

The Programme Organising Committee wishes to express its sincere thanks to Ian Pollard, Chairman of Flaxyard Environmental Development Company Limited, for making possible the publication and launch of the Conservation and Development Programme for the UK.

The Conservation and Development Programme for the UK

A response to the World Conservation Strategy

Sponsoring Organisations

World Wildlife Fund UK

Nature Conservancy Council

Countryside Commission

Countryside Commission for Scotland

The Royal Society of Arts

Council for Environmental Conservation

Kogan Page

First published 1983
by Kogan Page Limited
120 Pentonville Road, London N1 9JN

Copyright © The Programme Organising Committee
of the Conservation and Development Programme for the UK 1983

British Library Cataloguing in Publication Data
The Conservation and Development Programme
    for the UK
    1. Environmental policy — Great Britain
    383.7'2'0941   HC60.E5

    ISBN 0-85038-746-9 (Pb)

Printed in Great Britain by
Whitstable Litho Ltd.,
Whitstable, Kent

CONTENTS

PREFACE

The sponsors of this book are the World Wildlife Fund UK (providing finance), the Nature Conservancy Council (providing the central Secretariat), the Countryside Commission and the Countryside Commission for Scotland (providing advice and supplementing finance), CoEnCo and the Royal Society of Arts (providing coordinated voluntary effort and a forum).

The World Conservation Strategy (WCS), published in March 1980, called for an international and a national response. At its launch in this country the Secretary of State for the Environment welcomed its production and later, in the House of Lords, the Government said: 'the World Conservation Strategy is a realistic and unemotive restatement of the evidence that conservation of our natural and living resources is essential to the economic and social welfare of society and is entirely compatible with sustainable development'. In this country the lead was taken by the United Kingdom Committee for the International Union for Conservation of Nature and Natural Resources (IUCN). It invited the six sponsors to organise a UK response to the WCS: the Conservation and Development Programme for the UK.

The issues raised by the WCS in the UK go far beyond the sponsors' competence and they have therefore consulted widely. In early 1981, two Committees were set up: a Programme Standing Committee and a Programme Organising Committee. The former, which brought together a broad range of national interests, has been responsible for gaining commitment to the work from all sectors with an interest in resource-use. The Organising Committee has been responsible for ensuring that the content of the Programme takes full account of the complex interrelationships involved when applying WCS objectives in the UK. The memberships of these two committees are listed at the end of this book, pp 486-489.

To analyse these interrelationships involved, reports were commissioned on seven main subject areas from experts in the field of resource-conservation. They are the topics of Parts 1-7 of this book. A Review Group of professionals and practising experts was appointed to advise the author on the approach to and content of each report. Between autumn 1981 and summer 1982, some 180 individuals contributed to this process. The membership of the Sector Review Group is listed at the end of this book, p 490.

This broad base of advice was further extended in the last half of 1982 when the reports were circulated for consultation and debate. During this time — 'the Practitioners' Debate' period — 8,000 copies of the reports were issued to individuals, groups and organisations and some 330 single and collective written responses were received. There were also 35 seminars or conferences on the reports attended by over 1,000 people. Following this consultation the reports were revised to take account of comments received, and factual errors were corrected.

This extensive discussion was accompanied by the drawing together of the seven reports' analyses into an Overview report. In late 1982, the commissioned author began this work, assisted by the authors of the topic reports and the sponsoring organisations; that report, entitled 'Resourceful Britain', comes before the reports in this book.

Throughout all this work, the sponsors have recognised that, given the many and varied groups — some with specific vested interests — concerned with the topics considered, it would not be possible to produce reports which met with the full approval and agreement of every organisation and individual consulted. Therefore, the reports are not necessarily fully endorsed either by those who provided advice and commentary or by the sponsoring organisations themselves. The reports are primarily the work of the authors.

The production of the Conservation and Development Programme for the UK is not the end of the process. In many ways it can only be the beginning. Together, the seven topic reports and 'Resourceful Britain' contribute to a Programme for Action over a very wide range of fields and a considerable time span.

While some of the recommendations can be implemented straight away, others will be the basis of widespread public discussion. From the impetus generated by sound example, and from increasing awareness of the underlying advantages of the Programme as a whole, it is hoped that the next decade or so will be characterised by a great deal of activity in fulfilment of the essentials of the Programme, adapted, as necessary, in response to changing circumstances.

Dr F B O'Connor
Chairman, Programme Organising Committee

14 March, 1983

NOTES ON TERMINOLOGY AND NATIONAL LEGISLATION

This book covers the UK, that is, England, Wales, Scotland and Northern Ireland. Wherever possible, the terms UK or United Kingdom have been used, but on occasion, and in particular in relation to statistics, care should be taken to note whether reference is to England, to England and Wales (considered together for many administrative and other purposes) to Great Britain (which denotes England, Wales and Scotland) or to the UK (which is the same as 'Britain', that is, Great Britain and Northern Ireland) as a whole.

In each of the constituent countries of the UK there are not only important differences in the character and possible solutions to the resource-problems covered in this book but there are also significant differences in the legislation and the division of responsible agencies between Government and other organisations. Wherever possible, the authors have sought to recognise national variations, but inevitably, given the very broad scope of this book, important points of detail have been omitted. It is hoped that readers will accept this in the spirit intended and apply the arguments to suit appropriate national circumstances as required.

FOREWORD

What is the World Conservation Strategy about, and what does it mean for the United Kingdom? Ecological science shows how the rich natural resources of the Earth have developed over the millenia, through the workings of complex, self-regulated finely tuned processes within a global ecosystem or biosphere. During the latest stages of these processes the human species has not been content to function as a part of that ecosystem, but has broken away to create its own special role apart from it. That apartness has moved from a distinct ancillary role to a parallel and now dominant, although still basically dependent, role, forming an autonomous artificial system which we may call the technosphere. During the past few decades, the demands of this technosphere, on both renewable and non-renewable natural resources, have risen to a scale which cannot much longer be sustained without exhausting vital supplies, dislocating the delicate functioning of the biosphere, and inflicting permanent and irreversible damage to this planet as the home of all life, including human life. The gravity of this crisis is heightened by the fact that so many people remain unaware of it.

The challenge thus posed is rapidly to find a means of satisfying genuine human needs on a pattern compatible with the healthy survival of the biosphere. Responding to that challenge in 1980, the International Union for Conservation of Nature and Natural Resources, the World Wildlife Fund, and the United Nations Environment Programme together launched a World Conservation Strategy to show all people everywhere how to meet and live with this dire threat to mankind's welfare, and even survival.

The World Conservation Strategy is based on three main objectives:
   (a) To maintain essential ecological processes and life-support systems.
   (b) To preserve genetic diversity, which is being dangerously impoverished.
   (c) To ensure the sustainable use by us and our children of species and ecosystems.

These objectives require that broad conservation principles be incorporated henceforward in the whole fabric of society. Everyone must be able to say sincerely that we are all conservationists now.

The World Conservation Strategy was inevitably expressed in general terms. It needs reworking to fit the distinct requirements of each nation. The United Kingdom, for example, does not suffer from desertification or a population explosion but is so intricately enmeshed in international systems and affairs that, long before Earth's life support system totally collapses, the progressive erosion of that system could lead to poverty and misery for many British people, eventually making Britain's economy and society unsustainable.

The Overview and its seven accompanying special reports are not to be regarded as an isolated initiative; they follow on from a succession of earlier attempts to call public attention to the need for correcting our civilisation's collision course against its supporting biosphere. These attempts have already led to remarkable changes in attitudes, policies and legal restraints, which have begun to steer mankind in the right direction. The next stage is to secure broader complementary action in many aspects of development which are certain to lead to calamity unless redirected.

During the 1960s, the challenge to conservationists was on a narrow front: to learn where and how the most urgent threats to wildlife were arising, and how to mount fire-brigade operations against them. This piecemeal reactive response was clearly inadequate. It was rapidly superseded by an improvised strategy to anticipate, survey and counter pollution of land, air and water, the destruction of whales, big cats and other commercial target species, to build up networks of national parks and nature reserves, and to organise large support movements. On that basis, and with massive attention from the media, it was possible during the 1970s to secure widespread legislation, international conventions and agreements — such as at the Stockholm United Nations Human Environment Conference of 1972 — and to create official environmental agencies, scientific monitoring and public financial backing.

At the same time, well publicised Doomsday statements, and such analyses as those of the Blueprint for Survival and the Club of Rome, launched a strong challenge to the myths of unending exponential economic growth, and shocked the public into a recognition of the hitherto ignored limits of the Earth. (This was soon followed by the world-wide trauma of the 1973 oil crisis, which took governments and economists, but not conservationists, by surprise.) These bold initiatives reinforced the growing public disillusionment with the easy optimism of the 1960s and the erosion of public confidence in conventional wisdom and leadership. Fuller and more widely convincing ecological data, leading to a more balanced interpretation of ecological principles, converted influential people in politics, business and the professions to the cause of environmental conservation. On the other hand, some who had dismissed conservation as a passing fad took alarm at the groundswell and sought to polarise opinion to defend outmoded attitudes and rigid vested interests. The struggle broadened out, from the restraint of particular abuses and environmental injuries, into a campaign for the hearts and minds of people world-wide, and for profound changes in perceptions and lifestyles.

Conservationist thinking has moved towards reconciling enduring sustainable use of all natural resources with the continuing pursuit of prized social and economic values and goals, such as the abatement of world poverty and underdevelopment. These are being sought by people with fresh intellectual approaches in a climate of new awareness and conciliation.

The present scene has been set by the gathering of the fruits of enlightened public opinion, brought about by years of conservationist effort, together with the manifest failure of the mid-century economic regime which promised to deliver results: affluence, full employment, stable prices, tolerable interest rates, rewarding investment and the relief of world poverty. The thought that there must be more sensible ways of running our affairs than twentieth century politicians and economists have so far prescribed can no longer be prevented from spreading. In this situation, the alternative put forward in the World Conservation Strategy seems destined to win wide favour, and those who continue to contest this diagnosis run the risk of still further discrediting established beliefs and institutions. The worst enemies of established order are those who stubbornly obstruct its adaptation to fresh realities — while there is still time.

That is particularly the case in the United Kingdom, where the most recent failures to solve national problems are superimposed on decades of economic decline which can no longer be represented as anything but a failure to perceive and adjust to the realities of modern national management. Her Majesty's Government welcomed in broad terms the launch of the World Conservation Strategy, but instead of working out what it called for on its part, the Government preferred to turn to its official advisory conservation agencies and to the voluntary conservation movement to do the job. In response to that request from the Secretary of State for the Environment a joint task force was created, comprising Government and voluntary conservation organisations.

In order to convert the Strategy into practical British terms it was found necessary to scrutinise the linkages between conservation and the numerous other interests with which conflict has arisen, either through misunderstandings or contrary aims and practices. While it was impossible to cover every area, Review Groups, composed of widely representative and expert members, with picked authors, were commissioned to tackle rural, marine and coastal, urban, industrial and overseas considerations, as well as those of education and ethics. As will be seen in this book, the reports have brought into objective focus not only conflicts and problems but also the possibilities of reconciling and resolving them. It may be claimed that no other country has responded to the World Conservation Strategy in so much depth and breadth, and within this country no comparably comprehensive effort has previously been made to show the interactions and options for concerted advance over so wide a range of public affairs.

The many people who nowadays take great liberties with the term 'ecology' may be on shaky ground scientifically and semantically but they have sensed a great underlying truth. Ecology shows us how, when left to themselves, animals and plants can live together in equilibrium in their natural environment. The World Conservation Strategy insists that its principles can be translated to enable mankind to use the Earth's resources in a sensible and sustainable manner, instead of thoughtlessly pillaging and wasting them. But ecology offers more than such simple guidance. It also points the way to new and more rewarding lifestyles, affording greater harmony between the human species and nature, and consequently greater harmony among people. Once we recognise the existence of a human ecosystem in which we have to survive and evolve, with the continuous everyday support of a natural planetary ecosystem, it must be right to harmonise the human with the natural as fully as possible. Both share the same origins, co-exist on one earth, and respond to the same physical laws and forces. Whatever varying views and beliefs may be held concerning the supernatural, such an approach makes sense.

If the World Conservation Strategy is boldly and imaginatively followed through, intellectually, ethically and emotionally, that recognition can lead us to the missing principles and inspiration so desperately needed by our confused and frustrating civilisation. The World Conservation Strategy is right in placing the permanently sustainable use of natural resources in the human economy as the first priority, but the reports comprising *The Conservation and Development Programme for the UK* are right in now going further. The way we use natural resources must assure their continued availability and quality, and must also enduringly satisfy mankind's cultural and aesthetic requirements from nature. How far we fall short of these requirements is demonstrated most vividly in 'The Livable City', Part 2 but the theme also recurs elsewhere. It exposes the hollowness of the frequent assertion that conservation is against people.

Civilisations which persist in pressing too single mindedly for too long on a line of advance, however broad, end up in a blind alley. That happened, for example, to medieval Christendom just before the Renaissance, and it is happening to our lopsided technological modernism now, both in the East and the West. Human evolution builds up seismic tensions at great depth, which can only be resolved by eventual creative confrontation between apparently irreconcilable sets of values. Such was the role of the new scientific humanism in the Renaissance; it is now emerging as the role of our suddenly deepened and illuminated perception of our relation to planet earth and its natural resources. The World Conservation Strategy, however imperfectly, sets the stage for this great imminent and inescapable drama, in which the clash of conflicting beliefs and ideas has to be enacted against an inexorable background of rapidly vanishing resources, which subject the players to a tight time limit. It is perhaps appropriate that this should be spot-lighted in the British contribution to the Strategy, since the British have long been fascinated by the challenge of reconciling the irreconcilable, and have sometimes performed quite well at it.

We live in interesting times. Dramatic events dominate our daily news, but are mostly of less long-term consequence to us than the changes in our perceptions, in our knowledge and information, in our attitudes and ambitions, in our hopes, fears and tensions and in our satisfactions and deprivations — in other words of the kind of people we now are. We know we are no longer the same people as we were in the 1960s, whom we see portrayed in re-run films. Even the 1970s are becoming history, yet we have no reliable means of gauging just how we have come to differ from our previous selves. We are sadder and wiser through becoming more self-aware. Our age structure and social structure have changed; relations between men and women, young and old, have altered. The long period of British population expansion has ended. We are becoming inescapably more and more subordinated to the demands, constraints and imperatives of 'one world'.

Recently, many who used uncritically to welcome the advances of technology have turned against it on environmental or human grounds. If technology has earned a bad name, however, it is through its ham-handed and ill-advised applications and developments rather than through any inherent 'badness'. Once new guiding principles and attitudes prevail, scientists and technologists will again be seen to serve mankind's true interests.

Few world movements have participated more eagerly and more effectively in the new cosmos of the information revolution than the conservation and environmental movement, based on ecology, which is universal and which touches everyone, whether or not they know it or like it. The resultant rich fund of research, experiments, surveys, appraisals, reports, guidelines, appeals and campaigns underlies the World Conservation Strategy, and propels it into the mainstream of public debate. It is the sheer volume and quality of this well-focused work which is earning a hearing for the Strategy and its British version.

If the human species is to survive, it must sooner rather than later turn to evolving a wiser, worthier and happier pattern of life. That pattern will need, far more fully than is yet understood, to draw upon the principles of ecology and conservation.

To many well-disposed readers the greatest difficulty presented by the Strategy will be its many-sidedness. They will seek some central criterion to make clear just what would be involved in a transition from the existing mix of national policies to those which the Strategy calls for. In practical terms, the Strategy essentially demands a quite fresh, non-ideological, long-term approach to economics, and consequentially to life styles. It shows up the superficiality, subjectivity and instability of any brand of economics not firmly based on the physical systems analysis which underlies ecology.

Inflation arises through measuring everything indirectly in terms of money, and then allowing that yardstick to be cut adrift from the real physical resources upon whose accessibility, usability and renewability money's true value depends. This cutting adrift has been accompanied by a muddle over where economics leaves off and politics comes in. It gives rise to the current misconception of economics as a free-standing discipline, rather than as either a branch of applied ecology or else a servant of politics. The cutting adrift also leads to political confusion and conflict, by muddling the basic distinction between correct measurement of the sum of available resources for mankind — the 'cake' — and seeking the fair and rational division of those resources.

The power struggle between different interest groups over their sacred claims to resources which can only be supposed to exist by expressing them in false money would be comic if its consequences were not so tragic. Monetarism rightly tries to re-establish sound money, largely through the enforcement of market disciplines. Homo sapiens, however, is an incorrigibly inflationary animal, not to be enduringly disciplined by any instrument which it can sooner or later seize and subvert. Alleviating the symptoms is, in any case, no substitute for treating the underlying illness. Unhappily, despite the twice repeated demonstration by the oil crisis of the 1970s of the causal relation between over-commitment of limited resources and runaway inflation, the lesson has not yet been learnt.

The world today bears some resemblance to a gigantic Mexico, Brazil or Poland, too heavily in overdraft to be able to pay even the interest on it or to contain it at present excessive levels. The world's resource-problems are still misconceived as being peripheral to public policy; in fact they are fundamental.

In his Overview, Brian Johnson begins with the theme: 'An Idea Whose Time Has Come'. Britain has an unhappy record not only of failing to wake up to such ideas before it is too late, but also of continuously failing to spot and discard those other cherished 'Ideas Whose Time is Up'. Today, such ideas include those of indefinite *exponential economic growth* and of a return to *full employment in conventional full-time jobs* or of a carefree future for *the throwaway society*, indulging in waste and pollution. Too many people who strive for the adoption of new ideas and new attitudes are blind to the need for making room for them by identifying and discrediting such 'Ideas Whose Time is Up'. The processes are complementary and equally essential.

Until the essentials of the World Conservation Strategy are universally grasped, and substituted for outdated and bankrupt economic ideas, the world will not even have started on the long and arduous path to stability and honest dealing. A first selection of the required measures is outlined in this book. They can be applied flexibly and progressively without vast investment, revolutionary legal changes or unrealistic human responses. Indeed, there is evidence that important sections of public opinion are ahead of their leadership in thinking on these lines. Britain has the right traditions, skills, institutional resources and worldwide connections to show the way to the rest of the world. Will the nation act, while there may still just be time?

Max Nicholson
Chairman, Standing Committee

15 March 1983

SUMMARY

The World Conservation Strategy

The World Conservation Strategy, launched in March 1980, showed that over-exploitation of resources, loss of genetic diversity and damage to ecological processes and life-support systems have dangerously reduced the planet's capacity to support people in both developed and developing countries. It sought a new partnership between conservation and development, to meet human needs now without jeopardising the future, and called upon each country to prepare a national conservation strategy tailored to its own particular problems and characteristic cultural and economic conditions in order to achieve this.

The UK

The UK is fortunate in having an equable climate, resilient soils, a well developed industrial base, abundant energy supplies and a well organised society with sophisticated planning and decision making processes. This good fortune provides both the opportunity and the time to reconcile resource-conservation with the needs of society and economics.

The Conservation and Development Programme for the UK

Building upon and extending the objectives of the World Conservation Strategy to meet UK conditions requires action in three broad areas:
  (a) integrating conservation of both living and non-living resources with development;
  (b) developing a sustainable society in which both physical and psychological needs are fully met;
  (c) developing a stable and sustainable economy through the practices of resource-conservation in all spheres of activity.

Integrating Resource Conservation with Development

In the UK, this has a spectrum of components:
  (a) Preservation of genetic diversity and maintenance of essential ecological processes and life-support systems are in part served through the establishment and management of nature reserves and other protected sites; in part through the conservation of wild species of animals and plants on the land surface as a whole (both rural and urban). Both these elements require that the physical and chemical condition of the environment is maintained by preventing over-use and by control of pollution.
  (b) Conservation of non-renewable resources. A necessary part of the UK programme is to extend the lifetime of non-renewable resources, whether home-produced or imported, and to reduce polluting side effects on living resources from their use.
  (c) In the urban, rural and manufacturing spheres, a major aim is to develop less resource-intensive and less polluting technologies, accompanied by progressive

15

substitution of renewable for non-renewable sources of raw materials, and the use of physically inexhaustible energy sources rather than finite ones.

Social Sustainability

Success in this field both derives from and supports the integration of conservation with development and will depend on satisfying both the material and psychological needs of society. Thus:
  (a) Lack of knowledge about resources is a major barrier to the achievement of resource-conservation objectives.
  (b) Access to wildlife and good landscape is a powerful aid to education and the development of new perspectives.
  (c) More efficient use of physical and human resources, and improvement of local environments through conservation and enhancement of wildlife habitat, green-space and landscape in both the countryside and towns, fulfil a requirement for enjoyment and participation by an increasing number of people, offering opportunities for personal involvement, education and experience.
  (d) Social stability, quality of life and work satisfaction are enhanced by the kind of changed lifestyles required by conservation.

Economic Sustainability

This has both national and international components:
  (a) *nationally* — reduced demands, reduction in waste and pollution, and adaptability to less ample supplies of non-renewable resources challenge industry to become more efficient.
  (b) *internationally* — shifts in the composition of UK industries, and in the kind of goods and services upon which our external trade is based, reinforce the imperative to change.

'Resourceful Britain' — An Overview

'Resourceful Britain' attempts a reconciliation of economic resource-conservation and social well-being by setting the themes of the sector reports which follow in the context of some of the major problems facing Britain today.

The Seven Reports

Some principles which the seven major sector reports have identified are listed below.

Industry: 'Seven Bridges to the Future'
  (a) Identifying those sectors of the economy where economic growth will contribute to sustainable development;
  (b) identifying those which are inefficient in resource-use and obsolete in economic terms;
  (c) developing a coherent approach to a sustainable resource-use by increased investment in areas such as energy efficiency and cleaner, low waste technology.

Urban: 'The Livable City'
  (a) Achieving leaner resource-use by being low on energy, long in life, thrifty with land, resourceful with wastes, low on pollution and abundant in green and growing space;
  (b) becoming richer in the skills of doing more with less by thinking strategically towards resource-saving; acting locally for conservation with regeneration to

create jobs; and participating in and training for improving the environment;
and participating in and training for improving the environment;
(c) developing adaptable cities and citizens capable of taking advantage of present
opportunities to plan ahead for more livable cities.

Rural: 'Putting Trust in the Countryside'
(a) Optimising the use of the resources of the countryside so that they will be
permanently productive while minimising external inputs and environmental
damage;
(b) conserving visual beauty; protecting yesterday's heritage; and creating tomorrow's
heritage to give people a sense of belonging and identity, and the opportunity to
live satisfying and fully occupied lives.

Marine and Coastal: 'Conservation and Development of Marine and Coastal Resources'
(a) Protecting estuaries on account of their value to fisheries and other wildlife;
(b) reducing pollution of the sea, especially coastal waters, with persistent toxic and
other waste materials;
(c) avoiding over-fishing in order to maintain long-term yields.

International: 'The UK's Overseas Environmental Policy'
(a) Renewing and refocusing UK policies and programmes affecting global resource-use
and management;
(b) mitigating mis-use of resources by accelerating sustainable development assistance
to the poorer world;
(c) helping other countries to improve their knowledge and management expertise in
the environmental sphere;
(d) cooperating with international agencies and with other states to remove processes
destructive to the environment.

Ethics: 'Environmental Ethics and Conservation Action'
(a) Offering an ethical code, including recognition of humanity's interdependence
with nature;
(b) helping to achieve continuity between perception and action through education.

Education: 'Environmental Education and Sustainable Development'
(a) Creating an atmosphere of environmental concern in which decisions will be taken;
(b) requiring clear identification of values and priorities for resource-conservation
from which appropriate action can follow.

The Way Ahead

The seven reports contain the arguments underlying the objectives summarised here and
many recommendations to action in their support. Amongst these are actions which can
be taken now, others are for the medium-term, and some are for the longer-term.
Collectively, they offer a programme for a new and sustainable way of life based on the
careful use of resources.

The full implementation of the programme will require changes in public attitude and
policy to create a framework within which the recommendations of the reports can
flourish.

An Overview – **Resourceful Britain**

by Brian Johnson

RESOURCEFUL BRITAIN

*I am sure that the power of vested interest is vastly
exaggerated compared with the gradual encroachment of ideas*

J M Keynes (1936)
The General Theory – concluding notes

An Idea Whose Time Has Come

It is still easy to live in Britain in the early 1980s and yet to be unaware of a general
threat to our environment. Many of us are concerned about problems of pollution,
threats to the countryside, fouling of beaches, choking fumes, and even lead in children's
blood. Increasing numbers, through television and newspaper reports, are also aware of
great problems 'out there' — mostly, it seems, in Africa and India. Images of the hungry,
the diseased and the destitute have become, like the Oxfam corner-shop, a familiar fact
of life, as has the strife, bloodshed and calamity which this destitution helps to foster.
But it is hard for us to focus on these daily disasters. Few people in Britain are aware
how closely such realities touch the great majority of the world's people, and how closel
related they are to the mis-use of natural resources and environmental destruction. Even
fewer are aware of how such realities may affect us.

For the poorest in Britain, as in every other country, any threat of general environmental
disaster must seem irrelevant. It is dwarfed by their own immediate struggle for survival.
Meanwhile, for the more fortunate majority, amid a life which remains quite comfortable,
there are other immediate worries to keep our minds occupied — holding one's job — or
getting one, crime and violence in the streets and entering our homes, and, looming over
these, is the brooding threat of nuclear destruction — of annihilation happening perhaps
by accident, certainly against any sane judgement. A public opinion poll (MORI, 1983),
conducted in connection with the Conservation and Development Programme for the UK,
showed that these concerns remain uppermost in people's minds when compared with
future resource scarcities, pollution dangers or losses of amenity.

A New Fulcrum for Change

The theme of the reports comprising this book is that there is indeed a real and growing
threat to Britain's and the world's environment. This threat, however, need not overwhelm
us. Instead it beckons us on to a new phase in our evolution as an industrial society. It
offers an opportunity and a framework for solving some of our other immediate problems.

What is the threat? And why does it impinge upon our close-knit and energy-rich islands?
Elements of it are familiar to most people, and are commonplace to the educated
under-30s: over-population, resource-waste, pollution and, above all, some dangerous
distortions of the systems of nature.

Perhaps the most fundamental of these distortions, which is now becoming generally
recognised, but whose significance, like a hairline crack in a dam, is difficult to interpret,
is of the climate of the Earth. Mankind's industrial processes, especially energy use, and,
in the tropical forests, the quest for firewood and space to grow food, have released so
much carbon dioxide from burning that today there is general consensus among the
scientific community that the Earth's whole atmosphere is slowly warming up. The
process could affect the delicate climatic balance on which we in Britain rely for
producing our home-grown food.

Climatic modifications may turn out to be the most dramatic and far-reaching of the changes that people are bringing to their environment. But with a world population growing at almost 200,000 a day, and heading from the present 4.7 billion to six billion by the year 2000 (eventually levelling off, on the most optimistic of the World Bank's projections at something like eight to 10 billion), there are other very significant global threats. We are losing vast tracts of the world's fertile land as bad cropping and grazing practices strip immense quantities of fertile top soil from the land every year. World-wide, as papers prepared for the United Nations Conference on Desertification (1978) demonstrate, an area twice the size of Canada is on the brink of becoming desert. This process has been going on throughout the history of settled cultivation. But the rate in recent decades has accelerated remarkably, just when the remaining unused reserves of cultivable land are being used up.

If present rates of land loss and impoverishment are allowed to persist, the International Union for Conservation of Nature and Natural Resources (IUCN) warns us in the World Conservation Strategy (1980) that one-third of the world's remaining cropland will become useless in the next 25 years.

As we know, in Britain not much fertile soil is washed or blown away. But it disappears under concrete and tarmac and reservoirs. In England and Wales alone we have been losing some 15,000 hectares yearly to this process.

Other basic resources that have always been taken for granted are under increasing strain. As well as stabilising local climates, the world's forests remain one of the principal defences against soil erosion and are also a vital gene-pool for the maintenance of a host of plants and animals. These not only fascinate us in their rich variety and their extra-ordinary adaptation to their neighbourhood conditions, but, as we are learning continuously through new research, are also of incalculable potential importance in enabling us to adapt our science and our technology to changing circumstances. Yet these genetically rich forests are being consumed at a rate which the US Academy of Sciences has estimated at up to 50 hectares a minute: a rate which will halve the remaining area of productive unlogged forest by the end of this century.

Immemorial tracts of temperate forest in the Northern hemisphere are also dying or are stunted in growth, directly or indirectly, from rain made acid chiefly from the sulphurous and nitrogenous smoke of factory chimneys and oil and gas burning hundreds of miles away, while the same acid rain is a major factor in reducing the fertility of rivers and lakes, even making them sterile of fish and plant life.

The Food and Agriculture Organisation of the United Nations has documented the degree to which the oceans and seas are over-fished. The world catch has dropped back from a peak in 1970, despite much greater energy and effort spent on fishing.

Around the shores of Britain and elsewhere, many wetlands and shallows, the fertile breeding and feeding grounds that are 'support systems' of two-thirds of the world's fisheries, are being polluted or drained or filled by dredging, dumping, or shoreline 'improvement'.

Can Remote Disaster Touch Us in the UK?

It is true that the bulk of environmental destruction and degradation is happening in the poorer countries of the developing world. It is also true that it contributes yearly to the growth in flooding, refugee populations, tensions and destitution. But what effect can this really have on us?

The impact is transmitted through a combination of linkages generally summed up by the word 'interdependence'. The expression may be a useful shorthand, but is not in itself very enlightening. What are the linkages which create interdependence, and ties us to the resource-problems of distant parts? They are many, but three in particular involve the management and manipulation of resources.

The Economic Link

First is the direct economic link through trade and exchange. If Britain fails to stay buoyant economically and industrially, we will not command the means to purchase the manufactures and raw material resources on which we depend. These are likely to become more expensive as resource-bases deteriorate and demand expands with world population increase. In 1982, for the first time in our history as an industrial nation, we failed to export sufficient manufactured goods to pay even for our food and raw material imports — let alone for Hondas and Sonys and the rest of the myriad manufactured products which we import.

The Political Link

Second, and closely related, is the political link. If we are too dependent upon strategically located (especially non-renewable) resources, we are likely to experience other versions of the 'oil shocks' of 1973 and 1979. The oil shocks have passed, for the time being at least, thanks to the operation of energy-conservation and declining demand through international markets. Now the lessons of over-dependence must be applied to other scarce or potentially scarce resources. Three-quarters of the measured — or even indicated — reserves of six major metals or minerals used in industry — chromium, niobium, molybdenum, vanadium, platinum and asbestos — are found in just three countries. This political resource-problem is not primarily one of scarcity. The risk lies in insecure supply. No stockpiling on any scale that is economically feasible can eliminate the long-term insecurities of this dependence.

The Ecological Link

Third, there is the ecological link. We can call this the problem of the security of nature's supply. This, generally, is more uncertain and less visible than economic and political threats, but it is no less real. The ecological linkage produces direct effects upon supply, though often this will not affect Britain directly. We may feel the impact first through political instability and social strife overseas. In the Third World, famine and drought have, in the last decade, started or intensified political conflicts, for example between Ethiopia and Somalia in the 1970s and in India and Bangladesh. Closer to home we see not merely economic loss through ecological damage, for example in the loss of fisheries through over-fishing, but we also experience the political tensions that this can bring.

On a world scale, these tensions feed global instability, which encourages big power rivalries. This in turn fuels the arms race. The process loops back into the other linkages, intensifying our interdependence. The prospect of climatic warming which may well redistribute economic advantage in the production of food — the most strategic material of all — suggests that the ecological link could become the dominant connection in the interdependence of the coming century.

Resource Use and Values

Pressures on resources also threaten qualities which have non-economic value. Getting and consuming material resources threaten old values and produce new ones, forcing us to put price tags on abstract qualities that, until now, were, literally, priceless. Beauty, tranquillity, species variety (which also has a demonstrated practical and economic

importance) compete in scarcity, or, as objects of policy, with more conventional economic demands on resources. Often they cannot be priced, however, because they yield no financial return or, at least, none that can be readily identified. The linkage between resource-needs and these abstract qualities presents difficult and fascinating problems.

Britain, for example, has abundant coal reserves, but the cost of extracting coal (in both economic and social terms) increasingly includes the destruction of other resources such as in the Blackbrook Valley, Dudley, or the countryside around Corby. The same applies to other minerals. The transport cost of moving limestone and gravel, for example, makes it economically necessary to mine them close to sources of demand. That is why sand and gravel pits dot the populous Home Counties but, when exhausted, they can then often be made into lakes for water sports or for wildlife. Here is just one example of a potentially creative form of resource-substitution.

Elsewhere, however, the trade-offs between different uses are less possible or less benign. Indeed, they grow more frequent and starker: the early 1970s saw controversies over mining Snowdonia. More recent years have seen disputes over exploratory drilling for oil in the New Forest. Increasingly publicised and much more widespread are the common-place conflicts between food production and rural conservation in many parts of Britain.

Changing Perceptions: New Meanings for 'Development' and 'Conservation'

Understanding of the need for careful husbanding of physical and living resources has spread remarkably in the last two decades. As a result, new perceptions have changed the usage and meaning of words. Two decades ago, most British and other Western people understood the word 'development' to mean simply an urbanising alteration in the use of land. The change generally involved new building, or at least the spread of cement or concrete. It also connoted risk and potential profit. The word still retains that meaning. But since decolonisation of much of the Third World in the 1950s and 1960s, 'development' has come to mean something else as well: a whole modernising process of social, economic and technological change. The process has done much to promote first the idea, and now increasingly the reality, of an interdependent world society.

The understanding of conservation has also changed in face of these new perceptions. This is a more recent evolution. A decade ago, a conservationist was often seen as the natural opponent of the development process: a negative rather than creative influence. Now the economic expansion necessary for the new billions has forced resource-conservation to centre stage. At the same time, the range of resources needing to be conserved has expanded. No longer can we confine the term 'resource' to the coal, oil, copper or cotton of the old geography text book. It now embraces, for example, living resources, clean air and water, and stable top-soils. We can foresee the time when dependable climate may be the most critical question of all in resource-conservation.

By the early 1970s, conservation of resources and development were beginning to fuse together as an integral concept. Hence the growth of concern with 'environment' and the management of our surroundings as a whole. A much celebrated world conference was held in 1972 in Stockholm to mark this recognition. Still, however, a decade and more later, the habitual view of inevitable conflict between development and conservation more often than not prevails. Thus we have the extraordinary position in which sensible people see conflict between the interests of economic development and the health of a total environment that embraces the economy. Yet the idea of looking at the environment as an integrated whole has not faltered, despite much back-pressure in a decade of deep economic recession. Indeed, it has gained strength in the growing consensus over the need for 'sustainable' development.

The New Interest in 'Sustainability'

Clearly, the present course of resource-waste and destruction throughout much of the world is not sustainable, nor is Britain's present pattern of industrial development or decline. Interestingly, it was in 1982 for the first time that the word 'sustainability' was used in Government statements to define a new target for British economic development. However, the concept referred to sustainable economic expansion rather than the sustainable use of resources. The concepts are not necessarily opposed. A sustainable economy, and especially an expanding one, must imply a reliable supply of resources on which to draw.

How, though, should we define the idea of 'sustainability' for a country such as Britain? Certainly it cannot mean a fixed order of life, or any arrest in the course of society's development. If any such stability is sought, it inevitably implies one or other pattern of political control or behaviour. History teaches us that, over time, preconceived notions of social stability can never in fact be maintained for very long. Besides, it is difficult to embrace any such rigid concept when the conditions of life of so many people are, as at present, so miserably and unacceptably deprived.

The idea of sustainability, rather than stability, must relate to the reasonable prospects for any society, regardless of its social or economic organisation, in relation to its resource-base, especially the prospective availability of reasonably priced energy which is the prime economic mover in any modernising economy.

This sustainability is not yet much considered by Government in relation to the British economy. But many of the poor nations of the Third World are already finding their patterns of resource-consumption unsustainable because they are, too often, trapped in cycles of deprivation. Their population expansion gives them scant chance to reduce the handicap of initial poverty and lack of investment, and their proximity to the margins of survival force them into something akin to self-immolation — preying upon and consuming the living resources on which their long-term future depends.

Britain, however, has no such handicaps. It has, like its European partners, a stable and beneficent (if somewhat more sombre) climate for both human toil and food production. It has too readily been assumed that the supply of oil, as of other vital materials, could be and skill as most of its industrial partners. In the case of Britain, 'unsustainability' is not the result of resource-destruction through desperation, but of some more readily avoidable condition. In our case, it seems, the problem is faulty and short-sighted thinking about the husbandry of available resources.

With hindsight it is possible to see that, throughout the period since the Second World War, we in Britain have generally paid too little attention to the husbanding of natural resources both at home and abroad. It seems extraordinary, for example, how few — and how unheard — were the people who foresaw in the early post-war period that the supply of oil from the Middle East was remarkably insecure. But the interruption of its supply or the dramatic raising of its price through cartelisation was an odds-on prospect even in the 1950s, as political analysts at Political and Economic Planning (PEP) pointed out.

It has too readily been assumed that the supply of oil, as of other vital materials could be sustained in ever-increasing volume to meet world demand. Instead, the whole attention of political parties and the machinery of Government has been focused upon increased production and demand.

It's the Resource Links that Count — Not the Absolute Scarcity

It should be stressed at this point that the resource-problem, even when we refer to non-living or finite resources (basically metals and minerals, including oil, coal and natural gas, air and water) is rarely one of *absolute* scarcity for Britain or indeed for any other advanced industrial country. Only a very few metal ores traded in the international market are in danger of exhaustion without adequate prospects of effective substitution or re-cycling. The politics of supply could only in a few instances produce long-term deprivation, though the disruption which they can cause may prove economically costly and strategically dangerous. Moreover, in the case of oil and gas, the prospects are increasingly of major new discoveries, especially off the continental coastlines. These reserves are likely to extend, by several decades at least, the time in which to secure alternative sources of supply, whether from the sun or hydrogen or the more fully mastered atom.

Moreover, the shift towards a more efficient use of resources does not inevitably require cumbersome supervision or wholesale public intervention. The market system of adjustment in preferences and expectation is generally more effective and dynamic than it is given credit for. At the same time, as is indicated in the reports which follow, judicious planning and public investment that spawns a range of private initiatives in every neighbourhood could stimulate a variety of new industries. Such measures as improving the insulation of buildings have been shown, as in the urban and industrial reports, to be able to create many new jobs. At the same time, such conservation programmes can save hundreds of millions of pounds which might otherwise be devoted to extracting more costly oil and gas or constructing new power stations with all their implications of pollution and resource-use. Moreover, the employment created would be geographically spread, reducing our particularly intractable problem of regional and structural unemployment.

True, a chosen path of more resource-conserving development will require a considerable effort of discipline and restraint, and particularly of public education. But evidence is accumulating that the British public are beginning to become aware of the challenge and may be ready for new initiatives.

Do the British Understand the Challenge?

In the course of this initial phase in evolving a Conservation and Development Programme for the UK, a first attempt was made to find out, via a public opinion poll, more about British attitudes to resource-use and the environment. An important feature of this poll, conducted by MORI in early 1983, was that it attempted to find links in people's minds between conservation and resource-issues and other important topical questions of today. (MORI conducted the survey among 1,991 respondents aged 15+ across 171 constituency sampling points throughout Great Britain. The face to face interviews took place 20 to 26 January 1983.)

The first finding of the poll — that the immediate social and economic concerns of unemployment, inflation and law and order come well ahead of any public worries about pollution or resource-depletion — is hardly surprising. What is interesting, however, is that the proportion of people polled who put anxiety about pollution and resource-depletion at the top of their priorities almost doubled (to 25 per cent and 16 per cent respectively) when asked questions about their daily lives as opposed to problems of Britain or the world in general. While this can in no way be taken as definitive it does represent evidence that many people's level of concern with the issues is substantially raised when they are provided with the facts in ways which relate them to their daily lives.

People's responses to questions concerning the need to conserve resources so as to sustain development were of particular interest. Forty-nine per cent of the nationwide sample believed there to be a risk of using up the world's resources; 39 per cent and 37 per cent respectively were strongly in favour of recycling and other anti-waste measures. Well over half (58 per cent) said they would support an increase of a penny in the pound on income tax to pay for effective measures to reduce resource-waste.

Thus, initial indications are that the British public will respond positively if they are shown the possibilities for more conserving and sustainable patterns of development. This does not mean that they would opt for slower economic growth however. Indeed, economic growth scored high as a priority in the poll, but there was a strong interest shown among responses to the 25 questions asked in the values inherent in a different and more conservation-orientated pattern of development. Now, then, there is an opportunity to encourage the public to seek new ways forward, and new responses to our economic problems.

The last two decades, but especially the decade since the first world environment conference at Stockholm, have seen a quite remarkable increase in the number and membership of voluntary organisations in the United Kingdom that are concerned with conservation of species and their habitats, and with rural, urban, marine and international environmental issues. The concerns of these bodies tend to overlap, of course. But increasingly they also integrate with those of other private voluntary groups concerned with other facets of people's environments: with poverty, the well-being of children and the aged, with urban problems, problems of race and the plight of the poor in developing countries.

Living and working conditions are the most immediate and intimately experienced aspects of the human environment. It is perhaps understandable that heightened sensitivity regarding one aspect of environmental violation or decay should begin to link in people's minds with other areas of concern.

Beyond the interest of the paid-up membership of British conservation groups, which today stands at over three million, the MORI poll has shown that the environment ranks with many people as a major target of concern. A particularly interesting feature of the poll was that environmental concern shows remarkable uniformity across all sectors of the British public, whether defined by age, socio-economic class or political affiliation. Another, perhaps more surprising, feature is the more positive response shown by those questioned to issues of resource-conservation rather than to 'wildlife and environmental conservation'. Thus, against the background of a British floating vote of about 25 per cent, 12 per cent of respondents said they would consider switching support to a party committed to wildlife and environmental conservation, but 21 per cent would consider switching to a party committed to natural resource-conservation. This interest, if further tested and found to be solid, could have a marked effect on the centre in British politics.

Much further evidence is offered in the following reports to show that Britain has the capacity and that there is potentially the public will to see conservation incorporated on a more systematic basis into policies and plans for our future development. This desire and this evidence of a will to change is, however, impeded by four major obstacles.

Barriers to Making Conservation Part of Development

The Public Knowledge Barrier
The first of these obstacles is the absence of any clear public awareness of the fact that world resource-problems can affect our economic and social prospects as a nation. It was clear from the poll that many more people saw environmental problems as a world concern than a British one — the major exception to this being the urban (inner city) environment. By contrast, slightly more people saw inflation and unemployment as a British rather than as a world problem. In general, it may be observed that the MORI poll indicated that connections between developmental and environmental issues tend to be increased in people's minds when given further information which they could relate to their daily lives. Yet it seems that the notion that problems of the economy and conservation are two sides of the same coin is not yet accepted in the public mind. At the most basic level of domestic experience, it is understood that a thrifty household or business is one that thrives. The message that the same applies to whole countries and

economies when it comes to planning for resource-use is not one which has been taught widely in schools, discussed by the media or aired publicly in any other way.

The Ideology Barrier: The Fixation with Structure and Control

The tendency of those in public life to ignore issues of natural resource-management upon which economic growth depends has produced the second obstacle to public acceptance of an integrated approach: the polarised ideological positions of the country's intellectual and political leadership. This has had the effect of encouraging people to believe that, if only the structure of power in our society were altered, all our other problems would be readily soluble. It remains heresy to suggest that the policy mixes, offered by the right, left or centre, may be incapable of producing prosperity with full employment if the resource-dimension is ignored.

It has been said that all politics is at root about 'who gets what, how and when'. If so, we must become more concerned that the 'what' is not just more of the same material goods and services. As the first of the seven reports, which focuses on our industrial future illustrates, Britain has remarkable opportunities for expansion in pollution control and resource-conserving technologies as well as in the information-based industries. In fact, this report suggests that the contribution to our national wealth of seven 'sunrise' industries could rival that of North Sea oil by the mid 1990s.

The reason for a shift of emphasis to such industries may be both economic (in that Britain may be more competitive in them) and ethical, the latter particularly for the reasons already indicated by the world-wide environmental crises.

'Yes, Minister': The Institutional Barrier

The ideological barrier tends to divert us from framing the right questions. It is closely linked to an institutional barrier, which suggest that the new ideals and targets simply are out of our reach. The great inertia in the institutions of Government, business, commerce and organised labour interacts with the obstacle of ideology. Ideology, often bolstered by a single-minded concentration on consumption and economic growth, is used to defend the present role and nature of the institutions, whether they be great private corporations, or nationalised industries, trades unions, Government Departments or regulatory agencies, the CBI, the TUC, or, indeed, 'the Treasury view'.

Particularly striking examples of this institutional barrier are coming to light in the current Public Inquiry over the proposed construction of a pressurised water reactor nuclear power station at Sizewell. So far, in the course of that Inquiry, Government Departments have steadfastly refused to disclose documents revealing cost effective alternatives for investing £1,200 m in energy conservation for industry, commerce and homes as alternatives to the controversial proposed reactor. They have also sought to withhold other energy conservation documents which demonstrate that large scale employment opportunities exist in energy conservation industries.

Unless this sort of resistance and inertia yields to the pressure of conservation-minded interest groups, then little is likely to change beyond a slight tightening and perhaps broadening of the many piecemeal conservation measures that Britain has adopted or installed in the past.

Do we, perhaps, then, need a conservationist ideology to confront the major ideologies and their supporting institutions? The idea seems fraught with danger. First, it implies doctrinal rigidity regarding values, approaches and, indeed, measures. Such rigidity is inappropriate to the new directions indicated in this book. Second, it would also instantly confront a horizon ringed with opponents. The recommendations proposed for action in this book are of a kind which could be adopted by any of the major political groups which compete for power in Britain today.

But if we should avoid ideology in approaching a national strategy for conservation and development, we must be guided by a conserving ethic. A report on ethical issues in conservation and development follows the substantive arguments for action in resource-management. It discusses the nature of a conserving ethic, its importance, and how it might be introduced so as to permeate our individual and collective outlook.

The Financial Barrier: Can We Afford an Investment in Thrift?
Finally, there is finance: the fourth barrier to change. The recent mood of economic gloom is not conducive to any change which increases costs. When the going gets tough, environmental and resource-problems tend to be seen as luxuries to be dispensed with as we trim every possible ounce of fat from economic activity. Such desirable goals as environmental improvement must, it is claimed, be shelved until easier times yield a sufficient surplus to pay for the more costly procedures and investments which conservation-based development will involve in the short term. The reports do not avoid this fourth barrier to action, but the authors could not cost their proposals in any detail. This costing must be part of the follow-up to this programme. It is, of course, the first thing that any businessman or administrator will want to know about conservation today. However, it is a basic thesis underlying the whole of this programme, that resource-conservation will, in the longer term, be the only route to economic sustainability.

Values: Sorting out Costs and Benefits

The questions of costs — and of what is a cost and what is a benefit — raises another ethical issue. A change towards non-monetary values, on which all the reports inevitably focus, also implies a shift in the prices that are placed upon different goods and services by common consent. This is the point or 'no-man's-land' where intrinsic values and economic value interrelate. In fact, under market pressures, more conserving patterns of development are already producing changes in personal values. Ask anyone trying to sell a large uninsulated house. This is the positive aspect of the price mechanism: promoting changes of lifestyle. The uninsulated house, the thirsty car, etc, simply become less desirable. Thus, the notion of desirability is not just economic. It shades into social and moral considerations as well.

The price mechanism also operates eventually to embrace goods which were 'free' or unpriced before. When fresh air becomes scarce, people become prepared to pay for it through clean air technology. In a similar way, conservationists are challenging the use of a pricing system which puts into the national accounts on the credit side all the goods and services sold and leaves out the 'bads' and 'dis-services' produced.

Such radical reassessments of our pricing and accounting systems cannot expect to gain public assent in the immediate future. Today, there is an understandable reluctance to abandon any measures which encourage economic expansion. This is not just the result of materialism or greed. Now, as Britain strives to recover from the depths of a world slump, it is inevitable that measures that are seen to add to industrial or agricultural production costs, or increase the Public Sector Borrowing Requirement, or otherwise prejudice expansion, will be looked upon askance.

We must remember, too, as we examine opportunities for resource-conserving in our economy, that it is only by the production of a surplus within the national economy that Britain can afford to pay for and restore our dangerously dilapidated and depleted social welfare system, National Health Service, the State school system and other run-down areas of our public services. Besides, environmental costs, when added to the existing prices of manufactured goods, will, in many instances, raise those prices, and such rising costs could cut consumption.

These are familiar arguments, and the reports on conservation in urban Britain and in industry meet them squarely. They illustrate how a properly planned strategy could become a major feature of public investment that is undertaken to stimulate demand.

Such investment, by creating employment, could actually improve the social and economic equity in our society. The example already cited is that of energy conservation where, as a recent report by the consultants Environmental Resources Ltd demonstrates, over 150,000 new jobs could be generated if Britain were to adopt a major energy conservation-investment programme; a programme which would pay for itself within five years of completion and would save £2,800 m worth of fuel per year.

The urban and rural reports make a similar case for other investments in our national infrastructure — for example, reconstructing our decaying Victorian sewage systems or maintaining our priceless rural heritage while creating new landscapes for tomorrow. In most of the examples cited in the reports which follow, shifts in benefits (income) between groups in our society, and between this and future generations, would clearly be redistributive. Certainly it is vital that, when major schemes of investment for conservation are considered, the social cost is always counted.

Britain and the World Beyond

Several of the reports which follow call for measures to conserve Britain's environment and our territorial resources. But Britain is not an island in the management of its affairs. We have elected to be governed partly from Brussels. Almost equally important, we, more than any of our European partners, are enmeshed through commerce, politics and culture with the wider world beyond.

Through our membership of the Commonwealth, our various overseas associations and memberships, our treaty obligations and signatures on Conventions, Britain has, willy nilly, developed elements of an overseas environmental policy. In general it must be said that our international steps so far have been cautious and somewhat lacking conviction. True, on several major issues of international environmental concern, Britain has taken a positive line — especially in recognising the linkage between poverty and environmental destruction in the poorest countries. However on other policy questions such as over the Law of the Sea, the international impact of acid rain, or European proposals to require some form of environmental assessment for major development schemes, Britain has been among the more resistant to an open examination of the issues.

The report on Britain's overseas environmental policy argues that various emergent elements of a foreign environmental stance must be examined, clarified and brought into open relationship both to each other and to the scale of environmental problems which they confront. Only by identifying and assessing the environmental and resource-demands that we as a nation make on our overseas trading partners and those countries who receive our aid, can we begin to examine how far we must go to eliminate those practices which undermine the sustainable development of others.

It is the international report's contention — spelled out in some detail — that this exercise will reveal large opportunities for British expertise, services and products abroad, especially if Britain adopts a positive view of the need for a more conserving pattern of development both in the poorer countries and at home.

The Opportunity for a Resourceful Britain

The authors of the seven sector reports have identified many opportunities for British expertise and enterprise, both at home and abroad. These opportunities, if tested and found to be solid and real, will demonstrate that, for a relatively modest outlay, the return to be expected from more conserving patterns of development can in many instances rapidly become good business for the individual firm or entrepreneur and for the country as a whole; in others, controls and similar mechanisms will add costs, but even here as with clean air, technology can rapidly produce new economic opportunities.

At a less mundane level, the wider vista also suggests a role for British leadership. Perhaps because of their early embarkation into industrialism and thus early laying waste of so many of their own natural resources, some countries, and Britain in particular, have had a longer time to consider, and attempt to rectify, the results of this despoliation. As a result, they have played a leading role in the international conservation movement and in establishing principles for sound resource-management.

Through the world-wide knowledge of our culture and of our language, and through the reach of our communications systems, Britain has the means to play a role far beyond that implied by our present economic standing in shaping the world culture of ideas. It is a role not unworthy of a mature, increasingly post-industrial, nation seeking new avenues for its skills and for its remarkable resources of ingenuity.

INTRODUCTION TO
THE SECTOR REPORTS

The seven reports that follow are the product of a thorough and far reaching process of research, discussion and consultation. They provide a detailed analytical backcloth and reference point from which all those wishing to act to advance the creation of a sustainable and conserving society can draw.

Responsibility for this ultimately rests with all of us as individuals, especially if we are able to influence events through our roles in businesses, institutions or Government. Many of the proposals for modifying present policies and activities are for consideration by Government, and steps are being taken to establish a dialogue with those Government Departments and politicians to whom particular recommendations are mainly addressed. However, politicians and Government Departments do not act in a vacuum. If there is a clear expression of public enthusiasm for a more conserving society, this will provide a new perspective within which Government policy can be framed.

Much interest in this programme has already been shown during a period of debate in 1982, in which the ideas and recommendations of the seven reports were considered by several hundred professional practitioners in fields related to the reports' content. Partly as a result of this, initiatives are already being taken to implement aspects of the World Conservation Strategy within the United Kingdom context. But a thorough testing of the means of achieving the aims in the Conservation and Development Programme for the UK will have to be the subject of continuing efforts to secure public attention and action in many quarters.

The specific recommendations contained in the parts that follow will not all appeal to those with responsibility in the various walks of life upon which the reports touch. Alternative ways of redressing the imbalance in resource-use which the reports, both individually and collectively reveal, will be a matter for individual, institutional and political preference. More important are the objectives which have emerged from this major undertaking, both from and across the sectors covered in the reports.

The achievement of these objectives depends in the first instance upon the will to act existing within each of three broad groupings of 'actors'. These groups are central and local Government, business and institutions and other organisations, and individual citizens.

Thus, for example, central Government should accept responsibility for promoting optimum land-use through balanced support for food and timber production, rural communities and wildlife; for coordination of the policies for the marine environment to protect estuaries and coastal waters, manage fisheries and prevent persistent pollution of the sea; and for establishing a coherent overseas environmental policy. Local government should provide advice and incentive to local activities to encourage initiatives in various aspects of efficient and sustainable resource-use in both urban and rural areas. Above all, Government should foster, and be prepared to respond to, widespread public debate about the means of solving problems in achieving resource-conservation.

Businesses, public and private agencies, and other organisations should accept responsibility for building greater concern for resource-conservation and care of the environment into all their policies and activities. Greater emphasis should be laid on resource-economies in academic and business circles so as to construct resource-use models and to build resource-awareness into the national economy.

Individuals should adopt a conserving ethic towards the limited resources of the planet, including the natural heritage of wildlife and landscape; learn about the resource-implication of their actions and raise their awareness of the implications of resource-limitations for future life-styles; and ensure that their lives, whether urban or rural, become leaner on resources and richer in skills through individual action and through participation in community initiatives.

It is for all these groups to examine their objectives in the light of the need for resource-conservation and to see what can realistically be done now, and what can be done to prepare for future action.

This is the opportunity for all those who publicly endorse the World Conservation Strategy and wish to see its principles translated into practice in the UK to show the will to do so.

The remainder of this book consists of a detailed analysis of the present trends and prospects in relation to the goal of sustainable development. It also encompasses a body of discussion and consultation which has resulted in 169 specific recommendations for action.

There is an urgent need for a focus to provide information, and to initiate, coordinate and monitor action to bring about a shift towards a more conserving and resourceful society. It is a prime aim of this Programme to provide for such a focus.

PART 1
INDUSTRY

Seven Bridges to the Future
Industrial Growth Points for
a Sustainable Economy

A report by John Elkington

Acknowledgements

I should like to take this opportunity of thanking the sponsors of the Conservation and Development Programme for the UK: the World Wildlife Fund, the Nature Conservancy Council, the Countryside Commission, the Countryside Commission for Scotland, CoEnCo and the Royal Society of Arts. I also want to thank the members of the Programme Organising Committee and Liz O'Sullivan, Emily Duncan and James Robertson, who were responsible for the day to day running of the Secretariat — both during the report's preparation and during the ensuing practitioners' debate phase.

The seven authors of the other Parts of this book, together with the author of Resourceful Britain, have also made many suggestions which have helped shape the structure of 'Seven Bridges to the Future', and I am particularly indebted to Joan Davidson, Brian Johnson, Ann MacEwen, Professor Tim O'Riordan and Richard Sandbrook. While preparing the original report, I was ably assisted at various times by Marek Mayer, Georgina McAughtry and Helen Boutwood of Environmental Data Services (ENDS) Ltd — often in the thick of other projects and priorities. The original report also included a series of line drawings by Peter Clarke of the *Guardian*, which helped present a fairly complex set of ideas in a rather more digestible fashion, but which have been dropped from the present version for reasons of economy.

Whilst it may seem invidious to single out individuals who helped, given that the report drew on the experience of many companies, organisations and individuals (including the membership of the Industry Review Group), the following were particularly helpful during the production of the original report:

Frank Antrim (Wildlife Trade Monitoring Unit, Cambridge); Bert Bainbridge (British Reclamation Industries Confederation, Cambridge); Lennart Berggren (Du Pont, Geneva); Janet Barber (World Wildlife Fund, Godalming); Alan Bollard (Intermediate Technology Development Group, London); Timothy Cantell (Royal Society of Arts, London); Ray Dafter (*Financial Times*, London); Pamela Johnson (Green Alliance, London); Francois (Ecology Party, London); Dr David Everest (Department of the Environment, London); Mike Franks (Regeneration, London); Alan George (Unilever, London); Dr Peter Grant (Unilever, London); Pamela Johnson (Green Alliance, London); Francoise Nectoux (Earth Resources Research, London); Dr David Norse (Department of the Environment, London); Dr Alan Pickaver (Greenpeace, Amsterdam); Brian Price (Friends of the Earth, Bristol); Alison Pritchard (Turning Point, Ironbridge); Tim Radford (the *Guardian*, London); James Robertson (Turning Point, Ironbridge); Dr Heinz Schultheis (Bayer, Leverkusen); Dr Glyn Tonge (PATSCENTRE International, Melbourn); Nigel Tuersley (Earthlife, London); Professor Eberhard Weise (Bayer, Leverkusen); Peter Wells (Shell, London); Doreen Wedderburn (Unilever, London); and Sonia Withers (Centre for Extension Studies, University of Loughborough).

Members of the Industry Review Group took part not only in the preparation of the original report, but also in the practitioners' debate, as did many of those listed above. Among those who have not been mentioned so far, and who took a significant part in the debate are the following:

Viscount Arbuthnott (Chairman, Scottish Advisory Council, Nature Conservancy Council); Frank Bracewell (Director of Planning, Central Regional Council, Scotland); Ian Biggs (Deputy Director, Company Affairs, CBI); Robert Boote (Member of Council, IUCN); Edward Barbier (Earth Resources Research); C W Brierley (Managing Director, Economic Planning, British Gas Corporation); Dr Jean Balfour (Chairman, Countryside Commission for Scotland); Dr Morton Boyd (Director, Nature Conservancy Council, Scotland); M R Bartram (University of Salford); D J Bays (Association of County Councils); Dr David Clutterbuck (Managing Editor, International Management); Ronald Cook (Environmental Manager, United Glass Containers and Chairman, Environmental Committee, Glass Manufacturers' Federation); Fraser Cooke; Lord Craigton (Chairman, CoEnCo); Dr John Davoll (Director, Conservation Society); Baroness David (Chairman, Review Group on Education, Earth's Survival); John Davis (Intermediate Technology Development Group); John Davidson (Chairman, CBI, Scotland); D W Clement (Department of Education, Bangor); E D Dyke (Waste and Resource Management Services); Glyn England (Past Chairman, Central Electricity Generating Board); Gerald Elliot (Chairman, Christian Salvesen Managers); John Elias (Controller of Land Reclamation, Welsh Development Agency); Dr James Farquhar (Company Environment Protection Manager, Albright & Wilson); Dr Naylor Firth (Industry Department, Welsh Office); J M Fenwick (Community Relations Manager, British National Oil Corporation); John Foster (Director, Countryside Commission for Scotland); John Foster (Resources Project Coordinator, Ecology Party); Robin Grove-White (Director, Council for the Protection of Rural England); Paul Ganderton (Queen Mary's College, Hampshire); Trevor Harvey (Institution of Environmental Sciences); Dame Diana Reader Harris (Vice-President, Committee for Environment, Royal Society of Arts); Jim Hughes (Head of Policy and Research Division, Highlands and Islands Development Board); Harold Irving (Deputy Chief Planner, Scottish Development Department); J O Jones (Oxford University Institute of Agricultural Economics); Arwel Jones (Cynefin); Graham Knight (Alternative Heat Systems); A J Lebrecht (Ministry of Agriculture, Fisheries and Food); Sheila McKechnie (Association for Scientific, Technical and Managerial Staffs); Hamish Morrison (Chief Executive, Scottish Council); Lord Nathan (Vice-President, Committee for the Environment, Royal Society of Arts); Sir Arthur Norman (Chairman, De La Rue); Dr Howard Oliver (NERC Institute of Hydrology); David Potter (Huntingdon District Council); G S Parkinson (Institute of Petroleum); Dr John Potter (Institution of Environmental Sciences); Dr Ian Priban (British Consortium for Innovation); Dr Tom Pritchard (Director, Nature Conservancy Council, Wales); David Roberts (Industrial Programmes Development, Scottish Development Agency); Dr David Russell (Chairman, Tullis Russell & Co); Graham Roberts (Welsh Development Agency); The Rt Hon Timothy Sainsbury MP (Director, J Sainsbury); Graham Saunders (Area Secretary, Welsh Area Council, Association of Professional, Executive, Clerical and Computer Staffs); I G Simmons (Department of Geography, University of Durham); J K Smith (ICI); Dr Andrew Tasker (Director, Ecological Research Consultants); Dr E F Thairs (Secretary of Environmental and Technical Legislation Committee, CBI); J F Thomson (Managing Director, Material Recovery); Russell Turner (Assistant Director, Planning, Countryside Commission for Scotland); R Waller (Planning Services Division, Welsh Office); Andrew Warren (Director, Association for the Conservation of Energy); Brian Weller (Association of District Councils); and Christopher Wood (Department of Town and Country Planning, University of Manchester).

But the person who perhaps more than any other has served in the role of *eminence verte* in ensuring that the entire operation stayed on the rails is Max Nicholson, whose affiliations are too numerous to mention. Thank you Max.

Chairman's Introduction

Ten years after the United Nations Conference on the Human Environment in Stockholm, the role of industry and commerce in promoting the agreed goals of environmental policy remains pre-eminent. It is tempting to argue that environmental objectives will never be achieved without industry's full collaboration. It is even more tempting to argue that if only industry could rise to the challenges and opportunities of the kind identified in this report, then our environmental problems, which now seem to loom so large, would take on a different and less threatening dimension.

Realistically, of course, even a vigorous response by industry to the imperatives identified in the World Conservation Strategy cannot provide the whole answer. Take the issue of population growth, especially in the less developed regions of the world — but also in the industrialised nations, where environmental pressures are a function of both numbers and affluence. Population growth is undoubtedly the greatest environmental problem the world has ever seen. Industry can, and does, contribute to the search for better contraceptives and it is concerned with efficient systems of contraceptive supply and distribution. But it is idle to suppose that there are purely industrial solutions to the problems posed by human fertility.

Or, again, take the question of recycling and material recovery, a key element in the World Conservation Strategy. This report suggests many directions in which industry can economise on the use of materials and realise significant savings in the use of energy. Some of these suggestions can be adopted without further ado and, of course, where conditions are right (particularly market forces), many will be. But much will also depend on consumer choice and consumer action. Bottle banks are no good if nobody uses them.

Industry's part in this exercise must therefore be seen in conjunction with developments in other relevant policies and sectors. Government support and encouragement may be needed and, at times, the appropriate legislative framework will need to be established. That is why this report does not claim to be complete in itself. It needs to be taken together with the other reports in this book.

Almost all environmental policy can be related in one way or another to the goals of the World Conservation Strategy. Micro-effects add up to macro-effects. This report does not, however, set out to be a handbook covering all the interrelationships between industry and environment. It tries to focus instead on the three main objectives of the World Conservation Strategy, developing a series of suggestions and recommendations for industry and government.

One area which must be of special concern, if only because of the irreversible nature of so much of what is happening, is the accelerating rate at which species, both fauna and flora, are disappearing. This must, of course, be linked to the loss of habitat (eg the destruction of forests or the draining of wetlands for agriculture), where the inexorable pressures of economic and demographic growth play their part, but ecologically unsound trading patterns also have a great deal to answer for. One recommendation of this report is that industry should throw its full weight behind the implementation of the Convention on International Trade in Endangered Species and that it should press for a 'new emphasis to be given to the promotion of abundance, rather than just the prevention of extinction'.

Moral questions enter into the equation, too. Can the taking of whales, for example, be justified merely for commercial profit (no matter what the conservation status of the species may be) where there are perfectly acceptable substitutes — or where the end product is frivolous? There is no reason why industry should not be concerned with morality as well as conservation. They often go together.

A recurring theme in the report is the EEC dimension. The UK response to the World Conservation Strategy is inevitably part of the EEC's response. This is both right and proper. As Churchill said, if we do not hang together, we shall assuredly hang separately. While environmental policy was not specified in the Treaty of Rome, the EEC has evolved a relatively dynamic environmental policy and programme. Many of the recommendations in this report will only be properly implemented if they are carried out together with our European partners.

My Chairman's task was made especially agreeable by the knowledgeable contributions of the members of the Review Group and by the energy and imagination of its author, John Elkington. This report is essentially the product of his industry. In this he has set an example to us all. It is efficient, economical and environmentally benign.

Stanley Johnson, MEP
February, 1983

CHAPTER 1
INTRODUCTION

1. There has been a striking convergence between the interests of industry and conservation over the last decade, a convergence which is the subject of the present report. Our work broadly follows the guidelines suggested by the World Conservation Strategy (IUCN, 1980) which represents a bold attempt by a number of leading environmental agencies to sketch the outlines of new forms of development based on the sustainable exploitation of natural resources.

2. Genius, it has been said, involves seeing what everyone else has seen and thinking what no one else has thought. In study after study, report after report, the major world agencies responsible for economic development and environmental protection have concluded that many elements in today's development programmes are not sustainable, because they degrade the natural resource base on which their own future ultimately depends (Brandt Commission, 1980; OECD, 1979; Okita, 1980; US Department of State and the Council on Environmental Quality, 1980). Having seen the evidence of our current failures, the time is ripe for UK industry to display its natural genius by thinking new thoughts.

3. The World Conservation Strategy concludes that: 'Humanity's relationship with the biosphere, the thin covering of the planet that contains and sustains life, will continue to deteriorate until a new economic order is achieved, a new environmental ethic is adopted, human populations stabilise, and sustainable development becomes the rule rather than the exception'. As a starting point, industry could turn current logic on its head and view the Strategy as a market brief for the 1980s and 1990s.

4. Ironically, while environmentalists and many conservationists have opposed economic growth, and continue to do so, the evidence suggests that there is a growing need for fierce growth in those sectors of UK industry which offer products and services contributing to sustainable development. The first few paragraphs of Chapter 5 of this report succinctly describe the context within which industrial and technological change is taking place, while Chapter 4 identifies seven new industries, dubbing them the 'Sunrise Seven', all of which have made major strides in recent years — and will need to show exponential growth in the coming decades.

5. These clusters of scientific, technological, industrial and commercial activity (the 'Seven Bridges' of the report's title) will be vitally important in determining not only the sustainability of development in the Third World, but also in shaping the future prospects of the UK economy itself. Many other sectors will be equally important in making up our national income, but current estimates suggest that the overall contribution of the Sunrise Seven to our gross national product (GNP) could rival that of North Sea oil by the mid-1990s. And they are all based on a renewable resource, the nation's skills, rather than on a rapidly depleting capital account of fossil fuels.

Purpose of the Report

6. The purpose of this report is to review the opportunities for UK industry to achieve its own objectives of survival, profits and growth by fulfilling the objectives of the World Conservation Strategy. These are summarised in paragraphs 7 to 9 below.

7. The first objective involves the maintenance of essential ecological processes and life-support systems. These include such processes as the protection and regeneration of soils, the recycling of nutrients, and the natural cleansing of air and water. All of these are counted as 'free' services by economists and accountants, but we are a long way from learning how to reproduce them economically with technological systems — indeed, their scale is such that they are effectively irreplaceable.

8. The second objective involves the preservation of genetic diversity, the range of genetic material found in the world's organisms, on which depend the functioning of many of the above processes and life-support systems; the breeding programmes for the protection and improvement of cultivated plants, domesticated animals and micro-organisms; and a considerable volume of scientific and medical research, technological innovation and the long-term security of those industries — and this report argues that there will be a growing number of them — which exploit living resources.

9. The third objective is the sustainable utilisation of species and of ecosystems, many of which play a vital role both in supporting millions of rural and urban communities, and in sustaining major world industries. These three objectives are so closely intertwined that they have generally been taken as a single objective in the current report.

10. Industry is vital to our future, and has made some vital contributions to our understanding of all the problems outlined above, but it can impose strains on the biosphere by appropriating, and sometimes effectively sterilising, substantial areas of land in the winning of its raw materials; in harnessing energy and water resources; in producing, storing and transporting intermediate or finished products; and in disposing of the wastes produced in these processes. However, the most immediate impacts often come from those industries which directly exploit the living resource base itself, whether it be in the form of timber, agricultural crops, fish, or other wild animals and plants.

11. The four main industrial agencies of environmental change are the rural industries such as agriculture forestry and the outdoor recreation and leisure industries (covered in the rural resources report, Part 3); the fisheries industry (covered by the marine resources report, Part 4); the predominantly urban industries, such as construction, transportation and municipal waste disposal (covered by the urban report, Part 2); and the extractive, natural resource, energy, manufacturing and industrial waste disposal industries which, together with commerce and trade, make up the subject of the present report (Part 1).

An Accelerating Convergence

12. For better or worse, the world is becoming increasingly interdependent, however much some people might like to make ours a siege economy. The Organisation for Economic Cooperation and Development (OECD), which was originally established to promote economic cooperation and development, is now convinced that this interdependence covers 'not only population, migration, energy, food, financial transfers and technology, but also the environment and, increasingly, the ecological basis for development: renewable and non-renewable resources, the oceans, the atmosphere and climate, space and mankind's genetic resources and heritage' (OECD, 1981).

13. Simultaneously, however, there have been signs of a significant and, indeed, accelerating convergence between the thinking of those concerned to promote economic development and those concerned about the conservation of natural resources. Environmentalists have been shifting from essentially negative prescriptions (eg stop pollution, stop exhausting non-renewable resources and stop using renewable resources faster than they can regenerate) to a much more constructive approach — based, for example, on the promotion of environmentally sound technologies. Developers and industrialists, on the other hand, have been increasingly persuaded of the benefits associated with such techniques as environmental impact assessment (see Chapter 5 of this report).

14. Whereas environmental concerns were seen as largely synonymous with pollution problems 10 years ago, today most of the leading development aid agencies and many developing countries recognise that, while poverty may properly be described as 'the worst form of pollution', as it was at the 1972 UN Stockholm Conference on the Human Environment, development aimed at redressing social ills must be based on the sustainable use of natural resources — and on the avoidance of unnecessary environmental damage.

15. The role of national and international government agencies in meeting the real and growing needs of the developing countries for sustainable development is vitally important. Indeed, as the OECD itself suggests, a major implication of our growing economic and ecological interdependence is that 'the ability of governments to deal unilaterally with problems on a national scale will diminish. More and more economic, social, energy and other problems with an environmental or ecological basis within countries will be resolvable or avoidable only through increased cooperation among countries'. Examples of such problems would include the export of hazardous chemicals and wastes, acid rain and the build up of chlorofluorocarbons or of carbon dioxide in the atmosphere.

16. There is nothing inevitable, however, about such cooperation, especially with many national and international environmental agencies being starved of funds because of the recession or the political complexion of governments in such countries as the UK and USA. This problem has been addressed by the International Review Group. But it is easy to over-estimate the power of governments and, by implication, to downgrade the actual and potential contributions of industry, whether it be publicly or privately owned.

A Central Role for Industry

17. Industry's reaction to the Brandt Report, which provides the social and economic justification for many of the proposals put forward in the World Conservation Strategy, was perhaps best summarised in a critique published by the Trade Policy Research Centre (TPRC). This expressed concern about the Brandt Report's 'persistent, if implicit, belief in the efficiency and benevolence of governmental central planning and direction as the engine for economic progress and development' (TPRC, 1981).

18. The Brandt Report, the TPRC argued, displays a 'pervasive mistrust about the working of the market and an assumption that it will, almost automatically, produce "wrong" results'. Insofar as the problems identified by the World Conservation Strategy have been caused or aggravated by the workings of the market and by industry, there is convincing evidence that the wrong results are indeed being produced. But the basic point that development need not be a 'zero sum' game, in which only one side (ie the developer) wins, is worth making.

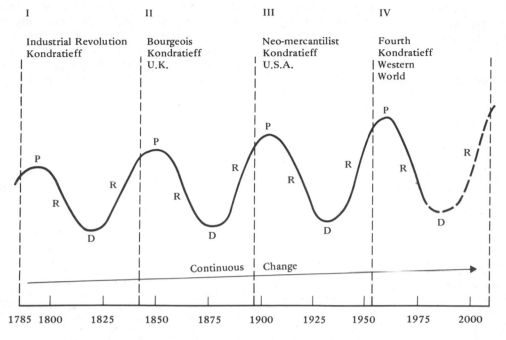

Figure 1. **Kondratieff cycles**
(source: Smith, 1982)

19. By contrast, a fundamental assumption in the present report is that industry will play a central role in the implementation of the World Conservation Strategy, but that it will need to extend considerably and upgrade its own internal environmental skills before it is able to do so effectively (see Chapter 5 of this report). One of the basic problems in this respect, however, is that the signals which the market generates about ecological problems are sometimes woefully inadequate. The market acts as a smokescreen, obscuring the environmental effects of industrial activities — particularly in relation to such trans-boundary problems as acid rain, or truly global problems such as the atmospheric build up of chlorofluorocarbons and carbon dioxide.

20. Similar problems are found in relation to international development. During the past decade, 60 per cent of the industrial development in the Third World originated outside those countries, and much of this investment was made by multinational enterprises. The OECD reports 'A large proportion went into the exploitation of natural resources (eg minerals, fuels, timber and fish) for use largely by the various OECD economies. This will continue'. The multinationals are also responsible for a major share of the growing volume of trade in minerals, manufactures and technology between the OECD area and the Third World. In 1978, for example, this trade represented 25 per cent of the total trade reported by OECD countries.

21. However, the OECD concludes, 'while this investment and trade plays an essential and beneficial role in development, there is no doubt that much of it has been associated with heavy inroads on exhaustible resources and avoidable damage to the environment and to the essential ecological basis for sustainable economic growth.

22. The export of hazardous industries to the developing countries, partly because their environmental controls are less stringent, is a cause of particular concern. As Chapter 2 of this report argues, the structural trends in the UK economy are tending to encourage the less environment-intensive industries at the expense of the heavier, more polluting and more materials hungry industries on which the Industrial Revolution was founded. But we must ensure that we do not simply export our problems, producing little net gain (or even a net loss) as far as the global environment is concerned.

23. Whether or not economists accept the concept of 'Kondratieff Cycles' (which proceed from prosperity via recession and depression to revival, over a 55 year period), our economy has gone through a number of major cycles — and gives every sign of being caught in another. Figure 1 summarises current thinking about the periods covered by some previous cycles, showing the Western world in a trough from which it is unlikely to emerge fully for well over a decade (Smith, 1982).

24. Whatever we call these major fluctuations in the fortunes of our economy, a number of basic facts emerge. The first cycle was based almost exclusively in the UK, the first industrialiser, and was based on cotton textiles, iron and steam power. The second cycle, also predominantly identified in the UK, depended heavily on the railways, while the third, most clearly seen in the USA, was based on electricity and the motor car. The fourth cycle, whose death throes we are now seeing, derived from a cluster of basic innovations

in the 1930s, including new transport technologies such as the jet engine, new communications technologies such as TV, and new materials such as plastics and synthetic fibres.

25. The question we now face is this: what new tech-nologies and new industries are going to pull the world economy in general, and the UK economy in particular, out of their depression? Some of the answers, we believe, may be found in the following chapters, while our recommendations both for industry and Government may be found in Chapter 7 of this report.

References

BRANDT COMMISSION. 1980. North-South: a programme for survival. The report of the Independent Commission on International Development Issues under the chairmanship of Willy Brandt. London, Pan Books.

INTERNATIONAL UNION FOR CONSERVATION OF NATURE AND NATURAL RESOURCES (IUCN), assisted by the United Nations Environment Programme and the World Wildlife Fund. 1980. The world conservation strategy. Available from the World Wildlife Fund. A popular version was also published as: Robert Allen. 1980. How to save the world. London, Kogan Page.

OKITA, S. 1980. Report to the Government of Japan on global environmental issues. (Mr Okita was previously Japan's Foreign Minister.)

ORGANISATION FOR ECONOMIC CO-OPERATION AND DEVELOPMENT (OECD). 1979. Facing the future: mastering the probable and managing the unpredictable. Report of the 'Interfutures' project team. Paris, France, OECD.

OECD. 1981. Report of the Director's workshop on selected global environment and resource issues. Held at the OECD, Paris, on 27-28 October. Published as Economic and ecological interdependence (1982). Paris, OECD. (2 rue Andre-Pascal, 75775 Paris CEDEX 16.)

SMITH, F M. 1982. Innovation: the way out of the recession? *Long Range Planning, vol 15, 1*, 19-29.

TRADE POLICY RESEARCH CENTRE. 1981. Global Strategy for growth: a report on North-South issues. Produced by a study group chaired by Lord McFadzean of Kelvinside. Available from the TRPC, 1 Gough Square, London EC4A 3DE.

US DEPARTMENT OF STATE AND COUNCIL ON ENVIRONMENTAL QUALITY. 1980. The Global 2000 report to the President: entering the twenty-first century. Three volumes. US Government Printing Office, ref 0-274-484. Also 1981, London, Penguin.

CHAPTER 2

THE NEED TO RE-INDUSTRIALISE

Introduction

1. We are no longer, many economists argue, an industrial nation. Industry contributes less than 40 per cent of the total UK gross national product. Manufacturing industry may still rank as the single most important sector in terms of its contribution to gross domestic product, but its lead slipped substantially during the 1970s — a process which has accelerated still further since the spring of 1979.

2. This trend is not a new development. The proportion of workers employed in the traditional blue collar occupations first dropped below the 50 per cent mark in the early 1960s, and the decline in the relative contribution of manufacturing industry to the economy has since been precipitate. Over the last 20 years, about 4.5 million jobs have disappeared, some 3.5 million of these having been lost in the manufacturing sector. Seventy-five per cent of these are thought to have gone within the last decade. As Chapter 6 of this report suggests, these job losses are often the result of structural change, rather than cyclical trends in the economy — so that a high proportion of them are unlikely to return even if the economy does recover. For the first time, too, the services sector has started to shed jobs, suggesting that it cannot be relied on to absorb those shaken out of core industries.

3. The challenge facing us in the 1980s, then, is to rekindle the industrial spirit and, perhaps surprisingly, the formulation of environmental policy will play an important role in shaping our industrial future. As the EEC's draft Third Action Programme on the Environ-

	1970	% of 1970 GDP	Rank	1979	% of 1979 GDP	Rank
Agriculture, forestry and fishing	1,266	2.8	11	3,792	2.2	13
Petroleum and natural gas	28	.0006	14	5,111	3.0	10
Mining and quarrying (excluding petroleum and natural gas)	611	1.3	13	2,696	1.6	14
Manufacturing	14,309	31.5	1	45,582	26.4	1
Construction	3,050	6.7	5	10,237	5.9	7
Gas, electricity and water	1,385	3.0	10	4,752	2.7	11
Transport	2,749	6.0	7	9,491	5.5	9
Communication	1,005	2.2	12	4,307	2.5	12
Distributive trades	4,603	10.0	3	17,146	9.9	3
Insurance, banking, finance and business services	3,097	6.8	4	14,891	8.6	4
Ownership of dwellings	2,368	5.2	8	9,837	5.7	8
Public administration and defence	2,962	6.5	6	11,752	6.8	5
Public health and educational services	2,363	5.1	9	11,030	6.4	6
Other services	5,665	12.5	2	22,267	12.9	2
Total	45,461			172,891		

Figure 2. **The contribution of different industrial sectors to GDP in 1970 and 1979** (source: Central Statistical Office, 1981)

ment (covering the period 1982-86) suggests, environmental policy must 'help in creating new jobs by the promotion and stimulation of the development of key industries [based on] products, equipment and processes that are either less polluting or use fewer non-renewable resources' (Commission of the European Communities, 1981).

A Post-Industrial Society?

4. The process of 'de-industrialisation' has been much more dramatic in the UK than in any other EEC country. There are many competing explanations, but some economists see de-industrialisation as an inevitable process, with the UK pioneering in much the same way that it pioneered the Industrial Revolution. Certainly, the statistics presented in Figure 2 (see p 43) show that the various service sectors had increased their share of GDP between 1970 and 1979. Public and private sector services, including transport and communications, now employ three out of every five workers. But how far can this process go?

5. The manufacturing sector has contracted for a number of reasons, but clearly a low demand for the products it was producing (at least in terms of quality and price) was at the heart of the matter. At the same time, however, we have been successful in the international trade in services. Our receipts from invisible trade — made up of services, plus investment income and government transactions — are still the second highest in the world, after the USA.

6. But the problem in making the transition to a service-dominated economy is that only exported services count as far as the balance of payments is concerned. A further problem is that the international market for services is only about 20 per cent the size of that for visible goods. In addition, the world market for manufactured goods has been growing faster than that for services. Even today, UK exports of services are still only half as important as those of semi-manufactured and manufactured goods.

7. The implication is that our service exports would have to increase by a phenomenal amount to provide the surplus we would need to pay for our imports of manufactured goods, energy and raw materials. We should, of course, do everything possible to increase our production of tradeable services, and the World Conservation Strategy should open up some new markets for UK expertise. But the idea that we can dispense with manufacturing industry, the engine which has fuelled the bulk of our growth to date, is an illusion.

8. Instead, we must re-industrialise, rebuilding some sectors of industry which continue to meet a real need and creating totally new ones, often building on small scale present day sectors, which will meet the needs not only of this country but of our changing export markets.

Despite the tendency to bewail any announcement that the total tonnage of our exports has fallen, because it generally provides an accurate indicator of value, we should aim to reduce that tonnage dramatically by concentrating on high technology, high added value sectors which even now are beginning to edge out some low added value, labour-intensive sectors. At the moment, the trade union movement is concerned about the deskilling of labour which could follow in the wake of automation, but the new industries demanded by the World Conservation Strategy will be skills-intensive.

The Real Limits to Growth

9. Setting up the 'Interfutures' study in 1976, four years after the publication of the Club of Rome's *Limits to Growth*, the OECD posed this question: 'Will growth in the world economy be halted, in the relatively near future, by the constraints resulting from the limited availability of the Earth's natural resources or the absorptive capacities of the ecosystem?' (OECD, 1979).

10. Funded by the Ford Foundation, the Toyota Foundation and the Marshall Fund, the Interfutures team worked on the problem for three years, reporting on 31 December 1978. It concluded that 'the economic growth of the countries of the world as a whole can continue during the next half century without encountering long-term physical limits'. But, it warned, there remain a number of vitally important problems, relating to energy, industrial raw materials and the environment, which need to be tackled effectively to ensure that such growth is not rudely interrupted.

11. The environmental problems identified by the Interfutures team are essentially the same as those identified in the World Conservation Strategy, albeit seen very much from the perspective of the industrialised nations. As for energy, the conclusion was that world energy resources would be sufficient to meet long-term consumption levels between 10 and 15 times higher than those in 1978 — at costs which would not be more than twice or three times as high as those prevailing in 1978. With oil prices tumbling early in 1982, there were those who felt that this conclusion was overly-pessimistic, but there remain very real dangers in the energy field, dangers which North Sea oil can insulate us against for only a relatively short period.

12. There is no disputing the fact that the UK economy is being weaned away from some energy-intensive industries, and the economy's overall energy consumption has been held to levels which were lower in 1980 than they were in 1973 (Figure 3, p 45). The growth in UK production of natural gas has also been spectacular (Figure 4, p 46) although this, too, is a limited resource and will soon need conserving more effectively.

13. As one of the world's leading oil producers, and with the largest coal reserves within the EEC region, the

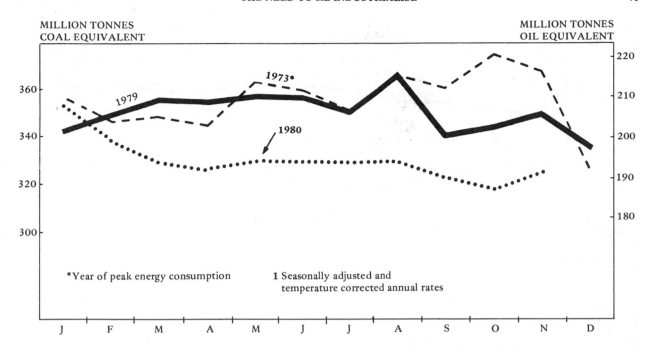

MILLION TONNES
COAL EQUIVALENT

MILLION TONNES
OIL EQUIVALENT

*Year of peak energy consumption

1 Seasonally adjusted and
temperature corrected annual rates

Figure 3. **Total inland energy consumption on a primary fuel input basis**
(source: Department of Energy, 1980)

UK has more of a breathing space than some of its European counterparts. But there is little room for complacency in a world whose energy market is so volatile and where energy-efficient products will command a premium in most important markets.

14. The Club of Rome's study considered both fuels and metals, arguing that all known reserves of 16 major metals would be exhausted within 100 years, with the exception of six: aluminium, cobalt, chromium, iron, magnesium and nickel. If exponential growth continued, it argued, then all except chromium and iron would be exhausted within 50 years — and these two survivors would only last for a further 40 years. The availability of such strategic metals continues to give cause for concern, although the exponential growth rates have largely evaporated.

15. The problem is likely to be not so much the physical availability of such metals as their concentration in a small number of politically volatile (or at least potentially so) countries. Taking seven major metals (chromium, columbium, manganese, molybdenum, vanadium, platinum and asbestos), the Interfutures team pointed out that more than three-quarters of the measured and indicated reserves are found in just three countries.

16. This theme has been taken up again by the Materials Forum, which has published a number of reports looking at the implications of this vulnerability. In a recent report it argued that the importance of eight metals (chromium, cobalt, manganese, molybdenum, niobium, the platinum group, tungsten and vanadium) to UK industry 'is impossible to overestimate . . . many of them are of vital importance to the automotive, electrical, aerospace and general engineering industries, among

others. If supplies were interrupted, in the short-term it would be very difficult to find substitutes in many of their applications' (Materials Forum, 1981).

17. The report went on to say that 'given a fairly lengthy lead time, substitutes may be found in several cases, perhaps at some sacrifice in quality and cost. It is noteworthy that in several cases, the more likely substitutes are to be found among the other seven metals of this group'. In almost every case, the UK is almost 100 per cent dependent upon imports.

18. Only tungsten, for which AMAX Exploration of the UK has been prospecting at Hemerdon, near Plymouth, would seem to offer any prospect of a domestic source of supply. The environmental impact associated with metal mines may yet prove to be an important constraint, particularly as poorer ores need to be exploited. AMAX have carried out extensive environmental impact studies (ENDS, 1979), but the potential social and environmental impacts likely to be associated with such major overseas metal mining projects as that proposed by Rio Tinto Zinc (RTZ) for the low-grade copper deposit at Cerro Colorado, Panama, are bound to be very extensive indeed (ENDS, 1981a).

19. An example of the political dimension of raw material availability has been the recent attempt to force up tin prices, which some observers have seen as a prelude to the establishment of an Organisation of Petroleum Exporting Countries (OPEC) for tin, or 'Tinpec'. However, tin consumption has been falling for some years, as more food is packaged either in plastic or in cans using alternative metals such as aluminium. The USA has also stockpiled 200,000 tons as a strategic reserve, so that any attempt to create an effective tin cartel may founder on some hard economic realities.

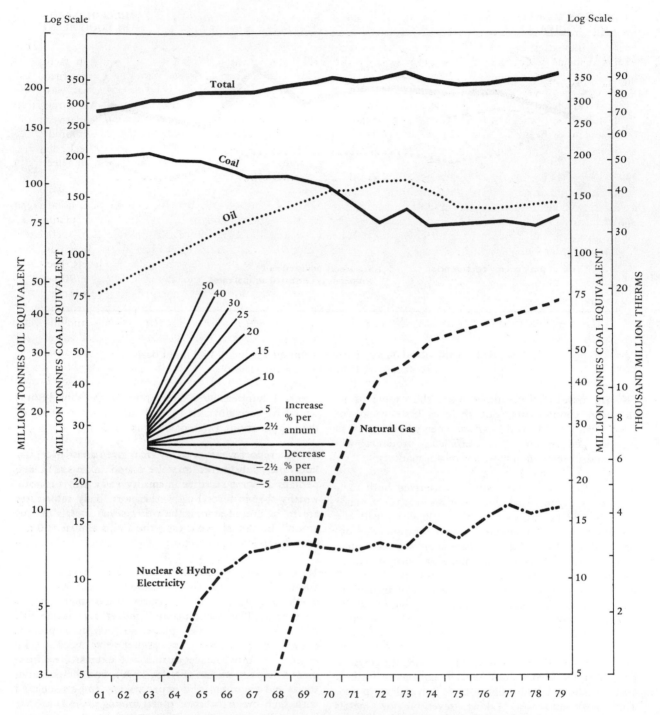

Figure 4. **Trends in the total inland consumption of primary fuels for energy use**
(source: Department of Energy, 1980)

20. Stockpiling, substitution and recycling are all possible approaches to reducing our vulnerability to such raw material shortages, of which the last two are technically the most difficult. The use of secondary (or recycled) raw materials varies widely from material to material, and from sector to sector. Some 60 per cent of lead is recycled, for example, while other strategic minerals, such as phosphate, are not recycled at all.

21. The various problem metals typically are used in alloys, which can be very difficult indeed to recycle. But a small number of companies are developing the specialised skills and technolgies needed. Ireland Alloys Ltd, for example, earned a Queen's Award for technical innovation in 1981 for two of its scrap recycling techniques. One of these techniques segregates solid scrap from other materials and assesses its value by means of spectroscopic assay, while the second permits the recovery of metals from alloys in particulate form — and the product can be of a guaranteed purity, a vital consideration for the melter.

22. Ireland Alloys deals with such metals as nickel, chromium, cobalt, molybdenum, tungsten and titanium,

all of which crop up in hundreds of different alloys used in growth sectors such as the aerospace and chemical industries. By early 1981, the company estimated that it had reprocessed alloy scrap materials which had saved the UK economy £22m in imports over three years, and £13m in manufacturing costs. Worldwide, it calculated that its operations have saved about 133 million kilowatt-hours of energy which would otherwise have been required to provide virgin metal from ore.

23. The recycling industry, whether it is recovering strategic metals or rather more mundane materials such as glass, will clearly be an important element in the industrial response to the World Conservation Strategy, and a review of the UK industry's current status may be found in Chapter 4 of this report.

The Implications of Structural Change

24. A number of existing trends in the UK economy promise to help reduce the environmental impacts associated with the earning of any given level of gross national product (GNP), although it is hard to be specific about the implied benefits in relation to the three main objectives of the World Conservation Strategy (see p 39). Interestingly, however, all three of the research reports commissioned recently by the Department of the Environment's Central Directorate on Environmental Pollution were fairly optimistic as far the pollution prospect was concerned (ENDS, 1981b; JURUE, 1982; PRU, 1981). What the researchers found surprising was the way in which the discernible structural and technological trends are almost uniformly tending to increase the economic output generated per unit of pollution discharged or, to put it another way, to reduce the pollution output for any given level of economic output.

25. The recession has knocked some significant polluters out of the industrial profile, although it has also ensured that some highly polluting plants, such as the National Coal Board's Aberaman Phurnacite works, are being propped up for employment reasons (ENDS, 1980a). The conclusions reached by Environmental Data Services (ENDS) Ltd for the economy as a whole were borne out substantially at the level of particular conurbations by the work carried out by the Joint Unit for Research on the Urban Environment (JURUE, 1982), based at Aston University, and by the Pollution Research Unit (PRU, 1981), based at Manchester University.

26. As PRU stated, in relation to the Greater Manchester region, 'it is generally those industries which have the lower emission ratings which are most likely to expand their output. Those industries with the most significant wastes, on the other hand, are most likely to experience a decrease in output. Thus changes in the composition of industrial output and stagnation in the general level of output (particularly in the manufacturing sector)

reinforce each other to reduce anticipated total emissions'.

27. Furthermore, PRU believes, 'emission factors, at least as far as industrial wastes are concerned, will continue to fall.. Thus it is possible that waste co-efficients and emission factors will change through an increase in the importance of new plant relative to old plant. In the case study industries, newer production plant was anticipated in the petrochemicals, battery, textile and plastics works, but not in electricity generation'.

28. Focusing on iron and steel production, non-ferrous metal refining, and on metal treatment, plating and finishing, JURUE found that the levels of metal contamination in the rivers of the West Midlands have fallen, largely due to lower production levels. The metal industries are directly responsible for over 90 per cent of the total metal load taken by the foul sewer system, and are responsible, directly or indirectly, for the great majority of the metal contamination found in water courses. However, JURUE found that 'total metal loads and effluent concentrations have fallen by an average of 10 per cent per annum for the previous four years. This appears to have been due to the reduced output from individual firms, rather than the wholesale closure of firms'.

29. Data from the Severn Trent Water Authority show that nickel and chromium levels fell by between 25 per cent and 50 per cent between 1979 and 1981. This decline in overall metal contamination has not, however, been sufficiently great to permit the resulting sewage sludge to be used for agricultural purposes. At the same time, however, cadmium levels have been rising, although the reason for this trend is not yet known — it may simply be that the cost of cadmium has fallen, making it a more attractive industrial raw material.

30. The environmental significance of the declining fortunes of the metal industries is illustrated by the fact that they are responsible for over two-thirds of the total volume of industrial wastes produced in the West Midlands — the main constituents being foundry sand and furnace slag. Clearly, the continued decline of these industries could reduce considerably the current demand for new landfill disposal sites for volume wastes.

31. Furthermore, as JURUE discovered, these industries are responsible for over 60 per cent of the hazardous wastes generated in the West Midlands, with the most important wastes including nickel liquors, plating solutions and other metal-bearing sludges from metal treatment and finishing, together with oils and greases from rolling mills. Again, poor prospects for the metal industries suggest that the demand for hazardous waste disposal sites may be reduced significantly.

32. What about those companies which survive? Inevitably, an economic recovery will bring something of a resurgence in pollution levels, given that many firms have not gone entirely out of business. However, an

Figure 5. **The FM21 membrane cell for producing caustic soda and chlorine**
(source: ICI, 1981)

example of what can be achieved in the metals sector is the clean-up effected by Metaltreat Ltd, which is principally owned by the Pillar Wedge Group, itself a subsidiary of RTZ (ENDS, 1981c). As the Angling Foundation argued in awarding the firm its Silver Medal, 'in its capacity as a hot dip galvaniser, Metaltreat could have met the Department of the Environment's statutory requirements for dealing with its effluent and atmospheric discharges by greatly increasing its intake of fresh water and by raising the height of its factory chimney — which would have created ammonium chloride fallout over a wide area'.

33. Instead, Metaltreat's management decided to seek ways to treat the effluent, so that the factory could achieve what approaches a closed water cycle by recycling (water consumption fell from 11,700 gallons a day to 1,129 gallons a day) and totally eradicating ammonium chloride emissions to the atmosphere.

34. In rebuilding the UK economy, we must build on the experience of such companies in developing, installing and operating cleaner, low waste production technologies. These technologies can bring significant benefits in terms of cutting pollution and of reducing the consumption both of renewable and non-renewable resources. A good example of what can be achieved may be seen in the case of Reed Paper and Board.

Cleaner, Low Waste Technologies

35. There is a Queen's Award for export achievement, but no comparable award for developments leading to the reduction of Britain's dependence on imported raw materials. If there were, Reed Paper and Board would have won it for its development work in de-inking technology, on which the company has spent over £6m over the last decade (ENDS, 1980b). Reed's newsprint, which is used by nearly 50 newspapers, now contains over 60 per cent of recycled fibre, reducing Britain's dependence on increasingly expensive imported virgin pulp by over 60,000 tonnes a year.

36. The UK packaging, paper and board industry has used waste paper for over 40 years, and much of the industry now has no economic raw material substitute. As the economics of paper and board making have changed, so waste paper has been exploited in a growing range of products, although the level of contaminants in recovered paper has been a barrier to its use for many higher quality applications. Reed researched and developed two main systems for removing ink: the washing system and the flotation system. Both systems are in operation at Reed plants, and at Aylesford, Kent, a washing system and a flotation system operate side by side. The effluent emerging from such plants is often very strong, but Reed has installed treatment equip-

ment which produces water clean enough to be re-used within the de-inking complex.

37. As part of the Industrial Review Group's activities, a number of case studies were undertaken, and a series of case reports have been published by ENDS. Among the companies visited were Bayer, in West Germany; Du Pont in Switzerland; AMAX, Boeing, Westinghouse and Weyerhaueser in the United States; and BP, Gould Foils, ICI, London Brick, Rockwool and R F Winder in the UK.

38. In the cleaner technology field, Bayer and ICI were of particular interest. ICI, for example, has developed a new technology for chlorine and caustic soda production, the FM21 membrane cell (see Figure 5, p 48), which could well replace the environmentally problematic mercury cell and the asbestos-based diaphragm cell. The FM21 is a simple, compact design, and has an important advantage in that it offers a relatively low power consumption. Compared to the mercury cell, which typically uses 3,000 kWh per tonne of sodium hydroxide, and the diaphragm cell, which uses 2,600 kWh per tonne, the FM21 cell uses only 2,300 kWh per tonne and further development work is expected to reduce this figure to about 2,000 kWh (ENDS, 1981d).

39. Bayer also provided extensive evidence of the introduction of cleaner production processes. Bayer faces many of the same difficulties in dealing with sulphuric acid wastes from its titanium dioxide plants as those which have plagued companies such as the Montedison subsidiary Sibit, in Italy, and BTP Tioxide and Laporte in the UK. But, whereas BTP Tioxide and Laporte have been making the transition from the sulphate process to the cleaner chloride route (ENDS, 1981e), Bayer has had difficulty in making the conversion in full — principally because of shortages of rutile, the raw material which guarantees that the production process generates fewer environmental problems.

40. Bayer has ceased dumping acid wastes in the North Sea, both because it has developed new recycling techniques and because its new Brunsbuettel plant, northwest of Hamburg, has been built around cleaner technologies. Bayer has been concentrating spent acids since 1962, and now recycles the equivalent of some 122,000 tonnes of 20 per cent sulphuric acid each year. This recycled acid, however, costs about five or six times as much as does acid produced from scratch. The use of cleaner, low waste production technologies is a much more economical approach. Indeed, of the first five plants built at Brunsbuettel, a 420 hectare site alongside the river Elbe, two are recycling plants designed to bring waste materials back into the production cycle (ENDS, 1981f).

41. Gould Foils, like Metaltreat, is a metal processing company, and like Metaltreat it is part of a large group of companies (RTZ in Metaltreat's case). Producing copper foils for, amongst other applications, electronic printed circuits, Gould Foils had a history of pollution problems, and the Southern Water Authority finally took the company to court in 1979. Since then, it has spent £500,000 on cleaner production technologies (ENDS, 1982b), a sum of money which would be quite beyond most medium-sized companies, let alone smaller companies. Gould, Inc has an annual turnover in excess of $1.5bn, which helps to explain how it was able to generate the resources, and it also controls around 50 per cent of the copper foil market.

42. Industry remains suspicious about the various proposals for promoting such cleaner, low waste technologies, with much of the impetus emanating from the UN Economic Commission for Europe (ECE) and from the Commission of the European Communities (CEC). In a large part, this concern stems from industry's conviction that organisations like the ECE and CEC have been converted to the US Environmental Protection Agency's now somewhat outmoded enthusiasm for 'zero emissions' and similar concepts. But, given that there is clear evidence that a wide range of companies are adopting such cleaner, low waste processes (Figure 6 — see p 50 — shows some of the longer-term trends, in food processing, as seen by Unilever) there is a strong argument for Government to promote investment in this area.

43. There is thus every reason to welcome the Department of Industry's decision to recruit UK companies into the ECE's clean technologies compendium, which could well serve as a 'shop window' for UK technology generally. The French have been the prime movers behind the ECE's efforts in this field, recognising that technologies with a low environmental impact are becoming as desirable as those with a high energy efficiency. Reading the compendium at face value, as it now stands, would suggest that France is light years ahead of the rest of Europe as far as cleaner, low waste technologies are concerned, simply because it has more entries. At the time of writing, the UK has none (ENDS, 1982a), but plans are afoot to ensure that a number of UK companies are represented by the end of 1982.

44. As Alvin Toffler argues in his book *The Third Wave*, 'the most basic raw material of all — and one that can never be exhausted — is information, including imagination' (Toffler, 1980). Through the exercise of imagination and the intelligent collection, interpretation and use of information as imagination's raw material, the limits to new forms of growth can be side-stepped. But, as the Bayer and Gould examples demonstrate, this is made easier if you have the money. A good deal of imagination will be needed to persuade the smaller companies and industries that they should invest in cleaner, low waste technologies. Some of the new growth sectors, which often side-step pollution problems entirely, are discussed in Chapter 4 of this report, but first we need to look at the future prospects for industry's biological resource base.

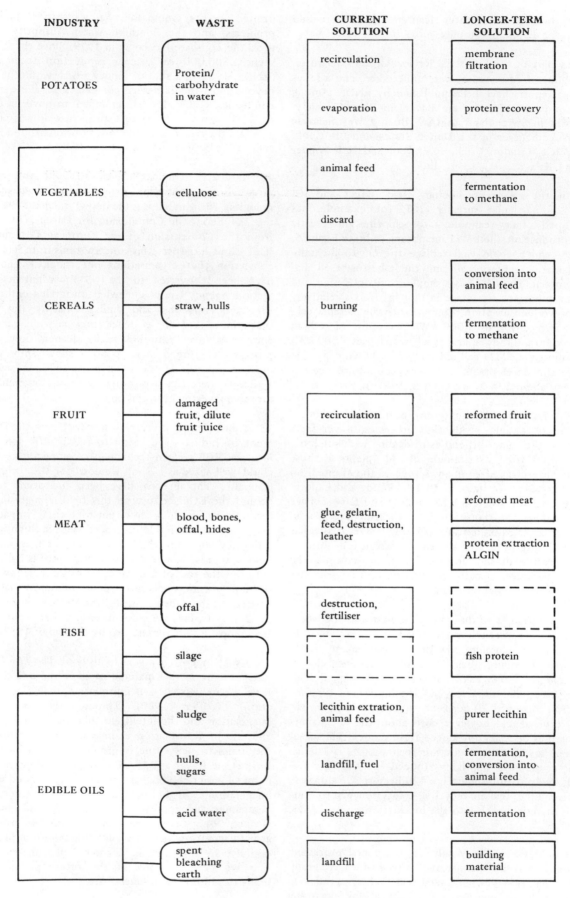

Figure 6. **Some trends in the management of food industry wastes**
(source: Unilever, 1980)

References

CENTRAL STATISTICAL OFFICE. 1981. Annual Abstract of Statistics, HMSO.

COMMISSION OF THE EUROPEAN COMMUNITIES. 1981. Draft third action programme on the environment, 1982-86. Unpublished.

DEPARTMENT OF ENERGY. 1980. Digest of United Kingdom Energy Statistics 1980, HMSO.

ENVIRONMENTAL DATA SERVICES (ENDS). 1979. AMAX exploration: the ecology of tungsten. *ENDS Report 36, October*, 11-19.

ENDS. 1980a. NCB discusses future of smokeless fuels plant after Government's refusal of aid. *ENDS Report 55, August*, 5.

ENDS. 1980b. Reed Paper & Board; yesterday's papers for tomorrow's news. *ENDS Report 50, May*, 10-12.

ENDS. 1981a. Will Rio Tinto think about the Guaymi? *ENDS Report 80, September*, 17.

ENDS. 1981b. Pollution 1990: the environmental implications of Britain's changing industrial structure and technologies. Report for the Department of the Environment. London, Environmental Data Services (ENDS) Ltd. (40 Bowling Green Lane, EC1R 0NE. 01-278 4745.)

ENDS. 1981c. Metaltreat Ltd: galvanised into environmental action. *ENDS Report 67, February*, 11-12.

ENDS. 1981d. ICI's new process eliminates mercury discharges from chlor-alkali plants. *ENDS Report 78, July*, 4.

ENDS. 1981e. BTP Tioxide and Laporte: pulling out of the TiO2 sulphate route. *ENDS Report 70, April*, 9-10.

ENDS. 1981f. Bayer, A.G.: buying time for cleaner technologies. *ENDS Report 82, November*, 9-11. See also: ELKINGTON, J. 1981. Chemistry's peaceful solution. The *Guardian, 3 December*, 15.

ENDS. 1982a. The Economic Commission for Europe's compendium on low and non-waste technologies. *ENDS Report 86, March*, 14-16.

ENDS. 1982b. Gould Foils: a step on the road to clean technology. *ENDS Report 86, April*.

JOINT UNIT FOR RESEARCH ON THE URBAN ENVIRON-MENT (JURUE). Environmental pollution and structural industrial change: a pilot study of the West Midlands. Birmingham, JURUE. (University of Aston, Gosta Green, B4 7ET.) Reviewed in *ENDS Report 87, April 1982*, 9-10.

MATERIALS FORUM. 1981. Strategic metals and the United Kingdom: a preliminary assessment. London, Institution of Mechanical Engineers. (1 Birdcage Walk, SW1H 9JJ.)

ORGANISATION FOR ECONOMIC CO-OPERATION AND DEVELOPMENT (OECD). 1979. Facing the future: mastering the probable and managing the unpredictable. Report of the Interfutures project. Paris, OECD.

POLLUTION RESEARCH UNIT (PRU). Report of 1981 study not yet published, covering structural change in the Greater Manchester region. For further information contact Chris Wood at the Pollution Research Unit, University of Manchester (061-273 3333).

TOFFLER, A. 1980. The third wave. London, Collins.

CHAPTER 3

THE BIO-ECONOMY

Introduction

1. Early in 1982, Japan and China agreed to launch a three year joint project designed to track down wild plant species in China's Yunnan Province, an area which is one of the world's last remaining reservoirs of little known or unknown plant species, including species related to such important crops as paddy rice, wheat, soyabeans and many other edible plants. The project, it is hoped, will turn up plants whose genes can be used to reinvigorate existing crops — or to produce totally new crop plants.

2. The breeding of plants for high yields, quality and resistance to disease and pests has been one of the really spectacular successes of agricultural research, but the other side of the coin is that the success of this approach depends on continuing inflows of new genetic material. More than 70 per cent of the crop production in the USA, for example, is based on plant species brought in from outside the country (OECD, 1981). A mere 10 plant species account for some 70 per cent or more of total cash receipts from crops in the OECD Member States.

3. Medicines and other pharmaceutical products are also heavily dependent upon plant and animal species. It has been estimated, for example, that more than 40 per cent of the prescriptions written each year in the USA contain a drug of natural origin, either from higher plants (25 per cent), microbes (13 per cent) or animals (3 per cent). It is also reported that the commercial value of all US medical preparations derived from natural products now surpasses $10bn a year. The most important applications of higher plants and animals in the bio-medical areas, according to the OECD, are as constituents used directly in therapy, as starting materials for drug synthesis, and as models for drug synthesis, for toxicity testing and for serum preparation.

4. These facts have encouraged some conservationists to make a case for conservation on the grounds, for example, that armadilloes may provide a cure for leprosy, that the albatross may contribute to the hunt for a cure for heart disease, that the baboon may lead to a cure for incontinence or that the manatee may serve us in identifying a cure for haemophilia. Perhaps so, but there is a much more fundamental message which has yet to be communicated effectively.

5. This is that the world's genetic resources represent our biological 'capital'. Wisely invested, this capital will yield important income in the form of new products and services, underpinning complete new industries. The current tendency in many countries, however, is to squander those resources, courting biological bankruptcy.

6. Meanwhile, the UN Food and Agriculture Organisation (FAO) is drawing up an international convention to protect the genetic resources on which the productivity of the world's crops ultimately depends. This will require the free exchange of germ plasm; the repatriation of some seed collections (most of the seeds stored in the developed countries were collected in developing countries), or at least of duplicate sets; and the establishment of a network of FAO-administered seed banks.

7. Seeds are fast becoming a major target for industrial investment. The London-based International Coalition for Development Action warned several years ago that the world seed market was increasingly dominated by multinational companies. Shell, for example, was the largest seller of seeds at the time and two-thirds of the US corn and hybrid sorghum seed market was controlled by just four companies: Ciba-Geigy, DeKalb, Pioneer and Sandoz. One concern that has been expressed is that such companies will breed crop plants selectively in such a way that they have a built-in dependence on the chemical pesticides and other crop protection products they market.

The Erosion of Genetic Diversity

8. Out of an estimated 250,000 plant species thought to exist on earth, only some 2,500 have been subjected to any sort of pharmaceutical study. At present, some 1,500 new compounds are reported from plants each year in scientific literature, of which perhaps 300 show some degree of biological activity. It is no surprise to find an increasing number of companies interested in carrying out a strategic screening of this biological capital for characteristics of possible commercial value.

9. At the same time, one of the world's species becomes extinct every day of the year. By the end of the decade, it is thought, this extinction rate will approach one species an hour. A million species may have vanished by

the year 2000, a loss of genetic and ecological diversity which will make the world a very much poorer place. 'Any species is expendable somewhere along the line', a lobbyist for the US pesticide industry recently argued, adding quickly, 'except man'. Man, of course, is industry's market and is therefore, within limits, worth conserving. But the time has now come for industry to consider seriously the implications of this dramatic shrinking of the world's gene-pools for its own long-term prospects.

10. Much of the recent concern about wildlife has focused on the international trade in wildlife-related products. The commercial trade in wildlife is based primarily on such products as meat, fur, feathers, hides and scales, rather than on the traffic in live animals. Live animals have, however, increasingly been exploited, not only for zoos, but for use in laboratory testing programmes or as pets and fashion accessories.

11. The developing countries of Africa, Asia and Latin America are, in effect, net producers of wildlife, while industrialised countries — including the UK — are net consumers (Inskipp and Wells, 1979). The international trade in wildlife products is monitored by, among others, the Wildlife Trade Monitoring Centre, based in Cambridge. The main mechanism for controlling the trade is the Convention on International Trade in Endangered Species of Wild Fauna and Flora, commonly known as CITES or the Washington Convention. Our imports of most products derived from endangered species have fallen dramatically, although a good deal more could be done to ensure that the UK is not used as a transit point for the international trade in such products.

12. As the attempts by the European Parliament to stop the Canadian seal hunt — or at least to prevent the resulting seal products from entering the EEC market-place — showed, there is growing concern that CITES only protects species when they are in danger of becoming extinct. It does little, it is felt, to promote the conservation of a range of populations, as distinct from the species as a whole, and it does nothing to promote abundance in such populations. Clearly, CITES was originally drafted with the problems of extinction in mind, but the time is rapidly coming when our definition of an endangered species must be broadened to take endangered populations into account — as well as the need to promote wildlife diversity and abundance. The definition of an endangered species in CITES needs to be revised, and the UK Endangered Species Import and Export Act of 1976 will need to be modified to suit.

13. This point was made by the European Parliament, which argued that protection should be afforded to stocks or populations which are 'depleted, threatened or endangered'. This argument is particularly significant in relation to the trade in such products as tropical hardwood, where the particular product may not be derived from a threatened species, but where the winning of that product disrupts or destroys the habitat of important species.

Industry's Biological Imports

14. Between 1971 and 1979, our agricultural self-sufficiency increased from 50 per cent to 56.9 per cent and, at the same time, figures published by the Central Statistical Office suggest that our dependence on many imported biological raw materials is actually declining (Central Statistical Office, 1981), largely because of the structural trends outlined in Chapter 2 of this report.

15. Our raw cotton imports, for example, slumped from 163,000 tonnes in 1969 to 99,000 tonnes by 1979, a 39 per cent drop; raw jute consumption fell nearly 60 per cent, from 107,720 tonnes in 1969 to 43,500 tonnes in 1979; imported softwood accounted for 8.5 million cubic metres in 1969, but was down to 7.4 million cubic metres by 1979; UK imports of hard-wood fell from nearly 1.1 million cubic metres to 950,000 cubic metres over the same period — and fell further to 768,826 cubic metres by 1980; and imports of natural rubber fell 32 per cent, from 202,100 tonnes to 137,900 tonnes.

16. Similar, if sometimes less dramatic, trends can be demonstrated for commodities such as sugar, cocoa beans and tea. But, at the same time, UK industry continues to depend on a wide spectrum of natural products, including resins and oleoresins, pectins, gums and other exudates, essential oils, flavourings, vegetable dyes, tannins, fats, waxes, insecticides (eg pyrethrin) and growth regulators. Also some biological products have been in increasing demand, including vegetable oils, coffee and, since we joined the EEC, wine — with consumption of wine rising from 33.7 million gallons in 1969 to 87.2 million gallons by 1979, approaching a 160 per cent increase.

17. The vulnerability of some of these imports was demonstrated by the Malaysian take-over of the rubber and palm-oil plantations of a number of UK companies, including Barlow, Dunlop and Guthrie. Malaysia, which produces 40 per cent of the world's natural rubber, has the idea of a rubber cartel firmly in mind, probably involving Indonesia and Thailand. Like oil, natural rubber is to all intents and purposes irreplaceable for some key industrial processes, being in many ways a superior product to its oil-based synthetic rivals.

18. However, of all the products mentioned above, probably the most sensitive in ecological terms are the tropical hardwoods, biologically the world's richest assets. Figure 7, pp 54-5, shows the distribution of the world's tropical moist forests: three nations, Brazil, Zaire and Indonesia account for 53 per cent of the world's tropical moist forests. Land clearance for farming continues to be the main cause of deforestation, but industrial logging is very significant in some areas.

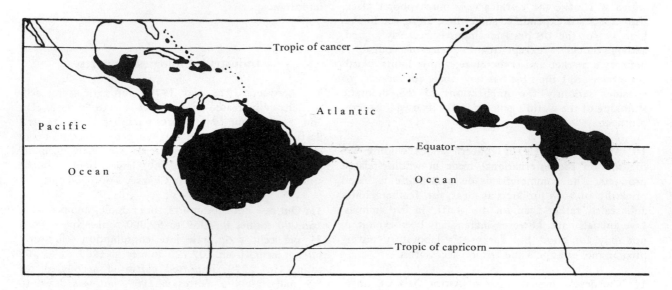

Figure 7. **The distribution of tropical moist forests, shown as shaded areas**
(source: Earthscan, 1982)

Since 1960, when exploitation of tropical hardwoods really began to take off, there has been a 16-fold increase in the volume of imports to the developed countries. Of the tropical hardwoods exported worldwide, some 53 per cent go to Japan, 32 per cent to Europe and 15 per cent to the USA (Earthscan, 1982).

19. UK imports of tropical hardwoods satisfy a wide variety of end uses, including construction; the manufacture of furniture, boats, caravans, coffins, engineering patterns, veneered panels and musical instruments; and DIY applications. Of a total of 2.98 million cubic metres of sawn tropical hardwood imported into the EEC in 1980, France accounted for 20.8 per cent, Germany for 21.3 per cent, Holland for 14.3 per cent, Italy for 16 per cent, Spain for 6 per cent and the UK for 13.6 per cent. Of 4.9 million cubic metres of tropical hardwood logs, the respective proportions were 35 per cent, 15.8 per cent, 3.2 per cent, 26 per cent, 15 per cent and, for the UK, 1.9 per cent (UCBT, 1981). So, while we are by no means the largest EEC importer of tropical hardwoods, we are certainly still very significant.

20. There is also evidence that the performance of UK-owned companies exploiting tropical hardwoods overseas could be improved. According to the Commission of the European Communities, for example, Levers Pacific Timbers Ltd, a subsidiary of UAC International which, in turn, is a subsidiary of Unilever, is the company exploiting and exporting most of the timber resources of the Solomon Islands and 'there is evidence of unnecessary damage resulting from the current logging operations that could be greatly reduced by more careful planning and operation of felling and extraction. The most severe effect is soil compaction by caterpillar tractors' (EEC, 1982).

21. The use of new harvesting technologies, particularly by Japanese firms, has meant that it has become economical to clear-fell the rain forest, which was not previously the case. Jant Pty Ltd, a subsidiary of the giant Japanese Honshu Paper Company, provides a striking example of this trend. At its 85,000 hectare (209,000 acre) timber concession in Papua, New Guinea, Jant has adopted what it calls 'total logging', in which every tree is bulldozed to the ground, regardless of its size or value, and fed into a mill which converts the trees into woodchips for export to Japan. Previously, the great diversity of species in the rain forest meant that it was relatively unsuitable for wood pulp production, but now even hardwoods can be rendered down economically into woodchips.

22. Japan has, in fact, been having considerable problems with such countries as Indonesia, which is insisting on more local investment to add value to timber before it is exported, and more replanting by the loggers. The replanting programme at Mandang, for example, has slipped badly behind, and experience in Indonesia is no different. The political initiative, however, in ensuring that such companies do replant (with performance bonds providing one way of enforcing replanting conditions), or establish commercial plantations, must come from the individual timber-producing nations, albeit supported by such agencies as the World Bank and, indeed, by the foreign policy of such timber-importing countries as our own.

Planting the World's Third Forest

23. The problems facing some of these companies are

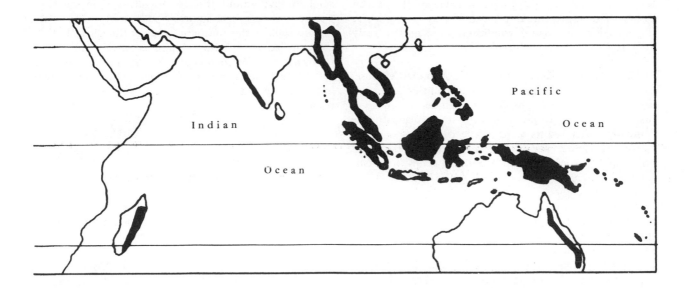

illustrated by Unilever's operations in Nigeria, where it conducts its business through another UAC subsidiary, African Timber & Plywood (ATP), the largest integrated timber business in tropical Africa. According to Mr Jeff Munson, General Manager of ATP, 'Our biggest problem, and the big question-mark hanging over the future, is the availability of resources. The species that can be used for plywood and lumber are fast disappearing. Provided we can keep resources at their present level, we believe that the future lies almost inevitably in restructured wood — and in particleboard (or 'chipboard') and possibly, in the future, in medium density fibreboard. It's the area in which, in the absence of raw materials, the business could still expand'.

24. But what about replanting? The timber trade is not the only reason the forest cover of Nigeria is disappearing, with 'timber bandits' and farmers also responsible in large measure, but surely an industry which is exploiting this type of potentially renewable resource should be ensuring that there will be a sustainable yield over the foreseeable future? Not according to Mr Munson. The cost of replanting, he says, is high, and the return on the investment far from certain.

25. Mr Munson argues: 'In reafforestation the minimum period for a return on your investment is 25 years, and for some species it can be as much as 80. Since land tenure for felling is only granted for a five year period, there is absolutely no guarantee that we would be given back, for our use, the area we had cleared, planted and invested money in'.

26. ATP, then, accepts that raw materials will be in increasingly short supply and that it will be forced progressively down-market, ending up producing fibre-

board from anything which comes to hand. This, in anybody's terms, is a poor apology for a business strategy.

27. The UK hardwoods industry, in fact, sees itself in something of a state of siege, with some governments (eg Holland and West Germany) having banned the use of hardwoods for some uses, Ghana having banned exports of 14 species and with Brazil having banned the sale of logs and cut timber over four inches thick. Other countries, such as Indonesia, Cameroon and Costa Rica are trying to establish local industries which will ensure a higher economic return from the exploitation of their indigenous timber resources. And, in addition, there is what the UK Trade Agency calls the 'ecologists lobby' (UK Trade Agency, 1982).

28. The UK Trade Agency says, perhaps slightly optimistically, 'The ecologist is a minority voice which can be controlled by the promotion of timber'. It is interesting to note that, at the round table meeting with representatives of timber exporting countries held in January 1982, the UK Trade Agency summarised the opinions of the timber industry as follows: 'it was felt that market forces will protect the resources'. Yet the evidence of ATP's problems and the fact that the timber importers, confronted with Brazil's Piranha Pine plantation experiment, retorted that the plantation approach was unworkable with hardwoods, would suggest that it is the current market approach which is unworkable in the long term.

29. No one disputes that new styles of plantation forestry will push the timber industry's skills and other resources to the limit. The collapse of Mr Daniel Ludwig's $1.2bn pulp farm at Jari, Brazil, which was based on

four million acres of rain forest (about the size of Belgium), provides an awesome warning of the vulnerability of such gargantuan projects — particularly where the prevailing ecological conditions were not properly understood before work began.

30. But there are success stories, too. Aracruz Cellulose, for example, has spent 13 years attempting to create 'the fastest-growing, homogeneous, high-density eucalyptus trees in the world at low cost', in Brazil. The company's first results were in the region of 35 cubic metres of timber per hectare, much better than had originally been expected and about 10 times the yields achieved in Scandinavia and North America.

31. Aracruz, which has planted a 'second generation' forest in Brazil, is hoping for yields in the range 50 to 60 cubic metres per hectare. The establishment of fuelwood and industrial timber plantations is a central theme in the World Conservation Strategy, and it is vitally important that UK companies do not simply quarry the world's forest resources with no thought for the future, although it may take a World Resources Tax (an idea proposed by the World Bank) to ensure that replanting is, in fact, carried out. It has been estimated, for example, that a 1 per cent tax on the current $5bn a year tropical hardwood trade would bring in a useful $50m — and the tax may well need to be set considerably higher.

32. Mr John Campbell, chief executive of the Oxford-based Economic Forestry Group, has distinguished between the world's primeval forest (the 'First Forest'), the natural forest cover of today (the 'Second Forest') and the artificially created plantation forests of tomorrow — the 'Third Forest' (Campbell, 1980). The fossil fuels derived from the decomposition of the First Forest, he argues, will be exhausted within a few generations, while wood supplies from the Second Forest will fall well short of demand by the end of the century. Given that it is estimated that we shall require 50 million hectares of fuel wood planting if we are to meet the increasing demands of the populations of the developing countries by the year 2000, Campbell calculates that a five-fold increase in current levels of planting and financial support is needed, largely in the Third World. This implies an expenditure of at least $5bn a year.

33. It is instructive to compare the UK with Japan, both being among the world's largest importers of timber. The FAO, in fact, predicts that Japan's imports will have doubled to 250 million cubic metres by 1991, or five times the projected UK figure. But some 60 per cent of Japan's land surface is afforested, compared with about 9 per cent of the UK land surface, and Japan intends increasing its planting programme — and hence its degree of self-sufficiency — from 30 per cent to 60 per cent. In addition, Japan has been investing in its own Third Forest in South America and South-East Asia, making very substantial investments indeed in industrial plantations to meet its long-term needs.

34. The time has now come when the UK must similarly give serious thought to investing in the Third Forest (although UK industry may well choose 'safe' regions such as the southern states of the USA), both to meet the needs of the developing countries and to meet its own needs for industrial raw materials. In doing so, the UK will be laying the foundations of new growth industries, based on the renewable use of natural resources.

The New Bio-Industries

35. Two examples of new bio-industries are the development of India's sal forests and the substitution of jojoba oil for oils derived from the endangered sperm whale. Sal seed is a forest crop collected by tribal peoples in some of the most backward areas of Orissa, Madhya Pradesh and Uttar Pradesh. Research by Hindustan Lever Ltd, another Unilever subsidiary, showed that the sal fruit, which contains about 14 per cent oil, could be used as a substitute for cocoa butter in chocolate manufacture. Growing exports of sal-derived fatty acid fractions now not only help India's balance of payments and provide work for the tribal people who collect the fallen fruit, but also provide an economic return from the sal forests, suggesting that they are less likely to be bulldozed flat and turned into woodchips or some other low value product (Thomas, 1978).

36. Sperm whale oil has been extensively used in such applications as sulphurised lubricants (including metalworking, cutting and quenching oils and high speed machine oils); high pressure gear grease and automatic transmission fluids; combing oils for worsteds; printing inks, crayons and soft-leaded pencils; cosmetics and pharmaceuticals; waxes for polishes; linoleum and oilcloth; and in leather dressing oils. Although substitutes have existed for most or all of these uses, industry has been slow to phase out the use of sperm whale oil — with a few exceptions, such as Clarks Shoes (ENDS, 1979).

37. Interestingly, the Transport and General Workers Union (1979) called for a total ban on sperm whale oil imports, with Mr Moss Evans arguing that, 'as a union, we are naturally aware that the banning of imports of any raw material could result in job losses, but if the sperm whale becomes extinct, any job losses will be permanent'. This, as Chapter 6 of this report suggests, is somewhat uncharacteristic of the UK unions (although the TUC also lodged a petition with the Prime Minister early in 1982, calling for an EEC-wide ban on seal products). But it does suggest that unions may yet be persuaded to think about the long-term ecological implications of any UK industrial strategy.

38. New industries are already emerging to replace the whaling industry, and it seems likely that the exploitation of jojoba — a bush which produces a seed which

has a 53 per cent oil content — will be among them. One plot of land in Arizona which a year ago had been worth only $500 an acre, recently changed hands at $8,000 an acre because it had been planted with jojoba. Some 500 American farmers have now planted over 20,000 acres with the plant, and African and Arab countries are increasingly interested, particularly because of the bush's ability to flourish in semi-arid conditions.

39. With the Sahara Desert spreading southwards at a rate of about three miles a year, jojoba could provide an invaluable — and economically productive — ally in halting or reversing desert formation, which is one of the major objectives of the World Conservation Strategy. To meet projected world demand for jojoba oil and wax, plantations covering at least 100,000 hectares (250,000 acres), yielding 2,500 kilograms of nuts per hectare (about one ton per acre), will need to be planted, laying the foundations for what the *Economist* has estimated as likely to be a $250 million a year industry (*Economist*, 1982).

40. With companies such as Unilever beginning to see their business as being in 'renewable chemicals', to quote that company's director of research, Sir Geoffrey Allen, there is a growing interest in the potential of the new biotechnologies to boost yields and improve products. Unilever, for example, is getting 30 per cent higher yields from its cloned oil palms, and is considering ways in which it might use new techniques such as genetic engineering and tissue culture to boost yields still further. The genetic implications of such techniques have yet to be considered seriously, however. Genetic diversity, properly exploited, offers the prospect not only of improved yields, but of better plant quality, environmental adaptability, disease and pest resistance, and added vigour (Prescott-Allen and Prescott-Allen, 1981). And in the longer term, it might well be possible to use cell culture to produce considerably greater quantities of natural products such as flavourings in a continuous fermentation.

41. Industry has been slow to recognise its dependence on the world's genetic resources, and has tended to favour gene-banks over *in situ* conservation of species. But one striking advantage of *in situ* conservation is that species continue to co-evolve with pests and diseases, providing a dynamic source of resistance — whereas the seed or germ plasm in a gene-bank is in a state of suspended animation. Gene-banks are vital, of course, but methods must be evolved to ensure that industry contributes more resources to the *in situ* conservatiion of genetic diversity. Another useful interim step could be to ensure that those exploiting the genetic resources of such systems as the rainforests actually pay some form of royalty — so that there is a visible source of income flowing from what might otherwise appear to be an uneconomic tract of woodland.

42. Biotechnology, meanwhile, is one of the new growth industries which offer some hope that we may be able to sustain our economy — and all the social requirements that it meets and will have to meet — while making considerably reduced withdrawals on the world's biological capital. These growth industries are the subject of Chapter 4 of this report.

References

CAMPBELL, J. 1980. The world's third forest. *Commonwealth Forestry Review, 59 (4)*, 527-536.

CENTRAL STATISTICAL OFFICE. 1981. Annual abstract of statistics. HMSO.

EARTHSCAN. 1982. Tropical moist forests: the resource, the people, the threat. Press briefing document 32, prepared by Catherine Caufield, Lloyd Timberlake, Jon Tinker and Shana Magraw.

ECONOMIST, THE. 1982. Stopping the desert: profitably. *13 March*, 89.

EEC. 1982. Official Journal of the European Communities, *no C47, 22 March*, 7-8.

ENVIRONMENTAL DATA SERVICE (ENDS). 1979. Clarks Shoes: a total approach to the production process. *ENDS Report 28, June*, 9-10.

INSKIPP, T and WELLS, S. 1979. International trade in wildlife. An Earthscan publication, with IIED and the Fauna Preservation Society.

ORGANISATION FOR ECONOMIC CO-OPERATION AND DEVELOPMENT (OECD). 1981. Maintaining biological diversity. Working paper no 3.1. Director's workshop on selected global environment and resource issues. 27-28 October. Paris, OECD.

PRESCOTT-ALLEN, C and PRESCOTT-ALLEN, R. 1981. Wild plans and crop improvement. World Wildlife Fund.

THOMAS, T. 1978. Can the less developed countries exploit multinational corporations? Paper written by a Unilever director while a Fellow at Nuffield College, Oxford.

UNION POUR LE COMMERCE DES BOIS TROPICAUX DANS LA CEE (UCBT). 1981. Importations europeenes des bois tropicaux. Edition 81. Bruxelles, UCBT. (Rue Royale 109-111, 1000 Bruxelles, Belgium.)

UNITED KINGDOM TRADE AGENCY. 1982. Report on the Marketing of Timber Round Table Discussion Group, held on 29 January at the London Chamber of Commerce and Industry building, 69 Cannon Street, London EC4. Unpublished.

CHAPTER 4

ENVIRONMENT'S GROWTH POLES

Introduction

1. Europe, which depends on outside sources for 55 per cent of its energy and 75 per cent of its raw materials, has been plagued with slumping growth rates, soaring unemployment and persistent high rates of inflation. A central plank in any policy designed to address these problems, whether for the EEC in general or the UK in particular, must be the development of what have been dubbed the 'sunrise industries' — which are perhaps best defined by their characteristic of producing a considerably higher value per ton of product than do the more traditional, and typically declining, industries.

2. In selecting seven such industries, or, more accurately, clusters of activity which are in the process of assembling themselves into industries, we are not suggesting that these are the only potential growth industries. But what we have dubbed the 'Sunrise Seven' are all, directly or indirectly, providing answers to the problems identified by the World Conservation Strategy. Some, such as the pollution control industry, are providing cures for environmental problems while others, such as the tradeable environmental services sector, increasingly deal in prevention. Whereas many environmentalists have tended to see appropriate technology as low technology, viewing anything else as a 'technological fix', we argue that there are a number of appropriate high technologies, most of which are represented among the Sunrise Seven.

3. Even without much government assistance, there is every reason to believe that these seven embryonic industries will contribute considerably more each year to the UK economy by the mid-1990s than will North Sea oil. Unlike fossil fuels, they are based on non-depletable, indefinitely renewable resources, including our imaginative, and other, skills. However, government support (both at the UK and EEC levels) will be vital in building up these industries, given that many of their markets are heavily shaped by government policies and spending, and because the lead-times associated with many of the technologies are rather longer than the private sector can comfortably cope with, especially in relatively fragmented industries.

4. Meanwhile, the question being asked by most industrial countries is whether the current period of much lower economic growth rates is a harbinger of prolonged recession or whether it is a symptom of a

transition to totally new forms of industrial development? (FAST, 1981).

5. An increasing, albeit as yet small, number of researchers believe that we are seeing the birth pangs of a new industrial order, what Alvin Toffler has called the 'Third Wave' (Toffler, 1980). The Worldwatch Institute suggests that: 'Designing an energy-efficient economy, shifting to renewable energy sources, arresting the deterioration of the earth's cropland, and stabilising the basic biological systems will perforce alter the structure of the global economy. New industries will emerge even as old ones fade' (Brown, 1981). The first such industry, which is enjoying an increasing degree of government support in the UK, is that based on information technology.

Sunrise Industry 1: Microelectronics and Information Technology

6. The electronics industry, including the microelectronics and information technology sectors, now constitutes one of the leading sectors of the global economy, with sales valued at over £100bn annually. Currently showing growth rates of something like 10 per cent a year, the industry will rival the motor car industry as the world's largest manufacturing industry by the 1990s.

7. The manufacture of integrated circuits is now worth about £10bn a year, and is reported to be growing at a rate of 30 per cent a year. The world market for computer equipment and services could double from £40bn in 1980 to £80bn by 1985, with sales of word-processors expected to increase from £1bn to £4.3bn over the same relatively truncated period.

8. The global market for information technology is expected to double from about £54bn in 1980 to perhaps £105bn a year by 1985 (at 1980 prices). The UK market for information technology is expected to grow from £2.1bn in 1980 to £6.2bn by 1990, with a trade deficit widening from £300m in 1980 to £1bn a year by 1990. These figures, and those given in later sections, are clearly indicative, representing a collation of the latest trade forecasts. They are not to be taken as accurate predictions: rather they suggest the relative

importance and prospects of the various sunrise industries.

9. What of the ecological implications of information technology? Will information technology reduce the demand for paper? The *Economist* predicts: 'The vision of the paperless office is future-gazing nonsense' (*Economist*, 1982). IBM is convinced that paper will still be needed in the office of the future, while the Xerox Corporation goes even further, arguing that automation will cut the cost of producing documents by up to 50 per cent, thereby stimulating demand. But, while it may be difficult to argue that the new information technologies will save the world's forests, they will entrain significant ecological and environmental benefits. The fact that the cost of paper, the basic office raw material, increased by 87 per cent between 1973 and 1979 suggests that opportunities to replace paper with electronic technologies will be taken up, eventually. (See Chapter 8, paragraph 17, p 91.)

10. It has already been found that the use of microprocessor controls in manufacturing and other processes can reduce their energy consumption, and there is every reason to believe that they can also be programmed to cut down on process emissions. A number of firms, however, have run into pollution problems in the production of the new semiconductor-based products. ITT Semiconductors, for example, was the source of a massive, accidental leak of caustic soda, which wiped out fish stocks in the river Cray (ENDS, 1979a). More recently, Fairchild Camera & Instrument and Intel, both based in California's Silicon Valley, have reported leaks of toxic chemicals — 1,1,1—trichloroethane, a degreasing agent, in the case of Fairchild, and the far more toxic trichloroethylene in the case of Intel.

11. These incidents aside, however, the electronics industry is incomparably cleaner overall than are such traditional industries as iron and steel making — and even food processing. The raw materials from which most microelectronic products are made are not generally in short supply, and their extensive use may well lead to a very significant saving of some of the raw materials whose winning has contributed to the problems identified by the World Conservation Strategy.

12. Recent interest in the 'Wired Society', based on cable TV, is a case in point. This may yet prove to be a prime case of an appropriate high technology. Harford Thomas, for example, has pointed out that cable TV and the associated technologies use little energy, either in manufacture or use, and are very economical with raw materials (Thomas, 1982). As with some solar energy technologies based on the use of silicon, the basic material is silica, which is the most abundant mineral. These technologies, it has been suggested, could side-step the need for a good deal of existing travel, permitting increased decentralisation, both organisationally and geographically. Whereas traditional electronic technologies used a great deal of copper, whose long-term supply is in doubt, the use of fibre optic technology is an excellent example of effective resource substitution.

13. The wiring up of 50 per cent of the UK with cable TV could provide a £2-3bn market for the cable and fibre optics companies, few of which would consider the objectives of the World Conservation Strategy in pursuing this venture, but most of which will be making an indirect contribution.. The problem for the Government is that the process may not move fast enough, not for ecological but for economic reasons.

14. In the microprocessor field, for example, a survey carried out by the Policy Studies Institute suggests that less than half of UK manufacturing establishments, based on a sample survey of 1,200, are currently applying microelectronics technology or are planning to do so in the near future (Policy Studies Institute, 1982). A UK policy for the electronics industry has now been published (NEDO, 1982), which will be discussed later in this chapter. Suffice it to say that we have problems: a trade surplus of £100m in 1975 was converted into a deficit of £300m by 1980. In the 'leading edge' businesses, such as consumer electronics and information technology, our performance was even worse, with a £500m deficit. As with biotechnology, which is discussed in the following section, information technology will need strong and continuing support if it is to make its required contribution in a sensible time scale.

Sunrise Industry 2: The New Biotechnologies

15. 'We envisage biotechnology — the application of biological organisms, systems or processes to manufacturing and service industries — as creating wholly novel industries, with low fossil energy demands, which will be of key importance to the world economy in the next century' was the conclusion of the highly influential Spinks Report (ACARD, 1980). It suggested that: 'Over the next two decades biotechnology will affect a wide range of activities such as food and animal feed production, provision of chemical feedstocks, alternative energy sources, waste recycling, pollution control, and medical and veterinary care'.

16. In many ways, the new biotechnologies are an archetype of the Sunrise Seven, being a cluster of extremely various activities with a real long-term potential of revolutionising a significant fraction of our industrial base. The new industries will require the skills of, among others, microbiologists, geneticists, biochemists, plant scientists and chemical and process engineers.

17. The Spinks Report argued that: 'It will shortly be possible to make a wide range of organic chemicals which either cannot at present be made economically on a large scale or, if they can be made, require extensive inputs of land, energy and capital plant for their production from feedstocks such as oil, which will become more expensive'. Biotechnology, in short, is an area of high technology which could play a key role in the renewal of various existing industries and in the creation of totally new industries.

18. While it is not possible to expand on the potential for biotechnology in any detail, it is worth pointing out some of the characteristics which make many of the technologies attractive within the framework provided by the World Conservation Strategy.

19. They will, for example, use alternative raw materials, including renewable feedstocks, waste feedstocks and other materials which are not currently exploited (including low grade deposits of minerals, such as spoil heaps). They will, typically, use less energy than more conventional production routes. They may also help boost recovery of North Sea oil (by digesting and liberating trapped oil deep underground). Some estimates suggest that oil worth £300bn will be left behind by conventional recovery methods (Moses and Springfield, 1982). They should produce fewer toxic by-products, and will, like microprocessor production, be sensitive to pollution generated either in-house or externally, suggesting that they will themselves require tight pollution control standards, and typically, at low pressure, reduce or eliminate the hazards associated with conventional process routes.

20. Despite the early nervousness about the safety implications of genetic engineering, particularly around the time of the 1975 Asilomar Conference, the evidence in hand to date suggests that these risks are very much less for most technologies developed to date than was originally expected, and, while human error or, indeed, malice cannot be ruled out, there should be no insurmountable difficulty in ensuring the safety of workers, the public and the environment. The environmental aspects of biotechnology, and particularly of the fermentation technologies likely to be used, are under constant review (ENDS, 1981a). An extensive review of the impacts likely to be associated with this developing area may be found in a recent report by the US Office of Technology Assessment (OTA, 1981). Clearly, even these new, cleaner technologies will need careful and continuous monitoring to ensure that they do not cause unexpected environmental problems.

21. According to one US firm of market analysts, the total market for biotechnology products during 1981 may have been little more than $25m, although a market potential of $64.8bn was predicted for the year 2000 (Sheets, 1982). Inevitably, there is a remarkable diversity in the various forecasts being made, even for the market size by 1990, depending on the assumptions being fed in. One recent estimate, however, forecasts a 50-fold increase in the current value of the world market (which it estimates at only $10m) to $500m by 1990, with the West European market reaching a value of about $175m by the same date (Information Research, 1981).

22. However, while the really significant economic impacts of these technologies may take rather longer to arrive than most analysts may hope, the increasing cost of energy and of some important raw materials over the next two decades will ensure that they will eventually make a major contribution to the UK economy. Figure 8 (see p 61) is a by no means inclusive listing of some of the applications currently being forecast for biotechnology: it does not, for example, include enhanced oil recovery.

23. Despite such actions as the formation of Celltech, the setting up of a new biotechnology directorate within the Science & Engineering Research Council (SERC), and the formation of biotechnology units at Cranfield Institute of Technology, Imperial College and the University of Surrey, the Government has not pulled out the stops to implement the recommendations of the Spinks Report.

24. The Government was forcefully criticised in evidence presented to the House of Commons Select Committee on Education, Science and the Arts' inquiry into this vital area, with a recurring theme being the argument that the drastic cuts suffered by many university departments are eroding the base on which these new industries would otherwise be built. The additional five year, £15m biotechnology programme launched early in 1982 was a welcome step in the right direction, but the fact that Biogen decided against setting up a new plant in the UK underscored fears that we will fail to develop the critical mass necessary to hold our own in what is becoming a fiercely competitive field.

25. Few other areas of technology are so disparate and in such need of careful integration and consistent support. Despite the current aversion to the idea of developing and pursuing a coherent long-term industrial strategy (the very concept being seen as simply a disguise for the continued support of 'lame duck' industries) biotechnology and the other embryonic industries represented in the Sunrise Seven would benefit considerably if the Government were to adopt and consistently pursue such a strategy. One area which would be a prime candidate for strong support would be the application of advanced biotechnologies in pollution control.

Sunrise Industry 3: Pollution Control

26. Successive waves of environmental legislation around the world have created new markets for what have been called the 'environmental industries' (Elkington, 1980). There are now some 6,000 companies involved in the development, manufacture and supply of pollution control equipment in Western Europe alone (European Directories, 1980), while until very recently US companies manufacturing equipment for air and water pollution control were growing twice as fast on average as the rest of US industry. President Reagan's cuts have dented this market considerably, but its long-term prospects are assured — although its value will tend to grow rather more slowly than information technology or biotechnology.

27. While the USA came to pollution control rather

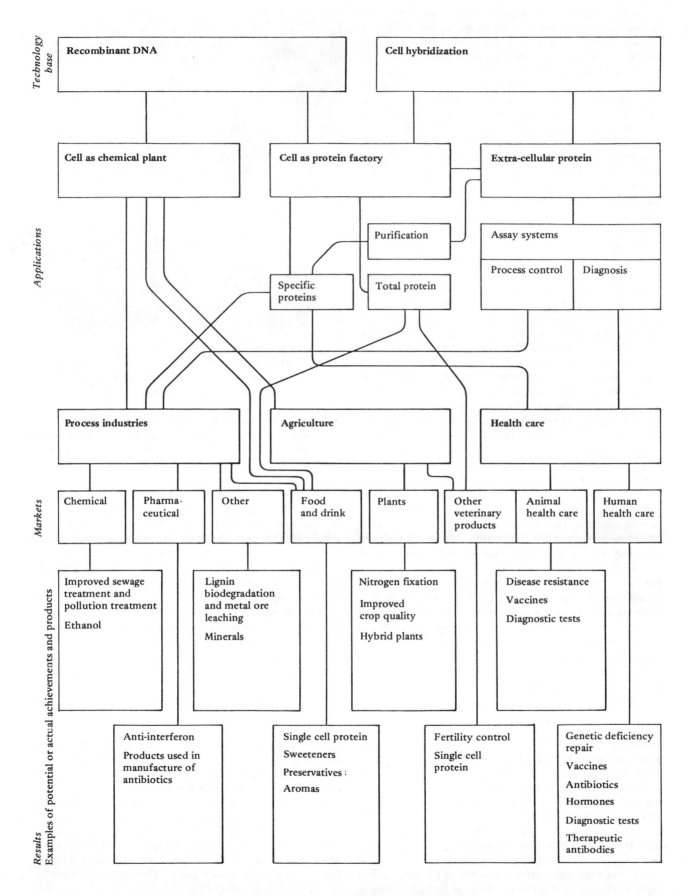

Figure 8. **Some potential applications of biotechnology**
(source: Celltech, 1981)

late and developed its legislation in a relatively short period of time, often producing legislation which was unduly costly in terms of the environmental results achieved, the UK has a much longer history of action in this field and, in direct consequence, the market for pollution control equipment here has been proportionately smaller. It has, however, been growing at an inflation-adjusted rate of between 6 per cent and 7 per cent annually, and annual sales are anticipated to grow from £138m in 1979 to £178m by the time the Conservation and Development Programme for the UK is launched in 1983.

28. Among the pathfinding companies in this field have been such companies as Simon Hartley Ltd, which has twice won a Queen's Award for Export Achievement, having quadrupled the value of its exports of sewage and effluent treatment plant between 1977 and 1980 (ENDS, 1981b); Johnson Matthey Chemicals, which won a Queen's Award for Technological Achievement for its development of sophisticated catalysts for use in controlling emissions from vehicle exhausts (ENDS, 1979b); R F Winder Ltd, which has built up a considerable business involving the removal and replacement of polychlorinated biphenyls (PCBs), used as dielectric fluids in electric transformers (ENDS, 1981c); and Biomechanics Ltd, which exploits biotechnology to treat a wide range of effluents, including those from pig farming and the production of gasohol, milk, whisky and starch (ENDS, 1979c; 1981d).

29. There is also Paramec Chemicals of Telford in Shropshire. While many of the early firms moving into the pollution control field simply produced add-on devices to control emissions, a growing number are concentrating instead on an approach which will make much more sense in the long term — the development of new forms of process engineering and of the cleaner, low waste technologies already discussed in Chapter 2. Paramec recently marketed a high pressure water cleaning unit which removes rust, scale, lubricants, coatings and other contaminants from wire —without the need for costly and potentially polluting acids and other chemicals. Paramec promptly landed a £100,000 order from China.

30. There is a real danger, however, that slowing the implementation of such legislation as the 1974 Control of Pollution Act will take the steam out of the UK pollution control industry, so that we simply end up licensing US or other foreign technologies. The announcement in early 1982 that the Government is adopting a four year timetable for the implementation of most of Part II of the Act will not only mean that we run the risk of being held to be in breach of several EEC Directives, but that a number of important pollution control markets will not develop as rapidly here as they will elsewhere in Europe.

31. To take just one example, a working party, including representatives of the Department of Energy, Environment and Industry, recently investigated the scope for the application of biotechnology to the treatment of

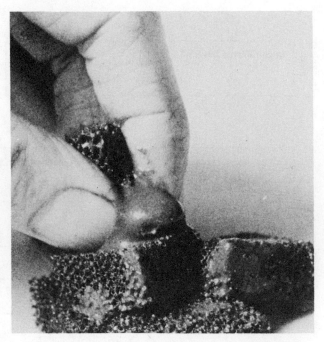

Figure 9. **An example of a biotechnology-based pollution control technology: Simon Hartley's captivated sludge support elements** (source: Simon Hartley, 1981)

farm, industrial and municipal wastes (see Figure 9). Although its report is unlikely to be published, it is understood that the working party concluded, early in 1982, that the agricultural sector was likely to be the most significant.

32. The working party concluded (ENDS, 1982) that the agricultural market for anaerobic digesters could be worth £200m over the next 10 years, and would be particularly helped if the Government could be persuaded to implement recommendations 47 and 48 of the Royal Commission on Environmental Pollution's report on agriculture and pollution (Royal Commission on Environmental Pollution, 1979). These would force the intensive livestock rearing industry, which has become a significant source of pollution, to treat its effluent. The use of anaerobic technology would yield a net energy gain in most cases, as well as reducing pollution, and the resulting market would give UK industry a springboard for exports.

33. The total UK market for anaerobic treatment technology over the next 10 years was estimated to be of the order of £350m. The working party suggested that the Department of Industry and the Science and Engineering Research Council's (SERC) Biotechnology Directorate (see paragraph 23, p 60) should carry out two surveys: one to identify which industrial effluent problems could be tackled by biotechnical means, and a second to identify specific developments in anaerobic digestion technology which would benefit from increased financial support. This approach needs to be more widely adopted in relation to all the new industrial sectors discussed in this chapter, as part of a coherent strategy and programme for the renewal of

UK industry. One sector which could benefit significantly is the recycling industry.

Sunrise Industry 4: Recycling and Substitution

34. The management of waste disposal is a critically important area, and the hazardous waste disposal industry has been scrutinised by the House of Lords Science and Technology Committee (House of Lords, 1981). The Committee concluded, *inter alia*, that: 'the scope for abuse is considerable and the waste disposal industry has sometimes been skating on thin ice'. This industry, it was concluded, 'depends vitally on good management' — a commodity which has often been in uncomfortably short supply. But, while the waste industry would do well to study Chapter 5 of this report, waste management does also offer a considerable number of opportunities.

35. A vital component in any UK conservation and development programme must be the recycling industry, which was also identified as an important sector needing to grow rapidly in *A Blueprint for Survival* (Ecologist, 1972). The industry has, in fact, taken some hard knocks in recent years, with the closure of a number of schemes designed to encourage higher levels of recycling and to focus thought on the rational utilisation of resources. Among the casualties have been the Waste Materials Exchange, the National Industrial Materials Recovery Association, the Waste Management Advisory Council and the National Anti-Waste Programme.

36. One survivor which is giving some thought to moves beyond immediate market imperatives is the British Reclamation Industries Confederation (BRIC). BRIC was established in 1977 to provide a new level of coordination to the several efforts of the various reclamation industries. BRIC represents the British Scrap Federation, the British Waste Paper Association and the Federation of Reclamation Industries. In arguing for a new and vigorous approach to reclamation and recycling, BRIC concludes that it would 'improve the competitiveness of British industry, reduce the extraction rate of valuable and diminishing natural resources, relieve the pressure on waste disposal services and decrease the need to import expensive raw materials'. BRIC points out that of the 56 million tonnes of industrial, commercial and household waste generated each year, only about 15 million tonnes are reclaimed and recycled by the reclamation industry and by manufacturing companies.

37. BRIC sees the energy savings which can be achieved by recycling as a particular attraction, stressing that it takes at least three times as much energy to convert imported iron ore into steel as it does to convert indigenous ferrous scrap into good quality steel. With the electric arc furnace depending almost entirely on scrap for its feed, the prospects for increased scrap utilisation should have been good — but for the plight of both the public and private sector steel-makers, whose problems have forced the scrap industry to reach record levels (over three million tonnes in 1981) in their exports.

38. Other potential energy savings would include those available in the recycling of aluminium, where the use of scrap aluminium saves 95 per cent of the energy used in producing the metal from virgin ore; in the production of copper wire bar from copper scrap in a reverbatory furnace, which uses only 3.2 per cent of the energy required to convert ore to metal; and in the recycling of glass, where it has been estimated that London alone could save 5.2 million gallons of oil equivalent each year simply by recycling its glass containers.

39. The Glass Manufacturers Federation has plans for some 3,000 bottle banks by mid-1984 (the current figure being about 900 bottle banks), to recover about 17 per cent (or about 250,000 tonnes) of the glass used in containers, while can manufacturers, worried by the prospect of an EEC Directive, have launched a £2m programme designed to recover tin from tinplate. Currently, something like 9bn food and drink cans are thrown away each year, representing a loss of an estimated 850,000 tonnes a year (out of a total of about 1.1bn tonnes).

40. The savings possible through recycling have been rather more obvious to governments elsewhere than they have to our own, with proposed legislation here typically foundering long before it is in sight of the statute book. The USA, for example, has its Resource Conservation and Recovery Act of 1976, which augmented an earlier Act of 1970, while West Germany introduced legislation in 1975 providing a framework for a waste economy programme. Amending legislation passed in 1980 laid even greater stress on recycling and energy conservation. The Federation of German industry, which concluded that energy costs and raw material price increases would, in any event, compel industry to improve its performance on the recycling front, has strongly supported moves to create a market for waste materials.

41. By contrast, the performance of our own government and of the CBI has been decidedly feeble, and the recycling industry has suffered accordingly. In 1978, BRIC's member associations (then also including the now defunct British Shipbreakers Association) had 800 member firms, employing nearly 20,000 people and paying an annual wages bill estimated at £64m. That year, too, 12.6 million tonnes of materials were reprocessed, with a sales value of £578m. But the recession has carved large slices away from the industry. The British Scrap Federation has lost about 30 companies, with its membership now in the region of 500, and the membership of the Reclamation Federation has dropped from 74 companies to 66.

42. As far as BRIC is concerned, the waste paper industry

is perhaps the best (or worst) example of what is wrong with the UK waste materials economy. To produce some 3.75 million tonnes of paper and board, BRIC points out, we import some 1.7 million tonnes of wood pulp costing about £500m, and we use around two million tonnes of our own waste paper. BRIC notes that 'The waste paper industry suffers from a very unstable price structure because it is almost totally dependent on commercial and industrial sources of supply, which are very sensitive to market forces both nationally and internationally. High prices tend to lead to a glut and severe falls discourage collectors, producers and local authorities. More coherent policies are needed if the collection of this valuable raw material is to be handled effectively'.

43. A small quantity of waste paper, possibly 50,000 tonnes, is already used for such purposes as loft insulation, moulded products, animal bedding and waste derived fuel, but BRIC believes that further research and development, coupled with new fiscal incentives, would produce many new applications and promote the diffusion of new technologies.

44. Among the recycling technologies announced while this chapter was being drafted were an oil-from-refuse pilot plant, developed by the University of Manchester Institute of Science and Technology (UMIST), which can transform refuse into oil at the rate of 10 tonnes of refuse to 26 barrels of oil (with a barrel of oil weighing 0.136 tonnes) in 10 minutes — with the UMIST team arguing that 3 per cent of the UK's energy could be produced from refuse; a new £6m pyrolysis plant in the West Midlands, to be backed by the Department of Industry and the EEC, which will be operated by Leigh Interests and will use about 50,000 tonnes of car tyres (ie five million tyres) a year to produce oil, solid fuel and scrap steel (at full capacity, in 1984, that would mean 20,000 tonnes of light fuel oil a year, 17,000 tonnes of coke-like solid fuel and 7,000 tonnes of scrap steel); and a new plant opened by Tarmac Roadstone which recycles bituminous road surfacing materials, producing cost savings as high as 25 per cent.

45. In order to give this vital, if fragmented, industry a boost, BRIC proposes that a comprehensive investigation into the reclamation and recycling prospect is needed urgently, to:

(a) identify and define realisable targets for improving the utilisation of wastes in each commodity sector;

(b) define the role of each of the major participants in waste management, including the roles of government, manufacturing industry, the local authorities, the reclamation and recycling industry, and of waste disposal contractors;

(c) consider the overall structure and legislative framework needed to achieve effective co-ordination;

(d) assess the areas of research needed to promote the use of waste materials in existing and new products — and the development funding required to take these products to market;

(e) create markets for the materials recovered by recycling technologies; and

(f) boost the fiscal incentives for the use of secondary materials, as the best way of creating these new markets.

Sunrise Industry 5: Energy Conservation

46. The Western world will have to spend about $10 trillion (ie million million) on new energy equipment in the next 20 years, according to estimates produced by the Dresdner Bank of West Germany. The UK may now be the world's sixth largest oil producer, and the only industrial country apart from Norway which is currently self-sufficient in oil, but at some point in the 1990s we will almost certainly become net oil importers again. We will then have what tends to be called a 're-entry problem' — and it could be crippling if we do not start planning the required transition away from oil at a sufficiently early stage.

47. According to forecasts produced by Cambridge Econometrics, energy demand in the UK will grow less than half as fast as the economy as a whole in the 1980s, reflecting structural changes in the economy itself as much as any successes in energy conservation. Nonetheless, the UK economy remains fairly energy-intensive. Of the eight major OECD economies, the UK rates second, behind the USA, in terms of how much energy we use per unit of GNP. This state of affairs must be a cause for concern.

48. Energy conservation, including the drive for greater energy efficiency throughout the economy, must be a major target in the Conservation and Development Programme for the UK — and, indeed, the urban report advances a strong case for boosting urban energy conservation programmes. In this respect, it is worrying to note that the House of Commons Select Committee on Energy found it necessary to criticise the Department of Energy during 1980 — expressing its dismay when it found that 'seven years after the first major oil price increase, the Department of Energy has no clear idea of whether investing around £1.3bn in a single nuclear plant . . . is as cost effective as spending a similar sum to promote energy conservation'.

49. An analysis commissioned from the Economists Advisory Group (EAG) by the newly-formed Association for the Conservation of Energy (ACE) during 1981 suggested that the Government should initiate a large scale programme of domestic energy conservation, arguing that 'such a programme would produce economic returns to the country up to three times as high as investment in an expanded programme for nuclear power or for other types of supplied energy'. The UK, ACE points out, has been spending far less than other major European countries on domestic energy conservation: in 1979, the total UK budget for the residential sector amounted to £35m, compared to £217m in West Germany and £130m in France.

50. The EAG calculated that a large scale and comprehensive programme of improvements to existing homes, at a rate of 500,000 homes a year, could eventually lead to a 3 per cent saving in UK primary energy consumption. Such a programme, which would treat nine million homes thought to have deficient insulation over a 17 year period, would be well within the capacity of the existing industry and could generate direct employment estimated at 27,500 jobs.

51. The domestic sector is only one among several energy-consuming sectors, all of which have been subjected to a thorough-going analysis in *A Low Energy Strategy for the UK* (Leach, 1979) — which will soon need updating, and should be. The need to improve the energy efficiency of all process industries will, for example, dominate the design of plant to be used in these industries over the next 20 years, according to the Process Plant Economic Development Committee of NEDO (NEDO, 1981).

52. About 2.5 per cent of our energy consumption, costing more than £500m a year, goes into a single industrial process: drying. The Electricity Council estimates that this energy could be halved by the judicious use of heat pumps across a wide range of industries, from the timber and paper trades, to sugar refineries, chemical plants and brick works. The heat pump market has shown considerable growth, albeit from a small base. According to the Electricity Council,

200-250 air-to-air external source heat pumps were installed in the UK during the period January 1977 to June 1978. At least 1,000 were installed in 1979, a number which was expected to rise to 2,000 in 1980 and to double again to 4,000 during 1981 (Electricity Council, 1981).

53. Even more substantial savings could be derived from a serious programme of work on district heating and combined heat and power (CHP) projects. In 1980-81, CEGB power stations, including nuclear stations, supplied 211.5 terawatt-hours of electricity from a total consumption equivalent to 97.6 million tonnes of coal. The energy dispersed as heat given that the stations were only 32.17 per cent efficient that year in converting that coal-equivalent into useable energy, was itself equivalent to 67 million tonnes of coal. Ten per cent of this heat went up the chimney, while nearly 60 per cent emerged in the form of heated cooling water. Some of this heat is already being used at the Drax power station, for heating greenhouses (see Figure 10) and a fish farm — but it is estimated that if a single 2,000 MW station were fully exploited, it would heat all UK greenhouses. The Marshall Report argued that we should follow the example of Denmark, Germany and Sweden by exploiting an increasing proportion of this wasted heat (Marshall, 1979). CHP, it suggested, could supply up to 30 per cent of our domestic and commercial heat load, at a saving equivalent to 30 million tonnes of coal a year.

Figure 10. **Combined heat and power approach to greenhouse management at Drax**
(source: Central Electricity Generating Board, 1980)

54. Marshall estimated that if the price of energy doubled over the 20 years from 1979 to the end of the century, then CHP would make good economic sense. The problem is that the capital cost would be very high for the entire programme: about £17 to 20bn to meet the 30 per cent target. It is perhaps easier to think in terms of a £500m outlay to provide a CHP system for a population of one million. No progress has yet been made on Marshall's recommendations that a National Heat Board be set up to expedite work in this area, but the CEGB, working with W S Atkins, has identified a number of possible sites for a demonstration scheme.

55. The success of the CHP scheme undertaken by the Midlands Electricity Board in Hereford has led to other Boards becoming increasingly interested, but the structure of the existing electricity supply industry is not entirely conducive to the efficient use of energy — as opposed to the economic generation of power.

56. Whatever the truth of the matter, the proposals advanced by the Secretary of State for Energy, Mr Nigel Lawson, for ending the state monopoly on electricity generation would be welcome if they accelerated investment in this important area — whether this was public sector or private sector investment. Proposals for changing the operating guidelines of the nationalised industry, including the electricity supply industry, are advanced in Chapter 5 of this report.

57. The possibility of an Energy Conservation Agency or Energy Efficiency Agency has also been advanced, to promote energy conservation more effectively than can the Department of Energy, which simultaneously has to satisfy the supply industries. Such an agency would face the problem of trying to do itself out of business, but there should be no difficulty in keeping it very busy indeed for at least 10 years. Unless some alternative means for invigorating our energy conservation effort can be developed, the agency idea is an attractive one — and should be supported.

58. What is the market size for the developing energy conservation industry? The investment in the EEC region in this area is expected to double by the end of the decade, at the very latest, and is already running at over $7bn a year for the larger process industries alone. The UK market for conservation related equipment services, and for equipment required for the switch from oil to coal, is currently estimated to be of the order of £1bn a year.

59. However, like several of the industries discussed above, the energy conservation industry is still highly fragmented, with about 1,500 firms producing equipment and 1,000 offering consultancy services. This fragmentation is highlighted by the fact that some 30 trade associations have interests in the field. This diversity may be a sign of strength. Whatever the case, the energy conservation industry has evolved a good deal further than the renewable energy industry, although the latter appears to be on the brink of a major take-off as far as the world market is concerned.

Sunrise Industry 6: Ecologically Tailored Energy Supply Technologies

60. The energy business is in a state of flux, with lower demand, increased efficiency of use and the recession leading to a radical re-assessment of past assumptions about the future direction of fuel and energy prices. Instead of needing a new nuclear plant every year, it is now argued that we only need one every three to four years. North Sea oil, at present rates of consumption, could last us well beyond 2040 — according to the Government's 'Brown Book', although Britain's self sufficiency in oil is unlikely to last beyond the late 1990s at best. Coal, meanwhile, is seen as winning a much larger share of industrial energy markets.

61. The UK has considerable strengths in a variety of energy supply technologies, with a particular emphasis now on coal technology, offshore engineering and, perhaps, nuclear technology. To meet the objectives of the World Conservation Strategy energy supply technologies should be ecologically sound: nuclear energy, with its continuing waste disposal problems, is some way from qualifying, while coal's increased use raises the possibility of acid rain or of carbon dioxide build up. The challenge for industry will be to come up with environmentally sound technologies for exploiting as wide a range of energy sources as possible — given that our future energy security, to a considerable extent, will lie in diversity of supply.

62. New and renewable sources of energy, according to Dr Ulf Lantzke, the Executive Director of the International Energy Agency, will supply the equivalent of an additional four million tonnes of oil a year by 1990, worth perhaps £28bn. Renewable sources of energy could produce the equivalent of 40 million tonnes of coal a year in the UK by the early years of the twenty-first century, according to the Department of Energy, which would be equal to 12 per cent of the current total UK energy consumption.

63. The total renewable energy resource in the UK has been estimated by the Department of Energy to be equivalent to over 200 million tonnes of coal a year, although it is likely that only a small fraction of that resource will be harnessed economically in the foreseeable future. As for the probable market size for renewable energy technologies, this is particularly hard to forecast. It is estimated that world sales of solar energy systems alone are running at well over $2bn a year, with the EEC market already worth more than £200m and expected to pass the £500m mark by 1988, despite the recession.

64. The UK solar industry is one of the largest in Europe. In 1980, it produced about 45,000 square metres of solar collectors. The value of our solar exports are estimated to be running at about £25m a year when photovoltaic cells and invisible exports are included. The long-term potential of solar heating is indicated by the fact that the Department of Energy is thinking about an annual saving, eventually, of about 10 million tonnes

of coal equivalent every year — worth £1bn at present prices.

65. The UK's solar export market is predicted to rise to over £100m by the end of the decade. Britain's prime contender at the moment in the export field is probably Lucas BP Solar Systems, which was set up early in 1981. The new company had delivered hundreds of systems to Algeria before the end of the year, as part of one of the world's largest solar contracts. What was claimed to be the largest contract ever, for $2.5m worth of solar photovoltaic systems for radio telephones in the remoter regions of Colombia, was also being handled by the company. World sales of photovoltaic cells have been increasing by between 80 per cent and 100 per cent a year, with projected unit cost reductions thought likely to open up a $100bn market by 1990. BP also owns 53 per cent of Sohio which part owns the US company Energy Conversion Devices which claims that it will be producing photovoltaic cells cheaply enough by the late 1980s to compete with fossil fuels and nuclear power even in the developed countries, thanks to the 20 per cent conversion efficiencies it expects to achieve with amorphous silicon cells.

66. Renewable energy technologies which are more applicable to the UK climate include tidal, wave and wind power. During 1980-81, wave power received the lion's share of government funding, at £3m, against £2.2m for geothermal energy, £1.4m for tidal energy — 1981 also saw the publication of the report of the Severn Barrage Committee (Severn Barrage Committee, 1981) — £0.8m for solar energy, £0.8m for wind power and £0.3m for biofuels. Only 3 per cent of the total energy Research and Development (R and D) budget went on the renewable energy sources that year, compared with 52 per cent for nuclear energy. This is in part because the renewables are still at an early stage in their development, but the point is rapidly coming where they will need considerably larger sums of money for demonstration projects — when they will begin to compete significantly with nuclear appropriations.

67. The Energy Technology Support Unit (ETSU) has calculated that biofuels, derived from biological feedstocks such as those considered in our section on pollution control, could contribute the equivalent of about three million tonnes of coal a year, although a considerable amount of energy could go into growing, harvesting, transporting and harvesting purpose-planted energy crops. Brazil is one country which has forged ahead in this field, spending at least £750m during 1981, and various UK companies have been angling for the new markets thrown up in the process — including Alcon Biotechnology, which pools the resources of Allied Breweries and Constructors John Brown. Brazil's first industrial scale ethylene-from-ethanol plant came on stream in 1981, beginning the transition away from hydrocarbon chemical feedstocks to renewable, biological feedstocks.

68. Some analysts see a $10bn a year wind power industry by 1990, which would rival the current US aircraft industry. In the UK, Dr Peter Musgrove of the University of Reading, and a pioneer of advanced wind energy systems, has estimated that offshore wind energy systems could provide up to 240bn kWh of electricity a year, compared with existing consumption of 260bn kWh a year. By the year 2000, he has argued, 20 per cent of the UK's electricity could come from the wind, compared with 12 per cent for nuclear power at present.

69. Many of the markets are going to be export markets, even if we concentrate heavily on renewable energy systems here — given that our resources are very different from those in countries such as the USA or Brazil, for example. In some of these markets, our strength may well prove to be the North Sea engineering and safety experience. A study carried out by the Marine Resources Project at the University of Manchester, for example, focused on ocean thermal energy conversion (OTEC) technologies, suggesting that while the UK might not be in the market for the construction of the platforms for what is essentially a tropical technology, we could make an impression on the likely requirement for ancillary equipment, including turbines, pumps and heat exchangers (Marine Resources Project, 1981).

70. Even more attractive, the report concluded, is the idea of breaking into the much more specialised market for monitoring and control systems, communications equipment, safety apparatus and so on, with the UK's technical sophistication giving it a competitive edge. Other technologies which may well represent markets for UK expertise include mini-hydro power generation, water turbines (such as those developed by the Intermediate Technology Development Group) and fuelwood combustion. Many of the products needed here, however, will need to be tailored carefully to local markets, rather than representing a target for the standardised design and mass marketing approach.

71. The final scale and duration of the transition away from non-renewable to renewable energy sources is impossible to predict. The development and deployment of the renewable energy technologies will tend to be episodic, reflecting the cost trends for (and availability of) fossil fuels and nuclear energy in particular. That said, however, the market for renewable energy systems looks sufficiently large even in the medium term to make it well worth addressing. And the failure of Government funding to keep pace with inflation, let alone the growing needs of the various research projects (1981-82 renewable energy budget, £13.6m; projected 1982-83 budget, £11-12m — worth perhaps £10.2-£11.1m in real terms), is particularly disappointing.

Sunrise Industry 7: Environmental Services

72. It is much harder to pin down precisely the commercial value of UK exports of environmental services, although they have made a significant contribution

to this country's invisible trade in recent years. But, again, the environmental service industry, whether operating domestically or overseas, is extremely diverse and fragmented. Yet its reputation remains considerable and, given that the UK's approach to environmental problems appears to have paid both environmental and economic dividends, the role of this emerging service sector will be vitally important in ensuring both future income for this country and professional, science-based advice for those involved in the development of natural resources.

73. Much of our expertise is to be found in the universities, a theme which is developed in some detail in the international report Part 5. Indeed, many private sector consultancy firms draw heavily on these university resources in their various domestic and overseas projects. New vehicles are needed to mobilise this expertise, such as the Joint Environmental Service recently established by the International Institute for Environment and Development (IIED) and the International Union for the Conservation of Nature and Natural Resources (IUCN).

74. Many universities and colleges run environmental courses, some having set up special departments or units, such as Imperial College, London, and the Universities of Bradford and East Anglia. Overseas students studying at these institutions are, in effect, consuming UK environmental services, and being exposed to the array of resources potentially on offer in the fields of environment and sustainable development. These relationships should be promoted, not least because they can boost the fortunes of the private sector in the longer term.

75. Private sector consultants have landed some impressive contracts: Environmental Resources Limited (ERL), which has done a great deal of work for the Commission of the European Communities, was also asked to help the Dutch government set up its new environmental impact assessment system, while Atkins Research and Development's environmental consultancy was asked by the United Nations Environment Programme (UNEP) to prepare guidelines and standards for environmental impact assessment for use by industrial developers, particularly in the developing countries.

76. Risk analysis services have been provided for a wide range of overseas clients by such firms as Cremer & Warner and Technica, while industry has often marketed the environmental skills it has been forced to develop to meet domestic legislation: ICI's Brixham Laboratory, Fisons' Environmental and Technical Service (FEATS) and Wimpey Laboratories' environmental consultancy are just some examples of this trend.

77. Companies such as British Aerospace, Hunting Geology & Geophysics and a new company called Programmed Neuro Cybernetics have been deeply involved in the development of remote sensing technology, which promises to provide much better data on the nature of our environmental resources — and on the trends, for example, in pollution or the felling of the tropical rain forest. Given the ever-increasing need to base important decisions on good science and reliable data, such activities are particularly important.

78. But there are also other, less obvious, forms of private sector environmental service which deserve mention, one of which is the development of wildlife-based tourism. By providing the governments and local people of some developing countries with a renewable source of income from their wildlife resources, the services offered by such organisations as Encounter Overland (based in London) or Town and Gown Travel (based in Oxford) can provide vital support to conservation efforts there.

79. The education report (Part 7) has developed a number of important proposals for the promotion of environmental education, but it is important that the providers of such private sector environmental services as those outlined above should be recognised in the Conservation and Development Programme for the UK. While a considerable amount could be done through such organisations as the British Consultants Bureau to promote some of these companies overseas, the Bureau has not yet featured environmental services in any of its export drives. It should.

Building Critical Mass for the Sunrise Seven

80. At a time when decentralisation and small scale organisation are seen as increasingly desirable, largely because of the poor cost effectiveness, administrative torpor and inflexibility of many big organisations, it may seem strange to argue for better coordination for these seven sectors, but their fragmentation and relatively undeveloped sense of identity makes this essential. For example, a recent Department of Trade report argues that the pollution control industry will need a good deal of governmental 'spoonfeeding' if it is to accept 'a more European diet' (Department of Trade, 1982). An example of the type of approach which is needed is the directory of UK energy conservation equipment suppliers compiled by the Department of Energy (Department of Energy, 1981).

81. The trade associations, such as BRIC or the Environmental Protection Equipment Manufacturers Association, are not particularly strong as far as resources and impact go. Such associations clearly have an important role to play, however, keeping their members abreast of developments and providing a 'shop window' for their goods and services, and the recent establishment of the British Water Industries Group is a particularly welcome initiative in this respect. The UK water industry has a great deal to offer, both in terms of basic water supply services and of the related environmental services.

82. Another approach which will need to be considered is the clustering of some of the new industrial companies

and organisations geographically. To some extent, this is already happening, with many advanced electronics firms tending to cluster along the M4, between London and Cardiff, in what has been dubbed Britain's 'Sunrise Strip'. Another form of clustering which is beginning to come into its own, long after it found favour in countries such as Japan and the USA, is the science park, with examples including parks at the Universities of Aston, Cambridge, Heriot-Watt, Salford and Warwick, and others in Bristol and Warrington.

83. An idea which deserves more Government support than it has so far had is that advanced by Earthlife Developments for a science park in London's Docklands. The scheme has been designed to promote most of the embryonic industries discussed in this chapter, and to encourage cross-fertilisation between them. The importance of this process can be imagined when it is recalled how biotechnology spills over into pollution control, recycling and renewable energy; how intimately linked are information technology and the provision of environmental services; and how the application of

microelectronic technology can contribute to improvements in the performance of industrial processes in terms of their energy- and environment-intensiveness.

84. This is exactly the type of exciting new focus which the Sunrise Seven need to break out of their traditional thought patterns and into the markets which will sustain the UK economy in the coming decades. There is growing support for a national policy promoting science and the new technologies, and the Conservation and Development Programme for the UK must underscore the need to switch investment away from the older, declining sectors of industry into the new, high technology sectors which will underpin the industries of the future. The NEDO policy for the electronics industry, for example, stresses the need for picking winners — and envisages Government, companies and the unions doing this together. This process will have major implications both for those who invest in and manage industry (see Chapter 5 of this report), and for those working in both the declining and potential growth sectors of the economy.

References

ACARD. 1980. Biotechnology: report of a joint working party. Advisory Council for Applied Research and Development, Advisory Board for the Research Councils and the Royal Society. Chaired by the late Dr Alf Spinks. HMSO.

BROWN, L. 1981. Building a sustainable society. W W Norton & Co.

DEPARTMENT OF ENERGY. 1981. UK energy conservation industry: a directory of British equipment for export. Department of Energy Conservation Division, London SW1P 4QJ. (01-211 5844).

DEPARTMENT OF TRADE. 1982. Guide to British pollution control equipment. Prepared by G de la Mer, Exports to Europe Branch.

ECOLOGIST. 1972. A blueprint for survival. Penguin Books.

ECONOMIST. 1982. Awash in paper? *30 January*, 93-94. See also Death sentence for paper shufflers? *27 December 1980*, 56-57.

ELECTRICITY COUNCIL. 1981. The UK air conditioning and heat pump market. June.

ELKINGTON, J B. 1980. The ecology of tomorrow's world: industry's environment. London, Associated Business Press.

ENVIRONMENTAL DATA SERVICES. 1979a. ITT semiconductors: coping with the unthinkable. *ENDS Report 26, May*, 14-16.

ENDS. 1979b. Johnson Matthey Chemicals: catalytic air pollution control. *ENDS Report 38, November*, 7-10.

ENDS. 1979c. Biomechanics: making waste treatment pay its way. *ENDS Report 37, November*, 8-9.

ENDS. 1981a. Pollution 1990: the environmental implications of Britain's changing industrial structure and technologies. Report for the Department of the Environment. London, Environmental Data Services (ENDS) Ltd. (40 Bowling Green Lane, EC1R 0NE. 01-278 4745.)

ENDS. 1981b. Simon Hartley Ltd: Queen's award for exporting environmental quality. *ENDS Report 73, May*, 7-8.

ENDS. 1981c. R F Winder Ltd: engineering solutions to PCB hazards. *ENDS Report 83, December*, 13-14.

ENDS. 1981d. Biomechanics: a progress report. *ENDS Report 71, April*, 12-14.

ENDS. 1982. Biotechnology in waste treatment: opportunities and constraints. *ENDS Report 88, May*, 10-12.

EUROPEAN DIRECTORIES. 1980. Directory of pollution control equipment companies in Western Europe. London, European Directories. (23 City Road, EC1Y 1RA.)

FAST. 1981. The old world and the new technologies. Michel Godet and Olivier Ruyssen, as members of the FAST team, for the Commission of the European Communities, Brussels.

HOUSE OF LORDS. 1981. Hazardous waste disposal. *Select Committee on Science and Technology, session 80-81, 1st report, July.*

INFORMATION RESEARCH. 1981. The commercial exploitation of the emerging biotechnics in Western Europe over the next 20 years. London, IRL. (40-42 Oxford Street, W1N 9FJ.)

LEACH, G. 1979. A low energy strategy for the UK. London, International Institute for Environment and Development and Science Reviews Ltd.

MARINE RESOURCES PROJECT. 1981. Ocean thermal energy: prospects and opportunities, Manchester, MRP. (University of Manchester, M13 9PL.)

MARSHALL, W. 1979. Combined heat and power generation in the United Kingdom. Department of Energy paper 35. HMSO.

MOSES, V and SPRINGFIELD, D G. 1982. Bacteria and the enhancement of oil recovery. London, Applied Science Publishers.

NATIONAL ECONOMIC DEVELOPMENT OFFICE (NEDO). 1981. Technology prospects in the process industries, parts 1 & 2. Process plant EDC. London, National Economic Development Office. (Millbank Tower, Millbank, SW1P 4QX. 01-211 3352 or 4717.)

NEDO. 1982. Policy for the UK electronics industry. Electronics EDC, April. London, NEDO. (Available free.)

POLICY STUDIES INSTITUTE. 1982. Microelectronics in industry: what is happening in Britain. London, PSI. (1-2 Castle Lane, SW1E 6ER. 01-828 7055.)

OFFICE OF TECHNOLOGY ASSESSMENT. 1981. Impacts of applied genetics: micro-organisms, plants and animals. OTA-HR-132. Washington, OTA. (Congress, Washington DC, 20510, USA.)

ROYAL COMMISSION ON ENVIRONMENTAL POLLUTION. 1979. Seventh report: agriculture and pollution. September, Cmnd 7644. HMSO.

SEVERN BARRAGE COMMITTEE. 1981. Tidal power from the Severn estuary. *Energy Paper 46, vol 1.* HMSO.

SHEETS, T A. 1982. The growth potential of the market for biotechnology worldwide. Ohio, T A Sheets & Co. (1654 Lee Road, Cleveland Heights, Ohio 44118, USA.)

THOMAS, H. 1982. Cable is a vision of the future. The *Guardian, 27 March*, 18.

TOFFLER, A. 1980. The third wave. London, Collins.

CHAPTER 5

THE MANAGEMENT AGENDA

Introduction

1. One of the most succinct summaries of the evolution of industry's environmental agenda emerged recently from the Organisation for Economic Co-operation and Development (OECD). According to Jim MacNeill, director of the OECD environmental programme, 'The first environmental debate focused on environmental pollution. It took off very quickly on a global scale and led, in a remarkably short period of time, to a wide array of institutions, policies and instruments, designed to correct past abuses, reduce pollution and preserve and enhance the environment. Its objectives and the means required to achieve them were both relatively straightforward. They retain their importance, and some evidence suggests that they may even become increasingly relevant in the mid-term future' (MacNeill, 1980).

2. The second debate, he argued, 'which is now under way, asks how the environment can be integrated into our society. It is characterised by an increased emphasis on policies that are anticipatory and preventive, reinforcing those that are reactive and curative. It reflects a heightened awareness in many quarters of the interdependence among economic growth, energy and resource management, product control and environmental quality'. This second debate has not taken off nearly as fast as the first, but it will be increasingly important during the 1980s.

3. MacNeill is not alone in seeing evidence of a third debate, which is 'even more profound'. This third debate 'is based on the view that even anticipatory environmental policies cannot attack the fundamental forces underlying the continuing degradation of the environment. It argues that these forces are set in the personal habits and cultural traditions of our society and in the institutional forms which serve it. It raises questions of alternative lifestyles and alternative growth patterns compatible with the maintenance of a healthy environment'.

4. The World Conservation Strategy encapsulates elements of all three stages of what Max Nicholson has called the 'environmental revolution'. To understand the implications for industry, it may help to consider the policies and guidelines which have already been published on industry's behalf, both nationally and internationally. Some of these go considerably further, it is fair to say, than most UK companies currently

seem minded to, but they do provide a useful series of reference points for assessing industry's current performance — whether that assessment is carried out within industry itself or by outside agencies.

Industrial Codes of Conduct

5. The International Chamber of Commerce (ICC) represents over 5,000 companies and 1,500 professional organisations from about 110 countries. It prepared its first set of environmental guidelines for industry in 1974, and has recently updated them (ICC, 1981). In devising environmental protection measures, the ICC argues, full account must be taken of the importance of human health; of the need to maintain the balance of ecological cycles; of the need to develop substitutes for non-renewable resources; of the cumulative effect on the environment of harmful wastes and other nuisances produced by industry; of the existence of transboundary pollution; of the law of diminishing returns; and of the need to minimise environmental risk, bearing in mind that 'a risk free environment is rarely feasible'.

6. In meeting its new environmental responsibilities, the ICC suggests that industry will need to adapt the ways in which it goes about long range planning, designing and locating plants, selecting processes and designing products. Industry, it stresses, 'should, in addition to the usual elements, take into account the vulnerability of natural ecological systems as well as the challenge created by the finite character of the earth's non-renewable resources. Industry should therefore regularly review its production processes, its procedures for the handling of materials and its products, in order to minimise the possibilities of pollution, to apply the most appropriate pollution prevention and/or abatement techniques, to decrease wherever possible the use of non-renewable resources, including energy, to develop substitutes, to maximise the recycling or re-use of its wastes, and to develop and utilise cleaner technologies'.

7. Interestingly there is no mention of the sustainable exploitation of renewable resources, a gap which needs to be filled in a revised version of the guidelines. As far as products are concerned, however, the ICC advises

that 'industry should assess the potential adverse environmental effects of these products when used by a consumer directly or incorporated by other industries into different products. Responsible efforts should be made to minimise any such effect'.

8. Furthermore, it suggests, 'industry should provide advice to its customers on conservation, [on] re-use and recycling, [and on the] handling, transport, use and disposal of its products. This should encourage the customer to exercise his responsibilities once he takes possession of the product, in full cognisance of its potential impact on the environment and human health'.

9. Industry also has a direct responsibility, the ICC concludes, both 'through its association channels and at company level, to support research into the prevention of adverse environmental effects of discharges on ecological systems and on public health'. Again, no mention of the impact of industrial development or operations on such aspects as ecological processes and genetic diversity.

10. Each company, the ICC insists, 'should promote among its employees an individual sense of environmental responsibility and should educate and encourage employees at all levels to be alert to potential sources of pollution and to sound resource conservation measures within their operations'.

11. In the UK, the Confederation of British Industry (CBI) has published an environmental policy statement urging industry (and trade) to:

(a) appreciate that the objective must be both economic and environmental progress;
(b) continue to minimise any adverse environmental effect of its activities through the appropriate location and design of industrial projects and allied services;
(c) apply good scientific and engineering principles, and to take account of the costs and benefits and international trade implications when assessing the environmental effects of its processes and services;
(d) continue to consult with, inform and assist those responsible for drawing up environmental policies and legislation to ensure that they understand their potential impact on any proposed industrial and commercial developments;
(e) work closely with those implementing agreed environmental policies;
(f) make those who are affected, directly or indirectly, by industrial and commercial activities aware not only of the importance of industry to society, but also of the measures proposed for the protection of the environment;
(g) take account of the views and interests of responsible conservation and environmental groups when planning or carrying out industrial activities; and to
(h) review periodically and update, as necessary, its environmental policies and practices (CBI, 1980).

12. Both the ICC and the CBI excerpts are extracted from longer documents, but it is clear that the ICC goes further towards meeting the objectives of the World Conservation Strategy at present than does the CBI policy statement, which is more tailored to buttressing the current UK approach to land use planning and pollution control. The CBI policy needs updating to take account of the World Conservation Strategy, too. Nonetheless, taken together, these two sets of guidelines represent a useful baseline for industry. In addition, the British Institute of Management has recently published a Code of Conduct for professional managers which includes a supporting guide to good management practice covering some environmental considerations. The manager is urged to:

(a) recognise his (or her) organisation's obligations to its owners, employees, suppliers, customers, users, society and the environment;
(b) make the most effective use of all natural resources and energy resources for the benefit of the organisation and with the minimum detriment to the public interest;
(c) avoid harmful pollution, and wherever economically possible reprocess or recycle waste materials;
(d) ensure that all public communications are true and not misleading; and
(e) be willing to exercise his (or her) influence and skill for the benefit of the society within which the appropriate organisation operates (British Institute of Management, 1981).

13. A rather more helpful checklist for management, however, was published by the BIM several years earlier (British Institute of Management, 1978). This asked the manager:

(a) Do you have an environmental committee or manager with overall responsibility for dealing with pollution problems, etc?
(b) Have you prepared an improvement plan, short- and long-term, concentrating on a limited number of identified priorities?
(c) Do budgetary allocations for environmental projects exist and have these been incorporated into company accounts with an indication of returns when these accrue?
(d) Are you trying to develop your own technologies and methods to overcome these problems?
(e) Have line management, operators and staff been sufficiently trained and educated in the implications of your recycling, pollution control and energy saving programmes?
(f) Do you operate suggestion schemes as a fruitful source of ideas for future improvements?
(g) Are you in contact with local authorities, water authorities and the relevant technical bodies able to advise on future requirements and technical problems?
(h) Are you in touch with international industrial associations and developments in international bodies such as the EEC?

14. Most of these guidelines and checklists are fairly general, however, so it may be helpful to look a little

more closely at the current industrial best practice in relation to policy formulation, product design, process selection and project planning.

Making it Company Policy

15. To give an idea of what an environmental policy can look like at the level of the individual company, consider that which was adopted by BP in October 1980. The policy statement begins: 'It is a primary and continuing policy of the BP Group that in the conduct of its activities it will endeavour to protect the health and safety of its employees, customers and others who may be affected by these activities and endeavour to limit adverse effects on the physical environment in which its activities are carried out' (BP, 1980).

16. To ensure that the policy is implemented, BP defines the following objectives for its management:

(a) to set standards which will at least meet the relevant local statutory requirements for health and safety, product safety and environmental matters, as these may affect its own employees, customers, contractors and their employees and the public at large;

(b) to review and, where appropriate, develop these standards in the light of changes in technology, industry practices and trends in legislation and to sponsor research and development to improve the rationale for the setting of standards;

(c) to cooperate with the appropriate authorities and technical organisations on the formulation of standards and the means for compliance;

(d) to ensure that the potential health and safety factors and environmental effects are assessed for all new products, projects, activities and acquisitions;

(e) to ensure that all employees are properly informed of their responsibilities for health, safety and environmental matters and discharge them effectively, and are encouraged to participate in the prevention of accidents and in the protection of health;

(f) to ensure that contractors working under the operational control of a BP company are informed of its relevant standards, and that appropriate procedures exist for monitoring compliance without detracting from the legal responsibilities of the contractors; and

(g) to ensure that these objectives are being fulfilled through the auditing of the Group's activities.

17. Clearly, as Britain's largest company, BP is in a category of its own, but the general principles underlying its policy can be applied to any industrial company or organisation. Any company considering using the BP policy as a model, however, should seriously consider incorporating further objectives covering the issues raised by the World Conservation Strategy. The nationalised industries, meanwhile, represent a special case and are worth discussing separately.

New Duties for the Nationalised Industries

18. Because of their pervasive influence on the UK economy, and the degree of Government involvement in their day to day running, the nationalised industries — whether they manufacture products or supply basic services such as water and energy — need new terms of reference, attuned to the needs of the 1980s and 1990s and including clear conservation objectives. For example, the revised terms of reference for the water and energy supply industries (which together have a very considerable ecological impact), should include variants of the following fundamental issues:

(a) a continuing basic duty to maintain secure and reliable supplies, although the likelihood of a prolonged period of relatively low economic growth suggests that existing 'planning margins' should be scrutinised carefully and, where possible, revised downwards;

(b) a duty to practice 'demand management' wherever possible, ensuring that water and energy, for example, are used more efficiently instead of automatically meeting new demand by building new dams or power stations;

(c) a duty to develop and market, or to ensure the development and marketing of, new generations of appliances which are more efficient in their use of water, energy and other environmentally significant materials; and

(d) a duty to promote conservation and recycling within the appropriate industry wherever it is economic to do so.

19. These industries should be encouraged to consider conservation before they turn to new supply options. In the water industry, for example, the rate of leakage from the water supply system may already be higher than 30 per cent in some areas, a problem which can only get worse as the water supply system continues to age. The water authorities need to be persuaded of the desirability of devoting more resources to the monitoring and prevention of leakage and other forms of avoidable wastage. Similarly, in the electricity supply industry, greater attention could be paid to conservation and to the more efficient use of fuel (eg by means of combined heat and power schemes) at a time when the Government is pushing forward with a major programme of nuclear power stations.

A New Focus on Product Quality

20. The vetting of the ecological, environmental, and health and safety aspects of both new and existing industrial products is becoming an essential element in the drive to promote product quality. The burden of responsibility on manufacturers and suppliers of products which are actually designed to have a biological effect — such as pesticides or herbicides — is particularly heavy.

21. Research carried out by Oxfam suggests that a number of UK chemical companies have failed to

observe the ICC guidelines in respect of their biocide sales in the developing countries, and it is clearly desirable that the controls on the export of potentially hazardous products such as these should be tight enough to ensure that the adverse impacts associated with such materials are minimised. But there are even more pressing reasons why industry is beginning to have to consider the quality of its products.

22. To survive, let alone flourish, industry is finding that it has to devote an increasing share of its resources to the broad spectrum of activities which cluster under the 'quality control' label. So far, however, progress has been relatively slow. A survey carried out in 1981 by Urwick Orr, management consultants, showed that 87 per cent of the money UK firms spend on achieving quality goes on paying for failures (ie wasteful rejects, rectifying faults and dealing with sub-standard goods returned by customers), while less than 3 per cent is spent on preventing failures happening in the first place (*Economist*, 1981).

23. It has been estimated that the cost of scrap and of defects in the production process is running at more than 10 per cent of the turnover of UK manufacturing industry — a cost penalty of more than £10bn (Lorenz, 1981). By spending 10 times more on preventing faults, Urwick Orr estimated, industry could raise its standards, capturing a larger share of the market, while still halving its expenditure on quality. A prime case of prevention being, in the long run, better (and cheaper) than cure.

24. Product quality is important not only because it implies a more resourceful use of raw materials, but also because the future of the UK economy is in large part dependent on its ability to move into high value-added goods and services, rather than relying on cheap, material-intensive goods for whose markets we shall be forced to compete increasingly with the newly industrialising countries. The car industry is a prime example of an industry which will need to adapt itself to the emerging requirements: for long life, low energy and low pollution products.

25. The evidence, however, suggests that the UK economy is moving in the opposite direction, a trend with worrying economic and environmental implications. Comparing the value per tonne of UK exports with that of our imports, the ratio for the economy as a whole has fallen from an already low 0.6 a decade ago to around 0.4 today. In West Germany, by contrast, the ratio is 1.2, while in Japan it is thought to be even higher.

26. Between 1970 and 1980, the cost of the material inputs to the UK economy rose by about 400 per cent, while output prices rose by less than 300 per cent, so that the ratio of material input prices to output prices rose (ie the position deteriorated) by about one third. The net value added by labour and by capital was, in direct consequence, squeezed — and real net value added is thought to have fallen by about 15 to 20 per cent (Maynard, 1981).

27. Clearly, the time has come for a thorough investigation of the economy's performance in terms of adding value, and for a new emphasis on doing more — and doing it better — with less. As part of this process of reviewing its intake of increasingly expensive raw materials and energy, industry will need to consider its dependence on both non-renewable and the (potentially) renewable resources.

28. The World Conservation Strategy points out that 'many businesses benefit from wild plants and animals, often in ways that may be easily overlooked. For example, alginate compounds from brown seaweeds are used in shampoos, soaps, cosmetics, paints, dyes, paper products, fire-extinguishing foams, building materials (including insulation products, sealing compounds and artificial wood), or the lubricants and coolants used in drilling for oil' (World Conservation Strategy, 1980).

29. Every industry, and every industrial company, should therefore, the Strategy continues: 'analyse its resource base to determine what living resources it uses, and for what purpose, and the extent to which each resource's combination of desired properties, cost and availability is unique to that resource. Each industry should then work with the governments and the other commercial sectors concerned to ensure that the particular plants and animals are exploited sustainably, that their genetic diversity is preserved, and that the ecological processes of which they are a part are maintained'.

30. Energy audits have been carried out by both government agencies (eg the Industrial Energy Thrift Scheme managed by the Department of Industry, and the series of industrial energy audits carried out jointly by the Departments of Energy and Industry) and industry itself, but there remains a considerable gap as far as raw materials are concerned. The Materials Forum has looked at some strategic minerals, as shown in Chapter 2 above but there is no equivalent body investigating future trends in our dependence upon less critical non-renewable or renewable resources. The International Institute for Environment and Development is probably the leading UK-based organisation in this area, but it does not typically focus on industry's performance and needs.

31. The tropical hardwoods trade, covered in Chapter 3 above, is a prime candidate for the development of such raw materials auditing procedures, and would itself benefit from the exercise of reviewing its resource-base in the light of projected future needs and resource availability. Once such raw materials have been acquired by industry, however, the emphasis shifts to the efficiency of their conversion into products.

A New Focus on Process Efficiency

32. A major breakthrough has been achieved in the more progressive parts of industry in moving beyond energy

conservation to a broader concern with energy efficiency — a transition which we have yet to make in relation to raw materials. That said, however, there are a number of companies which have achieved considerable progress in doing more with less and, often, doing it better than they did before. Among the examples covered earlier in this report are Bayer, ICI, Metaltreat and Reed Paper & Board.

33. In environmental circles, however, probably the best known and certainly the most striking example of what can be done to improve process efficiency is that provided by 3M's 'Pollution Prevention Pays' (or 3P) Programme. Recognising that add-on, pollutant-removal technology is unduly expensive and invariably constitutes a drain on industry's own scarce resources, 3M developed a very much more resourceful approach, based on the use of resource conservation oriented technology, where the aim is to prevent waste or pollution at source.

34. Placing the focus squarely on product reformulation, process modification, equipment redesign and the recovery of waste materials for re-use, 3M's employees are encouraged to examine personally the operations for which they are responsible for evidence of any pollution potential and, where this potential exists, to consider ways of dealing with the problem. In effect, 3M has set up the environmental equivalent of the 'quality circles', which are increasingly being used to upgrade the quality of industrial products, by involving all levels of a company's personnel. The criteria adopted for assessing the proposals emerging from these environmental quality circles include the following:
   (a) the project must eliminate or reduce emissions of a pollutant which is currently a problem or has the potential to become a problem;
   (b) the project must provide some monetary benefit to 3M, whether through reduced or deferred pollution control or manufacturing costs, increased sales of an existing or new low pollution product, or other reductions in capital or operating expenditures;
   (c) the project should exhibit, in addition to a reduction in pollution, additional environmental benefits through reductions in energy consumption, the more efficient use of raw materials, or improvements in the use of other natural resources;
   (d) the project should involve a technical accomplishment, innovative approach or novel element of design in meeting its objective; and
   (e) the individuals involved in the project should have made some effort to reach their objectives, rather than simply putting forward an idea.

35. If a project is accepted under the 3P Programme, then all the individuals involved receive an award at a special presentation ceremony. By late 1981, 505 projects had been accepted by 3M companies worldwide, involving a monetary benefit to 3M of over $80m and eliminating 115,400 tonnes of air pollutants, 2,800 tonnes of water pollutants, 870 million gallons of wastewater and 9,400 tonnes of sludges and solid wastes. A total of 44 projects had qualified in 3M's UK plants, contributing a direct monetary benefit of £1.5m and eliminating 1,950 tonnes of air pollutants, 630 tonnes of sludges and solid wastes, and 34 million gallons of contaminated wastewater.

36. Six 3M (UK) projects qualified in 1981: an improvement in solvent recovery, which cut hydrocarbon emissions by 93 tonnes a year and saved £23,000; a reduction in tape waste of 5.5 tonnes a year which saved £140,000 in landfill disposal costs; the elimination of carbon black in polythene bags, eliminating two tonnes of waste a year and saving £5,000; the direct gas firing of a tape coater, which reduced solvent emissions by 200 tonnes a year and saved £96,300; an upgrading of an etch tank, which cut particulate emissions by five tonnes and saved £7,030; and the substitution of a varnish which cut solvent emissions by six tonnes and led to a saving of £14,000.

37. So in 1981 3M eliminated 311.5 tonnes of pollutants and the company saved £285,330, having achieved comparable savings every year since it launched its UK 3P Programme in 1977 (in fact, it achieved savings of £387,634 in 1977 and £499,800 in 1979). Again, just as there is only one BP in the country, so there may be only one 3M, but the general principles of the exercise deserve to be much more widely known and adopted.

A New Focus on Investment Planning

38. The industrial use of environmental impact assessment (EIA) techniques has been another significant success story although, again, the approach has not been as widely adopted as some practitioners had initially hoped. The prospect of an EEC Directive requiring impact assessments for a wide range of industrial projects has served to concentrate the industrial mind, but industry is moving into this area not only because of the 'push' of legislation, but also because of the 'pull' exerted by the growing realisation that EIA can help industry meet its basic objectives of survival, profits and growth.

39. Two extremely useful guides to the experience gained to date have been published: one by the University of Aberdeen's Project Appraisal for Development Control research team (Clark, Bisset and Wathern, 1980) and the other by the Institute of Planning Studies at the University of Nottingham (Petts and Hills, 1982). Another source of detailed case studies of the industrial application of EIA procedures are the ENDS Reports which have investigated major projects undertaken by such industrial developers as AMAX, BP, the British Gas Corporation, British Nuclear Fuels Ltd, the Central Electricity Generating Board, the National Coal Board and the North West Water Authority. Review articles based on this work have appeared in the general literature (Elkington, 1981; 1982).

40. A clear illustration of the benefits which can accrue from a professional application of EIA is the experience of British Gas, which estimated in 1979 that the use of EIA had saved it £30m for a total environmental expenditure of less than £7m.

41. Those companies and other industrial organisations which have evolved EIA procedures have been increasingly conscious that EIA must be a dynamic process, with careful attention being paid to follow-up monitoring of the environment once the project is in operation, together with environmental audits and control systems. BP, which stesses the need for auditing in its environmental policy, recently translated this policy aim into practice with its first review of the environmental performance of a major project which had been the subject of an EIA at the planning stage — the Forties oil field (ENDS, 1982).

42. The purpose of the exercise was:
   (a) to assess the environmental performance of the Forties system in the light of current and anticipated legislation;
   (b) to advise management on the effectiveness of environmental measures, making recommendations for improvement, where appropriate; and
   (c) to comment on the effectiveness and value to management of the environmental assessment procedures applied during the design, construction and operation of the Forties system.

43. The review did not compare the actual impacts with those predicted during the EIA carried out in 1972, although this vital exercise is being undertaken for a wide range of industrial projects by the Project Appraisal for Development Control team at Aberdeen — an exercise funded by the Natural Environmental Research Council. The Aberdeen team is convinced that more must be done to convert EIA into a dynamic process which feeds back into the management process once a project is in operation.

44. Among the projects which will require EIA will be the proposed mining of manganese nodules and other materials from the deep ocean, with UK companies (BP Minerals, Consolidated Goldfields, Rio Tinto Zinc and Royal Dutch Shell, for example) involved in a number of the consortia which are keen to mine the nodules. EIA offers an opportunity for 'lateral thinking' during project planning and investment appraisal, and will need to be applied not only to projects, but also to Government and industrial policies and investment programmes which crystallise out in the shape of particular project proposals. The Commission on Energy and the Environment's analysis of the coal industry's future was a welcome step in this direction (CENE, 1981).

and methods have been developed which now mean that environmental restoration is almost always possible, given the will. Liverpool University's Environmental Advisory Unit (EAU) is a prime example of this new expertise, having helped a wide range of mining and quarrying companies to restore their old workings — and to avoid unnecessary dereliction when developing new projects.

46. Many of the projects undertaken by the EAU have involved areas contaminated with heavy metals, but even relatively uncomplicated land dereliction projects can raise taxing issues. The ARC Wildfowl Centre, for example, developed by Amey Roadstone (ARC) at its Great Lindford gravel workings, near Milton Keynes, started out as a problem: waterfowl introduced to the worked-out areas failed to thrive because the pits were essentially sterile. Such flooded pits can take up to 100 years to regenerate a viable ecosystem, so ARC has developed methods —with the Game Conservancy — designed to accelerate this process. The lining of the pit bottoms with barley straw, for instance, proved one effective way to stimulate invertebrate populations — a vital food resource for both waterfowl and fish (see Figure 11, p 77).

47. Other major industries must follow the same course, creating new wildlife habitats, promoting both wildlife diversity and abundance, with a view to providing new educational and leisure resources which will, in time, generate new flows of income. The Norfolk Broads, once extensive peat workings, show what can be achieved, given very long periods of time: the problem will be in ensuring that industry does what is necessary to speed up the process to cope with the pace of events today. (The Broads, incidentally, are not a happy example, given the way in which their ecological quality is now being eroded by agricultural, urban and recreational pressures.)

48. As a final example of what can be done to integrate conservation with development, consider the $500m chlor-alkali and petrochemical plant which ICI Australia has been developing near Point Wilson, in Victoria. A particular cause for concern was the fact that the nearby marshes and lagoons represented the major winter quarters of one of the world's most endangered species: the Orange-bellied Parrot. ICI, however, commissioned in-depth studies of the bird's distribution and feeding ecology and supported the World Wildlife Fund's project which successfully located the bird's remote breeding ground and, for the first time, studied its breeding habits. Serious, non-industrial threats to the parrot's future were also identified and are now being controlled — a clear illustration of the theme developed in the World Conservation Strategy.

A New Focus on Environmental Restoration

45. Although industrial development historically has been associated with extensive dereliction, new techniques

Educating the Rising Generation of Managers

49. There is a real and growing need for schemes designed to encourage industrial managements to focus

Figure 11. **Automatic grain feeder being adjusted at the ARC Wildfowl Centre**
(source: ARC, 1981)

on the environmental problems identified earlier in this report. We need award schemes; we need more effective dissemination of case histories of both successes and failures; and we need a much more effective environmental input into management training.

50. We also need much better mechanisms for ensuring that the guidelines described earlier in this chapter are adopted and enforced. So far, at least, the guidelines have no teeth whatsoever. They depend for their effectiveness on media pressure, yet it is often very difficult indeed to get reliable information on just what UK companies are doing overseas which could have an impact on the three main objectives of the World Conservation Strategy.

51. An equally worrying problem is the slow rate at which new skills and new perspectives are diffusing through industrial organisations. The work carried out by ENDS since 1978 suggests strongly that the degree to which a given company or industrial organisation adopts and enforces environmental codes of practice — or simply becomes more environmentally sensitive — is very much related to personalities. The right person with the right perspective and the necessary authority can work wonders: there remain all too few of such people. This is a theme which was taken up during the practitioners' debate phase of this report.

52. A recent study carried out by Professor David Norburn of the London Business School concluded that 'our [business] leaders are a product of the 1960s and 1970s, when the rules of the game were different. It can be argued that their management style is based on outdated experience' (Norburn, 1981). Norburn, in fact, went further than that, producing a good deal of survey data suggesting that the experience and inclinations of many senior managers are inappropriate to the needs of the coming decade. This finding represents a problem both in ensuring the rapid build up of the 'sunrise industries' and in converting industrial managers to new styles of operation based on the principles outlined above.

53. Sir Ieuan Maddock, who was chief scientist at the Department of Industry, has pointed out that 'the ability to forget — to shed past habits, attitudes, techniques and capital resources — is often at least as important as the ability to learn' (Maddock, 1982). Managers, engineers and scientists talk in terms of 'learning curves' when 'forgetting curves' can be just as significant for all levels of industry.

54. The rising generation of entrepreneurs, managers, corporate planners, research scientists, engineers, consultants and all the other skilled people whose commitment and expertise will be needed to effect the transition to more sustainable forms of economic activity, are typically — although by no means uniformly — more sympathetic to the goals expressed in the World Conservation Strategy. The problem will be to ensure that they are fed with enough information on the environmental implications of their professional activities and decisions — and in a climate of opinion which ensures

that they use that information to develop new, sounder strategies.

55. The business schools, management colleges, university and polytechnic courses and other training schemes which have grown up in recent decades only rarely use environmental themes in their course modules, despite the fact that there is now a wealth of material which could be tailored to suit their needs. A vital element in the implementation of the Conservation and Development Programme for the UK will be the development of such modules and their use in the training of those who will shape our industrial future.

56. At the same time, however, the 3M example shows that a great deal can be achieved at the level of the individual company and, in many respects, this approach may well pay much more immediate dividends than that outlined in paragraph 54 above, although short-, medium- and long-term strategies will all be needed to ensure that the message goes home and that the appropriate new management approaches are developed.

57. All the success stories outlined here have depended, ultimately, on the enthusiasm, commitment and expertise of the entire spectrum of industrial personnel, and it would appear that an increasing emphasis on workforce participation in industrial management, as in 'quality circles' or 'action learning programmes', will be vitally important in adapting our economy to the environmental constraints and opportunities identified earlier. The support of the trade union movement, which is discussed in Chapter 6, will clearly be indispensable in initiating and sustaining this process of transition.

References

BRITISH INSTITUTE OF MANAGEMENT. 1978. Environment – Management's responsibility. London, BIM. (British Management House, Parker Street, WC2B 5PT.)

BRITISH INSTITUTE OF MANAGEMENT. 1981. Code of conduct and supporting guides to good management practice. London, BIM.

BRITISH PETROLEUM. 1980. BP briefing document on environmental protection. BP Environmental Control Centre.

CLARK, B, Bissett, R and Wathern, P. 1980. Environmental impact assessment: a bibliography with abstracts. London, Mansell Bowker.

COMMISSION ON ENERGY AND THE ENVIRONMENT (CENE). 1981. Coal and the environment. London, HMSO.

CONFEDERATION OF BRITISH INDUSTRY. 1980. British industry and the environment. London, CBI. (Centre Point, 103 New Oxford Street, WC1A 1DU.)

ECONOMIST, THE. 1981. Getting British quality up to standard. 31 October, 91.

ELKINGTON, J B. 1981. Converting industry to environmental impact assessment. Environmental Conservation, vol 8, 1, Spring, 23-30.

ELKINGTON, J B. 1982. Industrial applications of environmental impact assessment. Journal of General Management, vol 7, 3, Spring, 23-33.

ENVIRONMENTAL DATA SERVICES. 1982. The forties environmental review: BP build environmental assessment into project management. ENDS Report 85, February, 9-11.

INTERNATIONAL CHAMBER OF COMMERCE. 1981. Environmental guidelines for industry. Paris, ICC. (38 Cours Albert 1er, 75008 Paris, France. 261-85-97; Telex 650770.) The CBI is the UK focus for the ICC, at Centre Point, 103 New Oxford Street, London WC1A 1DU (01-240 5558).

LORENZ, C. 1981. When survival depends on a quality product. Financial Times, 25 November, 16.

MACNEILL, J. 1980. Environmental policy in transition. OECD, 61. Observer, March 1979, 40-41.

MADDOCK, SIR I. 1982. Why industry must learn to forget. New Scientist, 11 February, 368-370.

MAYNARD, G. 1981. Why so many lost their jobs in the seventies. The Times, 1 September, 17.

NORBURN, D. 1981. British corporate leaders. London, Korn/Ferry International. (2-4 King Street, St James's, SW1.)

PETTS, J and HILLS, P. 1982. Environmental assessment in the UK: a preliminary guide. Nottingham, Institute of Planning Studies, University of Nottingham. (Paton House, University Park, NG7 2RD.)

WORLD CONSERVATION STRATEGY. 1980. ICUN.

CHAPTER 6
JOBS WITH A FUTURE

Introduction

1. The trade unions, both in the UK and in most other European countries, are in for a difficult decade. Long-term structural unemployment seems almost guaranteed for much of Europe, with even the West German economic miracle appearing slightly frayed at the edges. For the first time since the early 1920s, the unions are facing a significant shrinkage in their membership — and, consequently, in their income and political influence.

2. At least one million trade unionists joined the dole queues during the first three years after the UK Conservative government took office in 1979. Between June 1979 and January 1981, 1.3 million jobs were lost from the manufacturing sector, representing nearly 19 per cent of the workers in that sector. One-third of all metal workers and one-quarter of all textile workers lost their jobs during the same period. Between 1979 and 1981, the Transport and General Workers' Union lost 20 per cent of its members; the AEUW, which represents engineering workers, lost 16 per cent; and even the white collar conglomerate, the Association of Scientific, Technical and Managerial Staffs (ASTMS), lost 8 per cent. By April 1982, the Department of Employment was estimating that two million jobs had been lost since mid-1979, 60 per cent of these having been lost in the manufacturing sector — even though this sector accounted for only a quarter of total employment.

3. It is generally assumed that most of the jobs lost in the manufacturing sector will never return. By 1985, it is suggested, the UK will have more white-collar workers than it has blue-collar workers — a trend which is causing considerable concern to the major traditional unions. Having achieved a 10 per cent net increase in its penetration of the UK workforce during the 1970s, the TUC is now faced with the possibility that the 55 per cent penetration achieved by 1979 will, in retrospect, prove to have been its high water mark.

4. That said, however, the trade unions are by no means a spent force, although most of them will need to rethink radically their role as the UK economy undergoes profound structural change — a fact recognised in the TUC's plan for economic recovery, published in 1981, which focused on the need to promote the microelectronics and biotechnology industries, and to convert older, 'core' industries to the new technologies. The direction of structural change is tending to favour industries with non-unionised workforces.

5. Five years of little or no growth represent a major watershed in the history of the UK economy. The restoration of a high employment industrial manufacturing base seems highly unlikely, while the new industries will not offer the same 'commanding heights', to be fought over by the forces of capital and labour. And the new microelectronics firms, and other similar advanced technology exercises, may be light on the environment — but they will also be light on employment, too.

6. The implications of de-industrialisation and of (it is to be hoped) re-industrialisation for the traditional centres of union power are very significant indeed, yet evidence suggests that the very nature of most unions is such that they will feel happier reacting to events, fighting each change as it comes, rather than trying to get an overview of the direction of change and developing a strategy to ensure that their contribution is a positive one. Yet there are some signs that, embedded within some unions, there are centres of constructive — even visionary — thinking, and the central question is: how can these small seeds of change be nurtured?

An Uncertain Future

7. Environmentalists have increasingly been focusing their attention on the employment prospect, recognising that prolonged, high levels of unemployment could have a highly corrosive effect on the environmental achievements of the 1960s and 1970s. This concern was perhaps best summarised by Dr John Davoll of the Conservation Society when he argued that the industrial prospect may itself be so grave as to deny any chance of an orderly transition to more sustainable life styles. He suggested: 'It seems likely that industrial failure (at present very much on the cards for the UK) will not lead to a bland post-industrial future, but to a collapsed industrial society, sour, disillusioned and prone to political extremism' (ENDS, 1980).

8. Groups such as the European Environmental Bureau have held conferences to discuss ways in which an

increased emphasis on conservation could generate new forms of employment, while the Ecology Party, on the political front, has produced a policy document analysing the employment implications of a sustainable, steady state economy (Ecology Party, 1981). As the Ecology Party sees it, 'The challenge is to achieve an orderly transition to an era in which we can cope with substantially reduced opportunities for conventional employment. It is simply not an option at the moment to stand out against the introduction of the new technology . . . Moreover, there are considerable advantages to be derived from being able to generate increased levels of goods and services from significantly reduced inputs of energy and raw materials'.

9. The Ecology Party is not alone in seeing the rampant inflation which has afflicted most developed economies in recent years as a symptom of a wider problem: the pursuit of non-sustainable economic growth which, because it must ultimately consume the planet's natural capital, is inherently inflationary.

10. According to this view, 'all nations will have to learn how to manage the demands of their people in a stable-state economy. The characteristics of such an economy are clear: reduced industrial throughput, greater self-reliance and sustainability through largely decentralised economic activity, maximised use of renewable resources and conservation of non-renewable resources, a far-reaching redistribution of wealth, land and the means of production, with the possibility of more fulfilling, personally satisfying work, all set within a more cooperatively-based framework, and enhanced by the use of new technologies where they complement the above features' (Ecology Party, 1981).

11. This message is, in many respects, directly counter to the mainstream thinking of most trade unions, although occasionally it is possible to discern glimmerings of a new perspective breaking through in the pronouncements of some of the more forward thinking union leaders.

12. 'Quite clearly, the increase in the real price of energy has shown that raw material dependence is a reality and that [the] exhaustion of raw materials would be a tragedy', argued Clive Jenkins and Barrie Sherman of ASTMS in a recent book (Jenkins and Sherman, 1981). 'The time lag between the price increase and the use of alternative energy sources is also clearly a long one and when the stocks of iron ore, copper and even renewable resources, like trees, are taken into account, the future becomes alarmingly uncertain.'

13. Jenkins and Sherman stressed that: 'No government, indeed no industrialised society, takes its renewable resource policy seriously; nor, in the United Kingdom at least, are alternative energy sources fully explored or researched. The newer techniques, especially micro-electronics and genetic engineering, open up whole vistas in tapping renewable resources for fuel, energy and food and part of our thesis is that these are precisely the areas where their application will do the greatest good to the greatest number of people. Perhaps one of the slogans of a New Zealand fringe political party could help concentrate the mind: "We do not inherit the earth from our parents — we borrow it from our children". To encourage demand incessantly will only fulfil the doom-watchers' fears, even if, in the last analysis, the whole process grinds to a shuddering halt'.

14. ASTMS, however, dismisses the low growth, low output and low demand vision of the future out of hand, arguing that it 'would be an insult to those not needed and, furthermore, would be totally unworkable' (Jenkins and Sherman, 1981). The problem seems to be that, even if the various sectors described in Chapter 4 above enjoy very rapid growth indeed, as we argue they must, they are very unlikely to generate sufficient employment to make good the jobs lost in the increasingly obsolescent traditional sectors of the economy.

15. In fact, there is increasing evidence that the main areas showing employment growth will be well to one side of the mainstream economy, at least as traditionally understood. James Robertson, of Turning Point, has drawn on work carried out by a joint European-North American task force, based at the European Foundation for Management Development, to suggest that there will be at least four main sectors of employment, the more conventional of which will continue to shed jobs for the foreseeable future (Robertson and Pritchard, 1981).

16. The new production technologies, Robertson points out, including information technologies and the micro-processor, are likely to lead to more highly automated, more capital-intensive mass production processes. Simultaneously, however, they will almost certainly lead to more decentralised working and living, giving rise to at least four distinct sectors of employment. Sector A will be capital-intensive, highly automated and highly productive, including the large manufacturing industries and commercial services such as airlines, international banking and telecommunications. Sector B, on the other hand, will be the labour-intensive, large scale service sector, including such services as education and health.

17. Owing to automation, growing competition from both the newly industrialising countries and from other developed countries, and a continuing fall in demand for the products of many industries, Sector A is expected to continue shedding jobs, while Sector B — which includes not only the public sector services, but also the leisure industry and such information workers as computer specialists, scientific researchers, broadcasters and journalists — will almost certainly be constrained by cuts in public spending, suggesting that it would be realistic to assume relatively low aggregate growth at best, and possibly even a degree of contraction in the long term.

18. The expected growth in employment, in this formulation, will need to come from Sector C (a revived, small scale, entrepreneurial, local sector, supported by

new institutions and by local enterprise trusts) and Sector D (a revived household and neighbourhood sector, in which work is generally informal and either unpaid or marginally paid, and often difficult to distinguish from leisure).

19. Private sector industry is beginning to recognise this trend as both a problem and an opportunity. In March 1982, for example, the British Steel Corporation, the Co-operative Bank, Pilkington Brothers, Sun Life Assurance and Control Data UK, a subsidiary of the fourth largest US computer company, each subscribed £200,000 to set up a new enterprise called Worldtech Ventures. The idea behind the scheme is to set up and/or support new business ventures in areas which have been badly hit by de-industrialisation and the ensuing unemployment problems, such as the north-east, and the north-west of England, and Scotland and Wales. Control Data has already set up similar ventures in Sweden, Italy and Israel, providing financial support, management assistance, education and training, and access to technical and other services which might otherwise be beyond the reach of such small scale enterprises.

20. One of the new breed of companies set up to provide the infrastructure required by the new small scale, local industries is Regeneration, which has transformed old industrial buildings, a fair number of them owned by the British Steel Corporation, into complexes of low-rental small workshops for craftsmen and light industrial users. Apart from its base at the Clerkenwell Workshops in London, Regeneration has had a hand in the setting up of related projects in Acton, Wandsworth, Battersea, Camberwell, Spitalfields, Limehouse, Rotherhithe, the Isle of Dogs, Greenwich, Stratford, Islington, Hackney Wick, Ayrshire, Glasgow, Liverpool (Toxteth), Iron-bridge, Brynmawr, Cardiff, Southampton, Shoreditch and Teesside.

21. This new emphasis on local economies and small scale enterprise is showing every sign of succeeding, but the prospect of a new work order is presenting the unions with some fairly intractable problems. Typically, their major concern has been not with the interests of the employed as a whole, but with the narrow, sectional interests of their own members.

22. As James Robertson (see paragraphs 15-16 above) puts it, 'their goals have been to preserve employment, and to improve the pay and conditions attaching to employment. They have not campaigned for part-time employment for people who wanted it. Nor have they concerned themselves directly with the interests of people not in employment. It has never been their aim to enable people to undertake useful and rewarding work outside regular employment. Indeed, they have understandably seen that kind of work as open to exploitation by unscrupulous employers and as a threat to the interests of their members' (Robertson and Pritchard, 1981).

23. If, however, the trade union movement intends to stay at the forefront of the nation's decision making, it is going to have to take a much broader view of its constituency and of its best interests. At the same time, too, it will need to pay much greater attention to the small number of centres of progressive union thinking in this field, such as the Centre for Alternative Industrial and Technological Systems (CAITS), which arose out of the Lucas Aerospace Shop Stewards Committee's attempts to push through an alternative corporate plan.

Alternative Industrial Frameworks

24. CAITS has been a good example of what can be done to promote the involvement of workers in the development of alternative industrial products offering advantages in social, economic and environmental terms. CAITS has been involved, in one way or another, in a variety of workers' plans, developed in such companies as Lucas Aerospace, Vickers and Dunlop. Generally speaking, these plans have set out to identify socially and environmentally responsible products which could provide income for ailing industrial plants (CAITS, undated).

25. And that is part of the problem. So far, at least, trade union initiatives in this field have tended to occur at the eleventh hour, once it has been rumoured or announced that a factory is to close. Such initiatives are obviously battling against impossible odds from the very start. The real need is for a greater degree of industrial democracy, with the workforce involved in the development of a company's business on a continuous basis. If, in addition, sufficient thought is given to the design of new technologies at an early stage, avoiding the dehumanising and deskilling characteristics of many of the technologies deployed since 1945, then there is a good chance that industrial relations will improve.

26. There was no guarantee that the Lucas Aerospace Combine's alternative corporate plan would have turned the company's business prospects around, but the very fact that it was prepared underscores the real potential interest of the entire industrial community in ensuring that the UK economy has a future. But, so far at least, CAITS has had relatively little success — at least in terms of the scale of the overall problems — in denting trade union conservatism. The traditionally minded union leaders have not been enthusiastic supporters of the new wave of worker initiatives.

27. CAITS, at the time of writing, is looking around for a new base, and feels very much under pressure. But, at the same time, a new unit has been set up at Lanchester Polytechnic — the Unit for the Development of Appropriate Products (UDAP) — with some £140,000 in seed money. And there are other centres of excellence in related fields on which the trade union movement, if it was so minded, could draw.

28. One of these is the Intermediate Technology Development Group (ITDG), which has traditionally focused its efforts on the developing countries, but with an increasing eye in recent years to the possibilities for applying similar approaches in the UK. ITDG, for example, has been pioneering the development of Local Enterprise Trusts. It has also begun publishing a series of case study reports aimed at establishing a coherent framework for the transition to what has been called the 'conserver economy'. The first of these reports, which are seen as building blocks for an 'Alternative Industrial Framework for the UK', focuses on the brewing industry, an early form of biotechnology. In particular, it reviews the revival of craft brewing, with some 60 craft breweries (ie producing less than 10,000 barrels a year) now in operation (Bollard, 1982).

29. In addition, ITDG is pursuing its plans for a Schumacher Centre for Technology Choice, having launched an appeal during 1980. The aim of the Schumacher Centre will be to develop and promote new technologies and enterprises which reduce demands on raw materials and energy, and which open up possibilities for decentralisation. Examples of such technologies which are appropriate for the Third World may be found in a recent ITDG publication, 'Work from waste: recycling wastes to create employment' (Vogler, 1982).

30. To restore a modicum of growth and meet the objectives of the World Conservation Strategy, UK industry must learn to make more with less, involving increases in productivity which, all too often, is seen as a threat to jobs. To date, at least, the unions have allowed themselves to become locked into a decaying industrial economy, and, along with successive generations of investors, industrialists and managers, they have failed to come to grips with the need for real cooperation in laying the foundations for the industrial regeneration of the UK.

31. The vital role of the shopfloor in achieving real industrial change and progress in both economic and environmental terms needs to be recognised fully. Companies such as 3M (see Chapter 5 above) never could have implemented their pollution control policies without the willing and active support of their workforces. The management of UK industry will need to be much more imaginative if it is to succeed in recruiting the confidence and support of the shopfloor in achieving sustainable development and sustainable employment. But, for the relationship to be one between equals, the unions will need to absorb the messages which are coming out of units such as CAITS and Lanchester Polytechnic's UDAP.

Conservation Works

32. The TUC should consider ways in which it might improve upon recent calls for a new form of national

service, as a means of providing constructive work for those among the unemployed young who want it — emphasising not military service, but a wide range of direct and indirect community services. According to estimates produced by Enrico Colombatto of the London School of Economics, such a programme could provide between 847,000 and 1,768,000 jobs, easily accommodating the 900,000 or so young people who leave school every year (Colombatto, 1981).

33. Among the areas of activity which could be covered are the care of the elderly (providing a minimum of 250,000 jobs), hospital work and other health care (35,000), education (250,000), environmental conservation (52,000), conservation projects in urban areas (203,000) and skills development (37,100). Thus for the minimum level of programme proposed, nearly a quarter of a million jobs could come from conservation related activities.

34. The unions have tended to view such proposals as direct threats to their members, assuming that the Government and other employers would use such a scheme as a means of getting labour 'on the cheap'. But, at a time when the structural trends in the economy suggest that the emerging post-industrial society is unlikely to provide sufficient employment, at least as that word has traditionally been understood, the unions will need to recognise a wider responsibility to those who will find it near impossible to find work. Schemes such as these would also provide full-time employment for supervisors, team leaders and the skilled craftspeople who can direct, say, inner city rehabilitation projects.

35. As Ian Bradley recalls, 'one of the first actions of Franklin Roosevelt when he became President of the USA in 1933, in the midst of the worst depression this century, was to set up the Civilian Conservation Corps. The corps grew from zero to a quarter of a million in three months, and was responsible, among many other things, for planting two billion trees, covering 21 million acres, more than half the area now under forest in the United States. Nearly 40 million acres of farm land were saved from erosion' (Bradley, 1982).

36. The social, economic and environmental benefits of such a programme are such that it should be pursued as a matter of urgent national priority. But its long-term success will depend, to a considerable degree, on the extent to which it can win the support of the unions. In order to move towards such support, it is vital that the unions be closely involved in the implementation phase of the Conservation and Development Programme for the UK.

Some Unresolved Issues

37. In the final analysis, the trade union movement may well decide that there are specific details in existing proposals which it cannot live with. That is the nature of public discourse. But, if this is the case, then the onus

will lie rather more squarely on the TUC to come up with a viable alternative plan of action which will meet the same objectives.

38. Meanwhile, the promotion of the Sunrise Seven could well aggravate our structural unemployment problems, given that (except, perhaps, for energy conservation and environmental services) they have tended to be less employment-intensive than traditional industries. This report does not discuss the implications of this trend in any great detail, but recognises it as one of the most pressing issues of our time. To build a sustainable society split into two camps, ie, those who have work and those who will never have an opportunity to work, is clearly unacceptable. The new core industries will need promoting, whatever happens, but we must simultaneously think very seriously indeed about ways in which the social implications of this process can be resolved equitably.

39. And there is another issue here which has been drawn out in the practitioners' debate phase. The newer industries are showing a very marked preference, throughout Europe, to locate near new centres of technological and economic gravity which often do not overlap geographically with those areas experiencing industrial decline and structural unemployment. They seem likely, then, to accentuate the process of regional decline. Past attempts at persuading industry to locate or relocate in the depressed regions of the country have not been distinguished with any great success, and the question must be asked whether it might not be better to encourage these new activities to locate where it makes real economic sense for them to do so.

40. These new companies are looking for pools of skilled labour, for skills which the depressed regions typically do not possess in any great degree. If decisions are taken to push new industry into the regions, we must ensure that the skills infrastructure is there — which raises the question whether a greater proportion of regional aid might not be directed into the appropriate skills training. The Manpower Services Commission has about 100 skill-developing centres, each of which turns out perhaps 400 'graduates' a year from courses lasting 26 weeks. This is a vital exercise, but so far it is only scratching the surface of the problem.

41. Given the success of the Welsh Development Agency and the Scottish Development Agency in attracting new industries into their respective regions, should we not also have development agencies for the various depressed regions — such as in England in the north-west or north-east? This idea, of moving the development agency approach into England, has been fiercely resisted, but the structural unemployment problems discussed earlier in this chapter will make such innovative approaches increasingly indispensable.

References

BOLLARD, A. 1982. Pint-sized production: small firms in the brewing industry. *Alternative Industrial Framework for the UK, report no 1*. London, Intermediate Technology Development Group.

BRADLEY, I. 1982. A new national service: the way to find a million jobs. *The Times, 1 April*.

CENTRE FOR ALTERNATIVE INDUSTRIAL AND TECH— NOLOGICAL SYSTEMS (CAITS). Undated. A brief review of workers' plans.

COLOMBATTO, E. 1981. Nationwide social service: a proposal for the 1980s. London School of Economics discussion paper.

ECOLOGY PARTY. 1981. Working for a future: an ecological approach to employment. London, Ecology Party. (36-38 Clapham Road, SW9.)

ENVIRONMENTAL DATA SERVICES. 1980. Environmentalism into the 1980s. *ENDS Report 41, January*, 8-11.

JENKINS, C and SHERMAN, B. 1981. The leisure shock. Eyre Methuen.

ROBERTSON, J and PRITCHARD, A. 1981. The redistribution of work. *Turning Point paper no 1*. Ironbridge, Turning Point. (Spring Cottage, 9 New Road, Shropshire TF8 7AU. 095-245 2224.)

VOGLER, J. 1982. Work from waste: recycling wastes to create employment. London, Intermediate Technology Development Group.

CHAPTER 7

SUMMARY AND RECOMMENDATIONS

Introduction

1. Overall, the outlook for reducing the adverse impacts on ecological processes, genetic diversity and sustainable development associated with the operations of UK trade and industry appears to be fairly optimistic. However, much will depend on the climate of opinion within which industry operates. Given the nature of competition, there are limits to how far any given company or industrial organisation can move ahead of its competitors, at least where its achievements increase its costs in relation to those of its competitors.

2. But there is no question, meanwhile, that we face very considerable problems which will require our best efforts, over a considerable time span, to address with any hope of success. We have embarked on the transition sketched out in the introductory paragraphs of Chapter 5, p 71, but the process of moving from the first into the second and third stages is likely to be protracted and politically fraught.

3. The various mini case studies included in the previous six chapters of this report strongly suggest that environmental considerations can be taken on board by industry and can, in many instances, actually help in improving the efficiency of industrial operations against conventional accounting yardsticks. But the achievements presented here were in large part motivated by the body of legislation which has evolved both nationally and internationally: this has provided the brief to which trade and industry has responded. It is important that we maintain momentum in the environmental field, whether by way of legislation or other means.

4. It is vitally important that all legislation be based on sound science (which industry must do everything in its power to help make available) and that it should be cost effective. That said, however, UK industry should recognise its responsibilities in relation to the objectives of the World Conservation Strategy and do everything within its powers to ensure that economic development, whether it be in the UK or overseas, is carried out on a sustainable basis. In some instances, this inevitably will mean more controls, a high proportion of which will need to be evolved by means of international co-operation, through such agencies as the EEC, the OECD and the UN. Industry should play its part in ensuring that such controls do what they are designed to do, and in a cost effective manner.

5. Although many of the problems identified in the World Conservation Strategy are found predominantly in the developing countries, they may reflect economic relationships, sometimes built up over considerable periods of time, both within such countries and between them and the developed world. These relationships are in a constant state of evolution and will need to evolve further to reflect the imperatives defined in the World Conservation Strategy. There is no easy formula, however, for ensuring sustainable development and the conclusion of this report is that industry will need to play a central role if economic development is to be put onto an increasingly sustainable footing.

6. Overall, three main objectives emerge from the industrial Review Group's deliberations. These are outlined below, together with a number of recommendations designed to ensure that the objectives are met. Briefly stated, however, the recommendations relate to:
   (a) the need to ensure that all decisions and programmes are based on sound science and that the various problems and related environmental variables are kept under constant review;
   (b) the need to improve the performance of existing UK trade and industry in relation to ecological processes, genetic diversity and sustainable development; and
   (c) the need to provide strategic direction for the re-orientation of the UK economy, dropping environment-intensive industries and technologies in favour of those which are more environmentally sound, a process which (as Chapters 2, 3, 4 and 5 above have shown) is already under way.

Objective 1

7. The first objective is *to ensure the provision of accurate, up to date information on the nature and scale of environmental problems*, with a particular emphasis on any trends, especially where they affect, or could affect, the viability of ecological processes, genetic diversity and the potential for sustainable development.

8. The constraints in this area are considerable and growing more problematic as the recession continues. Government is cutting back both on its domestic

resources in the environmental field and on its international environmental commitments, as are many industrial organisations. The slowing pace of legislation and regulation in the environmental field is encouraging some industrial organisations to downgrade the priority accorded to some of the more conventional environmental considerations, while very few organisations have yet spent much time considering the implications of the issues, problems and opportunities identified in the World Conservation Strategy for their own operations.

9. To ensure that sufficient information continues to be generated on these known issues and problems, and that new issues and problems (including international transfers of hazardous wastes, the export of inappropriate chemicals, acid precipitation, the effect of chlorofluorocarbons and other materials on the ozone layer, and the build up in the atmosphere of carbon dioxide — a process illustrated in Figures 12 and 13, see p 86) are properly taken into account, we recommend that:

Recommendation 1
Industry should continue to invest in research on environmental issues, problems and opportunities, supporting and properly funding programmes both at the level of individual companies and other industrial organisations, and at the level of the trade and industrial associations.

Recommendation 2
Industry should collaborate with the appropriate international organisations and authorities to ensure that existing controls are met and that new controls are evolved in a rational, scientifically informed and cost effective manner.

Recommendation 3
Industrial companies and sectors whose direct or indirect influence is significant in relation to the three main objectives of the World Conservation Strategy should review their operations to identify existing and potential future issues, problems and opportunities, and undertake programmes of work designed to ensure that the issues are properly understood, the problems resolved over a reasonable time scale and the opportunities exploited.

Recommendation 4
The OECD should undertake a review of the implications of the OECD region's trade with all its trading partners, providing an up to date and statistically reliable database on the impacts on priority ecological processes, ecological diversity and on the potential for sustainable development.

Recommendation 5
The various pollution control agencies, including the Department of the Environment, the Alkali Inspectorate and local authority pollution control units should review the wider environmental implications of their strategies. They should adopt a best practicable environmental means approach, ensuring that local environmental

gains are not bought at the expense of remote environmental impacts.

Recommendation 6
Industry, through its own efforts, should help develop a climate of opinion both in the UK and, even more urgently, in the developing world, favouring patterns of investment and development which are compatible with the objectives of the World Conservation Strategy.

Recommendation 7
The initiative of the Department of the Environment's Central Directorate on Environmental Pollution in carrying out research on the strategic environmental implications of industrial and technological change (see Chapter 2 paragraphs 24 to 34, pp 47 - 48) is welcome — and this strategic perspective should be further developed through the 1980s.

Objective 2

10. The second objective is *to upgrade industry's environmental resources,* in order to ensure that its domestic and international performance is consistent with the objectives of the World Conservation Strategy.

11. The main constraint, again, is that the continuing recession and the reduced impetus behind environmental policy and legislation domestically have both contributed to a reallocation of priorities within industry, with environmental concerns slipping further down the rank order. This problem will only fully yield to pressure when the recession lifts, although, given that this may well take longer than most people would hope, it is essential that steps be taken immediately by all industrial organisations to ensure that their environmental performance does not deteriorate.

12. To ensure that the considerations outlined in this report are taken fully into account by UK trade and industry, we recommend that:

Recommendation 8
Industrial companies and organisations should revise their environmental policies to take into account the objectives of the World Conservation Strategy and, where such policies do not already exist, ensure that they are established and implemented. Some guidance on the drafting of such policies may be found in Chapter 5 (see paragraphs 5 to 19, pp 71 - 73).

Recommendation 9
Both the International Chamber of Commerce and the Confederation of British Industry should revise their environmental policies and guidelines (see Chapter 5 paragraphs 5 to 19, pp 71 - 73) to take into account the new responsibilities defined for trade and industry in the World Conservation Strategy. The OECD is also thinking of drafting a set of guidelines for adoption by

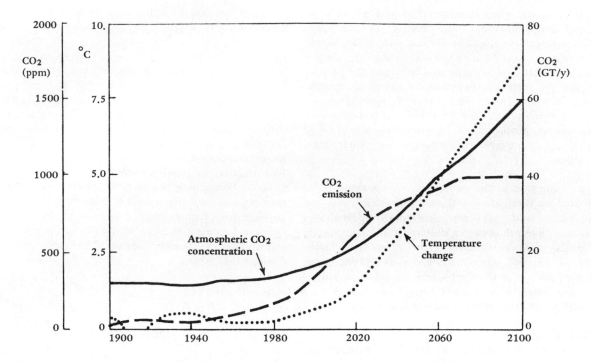

Figure 12. An estimate of the 'greenhouse effect' likely to be associated with a 'worst case' coal burn scenario, involving a seven-fold increase in the world coal burn
(source: Earthscan, 1981)

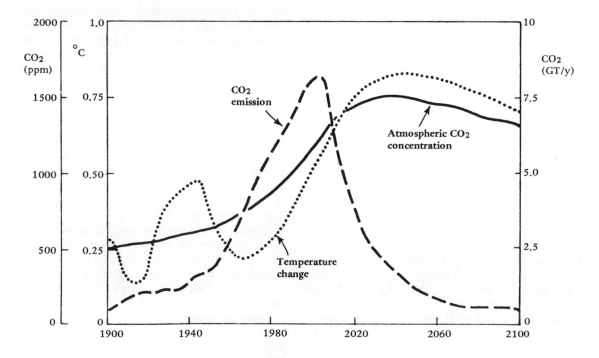

Figure 13. An estimate of the 'greenhouse effect' likely to be associated with a low fossil fuel, high energy scenario
(source: Earthscan, 1981)

(These diagrams are only indicative and it hardly needs pointing out that a nuclear future would not be without its environmental problems.)

its Environment Committee, possibly in 1984, a thought process which industry should encourage and assist. These guidelines, however, are conspicuously weak at present and require considerable effort on the part of all parties to ensure that their effectiveness is monitored, and that infractions are identified and stopped.

Recommendation 10
Industry should consider adopting new forms of environmental accounting, with regular statements published in the annual reports of companies and other organisations.

Recommendation 11
Industry should work with government, both domestically and internationally, to develop the concept of a 'resources tax', as proposed by the World Bank (see Chapter 3 paragraph 31 p 56), to be levied on ecologically sensitive industrial raw materials, with the proceeds being used to fund proper research and development work designed to put the exploitation of the appropriate resources onto a sustainable footing.

Recommendation 12
Industry should support the full implementation of the Washington Convention (CITES), and should press for its extension to cover endangered populations rather than only species, with a new emphasis on the maintenance of populations rather than just the prevention of extinction (see Chapter 3 paragraphs 8 to 13 pp 52 - 53).

Recommendation 13
Industry should review constantly its dependence on non-renewable and renewable resources and, in the case of renewable resources, should consider methods of ensuring that their genetic diversity is preserved, with an emphasis both on gene-banks and on *in situ* conservation — with the latter a prime candidate for industrial sponsorship (see Recommendation 17 below).

Recommendation 14
Industry should support the wider adoption of environmental impact assessment (see Chapter 5 paragraphs 38 to 44 pp 75 - 76) and product testing techniques (see Chapter 5 paragraphs 20 to 31 pp 73 - 74), recognising that they can bring significant environmental and economic benefits, and aim to ensure that impact assessments are dynamic processes, with a strong emphasis on post-development monitoring and environmental audits (see Chapter 5 above).

Recommendation 15
Industry, whether privately or publicly owned, should ensure that its environmental skills are appropriate to its developing needs and responsibilities, and that a higher proportion of all levels of industrial personnel are trained in such environmental skills, either before recruitment or in post, a requirement which will create increased demand for existing environmental training courses and for new modules in the business schools, management colleges, and in university and polytechnic courses on engineering, science and other appropriate disciplines (see Chapter 5 above).

Recommendation 16
Nationalised industries should be provided with new operating guidelines, as outlined in Chapter 5 (see paragraphs 18 to 19, page 73), with new duties in respect to demand management and resource conservation

Recommendation 17
Industry should review its sponsorship policies to see whether a greater proportion of charitable and other contributions could be made available to appropriate environmental conservation projects and programmes. Two vehicles for such sponsorship are the World Wildlife Fund and the newly formed Conservation Foundation.

Recommendation 18
Given the vital importance of the policy context within which industry operates, central and local government planners should give consideration to the impact of their industrial location policies on the objectives of the World Conservation Strategy, developing their plans and strategies within an ecological framework.

Objective 3

13. The third objective is *to promote and sustain the transition away from environment-intensive industries and technologies to cleaner, low waste industries and technologies*, always recognising that these new activities will account for a relatively small proportion of our national income for some time to come.

14. There are many constraints operating on this transition, as successive studies and reports on the process of innovation diffusion through the UK economy have demonstrated. Much of the evidence published by the National Economic Development Office suggests that, far from moving into higher value added sectors, we are actually slipping back into the vulnerable, environment-intensive lower value added activities.

15. The need is to ensure that scarce resources are ploughed into the industries of the future, industries which, on present evidence, would seem to offer a much improved performance in relation to the World Conservation Strategy's objectives, rather than into the declining, environment-intensive industries on which the Industrial Revolution was originally based and on which the prosperity of recent decades has been founded.

16. This transition will inevitably be a long one, and often highly politically charged (not least because of the employment implications sketched out in Chapter 6 above, but the development of a strategic perspective must help in ensuring that the requisite momentum is maintained. Since no country has yet made the transition to sustainable forms of development, the following

recommendations are intended to start the process and, where started, to accelerate it. They do not constitute a fully developed industrial strategy for the UK economy, which is currently conspicuous by its absence.

Recommendation 19
The Government, working closely with industry and other sectors of society, should evolve and adopt, as a matter of urgency, a national policy for science and technology designed to promote the re-industrialisation of the UK economy (see Chapter 2 paragraphs 4 to 8 page 44), emphasising new industries imposing reduced demands on finite natural resources, whether renewable or non-renewable, home produced or imported.

Recommendation 20
The Government should consider ways in which it can promote the development of the various industrial sectors identified in Chapter 4 above. Among other initiatives, it should consider the following with particular urgency:

(a) It should establish an Energy Efficiency Agency, taking into account the recommendation of the Marshall Report in relation to the need for a National Heat Board (see Chapter 4 paragraph 53 page 65).

(b) It should consider ways in which it can accelerate the implementation of outstanding pollution control legislation, particularly in relation to the agricultural industry, where this will help create new markets for potential growth sectors — such as the use of advanced biotechnologies in pollution control and waste or energy recovery (see Chapter 4 paragraphs 26 to 33 pp 60 - 62). It should consider implementing recommendations 47 and 48 of the Royal Commission on Environmental Pollution's report on agriculture and pollution (the rural resources report, Part 3).

(c) It should ensure that acceleration of plans already in hand within the Department of the Environment for a Pollution Abatement Technology award scheme, and consider the possibility of extending it to cover industrial activities bringing other types of benefit within the terms of the World Conservation Strategy.

(d) It should reinforce the Department of Industry's efforts to recruit UK companies onto the UN Economic Commission for Europe's Non-Waste and Low-Waste Compendium, which should be viewed as a 'shop window' for UK industry's achievements in the cleaner, low waste technology field.

(e) While recognising that some progress has already been made, with the setting up of the Science and Engineering Council's Biotechnology Directorate and of an Inter-Departmental Committee on Biotechnology, Government should consider giving further support to biotechnology in the UK (see Chapter 4 paragraphs 15 to 25 pp 59 - 60). The House of Commons Select Committee on Education, Science and the Arts will no doubt come up with some useful recommendations in

relation to educational support, but the Government should seriously consider appointing a Minister for Biotechnology.

Recommendation 21
The Department of Industry and the Science and Engineering Research Council's Biotechnology Directorate should undertake a survey of the effluent disposal and treatment problems which could be tackled by biotechnical means, supporting the necessary development work which will be needed — this recommendation running in parallel with recommendation 20.b above.

Recommendation 22
The Departments of the Environment and Industry should undertake a national survey, possibly as part of an EEC-wide programme, to identify opportunities for boosting the use of secondary, recycled materials and assessing the need for new fiscal incentives designed to promote recycling.

Recommendation 23
Government should, through its policies and day to day decisions, consistently and effectively support the development of the infrastructure needed by the new industries outlined in Chapter 4 above. This will involve both the encouragement of science parks (see the discussion in Chapter 4 paragraphs 80 to 84 pp 68 - 69) and the development of the new skills likely to be required (see Chapter 6 paragraphs 37 to 41 pp 82 - 83).

Recommendation 24
To ensure that these activities have a coherent focus, the Government should consider declaring 1984 as Conservation Technology Year, with an emphasis on UK technologies which offer an improved performance in environmental and resource terms and represent potential building blocks for sustainable development. The current downgrading of renewable energy R and D expenditure (see Chapter 4 paragraphs 66 to 71 page 67) is particularly short sighted. Support for such research, development and demonstration work should be a central plank in the Conservation and Development Programme for the UK.

Some Unresolved Issues

17. Even if all these recommendations were to be implemented promptly and effectively there would remain a number of critical issues and problems which have not been properly addressed in this report. In conducting the practitioners' debate (see Chapter 8 of this report), these issues were given a proper airing. Five of these issues are sketched out below, in paragraphs 18 to 22.

18. The first issue is this: *how can we monitor the overseas operations of UK-based companies more effectively, ensuring that they meet both the letter and the spirit of the guidelines outlined in Chapter 5?*

19. The second issue is a closely related one: *how can industry contribute constructively to the current debate about the exploitation of the global commons?* The often acrimonious debate about the Law of the Sea illustrates the way in which the allocation of natural resources can create international tensions — which can sometimes, as in the case of the Falkland Islands, spill over into open warfare.

20. The third issue permeates both of these issues and is proving a particularly difficult problem to resolve: *how do we ensure that all levels of UK industry understand the environmental implications of their activities — and take the appropriate action needed to reduce any adverse impacts?* A particular constraint on the diffusion of the required new perspectives and skills through industry is the state of the economy. Young people either do not get jobs or, if they do, do not move upwards as fast as they need to. As a result, the 'forgetting curves' discussed in Chapter 5 paragraphs 52 to 54 pp 77 - 78 are significantly slowed.

21. The fourth issue relates to the employment impact of the structural trends in the UK economy: *how can we ensure that all those who want employment can find it?* This issue, almost inevitably, will be made even more contentious if we actively set out to encourage structural change — as this report proposes.

22. The fifth, but by no means final, issue is this: *given the tendency of the new, advanced technology industries to locate towards the centre (a trend described in Chapter 6 paragraph 39 p 83), how can the economics of the depressed regions of this country be bolstered — without prejudicing the future of these new activities in the process?*

CHAPTER 8

THE PRACTITIONERS' DEBATE

Introduction

1. 'Pollution control and environmental protection are expanding world markets which British technology and skills are well placed to capture', said the Rt Hon Tom King MP, Minister for Environmental Services, at a CBI conference on Industry and Environment, held on 23 November 1982. He continued: 'We know all too well the problems of lost markets and the decline of traditional industries. But I do not want to look back in anger or sorrow, but to look ahead to those new markets and products that can help take the place of those we have lost. Future growth markets for this country are going to be significantly different — and they will go to those who adopt the right approach now'.

2. Mr King did not say, as this report does, that the World Conservation Strategy should be taken as a market brief for UK industry in the 1980s and 1990s, but he got closer to it than any other UK Government Minister had. He also pointed out that, 'as the revival of industrial growth takes place, both in the advanced countries and the developing ones, against a background of far higher standards of pollution control, we shall see far more comprehensive demands for environmental responsibility, and a new emphasis on the need to reclaim and clean up many of the areas devastated during an earlier industrial epoch'.

3. A related point was made at the same conference by Dr Martin Holdgate, Chief Scientist at the Department of the Environment, when he stressed that UK industry must increasingly carry the 'World Conservation Strategy standard', given that poor performance in this area can only rebound against the long-term interests of this country, perhaps closing important markets.

4. But the reverse side of the coin, also strongly evident during the practitioners' debate (see paragraph 5) on this report, was summarised by J F Thomson, Managing Director of Material Recovery Ltd. Pointing out that nearly half of the recommendations listed at the end of the report start with words to the effect that 'industry should . . .', Mr Thomson continued to say that 'it seems to me that industry is being asked to take on a burden of work which will almost certainly show no short-term return, but which will involve industrial companies in a great deal of expense. Whilst I am sure that most industrial companies respond to environmental needs

in a responsible manner, I think one has to take account of their current economic condition. Many companies are fighting for survival. Expenditure on long-term environmental projects may be difficult to justify to anxious shareholders'.

5. The formal practitioners' debate, during which the report's conclusions and recommendations were tested on a much broader range of individuals and organisations (see Acknowledgements for indicative listing) than were represented on the original Review Group, took place between June and December of 1982. Interest in 'Seven Bridges to the Future' (originally published separately from the other reports) was such that a second printing was required: over 1,400 copies were distributed and a series of workshops, seminars and conferences was held in England, Scotland and Wales. No formal response has been received from Northern Ireland at the time of writing.

6. An initial analysis of the responses received on the report was presented to a seminar organised by the Industry, Environment and Technology Group of the Institution of Environmental Sciences on 14 October 1982. Given the range of comments made by each of the respondents, a statistical analysis of the response to each conclusion and each recommendation was considered inappropriate. While some responses criticised specific elements of the report, criticisms which are discussed below, every single response received welcomed the report's central message — and supported its analysis of the industrial prospect.

7. A clear request emerged that a concise summary of the report's conclusions be included in the summary of the practitioners' debate. It soon became clear that a fair proportion of the queries and criticisms had been made by people who had not read the appropriate sections of the report and who were responding to what they thought it might say, rather than to what it actually did say. So paragraphs 8 to 14 below briefly restate the report's main conclusions.

The Industrial Dimension of Sustainability

8. First, it was accepted as a fundamental axiom that industry has a vital role to play in ensuring the implementation of the World Conservation Strategy, both in

the UK and elsewhere. Industrial technologies have enabled the UK to build up a population of over 55 million and this population is only sustainable through the continued use of industrial technology. Industry, as Sir Arthur Norman put it during the CBI conference (November, 1982), 'is in the business of wealth creation' — but the creation of real wealth increasingly depends on conservation-based development. A development process which destroys environmental resources will ultimately undermine its own economic base.

9. The UK economy is in the grip of a deep recession and the report suggests that any real, sustained recovery is unlikely before the late 1980s or early 1990s. Furthermore, it argues, there will be profound shifts in the patterns of employment and unemployment, with structural unemployment likely to persist at uncomfortably high levels for the foreseeable future. The growth of some elements of the services sector will help counter the decline in the share of the national income derived from the more traditional (and increasingly obsolescent) industries, but it is very unlikely to absorb more than a small proportion of those who have lost their jobs in the manufacturing sector.

10. The structural trends in the economy, it is argued, are tending to encourage the less environment-intensive industries at the expense of the heavier, more polluting and more materials-hungry industries which stemmed from the first Industrial Revolution. But, while these structural and technological trends will mean that the production of a given unit of GDP involves a decreasing 'take' of environmental resources, the current economic recession is now undermining vital environmental research, shrinking environmental budgets in industry and slowing the implementation of legislation.

11. The report argues that the UK needs to re-industrialise and identifies seven sectors whose future growth will help ensure an improvement in the economy's overall performance in relation to the World Conservation Strategy's three main objectives. The seven main sectors are: microelectronic and information technology; the new biotechnologies; pollution control and the development of cleaner, low waste process technologies; recycling, material recovery and substitution; energy conservation; ecologically tailored energy supply technologies; and environmental services.

12. The report stresses that: 'In selecting seven such industries or, more accurately, clusters of activity which are in the process of assembling themselves into industries, we are not suggesting that these are the only potential growth industries. But what we have dubbed the "Sunrise Seven" are all, directly or indirectly, providing answers to the problems identified by the World Conservation Strategy' (see Chapter 4 above). In no sense, then, is the report an attempt to produce an all-embracing industrial strategy for the UK. Instead, it identifies lines of cleavage whose development could help improve the environmental performance of our industrial economy as a whole.

13. The recommendations advanced in Chapter 7 of this report were intended as a 'shopping list', to be refined during the practitioners' debate. But three indispensable objectives were identified — and the practitioners' debate reinforced them. The first objective was to ensure the provision of accurate, up to date information on the nature and scale of environmental problems, with a particular emphasis on any trends affecting, or likely to affect, the viability of ecological processes, the conservation of genetic diversity or the potential for sustainable development. The second objective was to upgrade industry's environmental resources, to ensure that its domestic and international performance is consistent with the objectives of the World Conservation Strategy. And the third objective was to promote and sustain the transition away from environment-intensive industries and technologies to cleaner, low-waste industries and technologies.

14. The following section summarises some elements of the practitioners' debate, identifying a number of areas of consensus which can be built on during the implementation phase of the Conservation and Development Programme following its launch in June 1983.

General Level of Support and Specific Criticisms

15. The Welsh Office reported: 'We found the report to be a useful guide to current and potential progress in pursuing industrial developments that support conservation objectives. Its practical, problem solving emphasis is particularly welcome'. In fact, a considerable number of responses expressed surprise at how much was already being done to integrate conservation with industrial development — and many respondents felt that eventual publication of the report could help to encourage industry to overcome some of the information barriers to progress in this field.

16. None of the responses received suggested that the approach adopted in the report was out of key with the World Conservation Strategy, although a number recognised that the approach was different. The World Conservation Strategy, it was felt, distinguishes between sustainable and non-sustainable development patterns, but does so largely in respect of the less developed countries. In applying the same principles to the UK economy, a different approach had been required. We are dealing with mature (in some cases ageing) urban and industrial systems, rather than with rapidly growing urban and industrial centres in a relatively undisturbed environment.

17. Four factual errors were identified in the report, which have since been rectified: the number of bottle banks had been under-estimated, and the latest Glass Manufacturers' Federation figures are now included (Chapter 4, paragraph 39, p 63): a figure of £5m, as reported in the *Financial Times*, was given for a programme designed to recover tinplate, instead of the real

figure of £2m; the paper industry pointed out that the report quoted the *Economist* to the effect that paper prices had risen by 87 per cent between 1973 and 1979, suggesting that this be qualified by the fact that the Retail Price Index increased by 106 per cent over the same period — so paper became relatively cheaper (but the argument that electronic communication and storage methods are becoming more attractive was unaffected); and the Ministry of Agriculture, Fisheries and Food (MAFF) dismissed as 'completely false' a reference to it lobbying to prevent the publication of the working party report described in the pollution control section of Chapter 4 above. 'MAFF had disagreed with the report's estimate of £200m as the agricultural market for anaerobic treatment technology over the next 10 years and a MAFF disclaimer was attached to the report. At no time has MAFF attempted to suppress it.' Original statements have been altered to take MAFF statements into account. See Chapter 4 paragraph 31 page 62.

18. The quality of the data assembled was commented on favourably by a number of respondents, although the Institute of Petroleum cautioned in a written response that the data had come from 'many different sources' — Government departments, prestigious international review bodies, trade associations, environmental groups and individual companies quoted as case studies. It has largely been used uncritically and it had to be used selectively: there was little option to do otherwise if the report was to appear at all, and we are sure members of the Review Group know good data from bad. Nevertheless, in a field so emotionally charged as this, the same data, especially when used predictively, can be interpreted in quite disparate, yet equally honest and convincing ways by a trade association on the one hand and an environmental group on the other.

19. The Institute of Petroleum argued that: 'The ultimate constraint on human activity will be energy availability. The laws of thermodynamics provide a value free mode of assessment. If more energy has to be used in the extraction, refining and distribution of a new energy source than it provides, then the enterprise is thermally bankrupt'. The cost and availability of energy, it concluded, would be extremely important in determining the viability of particular pollution control or recycling technologies.

20. This point was buttressed by I G Simmons of the Department of Geography, Durham University, who argued that 'the procurement and use of energy is the great mediator between man and environment, and any strategy for resources and environment which ignores it is lacking the glue which holds all these disparate strands together'. Energy supply and conservation are discussed in Chapters 2 and 4 of this report. The most critical problem, and it is one addressed in 'Resourceful Britain', is that the availability of North Sea oil has blunted the drive towards greater energy efficiency in the UK. Whether or not oil prices increase as rapidly as was predicted after the first two oil shocks, energy efficiency must be a *leitmotif* in the design, manufacture, distribution and operation of industrial products and systems.

21. The most critical set of comments emerged from those involved in the drafting of Cynefin, the Welsh Conservation Strategy. While commenting that 'this report convincingly illustrates the urgent need to reconcile industrial growth and development with the maintenance of essential ecological processes, genetic diversity and species and ecosystem use', the Cynefin response expressed the hope that the practitioners' debate would involve 'practising industrialists, economists and others'. Interestingly, the industrial and employment workshop held prior to the launch of Cynefin in December 1982 attracted only one non-Cynefin person from industry — an information officer from the British Steel Corporation. By contrast, the debate on this report involved well over 100 people from industry, and related articles appeared in the Journal of General Management, International Management, the Environmental Data Services Reports, the *Guardian* and *The Times*.

22. A much more significant criticism was that the prospects of the 'Sunrise Seven' were over-emphasised at the expense of what Brian Johnson dubbed the 'Sunset Seventy' — the traditional, heavier manufacturing industries on which the Welsh economy has been so dependent.

23. Typical of this reaction was one made by Christopher Wood of the Pollution Research Unit, University of Manchester, whose work is reviewed in Chapter 2 above. 'The report is basically very optimistic but the evidence for its optimism is sporadic. It might have been more convincing if a survey of industrial pollution, pollution control and environmental management had been undertaken, at the very least among the firms represented on the Review Group. The weight of the (relatively) benign growth industries in comparison with the traditional industries is probably over-played. The effects of the recession on the environment are equally under-played. Nevertheless, the objectives derived are sensible and the recommendations worthy'.

24. Various respondents, including Glyn England (retiring Chairman, Central Electricity Generating Board) and Cynefin, pointed out that the 'middle ground' of UK industry, including component suppliers, will continue to play a vital role in the UK's economic future. They warned against a vision of the future involving only the ultra old and the ultra new.

25. As the Conservation Society's Director, John Davoll, said, 'it is difficult to form a clear picture of the general economy and way of life in which the "Sunrise Seven" industries will be embedded. For example, will a vast investment be made in cable TV and the "wired society" before or after the collapsing sewers, rotting housing and appalling mental hospitals have been remedied? Other "sunrise" industries are basically bolt-on jobs to an essentially unchallenged industrial system, and it can be argued that they do not form "bridges" to a sustainable future economy, since they leave the commitment to open-ended expansion intact and central to the functioning of the economy. The report admits that

government support for recycling has been cut back and that the lack of government commitment to energy conservation is "worrying". This is not surprising, in view of the in-built commitment of the expansion-dependent system to attack problems by redoubling, rather than abating, activity'.

26. But, while Dr Davoll concluded that the report followed the Brandt Report in 'severely underestimating the fundamental or even the minimum changes needed to make the economies of the industrial countries sustainable', Friends of the Earth put forward Edward Barbier, an economist, who was a good deal more positive. He concluded: 'Overall, I believe the report and its recommendations are a step in the right direction for achieving the World Conservation Strategy objectives. In particular, I was impressed with the sensible arguments in favour of genetic diversity, and by Mr Elkington's use of many examples from industry to illustrate his points. The identification of seven future growth areas (the "Sunrise Seven") provides an excellent basis for launching a debate over industrial strategy'.

27. Probably the most helpful argument put forward by Barbier, and it is one that is touched on in this report, was that the various growth sectors are not free-standing, but intimately linked with the rest of the economy. He pointed out that 'The important thing about "take-off" sectors is not that they are separate industrial entities but that they can pull the rest of the economy with them through multiplier and other indirect effects'.

28. Interestingly, the Cynefin workshop in 1982 ultimately decided in favour of encouraging just the sort of industrial concerns that Chapter 4 of this report suggests are so vital, both for economic and ecological reasons. The two main issues that emerged during that workshop were that many of these activities may be clean, but that they tend also to be land-hungry and do not provide large numbers of jobs immediately and, secondly, developers are able to pick and choose their sites — and are often able to demand 'green-field' sites. That said, however, both the Welsh Development Agency and the Scottish Development Agency argued that there was considerable scope for manoeuvring some of these new activities onto land which is already disturbed — or which has been reclaimed. The Scottish Development Agency commented that this report's vision of the future was very similar to its own.

29. A fundamental question came from the Countryside Commission: 'Is the world experiencing a cyclical downturn in a long run cycle, or are we experiencing a fundamental shift in the way we live? There is a fundamental difference between a Kondratieff Cycle and Toffler's "Third Wave" ' (see Chapters 1 and 2 above). The Commission continued: 'The former suggests evolution and the latter revolution'. The basic argument in this report, however, is that the two are not mutually exclusive: economic downturns in the longer-term industrial cycles have been followed, sooner or later, by upturns built on new technologies. Some of these technologies may appear

revolutionary, but they are part of the fundamental process of technological and industrial evolution. The seeds of the new industries which will underpin our economy (and offer an improved performance in environmental terms) already exist, but need to be planted in the right places and nurtured to maturity.

30. The Countryside Commission was also among the respondents who foresaw problems in resolving the potential conflicts between the proposals of this report and that of the Urban Review Group (Part 2). The Commission argued that the 'internationalist argument in "Seven Bridges to the Future" runs counter to the isolationism in "The Livable City", with its emphasis on self-sufficiency. Indeed, the gulf between the two reports is quite wide, with "Seven Bridges to the Future" wanting free-wheeling private enterprises to establish new growth poles on virgin land along the M4 and "The Livable City" wanting to protect the countryside from urban intrusion'.

31. At a seminar held at Earthlife on 16 December 1982, however, those responsible for preparing the industry (Part 1), urban (Part 2) and 'Resourceful Britain' reports discussed these areas of overlap with a small number of those who had responded to 'Seven Bridges to the Future', and concluded that the problem — one component of which is described in the discussion of the fifth 'unresolved issue' in paragraph 22, Chapter 7 page 89, was more apparent than real. Indeed, the report comments favourably on the Earthlife scheme for London's Docklands (see Chapter 4), which is seen as a model for encouraging the development of knowledge-based industries in the inner city. The Cynefin workshop was attended by many planners, most of whom said that incoming industry tended to be environment-conscious, and greenfield sites would be given to them if it encouraged them to put down roots in Wales. The problem, it was pointed out, is that it is not simply a question of Cardiff or the Welsh valleys competing with Birmingham or other UK locations, but of competition with rival European and even American locations.

32. The basic need now, the Earthlife seminar confirmed, is to facilitate the building of 'critical mass' in appropriate new sectors, whether this is done along the M4, in 'Silicon Glen' or in the declining areas of our major conurbations. The challenge today, as the British Consortium for Innovation said, is to find 'a means of developing new ways of doing things alongside the old, not in opposition to existing ways but in a complementary mode, thus providing a bridge between paradigms for those who need to cross step by step'.

33. The response from the planners was very positive, although the Association of District Councils (ADC) argued that the existing planning system was quite adequate to cope with the bulk of planning decisions, with no need for a new system of environmental impact assessment (EIA) (as suggested in Chapter 7 recommendation 14 page 87). Others disagreed and the ADC admitted that EIA is useful with major industrial projects. The Association of County Councils, on the other hand,

in a written response welcomed the report and its emphasis on the need for planning. 'The Association accepts that the current situation and the trend away from traditional manufacturing industries towards new technology-based jobs and some new public sector opportunities poses a role for local authorities in stimulating their local economies. County Councils can play a positive part in providing infrastructure for new industries.'

34. Overall, employment emerged as the main issue. Although it was never suggested that the 'Sunrise Seven' were to provide jobs for everyone who wanted employment (as is pointed out at the end of Chapter 7), the fact that these 'bridges' could not provide the required number of jobs was seen by a few respondents as a major failing in the report. As expected, a large number of respondents also reacted against the concept of a major programme of public environmental works (see Chapter 6) as a solution to youth unemployment. Instead, they argued, what is needed is reflation. The author, however, is still convinced that a major programme, particularly if aimed at renewing this country's collapsing Victorian infrastructure, could help significantly to provide employment and prevent environmental deterioration. This issue is discussed further in 'Resourceful Britain'.

The Priority Recommendations

35. Three main recommendations emerged in relation to the first major objective (see Chapter 8 paragraph 13 page 91), relating to the assembly and dissemination of information on UK industry's contribution to the problems identified in the World Conservation Strategy. The comment has been made that the problem often is not one of information availability but of the conflicting interpretations of the information which is available. Part of the purpose of the UK Programme is to breach some of these attitudinal barriers, but there are at least three areas where we need to ensure that we do assemble new information. These are covered in the following three recommendations:

(a) The OECD should undertake a review of the implications of the OECD region's trade with all its trading partners, providing an up to date and statistically reliable database on the impacts on priority ecological processes, ecological diversity and on the potential for sustainable development (see Recommendation 4 in Chapter 7 page 85). This work would build on that carried out by the Interfutures team. The Commission of the European Communites could help. (*Time scale:* 1983-1984, coupled with continuous monitoring thereafter.)

(b) The Government should ensure that the funding of research into the environmental impacts of industrial activity is maintained at a sufficient level both to maintain progress in the management of the UK environment and to assess some of the 'pollution transfer' problems identified

in the World Conservation Strategy — including acid rain and the build up in the atmosphere of such industrial pollutants as chlorofluorocarbons and carbon dioxide. (*Time scale:* 1983, with momentum maintained thereafter.)

(c) The Government has rejected the Royal Commission on Environmental Pollution's assessment that the existing UK pollution control system is failing to achieve the 'best practicable environmental option' — ie solutions to pollution problems which prevent pollution transfers between air, land and water. Instead of setting up a new central Inspectorate, the Government intends to encourage existing pollution control authorities to aim for the best practicable environmental option. In doing so, it should insist that such authorities consider not only inter-media transfers of pollution, but also trans-frontier transfers (see Recommendation 5, Chapter 7 p 85). (*Time scale:* 1983.)

36. The climate of opinion established by the World Conservation Strategy and the ensuing national initiatives will inevitably influence industrial decision making. Industry does not operate in a vacuum: the recommendations contained in the reports of the international (Part 5) marine and coastal (Part 4), rural (Part 3) and urban (Part 2) Review Groups, and in 'Resourceful Britain', will help shape the future business environment — partly through legislation and partly through voluntary agreements. As far as the second objective identified in paragraph 13 Chapter 8 p 91 is concerned, which focuses on the upgrading of industry's environmental resources, three recommendations emerged:

(d) UK companies and other industrial organisations whose business activities have a significant direct or indirect influence on the priority objectives identified by the World Conservation Strategy should review their operations to identify and tackle actual or potential problems. Where necessary, they should adopt new (or change existing) environmental policies to address these problems effectively. In implementing these policies they will need to consider the new environmental impact assessment and environmental accounting methods which are now available (see Recommendation 3, p 85, 8 p 85 and 10 p 87 in Chapter 7. (*Time scale:* 1983 for initial reviews, with periodic reviews thereafter.)

(e) Reduced recruitment of environmental staff by industry, coupled with redundancies and early retirements among existing staff, is slowing the 'forgetting curves' discussed in paragraphs 52 - 54 pp 77 - 78 of Chapter 5. Apart from the suggestions in Recommendation 15 (Chapter 7 page 87), all of which were supported during the practitioners' debate, industrial concerns should consider ways in which they could close the emerging 'experience gap' in their environmental units. One possibility would be a national scheme of secondments between companies, government and non-government organisations, and the universities. (*Time scale*: 1983 for planning and piloting, with development following as demand permits.)

(f) Voluntary groups in the environmental and conservation fields should consider ways in which they could collaborate to promote common objectives, including the monitoring of the environmental performance of UK companies operating overseas (see the first 'unresolved issue' in paragraph 18, Chapter 7 page 88). The voluntary sector will need to play a central role in ensuring that the third unresolved issue (paragraph 20, Chapter 7 page 89) is resolved, by mounting effective projects and campaigns. The proposed alliance between the environmental and Third World lobbies, discussed at an informal meeting on 2 December 1982, could prove a useful model. (*Time scale*: 1983 onwards.)

37. Various important initiatives were announced during the period covered by the practitioners' debate which were designed to promote various of the 'Sunrise Seven' sectors. The Department of Industry, for example, assumed responsibility for the promotion of UK biotechnology, and announced a £16m, three year support programme. During a two week tour of US biotechnology research institutes and companies in November 1982, the author was struck by the way that many biotechnology companies see their technologies as potential solutions for the environmental problems which have dogged the advanced industrial nations for several decades. In evidence to the House of Commons Education, Science and Arts Committee's inquiry into biotechnology in 1982, a number of those giving evidence also stressed this point (including Dr David Copsey of Prutec, the Prudential Assurance Company's new high technology venture capital unit).

38. Dr Copsey also stressed that biotechnological processes differ from recent microelectronic developments in that they can take tens of years and tens of millions of pounds to develop — characteristics which underscore the need for the type of Government support which the Department of Industry is increasingly offering.

39. The structural change arguments presented in this report were echoed both at Cynefin and at a very constructive seminar in Edinburgh, co-hosted by the Countryside Commission for Scotland and the Nature Conservancy Council. In fact, there have been a number of indications that the central message in this report — that this country's industrial prospects would be distinctly brighter if the markets identified in this report are tackled effectively — is gaining wider acceptance. As Tom King put it in relation to the pollution control industry during the 1982 CBI conference, 'Britain is now a potential world leader in pollution control technology and is in a very good position to take advantage of this growing world market. There are many countries, not least in the Middle East, which want their industrial growth to go ahead without the barbaric damage to their environment that has

occurred elsewhere. Some of these are countries with immense financial resources; they want our help, our hardware, our expertise, our design experience, and they are certainly willing to pay for it. Here then is a vital expanding market for our skills, a genuine new industry in its own right; an industry of the future'.

40. The investment institutions, such as Prudential Assurance, are not going to pursue environmental targets for their own sake, so legislation will continue to be an important factor in ensuring sensible long-term investment decisions. Given that a significant proportion of UK investment is currently going overseas, the recommendations contained in Part 5 on international affairs prepared by Richard Sandbrook are particularly important: by helping the less developed countries build up their own environmental resources and statutory frameworks, the UK can go a long way towards ensuring that UK companies operating in those countries behave responsibly.

41. As far as the third objective is concerned — that of promoting environmentally desirable structural and technological change in the UK economy — four main recommendations emerged from the practitioners' debate:

(g) The Government should urge the Departments of Energy, Environment and Industry to launch programmes designed to ensure that all levels of UK industry have access to information on the appropriate energy efficient, low waste, low pollution technologies. The Department of Industry's efforts in 1982 to recruit UK companies onto the ECE Compendium of Cleaner Technologies was a welcome development and should be sustained. Government should also ensure that the various Ministries have the resources (perhaps in the form of a counterpart of Denmark's Environmental Investments Support Act) to make these programmes work. (*Time scale*: 1983 onwards.)

(h) The CBI and the Department of the Environment should press ahead as soon as possible with the 'Pollution Abatement Technology Award Scheme (PATAS), which will help in promoting UK skills and technology in this important area. (*Time scale*: PATAS should be set up as soon as possible.)

(i) The relevant Ministries and trade associations should consider combining their forces and declaring either 1984 or 1985 'Conservation Technology Year' — to provide a launch platform for UK industry into the various markets identified in this report. This is seen as a particularly important recommendation, since it would provide a focus for many related activities in what are often highly fragmented industries. (*Time scale*: Planning during 1983, and possibly 1984, depending on launch date chosen.)

(j) Finally, as part of the build up to Conservation Technology Year, a study should be commissioned by Government of the economic and employment opportunities offered by the various conservation technology sectors. The Joint Unit for Research on the Urban Environment, for example, estimates that some 1.25 million people are employed in the EEC, Spain and Portugal in the environmental industry. The Association for the Conservation of Energy plans to publish the results of its study of the employment implications of a proposed major

energy conservation programme early in 1983. Over the last four years, the loss of jobs in the UK has been worse than in any other EEC country and the employment angle is therefore particularly important in selling policies which will be needed to promote the various conservation-based industries. (*Time scale*: Completion of initial study early in 1984.)

PART 2
URBAN

The Livable City

A report by Joan Davidson and Ann MacEwen

Acknowledgements

Many busy people gave willingly of their time and energy to help us. We are especially grateful to our Review Group members for their prompt and helpful reactions to all our late drafts, and we would like to thank in particular Gerald Leach of the International Institute for Environment and Development (IIED), Robert Davies of the National Council for Voluntary Organisations (NCVO) and David Hutchinson of the Greater London Council for the extensive comment and documentation.

We are grateful to colleagues at University College London, especially John Musgrove, Gerald Smart, Michael Edwards, David Banister and Richard Munton, for responding to our pestering with both material and good ideas, and to those at the College of St Paul and St Mary in Cheltenham, especially John Hancock and Erica Breuning, for a variety of support. Throughout, the secretariat at the Nature Conservancy Council and especially Liz O'Sullivan have responded to our queries in a most helpful way.

Our research assistant, Martin Halling, made a special contribution through his methodical analysis of a wide range of literature and by his continual — but very constructive — scepticism. Ziona Strelitz, Martin Stott and Richard Land prepared excellent papers upon which we have drawn for ideas and information. Adrian Phillips of the Countryside Commission and Solly Bursible made many helpful comments on various drafts.

For help at the consultation stage, we are indebted to the following who organised seminars and workshops: John Foster, and the Scottish Countryside Commission; Chris Baines and Birmingham Polytechnic; Robert Davies and NCVO; Ewart Parkinson and South Glamorgan County Council; Brian Lymbery and the Prince of Wales' Committee; Richard Allsop and the Transport Studies Unit, University College London; Patrick Harrison and the RIBA; David Massey and the Department of Civic Design, University of Liverpool. We are grateful to many others who wrote to us at length and most usefully.

But above all, our thanks go to John Davidson and Malcolm MacEwen for all their encouragement and intellectual support.

Chairman's Introduction

People have chosen to live in cities, or close to them, to enjoy the economic benefits of better jobs, a better chance of a good home and the many and varied advantages of good education, good shops, good transport and good opportunities for social and cultural enjoyment. These remain the benefits of city life hoped for by many in the developed countries and those, too, who flock to the urban centres of the Third World.

The price paid for all this seemed worthwhile until the side effects began to be too extensive to be comfortably ignored. Long-established communities suffer from cold and deteriorating homes, fewer jobs, traffic congestion, noise and a polluted atmosphere, from poor environments and crumbling sewers; parks created for public enjoyment are no longer safe at night and the burden of local taxes necessary to pay for the city services is becoming unbearable. Even the continuation of city life itself must be in question unless the style of living can be adjusted to be more caring and careful in its use of resources.

This report is essentially the work of Joan Davidson and Ann MacEwen, guided by a very helpful group of experts in many fields. We had a number of lively discussions, and, while some members would not agree with all that is said, the report does set out what we believe to be the major implications for urban areas of a conserving strategy for the use of our resources. None of its elements are likely to seem particularly revolutionary, but the bringing together of so many tough strands of logical thought should, I believe, lead most of us to the conclusion that we must mend our ways.

Audrey Lees
February, 1983

CHAPTER 1

NEW DIRECTIONS FOR URBAN CONSERVATION

The World Conservation Strategy

1. The World Conservation Strategy, the starting point for the British programme, is about matching the superficially conflicting goals of development and conservation; development being the means of meeting human needs and improving the quality of life and conservation being the use of resources, especially living ones, in a sustainable way, so safeguarding all their benefits for future generations.[1]

2. The Strategy sees both development and conservation as interdependent and draws upon many examples from around the world which illustrate where one has failed to keep pace with the other. It argues that development, the prerequisite for improvements in human welfare, cannot be sustained unless the resources it consumes are conserved. Some of these are finite and face depletion, but critical are the living natural resources on whose renewability all life support depends. So the Strategy is concerned with the better management of energy, land, air and water resources, with the preservation of genetic diversity upon which agricultural, industrial and medical advance will continue to draw and with the continuation of those systems, like food production, upon whose products health, well-being and economic activity depend.

3. In all this, the Strategy reflects the growing convergence over the last decade of environmental and development thinking: that both are about sustainability and that to succeed in realising their potential benefits, both must impinge upon the lives of people at the local level.[2]

What Relevance has the Strategy for Urban Development in the UK?

4. Since the Industrial Revolution, the growth of urban living has been the most tangible aspect of British development, reflected not only in the physical expansion of housing and industrial and commercial production but also in terms of ideas, innovation and human effort. Our high living standards, albeit with disparities between different groups, have been closely linked to an urban way of life. A great stock of physical and social capital is locked up in our cities.

5. But less and less do they seem to offer the advantages associated with urban living: ease of access and exchange of goods and services, opportunities to earn a living and participate in satisfying work and social relationships within a community. Some cities offer these in abundance, but changing national and international circumstances and many other factors have conspired to make some urban areas, especially the inner cities, offer the poorest quality of life possible in the UK. In increasing numbers, people are leaving the conurbations for smaller towns; but for those who remain, conditions of housing, services and environment deteriorate at an accelerating pace.

6. Conservation has never been seen as having a dominant part to play in the affairs of urban areas. Traditionally, it has been concerned with the protection of heritage and, although its scope has gradually widened to embrace more than the historic and visual aspects of environment, this kind of conservation is still applied in a local, piecemeal, and often inequitable, way during periods of relative prosperity. At times of severe social and economic difficulty, this kind of conservation is considered by some to be an irrelevant luxury — too much concerned with looks, too little with the affairs of people.

7. Conservation of natural resources has been seen almost wholly in the context of rural areas. But there is a new and growing movement towards the creation of wildlife habitats in cities which expresses genuine concern for promoting a quality of urban life in which natural things are important and may offer some way out of the alienation of city living. This movement, along with other community activities, illustrates the increasing enthusiasm for small scale participatory urban change, for initatives which can draw upon the active support of urban people where government and the private sector have been unable or unwilling to make improvements.

8. Rarely have questions of survival pervaded these conservation activities. Threats of scarcity, especially for energy resources, have erupted periodically but most often they have been referred to the future or to the global scale; they are seen as relevant, like the World Conservation Strategy itself, for the developing world rather than the UK. Yet the style of our urban living and its implications for natural resources, go beyond the protection of urban buildings and wildlife; it profoundly

affects survival — both the provision of basic needs for many in the Third World now and our own over the longer-term.

9. More immediately important, the failure to make a better match between resource-conservation and development, except in a handful of imaginative schemes, means that urban people are denied the benefits that could accrue from wider conservation action. There is a growing body of opinion that many changes in society — towards increasing unemployment, accelerating technological development and the desire for local participation and self-help — are of a quite different order from those of a decade ago.[3] They may indicate not only a turning point in the way society and the economy is structured, but offer new opportunities for creating jobs and wealth with social and environmental gain. Resource-conservation has many roles to play in these changes.

10. The following chapters try to show how and why this might be so and suggest some of the ways to a new approach to cities. Chapter 2 examines the resource-base for urban living, discussing questions of scarcity and waste, the wider implications of resource-consumption and the need to save. The next four chapters assess the opportunities and problems for resource-conservation offered by contemporary changes in the pattern of urban development, in the management of settlements and in the activities and attitudes of urban people. Chapter 7 sums up the findings and suggests some goals by which to guide a movement towards more sustainable urban living. Chapter 8 translates these goals into an eight-point strategy and Chapter 9 looks at some of the obstacles to achieving it. Chapter 10 summarises the report and lists recommendations.

11. Barbard Ward wrote: 'For an increasing number of environmental issues, the difficulty is not to identify the remedy because the remedy is now understood. The problems are rooted in the economy and society'.[4] Throughout, this has been the premise and, as a consequence, the report covers a very wide range of urban issues and policy areas. It has meant, for the authors, treading on some unfamiliar ground which needs to be explored much further. But this is the nature of a conservation approach to development: it cannot be segregated as a job for particular places, groups or times: it must pervade all urban activity.

Notes and References

1 IUCN. 1980. World conservation strategy.

2 See for example: ECKHOLM, E. 1982. Down to earth. Pluto Press; CLARKE, R and TIMBERLAKE, L. 1982. Stockholm plus ten. International Institute for Environment and Development.

3 See for example: ROBERTSON, J. 1978. The sane alternative. James Robertson; SHANKLAND, G. 1980. Our secret economy. Anglo-German Foundation; JENKINS, C and SHERMAN, B. 1979. The collapse of work. Methuen.

4 Foreword, Down to earth, op cit.

CHAPTER 2

THE RESOURCE PICTURE

Introduction

1. Every morning, most of Britain's 37 million urban dwellers wake to an alarm clock which has been assembled half the world away with components from around the globe. Many of the clothes they wear and much of the breakfast they consume will come from cash crops grown in Third World countries, perhaps in competition with local food production. They ride to factories, shops and offices on fuel from the North Sea, use paper from the trees of Northern Europe and work at benches and desks made from the wood of tropical forests where one species is extinguished every 24 hours. During one day, each individual will use 120 litres of water and together they will produce, from their homes alone, 50,000 tonnes of solid waste, most of which will be thrown onto the land around the cities where they live. Yet urban society remains largely ignorant of the scale, diversity and consequences of this resource-consumption.[1]

Resources in the Past and for the Future

2. Our larger urban settlements, with all their associated activities of production, consumption and exchange, are major consumers of natural resources. Buildings, for example, homes, schools, offices and factories (exclusive of their industrial process) account for more than 46 per cent of the total delivered energy consumed in the UK, which is still the most energy-intensive country in Europe. Homes alone take 28 per cent of the total energy supplied and 40 per cent of the electricity consumed (see Figure 1).[2] Although urban areas cover a fairly small proportion of the total land surface in the UK — 11 per cent is given by Best[3] — they are major consumers of the secondary resources, especially food and building materials, for which land is the foundation.

3. However, even for energy consumption, figures are hard to find. There is a profound lack of data about patterns of consumption, for resource-consciousness has so far played little part in urban decision making. It is unlikely that all settlements consume resources at the same scale: for vehicle fuels, it appears that large urban centres use proportionately less *per capita* for they are more likely to have public transport (which is energy-efficient) than smaller settlements. But there are

Sector	% of total delivered energy 1975	1980
Domestic	26.3	27.9
Industry (including buildings)	39.3	33.9
Transport	22.0	24.9
Agriculture	1.3	1.1
Other users	11.1	12.2
Total	100	100

Figure 1. **National energy consumption 1975 and 1980**
(Source: Digest of UK Energy Statistics, 1981)

no simple relationships here; resource-consumption depends upon a range of linked factors, including the density of development, the distribution of wealth and the position of a settlement in the cycle of economic growth and decline. These are issues which are explored in the next chapter.

4. As urban systems have grown in size and complexity, so has the level and range of resources they consume. In the past, cities were supported by their hinterlands which supplied food, fuel and raw materials to the growing economic centres as in many Third World cities today. Variations in the supply of resources were obvious and the implications of consumption could be seen. Many UK cities depended on local power stations and gas works: at least their source of energy supplies was obvious. Moreover, cities import most of their resources: the components of industries, offices, homes, shops and schools display amazing diversity and are drawn, not from urban hinterlands, but from around the world.

5. Cheap, abundant energy has been the key to urbanisation in its present form, and has led to the greater exploitation of all other resources and, in large part, to the growing sophistication of urban goods and services. But there is no constant relationship with population growth nor even with the increase of households for, as living standards change, yesterday's luxuries have become today's necessities. Over the life of cities patterns of resource-use have shown sudden leaps in consumption independent of the effects of release from war time restraints. Principal among the factors for the recent growth in consumption has been the change from

durability to obsolescence, from a demand for things 'built to last' to a concern for fashion.

6. Over the last decade there has been some slowing down in the growth of resource-consumption and even reductions where there has been the prospect of actual or perceived scarcity, such as followed the oil crises of 1973 and 1979. The effects of rising prices and political uncertainty at these times brought about efforts in resource-saving and re-use which have since been augmented by a levelling off of population and, with the recession, of economic activity generally. But growth of consumption still continues for many resources.

7. How sustainable is this resource-base? What are the prospects for scarcity and the implications of continuing to consume at present levels? It would be tedious, indeed impossible, to review the supply position for all supports to urban living, but a discussion of the key resources of energy, land, building materials and water can provide some clues about the resource-future for cities and suggest some principles by which to guide their management into the twenty first century.

8. It seems likely that urban areas will face not one but a number of diverse resource crises over the next few decades, and these will be reflected in fluctuating but generally rising prices coupled with increasing uncertainty of supplies, whether of energy, minerals, foodstuffs or timber. The resource-picture is not a simple one. There are no easy generalisations to be made about future supplies, approaching scarcities or the problems in using particular materials. Internationally, the picture is complicated by cycles of glut and shortage, and by the volatile economic, social and political forces involved in resource exploitation and the development of substitutes. But there is enough uncertainty to suggest that urban areas should start adapting now to a resource-tight future.

Energy

The Need to Save
9. Despite the present glut, oil, and later gas, will become more scarce with the prospect of critical shortages when the UK has once again to buy on politically uncertain world markets as North Sea supplies begin to decline after 1990. Therefore the UK has to anticipate and manage an energy transition. Extending the life of oil fields (by biological, chemical and thermal means) and exploiting new reserves (such as in Dorset and Hampshire) offer some scope for lengthening the timescale to depletion of our own supplies. But the costs, both financially and to health and environment, may be high. Sooner rather than later oil and gas need to be replaced by other energy sources for uses such as space heating, and need to be safeguarded for essential uses, in transport and as chemical feedstock, where few economic substitutes exist.

10. In the context of trying to match urban development with World Conservation Strategy (WCS) principles, two issues are important. First, how can this transition away from oil and gas be managed in a socially, economically and environmentally acceptable way? Second, what arguments should be made about energy supplies into the longer-term, when the requirement must be for production systems which are ecologically benign as well as safe and otherwise socially acceptable, secure and as cheap as possible?

11. Energy conservation is now widely accepted as a major means by which to bridge the gap that will be created by dwindling and increasingly costly oil supplies. After the oil crises of 1973 and 1979, some industries cut their fuel bills in half by energy saving measures. Overall, UK energy consumption fell by 4 per cent from 1973 to 1978, mainly through conservation, for this was before the deepening recession had reduced industrial output as well as energy use. By 1981, we were using 10 per cent less energy than in 1973.[4] Recent energy conservation efforts have shown that it is possible for Western countries to consume less energy yet still maintain (for some even to increase) their GDP.

12. The contribution of domestic (essentially urban) conservation measures to this saving is difficult to define. Although house insulation has been increasing, most of the older properties, and especially those without central heating, have not been insulated. Low fuel prices (relative to other items of household expenditure) have provided little incentive for urban dwellers to save, and they have enjoyed no comparable backing of advice or sufficient finance to stimulate action except in the few areas where neighbourhood energy conservation schemes operate.[5] (This is discussed in Chapter 6.)

13. But the scope for energy saving in urban areas is large. The European Commission (using national sources) has cautiously estimated that savings of 20 to 25 per cent are possible in the residential and tertiary sector between now and the end of the century.[6] Others have suggested the potential is much greater. By insulating and otherwise converting buildings and heating systems, using waste heat (especially from power stations and the incineration of wastes), improving the design of buildings and appliances and by introducing more energy saving transport systems and vehicles, the scope is there for, in effect, increasing the energy supply for urban areas. Moreover, a vigorous policy of conservation by these means could bring many other advantages for urban people, such as improving the environment of homes and neighbourhoods and providing new jobs. Energy saving is wholly consistent with WCS principles, for it is ecologically benign, producing no wastes, reducing pollution and involving no hazardous or uncertain implications for natural resources. Chapters 4 and 5 discuss in more detail the means and opportunities for urban energy saving.

14. Although the prospects look so good, in practice the commitment to domestic conservation remains low for many reasons, not least the lack of political interest.

A recent EEC report shows how poorly we compare, in practice and government expenditure, with some other countries in Europe, where investment in energy conservation is from four to 10 times greater.[7] In Britain, fuel prices, especially for gas, are not yet high enough for energy saving investments. Added to the lack of financial and other incentives to save, among so many small and scattered urban energy users, is the power of the major energy supply industries whose job it is to sell their fuel — whether gas, electricity or coal — rather than usable energy at least cost. Revised forecasts show that these industries have consistently over-estimated demand (compared with Department of Energy forecasts) and have planned for new supply to meet it. Yet the Department's conservation division has recently estimated that it would be more cost effective to invest £5,000m in conservation now than in new supply.[8]

15. Some parts of the electricity industry already have substantial over capacity;[9] on the basis of the latest Central Electricity Generating Board (CEGB) forecasts of a 1 per cent annual growth in electricity demand over the next seven years (and at best a 2 per cent growth), there seems to be little case for additional generating sources of any kind now to meet new demand, although some plant needs to be replaced. Yet the Government is committed to commission, from 1982, one new nuclear power station a year for 10 years. Instead, the statutory obligations of the fuel industries should be revised, together with their demand forecasting methods (and those of the Department of Energy), to take account of the need to promote and practice energy conservation by all available means.

Into the Longer-Term

16. So what of the future? So long as energy saving can be increased, there are two main routes by which to supply the bulk of UK energy needs into the longer-term (assuming a continuing move away from liquid fuels): from coal or nuclear electricity generation, supplemented by renewable sources, principally wind and wave power. The continuing downward trend of energy demand forecasts suggests that future electricity demands could probably be met either from coal or nuclear sources.

17. It is not appropriate here to rehearse in depth the arguments for and against an extension of coal-based or nuclear generation. Both present severe technical, economic and social problems. From the viewpoint of this report, the crucial issues are that an energy supply system, whilst being cost effective, should pose no serious threat to living systems. It should not undermine the imperative to conserve energy (for this offers so many advantages for urban living); it should allow a movement towards increasing emphasis upon renewable energy sources (for only these are sustainable into the longer-term) and recognise that a variety of energy supplies, maintaining options for the future, is both possible and desirable.

18. Britain has coal reserves for many generations but there are potentially serious global ecological consequences in the release of SO_2, oxides of nitrogen and CO_2. Techniques to reduce nitrous oxides (NOx) and SO_2 are known but they are at present expensive, although it is argued that non-polluting coal-based electricity generation could still be cheaper than nuclear power.[10] The effects of CO_2 release are more difficult to predict, but there is concern that the burning of more fossil fuels (together with the scale of present deforestation and desertification) will cause the further build up of atmospheric CO_2, leading probably to global warming.[11] There would be other consequences of more coal mining: the Belvoir inquiry confirmed fears that loss of crop land and environmental problems could be extensive without improvements in the speed and scale of coalfield restoration. But, as the Royal Commission on Energy and the Environment concluded, the environmental costs of coal use and means of alleviating them are largely known.[12] Those of nuclear generation are not.

19. The risk of serious reactor accident based upon known events is small (10^{-9}). But calculations take no account of dangers inherent in the transport and disposal of high level radioactive wastes (which must be protected and monitored for some 600 years), the export of nuclear technologies to countries which may not apply stringent safeguards, or the further production of plutonium from fast breeder reactors with the potential proliferation of nuclear arms. All these dangers threaten living systems on a global scale. But they are not reflected in the conventional accounting procedures (of CEGB and others) which claim a cost advantage for nuclear generation over coal and other alternatives. On financial criteria alone, recent studies, including that of the House of Commons Select Committee on Energy, have questioned these cost advantages, pointing to long delays and escalating costs in plant construction.[13]

20. With time, nuclear problems may well be surmountable — indeed, nuclear fusion could hold the key to cheap and virtually unlimited power. But although uranium, the fuel for existing nuclear stations and pressurised water reactors, may be plentiful, its mining will be increasingly costly and hazardous. Over the longer-term, a more sustainable nuclear fission programme depends upon the early introduction of fast breeder reactors using the plutonium cycle, but this seems unlikely to be soon for safety and other technical reasons. In all, there are sufficient present uncertainties over future demand, costs of supply, safety and the implications for other desirable directions for British energy policy, to argue against investing now in further nuclear generating capacity.

21. Important for urban areas is the fact that continuing government commitment to a nuclear future will divert effort and capital away from energy conservation and away from the conversion of coal-fired power stations to supply heat and power for urban areas. Marshall and others have argued that the low fuel efficiency of conventional power stations (around 30 per cent) could be substantially improved by their conversion to combined heat and power (CHP), meeting the heat load of cities (and reducing primary energy demand)

by one-third.[14] It is clear that further nuclear investment will also divert attention away from the
development and application of renewable energy
sources.

22. Although Britain is not well endowed with much of
the resource-base for renewable energy, research so far
(much of it in the Department of Energy) shows considerable scope for employing wind, wave and perhaps
tidal sources to back up coal or nuclear supplies.
Estimates of the future role of renewables vary widely.
Some have claimed that contributions of more than
20 per cent (even up to 50 per cent) of our energy needs
could be met from large scale, offshore wind and wave
generators supplying electricity to the national grid and
fuel from wastes with solar collectors contributing to
domestic and light industrial water heating. More
cautiously, the Department of Energy has estimated a
contribution of 12 to 15 per cent by the year 2025.
This compares with a present nuclear contribution of
12 per cent of primary energy demand, rising to a
possible 30 per cent by the end of the century.[15]

23. There are obvious environmental consequences to be
overcome in harnessing these renewable resources,
including demands upon land, visual intrusion and quite
severe ecological disturbance in the case of tidal barrages.
But their development offers many advantages — not
least sustainability — including more jobs, the potential
for developing and exporting more appropriate technologies for the rest of the world, and less tangible gains
of more varied means of supplying electricity to the
national grid. There are a number of other interesting
possibilities, for example, in the use of coppiced woodland for local fuel supplies. So long as pollution can be
avoided, such ideas may not be inappropriate for urban
edge environments where planting on waste land could
provide some timber for fuel and building and yield
wider amenity benefits. Indeed, there are already
practical demonstrations, for example, in some of
Sweden's local energy centres.

24. In 1981, the budget for all renewable energy R and
D was less than one-tenth of the sum (£130m) spent on
nuclear research. In part, this reflects the early stage of
the work on renewables, but it looks now as if the
Government (on the advice of the Advisory Council on
Research and Development for Fuel and Power) will
abandon further development of the most important
parts of its renewable energy programme at a time when
valuable basic research, on wave power for example, is
ready to be tested by experimental application. Britain
is one of the lowest spenders in Europe on renewable
energy projects; France, for example, is to treble its
budget by 1990.[16] Moreover, the UK is cutting back
just when its own embryonic solar energy industry needs
support, and when latest developments into simpler,
low-cost solar technologies offer the prospect of
widening the access to renewable energy sources.

25. For urban areas, then, to adjust sensibly to a future
of increasing oil scarcity and uncertainty, energy saving
must become a major component of any wider

conservation strategy. Along with many other
advantages for urban living, it allows time to develop
sustainable renewable supplies and find ways of reducing
the risks presently associated with these and with coal
and nuclear generation. Energy is a crucial aspect of
resource management for cities. Consumption is high, so
the effects of saving will be significant. Moreover, as
the neighbourhood energy conservation schemes are
showing, individuals can play a direct part in this. Caring
about energy consumption could prompt a more general
concern for resource-saving.

Land

26. Land not only provides space for physical development; it is also the foundation for many of the other
natural resources, including food, timber, building
materials, and water, upon which urban living depends.
Its remaining natural areas, in and outside the city, are
increasingly regarded as valuable for recreation and for
the regeneration of urban people. Land remains a
thriving commodity for trading, and the workings of
its market profoundly affect the fortunes of conservation (and development) in urban areas. (These issues are
explored later, especially in Chapters 3 and 9.) In all
these, land displays the characteristics of both resource-
scarcity and abundance so that it is in many ways more
difficult to arrive at the principles that should guide
the urban use of land than it is to argue for energy
saving. Open land, like oil, is ultimately finite although
much can be re-used. How much is sterilised and the way
in which the remaining area is managed conditions the
extent to which it can continue to supply all the many
resources which sustain cities over the long-term.

27. Urban and related activities annually consume
approximately 14,000 ha of open land and although
not all of this is physically built upon, nor is it all
biologically rich, this loss represents the sterilisation
of part of our stock of renewable living resources.[17] It is
true that low density development can retain productive
open land in large gardens. But biological diversity is
not easily or cheaply redeemed from most types of
urbanisation — soils alone take at least 150 years to
develop.

28. Even so, direct losses, through the physical development of open land for urban activity, do not constitute
the major threat to living resources. Rather does this
come from the way in which other supports to urban
living are won and how they are transformed in use.
Thus, in creating the market for most of the food now
produced in a highly intensive way on British farms,
society may be said to be contributing to the degradation
of many natural and semi-natural areas, to the loss of
species and to the critical genetic position of others. In
consuming more water and aggregates produced from
rural areas, urban systems have been indirectly
responsible for local losses of natural areas and of
cropland by the introduction and enlargement of

reservoirs and the creation of large areas of derelict and biologically impoverished land, especially at the margins of large conurbations.

Land for Food

29. For various reasons (discussed in the rural report 'Putting Trust in the Countryside', Part 3) pressure is now high to increase the self-sufficiency of our food supplies. Over the longer-term, circumstances suggest this is a sensible goal, in the face of such uncertainties about future population size and our capacity to import food in a world which has so few food exporters, so many rapidly growing nations and so many hungry people. More than a billion, a quarter of the world's population, go without enough to eat. Nearly all the major environmental studies of the last decade have concluded that access to food and agricultural products will become more difficult and expensive.[18]

30. There are many ways of moving towards greater self-sufficiency, depending upon how far land can be substituted by other resources including energy, chemicals and labour, on the mix of crops grown, on animals reared, and on diets. Most options would require much, if not all, of the present food producing land to be safeguarded from the sterilising effects of increasing, and high density, urban development with the best, most flexible, land reserved for food production. But there may be rather less need than is perceived to save every acre of open land for food production or to use every acre intensively.[19]

31. On a world scale, there is a sufficient food deficit for the WCS to argue forcefully, as others have done, for the conservation of all croplands, which implies that they should neither be permanently sterilised nor managed in such a way that essential life support processes, such as soil formation or genetic diversity, are jeopardised. The implication is that the potential for natural renewal should be enhanced rather than eroded (or sustained only by the costly application of further resources, especially oil and fertiliser).

32. There is evidence that parts of our present food production system may well be threatening some essential ecological processes. There have certainly been reductions in the 'wild' areas outside cities, which are the resources for the recreation and education of urban people.[20] Both the prevention of food shortages over the longer-term and the safeguarding of natural habitats in the countryside argue for a food production system which is generally more conserving — in all stages, from farm to city shop. A more conserving food production system could take a variety of forms.

What General Policy for Land?

33. The consequences of lengthening the supply lines of cities apply particularly to food which requires land, energy and other materials not only for its primary production but for storage, processing, transfer, marketing and promotion. Leach and others have shown that resource savings are possible at all stages.[21] Increasing the production of urban food closer to urban areas — in gardens, allotments and smallholdings as well as on larger farms — could make some contribution, even though the possibilities within urban areas may be slender. 'Saving land from urban development' then takes on a new meaning, for some of these kinds of food production are 'urban' activities, yet they could be quite compatible with the conservation and renewal of land resources.

34. If, overall, land is to be treated as a scarce resource, it must be wisely used to support the city. This suggests the positive use of much more open land, within and at the margins of urban areas, which at present lies idle, supplying neither food, naturalness, nor any other resource yet contributing, in a negative way, to poor environments. There are more than one-quarter of a million acres of city wasteland, part of which could be used not only to provide alternative development sites, but also for adventure playspace, trees and new wildlife habitats. The real issue, then, is not so much that urbanisation is, in any simple way, consuming too much land, but that we may not be making the best use of land resources available — both in and outside towns and cities. There are many obstacles here. Some see a major one as being the failure to solve the problem of escalating urban land values which have benefited a few investors at the expense of local communities who are denied both land uses in their interest and the profits from land betterment.

Urban Wildlife

35. Natural species and areas within cities can hardly be described as fundamental to the survival of cities. But there is a good deal of circumstantial evidence (and some empirical psychological research[22]) to suggest that experience and knowledge of natural things is an important part of urban well-being. While they are not major factors, it is difficult to dissociate the lack of naturalness in so many harsh urban environments from the rootlessness which breeds violence and vandalism. The strength of feelings aroused in opposition to the loss of local 'wild' spaces, together with the local support already shown for many city greening schemes, suggests that enjoying and caring for natural areas and wildlife are important elements in the livable city.

36. The WCS counts urbanisation among the most damaging of man's activities for natural life. Yet, paradoxically, some aspects of urban development in Britain have improved the lot of wild species and habitats whose non-urban environment is becoming increasingly hostile. Such is the case for foxes, frogs and many birds where new semi-natural areas have been created, and where large gardens (managed without chemicals), commons and wasteland have provided natural refuges. Even in the conurbations, a remarkable network of ecologically rich environments has been bypassed by development agencies, and is often protected along canals and railways and in the grounds of hospitals, schools and

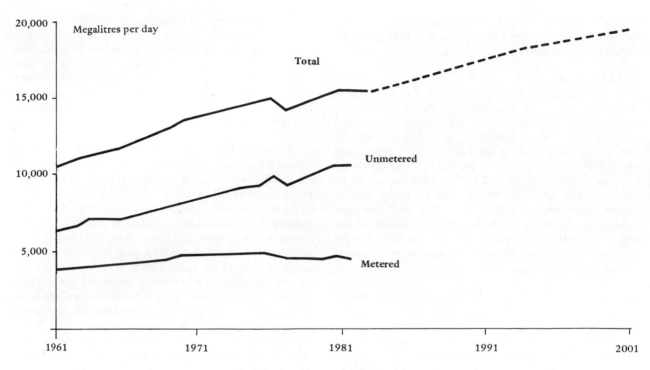

Figure 2. **Public water supplies in England and Wales: historic and forecast**
(Source: National Water Council, 1982)

churchyards. But the effects are highly localised: there is great potential for saving and creating more 'wild' land in cities which can 'touch so very many more people'[23]: in parks and playspaces, in urban woodlands and on land owned by public utility companies and the nationalised industries. More wild habitats could be created on a small scale: in school nature reserves, on land associated with housing developments, and in specialist nature gardens. Many cities in the Netherlands provide good models of what can be done.

37. The issue at stake is not only too little green and natural space, but a failure to make the most of the natural life in cities. Trees and shrubs are valuable not just to look at, but in their capacity to muffle noise, shade and aerate city streets, and absorb pollutants and dust. (Up to one tonne of dust can be trapped in a large urban tree.) They can provide working laboratories of extraordinary ecological diversity for city children to observe, so long as native species (for example, oak, birch and hawthorn) are planted rather than the trad- itional exotic urban trees, such as plane, sycamore and chestnut, which support so few native species. Continuing management, as well as planting, is important. Many city trees die for lack of water, because they are tied too tightly to their stakes. Chapter 6 looks at some of the recent work of voluntary groups in enhancing the wild- life resource-base of cities.

Water

38. In absolute terms, water for domestic, industrial and agricultural use is not scarce in Britain. But its exploitation, especially in reservoirs, commits other resources, including land of agricultural or ecological value, energy and construction materials, and there are also opportunity costs associated with the development of human and capital resources. The policy of the water industry has been to increase supply in response to steadily rising demands: total public supplies rose from under 11,000 Ml per day in 1960, to over 15,000 Ml per day by 1980[24] (see Figure 2). Trend- based forecasts exaggerated future needs and led to decisions about new supplies (like Kielder Water) which could not respond quickly to changing demands in a recession. Since reorganisation of the water industry in 1974, many regional water authorities have concen- trated on smaller schemes and have revised their analytical techniques of demand assessment. Even so, resource-saving has not been a prime objective.

39. Leakages from the system now account for about 25 per cent of total supplies, rising in places (the Lanca- shire coalfield area is one) to 50 per cent. There is a nationally agreed policy for greater waste control, and the National Water Council has reported progress. But implementation is slow, principally because of Govern- ment pressure to reduce expenditure and manpower levels in the water industry. Waste detection schemes, for example in Gloucestershire, suggest that a national programme of leakage detection and repair would be justified on financial grounds alone; it would also contribute to resource saving and new jobs.

40. Moreover, water conservation reduces the pressure to tap presently polluted lowland rivers to increase potable supplies. Water engineers are confident that polluted water can be treated satisfactorily, but, it is worth noting that, in the United States, more

Year	Plaster (1,000 tonnes)	Cement (1,000 tonnes)	Bricks (millions)	Plasterboard (1,000 sq m)	Mined gypsum (1,000 tonnes)	Sand and gravel (1,000 tonnes)
1949	258	9,382	5,227	36,617	1,106	37,288
1959	559	12,818	6,967	43,876	1,615	68,794
1969	942	17,460	6,734	82,824	2,855	108,783
1973*	1,125	19,986	7,183	112,801	3,689	129,150
1979	949	16,140	4,886	113,961	3,396	99,841
1980	960	14,806	4,562	108,915	—	—
1981 (Est.)	795	13,360	3,745	—	—	—

* peak year

Figure 3. **Production of building materials**
(Source: National Council for Building Materials Producers, 1981)

sophisticated methods of water treatment are now being imposed for supplies derived from rivers. Water pollution is discussed further in paragraphs 61 to 65 of this chapter, see pp 113 - 114.

41. Metering has acted as an incentive to conserve water in industry and there could be a case for an equitable pricing system for householders. Over 80 per cent of unmetered potable supplies are to the domestic sector: in the average home, 32 per cent of the water is used for WC flushing and a further 17 per cent goes in baths, showers and washbasins. The use of more efficient appliances (for which the technology exists) could also bring savings even if more extreme measures, like the dual supply system for potable and non-potable water, cannot readily be justified in the UK on cost grounds, except perhaps for major new developments. The development of WCs with greater hydraulic efficiency (and reduced flush volume) is being pursued by the water industry. In some areas, byelaws require the provision of dual flush WCs to reduce the volume of water used. The practice could be extended.

Building Materials

42. Presently declining production figures for most of the main building materials are a reflection not of their approaching scarcity but of the depressed state of the British construction industry, which is a sensitive barometer of the economic climate (see Figure 3, above). Apart from the timber and wood products used in construction, which are mainly imported, most building materials are produced here. The problems of supplying adequate resources for future building needs are indirect and are associated with the need to conserve other resources.

43. Even if materials are not generally scarce, their extraction represents a claim on land and upon its capacity to produce food and natural life. The south-east region, for example, has an estimated 600 to 700 years' supply of sand and gravel at current production rates, if all technical, economic and practical constraints are ignored. But it has been estimated that only 10 to 15 years' supply (20,000 to 25,000 acres) could be won in the south-east without conflict over the loss of agricultural or amenity values.[25] Shortfalls, perhaps as soon as 1990, would mean the transfer of crushed rocks from other regions or the use of more marine gravel, both at higher cost.

44. Restoration of land after extractive industry remains a major problem around British cities: there is too little, too late. Restoration to near the original quality is now feasible for most sites but this is time consuming and expensive; with ceilings on total public expenditure many LAs cannot afford to use the Derelict Land Grant. Most often, restoration simply does not take place: in the London Borough of Havering for example, no sand and gravel workings have yet been successfully restored to the intended grade of agricultural land. The extraction, production and transport of construction materials also consume energy and bring various, albeit temporary, environmental problems — of noise, heavy traffic, air and, sometimes, water pollution. It is desirable to minimise all of these, particularly (as the Verney Committee argued) by enforcing more rigorously the environmental conditions upon working.

45. Combined, all these resource effects of extraction argue for the better husbanding of building materials in urban construction. It seems probable that, over the long-term, the proper maintenance of all buildings to the end of their useful life will use fewer building materials than if the cycle of building is increased by new construction. Chapter 5 considers the arguments and progress in the debate over rehabilitation and 'new build'. Buildings could be more flexibly designed for easy internal adjustment to accommodate new activities and changing lifestyles. World Conservation Strategy goals would suggest using more materials that can be recycled (bricks rather than concrete, incinerated waste as hardcore, and perhaps compacted plastics) and more that are renewable.[26]

46. However, increasing the use of timber and wood products in construction raises other resource issues. Most are at present imported (Figure 4, p 110) mainly from Scandinavia. The future market is uncertain,

	Imports £m	Exports
Natural aggregates	3.9	12.4
Cement	3.6	24.2
Timber	498.1	3.1
Plywood, reconstituted wood, cork, hardboard, veneers, builders' woodwork	298.0	59.5

Figure 4. **Import and export
of building materials, 1980**
(Source: National Council for Building Materials
Producers, 1981)

because there will be more competitors for dwindling supplies as developing countries industrialise, and some exporters (notably Sweden) are known to be considering alternative energy uses for their forests.[27] World-wide, although Britain may not so far have been heavily implicated, the market for hardwood veneers has undoubtedly contributed to the rapid decline of genetic material in the tropical rain forests. Unless more timber can be produced here (and the Rural report 'Putting Trust in the Countryside', Part 3 considers this), there is little opportunity for substantially increasing the renewable components of construction.

Waste

47. Denis Hayes writes: 'at least two-thirds of all the material resources we now waste could be re-used without important changes in our lifestyles'.[28] Yet, unlike industry, where recycling is increasing as input costs rise, the re-use of domestic wastes has been declining. Of the estimated 28 million tonnes of waste dealt with by the waste disposal authorities (WDAs) of England and Wales in 1982, two-thirds will come from households and commerce (Figure 5, p 111). These authorities will dispose of 85 per cent of the waste as largely untreated landfill.[29] This will sterilise some land for long periods, often filling in, as in the West Midlands, the 'unofficial countryside' of local natural areas. Disposal by landfill consumes energy in transport and contributes to bad, often dangerous, environments, especially where hazardous wastes are disposed together with domestic refuse.[30]

48. Wastes are resources in disguise. Domestic rubbish can be sorted for valuable raw materials whose production from virgin supplies may become less certain (like paper) and is often high on energy consumption (like aluminium and glass). Recycling scrap aluminium requires only 5 per cent of the energy needed to smelt the metal from bauxite. Vogler estimated in 1980 that import substitution by reclaimed materials could save £275m on the balance of payments.[31]

49. In spite of the great cost advantages of untreated landfill over other methods (£2.41 per tonne, compared with £8.09 per tonne for landfill after shredding or pulverisation and £10.26 per tonne for incineration) there has been a small, but significant, shift away from untreated landfill towards other methods which reduce bulk (Figure 6, p 111).[32] Predictably, the trend is most pronounced in the metropolitan counties and the GLC, for these authorities face growing difficulty in finding suitable landfill sites within their areas and the rising costs of long hauls. Incineration is seen as the main alternative, accounting for almost 10 per cent of the total waste that WDAs dispose of. But their objective is to reduce the volume of waste rather than recover resources, although the two can be combined, and are, in the GLC's Edmonton incinerator which produces electricity.

50. Overall, very little domestic waste is reclaimed as energy or raw material, although there is considerable potential. Combustible materials (paper, textiles and plastic film) which make up one-third of the total can be turned into fuel of various kinds; paper-rich waste is suitable for board-making; ferrous scrap is acceptable to iron-founders and can be shredded and cleaned for re-tinning; the use of cullet in glass manufacture brings energy savings. In fact, public willingness to sort used bottles coupled with manufacturers' concern to prevent legislation on returnable containers have been responsible for one of the successes of domestic recycling: the bottle bank. Food and garden waste, which makes up one-fifth of the domestic load, can be pulverised and matured to make compost; it can be a feedstock for methane generation or for the growth of single cell organisms for use in animal feed.

51. There are several reasons for Britain's poor record on raw materials recovery. The capital costs of recycling plants are high and there have been many operating problems. But the technology for mechanical sorting, both to reduce volume and produce more than one raw material, is now being developed. The Government has contributed, both financially and technically, to experimental plants at Newcastle and Doncaster; other local authorities and the private sector have developed schemes, often as joint enterprises. There is a continuing debate over the relative costs and merits of post-collection recycling in these large, high technology plants and those of pre-collection sorting which relies upon the goodwill and efforts of individuals and community groups. Until the relative costs and advantages are better known after a good deal more experiment, it would seem sensible to pursue all avenues towards more waste saving, and particularly those combinations of methods that can bring a variety of benefits — in jobs and community participation as well as resource-saving. There are successful, labour-intensive waste disposal schemes in operation (Hamburg has one) which rely upon separation, at home, of the clean, dry recyclable materials from the rest. The contents of the 'green' bin are then carried, in special twin compactor vehicles, to plants where the re-usable materials are hand sorted to reclaim as much high value waste as possible.

52. In England, the divided responsibility between district councils as collection authorities and county

Waste category	England and Wales 1981/82 million tonnes
From collecting authorities (districts); mainly household and commercial	18.6
Industrial and commercial waste accepted by Waste Disposal Authorities (WDAs)	7
Generated by WDAs	2.4
Total disposed of by WDAs	28
	estimated annual figure for the UK
From building operations	3
From power stations	12
Mining waste	60*
Quarry waste	50*

* not subject to the Control of
Pollution Act 1974
all the rest are controlled
wastes under this Act

Figure 5. **Waste disposal in the UK 1981/82**
(Source: Gulley, B W. 1981. The way ahead. DOE)

	percentage of total waste	
	1979/80	1981/82
Landfill, untreated (WDAs)	71.3	67.0
Landfill, mainly untreated (WDAs and contractors)	16.9	18.8
Landfill after shredding or pulverisation	2.4	3.3
Incineration (mainly without separation)	8.7	9.7
Other methods	0.7	1.4

Figure 6. **Waste treatment in England and Wales 1981/82**
(Source: Waste Disposal Statistics 1981/82, Estimates for England and Wales; Chartered Institute of Public Finance and Accountancy)

councils as disposal authorities provides no incentive to sort wastes at either end. The internal organisation of the services which is geared to high productivity and bonus payments works against sorting and reclamation which will slow down the throughput of refuse.

53. A continuing problem has been the fluctuating market for waste materials, especially paper. Almost none of the 200 waste collection authorities that collected separated paper in 1974 now do so. Yet for newsprint alone, more than 80 per cent is imported and technically far more waste could be reprocessed. Guaranteed waste supplies and markets for recycled paper, for example from local and central government departments, could enable local reclamation firms to stay in business. That public agencies should use at least 10 per cent recycled paper would not seem unreasonable. Vogler estimates that a 20 per cent increase in the amount of waste paper used in UK paper and board manufacture could save 18 million trees a year.[33]

Pollution

54. Waste products can be so concentrated that they exceed the natural dispersal capacities of air, land or water causing pollution which can put at risk both human health and the capability of natural life to renew itself. Pollutants can also cause physical damage to the built environment and generally make urban areas less pleasant places in which to live and work than they would otherwise be. In all these ways, pollution limits the usefulness of many resources upon which cities depend. Its control to levels consistent with human well-being, good environment and the sustainability of natural systems implies complex trade-offs between these benefits and the costs involved in achieving them.

Air Pollution

55. Since the passing of the Clean Air Act in 1956, the urban atmosphere has improved dramatically. But there are still black spots. In some ways only the nature of the pollutants has changed: less smoke but more sulphur dioxide and other gases from domestic fires, industrial furnaces and power stations, and more lead in the air from vehicle exhausts. High SO_2 levels have been correlated with death and ill health, particularly among bronchitis sufferers; oxides of nitrogen are believed to increase susceptibility to respiratory diseases and, with hydrocarbons, they can form photochemical smog. Acid soot is discharged from the chimneys of oil-fired furnaces and can damage paintwork and fabrics. Smoke from oil and coal burning and from vehicles exacerbates the effect of all these pollutants, and soils buildings and clothes.[34]

56. It is now known that air pollution can be transported over long distances, from cities and industrial areas where the density of emissions is high, to fall as acid rain over a wide area. Although the process is not completely understood, there is mounting evidence of the effects in northern Europe. In German forests, the number of trees destroyed by diseases caused by acid rain are said to represent up to 50 per cent of the annual timber harvests and in Sweden 20,000 of the country's 100,000 lakes are affected.[35] Since Norway

Figure 7. **Wastes are resources in disguise**
Every day, 50,000 tonnes of solid waste is produced from British homes, most of it to be thrown onto
the land around our towns and cities. But there are more resourceful ways of dealing with waste
which could save land and raw materials and create jobs
Copyright: OXFAM

and Sweden claimed that the major part of the acid rain falling in their countries originated from elsewhere in Europe, the long-range transport of pollution has become a matter of international concern. Action so far has taken the form of resolutions and conventions on control, such as the 1979 Geneva Convention (of the Economic Commission for Europe) on Long-range Transboundary Air Pollution, but they lack the force of law.

57. In the UK, SO_2 emissions have been falling over the last two decades, with average urban concentrations measured at ground level now over 50 per cent lower than in 1960. Electricity generation accounted for over 55 per cent of SO_2 emissions at the end of the 1970s, and it is the CEGB's 'tall stack' policy (involving the release of pollutants as high as possible) that would appear to have contributed significantly to reduced SO_2 levels in British cities. But the same policy has led to environmental problems in the UK countryside as well as abroad. A recent study of the High Peak district suggests that peat erosion may have been prompted by nineteenth century air pollution, and that continuing high SO_2 levels are damaging the bog vegetation. Recent studies in Scotland show that most of the country has rainfall of at least 15 times greater acidity than would otherwise occur naturally. Yet research into air pollution in Britain, including the crop, forest and health effects of SO_2 and the monitoring of pollutants, is now to be cut.

58. The case made earlier in this chapter for an energy

policy based on conservation, coal and renewables rests upon pollution control at source, which is what the Geneva Convention recommends. But the CEGB estimates that to do so by means of a full scale programme of the flue gas desulphurisation (FGD) could increase generating costs by 25 to 30 per cent, and would involve an energy penalty of 5 to 10 per cent of the coal burnt.[36] In fact, there are other less costly methods than FGD of reducing sulphur emissions, such as fluidised bed combustion (FBC), but even with FGD, coal could still be a cheaper source of energy than nuclear generation.[37] An Organisation for Economic Co-operation and Development (OECD) study goes further to suggest that there could be net monetary benefits (increased crop and aquatic production, health improvements, and savings on materials erosion) with a programme reducing SO_2 emissions by 50 per cent over four years. The assumed measures include controls on oil combustion, the introduction of FGD to large plants and the use of low sulphur coal and gas. The analysis did not take into account the benefits of increased life expectancy and better environments.[38]

59. In 1980, the EEC issued a Directive setting 'limit' and 'guide' values for sulphur dioxide and smoke. The limit values are mandatory and to be complied with by April 1983 (although an extension period may be allowable). The guide values are intended as objectives for the longer-term.[39] In 38 British districts, mainly in the conurbations and the coalfield areas, there is evidence that SO_2 concentrations are in excess of one or more of the limit values, while in a further

GOOD	*Class 1:*	suitable for potable supply abstractions; high class fisheries; high amenity value.
FAIR	*Class 2:*	suitable for potable supply abstractions after advanced treatment; reasonably good coarse fisheries; moderate amenity value.
POOR	*Class 3:*	suitable for low grade industrial abstraction; fish absent or sporadically present; considerable potential for further use if cleaned up.
BAD	*Class 4:*	grossly polluted and likely to cause nuisance.

Figure 8. **River classification system**
(Source: National Water Council, 1982)

33 districts, the Department of Environment say more study is needed to find out whether excess concentrations of SO_2 and smoke are likely in future.[40] Parts of the central area of London will also fail to meet the EEC limits until there can be some reduction in the use of high sulphur fuels commonly burnt in office furnaces. There are also problems in meeting the limit values for smoke because of emissions from motor vehicles (especially diesels) in busy streets. Compliance with the EEC directive implies either tighter emission standards or measures to limit the use of fuel or vehicles; these are issues addressed in Chapter 4.

60. Although there is general agreement that too much lead in the bloodstream is bad for human health, and that children absorb it more easily than adults, there is still argument in this country about safe levels and about which sources of lead (from water pipes, contaminated food, vehicle emissions) constitute the most serious threat. However, there is mounting evidence that quite low blood lead levels (below the present DHSS safety limit) are associated with behavioural problems and impaired intelligence among urban children. The British Medical Association have said: 'Taking into account all the available evidence it would apear that the elimination of lead from petrol would reduce considerably the concentration of lead in the atmosphere . . . and produce a reduction in the burden of lead absorbed by individuals'.[41] The proposed reduction of lead in petrol to 0.15gm per litre by 1985 is an unacceptable compromise, providing no clear advantage but prolonging the pollution of urban areas and reducing their safety for many other desirable activities. It now seems likely (January 1983) that a decision in the European Parliament could bring an early ban on petrol lead in the member states of the EEC.

Water Pollution
61. There has been a substantial reduction in gross pollution of the rivers of England and Wales over the last decade mainly because of new and extended sewage treatment works and trunk sewers, a concentration of effort on 'black spots', industrial investment in the treatment of waste water and the connection of polluting trade effluent to public sewers. But the quality of many rivers has not improved, and some are now much worse. The latest findings of the National Water Council, employing a new classification of river quality

(see Figure 8), show that of the rivers, canals and estuaries of England and Wales categorised as 'poor' or 'badly polluted' most are in urban areas.[42]

62. The problems are more financial than technical. Although trade and farm effluent and leachates from waste disposal sites have all contributed to river pollution and the difficulties of improving water quality, within and around urban areas it is the lack of investment in sewers and sewage treatment that has been the major factor: spending in 1980 was less than half the 1974 level. The Regional Water Authorities (RWAs) are responsible for setting river quality objectives (following the Control of Pollution Act 1974) and for granting consents to discharge effluent subject to conditions. They are also the operators of sewage treatment plants. Most often, river quality objectives have been defined to maintain the existing quality rather than raise it over the short-term, even if longer-term objectives (beyond 10 years) are for improvement. For some urban rivers, the present quality of objectives is much lower than desirable on environmental grounds. But with outworn sewage systems, water authorities in many areas would be unable to meet their own consent conditions if quality levels and discharge standards were higher.

63. Years of under investment by local authorities before reorganisation in 1974, and subsequent limits on capital spending, have left urban sewage systems in an appalling state of disrepair. Sixty per cent of the treatment works inherited by the north-west Water Authority are in an unsatisfactory condition, and one-sixth of the mileage of public sewers is structurally unsound or close to collapse. Moreover, most urban areas have a combined drainage and sewerage system. During heavy rainfall, the rapid run-off means that storm overflows are necessary, discharging untreated sewage into rivers and estuaries. Some RWAs now operate separate drainage and sewerage schemes for new development but there remains an urgent need for more investment to increase the capacity of urban sewers and improve treatment works.

64. A number of major improvement programmes are planned: the north-west Water Authority is committed to a 15 year programme, costing £90m, to eliminate gross pollution from the Mersey Estuary, and the Northumbrian Water Authority is investing in major sewerage and sewage disposal schemes to improve water quality in the Tyne, Wear and Tees. A 10 year £43m sewerage and sewage disposal scheme in the Severn Trent Water Authority area is raising the quality of the urban streams through Birmingham and the Black Country. The Yorkshire Water Authority estimates that some £200m may have to be spent over the long-term to achieve water quality objectives, yet there is nothing in their current capital programme for this. In fact, many desirable projects are being deferred by the RWAs because of continuing cuts in public expenditure. For most of the authorities, the best they can hope for is to prevent rivers from deteriorating below their existing quality classes and to eliminate gross nuisance. But it may prove impossible to meet even these limited

objectives. In its 1982 Water Industry Review, the National Water Council states: 'Water authorities will find it difficult to maintain existing water quality . . . if present financial restraints continue. In some places water quality will deteriorate and in many it will not improve . . .'

65. Water pollution from industrial sources can be reduced by imposing tougher conditions on consents to discharge directly into watercourses, by connecting the discharge to the public sewerage system and by promoting more treatment of industrial effluent at source. Here again, there are difficulties. RWAs are encouraging more trade effluent to be discharged to sewers rather than directly to watercourses and this is now priced to take full account of handling costs, which should provide an incentive for more firms to reduce pollution by modifying their processes. Charging for direct discharge and applying more stringent conditions would act in the same direction. But this in part depends upon a much faster move towards meeting the long-term objectives of raised river quality — and the general obligations imposed by the 1974 Control of Pollution Act. For most RWAs the timescale for this, although beyond 10 years, is not specified.

Summing up on Resources: The Wider Implications

66. It is clear that British towns and cities will have to adjust to a leaner and more uncertain resource future, certainly for energy but also for other supports to urban living and perhaps especially for those imported from developing countries. The OECD Interfutures Study (and others) show that while the world resource-picture suggests no immediate shortages for Britain of any important raw material, rapid change is possible in international commodity markets and the future development of economic unions and cartels could bring unpredictable scarcities.[43] Besides, it is not necessary to forecast imminent critical shortages to show that urban living standards are threatened by continuing present consumption levels. Rising resource-prices, in energy and other materials, have a number of undesirable consequences for all sectors of the economy. Less capital is available for other public and private investments, including a wide range of urban improvements. Family budgets are strained, and even with support, which exists for fuel bills, the poorest, the old and the unemployed (whose energy costs make up a high proportion of total spending) are penalised.

67. There are many consequences for the natural world, here and abroad. The rising costs of oil and other raw materials will speed up the search for substitutes and prompt the exploration of lower grade and less accessible sources with potentially damaging consequences for environment and health. Without more water pollution control and less waste in water distribution, abstraction from lowland rivers will become increasingly difficult. Without making some of the

savings that are possible by the re-use of construction materials, extraction will continue to disfigure and pollute more landscapes. Most of our timber is imported, but on an increasingly uncertain and competitive market so that there is a strong case for recycling more wood products (especially paper) and for growing more trees.

68. These are some of the direct and immediate costs to us of continuing present resource consumption patterns. But the costs are also severe for the economies, societies and for the natural environments of developing countries — a key concern of the WCS. Inevitably, as Brandt and others have argued, the effects will rebound upon us; it is not only the consequences of scarcity and uncertainty at home that should guide our use of resources.[44] Although the implications of SO_2 emission, for example, are not wholly proven and may be indirect, there are sufficient links between our own resource-consumption patterns and the degradation of some of the world's major living systems to argue for a change in attitude and practice. One role must be to advise poor countries how better to manage their own environments, but we also have an obligation to reduce our own consumption of some resources and contribute to a greater sharing of the world's natural assets.

69. The UK uses more oil and gas than all of Africa and South Asia combined.[45] Such high levels of consumption of the world's oil supplies by the developed North means that less can be available at a cheap rate for the countries of the South, many of whom spend half their foreign income on oil imports. Yet Britain remains largely indifferent (notably in its lack of support for a two tier oil price system)[46] to the crippling economic effects of expensive imported fuel on Third World countries and their consequent inability not only to provide markets for British products but also to finance urban and rural development programmes which are more conserving of natural resources. For people in the major cities of the South, the scarcity and high cost of commercial fuels means they must continue to exploit dwindling forests at the edge of development for firewood.

70. By providing markets, but not ensuring sustainable yields, the UK is also implicated in the rapid exploitation of tropical hardwoods and in the damaging development of some cash cropping in Third World countries at the expense of local subsistence food production. By failing to recognise and employ all the means possible to safeguard natural systems and their genetic diversity the UK threatens not only the development prospects for the South, but also aspects of its own, in crop breeding and pharmaceuticals, for example. As the WCS states: 'The combined destructive impacts of a poor majority struggling to stay alive and an affluent minority consuming most of the world's resources are undermining the very means by which all people can survive and flourish'.[47]

71. Alone, reduced consumption here in the UK may have little direct effect on Third World countries whose fragile economies force them to exploit natural resources. But it will fit us better for a time when those resources

will be controlled and used locally and will no longer be available to us at such abundant, cheap rates. Whatever their development paths, most of the world's population cannot hope to live at the standards of urban society in developed countries. Such extreme imbalances in resource-consumption can only increase north-south tension and the potential for global conflict. This alone should make us question present patterns of resource-use and search for a more sustainable style of urban living that lends some credibilty to our belief in conservation. We need to develop ways of managing cities which could provide more appropriate models for our urbanisation advice to the Third World — on energy, waste treatment technologies and building methods, as well as community development. A British conservation strategy must reflect its global obligations.

72. Thus, the argument is for using fewer virgin materials in running our cities, for re-using existing supplies, for creating resources close to urban areas where possible and for developing a greater diversity of resource supplies. This does not imply isolationism or a siege economy. As the International report, 'The UK's Overseas Environmental Policy', Part 5, argues, we live in an interdependent world where increasing cooperation between nations (with trading as a part of this) offers the only real chance to solve global problems. Anyway, the prospect of total self-sufficiency in most of the natural resources the UK needs is impossible to foresee. However, in the UK we can still make better use of what we have — nationally, in our communities and in our homes. Chapter 3 looks at the effects of present patterns of urbanisation of resources.

Notes and References

1 'Resources' in this report means renewable and non-renewable, living and non-living natural resources, unless otherwise qualified.

2 Sources: DEPARTMENT OF ENERGY. 1981. Digest of UK energy statistics. HMSO; LEACH, G et al. 1979. A low energy strategy for the UK. International Institute for Environment and Development (IIED); GERALD LEACH. Personal communication.

3 BEST, R H. 1981. Land use and living space. Methuen. 11 per cent is the 1971 figure for England and Wales; 8 per cent is for the UK.

4 Digest of UK energy statistics 1981, op cit; DEPARTMENT OF ENERGY. April 1982. Energy trends.

5 Loft insulation grants now 90 per cent for most pensioners (to a maximum of £70); 60 per cent for other householders (to a maximum of £50).

6 GERALD LEACH. Personal communication.

7 In nine EEC countries $55 billion is presently being invested in new energy supplies, compared with $10 billion in conservation and other demand management technologies. Raising this to $33 - $35 billion could create an estimated 500,000 jobs (with eight million at present unemployed in Europe) and increase GDP by 1 per cent. Stated by Robert Shotton, Energy Directorate of the European Commission at an International Congress on Energy Use Management, Berlin 1981; EUROPEAN ECONOMIC COMMISSION. 1982. Investment in the rational use of energy. See also: ASSOCIATION FOR THE CONSERVATION OF ENERGY. 1982. Comparison of the energy conservation programme of the UK and other EEC countries. Part of the ACE evidence to the House of Lords Committee of Inquiry into energy conservation.

8 JANE CARTER of the Energy Technology Support Unit (Department of Energy) in a paper on energy conservation given to the Royal Institute of Public Administration/ Policy Studies Institute in November 1981.

9 The CEGB has a duty to meet demand, and its policy is to predict the demand likely to occur rather than a desirable level. Throughout the 1960s, the CEGB continued to assume that demand was increasing exponentially rather than, as was the case, linearly. This led to a large installed over-capacity to generate 28 per cent more electricity than is needed at peak demand.

10 COMMITTEE FOR THE STUDY OF ECONOMICS OF NUCLEAR ENERGY. 1981. Nuclear energy: the real cost. The Ecologist.

11 CLARKE, R and TIMBERLAKE, L. 1982. Stockholm plus ten. IIED.

12 COMMISSION ON ENERGY AND THE ENVIRONMENT. 1981. Coal and environment. HMSO.

13 HOUSE OF COMMONS SELECT COMMITTEE ON ENERGY. 1981. First report. Vol 1. HMSO; GERALD LEACH of IIED has also shown, reworking figures given in the Department of Energy Proof of Evidence for the Sizewell Inquiry, that nuclear generation does not appear to be unequivocably cheaper than alternatives.

14 MARSHALL, W. 1979. Combined heat and power generation in the United Kingdom. Department of Energy Paper 35. HMSO.

15 Energy Technology Support Unit, Harwell.

16 Nature, 296, 25 March 1982.

17 COUNCIL FOR THE PROTECTION OF RURAL ENGLAND. 1981. Planning — friend or foe? CPRE. The MAFF figure is quoted as the annual land loss to urban, industrial and mineral development over the period 1974-79. See also: Land use and living space, op cit.

18 Stockholm plus ten, op cit; BROWN, L R. 1982. Building a sustainable society. Worldwatch Institute; KENT, G. 1982. The poor feed the rich. Development Forum, May.

19 DAVIDSON, J and LLOYD, R. 1977. Conservation and agriculture. Wiley; See also: WISE, W S and FELL, E. 1978. UK agriculture: productivity and the land budget. Journal of Agricultural Economics, 29 (1).

20 NATURE CONSERVANCY COUNCIL. 1981. Annual report.

21 LEACH, G. 1975. Energy and food production. IIED.

22 MOSTYN, B. 1980. Personal benefits and satisfactions derived from participation in urban wildlife projects. Nature Conservancy Council.

23 BAINES, C. 1982. Urban wildlife — conservation and re-creation. *Natural World, Spring*, RSNC.

24 NATIONAL WATER COUNCIL. 1982. Water industry review — supporting analysis; NATIONAL WATER COUNCIL. 1982. The water industry in figures. See also: PARKER, D and PENNING-ROWSELL, E C. 1980. Water Planning in Britain. Allen and Unwin.

25 Evidence of the Institute of Geological Sciences and of the Department of Environment to the Verney Committee, 1977.

26 There is potential for increasing the production of aggregates of various kinds from colliery spoil, china clay waste, slate waste, pulverised fuel ash, blast furnace slag, fluorspar mine tailings and quarry wastes and for using slate quarry waste and tin mine tailings in brick manufacture.

27 JOHANNSON, T B and STEEN, P. 1977. Solar Sweden. Secretariat for Futures Studies, Sweden.

28 HAYES, D. 1978. Repairs, re-use, recycling — first steps towards a sustainable society. *Worldwatch paper 23.*

29 Estimates for 1981/82 by N Barnes of the GLC in *Energy from rubbish, November 1981.* See also: Merseyside structure plan. 1980; FRIENDS OF THE EARTH. 1981. Waste Midlands; GULLEY, B W. 1981. The way ahead. Department of Environment..

30 HOUSE OF LORDS SELECT COMMITTEE. 1981. The disposal of hazardous wastes. Report.

31 VOGLER, J. 1980. Muck and brass. Oxfam Public Affairs Unit.

32 Source of costs: The way ahead, *op cit.*

33 Muck and brass, *op cit.*

34 GREATER LONDON COUNCIL, LONDON BOROUGHS' ASSOCIATION, CEGB. 1980. Study report of the polluting matters working group — sub-group on air pollution.

35 Acid rain: diseases affecting Europe. *The Times, 16 February 1982.*

36 ENDS reports: Energy and environment. 21 March 1979; Coal's environment. 4 January 1981.

37 Nuclear energy: the real cost, *op cit.*

38 OECD. 1981. The costs and benefits of sulphur dioxide control — a methodological study.

39 Directive no 80/779/EEC. 1980.

40 DEPARTMENT OF ENVIRONMENT. Circular 11/81, WO18/81.

41 BRITISH MEDICAL ASSOCIATION. 1982. Evidence to the Royal Commission on Environmental Pollution. Quoted in *CLEAR Newspaper, 2.*

42 NATIONAL WATER COUNCIL. 1981. River quality — the 1980 survey and future outlook.

43 OECD. 1979. Interfutures: final report. Paris, OECD.

44 BRANDT COMMISSION. 1980. North-South, a programme for survival. Pan Books. See also: HIGGINS, R. 1981. The seventh enemy. Hodder and Stoughton.

45 FOLEY, G and NASSIM, C. 1981. The energy question. Penguin Books, 2nd ed. The EEC and USA together consume about half of all the world's primary energy.

46 Called for at the UN Conference on New and Renewable Sources of Energy, Nairobi, August 1981.

47 IUCN. 1980. World conservation strategy.

CHAPTER 3

URBAN CHANGE: OUTWARD GROWTH, INNER DECAY

Introduction

1. Declining populations now characterise all the major urban areas of Europe, irrespective of the size of a country or its stage of development. There are fewer employment opportunities in the central and inner parts of urban regions, reflecting both the economic climate and technological developments which have forced most businesses to shed labour and many to close down. These changes have been exacerbated by an increase in the number of people of working age.[1]

2. Since the 1950s, the pattern of urbanisation in Britain has been marked by two distinct stages. First there was gradual population decline from the large metropolitan areas, associated with the relocation of industry outside central and inner areas, with central area development for offices and shops, suburban expansion and the growth of new and expanded towns. Second, over the last decade, there has been a more rapid loss of population affecting the suburbs as well as the inner areas of large cities. In Birmingham, Leeds, Liverpool, Manchester, Newcastle, Sheffield and Greater London there was a 10 per cent loss between 1971 and 1981. The north-west region and the north of England have suffered the largest decline. More recently, medium-sized towns in the 80,000 to 160,000 range have also lost people: a 2 per cent growth in these settlements in the early 1960s had changed to a 3 per cent loss by 1970. It is the small market towns and parts of the remoter countryside, particularly the south-west, East Anglia and the East Midlands that have begun to grow. Overall, the decade up to 1981 saw a 1.9 per cent decline in the urban population and a 9.7 per cent increase in rural areas.[2] Population structure has also changed: there are now more households than 10 years ago, but they are smaller. Small household units account for 80 per cent of the growth in households in the south-east region during this decade.[3]

Decentralisation: Causes and Response

3. A number of factors have contributed to this outward flow from cities, including the controlled decentralisation from the conurbations which was enshrined in post-war planning policy. The movement of people and jobs to new and 'expanded' towns was one half of the strategy. The other was to transform the outworn and congested inner areas into better places in which to live and work by removing 'non-conforming' industry, creating green space and rebuilding homes and schools. In the event, the economy of these inner areas declined and much inner city renewal failed to create the kind of living environments people wanted. Conditions deteriorated for those most disadvantaged in job opportunities and housing. But rising incomes and increasing car ownership made it possible for some people to respond to the 'push' of worsening urban environments and the 'pull' of more spacious living by moving out to the greener suburbs and the countryside beyond.

4. The continuing out-movement of jobs reflects the disadvantages to modern industry of an inner city location (with its unsuitable premises, perceived high land values and rates, and poor access). New factory processes often demand large sites and new technologies, such as the manufacture of micro circuits and optical fibres, need clean environments. The highly accessible, low density industrial, office and science 'parks' on greenfield sites have been attractive to industrialists, developers and investors alike — in spite of inner area incentives, greenfield development has been easier and cheaper. Recent Government policy, in particular the streamlining of the planning system, has reinforced this trend. Good accessibility, large sites for storage and car parking and often pleasant surroundings, have also stimulated the development of out-of-town shopping centres. By 1980, there were some 250 superstores and hypermarkets, five times the number of 1972.[4]

5. With the exodus of much industry and the collapse of many small businesses, the decline of employment has been greatest in the inner city. The economic 'boom' of the 1960s, which provided the impetus for central area redevelopment and suburban growth, failed to revive the economy of inner areas or to solve their employment and environmental problems. In spite of renewal, the centrifugal forces have also affected city centres themselves. Problems which include transport and car parking, and the competition from new suburban centres for shops, head offices, administration and cultural facilities, are all helping to reduce the role of central areas.

6. The motor vehicle as an agent of decentralisation has reinforced other strong pressures that are leading to a

more dispersed pattern of land use. Dispersal is also being propelled by new communications technologies, in information retrieval and teleconferencing, which make it possible for people to work at home.

7. Since the mid 1970s there have been a number of responses to the plight of the inner city from central and local government, the private sector and community groups, all focusing on the need for economic regeneration. The initiatives have included three DOE-sponsored inner area studies in Liverpool, Birmingham and Lambeth, the 1978 Inner Urban Areas Act and a number of Government aided programmes relating to specified areas: the Enterprise Zones (with baits to private investment in the form of tax allowances, limited planning constraints, no rates) and Urban Development Corporations in the London Docks and Merseyside. A number of new organisations have emerged to foster small businesses such as the local enterprise trusts which seek to mobilise local resources, enterprise agencies formed by large companies and municipal enterprise boards.[5]

8. But there has been no consistent revival of the inner city economy, although a number of initiatives have taken hold at the local level (and are described in Chapter 6). Moreover, in the present period of acute recession and high unemployment, national economic recovery is seen to lie with modernised and automated manufacturing and the new high technology enterprises described in the Industry report 'Seven Bridges to the Future', Part 1. For most of these enterprises, neither their locational demands nor their labour requirements (for a small, highly skilled, non-manual workforce) favour the inner areas.

9. Examining some of the causes and consequences of the 'flight' from the cities, David Eversley concludes that, without a significant change in the economy and government policies, the process will continue.[6] The prospects for jobs and living conditions in the inner cities will continue to deteriorate: already poor housing will decay further; the population will remain older and relatively unskilled; and unemployment will rise. These trends will be exacerbated as housebuilding, industrial and commercial development resume in the growth areas (especially along the 'Sunrise Strip') leading, Eversley argues, to a more deeply divided society.

10. Quite apart from the consequences of decentralisation for the jobs and living conditions of those who remain in the inner cities, there are resource-implications of which the most significant are:
□ continuing land-take for development;
□ more wasteland both within cities and on their fringes;
□ lack of urban greenspace and reduced access to natural areas in the countryside;
□ empty and neglected buildings;
□ more travel (and more energy consumed in it) but poorer access in the city.

Land Take

11. Arguments for treating land generally as a scarce

resource have been set out in Chapter 2. Robin Best considers that, for so urbanised a country, the UK has been extraordinarily conservative in the use of land for building (indeed, he and others have suggested that too little land has been used in many settlements to provide adequate living conditions). His analyses show no sustained increase in the urban land growth rate since the early post-war years. In fact, the recession has so restricted residential and other types of development that 1978 saw the lowest level of annual land loss to urban uses — about 8,000 ha.[7]

12. But others are less optimistic about what has happened and the prospects for future change. The Council for the Protection of Rural England (CPRE) gives an annual average loss of 14,000 ha of open land in England alone (although this includes some non-urban industrial, recreational and mineral developments).[8] An upturn in the economy could see renewed pressure for suburban expansion: much land already has planning permission for development which has not been realised; household formation will increase to accommodate the late teenage bulge if jobs and incomes improve, and housebuilders will continue to press for the release of land to enable the building industry to revive. Even so, the building industry's priorities (in terms of the location and type of housing to be provided) may be wrong. Geoffrey Steeley has argued that the housing market is not responding well to the varied requirements of an urban population which is changing its structure and to the special needs of new households and elderly couples for smaller dwellings, both new and converted. Providing these within urban areas, rather than on their periphery, will ensure better access to a wider range of facilities for these groups, many of whom do not have cars. Indeed, it may be that sufficient land is already earmarked outside existing urban areas to cater for new housing needs over the next decade so long as the older housing stock can be rehabilitated to provide a greater variety of dwellings.

13. In 1980, the Secretary of State for the Environment urged planning authorities to ease restrictions on development in the interests of economic regeneration (DOE Circular, 22/80). The combined effects of new styles of industrial and commercial plant, existing planning permissions and the advice of the Secretary of State, may, as Elson argues: 'release a flood of development in areas within commuting distance of the main conurbations'.[9] It does not seem that inner city programmes will do much to counter these pressures while development is relatively uncontrolled outside urban areas. There are ways of influencing its location under existing policies, but the case is strong for a reversal of the principles of Circular 22/80 so that there is a presumption against greenfield building. The last part of Chapter 5 argues this case further.

Wasteland

14. The total amounts of vacant and derelict land in urban areas are not known, but they are likely to be large: Nabarro estimates at least 5 per cent of all

metropolitan land lies vacant, with the proportion rising to 6.6 per cent or one acre in 15 for the older inner cities.[10] There are more than 12 square miles of vacant land in the Merseyside Structure Plan area, and a further seven square miles which may in time become derelict, which will mean that 7 per cent of all land on Merseyside will soon become vacant.[11] Vacant land contributes to generally poor, often dangerous, environments. It represents an extraordinary waste of assets which could be used, as a number of recent reports have shown, in a great variety of positive ways.[12] But there is much debate over the type of development that should take place. London's Docklands provide a good example of opposing viewpoints.[13]

15. Land remains vacant in cities for many reasons. Some is caught up in the often lengthy process of development. Some owners hold on to it in the expectation of realising high development values. Inertia is also the cause of much land holding, especially among utility companies; public land registers may help to bring some of this onto the market. But despite the incentives that now operate (particularly in the Enterprise Zones and Inner City Partnership areas), peripheral and out-of-town locations, where there are relatively so few constraints upon development, will be preferred by investors and inner city vacant land will remain.

16. Most of this vacant land will stay out of reach of the less profitable but often desirable urban uses associated with conservation, unless arrangements can be made to release it (temporarily and permanently) at low rents. There are now a number of successful schemes where LAs have been willing to lease land for short periods — eg, the London Borough of Southwark and the William Curtis Ecological Park scheme, which is described in Chapter 6. But it needs to be made much easier for local groups and LAs to find out the ownership of wasteland and negotiate (if necessary, force) arrangements for interim management in the interests of the community — for housing, greenspace and food production.

Lack of Greenspace

17. The inner areas of many cities may contain large amounts of vacant land but this is neither green nor accessible. The relatively high housing densities and the poverty of open space in these areas reflect the renewal and infilling that has gone on since the late nineteenth century. It was the object of some post-war development to redress city open space deficiencies and to rebuild inner districts at lower densities than existed before. In London's Stepney-Poplar Reconstruction Scheme, for example, it was the aim to provide one-third of the homes with gardens; more greenspace was also part of the plan, but, sadly, this part of the concept remains unfinished.

18. Urban growth and renewal has also obliterated natural areas in cities, although, as noted in Chapter 2, many still remain. However, their future is not always secure. Only a vigorous local campaign, backed by the GLC, managed to save the Walthamstow Marshes, in the Lea Valley Regional Park, from gravel extraction. Near Swansea, the outstanding wildlife of the Crymlyn Bog is threatened by City Council plans for refuse tipping over the next 30 years. Chapter 6 looks at some of the positive schemes for urban wildlife conservation being developed by local groups.

19. Natural areas within the city are no substitute for access to them outside. The continuing outward spread of low density development separates inner urban residents from the countryside both physically and in terms of access: even for the inner London resident determined to visit the countryside, the time and cost involved in using public transport at weekends makes open land in the Green Belt virtually inaccessible. Those in the suburbs who benefit most from urban fringe countryside are already well provided with gardens and other types of open spaces. Following the activities of LAs and private owners using Countryside Act grants, some cities are now much better provided with open space at their margins. Getting to them remains a problem for many inner urban residents, although in some conurbations special public transport arrangements now operate: for example, promotion of public transport links between town and country is the objective of the Wayfarer Experiments in West Yorkshire and Greater Manchester, sponsored by the Countryside Commission and the two passenger transport executives.

Urban Fringe

20. In theory, this is the location which could play a more resource-supportive role for cities, providing not only recreation space, but also food, timber and construction materials more directly to serve urban markets. But suburban growth, and the expectation of it in spite of Green Belt designations, the fragmentation of ownerships and administration, and the density of urban services such as sewage works and refuse tips, make integrated land management difficult. Urban fringe farmland may be poorly managed where there is uncertainty about future land-use, and where there is severance from road developments and problems of trespass. Some farmers have adapted to the pressures of the fringe in ways which contribute further to the environmental decay of this zone: for example, by introducing intensive livestock units or leasing land for fly-tipping. Most British cities have no tradition of town woodland that characterises the margins of so many European cities. Where substantial urban forest areas do exist, they may be poorly managed and largely inaccessible by public transport.

21. There have been locally important environmental gains, notably in the tree planting, eyesore clearance and access improvements of various urban fringe management experiments.[14] But work in the London Barnet and Havering experiments indicates that, without

Figure 9. **Wasted assets**
The urban fringe of Greater Manchester by the Bridgewater Canal at Trafford Park. This area
will figure as one of a number of major environmental improvement schemes, involving the public, private
and voluntary sectors, as part of the Groundwork Northwest programme
Copyright: Planning Department, Trafford Metropolitan Borough Council

more attention to the arrangement and better management of land uses and a reduction in uncertainty, their improvements will remain piecemeal and largely cosmetic. Therefore, instead of a beneficial 'meeting place' between town and country, the fringe (albeit a transitional zone) represents wasted assets and often bad environments.

22. There are opportunities for creating new environments, in the style of Nan Fairbrother's 'man-made wild'[15] in a small way — in the grounds of existing developments and on a large scale. Many power station sites have nature trails open to the public and school parties, but all public utilities should carry obligations here — to make good, accessible environment available where this is not precluded by questions of safety or security. New urban forests could offer many benefits. The Ministry of Agriculture and LAs, in their smallholdings policy, need to cooperate on the problems of marginal fringe farming and develop ways of facilitating

the regrouping of land holdings to improve agricultural viability. Better links between the fringe and open land within the city are vital, not just through improved travel arrangements, but through the resurrection and application of green wedge ideas, using natural corridors where they exist along rivers and canals, and creating new corridors. Clearance of derelict land must be a priority in some of the older conurbations (see Figure 9).

23. In all, a mix of urban fringe policies, which involve many agencies, are required to tackle the problems of different areas. These include fiscal means of ensuring that land is in some positive use, the provision of advice, incentives and training for appropriate food production and more local management experiments.

Neglect of Buildings

24. If depletion of raw materials is to be minimised, there

must be husbanding of existing buildings. The process of urban change has allowed houses and other buildings over large areas to deteriorate: some of them are close to the point of no return. According to the latest English House Condition Survey, there are more than a million homes unfit to live in and a further million in disrepair. In Greater London, some 27 per cent of its 2,699,000 dwellings were surveyed in 1978 and declared as either unfit or needing substantial work to bring them up to local authority standards.[16] A programme of repair and continuing maintenance of the housing stock would bring resource as well as social benefits, as Chapter 5 explains.

25. Changes in the structure of industry over the last 30 years have left many empty buildings in cities. There are 20 million sq ft of empty industrial floor space in London alone. Factory space standing idle in England and Wales increased from 32½ million sq ft in December 1979 to 90½ million 20 months later — an increase of 178 per cent.[17] Although these figures reflect the economic recession and the collapse of firms, this decline was paralleled by the construction of 15½ million sq ft of new industrial floorspace, much of it in the prime greenfield locations. Firms' managers usually look for single-storey, wide span buildings covering only half the site area. They show little interest in older, multi-storey, multi-tenanted buildings which can be adapted for use by small firms, as Chapter 5 describes.

Separation of Activities and the Increasing Use of Transport Energy

26. While there has been some movement towards working at home and living closer to jobs, dispersal, in its various forms, has generally increased the separation of activities and the consumption of energy. Journeys have lengthened between home, workplace, shops and schools. Out-of-town shopping centres and greenfield industrial parks draw upon residential districts over a wide area; even in the new towns, designed to provide jobs close to homes, there is travelling both in and out to work.

27. It is now felt by many planners (and others) that land-use policies, in practice, have been too rigorous in seeking to separate jobs and homes. The approach sprang originally from a desire to improve the degraded environments inherited from the mixing of homes and workplaces in the last century and prevent them happening again. Now, for a number of reasons, the emphasis is again on reducing the physical separation of activities. People without access to cars greatly benefit from a close integration of land uses.

28. Nevertheless, recent work shows that a closer integration of land uses is not likely to reduce overall travel much so long as car ownership is high, fuel cheap and there are few basic disincentives to car-use. Only when family and business car-use is lower can land-use integration work better for the conservation of transport energy. This view is supported by Susan Owens in a study of energy and land use; she concludes that a reduction in travel requirements will not necessarily be achieved by the closer integration of activities unless people are motivated to seek the jobs and use the services which are close to their homes.[18] There is, so far, little evidence to show that decentralisation is bringing this about.

29. The strategic role of new development in exacerbating transport problems has been far greater than might be suggested by the small part new construction represents of the total building stock. Even though annual construction has accounted for only 1 per cent of the building stock, large scale, high density commercial development in city centres, low density housing in the outer suburbs, and commercial and industrial development on greenfield sites make up the major share of this 1 per cent.

Summing Up and Looking Ahead

30. It is impossible yet to discern what may be the real consequences of decentralisation in energy terms. The outward movement of people and jobs has contributed, both directly and indirectly, to inter-urban road construction and maintenance, the consumption of building materials, loss of agricultural land and natural areas and to much waste of land and buildings in and around cities. The form that decentralisation has taken in some areas had militated against the introduction of more resource-efficient technologies, for example, in the local supply of energy and in public transport. Continuing peripheral expansion has diminished the opportunities for many towns people, especially in the conurbations, to experience the open countryside, accepting that for others the liberation of car ownership has allowed access to rural areas and to many urban facilities formerly enjoyed only by a few.

31. Work in the UK on the relationship between urban land use, transport and resource consumption is particularly scarce.[19] Studies of the car-dominated cities of North America show, not surprisingly, that centralised, high density cities use considerably less transport energy than 'urban sprawl'. Emphasis is put upon the role of public transport, either as the means of servicing a concentration of activities in a central area or of linking local centres of commercial and medium-density residential development.

32. The situation in Britain is different. Towns here still have concentrations of activity in the centre; public transport still operates; and the low density spread of cities is much less pronounced. Greater linkage of homes and workplace, aided by communications technology, will become increasingly possible in small towns (and large cities) if development can be guided this way. Moreover, a loosening of densities in the inner areas of

conurbations provides scope for the environmental improvements they so desperately need. But the trend towards peripheral expansion and declining public transport is leading not in the direction of varied and resourceful urban communities but of wasteful and inequitable urban sprawl. Powerful forces are propelling this outward movement, but they are not all inevitable nor necessarily desirable: the extension of micro-technology and 'telecommuting' from home would save on energy and shop and office space but could bring intolerable isolation and may deepen, rather than reduce, the divisions in society.[20]

33. As British cities continue to change, the aim must be

to sustain those features that are resource-efficient and to resist extravagant trends, particularly as the urban pattern now being determined will last into the era of increasing fuel uncertainty and considerable social change. The location and density of new development, its mix of uses, and the modes of transport upon which it relies, will be critical to urban resource-consumption in the future. The last part of Chapter 5 draws all these strands of thinking together to make the case for more resource-conscious urban planning. Over the short-term, a major opportunity for resource-saving lies in rational-ising the urban transport system, which is the subject of Chapter 4.

Notes and References

1 DREWETT, R. 1981. Europe's urban problems analysed. *The Planner, 67 (6).*

2 OFFICE OF POPULATION CENSUSES AND SURVEYS. 1981. Census 1981 — preliminary report: England and Wales. HMSO; STOTT, M. 1981. Commissioned paper on recent urban change.

3 STEELEY, G. 1982. Land for housing — but for whom? *Town and Country Planning, 51 (6).*

4 *The Times, 22 June 1981* quoted in: COUNCIL FOR THE PROTECTION OF RURAL ENGLAND. 1981. Planning — friend or foe? CPRE.

5 STAFFORD, F and FRANKLIN, M. 1982. The techniques of industrial regeneration. *Architects Journal, 28.* See also: BURCHELL, M. 1981. Unemployment: the role of community-based emloyment initiatives. Unpublished MA dissertation, Trent Polytechnic.

6 EVERSLEY, D. 1982. Can planners keep up if the flight from the cities continues to accelerate? Paper delivered to the Royal Town Planning Institute Annual Conference, May.

7 BEST, R H. 1982. Land use and living space. Methuen.

8 Planning: friend or foe? *op cit.*

9 ELSON, M. 1981. Farmland loss and erosion of planning. *Town and Country Planning, 50 (1).*

10 NABARRO, R and RICHARDS, D with CHAPMAN, H. 1980. Wasteland. Thames Television Report. See also: BRUTON, M J and GORE, A. 1980. Vacant urban land in South Wales. Final report to the Land Authority for Wales and Prince of Wales' Committee.

11 MERSEYSIDE COUNTY COUNCIL. 1980. Merseyside structure plan.

12 COUNCIL FOR ENVIRONMENTAL CONSERVATION. 1981. Waking up dormant land. CoEnCo report.

13 LAND, R. 1981. Commissioned paper on London dock-lands. See also: Special issue of *Town and Country Planning, 51, 5, 1982* on Britain's docklands.

14 COUNTRYSIDE COMMISSION. 1981. Countryside manage-ment in the urban fringe. CCP 136.

15 FAIRBROTHER, N. 1970. New lives, new landscapes. Architectural press.

16 CONTROLLER OF TRANSPORTATION AND DEVELOP-MENT, GLC. 1981. Planning for London. Report to the Planning Committee.

17 HUTCHINSON, D. 1982. Urban form and resource require-ments. Paper prepared for Review Group.

18 OWENS, S E. 1978. The energy implications of alternative rural development patterns. Proceedings of the First Inter-national Conference on Energy and Community Develop-ment. Athens, July 10-15. See also: SUSAN OWENS. 1982. PhD thesis on this subject. University of East Anglia.

19 HUTCHINSON, D. 1981. Local authorities and energy planning — London. Paper delivered to conference on energy costs and conservation, Polytechnic of the South Bank, December 7-11.

20 LAVER, M. 1982. Microelectronics and tomorrow's communities. *Town and Country Planning, 51 (8).*

CHAPTER 4

A RESOURCE APPROACH TO TRANSPORT

Introduction

1. Transport is a major and growing user of energy in Britain, using a quarter of our total energy consumption. It is heavily dependent on a single fuel. Petroleum, the supply of which is not assured in Britain over the longer-term, accounts for 99 per cent of the energy used in transport. Moreover, while energy use in other sectors of the economy fell over the last decade, the amount supplied to transport in 1981 was not only greater than the amount supplied in 1971 but represented a higher proportion of all the energy used (see Figure 10, below). Furthermore, this growth occurred over a decade which saw two major oil crises, significant increases in the price of a barrel of oil, economic recession and growing unemployment. Road transport (passenger and freight) is by far the major user of transport energy, accounting for 79.2 per cent of the total petroleum consumed in transport in 1981, and showing an increase in both absolute and relative terms over the decade (see Figure 11, p 124).

2. In 1974, government responded to the need for energy conservation by calling for a 5 per cent reduction in oil consumption in all sectors of the economy, in line with other west European countries. Today, transport is the only major energy-consuming sector in which the demand for petroleum products is increasing. The interests of the national economy, as well as wider obligations, suggest that this trend should not be regarded as irreversible and that those involved in transport policy should now address the issue of energy conservation. This chapter argues that, because of the time needed to develop alternatives, planning should start now for a transition from an oil-based transport system to one which relies very much less on petroleum products. This could also bring social and environmental benefits.

The Growth and Consequences of Car Travel

3. 'Traffic in Towns' (1963) aptly referred to cars as the monster we love.[1] They cause death, injury and pollution but provide a magic carpet to almost anywhere and a door-to-door service of immense convenience. The distance people travelled in private cars and motor cycles increased by 27.8 per cent in the decade up to 1981, in spite of oil crises and the recession. The increase appears to be attributable to longer rather than to more journeys: over the last 30 years the tendency has been for the annual distance travelled to increase, with fluctuations related to particular events such as increased fuel prices. Over the last decade, distances by rail remained about the same and those by bus and coach declined by more than a quarter (see Figure 12, p 124).

4. There are a number of reasons for these trends:
□ Car ownership has increased steadily. The number of private cars and vans rose from 12 million in 1971 to 15.3 million in 1981, an increase of 26.6 per cent. In terms of households (whose number has also grown over the decade), just over half had the regular use of one or more cars in 1971; in 1981 the proportion had risen to 61 per cent.[2]
□ Fuel has remained relatively cheap. Despite the increasing price of a barrel of oil since 1973, the real price of petrol (after an initial rise) had fallen to the 1973 level by 1978. It then rose in response to the second oil crisis but started falling again in 1981.[3]
□ Market forces and economies of scale have meant that many smaller local facilities, such as shops, schools and hospitals, have closed and activities have been concentrated in larger, fewer and more widely spaced units involving longer journeys.

	1971 m therms	heat supplied %	1981 m therms	%	1971-1981 % change
Energy for transport	11,634	20	13,618	25	+17
Energy for other final consumers	45,367	80	41,302	75	− 9
All energy used by final consumers	57,001	100	54,920	100	− 4

Figure 10. **Energy consumption in transport**
(Source: Transport Statistics 1971-81, Table 1.25(b) Department of Transport, 1982)

Mode of transport	1971 m tonnes	%	1981 m tonnes	%	1971-1981 % change
Road	20.15	77.3	24.27	79.2	+20.4
Rail	1.10	4.2	.81	2.7	−26.4
Air	3.81	14.6	4.53	14.8	+18.9
Water	1.01	3.9	1.02	3.3	+0.99
All modes	26.07	100	30.63	100	+17.5

Figure 11. **Changes in petroleum consumption in transport 1971-1981**
(Source: Transport Statistics 1971-81. Table 1.25(a) Department of Transport, 1982)

☐ Continuing increase in the average speed of traffic has enabled people to live further away from work and other activities without increasing the time spent in travel.

☐ Journeys for shopping and for leisure between them account for about two-thirds of the distance people travel and it is here that most of the increase has occurred over the last 10 years.[4]

☐ Company cars travel on average more than twice as far as cars which are registered as household vehicles and have been estimated to account for between 42 and 70 per cent of new cars.[5]

5. There has been a spiralling decline in the use of bus services, as car travel has increased. A report by the Transport and Road Research Laboratory in 1976 estimated that, for every additional car that took to the road, 300 bus trips a year would be lost and that the resulting reduction in services and increase in fares would lead to further substantial loss of patronage.[6] Data for the 1970s illustrate the relationships: as mileage by private vehicles increased over the decade there was a 5 per cent decrease in bus miles, a 30 per cent reduction in bus journeys and a 30 per cent increase in the real level of bus fares.[7]

6. The growth in car travel and the transfer of people from bus to car have caused almost a doubling of road traffic over the decade. Goods vehicles make up only a small proportion of total flows and their number is increasing at a slower rate than for cars. In many towns, conditions have been moderated by traffic management and road schemes, but congestion is still a problem, particularly in the metropolitan areas, and is an important factor in the deterioration of bus services.

7. The trends in car travel have not been even handed in their social effects. For people who possess a car, it opens up opportunities in almost every sphere of life: it brings the countryside close to hand for the town dweller and makes it possible for the town worker to live in the countryside. But for those without cars, the cycle of decline in public transport, triggered off by the increasing use of cars, means that access to jobs and essential services is progressively reduced. Moreover, large parts of the countryside and many suburbs have become places where only car owners can live conveniently. Nor can all the members of car-owning households enjoy the accessibility the car provides. If it is used for work, the rest of the family have to rely on walking and the public transport system that the car is helping into decline.

Changes in Freight Traffic

8. Road transport dominates in the transport of goods as well as of people. Two-thirds of the goods moved in this country travel by road, a threefold increase over the last 30 years. The decline in rail freight since 1973, to the point where it now carries only 12 per cent of all goods moved, is in part because of the introduction of pipelines for moving oil products but is also related to competition between road and rail for general cargoes.

Mode of transport	1971 m passenger km	%	1981 m passenger km	%	1971-1981 % change
Road private (car and motor cycle)	330	78	422	84	+27.8
cycles	5	1	5	1	−
buses and coaches	51	12	38	7	−25.5
Rail	36	8	35	7	− 2.8
Air	2	0.5	2.8	0.6	+40.0
All modes	424	100	503	100	+18.6

Figure 12. **Changes in passenger travel 1971-81**
(Source: Transport Statistics 1971-81. Table 1.1 Department of Transport, 1982)

In this sector, the main opportunities for rail to compete commercially with road lie in the trunk hauls of over 200 miles or siding-to-siding traffic, such as coal moving from pit to power station.

9. The Armitage Report on lorries does not have a great deal to say about the energy consequences of the continuing growth in freight movement by road. But it does remark that: 'road haulage will continue to be dependent on oil for the foreseeable future and oil is going to be an increasingly scarce and expensive commodity'.[8] Armitage suggests it is in the interests of the haulage industry to improve its productivity in the use of fuel and argues that increased fuel prices should provide the main incentive. The report also sees scope for reducing oil consumption by a transfer of freight from road to modes of transport, like rail, that can use fuels other than oil. It suggests some transfers may arise from its own recommendations that the heaviest lorries should be taxed more highly (to cover road track costs) and that the grants available to British Rail for constructing private sidings should be increased.

Energy Performance

10. The trends show that car and freight travel by road are increasing, and that rail freight and bus travel are on the decline. How efficient are these forms of transport in their use of energy?

11. A number of researchers have made comparisons on the basis of the energy used per unit load (in passenger or tonne kilometre) from which there is agreement on the rank order of bus, rail, car: that is, buses are the most energy efficient, cars the least. A recent study which examined trends over the last decade has shown that, in the passenger sector, private transport (by car and motor cycle) is the only mode that has declined in efficiency.[9] It caters for the bulk of passenger travel, and nearly all the decline in efficiency can be attributed to the reduction, over the decade, in the number of people each car carries and the trend towards larger engines. It should be noted that a general indicator of performance of the kind used in these studies does not show up variations within the range. There will be areas and circumstances in which the car might be the most energy efficient way of travelling. But, in urban areas, conditions do not favour the car as the most energy efficient way of travelling.

12. Another measure of energy efficiency is the performance of the vehicle itself. Progress towards greater fuel economy is being made through improvements in the performance of the petrol-engine and the development of diesel-engined and electrically-powered vehicles. Overall, a diesel-engined car can be 28 per cent more efficient than a comparable petrol-engined one. Electric vehicles offer energy and environmental advantages if batteries with a high storage capacity can be developed, but the technology is not yet available for large scale application.[10] In the United States, research is being promoted to demonstrate that a four-seater fuel efficient car can be produced with a performance of 100 mpg in a diesel version and 80 mpg using a petrol engine. New models of the smaller cars now marketed in the UK show significant economies in petrol consumption which in some cases exceeds 60 miles per gallon at a constant 56 miles per hour. The main initiative for improving the fuel performance of vehicles rests with the manufacturers who in 1979 were committed to a 10 per cent reduction in fuel consumption by 1985.[11] But this is a slow progress. Over the next decade a 33 per cent reduction could be a practical target.[12]

13. A 17 per cent reduction in the energy consumption of road haulage vehicles is considered to be possible over the next 10 years as a consequence of improved engines, reduced drag and better tyres. The lorry fleet is largely diesel-engined, but a further transfer from petrol to diesel would bring fuel savings.

14. It is debatable how far rail electrification would save energy. Less oil would be consumed per passenger and tonne kilometre compared to a rail network operating on diesel fuel but, overall, energy consumption could grow. One view is that electrification would be accompanied by improvements in the service and better orientation to various markets; the increase in passengers and cargoes that could result would raise energy efficiency, outweighing the somewhat better energy performance of a comparable diesel system. Another analysis concluded that energy demand would grow by 22 per cent (on the basis of constant traffic) and that the rise in electricity consumption would be equivalent to the output of a 500 Mw power station running at full load.[13]

Worsening Environment

15. It is 20 years since the report 'Traffic in Towns' highlighted the effect of traffic hazard, noise, pollution, vibration and visual intrusion on urban life and the fabric of towns. Since then, the number of cars on the road has increased two-and-a-half times and the number of goods vehicles by one-fifth, the rate of increase being slower during the 1970s than during the 1960s. In all but one respect, conditions have deteriorated overall as traffic has grown, although environmental improvements have been achieved at particular places. The exception is road casualties. During the 1970s, when motor traffic increased by just over one-third, the number of all road users killed and seriously injured declined by 15 per cent as a result of improved management of traffic and campaigns to increase safety. However, with nearly 6,000 people killed on the roads in 1981, and over 78,000 seriously injured, the toll is still extremely high.

16. No annual surveys are made of noise levels, but noise from motor vehicles probably increased over the decade

in line with the growth in traffic. The former Noise Advisory Council, now disbanded, has suggested that road traffic is the biggest single source of noise nuisance, and that about 11 per cent of homes suffer more noise than the noise level standard used by Government for making grants to householders affected by noise from new roads. The problem of lorry noise, acute in some urban locations, is certainly perceived as a major nuisance: more complaints were made about lorry noise to the Armitage Inquiry than about any other aspect of nuisance from lorries. The phased introduction of noise standards for new lorries began in 1970, but the limit for maximum noise levels is still above the level recommended by Armitage.

17. With the exception of sulphur dioxide, the annual tonnage of all air pollutants emitted by road traffic rose by one-third over the 1970s. As air pollutants from domestic, industrial and commercial sources declined during the decade, the proportion attributable to road traffic rose. By 1980, pollutants from vehicles contributed 90 per cent of the carbon monoxide, 41 per cent of the hydrocarbons and 26 per cent of the nitrogen oxides.[14]

18. Although their effect on air pollution is not directly monitored, lorries make up only 8 per cent of total traffic flows and are not the main source of pollutants. Even so, according to Armitage, after noise, black diesel smoke and the smell of diesel engines are the most frequent causes of complaint about lorries. Diesel smoke is caused by incomplete combustion and results more from badly maintained and adjusted engines than from any inherent defect in their design. As diesel engines emit no lead they are, in theory, superior to petrol engines on environmental grounds. In practice, elimination of diesel smoke relies on the enforcement of regulations by means of smoke tests, but the standards used are subjective and there is, as yet, no means of testing at the roadside. There is a need for statutory objective standards and rapid development of the necessary smoke testing equipment.

19. Lorries bring other environmental problems. Traffic congestion is often caused by loading and unloading in the street and provision for lorries imposes extra costs on new road construction (estimated at 15 per cent). Nearly all the damage to existing roads, and other associated installations, is caused by lorries, although this is difficult to quantify. In many small but cumulative ways, for example, shattered pavements and damaged buildings, lorries erode the urban fabric.

20. It has not been possible for this report to examine the environmental and safety aspects of rail travel, but pollution figures show that emissions from railways are a small fraction of those from road vehicles. There is noise alongside railway tracks but the network in urban areas is limited and the nuisance intermittent.

Summing Up and Looking Ahead

21. Car ownership has extended to many more people all the benefits that greater freedom of movement can bring. For the majority, the car has already become indispensable to their way of life, for many others it is something to which they aspire. Yet over the last decade, the trends in transport, and car travel in particular, have not been moving in the direction of more livable or more resourceful cities. Transport is the only major sector of the economy where demand for petroleum is increasing in both relative and absolute terms; the car (which in energy terms is probably the least efficient way to travel in large cities) takes the lion's share of the resource. The growth in car travel and road haulage has meant continuing traffic congestion in the larger urban areas, worsening environment and, nearly everywhere, a deterioration in public transport.

22. Some observers regard the decline in bus transport as irreversible. Yet, in addition to the social reasons for reversing present trends, the superior energy efficiency of the bus suggests that, far from allowing its patronage to slide further, necessary action should be taken now to sustain and improve bus transport. The levels of public transport subsidy in the UK cities are far behind those in other countries. For example, in Rome it is 81 per cent, Paris 57 per cent, and New York 50 per cent, whereas London lags behind with only a 25 per cent subsidy.

23. The Transport Bill, currently before Parliament, seeks to curb the extent to which Metropolitan Authorities can support public transport from the rates. For the bus industry to develop as part of an overall strategy for low energy transport, the industry's basic requirements are the stability that would be provided by an investment programme lasting over several years, as well as higher levels of subsidy.

24. To recapitulate the wider context for transport change: at best, there is uncertainty about the cost, if not the availability, of oil over the next decade; at worst a supply crisis could catch the country unprepared, causing wholesale disruption to the transport system, to the economy and to personal lives. Over the longer-term, oil supplies will diminish and there is no guarantee of cheap or appropriate substitutes.

25. Looking ahead, a 10 to 15 year transition is needed to a less oil-based transport system. Priority aims for such a transition would be to arrest the increase in fuel consumption and later achieve absolute savings, stimulate new developments in fuel saving technology and eliminate pollution. The single largest contribution towards realising these aims would come from reducing the amount of petrol used in car travel. In spite of the difficulties of implementing such a transition (and the detailed questions this report leaves unanswered) the following framework sets out some of the interrelated measures that are required in central and local Government and in the car industry. Other important ways of saving transport energy and improving the environment — for example, some switching of freight from road to rail, or reducing the noise and diesel emissions from lorries — should also form part of a transition programme, but they are not discussed further here.

Ways and Means

26. The programme for a transport transition must start with progressive targets set by Government towards an absolute saving in transport fuel and a reduction in vehicle pollution. Starting now, but extending into the medium-term (10 to 15 years) there has to be a movement towards the 'green' car — lower on fuel consumption than present models and free of harmful emissions.[15] At present, the image of the capacious, fast car still attracts, particularly in the company car market which accounts for about half the sales of all new vehicles.

27. So far, rises in the price of petrol have not stimulated a mass demand for low consumption vehicles. An inducement to fuel economy is required as an incentive for manufacturers to produce, and for the public to buy, the 'green' car. Such a lever could take the form of increases in the real price of petrol at the pump (by raising the fuel tax), manipulation of the vehicle excise duty, regulatory measures (including fuel allocation) or a combination of these. For example, a recent paper on energy saving and the use of petrol suggests that gradual increases of 5 per cent per annum in the real price of petrol at the pump (by raising the fuel tax) could bring a 30 per cent reduction in consumption over 10 years.[16]

28. A price or regulatory lever of this kind is also needed to prevent extra travel by the users of 'green' cars from cancelling out the savings brought by greater fuel economy. Depending upon how strongly it was applied, the lever could persuade car owners to plan their trips more carefully to reduce their number and length. It could stimulate car sharing and a positive response to reduced speed limits. Higher motoring costs or fuel allocations (however liberal for the average consumer) may encourage some transfer to other, more fuel efficient, modes, such as walking, cycling and public transport. A price lever (or other device) would also help the implementation of management measures that would still be needed even if cars were smaller, quieter and pollution-free. Fewer vehicles in the central areas of cities would allow for more effective parking control, as well as better traffic and environmental management, with more space for pedestrians, cyclists and buses.

29. Assuming an effective and equitable lever can be devised to induce greater fuel economy, and that targets for progressive decreases in fuel consumption are set, then car manufacturers would be in a position to plan a production programme for the 'green' car. Over the short-term, the following measures are needed to bring about a reduction in fuel consumption:

☐ There should be the introduction of integrated measures for the inner and central districts of large cities such as area licensing, parking controls and bus priorities, to restrict the peak time use of cars and secure some transfer to public transport. Street closures may be needed and there is a place for computer-based integrated traffic control systems.

☐ There should be the creation of large pedestrian areas in city centres and pedestrian routes linking adjoining districts, making provision for the separation of people on foot from vehicles where routes cross heavily trafficked streets.

☐ For all urban areas there should be traffic and environmental management schemes and, where necessary, road works to improve traffic flows and conditions for pedestrians.

☐ There should be the provision of special facilities for cyclists, including cycle lanes on existing carriageways, the use of quiet streets as cycle routes, some shared facilities with pedestrians, and generally safer conditions, such as better signing and road surfaces.

☐ There should be increased subsidies for public and community transport (in association with changes in the legislative and financial base) to improve the standard of service.

☐ There should be reduced speed limits for inter-urban travel.

☐ There should be further limits on the use of company cars.

30. It is not possible to say, now, what form transport might take over the long-term when fuel supplies are less certain and probably more costly. What is clear is that the adaptation to these conditions must begin now.

Notes and References

1 BUCHANAN, C D et al. 1963. Traffic in Towns. HMSO.

2 DEPARTMENT OF TRANSPORT. 1982. Transport Statistics 1971-81. Tables 2.19, 2.28.

3 MOGRIDGE, M J H. 1982. A proposal to save energy. *Transport Policy Decision Making 2.*

4 DEPARTMENT OF TRANSPORT. 1979. Transport Statistics 1968-78. Table 14(b).

5 BANISTER, D. 1981. Town planning discussion paper 36. Bartlett School of Architecture and Planning, University College London; POTTER, S with RIEKIC, G.. 1980. Paper given to Motoring Cost Conference. Transport Studies Unit, Oxford; WOODMANSEY, M. 1979. Business cars, a survey of current practice, report 44, British Institute of Management.

6 OLDFIELD, R H. 1979. The effect of car ownership on bus patronage. Transport and Road Research Laboratory LR 872.

7 GOODWIN, P B. 1982. Essay on the role of the bus, the future of the bus. Bus and Coach Council; 1975/76: households with no cars: 3.85 bus trips/head/week; households with one car: 1.54 bus trips; households with more than one

car: 0.94 bs trips; BLY, P H and OLDFIELD, R H. 1978. The effect of car ownership and income on bus travel. *Traffic Engineering and Control, August/September.*

8 THE INQUIRY INTO LORRIES, PEOPLE AND THE ENVIRONMENT. 1980. Report. HMSO (The Armitage Report).

9 BANISTER, D and C. 1982. Travel and energy use in Great Britain 1969-79: trends and options. Department of Town and Country Planning, University of Manchester; The Department of Transport formula for assessing the economic cost of fuel implies that even at average bus occupancies of only 14 people, the fuel costs per mile travelled by each passenger on a bus are only one-third of those for cars; DEPARTMENT OF TRANSPORT. 1981. Traffic appraisal manual.

10 LEACH, G *et al.* 1979. A low energy strategy for the UK. IIED.

11 SOCIETY OF MOTOR MANUFACTURERS AND TRADERS. 1979. Under the terms of an agreement negotiated between the government and motor industry in 1979, the average petrol consumption of new cars was to be reduced by 10 per cent between October 1978 and October 1985. From 1970 to 1980 there was no change in the average fuel efficiency of c 30 mpg.

12 LEACH, G. 1979. *op cit.*

13 BANISTER, D and C. 1982. *op cit.*

14 HILLMAN, M. 1982. An evaluation of transport policy in the 1970s. *Policy Studies, October.*

15 The 'Green' car: no one style or colour is implied. This is shorthand for fuel economical, pollution free private vehicles.

16 MOGRIDGE, M J H. 1982. *op cit.*

CHAPTER 5

ADAPTING THE FABRIC

Introduction

1. Urban buildings are significant for resource-conservation in three ways: as consumers of raw materials, as consumers of energy and as consumers of land. The case for conserving all three was made in Chapter 2; in Chapter 3 the neglect of the existing building stock and land-take were identified as two of the main resource-effects of recent urban development. The structure and management of services associated with urban buildings, especially water supply and sewerage, also affect the rate at which resources are consumed — and wasted. This chapter argues the case for making buildings last and for saving energy by their better design and operation. It considers various means of improving the resource-efficiency of local heating and some provisional conclusions are drawn from the first five chapters of the report.

The Resource Case for Maintenance and Rehabilitation

2. The argument put forward here is that fewer building materials and less energy will be used if buildings are made and maintained to last as long as possible. The long life proposition is that, from the standpoint of resource-conservation, over the long-term it is better to have high quality buildings that require little maintenance and are renewed at long intervals than low quality structures involving high maintenance that are replaced more frequently. It is acknowledged that high quality, long life, low maintenance building will normally mean a higher capital cost. Nevertheless, there is a place for short life building, using renewable and recyclable materials wherever possible. Even for long life structures, maintenance will yield diminishing returns and there must come a point at which a building is 'worn out' and replacement is due. There may be overriding advantages in demolishing a building before the end of its useful life. A new structure may provide much better living conditions and be more suitable for the latest industrial processes. These are both conventional criteria employed in weighing up the balance of advantage between rehabilitation and rebuild. But in decisions on building options, the interests of owner, user and investor, which usually favour the short-term, have to be reconciled with the longer-term interests of society in resource conservation. The long life approach means that

this issue must figure in the building balance sheet, discussed futher at the end of this chapter.

3. Britain has a substantial backlog of neglected buildings. For those that still have some useful life, the question is whether to rebuild or rehabilitate. From a resource viewpoint, over the long-term it probably makes very little difference which option is adopted. Over the short-term (say 30 years) it is a matter of weighing up the relative consumption of resources in initial building work and in continuing maintenance (including heating and repairs). Rehabilitation employs fewer resources than rebuilding initially but the resource running costs of a new building should be lower.[1]

4. Placing the emphasis on rehabilitating the backlog has other resource-implications. There would be more building materials now for other purposes, although constraints upon building materials and energy might be greater in 30 years' time and the balance of advantage could lie with replacement now. Early rehabilitation would postpone a major rebuilding programme, allowing time for the technology of conservation to develop (in design, materials and construction). Rehabilitation would also spread the ultimate rebuilding load and the demand on building materials.

5. There are other reasons for conserving existing buildings. Buildings of architectural and historic interest are a valued part of the existing building stock. A general emphasis on rehabilitation rather than rebuild would not only reduce direct threats to the built heritage but make it more likely that historic buildings survive in a harmonious setting. Frequent rebuilding is also disturbing in social and functional terms. Townspeople have made it plain over the last few decades, in their opposition to redevelopment schemes and new roads, that familiar surroundings — the known network of schools, shops and community ties — are of intrinsic value. In all, it is likely that factors other than resource-conservation will be the decisive ones in the choice between rehabilitating or replacing the backlog of neglected buildings. But it is probably better on resource-grounds to make them last as long as possible.

Making Existing Buildings Last

6. At present, the older housing stock is deteriorating

faster than it is being either improved or demolished — with more than a million homes, in England alone, unfit to live in. Others lack basic amenities and some are in need of repair. The latest House Condition Survey shows that the number of dwellings in serious disrepair increased from 859,000 to 1,049,000 between 1976 and 1981 and each of these requires at least £7,000 to make good the damage.[2] A further three million homes need repairs costing more than £2,500. In all, five million dwellings (more than a quarter of the housing stock in England) need at least one essential repair.

7. The last quarter of 1981 saw reports from a number of organisations calling for urgent action and increased resources to deal with this backlog.[3] Concern was expressed at the severe cutbacks in the Housing Investment Programme over the two preceding years and the prospect of massive and costly clearance. In 1981, the Royal Town Planning Institute proposed a 10 year housing renewal programme for Britain, designed to remove the backlog and keep up with continuing obsolescence at an annual cost of £3.4 billion. The latest House Condition Survey gives £35 billion as the sum required in England alone over a 10 year period — a twofold increase over present expenditure on house repairs and maintenance.

8. A 10 year rehabilitation programme would undoubtedly serve the interests of resource-conservation. It would also be in line with social change and the needs of a growing number of younger and older households for a greater variety of housing. Implementation requires not only an increase in the Housing Investment Programme, but also a number of other measures. Several organisations have called for enough revenue and capital finance to implement area-based rehabilitation policies, the replacement of the present 'unfitness' standard by a minimum acceptable or 'tolerable' standard which would allow rehabilitation to be considered as an option, a unified grant system, the relief from VAT of all grant-aided work, the further relaxation of the rateable value limits on grants and the introduction of measures to encourage and, if necessary, compel the private landlord to act. A closer partnership between local authorities and builders over the supply of smaller converted dwellings would help. The building societies could play a much more influential role; housing associations already do (see Figure 13).

9. The scope for the re-use of redundant commercial and industrial buildings, most of which are located in the inner city, is limited. Many of them are multi-storey and it is improbable that they can be converted to accommodate firms of the size and type that abandoned them in favour of more floor space and a single-storey structure. The main hope lies with the small scale industries, particularly as inner districts contain a high proportion of these firms. A Department of Environment study of industry and employment in 1979 found that 76 per cent of companies in the inner city had less than 25 employees.[4] According to the Royal Institution of Chartered Surveyors (RICS) there is evidence from a Birmingham survey of an under-supply of units

Figure 13. **Community rehabilitation**:
The back courtyards at Black Road, Macclesfield, transformed by the local community in the pioneering Self-Help General Improvement Area; architect Rod Hackney
Copyright: Lisa Nobbs, Macclesfield

smaller than 250 sq m.[5] As many examples of successful schemes already show, redundant buildings can be converted into cheap, small workshops for new enterprises based, for example, upon craft industries such as furniture-making and printing, professional services and electronics. The next chapter discusses some of the prerequisites for action.

10. Regarding the financial costs and benefits of rehabilitation versus the rebuilding of industrial and commercial buildings, the Royal Institution of Chartered Surveyors (RICS) reports that although the costs of rehabilitation may be less, rebuilding offers a longer building life, more lettable floor space and a higher rent.[6] It has doubts about the willingness and ability of developers in the private sector to become involved in providing units for small firms and about the prospects for involving the major financial institutions. In its report on rehabilitation, the RICS emphasises the community enterprise approach whereby action is initiated by local people to generate economic development for the benefit of the local area.

Saving Energy in Existing Buildings

11. The heating, lighting and cooling of buildings consumes nearly one-quarter of the world's energy supplies

of which approximately two-thirds are obtained (directly or indirectly) from oil or natural gas. Forty-six per cent of the total delivered energy consumed in the UK was attributable to buildings in 1982, with housing as the largest single sector. Saving energy in buildings is therefore important to the national economy as well as to domestic consumers.

12. From the 1950s until 1973, efficient energy use in buildings was not considered important because it was assumed that technical developments would keep fuel prices low. It was a period of great construction activity during which time buildings became more and more energy extravagant. Lack of attention to climate-sensitive design and construction combined with energy-intensive heating, lighting and air conditioning has proved costly in both energy and financial terms. Christopher Flavin remarks that: 'The world's cities are full of buildings that will simply be too expensive to use in 20 years' time'.[7]

13. Rising fuel costs have forced government and the larger industrial and commercial firms to act: it is estimated that, since 1977, more than half a million dwellings have been improved under the Home Insulation Schemes and many householders have insulated their lofts without grants. The Neighbourhood Energy Schemes, launched by NCVO in 1981, are described in Chapter 6; other energy-saving schemes in progress are those sponsored by the Housing Development Directorate of DOE through its Better Insulated Homes Programme. The only Department of Industry scheme still operating provides grants for up to 25 per cent towards the capital cost of new energy saving equipment. The Department of Energy provides a small subsidy for one day consultant energy surveys of industrial, commercial and public sector buildings.

14. In the private sector, a number of the bigger firms are carrying out energy audits and are spending large sums of money on energy conservation in order to save on operating costs. British Leyland expects savings of £308,000 a year from its new microprocessor-based control system at Longbridge. For a capital cost of £500,000 the firm 3M estimates it has saved £2.5 million since 1975/76 through boiler replacement, hot water recycling and building insulation.

15. Most local authorities have appraised their energy requirements; some have major programmes of recording and monitoring consumption and have had notable success in reducing energy use by better building management. In South Glamorgan, for example, a programme of incentives for school caretakers, rationalising the use of educational premises after school hours and other management changes have all combined to reduce the LA energy use. However, careful monitoring and liaison with the local community is vital to ensure that public energy saving is not at the expense of local services or an overall rise in the use of energy in the domestic sector. Some authorities, such as the East Kilbride Development Corporation, have introduced crash insulation programmes for public housing with, in

this case, an estimated 23 per cent saving on fuel bills. However, cuts in expenditure are now inhibiting further public investment in energy saving measures.

Priorities

16. The prime target for energy conservation must be existing buildings. New buildings represent only 1 per cent of the stock, and according to the RIBA/RICS/CIBS policy statement on a national energy conservation programme, existing buildings constitute 80 per cent of the conservation target.[8] Housing is the largest single energy-using sector after industry (including its buildings), accounting for one-fifth of total energy consumption and offering enormous scope for saving. Loss of heat through the building fabric is one of the main reasons for this drain upon resources: it could be greatly reduced by insulation measures. A recent study[9] concludes that:

☐ to bring all lofts to a medium insulation standard (4" deep) would cost £1,599m (less than a power station) and would save 3m tonnes of oil equivalent annually;

☐ half of all homes have cavity walls but 89 per cent were uninsulated in 1981. To insulate them would cost £2,047m and save 3m tonnes of oil equivalent annually;

☐ insulating all lofts and cavity walls would reduce peak demands on winter days at a small fraction of the cost of providing equivalent generating capacity, saving 17 per cent of domestic energy consumption. On capital costs alone, an insulation programme could be four to 10 times as cost effective as investment in an equivalent supply of electricity.

The House of Commons Select Committee on Energy reports that a 20 per cent energy saving in domestic buildings alone would be worth more than £1,000m a year.[10] At present, £300m is spent annually in fuel allowances compared with an investment level of only £149m on energy conservation.

17. On the evidence, this report recommends a 10 year programme for the insulation and weatherproofing of all homes, along with the necessary incentives for implementation. But there are two main barriers to action. One is the lack of a perceived need to save energy at home: the average UK household spends only 4.5 per cent of its expenditure on fuels and light (the energy-intensive industries whose fuel costs represent 10 to 25 per cent or more of total costs have always taken energy saving seriously). If fuel prices rise faster than real incomes (and for domestic gas they have not) there should be an increase of interest in insulation measures. But those on low incomes who have most need to cut expenditure on fuel bills and can perceive all too well the cash benefits of insulation, cannot afford its installation. According to a National Council for Voluntary Organisations (NCVO) survey in 1981, the households most in need of help with insulation are the ones least likely to apply for a grant.

18. The second barrier is a lack of accessible advice about energy saving. Small businessmen, as well as householders, fail at any one of several decision points in acting to conserve: they do not know where or how worthwhile energy (and hence money) savings can be made, or how to tread the formidable technical maze of possible solutions. They lack the cash for investment and cannot easily obtain medium- to long-term financing to spread out the initial cost. In contrast, the decision maker in a large firm or institution is advised by a staff of energy managers. Government conservation programmes (advertising small grants for loft insulation and 25 per cent grants to industry) aim only at the investment hurdle and the person able to pay a share of the costs, and fail to provide the total service enjoyed by the big firm.

19. The answers lie partly with increasing both the limit on all grants for insulation and the percentage of the costs they cover (at the very least to 100 per cent for all households receiving social security payments as recommended by the NCVO) and combining this with energy advice and auditing from local authorities, voluntary agencies and the fuel industries, available perhaps at local energy advice centres. The fuel industries themselves might provide a total service covering audit, financing and implementation (with repayments on the fuel bill). Private consortia of building material firms, contractors and finance houses could provide a similar 'package'. Building societies (and banks) have a particular role to play, for conservation measures do not figure in mortgage conditions: well insulated homes should be given preferential treatment. Householders (and small firms) often need a stimulus to invest, such as can be provided by cooperative insulation schemes where bulk contracts for the work and materials can halve the costs per dwelling. But the critical requirement is for cheap, long-term finance. Most householders and small businessmen want a short pay-back time on the money they invest in energy saving. If they had the 15 to 20 year investment horizon of the fuel supply industries, a great deal of conservation would seem worthwhile. The need is for longer-term financing arrangements which can demonstrate that domestic energy consumers will be making regular cash savings.

20. The House of Commons Select Committee on Energy concluded that the evidence is overwhelming for sweeping changes to be made in the Government approach to conservation in buildings. Among the most important of their recommendations are that:
- □ similar criteria should guide investment in conservation as in supply, ie a 12 to 15 year payback period;
- □ the balance of public investment and government personnel should change in favour of conservation rather than supply;
- □ conservation grants and tax allowances should increase;
- □ specific funds should again be available for energy conservation in public sector buildings;
- □ there should be an insulation programme for the homes of those receiving fuel allowances.

(Neighbourhood energy schemes are discussed in Chapter 6 of this report.)
On the question of institutional change, the Committee recommend that:
- □ the statutory obligations of the gas, electricity and coal industries should be revised to require them to use fuels in the most economic and efficient way and encourage their customers to do the same;
- □ a new or existing, but strengthened, government agency should take the lead in promoting energy conservation.

Local Heating and Energy Conservation

21. There are a number of different technologies for local urban heating which operate at very different scales: combined heat and power (CHP) is capable of supplying a million people; small groups of homes can be served by one heat pump. Within this range, there are district heating schemes which supply several thousand houses using low grade fuel from refuse or sewage, and heat-only boilers which can service smaller groups of 100 to 200 homes. All these methods show energy savings over the heating of individual buildings. For future energy savings, heat pumps and substitute natural gas (made from coal) could be major competitors to CHP. Other possibilities include solar heat storage and the adoption of high insulation standards, combined with controlled ventilation.

Combined Heat and Power

22. Two-thirds of the energy content of fuel to a normal power station is discharged as lukewarm water and wasted. It is true that some CEGB power stations (such as Drax in North Yorkshire) exploit this heat in greenhouses or fish farming, but the extent is limited, with the electricity industry responding to requests rather than initiating such uses. Converted to CHP, a power station produces hot water which can be used for process heat in industry or for space and water (that is, district) heating in buildings. Provided uses can be found for very large quantities of hot water, overall fuel efficiency is greatly increased. According to the Marshall Report, if one-quarter of the population were supplied by CHP there would be a national fuel saving of some 20 million tons of coal equivalent. Applied on a large scale to high density development, CHP could, according to Marshall, save more energy and deliver cheaper heat than electricity or substitute gas.[11]

23. Although CHP requires a very large heat load for maximum economy of operation, the build up to the final load is incremental.[12] Local district heating schemes, based initially on heat-only boilers, are linked ultimately to a single CHP station when the load is

sufficient. Disused local power stations could have a part to play either in the provision of local district heating during the interim phase or possibly as final CHP stations. It is important that old power stations should not be demolished, or their sites developed for other purposes, until it is certain that there is no CHP/district heating role for them. This means a greater willingness on the part of the CEGB and local authorities to co-operate over local energy supply and the adoption of broader 'economic' criteria by the CEGB to assess the viability of CHP schemes and the retention of disused power station land. Some of these sites could be 'greened' under various interim arrangements, a topic discussed in Chapter 6.

24. But there are disadvantages in CHP. Unlike the use of substitute gas, it requires an entirely new distribution system which could be expensive. With the low fuel prices of 1977, it was not considered economic to begin converting city power stations to CHP. But nine cities have now been shortlisted from which one to two will be selected for pilot schemes.

CHP and Insulation: A Possible Conflict?

25. Local heating schemes are concerned with energy saving in supply. Good insulation reduces energy demand. But the more the demand is reduced, the less economic case there appears to be for CHP or other kinds of district heating for which a large and concentrated demand is essential. A 10 year insulation programme and a higher standard of thermal performance in new buildings may combine to limit the role of CHP and district heating on a large scale, although smaller CHP and other local heating schemes, for example those based upon renewable fuels such as refuse, could be integrated with home insulation and improvement programmes more easily.

26. In practice, integration will be difficult, for the existing institutional framework of fuel industries invites competition, not cooperation. No local agency exists to take on the integrating role. Elsewhere in Europe affairs are managed differently at the local level: in Denmark, for example, LAs have the sole franchise for selling electricity, gas and heat. This allows them to integrate local planning and development with energy distribution. As Marshall notes, high density housing development can be designated for district heating, intermediate areas for gas, and low density areas for electric space heating.

New Building: A Resource Approach

27. The concept of buildings as resources to be husbanded, and saving on materials and energy, is not new. Ten years ago the concept inspired the RIBA to look into the recycling of buildings in what became

known as the 'long life, loose fit, low energy' study.[13] Since then, two oil crises have focused attention upon energy saving, in which the RIBA and other building professions have been active.

28. Adaptability in buildings is central to this approach. The aim, according to Alex Gordon, initiator of the original study, is to combine maximum adaptability with minimum need to replace. As an illustration of adaptability, he took the permanent reinforced concrete multi-storey car park found in many city centres. If urban motoring declines, as Chapter 4 argued it should, many of these buildings will become redundant, but because of the way most of them have been designed — with low headroom — they are not suitable for other uses. It has been shown, however, that an initial expenditure of as little as 5 per cent extra would enable these structures to be built to allow for adaptation to other purposes such as offices.

29. Adaptability in fuel use is important for energy saving. It is one of the advantages of buildings (but not vehicles) that the low temperature heat energy they use can be provided by any of the four main fuels (coal, gas, oil, electricity), by district heating and by the sun. With the ability of switching from one fuel to another, buildings can buffer the effects of fuel shortages. Building designs which allow for the use of different fuels help to keep energy options open. Adaptability of function, to allow for different patterns of living and working, is also essential if new buildings are to be designed for long life.

30. Low energy building can take many forms, the main aim being to reduce the reliance on fossil fuels and make maximum use of natural energy sources. Traditional design principles include admitting sunlight (especially the winter sun), retarding heat loss through insulation, building in materials (like brick) which can retain heat, and using natural means of cooling and ventilation.

31. But energy savings can also be achieved by mechanically controlling the internal environment of a sealed building. A school in Kent has heavyweight construction to retain heat in winter and even out the solar gain in summer; the windows are small and permanently closed and the building is mechanically ventilated all year. A factory in Leeds has been designed on the same principles but uses a lightweight, highly insulated envelope wall with permanent artificial light in the production space. Its energy consumption, expressed as a cost/employee, is 30 per cent lower than other buildings operated by the same company.

32. Passive solar design provides another method of reducing purchased energy, even eliminating it. There are various ways of maximising solar gain; by having large areas of glazing on the south side (with insulation blinds to retain heat at night); a south-facing conservatory to collect warmed air for internal circulation; glazed walls to absorb and radiate heat into the building. Felmore housing at Basildon New Town illustrates what might be called 'resource-sensitive design'. The

scheme, for 430 units, exploits the natural features and micro-climate of the site. All houses, in three groups of parallel terraces, face south, with the larger windows on the south side. Careful spacing avoids overshadowing; prevailing winds blow along the terraces and are reduced by shelter planting between groups. The houses are brick built, with timber frames on the upper floors. A group heating scheme, based upon three coal fired boilers, allows easy fuel substitution, while the tenants' handbook shows how to derive most benefit from the homes with a minimum energy consumption.[14]

Resource Conservation and the Construction Industry

33. Although the construction industry has a key role to play in integrating resource-conservation and building, many other interests are involved: investors, developers, tenants, owners and users. The decisions of all these groups influence the quality of a building and how well it is maintained. The construction industry is diverse, including, at one extreme, large companies operating internationally and, at the other, small, local firms. The fragmented nature of construction — incorporating design, production and assembly — further complicates the application of a long-life approach, which would need to influence every sector and every stage in the building process. Some degree of long-term investment planning is needed, capable of surviving political change, to set the context for developing the design and technology of long-life building.[15]

34. Translated into costs, the long-life approach implies buildings whose capital costs are high in relation to their running costs in maintenance and energy use. At present, in the trade-off between capital and running costs, decisions favour low capital costs. The division of interest in the building process in part accounts for this. Investors and owners who are not users are unconcerned about running costs (unless these are so high that a building is unsaleable) and are more interested in keeping initial costs down. They are supported in this by the taxation system which allows relief on maintenance but not on new building. The public sector, for different reasons, is also under pressure to reduce capital costs.

35. Life cycle costing is a technique that helps determine the trade-offs between the capital and running costs of buildings and provides one way of encouraging those who commission buildings to build for long life, low energy and low maintenance. A study into a measurement method for life cycle costing is being undertaken by the RICS for one of the economic development committees of the National Economic Development Office (NEDO).[16] It is important that the balance sheet reflects the long-term value to society of conserving building resources and energy.

36. There is also a need to find ways of building resource-conservation into the thinking and practice of all sectors of the construction industry: the design professions, the producers of building materials, components and equipment, the small builders and the large construction companies. In the Practitioners' Debate of this report, architects suggested many means by which maintenance and repair could be emphasised within their profession and in the advice architects give on building husbandry.

37. The construction industry has been severely affected by the recession. More than two-and-a-half million people, some 10 per cent of the labour force, normally work in the industry and its associated professions. At the end of 1981, over 25 per cent of them were unemployed.[17] Professional, managerial and craft experts, stocks of materials and manufacturing capacity are all at a level that will make recovery and new approaches difficult to achieve.[18] A major programme of investment in buildings — for rehabilitation and energy conservation — could provide the stimulus for new thinking on resourceful building.

Summing Up on Urban Change

38. The study so far suggests that in much urban policy-making little or no thought is given to the resource implications of development or the sustainability of present patterns. Some urban changes have been extravagant in resource terms, yet the scope is there, especially in urban transport systems and in buildings, for adapting cities to be lower on energy consumption and longer lasting, which will engender other social, economic and environmental benefits. However, at the strategic level, there has been far too little research to draw firm conclusions about the resource (and particularly the energy) implications of different sized and differently planned settlements, or of alternative land-use arrangements and densities. What evidence there is suggests that choices have to be made.

39. From a resource-conservation viewpoint, the issue is not a simple one of dispersal or concentration or urban activity over which much recent debate has been polarised. Some types of dispersal are desirable in resource terms if work and residence can be more closely linked and resources (particularly land) can be managed in supportive, renewing ways. Quite low density development might be appropriate at the margin of (and within) some parts of settlements if more work could be home-based. In other places, the need is for more concentration so that opportunities for resource-saving and for resource-sharing can be realised, for example by district heating or by the provision of common services for a group of dwellings or by improvements in local transport. This concentration could be on a variety of scales and appropriate for settlements of different size.

40. The requirements of different types of resource conservation can pull in different directions. For

Figure 14. **High density — no tower blocks**
This scheme, by the London Borough of Camden's architecture department, in Harmond Street, NW1,
retains a human scale and gives every flat a private garden or roof terrace.
It received a Civic Trust award in 1981 as an outstanding high density development.
Copyright: Civic Trust

example, district heating and combined heat and power systems require high densities (20 to 40 dwellings per acre) for maximum efficiency, whereas low density development facilitates solar heating. Very different living environments would result. The higher density neither allows semi-detached suburbia nor dictates high blocks or close-packed flats without gardens or green-space. With skilful design, it permits an urban environment of terrace houses with small gardens and low rise flats. It reduces land-take and allows walking to become the way of getting from homes to schools, shops and public transport. The low density provides space for detached homes, for larger gardens and for growing food. It allows places for wildlife on a generous scale. At this density, not many will be in walking distance of local services but cycle routes, shared cars and community taxis, as well as economical liquid fuel and electric vehicles, can play the linking role.

41. Integrating resource-conservation with urban development requires a flexible and locally responsive approach to policy-making, and implementation which accepts a very varied meaning of what is 'urban', together with a breakdown of barriers between urban and rural.

A New Role for Planning

42. Britain's town and country planning system evolved over a period when fuels were cheap and land less developed and less valuable than it is today. In many ways, land use and transport planning still operate on old assumptions about resource-availability, especially energy. Moreover, successive circulars from the Department of Environment (notably 22/80) have sought to streamline the planning process, thereby reducing consideration of the obstacles to development.

43. At the strategic policy level, a new type of framework is now needed to guide the development of towns and cities into a future of more uncertain resource-supplies and to provide the basis for day to day urban management.[19] The new strategies would combine conventional Structure Plan policies for land-use, economic and social development, transport and environment with policies for the conservation of energy and other resources used and wasted by urban areas. This would require some statutory change in the present Structure Plan remit to allow policy-making on the use of resources other than land. Techniques

of resource-auditing and budgeting, already used by some LAs, would need to be developed further to provide an information base for new style resource-strategies.

44. Some Structure Plan authorities already do this. They not only express resource-constraints and opportunities in their policies but implement them. In Hertfordshire, for example, greenfield development has been approved only if it satisfies certain criteria which include the following:
- ☐ the land must be materially damaged;
- ☐ major environmental improvements must take place. Five yearly agreements are negotiated with site operators and there is regular inspection to ensure that the land is managed in ways that are environmentally acceptable.

Similar policies operate in South Glamorgan and probably in other planning authorities. The need is to disseminate much more widely the 'best practice' on linking development with resource-conservation.

45. More research is certainly needed, extending the work of Sue Owens and others, but there is already enough evidence for land-use and transport planners to take far more resource-issues into account. It is time that the Department of Environment guidance on Structure Plans, Local Plans and development control incorporated resource-saving (the current Memorandum on Structure and Local Plans should certainly do this).

Reversing the spirit of Circular 22/80, so that the presumption is against rather than for development of greenfield sites, would ensure the opportunity is there for assessing the 'conservation performance' of development proposals. The Royal Town Planning Institute should take a lead in promoting methods of resource-accounting in planning and stimulating the necessary training arrangements.

46. Resource-conservation strategies and the assessment of development applications on grounds of 'conservation performance' between them could help to guide urban change towards sustainability. But resource-conservation should not become just another Structure Plan heading: it must pervade all urban decisions and all levels of decision making, national to local. Chapter 3 identified the contradictions in present policy-making on urban change: there is no link, and much conflict, between the promotion of urban regeneration and the relatively uncontrolled dispersal of people, investment and jobs from the larger cities. It will take much more than the strengthening of Structure Plans to coordinate the approach to urban regeneration and the husbanding of resources. Without, among other changes, a new framework for planning and investment at regional level, it is difficult to see how many cities and most regions can arrest a continuing process of decline. For the moment, it is only at the very local level that there is much sign of development objectives being matched with conservation, as Chapter 6 shows.

Notes and References

1 In principle, high interest rates are bound to favour improvement rather than demolition and replacement. At a test discount rate of 10 per cent, and an assumed life of 30 years, it is worth spending about 75 per cent of the cost of a new house in modernising an old one to the standards of a new house of equivalent size. Recent studies, however, indicate that it may be worth spending much more on improvements, because this minimises the period of loss to the usable housing stock, whereas redevelopment may impose a sterile period of as much as five years. This represents a high cost to be added to that of redevelopment.

2 DEPARTMENT OF ENVIRONMENT. 1982. English house condition survey, 1976-1981. HMSO.

3 ASSOCIATION OF METROPOLITAN AUTHORITIES. 1981. Ruin or renewal? AMA report; ROYAL INSTITUTE OF BRITISH ARCHITECTS, INSTITUTE OF HOUSING. 1981. A housing brief; ROYAL TOWN PLANNING INSTITUTE. 1981. Renewal of older housing. RTPI report.

4 DEPARTMENT OF ENVIRONMENT. 1979. Industry and employment in the inner city. DOE Inner Cities Directorate.

5 ROYAL INSTITUTION OF CHARTERED SURVEYORS. 1981. Rehabilitation and associated economic factors. RICS report. See also: JOINT UNIT FOR RESEARCH ON THE URBAN ENVIRONMENT. 1979. Industrial renewal in the inner city. University of Aston, Birmingham.

6 ROYAL INSTITUTION OF CHARTERED SURVEYORS. 1981. Rehabilitation or new buildings? RICS report.

7 FLAVIN, C. 1980. Energy and architecture: the solar and conservation potential. Worldwatch paper 40.

8 ROYAL INSTITUTE OF BRITISH ARCHITECTS, ROYAL INSTITUTION OF CHARTERED SURVEYORS, CHARTERED INSTITUTION OF BUILDING SERVICES. 1981. A call for a national energy conservation programme.

9 LEACH, G. Personal communication December 1982. Costs assume bulk purchasing of insulation materials and street-by-street schemes. See also: LEACH, G et al. 1981. Insulating British homes. IIED; COYNE, P. 1981. Is it cheaper to save it? Energy Manager 4 (5).

10 HOUSE OF COMMONS SELECT COMMITTEE ON ENERGY. 1982. Fifth report: energy conservation in buildings. vol 1. HMSO.

11 MARSHALL, W. 1979. Combined heat and power generation in the United Kingdom. Department of Energy paper 35. HMSO.

12 COMBINED HEAT AND POWER GROUP. 1979. Heat loads in British cities. Department of Energy. Paper 34, HMSO.

13 GORDON, A. 1974. Architects and resource conservation. Journal of the Royal Institute of British Architects, 81 (1), January.

14 KASABOR, G. (editor). 1979. Buildings: the key to energy conservation. Royal Institute of British Architects.

15 HILLEBRANDT, P M. Personal communication.

16 BUILDING. 1981. Life Cycle costing. Editorial in *Building, 24 July*.

17 NATIONAL COUNCIL FOR BUILDING MATERIALS PRODUCERS. 1978. Building materials in perspective.

18 A housing brief, *op cit*.

19 These are not new ideas. The Council for the Protection of Rural England argued as long ago as 1975 that planning authorities should be obliged to take energy conservation into account. See: HOUSE OF COMMONS SELECT COMMITTEE ON ENERGY. 1982. Energy conservation in buildings, vol II, appendix 20; For additional ideas see: HALL, D. 1978. Energy options and planning. Town and Country Planning Summer School Main Paper.

CHAPTER 6

PEOPLE AND RESOURCE CONSERVATION

Introduction

1. In many parts of the developed world, urban people have become a powerful voice for conservation. But, as the WCS recognises: 'To win and retain as much . . . attention as possible, it is essential for conservation to be seen to be central to human interests and aspirations'.[1] The three previous chapters assessed the scope for urban resource-saving at the strategic level and in terms of the way the urban fabric is managed; this chapter looks at the role of individuals: acting at home, at work and in the local community. How can the very considerable human resources of time, energy, skills and commitment be more widely deployed for resource-conservation? The chapter examines some of the changing circumstances of urban people and how these affect their motivation and capacity to save resources.[2] It looks at the progress of community conservation activity and the new role for resource-saving enterprise.

Changing Urban Lives: The Prospects for Individual Action

2. It is possible to be both optimistic and cynical about current movements in society. Some have argued that the dominating trend towards less formal employment will release time in which lofts can be insulated, homes repaired and food grown. Although there are dangers in the notion that conservation is an activity best left to the informal economy, it is likely that more people in future will be able to participate in local action to improve their surroundings and they will have the time to acquire new skills. Earlier retirement, smaller families and the growth of free time among those in jobs all suggest the same scope for more individual and co-operative conservation activity. James Robertson offers the enticing prospect of resourceful city dwellers: 'More people will work on repairing, maintaining and servicing longer-lasting products and on recycling the components and materials they contain'.[3]

3. Indeed, there are signs of a move in this direction: the sale and hire of DIY equipment have soared. Allotment waiting lists have grown. More people now bicycle in cities. Although not motivated originally by questions of resource-saving, the efforts of self-build housing groups, in Lewisham and elsewhere, contribute to the conservation cause in a variety of ways.[4] The work provides jobs and satisfaction, the houses are built on waste land, they are 'low-energy and loose-fit' and use renewable materials (timber). But such schemes are still regarded, except by a few sympathetic local authorities, as an expedient, temporary, even bizarre approach to shelter, rather than, as in Denmark, a desirable additional means of providing urban housing. Local campaigns, and perhaps the influence of environmental education in schools, have contributed to the growing public willingness to use bottle banks and save waste paper.

4. But, in practice, the effort is not sustained. Fluctuations in the market for waste paper and the failure of most LAs to continue separate collections have brought domestic paper saving virtually to an end. Oxfam shops still collect waste aluminium but the earlier enthusiasm for voluntary recycling that kept the Huddersfield Wastesaver in business is waning.[5] For some people, restrictions are imposed (for example, on food growing and house repairs) by the nature of their housing tenure. Most homes are ill designed for the separation of wastes; there is no advice or incentive for people to bother. So, even among those who may be motivated to save resources, doing so is not easy. But how widespread is the underlying commitment?

5. There is little evidence to suggest that conservation is a pervasive popular concern in society. As Ziona Strelitz remarks in assessing such evidence as exists: 'it is in the air but is not broadly based . . . conservation views are usually those of experts or reformers rather than those from the heart of society'.[6] For the unemployed, and those on low incomes with falling living standards, most conservation activity, and the ways in which conservation messages are communicated, appear trivial and irrelevant. For a growing number of people, the potential more time available from formal work for individual and community activities which could bring conservation benefits will be constrained by low incomes and poor mobility.

6. Although high unemployment levels obviously reduce the capacity of families to consume, elsewhere in society changes in work patterns (towards more women working, for example) allow and often demand life styles which are more consuming of resources, with less time to sort and re-use wastes; to walk rather than ride. This is not to argue that unemployment should be condoned or that changes in work patterns should be denied, only that,

Figure 15. **Self-help in Lewisham**
Architect Walter Segal, who designed this timber house for construction on
wasteland by a self-build group, talks with his clients — the builders
Copyright: Architects' Journal

for conservation to work, it has to be linked into desirable trends in society, towards fuller employment, more female emancipation; it cannot succeed in competition.

7. For people to be motivated to save resources they must see the effort to be worthwhile. Conservation must relate to their daily experience and show some material benefit for them: in saving money, providing jobs, improving living conditions. conservation needs to involve people in shaping their surroundings where the impact is clear. This has been well shown in urban fringe tree planting schemes, where project organisers have had to overcome the apathy of those who are surrounded by large scale industrial dereliction. It is difficult for individuals to feel that an impression is being made in the face of powerful forces against conservation: the advance of highly packaged goods, bags with everything, throwaway products of every kind. Moreover, much resource-extravagance has been officially blessed — in medicine and food, for example, many wrappings signal more hygiene.

8. Above all, an ethos of conspicuous consumption must be the most potent force working against more individual conservation effort, particularly when consumption is perceived as being so closely linked to individual and family aspirations. Much effort amongst individuals in society is directed towards the acquisition of 'positional' goods — those (often high on resource-consumption) which provide pleasure partly because

other people do not have them. Hirsh's notion is of 'everyone standing on tiptoe but no one being able to see', an apt metaphor for the inevitable progression (but ultimate futility) of resource-extravagance.[7]

9. More personal free time — both enforced by and enjoyed by those in jobs — may not always pull in the direction of resource-saving. It may stimulate participation in activities which are high consumers of land and energy resources (*vide* the Sports Council Strategies of the last decade and their emphasis upon urban golf course and sports hall provision). This is not to deny society's need for the personal and community benefits that more leisure can bring, but rather to argue for the resource-implications of leisure choices to be assessed, working, where possible, towards providing opportunities in the least resource-expensive as well as in the most equitable manner. This kind of thinking has not been a notable feature of leisure policy-making so far.[8] Financial rather than conservation performance has dominated provision.

10. Over the short-term, the clues are that individual resource-saving will remain limited, unless there is a much stronger example set by other, more powerful groups in society — by industry and by government, both in their own activities and by their greater control and influence over resource-consumers. However, individual resource-saving can be achieved: there are good examples in Europe of developments which encourage individuals to conserve. Sweden and Denmark

have local urban energy advice centres to help citizens find their way through the maze of information about fuel saving. Denmark has banned the one trip soft drinks container; French supermarkets collect returnable bottles, and no extra disposal trip is needed. For home-based waste saving to work it must become physically easier, with consumer goods, kitchens and refuse collection services designed for it. Financial incentives would help as they do for the collection of bottles which require a deposit, or fiscal means as in the American Goodwill Enterprises (and in a similar anti-waste scheme in Glasgow). Here, consumers are encouraged to donate unwanted goods to collection depots where they are cleaned, repaired and sold in Goodwill shops generating a variety of jobs and training opportunities.[9]

11. Campaigns can be effective as 'SAVE IT' and the drought years demonstrated. But the results, particularly of national campaigns, are temporary; they are an adjunct to, but not the foundation for, a movement to greater individual resourcefulness. Measures which continually remind people of the need to save and create are probably more successful: energy consumption indicators, a 'reclaim' mark for all recoverable materials, more waste-collecting locations and special days for conservation activity. The Netherlands has a number of the latter, including an annual tree planting day and twice yearly neighbourhood exchanges of unwanted goods.

Community Action

12. More tangible results in resource-conservation seem at present to come from the actions of voluntary groups. The growth of interest in conservation matters and the rise in membership of environmental groups (now numbering more than three million) is a particular phenomenon of the 1970s. Since the Stockholm Environment conference, the concerns of these groups have widened and their means of dealing with issues have become more sophisticated. Earlier preoccupied with financing the protection of individual species, habitats and landscapes, many groups now question the underlying economic and social forces which threaten natural resources, and use their growing political muscle to promote the discussion of alternatives — in mining, energy, road and water catchment policy, for example.

13. One of the most significant recent developments in the environmental movement has been the progression of some groups away from the view that conservation is mainly needed elsewhere (in the Third World, or in the countryside) towards a concern to promote and sustain local action in resource-saving and creating better environments for living, especially in the city. There are some excellent examples — in the work of the neighbourhood energy schemes and in various greening initiatives — involving wildlife conservation, city farms and allotments. The examples described below do not represent the wide variety of community schemes now in operation but some of those which best illustrate the multiple values of resource-saving.

Neighbourhood Energy Schemes

14. In May 1981, the National Council for Voluntary Organisations initiated, with government backing, a Neighbourhood Energy Action scheme, extending to other areas the ideas pioneered in earlier projects by the FOE in Durham and Birmingham and, under a wider sponsorship of local groups, in Newcastle. There are now some 37 groups organising local schemes with Department of Energy and MSC funding and eight or nine are in operation; the plan is for 80 schemes during 1982/83 at a total cost of £5m.[10]

15. They focus on insulating and draught-proofing the homes of low income families — pensioners, the disabled and those on supplementary benefit — groups among which there is a good deal of fuel poverty. The schemes are centred mainly upon the low income end of the privately rented and owner occupied housing sectors, although some arrangements have been made, in New-castle, for example, to insulate public housing where this is not part of the council's programme.

16. These projects, like earlier ones, involve both volunteers and paid labour, and are funded under Urban Aid, Inner City Partnership and MSC schemes. The job creation element is strong, with work provided for school leavers and for the longer-term unemployed: 'Keeping Newcastle Warm' offers 14 jobs under the CEP programme. Some schemes, like 'Keep Warm' in Hammersmith run training workshops for local teams.

17. Community involvement at a very local scale has been a key ingredient, vigorously promoted by the NCVO in its coordinating role. Close contact between insulating teams and their clients has been the principal source of finding new homes to tackle; it has allowed advice to be given on many aspects of domestic conservation — and not only energy-saving but other services which can be organised locally such as gardening, home repairs and decoration. Local action of this kind can focus attention on wider issues of energy saving and the need to audit resources, in the home and in the community. 'A simple example of such accounting has been undertaken in Newport and Nevern in West Wales where local residents calculated that the community's total energy bill was of the order of £250,000. Concerned to retain this or part of this fund for their own economy, rather than let it be lost outside, the local community was galvanised to a broad-based scheme of energy conservation (and small scale power generation)'.[11]

18. The local advantages of an energy scheme are considerable — not just in terms of jobs but in the demand for insulation materials from local firms and in indirect

effects on the local economy: a pound saved on fuel bills means a pound more for spending. A notable strength of the schemes so far lies in the degree of co-operation achieved between so many voluntary and official groups with their: '. . . distinctive potential for forging inter-agency collaboration and drawing support from . . . charitable trusts, the private sector, central government agencies and departments, voluntary organis-ations, local government and trade unions'.[12] Trade unions, often suspicious and antagonistic towards job creation initiatives, have been closely involved, advising on wage rates, the skills required and communicating with local people.

19. Robert Davies argues that energy saving can offer a special focus for inner city regeneration because it combines many financial and manpower resources in a way which brings immediate social benefit, jobs and local economic gains. There may well be wider advantages, since the neighbourhood schemes have shown how immediately relevant conservation can be — homes are warmer and more people have jobs — and therefore these benefits will work better for the cause of conservation among many people than nationally-based exhortation. There is much scope for extending these neighbourhood schemes as part of a wider pro-gramme of Government support for home and public building insulation linked with more local advice on energy-saving and the stimulation of new enterprises. The Department of Energy expects to spend £300m in 1982-3 on fuel poverty allowances. The £5m promised for neighbourhood energy schemes seems far too low a figure for such a successful approach in keeping people warm and saving resources.

Urban Wildlife Conservation

20. The last three to four years have seen a growing movement towards conserving wildlife and natural areas in the city. Two strands of action have been at work. The first is to save threatened local areas, like Moseley Bog or the Walthamstow Marshes, from developments which would destroy their character and remove the vital association these areas have in the lives of local people — as playspaces for their children and of their own youth. A second strand of action comes from the disenchantment of young ecologists with much of the present greening activities of urban parks departments and others who manage urban open space, unsympa-thetic as they often are to the requirements of ecological diversity. Reacting against the spread of exotic trees and shrubs and manicured rosebeds, members of wildlife groups in some of the larger conurbations, particularly in Liverpool, London and Birmingham, have introduced a different approach to greening the city by converting vacant and derelict land of all kinds into new and varied habitats.[13]

21. One of the first was the William Curtis Ecological Park created, in the shadow of Tower Bridge, from a disued lorry park (see Figure 16, p 142). Within three years, after several loads of subsoil and much volunteer effort, a derelict urban site was transformed into an ecological oasis of great diversity. It is used for field studies by local schools; its management provides paid work for a warden and continuing opportunities for voluntary action. Another active group, the Liverpool-based Rural Preservation Association (RPA), has trans-formed some 26 inner area sites into new natural habitats since its 'Greensight' project began in 1979. Assisted by the Liverpool Inner City Partnership and MSC the project has employed over 70 young people in job creation schemes and uses children and adult residents where possible. Like other urban wildlife groups, the RPA is committed to the notion of community participation in conservation.

22. The London Wildlife Trust, now with a full-time conservation officer and a network of local member groups, is busy helping the groups to acquire and manage threatened sites by persuading owners to release land for wildlife conservation and by involving children and adults not only as learners but also as active conservers. In a recent 'trees-on-wheels' programme, children collected seedlings from urban fringe woodland and planted them in city plots. Another campaign 'loosen my ties' urged city dwellers to care for trees after planting, which is so often a neglected aspect of LA activity.[14]

City Farms

23. There is room for a greater variety of urban green-space and for using wasteland in ways which can involve city people in experiences normally associated only with the countryside. The 35 or so city farms have just such an aim. A product of the last decade, many are still in their early stages but they offer much scope for local participation in caring for animals, in growing food while learning (and developing the necessary skills to do this in an urban setting), in tree-planting and in general environ-mental improvements. In theory, the farms provide ideal vehicles for demonstrating all the main WCS principles, although they are primarily perceived as having educational and social roles. (A number, for example the Kentish Town farm, have facilities for the disabled and promote special activities for children and pensioners.) Some take on additional environmental tasks, the breeding of rare domestic plant and animal varieties and the production of flower seed. Deen City farm, for example, created from a derelict site in south London, has an 'interest garden', with more than 60 species of wild and garden flowers.

24. However, like other community initiatives, city farms face uncertainty over their funding. Charitable sources are small and the competition is high; urban aid monies and MSC support often last no longer than three years; city farms are unsure of the scope for marketing their produce and training services. Local authorities

Figure 16. **Nature in the city**
A lorry park transformed into an ecological park in the shadow of London's Tower Bridge
Copyright: The Ecological Parks Trust

Figures 17a and 17b. **Wasteland to vegetable growing**
Allotments in the London Borough of Redbridge cleared by the Redbridge Friends of the Earth:
before and after
Copyright: (17a) Civic Trust; (17b) Friends of the Earth

have had other priorities: LEAs, especially, with some exceptions, have displayed remarkably little interest in what would seem to be such an attractive educational tool, not only for school children but also for training others in wider community skills. Technical support is growing and is a key concern for the National Federation of City Farms which maintains a bank of advisers. Temporary and longer-term low rent leases on vacant sites are becoming easier to negotiate. Nevertheless, financial vulnerability remains, and some farms are having to think of new ways of becoming more self-sufficient: riding facilities are a common first addition. Other possibilities lie in the retailing of farm produce, craftwork and teaching facilities.

central and local Government funding, would be ecologically, socially and economically valuable. It would improve urban environments, promote a healthy recreation and nurture a community spirit. 'The additional potential benefits of supplementing incomes with fresh, home-produced food and creating jobs for unemployed young people and skilled tradesmen make an even stronger case for increasing the provision of allotments.'[15] Barbier calls for a national allotment programme to cover 50,000 acres of derelict land to meet estimated demand. This could be implemented by local authorities using extra funds under existing urban programmes and MSC labour to restore and service land with added powers to lease idle land for food growing.

Allotment Schemes

25. Renewed interest in allotment gardening has brought a number of new initiatives in urban areas (see Figures 17a and 17b, p 143). Some schemes (for example, the Adelaide Community Gardens, Camden) show that allotments can provide a focus for community interest in city districts where there are few gardens and perhaps a transitory population.

26. Some local authorities, which are the major providers of allotment land, still have an active allotment policy and have, like Leicester City or the London Borough of Brent, recently rationalised many of their holdings. But the plots are not always well distributed for those areas of the borough which suffer bad housing and a lack of public open space, which may account for the situation in which there are not only allotment vacancies but also a waiting list for accessible plots. The National Allotments and Garden Society have noted that under-use of allotments may be more a function of their position and poor quality — ill-drained and otherwise poorly managed — rather than of any lack of interest. In Brent, where many plots have deteriorated, they are offered rent-free for six months to encourage restoration. Local community management arrangements are encouraged and the borough offers an advisory service. In Hackney, local groups are paid to restore allotment land.

27. But the prevailing LA policy is to sell off allotment land for other uses. It is a policy born of the financial climate and of the changed national attitude to allotments: towards their leisure function rather than any welfare goal of subsistence food production. This trend towards changing the image with consequences, as in the leisure gardens of the Netherlands, for tool sheds to become second homes is hardly a movement for conservation. Patios and exotic flowers are not ecologically rich, nor do they seem to be the goal of many older people who presently rely upon the food and interest produced from their plots.

28. Barbier argues that an expanded allotment programme, with better management supported by more

Local Participation and Employment: What Prospects for Continuing Gain?

29. Behind much community activity lies the belief that for conservation to be a wider force in society, it must first be relevant, like energy saving, at the personal level, contributing to improved incomes, living standards and surroundings. The job creation issue is an important one. There are now more than three million registered unemployed; the number of jobless school leavers will rise to about a million by 1985. Most of the initiatives described have already created, and will continue to generate, more jobs, using MSC funding. Neighbourhood energy projects, urban wildlife schemes and city farms have all created jobs under the Youth Opportunities Programme and the Community Enterprise Programme for the longer-term unemployed.[16] This last capacity is encouraging, for the particular problems of this growing category of unemployed have been given rather less attention because job creation has concentrated on the immediate issue of reducing the number of school leavers without work. Yet, as the bulge of late teenagers passes after the mid-1980s, the number of older, longer-term unemployed will continue to rise. Their options and supports are fewer, responsibilities often greater and morale generally poorer than unemployed school leavers.

30. Barbier suggests that around 10,000 new jobs could accrue from an expanded allotment programme with perhaps one quarter of these organised under the Community Enterprise Programme (CEP).[17] The latest in a series of NCC reports on urban wildlife is enthusiastic about the scope for much more short-term youth and adult employment in this field, with MSC teams creating and managing more urban wildlife areas and running educational projects based on them.[18] But this will depend upon many more groups, in the private as well as the public sector, sponsoring job-creation projects and participating in good training schemes. Susan Kydd argues that the private sector could sponsor many more ambititious greening schemes, translating into larger scale action the wealth of ideas for environmental improvement that are emerging locally. The Shell 'Better Britain' campaign, which aims to inform and

award good schemes, is one example of how companies can augment voluntary action. But the scale needs to be much larger. The CBI Special Programmes Unit is working to promote private sector sponsorship of MSC schemes by assessing the capability of local firms to help and to benefit from participation.

31. There are other problems associated with MSC programmes — for conservation and for employment. The schemes are temporary, individuals work usually for no longer than a year and, while a great deal of good work has undoubtedly been accomplished, a constantly changing labour force and one which (it is acknowledged) has not always been well enough trained or supervised, is not necessarily the most efficient way of tackling conservation tasks. Those who have been through job creation schemes can rarely look forward to more permanent work in the same field. There simply are not the jobs yet available to absorb all the many young people emerging not only from MSC schemes, but also from college and university environmental courses.

32. The Youth Training Scheme, which replaces the Youth Opportunities Programme and aims to redress some of its obvious working deficiencies, proposes an entirely new training system for young people, both in and out of work. But a year is too short (particularly for many seasonal conservation skills) and unlikely to provide a 'conservation labour force' skilled enough to tackle the scale of problems that exist. Urban wildlife conservation, for example, is a new field, so more supervisors need to be trained quickly. The system ignores, once again, the longer-term unemployed; the community programme designed for this group needs to be expanded to include more conservation and resource-saving initiatives. But the training element must be improved and, with all temporary job creation schemes, some means found of providing more permanent jobs for the short-term experience to be consolidated. Resource-saving could provide a major new focus for the MSC to create and sustain work opportunities which combine post-school training, work experience and the transition to permanent jobs.

33. MSC funding extends mainly to labour costs, with only limited sums for project overheads and initial capital outlay. Sponsors must find the extra capital funding and the means to finance on-going management. Although there are now a variety of sources to be tapped, some are very short-term, and many emphasise capital but not running costs — a problem for conservation schemes which have no easy means of generating income. Moreover, negotiating for funds (and on other administrative issues such as insurance) requires experience and expertise which many voluntary groups do not have. More skilled intermediaries are required (by secondment and other ways) to put conservation spenders in touch with funders and also to help them to negotiate the release of land and buildings and assist with equipment, transport and administration. Some LAs already have special programmes to support community participation, providing seed corn funds, premises and information.[19] The Greater London Council has allocated £700,000 for environmental projects in 1983, including a London Ecology Centre to provide a base for voluntary groups in the capital. There are new ways of funding to be explored with scope for conservationists to be more entrepreneurial and to market the products of conservation schemes: plants, timber, food, tools and many other goods, as well as skills. Local resource and information exchanges could help here.

34. Technical advice is less of a problem: a number of specialist organisations, such as ComTechsa on Merseyside, InterAction in Kentish Town or the Intermediate Technology Development Group, can advise local groups. The British Trust for Conservation Volunteers plays a major role in training as well as carrying out urban conservation tasks. Some groups produce detailed local newsletters believing, like the London and Birmingham wildlife groups and the NCVO, that communication between volunteers and with sponsors plays a key part in facilitating and coordinating local action. There is scope for drawing more upon the resources of local education institutions.

35. Overall, voluntary action is a thriving force for more resource-conservation in cities. There is considerable scope for extending the efforts; with more certain funding, better coordination and inter-group learning and help on administration, much more could be achieved. But without this support, the danger is that efforts will be piecemeal, cosmetic and temporary. Voluntary action alone, even when backed by MSC labour, cannot be the only means by which conservation is integrated with development at the local level. Coverage of voluntary action is patchy and commitment may be short-lived. Nor do MSC temporary job creation schemes alone offer a satisfactory way of realising the employment potential of more urban conservation activity.

Community Enterprise

36. An increasing number of small businesses are working, both directly and indirectly, in the urban conservation arena. Of particular relevance are those which may be described as community enterprises, businesses which (varied though they are in structure) aim to combine local community and urban regeneration objectives with profit making in a sustainable way. It is possible to see this kind of initiative, that is enterprise with a community and a resource-saving face, as having a major part to play in integrating conservation with development, and so implementing the WCS at the local level.

37. There are a number of good examples in practice. Various workshop enterprises, like those developed by Regeneration in Clerkenwell (and now elsewhere in London and other cities) combine a number of aspects of resource-saving with the goal of local economic

revival by creating space at low rent, under informal arrangements, for new and permanent jobs.[20] Local incomes are raised, trade and exchange are improved and these small businesses begin to expand.

38. David Rock in *The Grassroot Developers* describes a wide range of community enterprises, each at present operating as a town development trust which he describes as: '. . . a people's entrepreneurial organisation (probably taking the form of a charity owning a trading company), created by a local community — whether that be a street, part of a town, a whole town, a village or part of a region — to revitalise, by building or renovating, that community's physical surroundings and in so doing, the community spirit itself.'[21]

39. However, community enterprises can take many forms: some are cooperatives, owned and managed by the employees; some are companies with residents as 'shareholders'; others are voluntary charitable organisations which have established trading companies to run shops and other associated businesses. Many community enterprises also involve trade unions, local government and the private sector. Whatever their structure they have the following aims in common:
   □ creation of permanent jobs;
   □ provision of other community benefits;
   □ collaboration between different local interests;
   □ broad community control;
   □ profits directed towards social and community benefit rather than private gain.
With such aims, community businesses can provide 'a valuable "third arm" of enterprise . . . which operates alongside the public and private sectors.'[22] But what is the scope for building in resource-saving?

40. The rehabilitation of vacant buildings, a common first stage of community enterprise, is clearly a conservation gain. Most of the Regeneration schemes have involved the repair and adaptation of vacant buildings into a range of workshop premises through which small businesses can progress as their fortunes change. Mike Franks, a director of Regeneration, also sees the workshop development: '. . . as a catalyst to trigger a number of associated projects ranging from involvement in training schemes and educational projects within the Workshops to tree planting [and] the reclamation of adjacent derelict sites for community gardens. . .'[23]

41. A close match between conservation and development has sometimes occurred in tourist enterprises which, like the Ironbridge Gorge Museum Trust, combine commercial success with the conscientious restoration of buildings, general environmental improvement and a widening role in education and interpretation.

42. Some small businesses are themselves directly resource-saving: they are concerned with the repair of goods or the manufacture of spare parts. The Hackney Brass Tacks workshops, for example, recycle furniture, electrical goods and bicycles. There is a workshop where local people can do their own repairs and a call-out service to help elderly and housebound people in the locality with small scale repairs. Training and work experience has been provided for some 20 previously unemployed people; the workshops emply 11 full-time staff. The provision of shared services (secretarial and accountancy, for example) is a common theme in the Regeneration schemes, in Hackney, and in other community enterprise units. Sometimes other helpful links can be made within a workshop complex: at the Old Bakehouse Trust workshops in Oxford, for example, the upholsterer makes seats for the motorcycles restored in a neighbouring enterprise.

What Future for Small Businesses and Conservation?

43. The work already in progress on many aspects of resource-saving suggests there are opportunities for businesses to expand and for more enterprises to start up, not only in building, insulation and repair, but also in the restoration of derelict land and the greening of urban areas, in the processing of domestic wastes and in the development and production of electronic control and monitoring devices which could help people to know more about, and reduce, their resource-consumption. But all small businesses, community-based and otherwise, face a number of problems which limit their potential, both for urban regeneration and for bringing conservation benefit.

44. The importance of the small business sector to the British economy, and to the regeneration of the inner cities in particular, is widely acknowledged. Small enterprises contribute about 20 per cent of GNP; they are more labour- and less capital-intensive than larger companies and are the prime creators of new jobs. They are often innovative and benefit from the 'sweat equity' of independent entrepreneurs. John Bolton, one time chairman of the Committee of Inquiry on Small Businesses, argues: '. . . the scale of the economic and social problems facing the country in the 1980s is so enormous that no solution is likely without a very substantial expansion in the number of small businesses, and in the growth of existing small businesses, in the future.'[24]

45. Yet the record, of few start-ups and a relatively large number of closures, shows that British small businesses fare rather less well than those in Europe or the USA. In spite of government support, through the Small Firms Division of the Department of Industry and more recently through the Business Opportunities Programme and the Loans Guarantee Scheme, many enterprises find it difficult to get initial funding, suitable premises and proper business advice. There is continual uncertainty about all of these issues and a lack of contact between those who face common problems.

46. All the major lending banks and a number of the larger companies have business support schemes, but deteriorating economic conditions and high interest rates discourage investment. Lending from pensions and insurance companies has grown, but, for most, probably no more than 1 to 2 per cent of their funds go to the small business sector.

47. One recent urban initiative is designed to improve on this. Advised by the Financial Institutions in Government Group (FIG) Michael Heseltine announced in 1982 a new £70m grant scheme as part of the Urban Programme to lever private investment into funding partnerships for new enterprises in designated inner city areas.[25] This could amount to a substantial sum but, in practice, it may be thinly spread and unable to compensate for the overall reductions in public spending on the inner cities of recent years. Moreover, it looks unlikely that much investment will be attracted to the very small scale, less profitable and less proven enterprises, characteristic of resource-saving. It appears that the funds will be (as is the rest of the Urban Programme) for capital projects, whereas a major problem, both for voluntary and business initiatives in resource-saving, has been getting enough support to sustain the work until projects can generate some income. More funds are also needed for feasibility studies — to identify local markets for products and services and to explore alternative means of operation and the possibilities for local co-operation.[26] There should be more opportunities, perhaps through special local units, for investors (both large and small) to support small enterprises in their locality, including innovative schemes in their early stages when risk capital is so hard to get.

48. In many ways, the need is not just for more public and private investment in small businesses but, as the community schemes have shown, it is for more for 'facilitators' to pull together cash, expertise and other support from all the many resources of a local community. The need is to identify and organise local exchanges, for example, between those who produce usable wastes and those who can recycle and repair them, and between those who have expertise to offer and those who need it: for example, Hackney Brass Tacks benefits from the business advice available from an economic manager, seconded from Marks and Spencer. A major requirement is for the better exchange and development of skills — technical, administrative and social — through local training schemes.

49. A number of public and private organisations, in the shape of environmental and enterprise trusts, have emerged to play this catalytic role. Groundwork North-west, extending the work begun by the St Helen's Groundwork Trust, aims to orchestrate the restoration and management of much degraded urban edge land by mobilising the resources of voluntary organisations, local councils, industry, landowners and the Countryside Commission. Some LAs, like Hackney, promote small businesses through special development units.[27] More are needed.

Local Action for Conservation with Development

50. This chapter has looked at some conservation and regeneration initiatives which involve a wide range of environmental and entrepreneurial organisations. All have rather different structures, responding to local circumstances and personalities, but they face a number of common problems in stimulating and sustaining local action, especially in the inner city. Financing, both of feasibility studies and subsequent development work, is often difficult. Local community groups and local businesses cannot easily secure land and buildings, which are the hardware for their environmental or entrepreneurial activities, whether they are running city farms or repair workshops. Raising funds, finding and training staff and negotiating through often complicated bureaucracies make demands upon limited time, money and effort before the action can begin.

51. It is difficult to generalise about the critical ingredients for success. For some groups, success has depended upon a charismatic style of leadership. For others success has been in the past, and still remains, a dependence upon money, although there are now encouraging signs that groups can lever funds from the private sector as well as from central Government and local authorities (under grant, partnership and urban aid schemes) and from charitable sources. Many groups have no lack of technical expertise, though others could learn from practical experience elsewhere and by having better knowledge of the latest materials. Yet the limiting factor for local action may not be money, land, buildings or advice, but the negotiating skills to find and make use of these things. Successful and sustained conservation and economic regeneration at the local level have relied much upon the coordinating skills of those who can make the most of local resources — in physical, financial and human terms. The need is to find ways of increasing the catalysts without stifling local spontaneity.

52. There is still far too little integration of conservation and development at the local level. Resource-saving, environmental improvement activities and small business developments most often remain separate. Both environmental and business ventures share common interests — in realising community benefits, or in creating jobs or better surroundings. Yet their two approaches have appeared distinct and superficially opposed: entrepreneurial activities trying to attract risk capital, aiming for permanent jobs and profitable economic regeneration (which often cannot accommodate the expense of environmental improvements); environmental initiatives relying mainly on public support, being non-profit making and finding it hard to provide permanent jobs or secure enough finance for long-term improvements. It is the particular skills and actions of both groups that need to be combined for a sustainable approach to conservation and development in the city. Local authorities and community groups who face continuing management costs — of greening, for example, or waste disposal — need to look not only

at cheaper techniques but also for ways of generating some income from their activities. Likewise, companies must recognise some public obligations in their use of resources and local environment.

53. Such a linkage of approach needs help. This could take the form of a new programme for local conservation and regeneration to focus on the presently disparate opportunities for linking resource-saving with the creation of permanent jobs and new enterprises. The aims of a new 'Resourceful Cities' programme would be to:

☐ mobilise funds under existing, and new, public programmes and from the private sector towards urban conservation with development initiatives, particularly innovative schemes;

☐ promote and assist local organisations to co-ordinate action in their area;

☐ provide or arrange for information exchanges of experience and skills;

☐ publicise and award good practice;

☐ support, advise on and run training workshops.

54. At the very least, the Urban Programme, the Loans Guarantee Scheme for small businesses and the MSC should be given an explicit brief to include conservation as a priority alongside economic regeneration and community participation. Revised funding arrangements should reflect the need to break down barriers between wholly voluntary action and schemes that can eventually become self-financing. The Small Grants Programme, with an annual budget of less than £300,000, is the only national source of Department of Environment funding for the voluntary sector, but this has no legislative base, has to be agreed from year to year, usually contributes only 50 per cent of costs, and seldom lasts longer than four years. Promising conservation schemes

should be capable of being assisted at higher levels and for a longer period. The MSC needs greater flexibility to fund longer-term posts and to allow projects to shift from temporary job creation to self-sustaining enterprises. Although the priorities for more support lie in the inner cities, a conservation for development programme should also promote new initiatives in other urban areas.

55. A programme of conservation for development probably needs an organisation to back it. This could take a variety of forms as a 'facilitating' unit working in the interstices of existing agencies as, for example, the NCVO does for neighbourhood energy schemes, or the NCC for urban wildlife conservation, or the Countryside Commissions for area management on the urban fringe. It may be that an existing organisation could take on the role, but not without a substantial widening of the remit of those most appropriate. Joint funding and independent status would seem sensible goals.

56. A 'Resourceful Cities' programme of local action for conservation and regeneration could combine and realise many different objectives for urban areas and provide a focus for many different types of voluntary action and enterprise: the restoration of vacant land, energy saving, home improvement, historic building repair, the creation of wild habitats and many more. Better coordination between voluntary, business and government action could ensure the synergism that is needed rather than a piecemeal separation of independent interests. The programme could provide a key means of implementing the WCS for urban Britain and a unifying theme for revitalising many cities to set alongside the dominant decentralising trend. This, as Chapter 3 argued, signals no great advantage for many inner urban areas or their environments.

Notes and References

1 IUCN. 1980. World conservation strategy.

2 This chapter draws upon a paper commissioned for the study from: STRELITZ, Z. 1982. Resource conservation: changing activities and attitudes of urban people.

3 ROBERTSON, J. 1981. The redistribution of work. Turning Point.

4 STEAD, P. 1978. Self-build housing groups and co-operatives — ideas in practice. Anglo-German Foundation report.

5 VOGLER, J. 1980. Muck and brass. Oxfam Public Affairs Unit.

6 Resource conservation: changing activities and attitudes. op cit.

7 HIRSH, F. 1977. Social limits to growth. Routledge and Kegan Paul.

8 See for example: GREATER LONDON AND SE COUNCIL FOR SPORT AND RECREATION. 1982. Prospect for the eighties — regional recreation strategy.

9 NEWNHAM, R. 1980. Community enterprise: British potential and American experience. University of Reading School of Planning Studies report OP3.

10 DAVIES, ROBERT. Personal communication.

11 Quoted in: Resource conservation: changing activities and attitudes. op cit.

12 NATIONAL COUNCIL FOR VOLUNTARY ORGANIS— ATIONS. 1980. Energy — a programme for the inner city. NCVO Inner Cities Unit.

13 KYDD, S. 1982. Urban nature conservation and youth employment. Nature Conservancy Council.

14 LONDON WILDLIFE TRUST. 1981. Wild London, 2, September.

15 BARBIER, E B. 1981. Earthworks: environmental approaches to employment creation. Friends of the Earth.

16 Now the Community Programme. In numerical terms YOP dominated, providing 360,000 temporary jobs in 1980/81 compared with 18,400 entrants to the programme which

became CEP. But the majority of YOP places were for work experience on employers' premises; only 6 per cent (20,100) involved project work which in some cases involves conservation. See: MANPOWER SERVICES COMMISSION. 1981. Review of the third year of special programmes. MSC.

17 Earthworks, *op cit.*

18 Urban nature conservation and youth employment, *op cit.*

19 TOWN AND COUNTRY PLANNING ASSOCIATION for the Calouste Gulbenkian Foundation. 1981. Community initiatives in urban renaissance. European Campaign for Urban Renaissance Conference paper. University of Durham. December.

20 ALDOUS, T. 1980. Urban regeneration. *Building, 18 April.*

21 ROCK, D. 1979. The grassroot developers. Royal Institute of British Architects. See also: FALK, N. 1981. New communities and development trusts. *Town and Country Planning, 50 (11 and 12), November/December;* WINDASS, S. (editor). 1981. Local initiatives in Great Britain. Foundation for Alternatives.

22 COMMUNITY BUSINESS VENTURES UNIT. 1981. Whose business is business? Calouste Gulbenkian Foundation.

23 FRANKS, M. 1980. Description of the Clerkenwell Workshops for European Urban Renaissance Year Handbook.

24 BOLTON, J. 1982. The future of small business. *Journal of the Royal Society of Arts, cxxx (5310), May.*

25 FIG was established in 1981, operated from the Department of Environment, and comprised staff seconded from 25 financial institutions (banks, building societies, pension funds and insurance companies). It is acknowledged that their ideas drew upon experience in the US where small businesses have been supported by a Federal grant aid programme (UDAG) as well as by Federal tax incentives and local community banks. Under the £70m scheme announced for British cities, it is expected that for every £1 of public money, at least £4 can be levered from the private sector.

26 Feasibility studies and planning work are supported by the Department of Energy in the neighbourhood energy schemes.

27 BURCHELL, M. 1981. Unemployment: the role of community-based employment initiatives. Unpublished MA dissertation, Trent Polytechnic.

CHAPTER 7

TOWARDS SUSTAINABLE CITIES

Introduction

1. This report has looked at the limits natural resources place upon city living and how benefits might be enhanced and widened by a different approach. There is much evidence to support a change of direction. It is the aim of this and the next chapter to sum up the findings and suggest some goals and methods by which to guide a movement towards more sustainable urban development.

The Need to Adapt Now

2. It is clear that British towns and cities will have to adjust to a resource future which is generally leaner and more uncertain and the need is to speed up the adaptation begun, in a largely unplanned way, over the last decade. Yet some aspects of contemporary urbanisation — the style of much decentralisation, the neglect of land and buildings within cities — is leading to greater resource-extravagance and the implications of this are not confined to Britain. At the same time we are wasting assets which offer much scope for improving urban living conditions.

3. Many of the existing and approaching resource-problems, especially those which impinge upon far off natural systems, are masked by our preoccupations with the short-term and the obvious. First lulled by the comforting prospect of apparently abundant North Sea oil, and now confused by the complex messages of fluctuating world prices, the danger is that Britain will not react quickly enough to make the most of a transition to resource-saving.

4. It is easy to be falsely encouraged about the long-term by recent conservation efforts, particularly in energy saving, since 1973. Indeed, industrial conservation, stimulated by soaring oil prices, has shown that growth in output (for some industries at least) can occur without increasing energy use — an attractive message for countries struggling to reduce inflation and emerge from recession. Domestic consumption, too, has come down but it now seems unlikely that energy prices will rise fast or high enough to bring the future savings that are possible or necessary. Moreover, the pricing mechanism alone, as a way of achieving more energy conservation, is an unpredictable and often inequitable tool. The signs are that periodic falls in the relative price of crude oil (although they are probably temporary) will stimulate more demand for energy-based goods yet will weaken both the industrial and domestic imperative to conserve. The urge to move quickly out of recession could push the UK back into renewed energy consumption, and the fundamental advantage for resource-conservation of decoupling energy from economic growth will be lost — unless there is a much greater commitment to energy saving now, both in industry and also in the domestic, essentially urban, sector. The same is true of pollution: Eric Eckholm quotes an OECD warning: 'Total pollution emissions in a number of sectors, assuming present quality standards and technology, could rise 30 per cent or more between 1978 and 1985.'[1] He argues that, in the absence of more stringent pollution control regulations and stronger efforts to recycle materials and conserve resources, economic growth will inevitably mean increased degradation.

5. It is possible to be equally uneasy, from a resource viewpoint, about the longer-term future forecast for Britain and other OECD countries. Many of the remaining growth industries of Europe, upon which fragile economies can be restructured, are those, based upon electronics or biotechnology, whose products are high in value but generally low on natural resources. This is good news for conservation: again the potential is there for decoupling economic growth from resource-extravagance and shaking off the political straitjacket which has always worked against conservation. But this may herald no advantage for living natural resources on a global scale if the products of high resource-consuming industries are imported to serve expanding European markets from the newly industrialising countries of the Third World. It is only the location of heavy resource-consumption that will have shifted and not the scale or style of urban development that supports it. Indeed, the overall effects of this redistribution of the industrial base may be worse, for there may be fewer restrictions on resource-development and the discarding of waste.

6. As the International report, 'The UK's Overseas Environmental Policy', Part 5, argues, Britain has a responsibility for the transfer of advice and skills abroad to see that resources and environments are well husbanded. But it must also organise an urban living style which, in its demands for a whole range of industrial and consumer products, contributes to less

resource-depletion and more durable means of national and global conservation.

7. All of these arguments point to a major problem of 'resource-blindness' — a symptom of urban society which has become cushioned against the nature of its natural resource-base and which is unable to appreciate the consequences of its activities. It is easy to think that enough resource-saving is in hand to both protect us from future scarcities and to safeguard our long-term interests in the world's living systems. In fact, the case is for being much 'leaner on resources'. We need to act now, in ways which improve awareness and allow urban dwellers to take more 'resource-responsible' decisions.

Benefits of Resource Saving

8. Earlier chapters have argued that there is scope for adapting both the strategic pattern of urban development and the way urban land and buildings are managed locally to bring about resource-saving. In doing so, other, wider, benefits accrue. The conclusion is that adjusting to a resource-tight future need not require a course of austerity. A resource-tight future presupposes some changes in the way individuals and urban groups operate, but it offers, through a variety of economic, environmental and social gains, scope for building more sustainable and satisfying urban societies. As well as the reduction of uncertainty about future resource-supplies that could come from a more conserving approach to development, there are four other major benefits: in terms of money, jobs, environments and community involvement.

Resource Saving is Cost Effective
9. The growth of industrial recycling is evidence of the savings possible on raw material imports and energy; it is likely that urban groups could play a greater part in supplying reusable materials for industry, especially paper. So long as the coordination between Departments can be improved, local authorities (and central Government) could save by recycling more of their wastes. The Edmonton incinerator of solid domestic waste makes more than £3m a year through the sale of electricity to the public supply system.

10. The Department of Energy's conservation division (and others) believe that it is more cost effective to invest at least £5,000m in energy conservation now than in new supply. Gerald Leach argues that it would cost less to insulate the roofs and cavity walls of homes (£3 billion) than to install three power staions to supply the energy that could be saved.[2] A number of recent studies estimate that substantial savings can be achieved in other ways: in Southwark, for example, CHP for district heating could supply heat more cheaply than any other means.[3] Although the annual sum for a programme of house rehabilitation is high (£3 billion), the difference in cost between rehabilitation and new building can be substantial — £5/sq ft compared with

£20/sq ft has been quoted.[4] The problem is to find ways round the short-term financial, institutional and attitudinal barriers to making these savings.

11. Individuals can cut fuel bills by a variety of home insulation measures and the neighbourhood energy schemes have shown just how relevant this can be for low income families. Home food growing, DIY repairs can all save money and, like many resource-saving activities, they can lead to other non-monetary advantages, such as improved health. The need is to stimulate the will to act and provide the financial ability and skills to do so.

More Jobs
12. Unemployment is now a major urban (and rural) problem; even with some national economic recovery it is likely to continue at high levels, especially in the older industrial centres. Industrial scenarios for Europe — an increase in specialised electronics, chemical enterprises and high level financial services, and a corresponding decrease in heavy industry — do not suggest a future of full employment. Joblessness means a declining quality of life for more and more people: it represents a profound waste of human resources.

13. A resource-conservation approach offers no instant panacea. However, it could make some contribution, both in the provision of new jobs in the formal economy (so long as this was coupled with more training) and by creating conditions for more work in and around the home and in the local urban area which could be organised in different ways. Most conservation jobs are highly labour-intensive, and many offer satisfactions that could increase individual and community wealth although this will not be measured only in monetary terms.

14. Over 10 years, 50,000 or more new jobs could be created in the field of domestic insulation. At least that number, probably more, could be employed on a programme of rehabilitating and repairing buildings. New jobs could accrue from the greater recycling of domestic wastes in local authority processing plants, in the separate collection and baling of paper and other wastes from homes and for groups involved in the repair and sale of second hand goods. All the estimates must be conservative, for they do not include induced employment in the local economy stimulated by these tasks. However, there is little statistical case study material to draw upon and it is difficult to estimate job losses elsewhere that might be brought about by resource-saving.[5] Existing area management experiments employing MSC teams show there is considerable potential for permanent jobs to be created in the rehabilitation of urban and urban fringe wasteland. A concentrated programme of greening cities in many different ways — by more tree planting and care, more allotment and smallholding management — would also bring new jobs.

15. New employment opportunities are unlikely to arise without more government support for the conservation

programmes required, but the overall support costs need not be high. Some jobs could be financed out of resource-savings (as in materials recycling), others would rely upon new public and private investment and, especially over the long-term, the stimulation of more general local economic regeneration. Other mechanisms of financing are possible, for example, the diversion of unemployment (and other) benefits into wages for resource-saving jobs. Existing job-creation programmes need augmenting as was argued in Chapter 6, but these are not the only ways in which to harness the potential that conservation offers for new employment.

Better Environments

16. Chapter 2 argued that more resource-saving in urban areas could indirectly reduce the pressures which lead to environmental damage of the UK countryside and of natural areas elsewhere in the world. Many kinds of resource-conservation also bring direct and often rapid local environmental improvements — by the transformation of wasteland, the greening of stark neighbourhoods and the saving of wildspace, by the reduction of litter and the rehabilitation of crumbling buildings. That urban people perceive these (largely visual) improvements as important has been shown in a number of studies. They are beginning to be alive to the less obvious, and more insidious, environmental degradation (like lead pollution) and recognise the benefits that come from traffic and pollution control. There is more and more circumstantial evidence that bad environments are associated with urban alienation and violence, and that good environments could be a decisive factor in fostering local investment and regeneration.

Community Involvement

17. Increasing pressure by individuals and community groups to participate in decisions that affect their locality has been a notable movement of the last decade. Some of the commitment is armchair and passive, but there is increasing enthusiasm for local action which offers great scope for building a resource-saving society: here is a unique opportunity for showing how individual practical actions can count — in planting trees, repairing buildings or re-using wastes. The need is to find ways of harnessing community skills and the capacity for work, and of reducing apathy and the frustrations which limit participation so that local involvement can improve the satisfactions of urban living and make real resource-savings.

The Importance of Skills: Thinking Globally, Acting Locally

18. How can these benefits be realised? Many levels of action are required to build a more sustainable urban society. No one group holds the key. Individual and community efforts will remain piecemeal and limited, unless there is much greater commitment towards resource-saving in central and local Government and their agencies, in large industries as well as small businesses,

and in the major institutions. Self-help can achieve much, as Chapter 6 described, but its promotion is only one ingredient of a conserving strategy; it should not legitimise a lack of action by Government. 'Bottom-up' enthusiasm will have to be supported at the top, especially in energy saving, the rehabilitation of buildings and control over development and pollution.

19. However, the need is not only for different legal, financial and institutional arrangements to do these things, but also for new skills. There is a need for new ways of looking at issues so that resource-saving becomes a key element of decisions, whether these are to do with trade and aid, national and local economic management, energy, transport, industrial investment, planning or any other major area of policy-making. Only by being richer in skills nationally and locally can the UK adjust to a leaner natural resource future by making the most of the human and physical resources it has.

20. There are crucial weaknesses in present Government machinery, both centrally and locally, which block such an approach. Action is very fragmented among many different ministries, departments and committees, and, while some have an environmental remit, rarely does this extend to a role in evaluating the total natural resource-effects of activities. In practice, environment and resource-conservation (where it plays any part at all) are still side issues for most arms of Government, and are last minute considerations which rarely influence the conception or implementation of public programmes. There is still too much emphasis upon large, prestigious projects and too little concern and support for small scale schemes which, like neighbourhood energy action, bring wide-ranging and durable benefit. New mechanisms within central and local Government are needed to ensure that individual institutions are themselves more conserving (for example, in the use of heating and paper) and that the overall resource-effect of their policies is monitored and influenced — as spending is by treasury departments. Annual reports should be required to report on 'resource-accounting'.

21. At the local level, local authorities, area electricity and gas boards, local branches of commercial companies, finance houses (especially banks and building societies) and voluntary organisations need to respond by monitoring their own activities with regard to both the opportunities for internal resource-saving and their influence, through investment and otherwise, on resource-use in the locality. A regular discussion and the generation of cooperative action — for funding, sponsorship, advice or shared premises, perhaps — could ensure that more good ideas get translated into practice.

22. But there is a need for training to change attitudes sufficiently for this to happen. There may be no lack of able, environmentally skilled graduates for junior posts, but there is a great need for in-service training of decision makers who qualified at times when natural resource-limits were perceived as unimportant. The Industry report, 'Seven Bridges to the Future', Part 1, discusses opportunities for environmental training in

business schools; likewise, Civil Service and LA training programmes[6] must respond to the requirements for new skills — in resource-accounting and in the promotion of local initiatives in conservation. Earlier chapters have pointed to the poverty of ecological skills among open space managers. Yet the experience of urban wildlife groups and of Warrington and Telford Development Corporations, for example, show that open land management, using native species and natural landscape methods, can be cheap and successful. More secondment between LA departments and conservation organisations such as the BTCV could improve these practical skills. Relevant professions should take a lead here in promoting in-service training, by introducing new awards and encouraging university and polytechnic environmental departments to organise special courses. Many conservation organisations could market their skills in the new training programmes.

23. Chapter 6 looked at the potential for harnessing the many practical and organisational skills of local urban groups which can contribute so much to economic and environmental regeneration. It identified the need to support their initiatives in different ways and help groups and individuals to develop the negotiating skills necessary to make the best use of local resources — in physical, financial and human terms.

24. Practical skills are also required for most resource-saving tasks, especially in repairing and insulating buildings and in growing food and trees. Urban areas have many people who can do these things, but they need to be sought out, their skills revived, augmented and passed on not only to young people but also to the longer-term unemployed and to the old (an increasing proportion of the population). In a society beset by the prospect of further de-skilling, finding new outlets for

expertise and the kindling of new skills add up to a major challenge. The work that is so obviously required to be done in urban areas should not be available only to the already skilled or for the leisure time pursuits of those who remain employed. Widening the access to paid jobs will demand a much greater emphasis (and not a reduction in Government support as recently announced) upon adult training in resource-management, using all parts of the formal and informal education system, trade unions, professions and the media. Chapter 6 identified a major role for the MSC in community resource-saving and environmental improvement.

25. Resource-saving at home demands new skills which must be introduced and practised in schools and continued in a community education programme which equips individuals to manage their own lives in a more sustainable and satisfying way and to play a more responsible part in urban decision making. While there are some good examples of practice and support (in the Open University Community Education Programme and the Royal Society of Arts Education for Capability Award Scheme), the scale is not large enough, nor do the opportunities for skills development impinge upon most people. The resources of local education institutions remain largely untapped: children are generally taught about the environment but not to play an active part in shaping it. There is scope for schools and colleges not only to teach new skills, but also to become local centres for resource-saving in the community.

26. In all, a movement towards resource-saving requires, but can also stimulate, the development of new skills, and this must be a major means by which urban society can be equipped to deal successfully with the various transitions to the twenty first century.

Notes and References

1 ECKHOLM, E. 1982. Down to earth. Pluto Press.

2 LEACH, G et al. 1981. Insulating British homes. IIED.

3 Town and Country Planning, April 1982, 51 (4).

4 MACDONALD, K. 1982. New communities project. draft report prepared for the Town and Country Planning Association, February.

5 For a discussion of the potential for conservation jobs and an appraisal of the various estimates that have been made, see: HALLING, M. 1982. Employment in conservation. Unpublished paper prepared for this study.

6 Involving, for example, the Institute of Local Government Studies, Birmingham, the School of Advanced Urban Studies, Bristol, and LAMSAC.

CHAPTER 8

AN EIGHT-POINT STRATEGY FOR ACTION

Introduction

1. The strategy for integrating urban development with resource-conservation for creating livable cities rests, then, upon two principles: being 'leaner on resources' and 'richer in skills'. To be leaner on resources, urban areas must be:

☐ low on energy
☐ long in life
☐ thrifty with land
☐ resourceful with wastes
☐ down on pollution
☐ abundant in green and growing space.

To become richer in the skills of making the most of resources, urban people need to:

☐ think strategically towards resource-saving
☐ act locally for conservation and regeneration.

Each of these programme areas is developed in the rest of this chapter which pulls together a number of suggestions made earlier in the report. The priorities for action are given in Chapter 10.

2. Three points of context must be made. First, there are no easy 'right' answers for resource-saving. There is no one style of settlement that is 'best' for resource-use and also offers the range of urban benefits we expect. Resource-conservation does not, for example, suggest an automatic choice between high and low density development, but implies ways of making the most efficient use of both. While as a general principle, buildings should be made to last, in practice the choice between rehabilitation and replacement will depend on local circumstances. For example, the choice in matching conservation with development is not between low technologies rather than high, but between the most appropriate. A variety of technologies will be needed in energy. There should be less reliance upon nuclear generation and more direct use of local renewable supplies but wider use of more sophisticated control mechanisms. Parts of this strategy are concerned with equipping urban decision makers (at different levels) to make the right choices.

3. Second, the strategy programmes cover a wide range of urban issues. Where appropriate, the authors have drawn upon the recommendations made in recent reports of a number of the professional organisations specifically concerned with these policy areas.

4. Third, it is tempting to look for a single new innovative approach to urban management which will quickly bring about a redirection to resource-saving. Yet the ideas are all around and there are many vigorous examples of urban conservation activity. There is much research in progress, and for many aspects of urban conservation the problems seem to be less technical than administrative. The major issue over the short-term is how to extend and implement more conservation ideas. The following programme areas set out some ways and means for the short- and medium-term 10 to 15 years ahead.

Programme Areas

> **Energy saving:** develop a benign and non-wasteful system of energy supply based upon energy conservation, the non-polluting use of coal, fuel from urban wastes and other renewable sources with no further investment now in nuclear generating capacity. Priority for energy conservation through low-energy buildings, transport and equipment, appropriate energy pricing and increased awareness of the need for conservation.

Energy supply: increase investment in energy conservation, develop clean coal combustion technologies and retain suitable local power stations and sites for district heating and CHP. Use fuel from urban wastes and waste heat from industry and incinerations and other local energy centres for space heating. Experiment with other renewable energy sources for towns.

Existing buildings: set a 10 year target for the insulation and weather-proofing of all homes. Stimulate more private investment in energy conservation through long-term loans, increased grants, extension of funding for neighbourhood energy schemes, more advice and by making available to householders and small firms 'conservation packages' (covering advice, financing and implementation). Introduce special arrangements for privately rented dwellings. Increase investment in the insulation and weather-proofing of public buildings, and promote energy saving through better management.

New and rehabilitated buildings: reduce energy consumption by resource-sensitive design and layout and the use of energy efficient building materials and components (those that are thermally effective in use and whose energy costs of production are low). Minimise the use of fossil fuels in space and water heating, using natural energy sources where possible.

Low energy transport: reduce the amount of fuel used in transport over a decade and accelerate the production of fuel-economical and non-polluting vehicles. Manage land use change, traffic and public transport so that journey lengths are minimised, the potential of public transport for energy efficiency is realised, wasteful and polluting traffic congestion is reduced and quieter and safer environments are created for more walking and cycling. The integrated measures include: price and regulatory means of reducing petrol consumption, attracting more people to public and community transport, managing traffic to improve flows and safeguard the environment, and making provision for walking and cycling.

Energy efficient equipment: set target dates for the introduction of mandatory performance standards for a wide range of energy-using machines and equipment, including vehicles, household electrical and gas appliances, and lighting. Develop energy monitoring and control devices for use in buildings.

Energy pricing: by means that allow oil prices to remain high enough to maintain the imperative to conserve, but with protection for those on low incomes and for industries whose competitive position is threatened by high energy costs.

Awareness: promote energy saving by a revived national campaign implemented through the media, companies, schools, local advice centres and by extending the use of monitoring devices.

> **Long in life:** make the most of built resources by increasing investment in the rehabilitation of much of the rapidly deteriorating housing stock, and in maintaining all buildings to the end of their useful life where possible, rather than accelerating the cycle of replacement; by designing and constructing new and rehabilitated buildings for long life and adaptability; replacement, repair, maintenance of water mains, sewers and roads; improving the capacity and performance of the building industry.

Neglected homes: set a 10 year target for the rehabilitation (and replacement as necessary) of older housing. This implies increasing the Housing Investment Programme, stimulating more private investment, relating minimum housing standards more closely to the choice between rehabilitation and rebuild, building in resource-conservation criteria to the assessment of alternatives, surveys of the housing stock. Provide incentives to maintain the fabric of homes including: measures to ensure Landlords Act, reform of public housing mainten-

ance arrangements, information easily available for consumers to repair and adapt homes, support for local groups to rehabilitate.

Redundant commercial and industrial buildings: find users and orchestrate public and private funding, advice and manpower for conversion. Where possible, offer as alternatives to greenfield development and combine them with environmental improvement on vacant land. Facilitate community use of appropriate buildings.

New and rehabilitated buildings: design, construct and use materials appropriate for long life, low energy and adaptability (for different heating systems, for work at home and for waste separation). Research, development and application of resource-saving building, in association with consumers, professions, construction industry, materials and components firms.

Utilities and roads: save water by renewing water mains. Secure long life for sewers and roads by increased investment in renewal, repair and maintenance and the use of long life, low energy methods of replacement. Avoid waste of resources by integration of road and utilities improvement with the rehabilitation of buildings and area renewal.

Building: enable the building industry to increase capacity, assimilate the techniques of resource-conserving building and improve its performance by resource, expenditure and manpower planning, the development of training and re-training facilities and by measures to foster and improve the efficiency of small businesses in building and building materials.

> **Land thrift:** make the most of land resources for conservation and development by promoting urban regeneration, by positive management of vacant and underused land for resource-saving and community benefit, by controlling urban development to avoid building upon or otherwise sterilising natural areas and food-producing land and by effective management of the urban fringe.

Urban regeneration: combine efforts to retain and create employment with environmental improvement, especially for the inner cities. This could make a contribution to reducing the outward flow of people and jobs as well as the demand for greenfield development sites and make better use of urban wasteland. Present progress suggests the need for more measures to release and support local entrepreneurial initiatives, to encourage redevelopment and modernisation of existing business premises and the rehabilitation of vacant land and buildings and to speed up environmental improvements on wasteland.

Vacant land: release appropriate vacant land for less profitable and unprofitable uses (especially greening). This implies more registers of public and private land, means to encourage the permanent and interim release of private and public land, increased public and private spending on reclamation and site preparation and bringing about appropriate uses, including sponsorship of local initiatives, in the community use of vacant land.

Control over development: strengthen control over peripheral development which increases resource-extravagance (especially in land and energy) and draws investment away from inner areas. Include resource-criteria in the assessment of development proposals. Make resource-saving schemes the practical option for developers and investors by, for example, intervention to make a serviced inner city site available for redevelopment, by integrating developments with improved public transport and other means.

Urban fringe: organise development (including waste disposal and public utilities) to reduce the uncertainties, severance and trespass characteristic of this zone, enabling more effective management of farm land and natural areas. Find ways of assembling fragmented and underused holdings for appropriate purposes. Plan for greenspace wedges, linking the fringe to the city centre and separating development corridors.

Making wastes work: save on land and energy (in transport), reduce pollution and augment the supplies of energy and other resources by treating and re-cycling urban wastes and re-using cast-off goods. Work towards reducing packaging.

Maximise the treatment of wastes to reduce landfill requirements and produce waste material that is inert (or unattractive to pests) and capable of being used, for example, as load-bearing landfill, fuel or aggregate. Permit untreated waste disposal only on sites that cause no damage to existing developments and environment. Treat hazardous wastes by incineration or chemically to reduce the hazards of co-disposal as landfill.

Pre-collection separation and recycling of municipal solid waste with financial and other support for local authority and community collection of sorted household wastes (especially paper, but also glass and aluminium) and for recycling plants run by local authorities, community groups or private enterprise. Central and local Government Departments and other public bodies to sort their own wastes, and cooperate with local recycling enterprises, guaranteeing markets for recycled products. All central and local Government Departments to use at least 10 per cent recycled paper. Research, development and application of technical improvements in local waste processing plants and vehicles and home recycling.

Post-collection recycling of remaining municipal solid wastes by pulverisation, incineration and mechanical sorting to recover metals. Use waste process heat for industrial and district heating, produce waste-derived fuel and hydrocarbon fuels by pyrolysis. This implies financial incentives, coordination between collection and disposal authorities, joint working with companies (for example on the use of heat) and higher prices for waste-derived electricity supplied to the national grid.

Repair of cast-off domestic goods: lengthen the life of goods and create jobs by setting up local collecting points with staff to sort for waste-processing, repair or resale. Establish workshops for repair and retailing. Introduce financial and fiscal incentives for the donation of second hand goods, promotion of repair and resale enterprises by MSC job creation and training programmes. It may be appropriate to combine all waste collection at accessible local points ('Saver Skips').

Awareness: revive public campaigns on the need for recycling, linked with advice on home separation, storage and re-use of wastes and the location of collection points. Extension of composting schemes for school and domestic food and garden waste.

Packaging: devise and implement a programme for the progressive reduction of packaging in the transport and marketing of consumer goods to include, for example, mandatory statements about recycling and recycled materials used, reductions in VAT for recycled packaging, and codes of conduct promoted through the Advertising Standards Authority.

Reducing pollution: in order to safeguard human health and encourage natural life, establish and move faster towards meeting stringent quality objectives for air, water and soil. Control emissions of pollutants in urban areas in accordance with these objectives through a system based upon consents, orders and emission performance standards.

Air — fossil fuels: work towards meeting the EEC guideline values for ambient smoke and SO_2 concentrations (and introduce values for other pollutants) by extending the areas covered by local authority smoke control orders (Clean Air Acts) and orders restricting the sulphur content of fuel oils (Control of Pollution Act), and investigating the case for giving powers to control the selection of fuel in buildings. Implement an integrated programme (of coal washing, fluidised bed combustion and flue gas desulphurisation in power stations) to reduce smoke and SO_2 emissions from coal combustion and introduce more CHP and district heating schemes where economically feasible.

Air — long-range transport of pollution: commitment by the UK Government to the Convention on Long-Range Transboundary Air Pollution (Geneva, 1979). Continuation of international monitoring and modification of UK measures for reducing air pollution as necessary.

Air — vehicle emissions: make available lead-free petrol now for vehicles capable of using it. Set an early target date by which all new vehicles must run on lead-free petrol. Government, in consultation with the motor industry, to set progressive target dates by which mandatory standards for the manufacture of low-energy and pollution-free vehicles must be met; the standards should cover fuel consumption and emissions of smoke, carbon monoxide, and oxides of nitrogen.

Water: Regional Water Authorities to move faster towards meeting objectives for the improvement of river quality, particularly of those watercourses categorised as 'badly polluted' or 'poor' in urban areas. Regional Water Authorities, with government backing, to increase investment in the replacement of inadequate or obsolete plant, apply more stringent conditions to consents to discharge pollutants and encourage more trade effluent treatment in sewage works to reduce direct discharge to watercourses. Waste Disposal Authorities to minimise the risk of water pollution from waste leachates by using methods for the disposal of wastes already described.

Land: aim to enable urban land to be capable of supporting diverse natural life and the safe production of food, by reducing emissions of lead and other heavy metals (from vehicles and industrial sources) and taking action to restore grossly polluted sites.

Greening and growing: protect existing greenspace and create much more of different kinds in and around urban areas to increase wild habitats, enhance the visual environment, and provide for recreation and education. Make the most of opportunities for growing food and trees for a variety of purposes.

More greenspace: save, rehabilitate and create natural areas, linking where possible to existing open spaces and to urban fringe countryside (along waterways, old railways, and new cycle routes). Increase diversity in open space management to create community gardens, more natural areas within formal parks, city farms, ecological parks and local nature reserves, each with a variety of purposes including promoting awareness of the resource supports to city life.

Organisation and management: notify and protect many more sites of wildlife interest in urban areas. Public and private landowners to be persuaded to release land for temporary and permanent greenspace management. Foster appropriate groups to initiate and manage neighbourhood and settlement-wide greenspace schemes, such as urban wildlife groups and environmental trusts, public and private partnership arrangements to provide help at initial stages and continuing support. Enhance cooperation between groups and users (with nature centres, newsletters, demonstration sites). Local education authorities to stimulate greater school use of local greenspace for learning and action. Management of public open spaces to include more natural areas with appropriate ecological training for LA staff. Negotiate environmental management agreement with private landowners.

More trees: increase planting in association with many activities, by incentives to groups and individuals (free trees, labour, sponsorship schemes) and by placing conditions upon development permission. Promote more tree banks and better aftercare of planted trees.

Woods and forests: survey town woods, and assess the need for action and the scope for profitable uses and local timber markets. Investigate the potential for large scale public and private planting of multi-purpose woods within and at the edge of cities, for recreation and education, and timber for construction and energy. More cooperative schemes of tree and woodland planting on the urban fringe (involving local authorities, Forestry Commission, water authorities, farmers, smallholders and others).

Food: stop the further sale of public allotments and smallholdings and increase the supply for local use. Organise the provision of support services (refuse collection, fertilisers, labour, and training). On the urban fringe, promote more food and timber production for local urban markets, adjusting national agricultural and local policies to deal with the special problems of this location.

Awareness: promote active financial support through campaigns linking initiatives aimed at individuals, community groups, schools and colleges, local businesses and finance houses.

Strategies for urban resource-management: central and local Government to manage urban change in line with the principles of the World Conservation Strategy by integrating the economic and physical development of towns and cities with resource-conservation.

Central coordination of resource-conservation and development: at central Government level, commitment to resource-conservation will require new mechanisms to coordinate the policies and decisions of various Departments, agencies and public authorities concerned with urban development and resource-management.

Integration of urban development and resource-management: at local government level, the means include the preparation of strategies for urban development and resource-management that could guide the development of towns and cities into an era when resources will be tighter, and provide the basis for managing urban change now. The strategies would combine policies for energy conservation, the use of wastes and wasteland, husbanding built resources, protecting and extending natural green and growing areas with policies for economic development, land use, environment and transport. Central Government to initiate low-resource transport studies for the longer-term.

Resource audits and budgets: the information base for strategies should include some form of resource-auditing.

Local authorities (in association with the DOE) need to investigate methods of assessing resource-supply and consumption, the potential for savings and making use of wastes. The start already made in the public sector with the inventory of vacant land could be extended to cover public sector use of energy in public transport and LA housing and go on to cover other resources.

Conservation performance: the Department of the Environment and local authorities should develop a checklist of resource-criteria against which development applications and public developments can be judged and compared with alternatives.

Local action for conservation and regeneration: increase initiatives in local economic and environmental regeneration which combine resource-saving with job and wealth creation for community benefit.

Community enterprise: many kinds need to be fostered (by partnerships between LAs and commercial and community groups) which link new jobs with energy and resource-saving, the rehabilitation of old buildings (or interim use of short-life properties), and re-use of wastes and vacant land. All this requires:

Financial support: for feasibility studies (assessment of local skills, markets and competition), for conversion of buildings and upgrading of land and for later development work. Government support to be increased under the Small Business and Urban Programme funding arrangements and an expanded Small Grants Programme to be directed specifically to resource-saving, job-creating local initiatives. These central funds to be augmented by LA loans and provision of low-rent buildings and land. Means must be found of attracting more private investment to small scale inner city enterprises — procuring funds by negotiation and by increasing the influence over finance houses and individuals to invest locally.

Manpower Services Commission: to extend its funding for longer-term and on-going management jobs, and for schemes which can become self-financing. The MSC to organise the better training of participants and supervisors.

Other supports: development of initial services (in funding, acquiring and converting premises) and continuing services (business and technical advice units, training, secretarial) to encourage community enterprise.

Information exchanges: organise registers of local product and service needs, of locally produced goods, services and skills available and of enterprises, schemes and individuals working locally for conservation with development.

Coordination: the need is to bring together local economic regeneration, resource-saving and environmental improvement, to exploit the scope for working together, for the profitable enterprises to subsidise the less profitable, for the sharing of common services and for linkage between producers and users (for example, in the collection, repair and retailing of recyclable goods, and the provision of allotments and shops for their produce). At present, coordination is being successfully achieved for some urban areas by enterprise trusts (for businesses) environmental trusts (for greening), by those LAs with special units, and by voluntary groups. Environmental and entrepreneurial activities are rarely combined. The need is for more local coordination, experiment, and sharing of experience and training in various skills.

New action programme for Resourceful Cities: to call for, promote and support initiatives, mobilise funds, and arrange information exchanges and training. The programme to be based in central Government and guided, if appropriate, through a new facilitating organisation with powers and a budget to support innovative schemes.

CHAPTER 9

PROSPECTS FOR ACHIEVEMENT: THE OBSTACLES AND OPPORTUNITIES

Introduction

1. There is relatively little time left before resource-crises of various kinds may provoke expedient and ill-conceived responses. The need is to adapt now to more resourceful ways of living. Yet speeding up the adjustment in Government to an inevitably leaner resource-future, and realising, much more effectively, the local potential for building better cities, is bedevilled by a number of prevailing attitudes and practices.

2. It is true that some of the policies set out in the eight-point strategy of action imply no radical change of direction. A number are cheap; many require no new legislation. They build upon ideas and work in hand and would be supported by trends that can be discerned in the economy, in technology and in the pattern of urban social life. But we cannot be deluded into thinking that a package of easy short-term, piece-meal conservation efforts will work by itself. Many elements of the strategy cannot be implemented unless some of the more fundamental yet so far intractable problems working against conservation are tackled. What seem to be the most important obstacles are summarised in this chapter, moving from the more specific problems of institutional inertia, the lack of investment and the nature of the urban land market, to the wider issues of Britain's social and economic future including attitudes to the car, the production of consumer goods and patterns of work.

Lack of Awareness

3. 'Resource-blindness' pervades urban society at all levels: in the lack of attention to saving at home, the disregard for wastes once they are out of sight, the lack of information about the true resource-costs of goods and services consumed, the apathy of urban decision makers towards taking account of resource-issues. Unless awareness is increased dramatically, there will be too few incentives to reduce resource-consumption or to reap the benefits of it. More realistic resource-pricing must be supplemented by direct campaigning at all levels (with methods and a language designed to motivate all sectors of society) and by the extension of devices, in buildings and vehicles and in other goods, which give direct messages about resource-consumption. Conventional environmental education in schools and the media has worked well to increase public awareness of many resource-issues in the UK and the world, but it has failed to show how individuals are themselves impli- cated — as resource-consumers, improvers, investors and voters. (See Chapter 2, paragraph 1, p 103; Chapter 5, paragraph 17, p 131; Chapter 6, paragraphs 7 - 11, pp 139 - 140; Chapter 7, paragraphs 2 - 7, pp 150 - 151.)

Institutional Inertia and the Fragmentation of Responsibilities

4. More rapid implementation of many conservation ideas, even those where cost effectiveness has been demonstrated, seems bedevilled by existing institutional structures and attitudes. Energy policy provides a particularly good example. The CEGB is committed to a scale of nuclear generation which seems highly questionable on the evidence of need, cost and safety. The Board's avowed preference for large power stations on greenfield sites, its tardiness on energy conservation and lack of enthusiasm for cooperating with local authorities on smaller CHP schemes (which, as experi- ence in Denmark shows, can be economical) all run counter to the wider and longer-term energy and resource needs of society. Competition between the gas, electricity, coal and oil industries for their market share has traditionally been encouraged to keep prices low. However, with recent moves to raise the price of gas to conserve reserves, there is little justification for continued competition. The energy supply industries should work together in the national interest so that the most appropriate fuel is used in the most economical way. But a lead agency, such as a strengthened Depart- ment of Energy Conservation Division, is needed to push this.

5. There are other examples of inertia, not least in the financial institutions discussed below. Greater recycling of domestic urban wastes is complicated not only by the divisions of responsibility between collection and disposal authorities, but also by their complacent attitudes. There is a need for public bodies to take a lead in resource-conservation yet few display exemplary practice — in recycling their own wastes for example. (See Chapter 2, paragraph 14, p 105; Chapter 2, para- graph 15, p 105; Chapter 2, paragraphs 51 - 53, pp 110 - 111; Chapter 5, paragraph 26, p 133; Chapter 7, paragraph 20, p 152.)

Lack of Investment

Public

6. Cuts in public spending (for local government, the ceilings imposed on expenditure and the removal of special grants) mean that little or no funds are available for tasks requiring substantial investment now (like home insulation) despite the fact that cost effectiveness has been proved. Yet the levels of public subsidy for resource-saving in British cities are far behind those of other EEC countries — on public transport and energy conservation for example. (See Chapter 2, paragraph 14, p 105; Chapter 2, paragraph 24, p 106; Chapter 2, paragraph 39, p 108; Chapter 2, paragraphs 62 - 65, pp 113 - 114; Chapter 4, paragraph 13, p 125; Chapter 4, paragraph 16, p 126; Chapter 5, paragraphs 15 - 19, pp 131 - 132; Chapter 7, paragraphs 9 - 10, page 151.)

7. Many of the programmes suggested in the last chapter do require more public spending but this will often be small and need not be inflationary. Experience has shown, for example, on the neighbourhood energy schemes that substantial benefits can result from small amounts of funding. While these may be available, under the Urban Programme, for small scale conservation initiatives in parts of some cities, this support does not extend to all the urban areas that need them, nor in general is it available for revenue expenditure. (See Chapter 6, paragraphs 14 - 19, pp 140 - 141; Chapter 6, paragraph 24, p 141; Chapter 6, paragraph 33, p 145; Chapter 6, paragraphs 48 - 49, page 147; Chapter 6, paragraph 54, p 148.)

8. To finance more schemes, funds can be diverted from other areas of expenditure, for example by redirecting unemployment benefit (at least £5,000 per person per year) into conserving programmes which create jobs. Much of the sum presently paid in fuel allowances (£300m each year) could be redirected to home insulation schemes. Higher charges for the discharge of polluting wastes could contribute to financing a major renewal of the sewerage system. Rating idle urban land could provide the revenue for positive management. Over the longer-term, new sources of national and local finance are possible associated with the development values of land and taxes on the production and sale of high waste goods.

Private

9. Many resource-saving measures are perceived only in terms of increased costs for little or no return. Either the benefits cannot easily be quantified (such as improvements in health and well-being, or the reduction of litter) or they fall to other groups outside the accounting, elsewhere in the world, or in the future. Not surprisingly, cost effectiveness is often hard to demonstrate and spending on resource-saving limited. High interest rates discourage individual investment even in activities like home insulation which have a playback time of one to two years. In general, householders have few incentives or the ability to go for energy conservation measures. (See Chapter 5, paragraphs 17 - 19, pp 131 - 132.)

Likewise, small resource-saving initiatives, even in the inner cities, cannot easily attract funding for on-going running costs.

10. With a few notable exceptions all the major urban investors (building societies, banks, pension funds and insurance companies) are exacerbating the trend away from resource-saving. Most of these investors (especially those concerned with pensions and insurance interests) adopt short-time horizons, have no local affiliation and are unwilling to widen their investment criteria beyond the traditionally conceived 'prime site'.[1] There activities are working against conservation and urban regeneration, drawing the wealth out of inner areas and leaving land and buildings vacant. Yet increasing levels of private saving are being directed through these institutions to enterprises which, by their scale and location, intensify resource-consumption. (See Chapter 3, paragraphs 4 - 24, pp 117 - 121; Chapter 5, paragraphs 9 and 10, page 130; Chapter 6, paragraphs 45 and 46, pp 146 and 147.) A few of these enterprises may well cancel out the effects of many small scale resource-saving activities in the city. There is a need to find ways of promoting much more investment in desirable inner urban schemes that looks less to the standard criteria and more towards longer-term benefits in jobs, resource-saving and community building. It is clear from the Industry report 'Seven Bridges to the Future', Part 1 that new, ecologically benign, opportunities for consumer spending and wealth creation are being overlooked by investors; the potential UK market for energy conservation goods could approach £20 billion over the next decade. However, there are many other markets to be exploited locally if repair and renewal of urban land and buildings are increased and homes and goods are designed better for resource-saving.

11. The experimental £70m urban programme grant introduced by Michael Heseltine on the advice of the Financial Institutions in Government Group (FIG) is designed to attract private investment into funding partnerships for inner city enterprises. But, as Chapter 6 argued, this may be too thinly spread and concentrate, as other programmes do, on capital funding.

12. Urban areas also require more skilled local 'facilitators' who can negotiate and procure funds and also more locally responsive banks and building societies channelling local investment through long-term, low interest loans into home and business conservation activities and making conservation performance a condition of mortgages and other lending.[2] These are essential steps to greater community control over local investment.

Ideologies

13. The objectives and practice of many groups which influence the way cities are managed are now, reluctantly or willingly, dominated by narrow market criteria.

The multiple values of many conservation schemes — in terms of jobs, environments and community strength — do not carry the schemes into implementation unless cost effectiveness can be shown over the very short-term. In energy management, urban transport, new building, rehabilitation and support for small businesses, the market needs adjustment to respond much better not only to the social and environmental needs of many urban people, but also to safeguard our future resource-position.

14. The problems run deeper. There is such a polarisation of attitude on some of the issues that most closely affect resource-use that inaction is the result. For example, 'realistic' resource-pricing as a tool for urban conservation, has not so far been successful either in energy-saving, the re-use of buildings or waste recycling. Other mechanisms — regulatory, fiscal and otherwise persuasive — are also needed. Chapter 3 described the conflict between those who favour 'running down' large cities and those who argue against dispersal. Both extremes are unrealistic: dispersal cannot necessarily be contained, but it can be influenced. There are those who believe that creating greener urban areas should be the prerogative of the local authorities (with central Government supporting their continuing revenue costs). Others argue that the job should be left to volunteers and the public sector role contained. Few nationalised industries or commercial companies would willingly accept a continuing obligation to green their holdings. But the way forward is through greater cooperation between all these interests: local authorities need to be more innovative and entrepreneurial in their approach to urban regeneration, private investors must be persuaded (or otherwise influenced) to fulfil a variety of environmental and social obligations and support less conventional city enterprises. The adoption of rigid ideological positions — public versus private, central versus local, urban versus rural, regulation versus persuasion — are proving to be particularly damaging to the cause of urban conservation. The most resourceful, adaptable ways forward seem not to be so easily pigeon-holed but come from better harnessing the energies and commitment of a whole range of urban groups in many different ways.

Land

15. The urban land market is important in two ways: its transactions condition the possible uses of space in the city and, in theory, land offers a source of wealth for community benefits.[3] In neither way does the present situation work well for the interests of conservation with development.

16. High land prices (or the expectation of them) have prevented the use of many urban areas for less profitable yet desirable conservation activities which cannot compete with large scale commercial and industrial development for the permanent use of expensive urban land. Progressive repeal of the financial provisions of the 1947 Town and Country Planning Act has removed the possibility of public authorities acquiring land relatively cheaply for less profitable uses in the public interest. Moreover, the confidential nature of most transactions and the lack of information about ownerships have worked against even the temporary use of vacant lots. Although the expectation of high values may be misplaced for some inner city land, idle sites (both large and small) are held for long periods attracting rubbish, vandalism and crime. The release of more urban land for conservation may flow from the current round of land registers (if pressure is brought to bear on public bodies to make plots available) but the registers need to cover small areas as well as large, and they need to apply to more authorities and to private land.[4] There is little chance of realising the opportunities for resource-saving and environmental improvement now offered by the loosening of city densities without a combination of reforms in the land market. Temporary use has to be easier to negotiate. Local authorities and other groups should be able to acquire land for a wide range of purposes at a price which reflects its existing use value. But these measures are not enough.

17. Urban land values have risen throughout the recession and in spite of sluggish development. They display investors' continuing confidence in land as a commodity for trading where most other investment media have shown declining interest. Yet almost nothing of this rise in value has been captured for local economic or environmental regeneration. Local funds for resource-saving (and other urban improvements) could be raised by taxing idle land and by increasing the rate of development land tax (although this will make a small contribution while development is slow and there are so many exemptions). But these are only temporary solutions. Ways must be found of vesting more of the urban land asset in the hands of local urban communities. (See Chapter 3, paragragraphs 14 - 16, pp 118 - 119.)

Lack of Skills

18. Few of the programmes recommended in Chapter 8 can be implemented without more emphasis upon training: moving slowly on training could be a major obstacle to progress. More skilled people are urgently needed to carry through the repair and insulation of buildings, the greening of cities, the better management of open land and the matching of conservation with development in local enterprises. More emphasis on conservation training is required now in job-creation programmes. Policy-makers have to be trained in the skills of building in resource-saving in all aspects of urban activity. Chapter 7 argued for the development of personal skills in resource-saving among children and adults. Yet few of the established education and training media are prepared for any of these tasks. (See Chapter 6, paragraph 32, p 145; Chapter 7, paragraphs 18 - 25, pp 152 - 153.)

Control of the Car

19. The car is central to many people's lives, to the national economy and to local trade. Measures to reduce the amount of fuel used in motoring are bound to be resisted by many groups, including the car industry, retailers, and car owners themselves who regard their cars as indispensable for most of their work, social and leisure journeys. Inducing fuel economy by price rises alone will not be equitable; this will hit hardest at those who can only just afford a car, and contribute to inflation. A combination of measures is needed, including manipulation of price and fuel allocation. The major problems are how to ensure accessibility for car owners who will be disadvantaged and how to persuade motorists that resource-conservation must become a major factor in transport policy. In the long run the transition to a less oil-based transport system is inevitable, but the sooner it begins the less painful it will be.

Technology and Standards

20. Many new technologies are working for resource-conservation: microelectronics especially offers the prospect of rapid, detailed and cheap environmental monitoring and control at many different scales. Micro-electronics will, for example, be a major means by which twenty first century homes and vehicles can save energy; it should simplify the preparation of resource-audits and budgets on a city-wide scale and improve the detection and control of pollution. But more backing is needed for the research, development and application to come quickly enough to help resource-saving and to enable Britain to take a lead in home and export markets.

21. There has been, and there remains, a notable government reluctance in the UK to stimulate technology to respond to environmental needs: control of SO_2 and now lead emissions from vehicles has followed rather than forced the development of economically-sound technologies, whereas in other countries, the US especially, the imposition of more stringent environmental standards — first on air emissions, and more recently on fuel consumption — has accelerated technical innovations to meet them. It would seem sensible for British industry to operate to standards at least as stringent as those of her main competitors and to press for EEC agreement on them.

22. The reluctance to act stems, in part, from a prevailing attitude that pollutants are presumed acceptable unless proved otherwise. Dr Michael Rutter argues in the context of lead) that it would be safer and more scientifically appropriate to act as if the reverse were true.[5] The widespread acceptance (and official encouragement) of 'best practical means' in pollution control, which take no account of wider environmental effects, continues to block improvements in air and water quality. It is also widely assumed that pollution control means economic penalties. Yet the environment ministers of OECD countries said in 1979 that the environmental measures of the 1970s: 'had generated significant benefits without, in most cases, negative effects on the economy'.[6] Part of the problem now is that the benefits of pollution control (like a reduction in acid rain or CO_2 emissions) are much more remote. Creating the imperative for action depends upon dramatically raising the national awareness of global resource-problems.

Durability, Obsolescence and Waste

23. Earlier chapters have argued for a much more resourceful approach to wastes, making use of them by recycling and repair. However, the long-term aim must be to reduce waste. One priority is to reduce the amount of wood fibre and non-degradable materials used in packaging, where consumers' awareness of the resource-costs of production and disposal (and of the indirect costs to them through LA expenditure) is very low. (See Chapter 2, paragraph 47, p 110; Chapter 2, paragraph 53, p 111.)

24. Resource-conservation over the longer-term will also depend upon the production of more durable, repairable, useful goods and far fewer throw-away, high resource-consuming, waste-producing products with incentives against, and penalties for, their manufacture and advertising. Various financial means should be explored, including levies on virgin materials used, amortisation taxing which favours long-life products and the building into insurance calculations of values for repairability rather than depreciation.

Employment and Work

25. The production of more durable, repairable goods and resource-saving by recycling and repair are implied in many programmes of the Strategy. They are labour-intensive activities.[7] A move towards durability will require much greater willingness by Government, trade unions and investors to support enterprises which place less reliance on natural resources and capital inputs and more on labour and skills, and see productivity in terms of return per unit of (renewable) resource and not only in output per person with its consequences for job loss and resource-extravagance.

26. In addition, the prospect of high unemployment levels for at least a decade and probably longer, demands increasing recognition, in the policies of central and local Government, employers and trade unions, of the changing structure of work, with more positive support for movements towards breaking down the divisions between formal employment and other types of work in the home and local community, and towards part-time and shared jobs.[8] Some see expansion of the informal

economy as an answer. But there are dangers here — for example, of a return to exploitive conditions of work and the emergence of a more polarised society. The growth of local enterprise offers a more attractive prospect for the future, in which not only is work better distributed but also everyone will have time enough to be more resourceful. Unless employment structures change, new opportunities for permanent conservation work will continue to be organised through temporary job-creation programmes, with all their attendant disadvantages. (See Chapter 6, paragraph 31, p 145; Chapter 7, paragraphs 12 - 15, pp 151 - 152.)

Confronting the Future

27. Saving resources and matching conservation with development, both nationally and locally, demand new thinking and a reassessment of established values, particularly about what constitutes wealth. Arguments throughout this report have linked resource-conservation with economic regeneration, particularly at the local level. Wealth earned from production and exchange will be needed to finance conservation activity; but if increased production and turnover of wasteful consumer goods and the level of cash exchanges remain the main measures of economic growth then this must always run counter to the requirements of resource-conservation. In a 'renewable' society other goods and services must make up the definition of a healthy economy.

28. The scenarios of James Robertson, Hugh Stretton and others link many of these issues to alternative visions of a post-industrial society.[9] But a willingness to confront the future is not widespread. There is a need for many more people to realise that what happens is not inevitable, to be persuaded to consider alternative courses of action and to be helped to make more resource-conscious decisions. All this is unlikely to be achieved through formal education alone, nor can it wait that long. Too many opportunities are being missed to expose the choices that exist for discussion and resolution.

29. Some of the major obstacles to be overcome in the redirection of action towards more resourceful, sustainable and livable cities have been considered in this chapter; the recommendations set out in Chapter 10 include some means of tackling them.

Notes and References

1   CADMAN, D. 1981. Urban renewal in inner London — the development process. Paper presented at a Thames Polytechnic Conference on 'Economic regeneration in the inner city'; 25 March, London. See also: CADMAN, D. 1980. The private property sector in an era of low growth. Paper presented to the Department of Land Economy, University of Cambridge; 13 November.

2   The Abbey National Building Society is becoming involved in these activities.

3   For a much more detailed discussion of the land issue, see for example: LAND VALUES WORKING PARTY. 1979. Land values and planning in the inner areas. Final report. London, Royal Town Planning Institute.

4   Under part 10 of the Local Government Planning and Land Act 1980, registers of unused and underused public land holdings of one acre or more are being prepared, in the Department of Environment, for all districts in England (and the London Boroughs). By May 1982, 360 registers had been published (for all but five of the districts concerned) showing a total of 87,280 acres of unused or underused public land.

The Secretary of State for the Environment has the power to direct public bodies to dispose of sites where appropriate.

5   RUTTER, Dr M. 1982. Summing up at the CLEAR Symposium on lead pollution, London. May.

6   Quoted in: ECKHOLM, E. 1982. Down to earth. Pluto Press.

7   STAHEL, W R and REDY-MULVEY, G. 1981. Jobs for tomorrow — the potential for substituting manpower for energy. New York, Vantage Press. Quoted in an unattributed article in the November 1981 issue of Development Forum: Labour saves energy.

8   See for example: ROBERTSON, J. 1981. The redistribution of work. Turning Point; SHANKLAND, G. 1980. Our secret enemy. Anglo-German Foundation.

9   ROBERTSON, J. 1978. The sane alternative: signposts to a self-fulfilling future. James Robertson; STRETTON, H. 1976. Capitalism, socialism and the environment. Cambridge University Press.

CHAPTER 10
SUMMARY AND RECOMMENDATIONS

Introduction

1. The better management of cities offers great scope for saving resources. Looking ahead, in the wider context of an obligation to safeguard the environment and resource-position of other countries (particularly those of the Third World), to the prospect of an uncertain resource-future for Britain, this report concludes that urban society has to become 'leaner on resources' and richer in the skills of doing more with less. Far from implying an era of austerity, this could bring about many benefits: more jobs, greener, less polluted environments, buildings that are cheaper to heat and maintain, more efficient and more equitable transport and scope for rekindling skills and community participation.

2. A commitment to resource-conservation means saving energy, being more thrifty with land, making the most of existing buildings and creating new ones to last longer, using wastes to augment resources, reducing pollution and increasing the green and growing space of urban areas. For townspeople, commerce and industry, central and local Government, resource-conservation will demand new ways of thinking ahead at the strategic level and new ways of acting locally to make the most of all the human and physical resources that exist in towns and cities. Failure to arrest the growing dependence of urban life on an increasingly uncertain resource-base will bring about escalating costs and a further deterioration in the quality of life for many people.

3. An eight-point strategy for integrating urban development and resource-conservation along these lines was outlined in Chapter 8 of this report. Its implementation depends upon building on the forces now moving towards resource-saving but also on tackling some of the more fundamental problems (discussed in Chapter 9) that pull in the opposite direction.

4. Above all, the need is for adaptable towns and cities to ease the adjustment to an uncertain future. But the action must be now, taking advantage of present circumstances to plan ahead for more livable cities before expediency dictates measures which will destroy the prospect of ever reaching them.

Recommendations

5. The strategy in Chapter 8 sets out some requirements for the short- and medium-terms. Not all its elements are listed below as recommendations; they are *priorities for action*, which include those that:
   - □ would make a clear and early contribution to resource-saving (like home insulation);
   - □ are likely to be cost effective;
   - □ are needed now, because the opportunity for conservation will be lost if action is delayed (as with the rehabilitation of older housing or the sale of small power station sites suitable for local energy centres);
   - □ could make some contribution to alleviating pressing urban problems, especially bad environments and the need for jobs;
   - □ would work together and augment conservation efforts;
   - □ would improve the awareness of resource-issues;
   - □ could establish the preconditions (for example, in training and methods of working) for a new approach to the continuing management of urban activity for conservation and development.

All these programmes of action need to start now for implementation over the next 10 to 15 years. Although the benefits of some will not be immediate, they are essential for a movement towards anticipating and adapting to a leaner, uncertain resource-future and avoiding the costs of crisis management.

Priorities for Action

GOVERNMENT COMMITMENT

Recommendation 1
The Government should state its commitment to intgrate resource-conservation with urban development and secure appropriate investment in the sectors identified in Chapter 8 of this report, which gives priority to:
   - □ energy saving in supply, buildings and equipment;
   - □ long-life buildings and infrastructure;
   - □ managing the transition to low energy transport;
   - □ safeguarding undeveloped land and promoting the use of vacant sites;
   - □ recycling wastes;
   - □ reducing pollution;
   - □ greening the city;
   - □ promoting local conservation and regeneration;
   - □ necessary training and research.

An early White Paper on environmental resources should set out Government policy for the next 10 to 15 years, identify lead agencies to promote and coordinate resource-saving activity in these sectors and show how urban policies and programmes (and associated financial provisions), administered mainly through the Department of Environment, will be adjusted to make resource-conservation an explicit objective.

ENERGY SUPPLY

Recommendation 2
The Government should commit itself to a national energy policy which gives priority to energy conservation, the non-polluting use of coal, fuel from urban wastes and other renewable sources (especially wind and waves), with no further investment now in nuclear generating capacity.

Recommendation 3
This report supports the recommendations made by the House of Commons Select Committee on Energy in its Fifth Report (1982), in particular that:
- ☐ The statutory obligations of the nationalised energy industries should be revised to include the duty to ensure, firstly, that they use fuels in the most economic and efficient manner and, secondly, to ensure that they use every available means to encourage their consumers to do the same. (For the arguments in this report see Chapter 2, paragraph 14, p 104; Chapter 2, paragraph 15, p 105; Chapter 5, paragraph 20, p 132; Chapter 9, paragraph 4, p 159.)
- ☐ There should be new institutional arrangements to coordinate and lead the national conservation effort. This report favours strengthening the existing Department of Energy Conservation Division.

Recommendation 4
The energy industries, through their marketing priorities, and the Government, through its research and development programmes, should stimulate quickly the design, manufacture and use of more energy-efficient domestic equipment, including consumption indicators and controls.

Recommendation 5
Local authorities and industry should be encouraged to make use of heat derived as a by-product from the incineration of wastes and other processes for space heating and/or electricity generation for sale to the national grid. (See Chapter 2, paragraphs 13 - 14, pp 104 - 105; Chapter 2, paragraphs 49 - 50, page 110; Chapter 5, paragraphs 21 - 26, pp 132 - 133.)

Recommendation 6
Before they are released, CEGB power station sites should be considered for local energy supply, as district heating or CHP centres, with appropriate interim management. (See Chapter 2, paragraphs 13 - 14, pp 104 - 105; Chapter 5, paragraphs 21 - 26, pp 132 - 133.)

BUILDINGS: ENERGY CONSERVATION

Recommendation 7
Central Government, local government and the private sector to develop and implement a 10 year programme for bringing all homes up to a minimum standard of insulation and weather proofing. For the older housing stock, an insulation programme should be integrated with a 10 year programme of rehabilitation, incorporating necessary utilities improvements, as recommended in Recommendation 12. (For arguments in the report see Chapter 2, paragraphs 11 - 15, pp 104 - 105; Chapter 5, paragraphs 16 - 21, pp 131 - 132.)

Recommendation 8
This report supports the mechanisms recommended in the House of Commons Select Committee Report on Energy Conservation in Buildings, in particular that:
- ☐ The homes of all those receiving fuel allowances should be fully insulated, diverting £300m from the current to the capital account by the end of 1983.
- ☐ Specific funds should be available for approved energy conservation projects in public sector buildings with clear guidance on the targets to be achieved.
- ☐ Increased levels of grant and tax allowances should be available to stimulate private sector cost effective investment in conservation.

Recommendation 9
The following means of implementation are recommended here:
- ☐ Department of Energy funding for Neighbourhood Energy Schemes should be increased to allow the programme to be extended. (See Chapter 6, paragraphs 14 - 19, pp 140 - 141.)
- ☐ Fuel companies, finance houses (especially Building Societies), building firms and LAs to make available 'energy conservation packages' covering advice, finance and implementation. (See Chapter 5, paragraph 19, p 132.)
- ☐ Consideration should be given to providing, in local centres, specialist advice on energy-saving, along with building repair and maintenance, using existing local advice centres where possible. (See Chapter 5, paragraphs 18 - 19, page 132.)

Recommendation 10
Energy-saving — in buildings, transport and equipment — should be the focus of a large scale publicity and information campaign linked to an overall programme to improve public awareness of resource-issues.

BUILDINGS: LONG LIFE

Recommendation 11
As a prerequisite for the development of resource-sensitive buildings, a long-term investment programme for the construction industry should be prepared to command the support of all political parties and the industry. (See Chapter 5, paragraphs 33 - 37, page 134.)

Recommendation 12

Central and local Government and the private sector to initiate a 10 year rehabilitation programme, incorporating the repair and replacement of utilities, especially damaged sewers. The means include:

☐ raising Housing Investment Programme levels;
☐ changes in local government financing to allow forward planning of capital spending programmes and to raise the limits on revenue spending.

Recommendation 13

Introduction of fiscal and legal reforms to encourage maintenance, repair and rehabilitation, for example:

☐ removal of value added tax now chargeable on maintenance and repair work and on architects' fees for this;
☐ the further relaxation of rateable value limits on improvement grants;
☐ mandatory and regular inspections of all public sector buildings or any building in which public money has been invested, in order to identify early essential maintenance work;
☐ introduction of measures to encourage, and if necessary force, both private and public landlords to act; for example, amendment to Section 32 of the Housing Act 1961 to require landlords to remedy basic defects as well as do repairs (suggested by the National Consumer Council in 'Cracking Up', 1982).

Recommendation 14

Initiatives to be taken to develop the techniques, skills and practice of resource-sensitive buildings in the building industry and its professions, financial institutions and among developers, owners and users (both private and public). The means include:

☐ Research and development in the building industry into recycled building materials and the implications of their use for building design.
☐ The building industry to develop the training and apprenticeship systems for skilled tradesmen.
☐ The building professions to develop techniques for taking into account the long-term benefits to society of resource-conservation, perhaps as part of life cycle costing and for use in decision making on building options.
☐ The building professions to take the lead in educating all sectors, including the professions, owners and users in building husbandry.

Recommendation 15

Central and local Government, working with the private sector, to investigate and advise upon ways of preventing the destruction of commercial and industrial buildings which still have a substantial useful life, persuading applicants for development to adapt existing buildings where possible. (See Chapter 3, paragraph 25, p 121; Chapter 5, paragraphs 9 - 10, page 130.)

TRANSPORT

Recommendation 16

Government, in consultation with relevant interests, should publish a discussion document which states its programme for the transition to a less oil-based, less polluting transport system. The programme should incorporate:

☐ progressive targets towards an absolute saving in transport fuel over 10 years;
☐ progressive targets towards the elimination of pollutants from cars;
☐ fiscal and regulatory mechanisms to induce fuel economy in transport;
☐ the phased production and sale of pollution-free, fuel economical 'green' cars which could reduce petrol consumption by 30 per cent within a decade;
☐ other mechanisms to bring about fuel economy including revised speed limits for inter-urban travel and residential districts, and further limits on the use of company cars.

(For all arguments see Chapter 4 of this report.)

Recommendation 17

Immediate action by central and local Government and the transport interests to:

☐ halt the further decline in public transport by long-term investment planning, increased financial support and other measures;
☐ improve the environment and conditions for walking, cycling and vehicles through transport and environmental management schemes.

Recommendation 18

The noise limit for new lorries should be reduced to 80 decibels (a recommendation of the Armitage Inquiry into Lorries, People and the Environment, 1980).

GUIDANCE AND CONTROL OVER URBAN DEVELOPMENT

Recommendation 19

The development plans machinery should be revised to take account of resource-issues, particularly energy and more aspects of land. As an interim measure, the Department of Environment should require (through a circular) that Structure Plans and Local Plans state the resource-implications of their proposals and show how resources will be conserved consistent with other development plan objectives and over the short- (three to five years) and medium-terms.

Recommendation 20

The Department of Environment, in association with LAs, to enable this to be done by:

☐ developing techniques of resource-auditing and budgeting to be tested in pilot studies;
☐ refining a checklist of criteria against which proposed developments can be judged for their 'conservation performance'.

Recommendation 21

The principles embodied in the Department of Environment Circular 22/80 should be reversed so that the presumption is clearly against the development of green-field sites. (See Chapter 3, paragraphs 11 - 13, page 118; Chapter 5, paragraphs 42 - 46, pp 135 - 136.)

VACANT LAND

Recommendation 22

Promotion of the positive management of presently underused and vacant urban land for resource-saving and community benefit, starting with:

☐ more negotiated release of sites under leasing and licensing arrangements (local authorities acting, where appropriate, as intermediaries);

☐ Department of Environment requiring the public holders of vacant land to state, within three years, their proposals for use that combine resource-conservation with development;

☐ extending land registration to cover all urban areas and private land.

(For the arguments, see Chapter 3, paragraphs 14 - 16, pp 118 - 119; Chapter 9, paragraphs 15 - 17, page 161.)

Recommendation 23

The Compensation Code should be amended to allow public acquisition of land at existing use value, and net of development land tax.

Recommendation 24

Government should initiate an independent review of the statutory and other instruments whose working affects the management of vacant urban land for resource-saving and environmental improvement. The review should examine the case for rating vacant land and adjusting the scale to favour uses which combine job creation, resource-saving and environmental improvement.

RECYCLING WASTES

Recommendation 25

Central Government to set an early target date for plans to be submitted by Waste Disposal Authorities for dealing with wastes in ways which:

☐ maximise treatment and recycling;

☐ create jobs;

☐ promote waste exchanges and arrangements with local firms and community groups for collection, recycling and, if appropriate, repair and sale.

(See Chapter 2, paragraphs 47 - 53, pp 110 - 111; Chapter 6, paragraph 10, p 139.)

Recommendation 26

Government to introduce the necessary financial and administrative adjustments to make these improvements possible and to step up research and development on the recycling of domestic wastes.

Recommendation 27

Central and local Government to use at least 10 per cent recycled paper, and to sort and grade paper waste for recycling. (See Chapter 2, paragraph 53, p 111.)

Recommendation 28

Manufacturers to collaborate with Government, retailing, consumer and advertising organisations to devise and implement a programme for the progressive reduction of packaging to include:

☐ the use of a 'reclaim' mark on goods which can be recycled or are made of reclaimed materials;

☐ reductions in VAT for recycled packaging;

☐ codes of conduct promoted through the Advertising Standards Authority.

REDUCING POLLUTION

Recommendation 29

Lead-free petrol to be available now. Central Government to adopt an early target date (not later than 1985) by which all new vehicles must run on lead-free petrol. (See Chapter 2, paragraph 60, p 113.)

Recommendation 30

Government should introduce, at the earliest opportunity, statutory standards for smoke emissions from vehicles and develop equipment for measuring smoke at the roadside.

Recommendation 31

Regional Water Authorities, with Government support, to move faster towards meeting their objectives for the improvement of river quality in urban areas by:

☐ increasing investment in the replacement of obsolete sewage treatment works and other plant;

☐ applying more stringent conditions to consents to discharge pollutants;

☐ encouraging more trade effluent treatment in sewage works to reduce direct discharge to watercourses.

(See Chapter 2, paragraphs 38 - 41, pp 108 - 109; Chapter 2, paragraphs 61 - 65, pp 113 - 114.)

GREENING THE CITY

Recommendation 32

Greening to become a major focus for urban action, involving voluntary groups, the private sector, central and local Government. Priorities are:

☐ in the context of city-wide greening strategies, local authorities (or other appropriate groups) to coordinate the retention, creation and management of greenspace, taking this into account in development control and in agreements with private landowners;

☐ more support for local organisations to initiate and manage neighbourhood greenspace, including funding but also technical and administrative advice and tools;

☐ campaigns to double the number of trees in towns and cities, backed by sponsorship schemes, school and community projects, paying particular attention to the need for more urban woodlands to be managed on ecological principles and for better aftercare of planted trees which should be native species.

(See Chapter 2, paragraphs 35 - 37, pp 107 - 108; Chapter 6, paragraphs 20 - 28, pp 141 - 144.)

Recommendation 33

All registered public and private land holders in urban

areas should be obliged to manage their land in defined environmentally acceptable ways and report on this.

LOCAL CONSERVATION AND REGENERATION

Recommendation 34
Central Government to introduce and fund a new urban action programme to promote and support local initiatives in resource-saving, job creation, training and environmental improvement. This 'Resourceful Cities' programme, backed by funds in the Department of Environment, should be administered by one local agency which could assess schemes for support, mobilise funds from all sources, and arrange information exchanges and training. (See Chapter 6, paragraphs 53 - 56, page 148.)

Recommendation 35
Resource-saving should be included among the specific objectives of the following Government programmes: the Urban Programme, Loans Guarantee Scheme, Business Start-Up Scheme, Small Grants Programme and those of the Manpower Services Commission. (See Chapter 6, paragraph 54, p 148.)

Recommendation 36
The resources of the Manpower Services Commission should be available for a new 'Resourceful Cities' programme to promote jobs in resource-saving. This should allow funding over longer than one year, for on-going management jobs and for schemes which can become self-financing. (See Chapter 6, paragraph 32, p 145.)

Recommendation 37
Financial institutions (including building societies, insurance companies and pension funds) should be enabled, through special units, to invest in small, local enterprises paying particular attention to those which combine resource-saving, job creation and environmental improvement. The local investment units should also coordinate the exchange of business skills and otherwise participate in a 'Resourceful Cities' programme. (See Chapter 6, paragraph 56, page 148.)

Recommendation 38
Urban groups should consider promoting, for their area, a local 'Resource Forum' for the exchange of ideas and progress on resource-saving between public agencies (including local authorities, area boards of the fuel and water industries), local finance houses and voluntary groups (See Chapter 7, paragraph 21, p 152.)

SKILLS

Recommendation 39
The need for skills in urban resource-saving should be explicitly recognised in the training programmes of the MSC, in LEA policy for school and adult education, in community education programmes (of, for example, the Open University and Workers' Education Association) and in educational award schemes. (See Chapter 7, paragraphs 18 - 26, pp 152 - 153.)

Recommendation 40
The urban professions, notably those led by the RTPI and the RIBA, should give priority to the promotion of training in resource-conservation.

AWARENESS

Recommendation 41
Government, in association with many public and private organisations, to fund in 1984 (as part of its response to the World Conservation Strategy) a national campaign on livable cities to stimulate local action and award and publicise innovative schemes. (See Chapter 9, paragraph 3, p 159.)

Recommendation 42
Communication of the ideas and opportunities of resourceful urban living, promotion of action at all levels, backed by demonstration, research and training, should be considered as major tasks for a new organisation (funded from a variety of sources) to sustain public interest in working for livable cities. (See Chapter 6, paragraph 55, p 148.)

CHAPTER 11

THE PRACTITIONERS' DEBATE

1. The consultation draft of this report stimulated a wide ranging debate among people involved in many different aspects of urban living. The linking together of so many strands of city management from the viewpoint of resource-use was welcomed as an essential first step towards identifying the requirements for more resourceful and adaptable towns and cities. Almost everyone who participated in the consultation thought that this was a much neglected field of urban policy-making and action, and that changes were needed — some urgently. For the authors, the practitioners' debate proved to be a useful way of testing ideas and finding out more about urban resource-saving, especially the obstacles to good practice. Discussions confirmed that a great deal of enthusiasm and energy exists, especially at the local level, which could be harnessed better for conserving development.

2. More than 1,000 copies of the report were circulated to Government Departments and agencies, local government associations, nationalised industries, professional institutions, non-Government organisations, special interest groups, political parties and a large number of individuals. In numerical terms, the written response was not impressive. Moreover, it was heavily biased towards individuals rather than organisations, perhaps predictably in view of the timescales on which most organisations operate for the processing of documents. But what they lacked in number, the letters received made up for in length and value — they were much quarried when amending the report.

3. Nine workshops (of some 20 to 50 participants each) were organised at the authors' request by other people, with the support of their own specialist organisations, and their help is gratefully acknowledged in the Acknowledgements at the beginning of this report. Three workshops, in Edinburgh, Cardiff and Liverpool, explored many local achievements in urban resource-conservation and identified a number of parts of the report which needed strengthening. Three workshops related to specific themes — greening, transport and local initiatives — in resource-saving and regeneration. A final three workshops were held with specialist groups, including the RIBA. All these meetings were stimulating and valuable for the authors, not least because so much lively argument took place between the participants.

4. Over the debate as a whole, although there were strongly opposing views expressed on certain issues, nothing was said or written which suggested a radical change in the approach adopted. Many amendments have been made to illustrate and update the text and correct inaccuracies. Chapter 4 of this report has been substantially redrafted to put the case more strongly for a low resource-approach to transport.

5. This report refers, all too briefly, to many specialist fields of urban planning and management. Much of what it says is familiar to those working in these areas (though not to their counterparts with a different specialism) and it is inevitable that they should feel the analysis does not go far enough in identifying what should now be done, by whom and at what cost. Most of the recommendations in Chapter 10 of this report are now more specific, but it has not been possible, in the time allowed, to cost them — nor could this have been done without further consultation and a greater contribution from specialists. A number of professional institutions have now set up working groups to consider the report further and the RIBA have formally welcomed it in a preliminary comment.

6. Several important themes recurred during the debate, some relating to the feasibility, political and otherwise, of implementing the strategies for resource-conservation, and some to specific issues such as decentralisation, restraining car use and arresting the decline in public transport, the roles of central Government and local self help and of the public and private sectors. The views expressed were highly polarised and often reflected extreme ideological stances. Chapters 3, 4 and (especially) 9 of this report have been amended to reflect the debate on these issues.

7. Since June 1982, when the draft report was completed, a number of policy changes have taken place which impinge upon the issues discussed. The Manpower Services Commission has launched its Community Programme, and Government has urged local authorities to increase their capital spending and has introduced the Transport Bill, which seeks to restrict local authority spending on public transport. A number of relevant reports have been published, including the fifth report of the House of Commons Select Committee on Energy (Energy Conservation in Buildings) and the English House Condition Survey. Where appropriate, these have been referred to in this revised report.

8. It has not been possible to take account of all the information, ideas and case studies that emerged during the consultation, nor to do justice to the wealth of experience that many urban 'practitioners' made available to the authors. It is important now to sustain the interest generated and to widen the audience.

PART 3
RURAL

Putting Trust in the Countryside

A report by Timothy O'Riordan

Acknowledgements

In every sense of the word I have acted as a rapporteur when preparing this report. I have received the benefit of advice from a great number of people, many of whom spent hours commenting on early drafts and ferreting out valuable information. There is no doubt that this report would not have been written without all their help and cheerful assistance.

All members of the Review Group and the Programme Organising Committee were enormously considerate and supportive in this endeavour. It must be stressed that throughout the exercise they acted as individuals and did not represent their organisations. Naturally, any interpretation and recommendations are my own responsibility. I would like to pay tribute to Clare Stimson for preparing a number of invaluable briefing documents and for chasing up a whole host of references, to Michael Usher for coordinating much of the ecological material so very relevant to this analysis and to Ken Parker for providing some especially pertinent comments. Other people who commented on early drafts or sent me material include John Andrews, John Barkham, Richard Evans, Malcolm MacEwen, Malcolm Mosely, Norman Moore, Richard Munton, John Tarrant and Peter Wright. To all of them I am enormously grateful. Finally, a special note of thanks to Barbara Walker and Jill Baker who converted my almost illegible manuscript into typescript, with remarkable speed and accuracy, and to Bixie Nash for much painstaking work on the wordprocessor.

Chairman's Introduction

As public concern for care of the countryside has been growing over recent years, so has the controversy. The Review Group which has been guiding Professor O'Riordan has reflected this controversy, both in its membership and in its discussions. It was therefore inevitable that the report itself would be controversial and that members of the Review Group would not individually feel themselves committed to all the solutions it proposes.

Nevertheless, I believe that Professor O'Riordan is to be congratulated for assembling a great deal of important and relevant factual material, for his lucid analysis of some of the problems and conflicts and, not least, for putting forward for further discussion a number of interesting proposals.

I myself am optimistic that Britain's rural beauty and wildlife, the quality of life of those who live and work in the countryside and the enjoyment of those who visit it, can be not only preserved but enhanced. Much has already been achieved since the war. Some of the earlier mistakes such as unwise use of pesticides, neglect of woodlands, pollution of coasts and inland waters, loss of hedges, careless straw-burning and denial of public access are already to some extent being corrected — albeit not as rapidly as some of the protesters would demand.

Those who farm the land have been made aware that, in return for that privilege, they have an obligation to cherish the countryside. This obligation applies not only to national parks, areas of outstanding natural beauty or scientific interest, but also to the remainder — what Professor O'Riordan in his new system of countryside classification describes as 'agricultural and forestry landscapes'.

A failure to meet these obligations will inevitably result in the imposition of some form of external controls which may be clumsy, bureaucratic and/or costly and thus, to many, not acceptable. Professor O'Riordan advocates some controls, while others have been urged on him. Equally, conservation costs money and thus incentives, particularly through the tax system, also play a major role in his proposals.

Conservation in general, and rural conservation in particular, is a growing political issue in Britain. Thus the conservation movement can be expected to gather an increasing number of votes which none of the political parties can afford to ignore. It is against this background that the controversies are likely to be resolved.

Mark Schreiber
February, 1983

CHAPTER 1

A SUMMARY OF THE REPORT

The purpose of this report is threefold.
  (a) To promote understanding of why conservation principles and practices must be fully linked in to all aspects of development of rural resources in the UK.
  (b) To analyse why key principles of sustainable utilisation of rural resources are not at present being properly taken into account.
  (c) To make a series of recommendations so as to ensure that all future rural resource-development in the UK is ecologically sustainable, protects heritage values and ensures the long-term survival of rural communities.

Chapter 2 outlines the wider philosophy of modern conservation principles as they apply to the UK of the late twentieth century. The cardinal principle is to strike a proper balance between the economic productivity of rural resource-development and the aesthetic, emotional and scientific aspects of sustainable resource-utilisation. In this report, sustainable resource-utilisation refers to the use of the nation's mineral, soil, water and wildlife resources in such a manner that:
  (a) long-term economic wealth from these resources can be guaranteed;
  (b) the amount of resource inputs into the UK necessary to maintain this productive wealth is limited so as not to impair the long-term resource wealth of countries exporting their commodities to the UK;
  (c) features of landscape beauty and wildlife interest which are widely cherished by the citizens of the UK for their beauty, inspirational and educational values, and which have international significance because of their representativeness and typicality, are suitably protected and managed;
  (d) jobs are created and expanded to cement socially viable community life, and economic enterprise is linked to land management and care.

It is argued that the UK is not in a position to be complacent about the scope for increasing economic wealth arising out of new technological developments and improved management practices in agriculture, forestry, mining and rural industry. Not enough is known about the long-term effects of modern management practices on soil fertility, water availability and wildlife survival for anyone to be other than cautious and watchful. In particular, the UK must be careful to examine the demands rural industries (including agri-culture and timber production) make on the resources of other countries to ensure that these resources (minerals, timber, food and energy fuels) are not being drained away.

Chapter 3 summarises the economic contribution to the UK economy of each of the major rural industries: agriculture (worth about £4.5bn annually, or 2.2 per cent of the UK GDP), forestry (worth about £400m annually, or 0.2 per cent of the UK GDP), tourism and recreation (worth in total some £6.6bn annually, or 3.5 per cent of the UK GDP — though not all of this is spent in the countryside), and mining and quarrying (worth £7.8bn, or 5 per cent of the UK GDP). In all, rural resource-development accounts for about £18.5bn annually, equivalent to nearly 10 per cent of the UK GDP.

The chapter then outlines how nature conservation and landscape protection and enhancement are organised and managed in the UK. The main argument here is that the obvious relationship between nature conservation and landscape beauty is *not* adequately made, partly because different official and non-governmental agencies are involved (and they rarely coordinate policy and practice), and partly because landscape protection classifications vary greatly from country to country and according to purpose. This mish-mash of protective designations is too dependent on the whims of local authority and regional agency budgets and expertise, inevitably resulting in variable quality of management, inconsistent policies, wasteful practices in both resource and cash terms and much public confusion.

Finally, Chapter 3 describes the scale and rapidity of habitat loss in the UK due to thoughtless agriculture, forestry, mining and land use planning practices. This loss and associated damage, both to wildlife and characteristic scenic beauty, are arguably too much for UK citizens to tolerate and if nothing is done to stop the rot it could result in very serious alterations to plant and wildlife populations within a generation. Without being too alarmist, the chapter concludes that the future of the nation's scenic and wildlife heritage is very much in the balance: the potential for protecting key habitats and landscapes and for creating new habitats and landscapes for future generations to enjoy and marvel at is very great indeed. But it will require a tremendous concentration of national will to undertake this task and a radical change in attitudes and policies. No tinkering with present arrangements and procedures will be sufficient.

Chapter 4 looks at the economic history of UK agriculture, noting that, for almost a century prior to 1939, UK agriculture was neither profitable nor technologically advanced. Today the picture is very different. UK agriculture is one of the most productive and wealth-creating industries in the UK, supplying over 75 per cent of temperate food requirements. This tremendous achievement, which should not be underestimated, nevertheless has been won at a great cost. That cost involves the loss of farm-related jobs, the virtual elimination of the small family farm operating largely as a self-sufficient unit, the requirements of enormous amounts of energy and chemicals plus foodstuffs, nearly all of which are imported, and the tremendous economic burden of highly expensive land and machinery. All of this means that modern agriculture is more a business than an enterprise. It is also supported by a vast array of subsidies and price guarantees to maintain its economic viability. One estimate is that UK agriculture is subsidised to the tune of £3.35bn annually: through price supports, subsidies for storing and selling off cheaply surplus foodstuffs, grants for agricultural improvement and machinery, tax concessions on income tax, VAT, capital gains and capital transfer tax, and relief from the rates for all agricultural land. This subsidy works out at about £13,000 annually per working farm and appears to be rising in real terms every year. It is also estimated that the price of food in the UK is 10 per cent higher than would be the case if a freer agricultural market operated.

Subsidies in themselves are not bad so long as they lead to real advances in efficiency and productivity. Chapter 4 examines this claim and suggests that the present mix of agricultural support leads not only to wasteful surpluses but to inappropriate use of marginal land whose conservation value is being lost for unnecessary food production. In addition, excessive use of chemical fertiliser and farm machinery, plus inappropriate use of chemical pesticides and herbicides are creating, in some places, unacceptable environmental damage to water resources and wildlife with real health dangers for some people (particularly through nitrogen-rich water supplies and diseases associated with the use of chemicals). In terms of ecological substainability, the protection of heritage values and the maintenance of viable rural communities, these blunt economic forces and modern tillage practices appear to be counter-productive — at least in some important conservation areas. Too little is known about the long-term viability of the nation's soils and water resources to withstand modern agricultural techniques, especially marginal soils not ideally suited to advanced tillage practices. If there is to be any fundamental change an herioc change will be required in both attitude and management approaches, together with a radical shift in the way in which financial and tax incentives are deployed. Chapter 4 also describes the inconsistencies in policy underlying the Wildlife and Countryside Act, the unnecessary demands on public expenditure which it will likely entail, and its false premises with regard to the ethos of conservation for development.

Chapter 5 looks at the ecological aspects of large scale coniferous afforestation in upland UK, notably the effects on bird life, water supply and the use of chemicals on soils and wildlife. The general conclusion is that large scale even-aged coniferous afforestation could result in unfortunate damage to some bird life and water availability, but that the scope for linking creative afforestation to conservation is enormous. This would involve multiple aged stands of a variety of species planted in carefully planned and thoughtfully shaped blocks, interspersed with open space. Already there are some good examples of this approach. Currently, forestry interests are working assiduously to improve this balance, but there may still be a conflict between maintaining open moorland in some parts of upland England and Wales (and to a much lesser extent in Scotland) and the requirement for more trees. This kind of conflict can only be determined at a political level in relation to a national land use strategy and informed judgement.

The chapter also looks at the ecological significance of broadleaved woodland, especially for harbouring ecologically important bird and plant life as well as adding to the attractions of lowland landscapes. It points out that it is very difficult to make broadleaved woodland pay unless there is considerable economic assistance through investment grants and tax concessions. Yet the saving on the world's hardwood timber resources may well justify much greater financial encouragement of broadleaved planting and management.

The controversial issue of the economics of softwood forestry is also examined. The problem here is the lack of a sound economic analysis of both the productive and conservation-related gains of modern coniferous afforestation. Such an analysis needs to be undertaken both in a national and in an international context. As things stand now, there are major gains to be made out of very generous tax concessions already available to large estate owners, though these may encourage too much coniferous planting at the expense of broad-leaved planting, despite recent improvements in grant aid and management advice for hardwood timber production. Better advice and more suitable economic incentives to encourage mixed forest planting, coupled with recreation access and sound conservation measures, need to be encouraged.

Chapter 6 looks at the changes taking place in rural communities in the remoter areas of the modern UK. These changes reflect the long-term economic decline of the nation and the shifting economic fortunes of many rural areas. Population shifts are tending to encourage settlement in middle-sized towns rather than remote villages which are not only shorn of people but which are losing many local services such as shops, schools, pubs, post offices and welfare facilities. Accessibility for those without a car is a major problem, while the relatively wealthy urban retiree immigrant thrives. Most modern rural communities are far from being socially cohesive (if they ever were); many display a mixture of poverty and plenty, security and uncertainty, influence and powerlessness, none of which is conducive to social harmony or long-term economic stability. There is a desparate need to keep young, family forming couples in their own rural communities, to provide them with adequate housing, land and employment and to encourage job sharing, job complementarity (for example, working on the land in winter and in tourist-related jobs in summer) and encourage community enterprise via individual and collective initiative.

The highly successful 'tit-for-tat' informal economy which still characterises many rural areas needs to be further strengthened: it is likely to be an essential source of wealth for many rural families in future years. It is important to note here that the informal economy which usually involves sharing services or paying in kind rather than in cash should not be confused with the 'black economy' which, though technically illegal, nevertheless plays an important economic role in rural communities.

Chapter 6 also illustrates the modest, but not insignificant, economic importance of game management in both upland and lowland UK and the limited but potentially significant spin-off for conservation. It also discusses the problem of modern recreational use of the UK countryside, notably the growth in leisure walking and some water sports with attendant problems of access to suitable land and water resources and management of use to safeguard delicate sites. It concludes that there is scope for more initiative in recreational management and that the whole matter of public access to land, especially common land, should be carefully examined and improved. This may well involve further amendments to existing legislation.

The chapter looks at a series of attempts to integrate rural development with conservation and rural employment. The examples examined include the upland management experiments in Snowdonia and the Lakes, the East Fellside project in Cumbria, the Somerset Levels and Moors Local Plan, the Peak District alternative grant aid project, and the Integrated Development Programme in the Outer Hebrides. All of these noble efforts are shown not to be as successful as they are intended to be, largely because national economic incentives to various agencies concerned with development and conservation are not well integrated — indeed they frequently work at cross-purposes — and because local coordination at the grass roots level is not easy to achieve. It invariably involves an enormous amount of consultation, give and take, and a budgetary flexibility, all of which depend upon the enthusiasm, competence and availability of local officials and residents. The chapter continues with the observation that, unless financial assistance and tax incentives are altered to focus more efficiently on agreed management priorities, it is unlikely that integrated rural resource-development in key areas will be successful in terms of minimising public expenditure and maximising conservation for development objectives. The chapter also emphasises the essential role of local initiative and commitment

if the objectives enshrined in the report are to be met. Management through partnership may well become a key concept.

Finally, Chapter 6 assesses the state of environmental assessment of major development projects such as roads, reservoirs, airports and mineral extraction in the UK countryside. It argues that while UK planning procedures permit the use of environmental assessment for major projects, this is not done to any set standard. Environmental assessment is frequently not properly appraised in public and final decisions do not always reveal precisely how it was taken into account. The chapter endorses the procedures enshrined in the proposed European Community Directive on Environmental Impact Assessment, though it warns of the dangers of making the requirements too cumbersome, time consuming and inflexible. The chapter also argues for better safe-guards over the taking of prime agricultural land for development, and recommends that all mineral workings be approved only when restoration guarantees are provided.

Chapter 7 brings all these arguments together. It reiterates the potentially alarming extent of scientific and practical ignorance about the ecological bounds to sustainable resource-use in the UK, particularly if the total resource input-output budget is calculated (ie involving imported goods and materials as well as UK resources). It argues for a concentrated effort to estimate what would be the limits to ecologically productive use of the nation's soils, water and wildlife, bearing in mind that aesthetic and emotional requirements on landscapes and wildlife habitats may well reduce even further the productive potential of some areas. The chapter also calls for a national inventory of threatened habitats and landscapes to form the rationale for the protection, management and enhancement of representative habitats and landscapes.

Chapter 7 also observes that, despite the modest achievement of the Wildlife and Countryside Act to focus attention on cherished conservation areas and to improve the chances of their protection, albeit at unnecessary public cost, there is still an imbalance of effective power between the interests of land development and land conservation. Far from being united, these interests are in combat and are deeply suspicious of each other's motives. The Act may well worsen this division despite its philosophy of voluntary cooperation and, unless something quite drastic is done, this gulf of misunderstanding may widen even more.

The arguments for and against extending the present system of development control to agriculture and forestry operations are thoroughly examined. The conclusion is that comprehensive extension of such powers would neither be practicable nor would achieve the desired purpose of guaranteeing appropriate management. Such an outcome could only be achieved with a wholesale revision of present grants in aid and tax arrangements, plus the employment on the ground of many more qualified advisors (whose training at present is insufficient for the task involved). In any case, the price supports inherent in the Common Agricultural Policy (CAP) would preclude any effective tampering with an already complicated national grants system.

The proposal advanced in this report is to establish, first by a rather general procedure and subsequently through a change in the whole system of landscape designation, a new pattern of countryside classifications. The principle involved is to identify areas of land and water which are particularly suitable for conservation *over* development (heritage sites), areas more appropriate for conservation *with* development (conservation zones), and areas where development *with* conservation would be most acceptable (agricultural and forestry landscapes). It must be emphasised that, in this third category of the UK countryside, development would not be encouraged without adherence to the principles of sustainable utilisation and local authorities would have duties to establish areas of local conservation interest which would enable them to protect important areas locally for nature conservation and landscape beauty. In short, the new classification would emphasise different priorities of conservation and development, and would channel money and tax incentives accordingly.

Ideally, the fundamental objective should be to link conservation to development throughout the UK and for all rural resource-uses. However, it is argued that precise practical applications of conservation and development are almost impossible to achieve given the current state of knowledge and technology, let alone attitudes of mind. In any case, it is only sensible to highlight those areas where existing conservation values are clearly very great and ensure that these values are appropriately maintained, and to identify areas where potentially new conservation values could be created in an imaginative and exciting fashion. In both cases, the way forward is to fashion education, advice and economic incentives towards agreed management priorities and to ensure that no public funds are available for practices that would be detrimental to such objectives.

Nevertheless, the nettle that still must be grasped is what to do about private use of private land which may lead to outcomes which are not in the public interest. Ploughing and reseeding moorlands, over-grazing herb-rich upland or coastal wetlands, felling ancient broadleaved woodlands in favour of commercially more attractive conifers are all examples. Here, two possibilities open up. One is the extension of planning controls to ensure advance notification of any intention to change existing land-use. This would have to be a compulsory requirement in key sites because voluntary notification arrangements can break down and one miscreant can destroy a vital piece of heritage. The other possibility is to devise a single compensatory payment scheme to buy out the private right of development on such lands, and subsequently place a restricted covenant covering all future land-use so that it conforms to agreed management priorities. In this way, no further compensation would be required to guarantee the public interest in the use of that particular piece of the nation's heritage. Naturally, owners would be encouraged to sell or to lease to official or voluntary bodies eager to manage such sites according to conservation/development principles. In the last resort, for the really key sites, the heritage sites and some areas of local conservation interest there would have to be a reserve ministerial power requiring the owner to sell the land to a suitable body where the owner would not guarantee to manage the site according to ministerially determined management priorities. It should be stressed that such a power already exists for the Nature Conservancy Council (NCC) with respect to Sites of Special Scientific Interest (SSSIs), and, given the new pattern of incentives and tax arrangements, there should be less reason for unwilling owners either to want to destroy a heritage site or to hold on to such land.

It is essential to avoid the principle of compensation for not doing something to the land, which is neither justified on sustainability grounds (whether ecological or aesthetic according to agreed land use priorities) nor wasteful of public and private expenditures. Awards or rewards should be available for managing land according to principles acceptable to a conservation for development approach. There is nothing wrong with a land maintenance grant for undertaking a specific form of husbandry; there is everything wrong for a compensatory payment for not undertaking a land use which would not be economically, ecologically or aesthetically justifiable.

This new pattern of countryside classification looks cumbersome, bureaucratic and confusing, and many rural resource-users are alarmed by the proposal. But it is argued that some kind of agreed management priority must be established for key areas, that the rechannelling of public funds can only be practically deployed with respect to certain areas, and that landowners should not be any worse off than they are now because agricultural and forestry grants would be available for appropriate conservation practices. Thus, new arrangement of economic incentives should *redistribute and redirect* public money towards landowners and tenants who wish to use the land for agreed public purposes drawing money away from expenditures which are neither environmentally nor economically productive. There need be no additional expenditure of public money to achieve the objectives of this report.

Management of the new countryside categories would be the responsibility of existing agencies or local government bodies already charged with the management of such areas. Coordination of management would be achieved through support for local voluntary conservation organisations and farming and wildlife advisory groups. These would be encouraged to participate through the establishment of local rural management advisory panels composed of a representative cross section of development and conservation interests. The local level approach, based on sound knowledge, good personal relations and plenty of give and take, must be the basic point of departure for any programme of rural management in trust.

The principal recommendations are laid out in Chapter 8.

CHAPTER 2

STRIKING THE RIGHT BALANCE

Introduction

1. The most profound ideas are often the most simple to express. The central concept of the World Conservation Strategy (WCS) (IUCN, 1980) is that improvements in economic development and human happiness cannot be maintained unless conservation of living and material resources is specifically drawn into the developmental process. The logic is inescapable: without due attention to environmental conservation future pathways for development will be closed. Either the resources will not be there or it will prove too expensive to utilise them. Sound conservation, therefore, is not only sensible development but wise economics. The common origin of the words 'economics' and 'ecology' is *oikos*, meaning household: society must treat the global economic and ecological household with great care and understanding if it is to survive.

2. The relationship between development and conservation is really one of mutual dependence, or synthesis. In this report, this linkage is one of the two meanings given to the term 'the right balance' which is the subject of this chapter. The second meaning is introduced in paragraph 9 below (see p 181). As an approach to striking the right balance between development and conservation, the WCS introduced the term 'sustainable utilisation' of resources. In the context of the WCS this phrase has a very precise meaning relating to the conservation of living matter and life-support systems. It demands that development can only proceed if it fully takes into account both the opportunities and limitations imposed by ecological processes, and preserves the genetic diversity of living things.

3. Striking the right balance between development and conservation through the mechanism of sustainable utilisation therefore forms the philosophical foundation of this report, which suggests new signposts for the sustainable development of the rural resources of the UK. As such, it is also designed to be complementary to the six companion reports which, together with 'Resourceful Britain', form the Conservation and Development Programme for the UK (see the Preface).

4. Rural resources refer to land and water in terms of their living (soil, water and wildlife) and non-living (mineral) constituents, capable of being managed both for productive use (generating economic wealth) and for their inspirational values embodied in wildlife and scenic beauty. In geographical terms, rural resources are found outside of all settlements right up to the high tide line on all coasts. However, since 'Conservation and Development of Marine and Coastal Resources', Part 4 of this book, covers both marine and coastal resources, this report will only make passing reference to coasts, though its philosophy and recommendations encompass all rural land in the UK. This report will largely devote its attention to resource-uses: agriculture, forestry, mining, tourism, rural settlement and associated economic activity, nature conservation and landscape management. Resource-use, however, cannot be separated from the motivations and aspirations of resource-users: farmers, foresters, planners, tourism providers, and those who enjoy the countryside for recreation and for nature conservation. In many ways we are all rural resource-users. Whether we live in the towns or the countryside we eat the food produced on the farms, use the timber products derived from woods and forestry plantations, consume energy in part drawn from, or generated in, rural areas and travel through the open countryside on roads or footpaths to enjoy its scenic beauty or attractive wildlife. Rural resources, like all resources, provide wealth, usefulness and beauty for all of us in a myriad of ways: we all have an obligation to see that they continue to do so.

Placing the WCS in the UK Context

5. The WCS was written to focus debate on the future management of the world's resources, particularly its living resources. Interpretation for a UK context must bear in mind that the UK does not presently face many of the development dilemmas (such as expanding deserts, widespread soil erosion and loss of forest cover) affecting most developing countries. This does not mean that the WCS has no relevance for the UK. Indeed, because of some very specific conditions that apply to the UK, this country could establish a lead for many other countries. Some key points relating to the UK which suggest this are:
   (a) The UK has very few virgin natural resources. Virtually every habitat is influenced by humans to a greater or lesser extent. The scope for artificially creating new habitats which should become cherished conservation sites in the twenty first century and beyond is enormous.

(b) The UK is a net importer of many natural resources: food, timber and minerals. At present, the UK makes excessive demands upon the world's resources. As the world's population grows and Third World cities explode, other countries may not be willing or able to supply UK needs. Alternatively, security needs may increase commodity prices with considerable effect on the UK economy.

(c) The UK has already developed an impressive organisational framework for dealing with rural resource management. While not perfect, these procedures provide a model which other nations copy. The UK is poised to set a crucially important example on a global scale.

(d) Many countries send students to the UK. Some of these learn how to manage rural resources so as to balance competing demands. Example through wise rural resource-management should be a powerful teaching aid.

(e) Many developing countries would like to industrialise and to use their rural resources to meet five basic requirements: (i) for food, water and shelter to meet basic human needs; (ii) for industrialised raw materials, that is, timber, minerals, water supply and disposal; (iii) for recreational use, ranging from traditional country pursuits to a wide variety of uses by urban populations; (iv) as a repository for a nation's scenic and wildlife heritage, including elements of how society lived and worked in the past as well as representative habitats harbouring the national variety of living species and scenic, historical and archaeological features. All this is valued both as a tourist resource and in its own right so giving the nation a sense of identity; (v) as the basis for economically and socially cohesive rural life, where people's livelihoods depend upon the commodities and the services created out of wise rural resource-use.

6. The UK, therefore, has a very important role to play in showing how the WCS can be made to work in an industrialised, densely populated country. It is important to look at how the three basic tenets of the WCS apply to the UK.

(a) *To maintain essential ecological processes and life support systems.* The UK must ensure that its soils remain fertile, its water resources are replenished with potable water, and that nutrient cycles remain unbroken. All its basic natural resources should be managed so that renewability' is at least maintained and, where possible, extra yield obtained.

(b) *To preserve genetic diversity.* This has two aspects. First, in general, the more diverse an ecosystem the more stable it is. The UK must protect and maintain a representative variety of habitat types; it must ensure that gene-banks, both in living environments as well as in specially protected conditions, are maintained; and it should not rely too extensively on monocultures dependent on a few genetic strains and

unprotected from 'natural' conditions where normal biological controls no longer operate. Second, genetic diversity in wildlife and cultivated plants has not only many ecological advantages (including provision for future strains) but may well have important commercial value as well. The greater the variety of genetic material the more scope for the new biotechnologies — in agriculture, forestry, pharmaceuticals and new industrial applications (see Part 1 'Seven Bridges to the Future').

(c) *To ensure sustainable utilisation of species and ecosystems.* This is such a central concept for this report that it is discussed at length in the following paragraphs.

Defining Sustainable Utilisation

7. The WCS defined sustainable utilisation largely in terms of ecological principles, though it was at pains to emphasise that the purpose of sustainable utilisation was to improve the well-being of people as well as all living matter. In this report, sustainable utilisation is given three specific meanings each of which is valued by society for different reasons. Figure 1 illustrates the linkages between these three meanings. From a glance at this diagram it will be seen that two of the definitions stem from ecological principles while the third is rooted in social and economic factors, though all are interconnected.

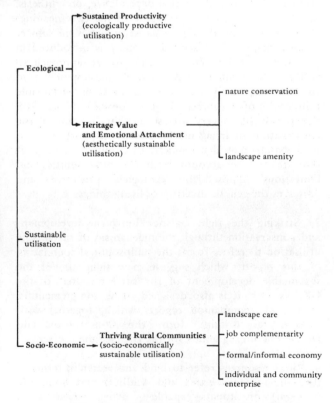

Figure 1. **The three meanings of sustainable utilisation as used in this report**

Sustained Productivity as a Component of Ecological Sustainability

Sustained productivity is a component of ecological sustainability. Rural resources must be managed so that their inherent productivity is not diminished; indeed, where possible their productivity should be increased. Soils must be cared for in order that they remain productive, woodlands managed so that their ecological functions are retained, water resources used so that their hydrological processes and ecological functions are not impaired. The boundaries to sustained productivity depend upon the relationship between inputs and outputs over long periods of time. There are no absolute boundaries. For instance, it is technically possible to grow bananas on the top of Ben Nevis, but this would require massive amounts of energy and materials and so would only be sustainable if energy and materials were indigenous, abundant and cheap — which they are not. Modern agriculture and forestry depend upon large quantities of chemicals and energy and imported foodstuffs. What is not known is whether the UK will always be able to afford to import such commodities, whether it should deny these resources to the nations which currently export them, and whether soil and water productivity and their associated nutrient cycles can be maintained indefinitely with these inputs (or more or less of them). Sustained productivity of natural resources is a slippery concept because it depends so much on scientific confidence, economic appraisal and moral obligation — all of which involve a very long-term approach to the subject. This is why so much emphasis is placed upon profiting from what is already known about this concept and on the need for more systematic research.

Heritage Values or Aesthetically Sustainable Resource-Use

Heritage values or aesthetically sustainable resource-use, refers to the maintenance and enhancement of the scientific, the aesthetic, the inspirational and the educational qualities of wildlife and scenery, together with historical associations of life and times past in archaeological and historical landscape features. All of these factors contribute to our sense of emotional attachment to our countryside, an attachment which contributes profoundly to that elusive concept, the 'quality of life'. They also add to our sense of being 'British' with its distinctive cultural traditions. The immense regional variation in many heritage features gives the UK an almost unique assemblage of countryside characteristics. As a nation, we surely have a duty to pass on to future generations both the best of our past civilisations and some testimonial to our own achievements. It is important to stress that heritage does not mean 'fossilisation' or 'museumisation' of treasured countryside features. It means custodianship of a wide variety of management practices to create living landscapes moulded through individual enterprise and community support. Although these important qualities can only be guaranteed if the principle of ecologically productive sustainability is applied (see above) — hence the connection to ecological sustainability in Figure 1 (see p 180) — nevertheless, heritage values encompass more

than ecological principles, for they embrace emotional and cultural values which pass beyond such principles. However, certain heritage values can be damaged even when there is productive sustainable use, and this is especially true of cherished nature conservation sites and certain scenic landscapes. Also, while the word 'aesthetic' is applied to this notion of sustainable resource-use, its sense as used in this report is not confined to beauty; it encompasses emotional connotations associated with scientific, educational and ethical inspiration. In common language, it means nature conservation and landscape appreciation (see paragraphs 17 and 18 below, page 183).

Thriving Rural Communities

Thriving rural communities refer to countryside settlements whose inhabitants have local loyalties and a sense of affinity to the land and features surrounding them. Such settlements require an appropriate size and age distribution of population, supported by local economic enterprises and justifying a wide range of local community services such as schools, shops, health care, other social services and cultural activities. A well managed countryside requires the presence of happy active people who are concerned about their surroundings and proud of the rural environment in which they live and work.

8. Figure 1 (see p 180) suggests that, for each of these three concepts of sustainable rural resource-use, two management principles can be applied. One is to *maintain* existing features or processes simply because they are productive or attractive and/or cherished as they are. The other is to *enhance* existing features and processes through scientific and managerial efforts to increase levels of productivity, or to create different landscapes through shaping and designing new landscape features. Many of the most cherished countryside areas of modern Britain were created less than 200 years ago; some of the most important inland bird sites are the result of considered interference by human beings. The twin managerial concept of maintenance and enhancement will form a continuous theme throughout this report. The notion of 'heritage' applies as much to what we can achieve now to create a legacy for the future as to what we can do today to preserve the legacy of the past.

9. The daunting task of this report is to devise a series of proposals for the utilisation of the rural resources of the UK which unite all three concepts of sustainability. This is a second feature of the concept of 'right balance' which has to be struck. But the report also seeks to build bridges between the competing interests which are currently in dispute as to how the countryside should be managed so that it is economically productive, aesthetically inspiring and socially viable.

10. This is why this report is entitled 'Putting Trust in the Countryside'. The concept of trust is also given two meanings in this report. The first is the notion of heritage. The rural resources of the UK must be managed in trust for both the present and the future. The

enjoyment of private rights — in land-use, in recreation, or in economic activity of whatever kind — must always include a sense of public obligation, a commitment to management in trust. The other meaning of trust relates to a sense of self-motivated responsibility born of understanding and concern. We all must be trusted to care for the land, whether we are landowners and/or managers or users of rural resources. A permanent commitment to caring for the land cannot merely be imposed by laws, regulations and financial incentives backed up by inspections. *This statement must not be misinterpreted*: a conservation-development plan for rural use cannot survive on the old fashioned notion of trust alone. Chapters 4, 5 and 6 of this report document why, and Chapter 3, paragraphs 20 to 38 (see pp 190 - 195) displays the evidence of this failure. The second notion of trust must encompass enlightened management of rural resources in partnership with the community and in accord with conservation/development principles. Such a commitment must come from personal conviction and a communal sense of trust. It is in both contexts that this report should appeal to all who are rural resource-users.

11. This report shows that there is insufficient evidence, indeed a worrying ignorance, as to whether agriculture, forestry, mining and other rural resource-development practices are breaching the principles of ecologically sustainable utilisation. Yet the conflicts between the development practices, nature conservation and/or landscape amenity and community enterprise are currently attracting more publicity. These incompatibilities need not continue. It is in the interests of both those who own and manage the UK countryside and those who enjoy its beauty as a place in which to live and work to recognise their common purpose in uniting the threefold concept of sustainable utilisation as outlined in paragraph 7 above (see pp 180 - 181).

12. Figure 2 puts these points together in simple diagrammatic terms. The ultimate objective of a rural conservation/development programme is to ensure social and economic community enterprise tied to the economic and aesthetic enjoyment of rural resources.

The Philosophy of This Report

13. Some readers will expect too much of this report. They will wish to see not only a clear philosophy of conservation for development in the UK context but practical advice as to how specific rural resources ought to be managed in the future and what they as individuals should do. This report cannot meet their expectations because its author does not have the knowledge or the competence to offer such detailed prescriptions. These are tasks which the continuing Conservation and Development Programme for the UK must tackle and which must rank high on its medium-term priorities. This report can only point out some of the reasons why conservation must be meshed with development,

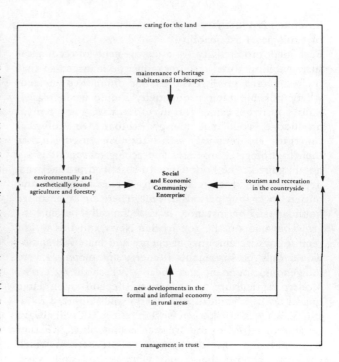

Figure 2. **Putting together the three strands of sustainable utilisation**

indicate the obstacles to achieving better integrations of these twin objectives and suggest certain recommendations to encourage official and non-governmental agencies and other interest groups to take note of the issues raised and respond in a constructive manner.

14. This report takes the view that any conservation-development plan for rural resources must strike a balance between more productive output and more efficiency in resource-use (ie less total demand for resources). This means that all major rural resource-uses, notably agriculture, forestry, mining and recreation, must not be so ambitiously developed as to supply more than the nation requires, and, above all, that land and water should be utilised only in ways for which they are most suited.

15. Equally important are the protection and proper management of land and water so that their nature conservation and scenic values are not unnecessarily destroyed. These aesthetic qualities of the UK countryside are part of that ill-defined concept 'the quality of life' which many UK citizens share. How many is not known, but it is probably at least half of the population and could be much more if environmental education takes a proper hold in school and adult educational curricula — see Part 6 'Environmental Ethics and Conservation Action' and Part 7 'Education for Commitment: Building Support in Society for Conservation and Development'. These qualities have an inspirational significance that many believe have important psychological functions in maintaining the wholeness of the human personality. Ecological health embodied in sustainable development marries with psychological health in human development to produce environmental health for the nation as a whole.

16. The love of beautiful landscapes and wildlife in its natural setting have a firm hold on British culture. Goyder and Lowe (1982) estimate that there are about three million members of environmental interest groups in the UK today. In Northern Ireland there are at least 15,000 members of voluntary conservation organisations (Cruickshank, personal communication, 1982), and membership continues to increase. Because public interest in both nature conservation and landscape amenity is increasing, and because, as will be discussed in Chapter 3 of this report, these interests are increasingly seen to be in conflict with certain agricultural, forestry, mining and industrial development practices, it is important to look at why these two aesthetic qualities of the UK countryside are so highly valued. Two reasons stand out. First, the extent and rapidity of habitat loss and landscape change are now so well documented as to shock many people and cause ecologists to worry lest the pace of alteration is too rapid to allow certain plant and animal species to adjust. Second, these changes are occurring too quickly for many people to tolerate. For a majority of the British public 'the countryside' evokes an image of beauty, peacefulness and harmony, and there are still some parts of the countryside where such images are real. But elsewhere, as the image is realised to be an illusion, people react with anger and despair.

17. Nature conservation serves two purposes. First, there are the interests of scientists who require a wide range of wild and semi-wild habitats in order to study ecological processes and physical features so as to understand not only how non-human existence functions, but also how society can better utilise living and non-living resources for its collective benefit. In addition, it is widely believed that varied and self-sustaining ecosystems are vitally important for maintaining ecological balance and diversity and for acting as barometers (signposts) of ecological change. It can also be argued that the greater the diversity of genetic material the greater are the opportunities for evolution and the deliberate breeding of plants and animals by human beings. Second, there is the interest of the general public who share with scientists a concern for the welfare of wild plants and animals, and who also have a moral conviction that some natural species, communities and ecosystems should be allowed to exist in their own right — a kind of natural trust. Hence, people are becoming more and more distressed if they see wildlife thoughtlessly or unjustifiably destroyed. As a consequence there is broad public support for the official nature conservation agency, the NCC, and a range of non-Governmental conservation organisations, in pursuing a two-fold conservation strategy:

    (a) the protection, including appropriate management, of the most important areas for wildlife and physical features;

    (b) the persuasion of all other resource-users to take as much account of the needs of nature conservation as they are able in the practice of their professions and interests. This involves advice at all levels both to organisations and individuals.

The NCC is currently preparing a Great Britain Nature Conservation Strategy which should complement this report. In Northern Ireland, nature conservation is the responsibility of the Conservation Branch of the Department of the Environment, advised by the Nature Reserves Committee.

18. While the reasons for supporting nature conservation are probably widely recognised, there is less agreement about the importance of protecting and enhancing landscapes. Landscape protection and landscape enhancement are not the same thing. The former aims at creating living landscape museums whose characteristic scenic beauty and heritage value, associated with a particular period and quality of management, render them unique or typical of a region. Aesthetic appreciation of the countryside also involves emotional attachment associated with a concern for history, regional industry and a sense of place, revealed through patriotic and parochial feelings. Such landscapes are ideally left broadly unchanged (though this usually involves very careful management). The objective of landscape enhancement is to improve visual attractiveness through creative landscape design. This requires a different kind of management from that associated with landscape protection and includes landscape rehabilitation (see Leonard, 1981). It may be reasonably easy to obtain agreement over what constitutes a heritage landscape, but people will argue endlessly over what is attractive.

19. There are important differences between the philosophy and practice of nature conservation and those of landscape protection and enhancement. Nature conservation is a more scientific discipline, with a greater educational value, dealing with natural systems. Landscape appreciation involves more aesthetic sensitivity, and encompasses (in the UK) artificially created scenes which may include semi-wild vegetation. Yet in many ways these two qualities of the UK countryside — and, indeed, the urban scene — are very closely united. It is not uncommon to experience landscape beauty in nature conservation sites and important nature conservation features in protected and restored landscapes (see Westmacott and Worthington, 1974; Mabey, 1981). About 14 per cent of the land area of national parks and 6.3 per cent of areas of outstanding natural beauty have special nature conservation value. This report argues that nature conservation and landscape protection and enhancement should largely be treated as one and the same thing, and that future policies and management methods should reflect this.

20. The WCS recommended that each national report proceed, where possible, along the following lines.

    (a) Review appropriate sectoral development objectives (in this case relating to rural resources) in relation to key conservation objectives (as defined here under the three concepts of sustainability).

    (b) Identify the main obstacles to achieving these conservation objectives and argue a range of opportunities for overcoming these obstacles and the resulting implications of any actions advocated.

(c) Estimate the financial and other requirements, including legislative and administrative measures, to carry out such actions in the most cost effective manner, and, where necessary, to propose priorities for attention.

(d) Identify lead agencies to execute and monitor the required actions and to increase public understanding.

In Chapters 4 to 6 of this report these themes will be followed with respect to three major categories of rural resource-use in the UK: agriculture, forestry and tourism, plus other economic activity.

References

GOYDER, J and LOWE, P. 1982. Environmental groups in British politics, London, George Allen and Unwin.

IUCN. 1980. World conservation strategy. Geneva, International Union for the Conservation of Nature.

LEONARD, P. 1981. A public role in landscape conservation. *The Planner, January*, 19-25.

MABEY, R. 1981. The common ground: a place for nature in Britain's future? London, Hutchinson.

WESTMACOTT, R and WORTHINGTON, T. 1974. New agricultural landscapes. Cheltenham, The Countryside Commission.

CHAPTER 3

DEVELOPMENT AND CONSERVATION OF RURAL RESOURCES

Introduction

1. This chapter documents the importance to the UK economy of the principal resource-uses of the UK countryside, namely agriculture, forestry, tourism, and, where identifiable, rural industrial activity, describes the existing policies which relate to these uses, and also outlines how certain aspects of these uses adversely affect nature conservation and landscape appreciation.

Agriculture

2. Although the UK is a densely populated, industrialised country relying on imports for about 40 per cent of its food supply (including agricultural factors of production), agriculture remains one of its most important industries. (Note: some of the data which follow exclude Northern Ireland.) Agriculture provides employment for about 639,000 people of whom about 205,000 are full-time and 90,000 are part-time farmers, partners and directors — 66 per cent of whom are owner occupiers and 34 per cent are tenants (Ministry of Agriculture, Fisheries and Food, 1982). An additional 237,000 work directly on farms (175,000 full-time and 62,000 part-time), 99,000 are casually employed and about 230,000 have jobs in the agricultural service industry. The 639,000 employee figure represents 2.8 per cent of the total civilian working population. In 1981, the value of all agricultural output in the UK was £9.6bn and its contribution (ie final output less the sum of net input and depreciation) to the GB gross domestic product (GDP) was £4.5bn or about 2.2 per cent. In Northern Ireland, approximately 10 per cent of the labour force is employed in agriculture and forestry, contributing about 5.6 per cent of the Province's GDP. The agricultural industry also plays its part in the export drive, though some of its exported products are processed from imported goods: in 1979, exports of livestock and agricultural products amounted to £3.0bn while exports of agricultural machinery were worth £830m. Associated with agriculture are the ancillary industries of food processing (employing 600,000 in March, 1980 — though much of this industry deals with imported food products), food distribution and retailing (employing 187,000 in March, 1980) and the manufacture of machinery (employing 60,000) and chemicals (employing 12,000 for fertiliser production alone). Farming,

therefore, has great significance for other sectors of the economy. In 1981, farm businesses purchased goods to the value of £5.5bn from domestic industries, while some £7.0bn of agricultural output formed vital inputs for several domestic industries. Altogether, it is estimated that about 215,000 jobs in the food and drink, textile, leather and parts of the chemical, industries are directly dependent upon UK agriculture (Rickard, 1982).

3. Since the war, agriculture has become a highly efficient industry in terms of output per unit of labour input. Over the period 1969 to 1979, labour productivity in agriculture rose by 3.8 per cent per year, while between 1969 and 1981 the volume of agricultural production rose by 28 per cent. This remarkable achievement has largely been the result of considerable advances in plant and animal breeding, developments in fertiliser and pesticide use and investments in mechanisation. But it has meant the shedding of agricultural labour and the amalgamation of farms into larger units. (Note: the data which follow refer to GB.) Between 1949 and 1981, the number of full-time agricultural workers fell from 540,000 to 175,000. The total number of 247,300 farming units was about 5 per cent lower in 1981 than in 1976. About half of these farms are very small units, some of which are farmed part-time, and account for only one-tenth of the industry's output. The 30,000 large farm businesses (capable of employing four or more full-time workers), which represent only 12 per cent of all holdings in terms of numbers, produce about half the total output on less than half the total agricultural land. There are about 45,000 medium-sized (employing two to three workers) and 50,000 small farm businesses (employing one worker). Part-time holdings (with under 275 standard man days) contribute only 5 per cent of total output, account for 10 per cent of total area, yet represent 40 per cent of all agricultural holdings. Between 1968 and 1975, the number of small arable farms fell by 25 per cent, while between 1965 and 1975 the number of land holdings in excess of 120 ha increased from 33 per cent to 45 per cent (Northfield, 1979).

4. Modern agriculture in the UK is a highly diverse industry in its use of the land, its management practices, its income and its employment. An important distinction should be made between upland and lowland agriculture. For example, of the 19 million ha of land in agriculture (79 per cent of the 24 million ha of land in the UK) 6.3 million ha are in rough grazing and 264,000 ha are

	England and Wales		Scotland		Northern Ireland		United Kingdom	
Total area of agricultural land	11,580		6,133		1,115		18,828	
Percentage of total land area	70		70.7		77.7		72.2	
Arable land	5,449	(47%)	1,106	(18%)	340	(30%)*	6,895	(37%)
Pasture land	4,054	(35%)	565	(9%)	507	(45%)	5,126	(27%)
Rough grazing	1,738	(15%)	4,367	(71%)	224	(20%)	6,329	(37%)

*Note: Most of this is still under grass: only about 7 per cent of all improved land in Northern Ireland is not in grass.

Table 1. Use of agricultural land in the UK, June 1979 data (000 hectares)
Source: Annual Census of Agricultural Statistics, 1980. Table 2.

woodlands. However, in southern England only one-tenth of agricultural land is in rough grazing while in upland England this constitutes one-third, and in Scotland three-quarters. These regional land-use variations are reflected in the differences in the value of total agricultural production per ha. In 1976-77 this ranged from a high of £633 in East Anglia to £456 in the south-west to £387 in Northern Ireland, £297 in Wales, £218 in lowland Scotland to only £29 in highland Scotland — the average for the UK as a whole being £363 (Marsh and MacLaren, 1981). Any conservation/development programme must take these regional variations fully into account, as well as the relative economic importance of agriculture to a locality. Table 1 (see above) lists the area of agricultural land in various uses in the UK.

5. The consequence of the general improvement in agricultural productivity is that, during the past 10 years, UK agriculture has increased its contribution of home-produced temperate foods from 61.5 per cent to 75 per cent of an expanding market. While this represents a value of nearly £8.0bn, the nation still imports some £6.0bn of food and feed. Successive governments have believed that much more can and should be done to improve agricultural productivity. This is the principal argument contained in the most recent White Paper 'Farming and the Nation' (Cmnd 7458 1979, p2): 'The productivity record of our agriculture and its potential for further growth in efficiency provide a sound base on which to promote expansion. The necessary investment is already assisted by the Government in a number of ways, including capital grants and taxation policies, but there will need to be further investment by those engaged in the industry. This will be forthcoming only if there are sufficiently stable conditions and sufficient incentive and confidence in the future of the industry. If the country is to continue to benefit from gains in agricultural productivity, therefore, the progressive farmer needs a reasonable assurance that his production will continue to be profitable.' This is the view of the previous Labour administration but the present Government appears equally enthusiastic about encouraging more agricultural productivity and food self-sufficiency, and is keen to improve the marketing of surplus UK agricultural products at home and abroad. (Note: in England agri-

cultural affairs are handled by the Ministry of Agriculture, Fisheries and Food (MAFF), by the Welsh Office Agricultural Department (WOAD) in Wales, by the Department of Agriculture and Fisheries for Scotland (DAFS) in Scotland, and by the Department of Agriculture for Northern Ireland (DANI) in Northern Ireland.)

Forestry

6. The UK forestry industry operates in both the public and private sector. The public sector is owned and managed by the Forestry Commission, a quasi-autonomous governmental body which complies with directions given by forestry ministers. In Northern Ireland, forestry matters are the responsibility of the Forest Service of DANI. The Forestry Commission is a nationalised industry producing timber. The Commission has three other roles. It advises and assists private owners on the management and production of timber; it furthers the aims of nature conservation and landscape amenity in all woodlands in the UK through various means of consultation, advice and grant aid; and it is responsible for research on behalf of the whole of the UK forestry industry. This includes detailed studies of the effects of forests on soils and wildlife.

7. The estimated total area of woodland in the UK is 2.1 million ha or about 9 per cent of the total land area (see Table 2, p 187). About 1.7 million ha are regarded as productive forest of which half (884,000 ha) is managed by the Forestry Commission. The Commission plants about 11,800 ha of new productive forest annually (mostly in Scotland) while private woodland owners plant an additional 8,100 ha per year. In Northern Ireland less than 1,000 ha of new forest was planted annually by DANI in 1979-80. Estimates for total afforested area in Northern Ireland by the year 2000 optimistically aim at an additional 40,000 ha (a doubling of the 1980 total planted area) of State planting and some 28,000 more ha of private planting (also a doubling of the 1980 planted area). It is unlikely that these targets will be reached. At present, the UK imports all but 8 per cent of her softwood requirements,

Forest type	Great Britain			Northern Ireland		Total
	FC	Private	Total	DANI	Private	
Broadleaved high forest and coppice	50	345	395	3	6	404
Conifer high forest	806	506	1,312	47	3	1,362
Total productive area	856	851	1,707	50	9	1,766
Unproductive or partly productive	7	283	290	0	6	296
Total	863	1,134	1,997	50	15	2,062

Table 2. Area of forest in the UK in 1977 (000 hectares)
Source: Centre for Agricultural Strategy, 1980, p 46

worth £2.8bn in 1979. About one-third (1.0 to 1.2 million cubic metres) of the nation's hardwood requirement of three million cubic metres is produced from domestic forests. In all, the UK wood industry is worth around £400m, which is about 0.2 per cent of the GDP. In 1979, 21,000 workers were employed directly in the UK forestry industry, but an additional 15,000 out of a total of 236,000 people employed in timber-based industries, utilising both imported and home produced wood, owe their jobs to the domestic timber industry.

8. The present and future demand for industrial wood has been estimated by the Forestry Commission (1977) and revised by the Centre for Agricultural Strategy (1980) as described in Table 3, see p 188. These data are based on best estimates, taking into account changes in the technology of extraction, and medium to low forecasts of economic growth, but not any substantial change in the scale of recycling. The Forestry Commission suggests that, assuming the present planting programme, the increased quantities of home grown timber in the years 2000 and 2025 would have a potential import saving of about £800m and £1,500m respectively at current prices. This will clearly depend upon the relative cost of imported and home produced wood and the cost and scale of recycling wood products.

9. In 1978, the Commission sought to estimate how much land not in agricultural or urban use was capable of being forested in GB and how much in turn of such lands should not be forested on the grounds of conservation and amenity and other factors. Its conclusions were that about another 1.8 million ha were capable of being planted. Of this, the Commission felt that about 40 per cent may prove unsuitable when ground surveys are complete and when nature conservation and landscape beauty are taken into account, leaving (by its calculations) about 1.1 million ha technically suitable for afforestation. This is not an estimate of likely planting, which will depend upon future Commission budgets and official policies; it is merely a desk calculation of possible afforestable area.

10. These estimates are controversial (as discussed in paragraphs 14 and 15 of Chapter 5 of this report) for they are based on assumptions about the state of future wood product markets, the net benefits of afforestation and the relative importance of conservation and amenity about which there is much dispute. Nevertheless, following his review of forestry policy announced in Parliament on 10 December 1980 (Col 1405) the Secretary of State for Scotland announced that the present Government was confident about the future of the industry. He stated that the Government: 'look for a steadily increasing proportion of our requirements of timber to come from our own resources. A continuing expansion of forestry is in the national interest, both to reduce our dependence upon imported wood in the long-term and to provide continued employment in forestry and associated industries. There should be scope for new planting to continue in the immediate future broadly at the rate of the past 25 years while preserving an acceptable balance with agriculture, the environment and other interests'.

Tourism and Recreation

11. The distinction between tourism and recreation is blurred. Conventionally, tourists are those whose home is some distance (often abroad) from a particular locality which they visit for recreational enjoyment, who spend at least a whole day in the area and normally stay one night. Recreationists are characteristically those who visit an area for not more than a day. Tourism is a major economic activity in the UK. Expenditure by overseas visitors in 1979 made a net contribution of £673m to the nation's balance of payments, while total tourist spending by both British and overseas visitors in 1981 amounted to £8.4bn or about 3.5 per cent of the UK GDP. Admittedly, overseas visitors do not come specifically to visit the countryside, but there is no doubt that the beauty and historic interest of the landscape and cultural heritage in rural areas are important attractions. Although only 10 per cent of tourists are overseas visitors, they contribute 45 per cent of total tourist spending. Of UK residents, 75 per cent visit the countryside at least once per year and 54 per cent at least once per month, mostly in the form of day trips. About 82 million trips were made to the countryside in England and Wales during an average summer month in 1977 (Countryside Commission, 1979). In Scotland, some six million trips were made to the Scottish countryside by Scottish residents and a

	Sawn wood	Paper and board	Wood panels	Adjusted total
1972	10.0	7.3	2.8	20.1
1985	17.4	23.5	7.5	46.0
2000	17.9	31.3	12.4	55.0
2025	18.4	50.3	19.6	75.0

Table 3. **Estimate of UK demand for wood products (million cubic metres wood raw material equivalent)**
Source: Centre for Agricultural Strategy, 1980, p 29

further two million trips were made by visitors on a typical summer month in 1981; almost 40 per cent of Scottish holidaymakers regarded the Scottish countryside as a major reason for coming to Scotland (Scottish Leisure Survey, 1981). In addition, about 20 per cent of all holiday nights by British residents in England were spent in the countryside (ie 70 million person-nights) while a further 15 per cent of all holidays nights were spent in small country towns (Borley, 1982). No equivalent figures are available for Scotland but about 35 per cent of all holiday nights are spent in the Scottish countryside.

12. It is difficult to estimate precisely how many jobs are created by the tourist industry as much of the work is part-time and seasonal, but one guess is as high as 1.5 million or 7 per cent of the working population (English Tourist Board, 1981). In the hotel and other residential establishments tourist sector employment now stands at some 290,000. In Scotland 92,000 are employed full- or part-time in the tourist industry — some 3 per cent of the Scottish working population. Locally, tourism can provide jobs and incomes in areas where it is difficult to generate alternative forms of employment. Apart from jobs, tourism also helps to support a variety of community services ranging from shops to theatres and encourages the restoration of old buildings, thereby maintaining the historic fabric of many towns and villages throughout the country.

Mining and Quarrying

13. Mining and quarrying refer to the extraction of coal and non fuel minerals plus sand and gravel and limestone for construction and agricultural purposes. In this sector coal mining has a special economic significance. Of the 335,000 employed in the mining and quarrying sector in 1980, 286,000 worked in the coal industry leaving 49,000 in the rest of the industry. This sector generally provided £7.8bn to the UK GDP in 1979, of which about £6.4bn was due to coal production. This combined figure represents a contribution of about 5 per cent to the UK GDP.

The Economic Contribution of Rural Resource Development

14. It is not possible to isolate the 'rural economy'

from the national economy because so much of the rural economy is immersed in general economic activity. Table 4 (see p 189) summarises the contribution of certain of the key rural resource-development sectors as a proportion of the national economy and labour employed. These are rough and ready figures based on the best data available for the period 1979-80. They suggest that, at the very least, rural resource-developments account for £18.5bn of economic output equivalent to about 9 per cent of the UK GDP, and provides jobs for at least 2.5 million people, or about 10 per cent of the employed labour force of the nation.

Nature Conservation

15. As part of its remit to protect the most scientifically important areas for wildlife and geological features, the NCC has identified a national network of areas representing all the principal types of wildlife and habitats through notification of SSSIs and National Nature Reserves (NNRs). The scientific justification for this approach is outlined in the publication *Nature Conservation Review* (Ratcliffe, 1977), though a more accessible reference has been prepared by Moore (1982) and controversially criticised by Rose and Grove (1982). At present, there are about 3,900 SSSIs (of which 3,000 are designated for their biological interest and the remainder for their geological and other physical features) covering some 5.9 per cent of Scotland, England and Wales, and 182 NNRs encompassing 139,000 ha or 0.5 per cent of the same land area. In Northern Ireland there are 36 NNRs (covering about 3,000 ha) and 47 Areas of Scientific Interest (covering about 74,000 ha). Of the NNRs, only 14 per cent by area are owned, the rest being held under lease or under a nature reserve agreement with the landowner. In its *Nature Conservation Review* the NCC listed 735 of the most outstanding biological SSSIs (representing about three-quarters of the area of all SSSIs) as 'key sites' which are all regarded as equivalent to NNRs in nature conservation value and which include nearly all existing NNRs.

16. The voluntary conservation organisations have established a total of some 1,300 non-statutory nature reserves covering about 80,000 ha. Many of these reserves are SSSIs and some are key sites. There is also a

		Agriculture	Forestry	Tourism	Mining
Net contribution to GDP	(£)	4,493	400	8,400	7,807 (1,300)*
	(%)	2.2	0.2	3.5	4.0 (0.6)
Labour employed directly	(N)	639,000	21,000	1,500,000**	335,700 (49,100)
	(%)	2.8	0.01	7.0	4.0 (0.2)
Labour employed indirectly	(N)	246,000	14,626	—	—
	(%)	1.0	0.006		

* excluding coal
** involves part-time and seasonal employment

Table 4. **Contribution of rural-related activity to the UK gross domestic product**

small number of Local and Forest Nature Reserves established by local authorities and the Forestry Commission. Many National Trust properties are nature reserves when managed in sympathy with wildlife interests. Nature conservation is also furthered to varying degrees by some farmers and landowners, and by local and central Government agencies such as the Countryside Commissions, the National Park Authorities, the Agricultural Development and Advisory Service in England and Wales and the Agricultural Colleges in Scotland. (These last two agencies, together with Regional Water Authorities and internal drainage boards, have a statutory duty to further the cause of nature conservation and amenity under the Wildlife and Countryside Act 1981.)

17. For wildlife, the lands managed as SSSIs or NNRs have a value out of all proportion to their relative area in the nation. The biological SSSI and NNR system is a mutually supporting network of representative samples of the main vegetational types in Britain — woodlands, heathlands, grasslands, moorlands and various kinds of aquatic habitats. Their absolute protection is vital, for they contain the national biological treasury which should be preserved both for its own sake and in the public interest. This is one reason why the NCC has powers to acquire land compulsorily should its scientific interest be threatened (though in practice this power is very rarely used), and why SSSIs are given special protection under the Wildlife and Countryside Act 1981 (which does not apply to Northern Ireland).

18. Approximately 80 per cent of the UK land surface is devoted to agriculture, 9 per cent to forest (about half of which is conifer plantation) and 11 per cent to urban land. Most croplands (including grass leys) have very little nature conservation interest and contribute almost nothing to the maintenance of genetic diversity. That is to be found in deciduous woodland, wetland, bogs, moors and heaths, coastlands and mountain tops, hedges and unimproved grasslands. According to the Chief Advisory Officer of the NCC, the UK still contains a wealth of wildlife from the world point of view. Its outstanding features are:

(a) The humid deciduous woodlands of the west with their exceptionally rich bryophyte flora.
(b) The wide range and extent of heathlands, several types of which are confined to the UK.
(c) The immense variety of habitats in a very small area due to the unusual variations in geology and climate.
(d) The numbers and diversity of wintering birds which visit UK shores and marshes because of the relative mildness of UK winters.

Unfortunately, many of these habitats have already suffered damage and destruction and continue to be threatened. In the interests of both heritage protection and as part of the UK obligation to maintain genetic variety, generous amounts of representative portions of these habitats must be protected as a key element in the Conservation and Development Programme for the UK.

Landscape Protection and Enhancement

19. The official agencies responsible for landscape protection and enhancement and the creation of new landscapes are the two Countryside Commissions (in England and Wales, and in Scotland). In Northern Ireland, amenity matters are the responsibility of the Department of the Environment for Northern Ireland, advised by the Ulster Countryside Committee. All these agencies work closely with the 10 National Park Authorities (a term covering the various local government bodies responsible for National Parks) in England and Wales, and local government planning departments throughout the UK. Unlike the NCC, the Countryside Commissions do not own land, nor do they have powers of compulsory acquisition in order to protect landscape beauty. Their task is to persuade and their method of operation is that of partnership, mainly with local authorities through a variety of grant-aided schemes, but also with landowners and nature conservation interests through their imaginative programme of demonstration farms, tree planting schemes, the protection of heritage

coasts and the promotion of upland management experiments. From April 1982, the Countryside Commission for England and Wales was granted a status making it more independent within the civil service and freer to criticise Government policies, and is now financed by separate grant-in-aid. (Its Scottish counterpart has been independent since it was set up in 1967.) It is likely that the Countryside Commission for England and Wales will continue to pursue its consultative, persuasive approach. Its Chairman stressed this point in his introduction to the Commission's new Prospectus, published in 1982. 'Open partnership is our style. From now onwards we are taking our countryside partners more into our confidence, showing them in advance what we plan and asking for their comments before we make firm decisions.' Broadly speaking, the aims of the two Commissions are:

(a) the conservation and enhancement of the natural beauty and amenity of the countryside;
(b) the provision and improvement of facilities for the enjoyment of the countryside;
(c) to secure public access to the countryside for the purpose of open-air recreation through encouraging and grant aiding access agreements with private landowners and cooperating in the provision of long-distance footpaths.

20. The Countryside Commissions assist financially and advise relevant local authorities on a variety of officially designated areas which are discussed below.

The National Parks

The National Parks (restricted to England and Wales) were designated because of their natural beauty and the opportunities they afford for open air recreation. There are 10 national parks covering 1.36 million ha or about 9 per cent of England and Wales, mostly confined to the uplands. Each national park authority (with its own budget financed approximately 75 per cent from central Government and 25 per cent from local rates) has prepared a management plan, a flexible but statutory document designed to promote the conservation and enhancement of landscape beauty and public enjoyment through access, while taking into account the legitimate concerns of agriculture, forestry and other economic and social interests of the area. (For an up-to-date analysis of national parks see MacEwen and MacEwen, 1982.)

Areas of Outstanding Natural Beauty

Areas of Outstanding Natural Beauty (AONBs) are also denoted primarily for their natural beauty (which, as in national parks, includes protecting flora, fauna and geological sites as well as scenic landscape features). However, in a recent policy statement, the Countryside Commission (1980) concluded that recreation be recognised as an objective of designation when it is consistent with the conservation of natural beauty, though account must also be taken of the need to safeguard agriculture, forestry and other rural industries and the economic and social needs of other communities (see also Himsworth, 1980). Planning within AONBs is the responsibility of local planning departments, occasionally through a joint advisory committee where more than one local authority is involved, and infrequently with a named officer in charge. The Countryside Commissions grant aid approved projects up to 50 per cent. Currently, there are 33 AONBs in England and Wales covering 14,493 sq km (about 10 per cent of the land area); four more have been designated but await ministerial confirmation, and three others are in the pipeline. In Northern Ireland, eight AONBs covering 18 per cent of the total land area have been designated, with two additional AONB designations pending.

National Scenic Areas

National scenic areas (NSAs) are confined to Scotland where there are neither national parks nor AONBs. At present, there are 40 national scenic areas covering one million ha (some 12.7 per cent of the land and inland water surface). Landscape protection is achieved through policies in structure and local plans and through planning control. This new designation, established in 1980, replaces five National Park Direction Areas (1948-1980) which covered 486,000 ha.

Green Belts and Areas of Great Landscape Value

Within county structure plans are various designations again designed mainly to protect scenic attractiveness and/or encourage recreational access. Most well known are the Green belts which surround all the major conurbations where planning controls are especially severe. In addition, local authorities may designate areas of great landscape value, based on a varied (and often inconsistent) set of criteria where proposed development may occasionally be more strictly controlled than elsewhere. These are non-statutory designations, but in total they encompass some 20 per cent of England and Wales and about 12 per cent of Scotland.

Heritage Coasts and Preferred Coastal Conservation Zones

Also non-statutory but equally important are the heritage coasts which are protected by local authorities. In England and Wales there are 33 of these covering 1,084 km (or 25 per cent of all coastal frontage), while in Scotland nearly two-thirds of the coastline is designated (again on a non-statutory basis) as preferred coastal conservation zones.

Footpaths and Bridleways

The many footpaths and bridleways which criss-cross the length and breadth of the UK are managed in an inconsistent manner by local authorities in cooperation with landowners. Sadly, the main problems are neglect and lack of enthusiasm. Many rights of way, both ancient and new, are only kept open by the steadfast activities of ramblers' groups and particularly by members of the Ramblers' Association. Mattingly (1982) notes that footpaths (numerically) are disappearing at a much faster rate than they are being created. In 1979, for example, there were 341 orders for the closure of public paths, 1,281 orders for diversions and only 75 orders for path creations. These figures are similar to those for previous years. Walking in the countryside is an increasingly popular activity. About one-fifth of all

Pistyll Rhaeadr in the Berwin Mountains:
an area over which there was dispute
over the extent of designation of
a site of special scientific interest.
(By courtesy of the Director of Aerial Photography,
University of Cambridge,
and the Nature Conservancy Council)

visitors to the countryside walk at least two miles (Mattingly, 1982). The Countryside Commissions have assisted local authorities to designate a system of long-distance footpaths. Currently, there are some 11 long-distance routes covering some 2,700 km, with four more paths in preparation. However, designation of long-distance and other recreational paths is often a painstaking process which requires much tact and diplomacy, for many landowners are very hesitant about permitting public access to their property.

The National Trust and the National Trust for Scotland
21. The National Trust (NT) and the National Trust for Scotland (NTS) play a vital role in purchasing tracts of important landscape and holding them inalienable for the public to enjoy. In Scotland, some 44,450 ha are owned by the NTS, though considerable additional areas are managed by, or in conjunction with, the Trust. The NT owns about 182,000 ha in England and Wales of which public access is available to about half, and 2,633 ha in Northern Ireland. These holdings include some of the most beautiful vales, downs, moors, heath and coast in the UK. In many cases the Trusts own lands which are already designated for other purposes, so they work closely with the two Countryside Commissions and the relevant local authorities. The properties of the two National Trusts are immensely popular with the British public. In 1978, 6.2 million people visited National Trust lands and buildings (up from 3.1 million in 1970) while 1.3 million visited Scottish properties (up from 379,300 in 1970).

Farmers, Landowners and Volunteer Groups
22. It should be observed that individual farmers and landowners play their part both in enhancing the landscape and in enabling public access to their property. The proportion who conscientiously and willingly do this is not known though a recent survey (which may not be truly representative) undertaken by the Country Landowners Association (CLA) suggests that owners of medium to large estates are most enthusiastic. Mention must also be made of the much underpraised work of the county farming and wildlife advisory groups, plus the conservation corps and other volunteer groups which collectively do so much to save the countryside (see Gundry, 1981).

Summary
23. Nevertheless, the UK conservation lobby and the land managing interests both believe that more can and should be done to instil conservation-mindedness amongst all land managers and users. The present pattern of countryside designation in the UK is complex, inconsistent and ambiguous. Only England and Wales enjoy the same arrangements; elsewhere the picture varies greatly as do the powers of management. The picture is summarised in Table 5 (see p 192). In Chapter 7 paragraphs 18 to 28 of this report (pp 242 - 245), it is argued that this system is unnecessarily cumbersome and misleading and that a simpler, more uniform pattern of classification should be sought. Table 6 (see p 193) outlines the areas of land by country in the UK identified for conservation, recreational and scenic purposes.

Ecological Aspects of Habitat Change

24. One aim of this report is to document, as far as is known, both the nature and scale of ecological changes presently taking place in the UK countryside. This reflects the controversy currently raging over the apparently accelerating destruction of the conservation/amenity qualities of rural resources, a controversy which is now a matter of considerable political interest.

25. In response to a request by the author, members of the British Ecological Society (BES) have attempted to summarise what is known about species and habitat loss in modern Britain. 'Habitat' tends to have two meanings. Its biological definition is simply a place where a species exists. However, in social terms it refers to lands or waters on or in which live plants, insects, animals and birds which are scientifically, emotionally and aesthetically cherished.

26. The view of BES members is that while there are good records regarding species loss and habitat change for birds (kept by the British Trust for Ornithology and the Royal Society for the Protection of Birds — RSPB) plantlife (kept by the Botanical Society of the British Isles and the Biological Records Centre and monitored through the recently initiated National Vegetation Classification located at the University of

Country	Nature Conservation	Landscape Amenity
England, Wales	SSSI, NNR	National Park, Heritage Coast AONB
Scotland	SSSI, NNR	National Scenic Area
Northern Ireland	Area of Scientific Interest, NNR	AONB

Table 5. **Official countryside designation within the UK**

Lancaster), and some insects (notably butterflies as monitored by the Institute of Terrestrial Ecology — ITE), nevertheless the picture is a patchy one (though a fairly complete reference can be found in Hawksworth, 1974). Locally, some very good data exist (particularly in Scotland) but nationally no comprehensive appraisal can be made of what species and habitats may be disappearing. According to Mellanby (in Hawksworth, 1974, p 420) not enough is known about the factors limiting the occurrence of Britain's rarest species (often important barometers of environmental change). He claims that more research on these species is necessary as accurate knowledge of a species' requirement is essential before attempting to preserve it. *A systematic programme of ecologically effective monitoring (ie monitoring that takes into account the ecological implications of land use changes and management methods) is urgently required.* In this respect, the view prevails that the NCC and the ITE should take a lead, though this will require an injection of funds and trained personnel, since both organisations are desperately short of manpower and research/management budgets. This lead should be accompanied by complementary studies at the local level, tailored to suit local requirements, so that meaningful planning decisions and management agreements can be pursued.

27. Data on long-term trends in species numbers are even more patchy. The Rothamsted Insect Surveys have uncovered some valuable evidence on the population dynamics of certain insect species; there is some work on woodlands (eg Peterken and Harding, 1975; Ford *et al*, 1979; Peterken, 1981) and there are some long-term observations of birds by a variety of ornithological enthusiasts and organisations. But, again, no systematic or comprehensive picture is available. Yet, if a UK rural conservation programme is to have any proper meaning it is essential that it should be possible to predict changes in wildlife populations in relation to various land management activities. Some critics within the BES believe that conservation planners seem to spend too much of their time attempting to safeguard species and habitats only when these are threatened, and only concentrate upon a mosaic of key representative sites; conservation officials do not appear to be able to develop a more constructive understanding of the relationship between land-use change and ecological health. Any new initiative will require careful attention, for ecological modelling is a difficult, expensive

and time-consuming business fraught with scientific hazards. *It would be desirable to ensure that before any major new programme of ecological modelling is contemplated a lead institution or institutions establish priorities for investigation and comparable methodological approaches.*

28. The claim amongst both the official and the voluntary conservation movements (see, for example, King and Conroy, 1981; various issues of *ECOS*; and recent annual reports of the NCC) is that habitat change is frighteningly rapid both in the absolute sense of irreversible destruction and in the relative sense of ecological alteration through which remnants become worthless. One of the more startling revelations was the evidence presented by the NCC in their Seventh Annual Report (1980-1, pp 18-19) that at least 13 per cent of a random sample of 399 SSSIs had suffered significant damage to their features of interest. In terms of area of SSSIs affected, about half the damage was a result either of agricultural 'improvement' (drainage or ploughing) or of a cessation of traditional management practices. Fire and road and/or pipeline works accounted for another quarter of the area lost. What is giving rise to concern is the scale and accelerating pace of these changes and the seeming impotence of the conservation interests to stop this loss.

29. *As a matter of urgency, surveys must be completed to identify the extent and range of broad habitat types.* The lead agency here should be the NCC in collaboration with ITE and appropriate university departments. Experience by the NCC in England shows that a team of two experienced people can undertake a survey of all the habitats of a county within one year. So it would not be a major undertaking to survey the nation, though this would be confined initially to botanical information. This work should be coupled to existing NCC surveys of changes of SSSIs and to the Great Britain Nature Conservation Strategy. Ecological judgements must be based on sound knowledge, not informed estimates, of the total resource. If current work is not speeded up it will take 20 years to complete this task, by which time much irreparable damage might have occurred out of ignorance rather than mischief.

30. As to the causes of these changes there is no single culprit. The most popular candidate is agriculture, which has undergone a revolution in both technology and management over the past 30 years. But the trend towards coniferous afforestation and the removal of broadleaved woodland also has taken its toll (see Reed, 1982 for a summary of the effects of afforestation on bird life; Hill and Jones, 1979 for an account of the ecological effects of afforestation on rough grazings; and more generally Ford *et al*, 1979; Peterken, 1981). Another major cause of habitat destruction is the loss of farmland and semi-natural moors to urban and industrial development including roads, reservoirs and oil and electricity generating stations. This loss amounts to some 15,000 ha per year for England alone and could be twice that for the country as a whole (Strutt Committee, 1978; Council for the Protection of Rural

	England	Wales	Scotland	Northern Ireland	UK
National Parks (sq km)	9,500	4,100	N/A	N/A	N/A
% land area	7.2	19.7			
NSAs	N/A	N/A	10,015	N/A	N/A
% land area			12.1		
AONBs (sq km)	13,810	680		2,595	17,085
% land area	10.3	3.3		18.4	6.0
NNRs (ha)	29,364	9,955	94,321	3,000	136,640
number	83	32	56	38	171
SSSIs (ha)	655,091	136,276	570,037	N/A	1,364,404
number	2,606	435	836		3,877
Areas of Scientific	N/A	N/A	N/A		
Interest (ha)				74,000	
number				47	
Local nature reserves (ha)	5,870	880	1,169	66	7,985
number	49	9	3	5	66
County trust reserves (ha)	22,009	1,628	8,773	320	32,730
number	108	928	47	9	1,092
RSPB nature reserves (ha)	7,611	18,370	8,191	312	34,484
number	6	40	26	5	77
Nature trails (N)	153	97	98	21	369
NT properties:					
owned (ha)	133,900	29,500	44,450	2,633	210,483
covenanted (ha)	52,300	23,000	6,700	22,400	200
Country parks (ha)	16,413	2,399	2,484	N/A	21,296
number	130	17	10	7	164
Picnic sites (ha)	981	67	N/A	N/A	1,048
number (ha)	166	28			194
Long distance routes (km)	2,528	200	N/A	N/A	2,728
Water resources:				N/A	
*navigable canals (km)	1,596	16	50		1,602
*navigable rivers (km)	432	N/A	N/A	N/A	432
Other navigable					
waterways (km)	N/A	1,783	68	96	1,947

*Owned by the British Waterways Board
Note: these figures are derived from various sources and are based on the latest evidence available

Table 6. **Distribution of areas designated for conservation and natural beauty**

England, 1981). Industrial Activity must not be excluded from blame, however. Indeed, the BES is currently pressing the Royal Commission on Environmental Pollution to instigate a comprehensive survey of the effects of pollution on wildlife, a topic about which all too little is known, despite the good work done by the Pesticides Safety Precautions Scheme (PSPS).

31. From an ecological perspective, there are two viewpoints on habitat change. On the one hand, there are some species (usually the less common) which do not adapt to habitat alteration and which are likely to become extinct when their habitats are destroyed. For example, in 1970 the ITE estimated that there had been a 30 per cent reduction in the distribution of the rarer species of flowering plant and fern between 1930 and 1960, and that between 1900 and 1970 the number of very rare species had more than doubled (as reported in NCC, 1977). The ITE attributed 50 per cent of the changes in rare plants generally since 1800 to agriculture, 26 per cent to natural causes, 9 per cent to collecting, 8 per cent to changes in scrub and woodland management and 7 per cent to building or other changes. Where the habitats containing such species are destroyed it may prove impossible to recreate them. This is a controversial point because some ecologists accept that, through succession, 'new habitats' can produce 'new' ecological mixes. For example, natural colonisation of many mineral extraction sites, waste heaps, subsidence areas, railway cuttings, canals and reservoirs has produced numerous habitats of biological importance. Of particular interest are limestone quarries, chalk pits, clay workings, alkali waste, blast furnace slag and pulverised fuel ash. (See, for example, Chadwick and Goodman, 1975; Bradshaw, 1977; Gemmell, 1977; Johnson, 1978; Bradshaw and Chadwick, 1980 on the restoration of derelict industrial land and waste tips; and Davis, 1979 on the rehabilitation of industrial sites and chalk and limestone quarries.) Nevertheless, destroyed habitats do result in an irreplaceable loss of species diversity and the total area of recreated habitats is usually trivial compared with the scale of losses. *Thus at the very least the NCC and ITE must be encouraged to continue to identify rare species adapted to particular habitats and should be enabled to protect such habitats according to specified scientific priorities through acquisition and appropriate management.* However, these bodies should not lose sight of the great potential of abandoned industrial sites and other derelict land as refuges for important species of wildlife.

The Pattern of Habitat Change

32. The pattern of habitat alteration in recent years is an enormously varied one, in terms of both biotype and locations. The generalisations that follow (drawn largely from data supplied by the Chief Scientist's Team of the NCC) must be seen as indicative of the nature and scale of change only and as such they will inevitably mask important regional variations. There is very little specific data available for Northern Ireland. It also must be stressed that losses of environmental features only have meaning when quality is related to quantity. Not all hedges are important either for ecological or for landscape reasons, though neglected hedges can be ecologically very interesting; mismanaged hedges, however, are often ecologically worthless. Similarly, an even-aged heather moor may look as visually pleasing as a multiple-aged heather moor with its variety of micro-habitats, but it cannot be compared for its ecological interest. In general, public attention has been concentrated more on changes in lowland areas due to the possibly greater incompatibilities between the demands for productive agriculture and certain nature conservation and landscape amenity needs and because of more widely publicised research. But the *Uplands Landscapes Study* recently published by the Countryside Commission showed rapid changes in the uplands — mainly caused by afforestation, abandonment of marginal farms, more intensive agricultural management, field enlargement and the loss or dereliction of many characteristic landscape features (Mabey, 1981).

Hedgerows and Amenity Trees

33. In 1962, there were approximately one million km of hedgerows in Britain encompassing 200,000 ha, an area greater than all nature reserves at that time. Between 1945 and 1970, it is believed that about 1 per cent of hedgerows (some 8,000 km) disappeared each year amounting to a cumulative loss of 225,000 km of hedgerows (King and Conroy, 1981). Since then, the rate of loss has slowed, but hedgerow disappearance continues. Loss of hedgerows, depending upon the history of their maintenance, can mean loss of an important wildlife sanctuary at the field margin; the effect is greatly amplified if nearby deciduous woodland is also removed. About 280 species of plant are particularly associated with hedgerows. It has been suggested that further hedge destruction would relatively quickly affect the total population of about 20 species very seriously, a further 20 species quite seriously and another 30 to 40 species to a marked extent (Pollard, Hooper and Moore, 1974). Concern over hedgerow loss amongst the conservation-minded public is now so great that a private member's bill was recently but unsuccessfully prepared to protect certain prominent hedges through statutory controls. Amenity trees are the characteristic hardwoods associated with hedgerows and fields, many of which date back to the enclosure period of 1750 to 1850. Many are now overmature. Control of removal can be exercised through tree preservation orders and felling licences, though these should be more clearly designed to maintain an acceptable range of amenity trees than is the case at present.

While in some areas considerable replanting is being carried out (mainly through voluntary schemes and grants from the Countryside Commission to local authorities and to individual landowners) this does not compensate for the loss of mature trees. There appears to be no systematic survey of post-planting care of new amenity trees, though in some counties this is being done. However, the Forestry Commission is looking at the follow up management of new woodlands. Preliminary results for some of the lowland counties are most encouraging for the replacement of new trees and the natural regeneration of small broadleaved woodland. *Nevertheless, the whole question of post-planting care requires more attention, probably through regular surveying by local voluntary organisations in co-operation with the local authorities and the Countryside Commissions.*

Wetlands

34. Wetlands range from estuaries, saltmarsh and fresh-water meadows where the water table is at or above ground level, to peat bogs and raised bogs where water tables vary slightly but are usually at ground level, to drained marshes where water tables are normally down to about 75 cm below ground level. Some of these last areas provide seasonal pasture yet can be of great ornithological interest if allowed to flood in the winter. Many of these water meadows, of considerable botanical and entomological interest because of a long, unbroken record of traditional management, are now threatened by improved drainage and/or by the addition of artificial fertilisers. Although some of these areas are designated as SSSIs or voluntary trust reserves, by no means all of the important sites are so protected, though their existence is probably known to the relevant county naturalists trusts. *A proper inventory of all ecologically important wetland sites should be drawn up to supplement the excellent coverage already provided in the Nature Conservation Review.*

Lowland Bogs

35. The lowland bog is also an endangered habitat. Once commonplace in ill-drained areas, lowland bog habitats have been reduced to less than 15 per cent of their estimated occurrence 100 years ago throughout northern England and Scotland. The current demand for horticultural peat has been a major cause of this loss in recent years. Since planning controls do not always apply to peat cutting, much of this has been undertaken in a manner that destroys the ecological integrity of the bog community without anyone being informed beforehand. Many of the remaining bogs are SSSIs; as things now stand their future may depend upon the ability of the NCC to compensate landowners for loss of potential income should further peat cutting and drainage be stopped.

Chalk grassland

36. Until the late eighteenth century, vast areas of chalk downland were used for sheep pasturage: the close cropping animals encouraged a remarkably varied mixture of grasses and herbs. Nowadays, such lands have either reverted to scrub because sheep grazing

using traditional low stocking levels is less economic and rabbit populations have been depleted, or they are fertilised and reseeded for more productive grazing, or they are ploughed. Between 1966 and 1980, some 21 per cent of this grassland disappeared: of this, 61 per cent was due to arable conversion and 32 per cent to the development of scrub in the absence of grazing. Many downland SSSIs have been ruined owing to widespread application of fertilisers sprayed from both ground and air: in Wiltshire 29 out of 50 SSSIs have suffered significant loss of scientific interest in recent years as a result of agricultural 'improvement' practices which, until 1980, were not notifiable in advance to the NCC.

Heathland

37. Heathland, like bogs, is a biotype that does not need to be eliminated to be ecologically destroyed. Fragmentation is as much a harbinger of death as total conversion. It has been claimed that, by 1990, no heathland will be left in Dorset except that contained in designated reserves and SSSIs, and, in the latter, protection is by no means guaranteed. The Dorset heaths are of particular interest for they provide the major sites of the sand lizard, the smooth snake and the Dartford warbler, all national rarities. Yet today, the heathland is reduced to 15 per cent of its 1760 figure and about half of its 1962 acreage. Heathland loss in Hampshire and East Anglia is of a similar magnitude again mainly through arable conversion, though afforestation and different grazing practices can also be damaging.

Moorland

38. The ecological and scenic importance of the artificially created upland moorland is very great. Because of improved drainage and reseeding techniques, much of this area is now convertible into coniferous forest and more productive pasture. The loss of this habitat (for scenic and ecological interest) has recently been estimated at 5,000 ha annually for England and Wales alone, or about one-third of the area at which farmland is being lost to urban use (Parry et al, 1981). Parry and his colleagues also calculated that about 46,000 ha, or 10 per cent of all moorland and roughland in National Parks, have been lost to reclamation since 1950. Most of this loss is in moorland core, a finding which led the Government to require National Park authorities to publish maps of all important moorland and review them annually. Under section 42 of the Wildlife and Countryside Act 1981, ministers issue moorland protection orders under special circumstances. While there has been much public outcry over the loss of moorland in recent years, notably in Exmoor (Porchester, 1977; MacEwen and MacEwen, 1982), one must not lose sight of the fact that moorlands are degraded ecosystems and so require special attention if they are to survive in their present state. In this context, the work by the North York Moors National Park moorlands research programme is helpful in indicating what can happen to moorlands as a result of various landscape changes (Statham, 1982). Gimingham (1972) is also a valuable reference. In Scotland, evidence presented to the Commons Select Committee on Scottish Affairs (1972) summarised research into the management problems of upland moors (see also McVean and Lockie, 1969), though informed BES correspondents allege that relatively few of the recommendations of that report have been acted upon. Like many of the threatened habitats described in this section, moorlands are the product of generations of a particular form of agricultural husbandry and sporting practices. Their survival can only be guaranteed if the land managers are persuaded · to continue their traditional grazing and land use practices such as controlled heath burning on grouse moors.

Ancient Deciduous Woodland

39. Remnants of the natural vegetation of lowland Britain support a remarkably rich fauna and flora which owe their survival to the continuity of woodland cover over many centuries. Such woodlands have a very special significance for nature conservation, yet the NCC estimates that between 30 and 50 per cent of all this remaining woodland has been lost since 1947, an extent of loss that took 400 years to complete prior to 1947. The NCC believes that many of these changes have been brought about by conversion to conifer plantations or to unmanaged grazing, though more comprehensive field surveys are required.

Limestone Pavements

40. Limestone is used for established rural activities such as the building of dry-stone walls and for modern activities such as rock gardening. Damage to limestone pavements is regarded as serious, since they support a very rich and all but irreplaceable plant life. How serious this loss is, however, remains a matter of conjecture. Usher (1980) has sought to apply the criteria for determining conservation value to some limestone pavements in the Yorkshire Dales National Park. The current anxiety over the floristic value of limestone pavements is reflected in the new powers available to relevant ministers to enable them to issue limestone pavement protection orders under section 34 of the Wildlife and Countryside Act 1981.

Habitat Loss and Landscape Change in Perspective

41. Not all change in the countryside has destroyed wildlife or scenic beauty. Already there are signs that new habitats, both in forestry operations and reclamation schemes, are establishing new niches for wildlife. Nevertheless, recent publicity over the scale and the rapidity of habitat changes and species losses has alarmed many people who had not previously seen the picture as a whole. These statistics are also worrying many ecologists who frankly do not yet know what effect fragmentation and mutilation may have on dispersal of species and eventual equilibrium numbers of species on different areas of land. Indeed, the rate of change may be too great to permit many species to adapt. The necessary interconnecting scientific investigations are yet to be done. Yet it would be foolhardy to

await the results of all necessary research. The loss of these features is far too serious to permit any further delay. *Since society has created both the economic forces and the accompanying fragmented attitudes and knowledge which shape the modern pattern of rural resource utilisation, so society should be able to create a new mix of incentives and penalties, coupled with a greater depth of awareness and moral concern, to counter these trends.* However, a clearly defined strategy based on scientific understanding, total safeguarding of key conservation sites, various mixes of conservation and development in other areas, all in the context of Britain's global commitments, **will require:**

(a) A basic knowledge of ecology and the principles and practices of conservation management amongst *all* rural resource-users: farmers, foresters, planners, developers and ordinary citizens. This, in turn, will mean that *the curricula in agricultural and forestry colleges will need to be broadened to improve both the understanding of basic ecological concepts and the practices of conservation. Likewise, the planning profession will require these elements in its training.* On the other hand, it is also important that conservation bodies and ordinary citizens are made aware of the principles and economics that lie behind agriculture and forestry and the water and mining industries which should lead to better mutual understanding.

(b) Detailed scientific investigation of the mix of species and habitats that require total protection or special management for their survival. This is vital to justify, both on scientific and moral grounds, any new measures (such as enlarged funds for acquisition, or new patterns of incentives for management agreements) for safeguarding such areas.

(c) *A fresh look at the scientific and aesthetic values of new or recreated habitats and landscapes from derelict, relict or degraded lands and waters,* notably in the context of their long-term outlook. This work must be done with patient care and attention, for the rewards may only become evident a generation or two hence.

(d) *A reconsideration of the implications of increasing food, timber and mineral productivity from the rural resources of the UK in the light of Britain's trading obligations and demands upon the resource sustainability from exporting countries.* This reconsideration may have to take place in a series of stages, taking into account the various environmental and socio-economic implications of different productivity mixes both at home and abroad over periods of, say, 20 years. It is important that a future Conservation and Development Programme for the UK be set in terms of a commitment to international trade on the one hand or self-sufficiency on the other. Over the course of time it is possible that the balance of this commitment will shift from the former approach (which is now prevalent) to the latter perspective, depending in part upon how Third World countries act upon their own strategies for survival. This point is developed further in Chapter 7, paragraph 6 (p 239) and in Chapter 8, Recommendation Group 6 (p 253) of this report.

References

BORLEY, L. 1982. Tourism means jobs. Paper presented to Royal Society of Arts Conference on 'Town and Country: Home and Work'. London, English Tourist Board.

BRADSHAW, A D. 1977. Conservation problems in the future. *Proceedings of the Royal Society of London B, 197,* 77-96.

BRADSHAW, A D and CHADWICK, M J. 1980. The restoration of land. Oxford, Blackwell Scientific Publications.

CENTRAL OFFICE OF INFORMATION. 1980. Agriculture in Britain. Reference Pamphlet 43. London, HMSO.

CENTRE FOR AGRICULTURAL STRATEGY. 1980. Strategy for the UK forest industry. CAS Report 6. Reading, Centre for Agricultural Strategy, University of Reading.

CHADWICK, M J and GOODMAN, G T. 1975. The ecology of resource degradation and renewal. Oxford, Blackwell Scientific Publications.

COMMONS SELECT COMMITTEE ON SCOTTISH AFFAIRS. 1972. Land resource use in Scotland. HC 511. London, HMSO.

COUNCIL FOR THE PROTECTION OF RURAL ENGLAND. 1981. Planning — friend or foe? London, Council for the Protection of Rural England.

COUNTRYSIDE COMMISSION. 1979. Digest of countryside recreation statistics 1978. CCP 86. Cheltenham, Countryside Commission.

COUNTRYSIDE COMMISSION. 1980. Areas of outstanding natural beauty: a policy statement, p 3. CCP 141. Cheltenham, Countryside Commission.

DAVIS, B N K. 1979. Chalk and limestone quarries as wildlife habitats. *Minerals and the Environment, 1,* 48-56.

ENGLISH TOURIST BOARD. 1981. Planning for tourism in England, p7. London, English Tourist Board.

FORD, E G, MALCOLM, D C and ATHERSON, J. (editors). 1979. The ecology of even-aged forest plantations. Cambridge, Institute of Terrestrial Ecology.

FORESTRY COMMISSION. 1977. The wood production outlook in Britain — a review. Edinburgh, The Forestry Commission.

GEMMELL, R P. 1977. Colonisation of industrial wasteland. London, Edward Arnold.

GIMINGHAM, C H. (editor). 1972. Ecology of heathlands. London, Chapman Hall.

GUNDRY, E. 1981. Helping hands: a guide to conservation. London, Unwin Paperbacks.

HAWKSWORTH, D L. (editor). 1974. The changing fauna and flora of Britain. London, Systematics Association and Academic Press.

HILL, M D and JONES, E W. 1979. Vegetation changes resulting from afforestation of rough grazing in Caeo Forest. *Journal of Ecology, 66*, 433-456.

HIMSWORTH, K H. 1980. A review of areas of outstanding natural beauty. CCP 140. Cheltenham, Countryside Commission.

JOHNSON, M S. 1978. Land reclamation and the botanical significance of some former mining and manufacturing sites in Britain. *Environmental Conservation, 5*, 223-228.

KING, A and CONROY, C. 1981. Paradise lost? The destruction of Britain's wildlife habitats. London, Friends of the Earth.

MABEY, R. 1981. The common ground: a place for nature in Britain's future. London, Hutchinson.

MACEWEN, A and MACEWEN, M. 1982. National Parks — conservation or cosmetics? London, George Allen and Unwin.

MAFF/NFU. 1981. Energy in Agriculture. London, MAFF.

MARGULES, C and USHER, M B. 1981. Criteria used in assessing wildlife conservation potential: a review. *Biological Conservation, 21*, 71-109.

MARSH, J S and MACLAREN, D. 1981. Regional impact of the community agricultural policy: UK report, Table II, 7. Brussels, Commission of the European Communities.

MATTINGLY, A. 1982. Recreation and access to the countryside. London, Ramblers' Association.

MCVEAN, D N and LOCKIE, J D. (editors). 1969. Ecology and land use in upland Scotland. Edinburgh, Edinburgh University Press.

MINISTRY OF AGRICULTURE, FISHERIES AND FOOD. 1979. Farming and the nation. Cmnd 7458. London, HMSO.

MINISTRY OF AGRICULTURE, FISHERIES AND FOOD. 1982. Annual review of agriculture, p 19. Cmnd 8491. London, HMSO.

MOORE, N. 1982. What parts of Britain's countryside must be preserved? *New Scientist, 28 May*, 550-551.

NATURE CONSERVANCY COUNCIL. 1977. Nature conservation and agriculture. London, Nature Conservancy Council.

NORTHFIELD, L. (Chairman). 1979. Report of the Committee of Inquiry into the Acquisition and Occupancy of Agricultural Land, pp 32-34. London, HMSO.

PARRY, M, BRUCE, P and HARKNESS, C. 1981. The plight of Britain's moorlands. *New Scientist, 28 May*, 550-551.

PETERKEN, G F. (editor). 1981. Woodland conservation and management. London, Chapman and Hall.

PETERKEN, G F and HARDING, P T. 1975. Woodland conservation in eastern England: comparing effects of changes in three study areas. *Biological Conservation, 8*, 279-298.

POLLARD, E, HOOPER, M D and MOORE, N W. 1974. Hedges. London, Collins.

PORCHESTER, L. 1977. A study of Exmoor. London, HMSO.

RATCLIFFE, D. (editor). 1977. Nature conservation review. Cambridge, Cambridge University Press.

REED, T M. 1982. Birds and afforestation. *ECOS, 3 (1)*, 7-10.

ROSE, C and GROVE, R. 1982. On 'representative' without 'protection'. *ECOS, 3 (1)*, 30-32.

RICKARD, S. 1982. Agriculture and employment, p5. Paper presented to the Royal Society of Arts Conference of 'Town and Country: Home and Work'. London, National Farmers Union.

ROYAL COMMISSION ON ENVIRONMENTAL POLLUTION. 1979. Agriculture and pollution seventh report. Cmnd 7644. London, HMSO.

SCOTTISH LEISURE SURVEY. 1981. Edinburgh, Scottish Tourist Board.

STATHAM, D C. 1982. The future of the moorland. Helmsley, Yorks. North York Moors National Park Authority.

STRUTT, N. (Chairman). 1978. Agriculture and the countryside. Report of the Advisory Council for Agriculture and Horticulture in England and Wales. London, HMSO.

USHER, M B. 1980. An assessment of conservation values within a large site of special scientific interest in North Yorkshire. *Field Studies, 5*, 323-328.

CHAPTER 4

A CONSERVATION/ DEVELOPMENT PROGRAMME FOR UK AGRICULTURE

Introduction

1. Throughout history, land has always been a peculiar form of capital. It is inherently scarce and fixed in place; its ownership confers a certain social prestige and economic security. While short-term returns may be modest and sometimes uncertain, ownership of land provides a secure long-term economic investment. It is hardly surprising, therefore, that land ownership generally, and agriculture in particular, have long been associated with social influence and political power. Norton-Taylor (1982) reinforces this point with statistical information. After the First World War, many ennobled leaders of industry bought large estates, and land ownership is an important feature in the private assets of many leading national figures of finance, industry and politics. It should also come as no surprise that land is regarded as a peculiar mix of private right and public obligation by both owner and tenant. The right to do what one likes with one's own land is a deeply cherished ideal, but, in many cases, that right has been linked to a social duty to safeguard an element of public interest in the present and future qualities of land. It is this mix of private right and public responsibility which lies at the heart of a conservation/development plan and which is so central to the notion of trust that pervades this report.

2. In mid-Victorian times, some 7,000 landowners owned about 80 per cent of the nation's land; today, about 250,000 individuals own nearly 60 per cent of England and Wales (Newby, 1980). It has been estimated that 1,500 individuals own one-third of England and Wales, and 100 landlords own one-quarter of Scotland (Norton-Taylor, 1982). Until the turn of the century, politics and landownership were totally intermingled, with both Parliament and Cabinet dominated by the landowning classes. The political influence and social importance of major landowning individuals is still evident today. The major three interest groups representing landowners and farmers, namely (i) the Country Landowners Association (CLA), (ii) the Scottish Landowners Federation, and (iii) the National Farmers Union (NFU) and the National Farmers Union of Scotland (NFUS), are widely respected for their thoroughness and professional expertise in getting their views across to the people who count (for an analysis of the tactics of the NFU, see Self and Storing, 1974).

3. While modern agriculture in the UK is a relatively

prosperous industry (but with considerable regional variation), this economic good fortune is fairly recent. Throughout much of the period 1873 to 1945, UK agriculture suffered a series of economic depressions, shorn of investment capital and swamped by cheap food imports from the Empire. One outcome was a long period of relatively few owner-occupiers (in 1936 over two-thirds of farmland in England and Wales was tenanted). Another consequence is that the landscapes and conservation sites, which are nowadays so highly valued, are in part the product of labour-intensive husbandry, of low productivity agriculture and in part the outcome of investment in attractive landscape design by some of the wealthy landowning classes. It is a paradoxical combination of affluence and poverty that has helped to shape the UK agricultural landscape.

4. Until the late 1940s, few people saw anything other than harmony between agriculture and conservation. For example, John Dower (1945), the architect of the national park, singled out agriculture as a key ingredient in maintaining landscape beauty. He wrote: 'Efficient farming is a key requirement in National Park areas; and, to be efficient, farming must be given generous scope for changes in methods and intensity of cultivation, cropping and stocking'. Indeed, the Scott Committee (1942) sought to encourage rural economic renaissance through profitable agriculture and the provision of essential services and small industry to otherwise deprived rural communities. Only a handful of people at that time saw that a transformed and highly efficient agriculture might not foster the economic interest of remote rural areas and that it might be prejudicial to conservation interests as broadly defined.

5. Both world wars demonstrated the strategic vulnerability of the UK to food imports, and displayed the amazing potential for vastly increased output when farmers are given the appropriate incentives. It was politically unpopular to place land-use changes arising from agriculture and forestry under the public controls over private property interests which were enshrined in the Town and Country Planning Act of 1947. To this day, land-use alterations, associated with both agriculture and forestry, remain essentially free of planning controls (though there are some controls over agricultural buildings). It was also accepted that, if agriculture was to prosper and food supplies were to be plentiful and stable, the free market had to be

manipulated in favour of guaranteeing prices to farmers. This was one of the key features of the Agriculture Act of 1947, an Act which also established a network of professional advice aimed at improving agricultural productivity.

6. As indicated in Chapter 3, pargraphs 2 to 5 of this report (pp 185 - 186), modern agriculture is a highly mechanised industry, dependent on vast amounts of energy and capital. The degree to which these resources are exploited depends upon such factors as climate, topography, soil conditions, drainage, cash flow and capital indebtedness, the nature of ownership and entrepreneurial skills. Successive UK governments have supported policies aimed at providing adequate and secure supplies of food at reasonably stable prices. In 1981, the average British household spent 20 per cent of its income on food and drink, about one-quarter of the proportion spent by its urban counterpart in developing countries. Apart from temporary disruptions caused mainly by adverse weather, plentiful food supply is taken for granted by the British public and it is generally assumed that there would be political trouble should this no longer be the case. A conservation/development plan for UK agriculture must guarantee an adequate supply of home-produced food, but equally must ensure that this is produced in a manner that does not use up unnecessary energy and environmental resources and public money, safeguards the aesthetic qualities of the countryside, and is integrated into community enterprise initiatives.

Modern Agriculture and Ecological Sustainability

7. An important theme of the WCS was that managing the land without regard to long-term ecological sustainability would result in economic as well as environmental calamity. So what aspects of modern agriculture, if any, are adversely affecting the fertility and structure of soil in this country? These were last studied in some detail by the Agriculture and Horticulture Advisory Council 12 years ago (Strutt, 1970), when the Council concluded that there was no evidence to suggest that inherent (as opposed to natural) soil fertility was being reduced as a result of intensive farming and the use of chemical fertilisers. The Council was more concerned about the effects of heavy machinery and tight cropping sequences on unstable soils, particularly those with poor drainage. It recommended that more attention be given to the need for improved drainage and the proper maintenance of existing drainage on all soils. It also warned of the dangers of overstocking in areas of high rainfall but was unable to find evidence to suggest that the use of chemical pesticides has any deleterious effect either on soil fertility or on soil structure. However, throughout its report, the Council emphasised the lack of reliable research data on many of the points examined. Even today, too little is known about the ability of pesticides to attach themselves chemically to organic matter in the soil and the consequences for

crop yield losses many years after application. The Committee was careful to stress that more attention should be given to regional variations in soil conditions and appropriate management practices. More recently, Stewart (1981) has commented that the loam soils, which cover about 75 per cent of the UK, maintain their granular structure, vital for good drainage, largely because of the agency of plant roots and earthworms. He notes: 'This type of aggregate structure, though stable to the impact of raindrops, cannot be other than vulnerable to collapse, returning to a compact, totally micropore state, prone to waterlogging, if abused physically by excessive cultivation, treading or wheel traffic'. The work of the Strutt Committee should be brought up to date, and should include evidence from organic farming and other research groups with long experience of the effects of chemical additions in soil structure and productivity.

8. Members of the BES note that even today there is still insufficient evidence to make an adequate assessment of the long-term ecological sustainability of modern British agriculture (see Chapter 3, paragraphs 26 and 27, pp 191 - 192 of this report). At best, only episodic information is available. For example, from limited experiments, it seems that there may be a long-term deleterious effect on grass swards (particularly in hill-farming areas) and possibly other crops if chemical fertiliser is used to the exclusion of organic fertiliser. The optimum balance between the needs of agriculture and conservation of herb-rich pastures can be obtained by using organic fertilisers or nitrogen-free chemical fertilisers (Grime, 1979; Fitter, 1982). Where ecologically important pastures are to be kept botanically rich, farmers should be discouraged from applying nitrogenous fertiliser (see Thurston, 1969, for a review of the Rothamsted Park Grass experiment). But not all change is necessarily detrimental in ecological terms. For example, Gray (1979) reports that land reclaimed from saltmarsh can, if skilfully managed, support a unique and interesting assemblage of plants and animals. Needless to say, if reclamation is not skilfully done, impoverishment of species will occur. For example, the vegetation of much of the reclaimed saltmarsh of the Wash consists of only five to six species with the loss of a number of characteristic plants. Thus, representative sites must be safeguarded and, where reclamation does take place, ecologically important small scale habitats protected.

9. Equally uncertain is the evidence of the long-term effects of insecticides and herbicides on birds, plant and insect life which are not regarded as pests. Following the scares over the loss of certain raptors and other wildlife species as a result of the uncontrolled use of pesticides, the PSPS was established in 1957 as a non-statutory but formal agreement between eight Government Departments and member companies of the British Agrochemicals Association and the British Pest Control Association. In 1970, the Scheme was extended to Northern Ireland and in 1975 it was enlarged to cover all non-agricultural use of pesticides. The essence of the Scheme is that manufacturers, distributors and importers

who propose to introduce new pesticides or new uses for pesticides voluntarily seek prior official agreement and submit appropriate scientific information to Departments who, in turn, are advised by the Advisory Committee in Pesticides supported by its Scientific Sub-committees. These Committees make recommendations to appropriate Government Departments, both as to the suitability of the product to do the job intended without undue environmental side effects (the notification procedure), and as to how each chemical formulation should be applied and on what crops (the clearance procedure) (see Royal Commission on Environmental Pollution, 1979). Nearly all products then pass through the Agriculture Chemicals Approval Scheme, which is also voluntary but which forms the basis of official guidance as to choice and use of pesticides. In general, it seems that a combination of much greater research and development by agrochemical manufacturers into the environmental aspects of new chemicals, plus the cooperation of the NCC and the various voluntary organisations interested in the subject, have led to a significant reduction in bird deaths over the past 20 years, removing the threat of wholesale species loss. However, the PSPS is a voluntary scheme and some chemicals might slip through the net (though it is arguable whether a statutory scheme would close all the loopholes). Also, any scheme relies on farmers using products exactly as labelled and misuse can result in unfortunate ecological consequences. The recent decline of certain raptor species is a matter of much concern to the RSPB and other conservation bodies. Poorly applied spraying in unsuitable weather conditions can result in spraydrift damaging non-target insects in nearby woods and fields. Like the perennial problem of stubble burning, an unquantified but possibly small number of thoughtless accidents can give both the farmer and the management practice a bad public image.

10. It is tempting to conclude that better information and advice will overcome the problem of pesticide misuse, but this ignores the fact that the ecological connections between pesticide applications and biological communities are not known, and that many farmers have become trapped in a treadmill of increased pesticide usage (Tait, 1980). This is because, no matter how specific the target, almost all chemicals have adverse reactions on benign species of plants, insects and birds, whose subsequent loss opens the way for pests (some of which become resistant to certain chemical formulations) to become more ecologically dominant. The trouble is that the ecology of the 'natural' state of benign species is generally not known before the disturbances caused by pesticide applications are observed. Because most ecologists support the Elton principle that more complex ecosystems are generally more stable, they are not happy about the growing dependence by farmers on the 'chemical economy'. The prestigious Royal Commission on Environmental Pollution (1979) encapsulated this alarm in its comment: 'Pesticides are by design biologically active and hence hazardous chemicals; however stringent the tests applied to them, there is the possibility of unforeseen and unforeseeable effects. They should be

used with care, in the minimum quantities needed for effective pest control, and increasing usage should be questioned. The wise use of pesticides is not ensured by the restraining effect of cost'.

11. The Commission took the view that official policy should be changed to one of reducing pesticide use to a minimum consistent with agricultural objectives. The Commission was particularly concerned about the development of resistance in pests and favoured a more balanced and integrated pest management strategy. Unfortunately, the use of larger amounts of more target-specific chemicals undermines the introduction of better crop management techniques. Furthermore, unless the advisory services are appropriately trained and committed, they cannot assist farmers to improve their pest control practices. Corbett (1981) proposes a shift in funding research to large grants to competent teams of applied scientists rather than small grants to individual researchers. From a psychological point of view, Tait (1981) has shown that farmers in eastern England tend to apply pesticides on brassicas even when they know there may be ecological dangers. Farmers claim they are almost forced into doing this because of the economic consequences of crop failure or blemishes in appearance. The cost of additional spraying is minuscule compared to the economic loss of a crop that cannot be marketed. Because both the public and the food regulation agencies demand (or appear to demand) high cosmetic standards, integrated pest management methods are often jettisoned in favour of 'safe' pesticide applications that ensure an undamaged crop (Corbett, 1981). This probably accounts for the growing cost and use of pesticides in UK agriculture. Weed control alone cost farmers £117m in 1982 yet there is no evidence that any major pest has been successfully controlled. Indeed, the problem of mutating pest species rendering them resistant to known chemical sprays is a serious one. There is no doubt that the barriers to reduced pesticide usage are so formidable — encompassing commercial commitments, conservative attitudes amongst users and regulators, laws that encourage high cosmetic standards in food, and an imbalanced cost-benefit relationship favouring increased pesticide usage — that a *major effort on a number of fronts will be required if the pattern of pesticide use is to be altered*. Meanwhile, ecologists will have to redouble their efforts to demonstrate that *ad hoc* chemical control can prove both agriculturally and ecologically counter-productive in the longer run and chemical manufacturers will have to show more explicitly, to both official and independent bodies, that their products are environmentally safe for employees, consumers, the soil and the nation's wildlife. Otherwise, attempts to persuade farmers to adopt practices that harness those elements of the crop ecosystem which are sympathetic to the natural control of crop competitors will meet with stout resistance. In this context, the work of Potts and Vickerman (1975) is instructive. They have looked at the effects of fungicides and insecticides on cereal aphid populations and predator arthropods. Their pioneering work indicates that *ad hoc* use of pesticides can result in significant kills of aphid and predator

species (which may result in explosive populations of aphids), and in the loss of partridge chicks.

12. Evidence on the ecological and health effects of fertiliser application is also inconclusive, but there is more cause for concern here than there is regarding the ecological and health effects of pesticide usage. One of the main danger substances is nitrate which gets into agricultural drainage from field run-off (where inorganic nitrogen has been added), from slurry (especially from the discharge from concentrated livestock units, another feature of modern agricultural practice), and from mineralisation of nitrogen in soils notably following conversion from pastoral to arable use. The actual concentrations of nitrogen depend upon soil type, topography, drainage characteristics, agricultural use and fertiliser application, but in some parts of the UK nitrate levels in the water supply equal or exceed the 50 mg per litre concentration recommended as safe by the World Health Organisation (WHO). Indeed, the National Water Council estimate that this level has been reached either continuously or intermittently at over 100 public water sources in the UK. At these concentrations there is a danger of young babies suffering from the blood oxygen deficiency disease methaemoglobinaemia. In addition, application of inorganic nitrogen to soils can result in concentrations of nitrate in leafy vegetables, such as spinach and beet, sufficiently high to be possibly dangerous for some exposed people (especially young people), though research results are not clear as to whether appropriate mixes of organic manures can lower these concentrations. Clearly this is an area where more research is required. Eutrophication of waterways (which is a condition of excessive nutrients stimulating the growth of phytoplankton [algae] over macrophytes [broadleaved plants]) is not caused so much through nitrate concentrations as through high phosphate levels; by reducing the concentration of phosphates much of the adverse ecological consequences can be controlled. Phosphates do not enter watercourses so much from fertiliser (especially from grasslands) as from human and animal wastes discharged in a concentrated form from sewage treatment works or slurry pits. *The technology for removing phosphates from sewage treatment works is now well tested and should be used where conditions demand.*

13. Fertiliser manufacturers are currently investigating how to manufacture chemical fertilisers which break down in the soil much more efficiently. This work should be encouraged. Nevertheless, there is scope for increasing the use of organic manure. Recent advances in crop genetics and biotechnology can be compatible with ecologically sustainable agriculture. One example of this approach is that followed by the Real Growth Farmers (RGF) who claim to invest less than half the £40 to £100 per ha spent by high energy-chemical using farmers on approved preparations which will not harm the organic nature of the soil. RGF embraces 80 farms covering 4,000 ha in the UK, producing foods — flour, muesli, dried fruit, apple juice and potatoes. They are determined to show how an organic-chemical mix of inputs sustains the long-term health of the soil, even though in the short-term their prices are 10 per cent higher than those for conventionally produced foods.

14. A recent study of the economics of organic farming practices compared to conventional farming (Vine and Bateman, 1982) concludes that, although practices vary greatly, organic farming is less profitable by standard economic measures. Although inputs of fossil fuel energy and chemicals were lower, outputs were lower still, both in quantitative terms and when calculated as net farm income. The differences were sufficiently large to suggest that organic farming would not expand unless prices for both inputs and outputs were altered to take account of the long-term resource conserving benefits of organic farming and the ecological advantages for the soil. The study also revealed that organic farming did not employ more people per unit of output than its conventional counterpart, but found that the official advisory services were not providing suitable assistance to the organic farmers, nor did the officials appear to be learning from many of the beneficial aspects of organic husbandry which would be of use to conventional farmers. These results however must be regarded with caution. The investigation covered only a small number of unrepresentative farms and lasted for only a year. Organic growers estimate that it takes over five years for soil conditions to stabilise following a switch from inorganic to organic fertilisation methods. They claim that, after an initial period of lower yields and disease problems, yields are above average compared with conventional farms in their locality with fewer pest and disease problems. Economics should not be the only criterion of the advantages of organic farming, nor can it be assumed that the UK can or should afford to rely on expensive imports to provide the benefits that organic manures can also produce. Organic farming interests claim that organic husbandry is not only vital to long-term sustained production but should encourage more jobs and promote a more 'steward-like' approach to land management. Without appropriate financial encouragement and better advice there is a danger that organic agriculture will not be in an exemplary position to influence conventional agriculture with more ecologically sustainable practices.

15. Another area of controversy is the apparent inefficient use of energy in agriculture (see Leach, 1975). Attempts have been made to demonstrate that, for some crops, food output in energy terms is lower than the energy inputs required to produce, store, transport and market it. For example, a recent MAFF/NFU (1981) report has calculated that the energy output/energy input ratios for the production sector alone vary from 3.12 for wheat (ie three times as much energy is available in wheat as went into the production of it) through 0.57 for milk to 0.05 for tomatoes grown in a heated glasshouse. While this may be true, energy analyses of this kind have relatively little bearing on the costs and benefits of food production and consumption and only in terms of conventional economics and the narrow definition of price in relation to value. In the UK, only 3.6 per cent of natural energy is consumed

directly by the agricultural industry. If food processing, storage and transport are included, the total requirement rises to 16 per cent of total energy use. Of direct agricultural energy inputs, 32 per cent was in the form of fuel and electricity, 28 per cent in fertiliser, 12 per cent in machinery manufacture and 16 per cent in off-farm foodstuff processing. According to MAFF (1982), of a gross input of £5.2bn absorbed by British agriculture in 1981, only £326m (6 per cent) was spent on fuel and oil. The MAFF/NFU report provides a number of suggestions for energy conservation in agriculture which would reduce energy usage by up to 30 per cent, but the authors stress that, because inefficient energy usage often results in profitable productivity gains, few farmers are tempted to conserve energy. The problem of energy conservation in agriculture will have to be tackled in the context of price supports for inputs and outputs and through a pricing policy that reflects the scarcity of non-renewable resource-use if any real progress is to be made. Any conservation/development programme for modern agriculture must also consider how energy waste can be converted into an energy gain. The use of biogas, biomass conversion and a switch to less energy-intensive inputs all hold possibilities that are already technologically possible. Price incentives, together with better information and advice, should help, but a concerted effort will be required.

16. An important objective for ecological sustainability is to relate land-use management to ecological and other environmental constraints. This is the basis of the technique of land-use assessment and land capability classification which have been developed over many years. It would be helpful if ecologists and soil scientists continue to improve classification and assessment techniques. (For a good recent example for Scotland see Thomas and Coppock, 1981.) A useful proposal (see Table 7) for the Scottish Highlands has been advanced by McVean and Lockie (1969) (though this approach is currently being improved upon).

17. This type of classification does not necessarily dictate land-use, but at least it provides a guide to the ecological and other environmental dangers should land-use guidelines be transgressed for other reasons. Moor burning, for example, is now a widespread practice in upland moors, but in wet areas it tends to eliminate heather in favour of its competitors: deer hair sedge and cotton grass. These provide poorer grazing than heather, they do not form suitable cover for grouse, and exposed peaty areas tend to become rubbery in texture and liable to erosion through sheetwash (McVean and Lockie, 1969). Repeated moor burning reduces floristic variety which, in turn, impoverishes dependent animal life and can lead to violent fluctuations in animal populations. This, in turn, can result in pest explosions and considerable damage. Hence on Grades 6 to 8 lands moor burning is not advised. The Guide to Good Muirburn Practice (Gimingham, 1977) provides an exemplary statement of how moor burning should be tackled according to ecological principles.

Land capacity and precautions in use	Primary uses	Secondary uses
Grade 1 Suitable for retention or reclamation as cropland. *Note:* This would not imply that reclamation was economically feasible but only that it was ecologically valid.	Agriculture	Recreation, wildlife, grazing
Grade 2 Suitable for improvement as grazing by cultivation and reseeding. Sub-class (a) mineral soils (b) peats	Grazing	Recreation, wildlife
Grade 3 Suitable for improvement as grazing by methods other than cultivation. Sub-class (a) mineral soils (b) peats	Grazing	Recreation, wildlife
Grade 4 Suitable for retention as unimproved rough grazing in association with Grades 1 to 3. Position with respect to surrounding areas of the other classes would have to be taken into account. Careful moor burning possible.	Grazing	Recreation, wildlife, watershed-management
Grade 5 More suitable for commercial afforestation than grazing	Commercial	Recreation, forestry wildlife, grazing, watershed-management
Grade 6 Suitable mainly for protection, afforestation and wildlife. Moor burning not permissible	Protection, afforestation, wildlife	Recreation, grazing, watershed-management
Grade 7 Suitable only for wildlife: moor burning not permissible	Wildlife	Recreation, watershed-management
Grade 8 Any areas requiring urgent counter-erosion works, including areas of severe peat hagging, badly gullied or sheep eroded slopes, landslips and river bank failures.	Erosion control and watershed-management	Wildlife

Table 7. **A land capability classification for the Scottish Highlands**
Source: McVean and Lockie, 1969, p 109

Merging Ecological with Aesthetic Sustainability: the Case of Hedgerows

18. So far, the discussion has focused on the relationship between agriculture and the productive aspects of sustainability. When the aesthetic and/or heritage components of sustainability are taken into account, the impact of agriculture is considerably greater and more likely to result in public concern. In practice, the distinction between these two major strands of

sustainability is a little misleading, since there are ecological implications when amenity issues are involved. By way of illustration, let us look at the ecological and aesthetic factors associated with the loss of hedgerows.

19. As indicated in Chapter 3, paragraph 33 of this report, hedgerows are disappearing in Britain at the rate of around 0.5 to 1 per cent per year. In their excellent study of changes to lowland English landscapes, Westmacott and Worthington (1974) document why farmers wish to remove hedges:

    (a) to facilitate mechanisation and to intensify production;

    (b) to facilitate changes in grazing management;

    (c) to reduce the burden of maintenance;

    (d) to remove untidy hedges which have no further agricultural function;

    (e) to facilitate drainage;

    (f) to gain land; and

    (g) to control weeds and rabbits.

Westmacott and Worthington found that, in their seven study areas, the removal of only 16 per cent of hedges was grant aided, though current MAFF/WOAD policy is to concentrate on incidental removal of 'minor' hedges as part of other eligible improvement; the vast majority were taken out by farm labour in their spare time. A large number of hedges were also grubbed up, having been effectively destroyed by 'negligent' stubble burning. They also found that, during the severe agricultural depression of the 1930s, many hedges were left unmanaged since there was not the labour available to look after them. Subsequently, many hedges were cut back by fairly crude methods thereby reducing their ecological interest. Yet hedgerows provide important habitats for 'edge' species who thrive on the field/hedge margin, many of which prey on insects which otherwise might explode in numbers and damage a crop. (For a comprehensive statement, see Pollard *et al*, 1974.) In addition, some pests are transferred through a crop by wind, but this would be less likely if good quality hedges were available to provide a wind break. (For a comprehensive review of these issues see Terrasson and Tendron, 1981.) Furthermore, hedges provide important benefits, such as reducing soil erosion and windblow, cutting down evapotranspiration losses and capturing precipitation. These factors will vary in significance depending upon field size, soil and climate conditions, crops grown and crop management techniques. Some hedgerows have considerable historical and aesthetic significance. Many parish boundaries are marked by hedges which are older than any buildings on the landscape, and the pattern of hedge-enclosed fields is one of the most distinctive features of the lowland countryside. The interesting question is how far the advantages of hedges kept in good condition by expensive means outweigh the costs of their restriction of field usage and cropping practices. The answer depends not only upon local conditions and the pattern of subsidy (favouring hedge removal at the expense of hedge maintenance), but also upon the environmental knowledge of farmers and their interest in protecting landscape amenity. This, in turn, will depend upon the nature of their holdings, the kind of advice they receive, and the ways in which they come into contact with the conservation ethos. It seems that there are no great economic advantages in having fields greater than 40 ha (100 ac), economies of scale becoming less evident in fields greater than 18 ha (40 ac). Removing hedges to create very large fields, therefore, does not even make economic sense, irrespective of the conservation damage.

The Economic Momentum Behind Modern Agriculture

20. Behind the observations that follow is the belief that the economic and managerial forces that presently shape modern agriculture make it very difficult for a landowner or farmer to observe his or her public obligations towards the stewardship of his or her land even if he or she is morally committed to doing so. Those forces also encourage landowners or tenants to damage or destroy certain conservation/amenity features that otherwise they might wish to safeguard and/or enhance. Hence the call made in Chapter 7 for a reform of the pattern of incentives and advice in favour of a more balanced conservation/development approach to rural resource-use.

21. A growing cause of public and political concern is the already high, and apparently endlessly increasing, cost of subsidy to modern agriculture. This is partly a feature of favourable tax concessions and principally an outcome of price support guarantees and food tariff protection measures contained within the Common Agricultural Policy (CAP) of the European Economic Community (EEC). The original philosophy of CAP was to support incomes of farmers so as to keep them on the land, to encourage small and/or part-time farmers either to expand production or to become less dependent upon agriculture as a source of income and to give Community consumers plenty of food at reasonable prices. In practice, CAP has served, by and large, to protect farmers' incomes, especially for the larger and more capital-intensive farmers on the more productive lands. Small farmers, with less than 250 standard man days (SMD) equivalent, have not fared so well, yet many try to continue in farming. Although, in real terms, average farm incomes have fallen by about 20 per cent between 1974 and 1981, this varies by size of operation, land productivity and level of investment, and the fall is comparable with the drop in income of most small to medium businesses. The CAP has, however, increased the price of food — by at least 10 per cent for the UK consumer. This is the result of expensive levies on many imported foodstuffs (to protect European surplus production from cheaper produce) and the high cost of guaranteeing prices of most produce and of storing and/or selling off cheaply surplus foodstuffs. The support price for all European protected commodities, with the exception of milk (ie wheat, barley, maize, paddy rice, soyabeans and butter), exceeds US support prices by at least 40 per cent. One must also consider the distributional effects

of such high tariffs. The Institute of Fiscal Studies (1982) estimates that these tariffs represent a transfer of cash from the consumer to the farmer worth about £1.05bn (or around £50 per family) in 1978. The poor pay proportionately more of this than the rich. In 1981, the total cost of CAP to the Community was 11.5 billion ecus (European Currency Units, equivalent to about £7.9bn) or about 75 per cent of the total Community budget; of this, about 5.5 billion ecus (or 48 per cent of CAP spending) was deployed in subsidising food exports. As will be discussed in more detail in paragraph 30 of this chapter below (see p 206), price guarantees encourage high yields and surplus production. For example, the Community produces nearly 40 per cent more milk powder than it needs, 12 per cent wheat and 10 per cent barley. The cost of disposing annually of some four million tonnes of surplus wheat alone costs the European taxpayer over £800m. This is because it is too expensive for feeding to livestock, but not good enough for making into bread. It is dumped on the international market with subsidies equivalent to between a third and a half of the EEC market price (Gardner, 1982). (For good data on CAP, see the *Economist*, 23 October 1982, pp 54 to 55 and 8 January 1983, pp 66 to 67.)

22. CAP, together with national agricultural support prices (see paragraphs 33 to 35 of this chapter, pp 207 - 208), not only absorb too much scarce public money, but they also encourage wasteful resource-use and environmental damage. This is because it now pays farmers to invest expensive energy, chemicals and machinery to produce subsidised crops from unsuitable land. With advances in plant genetics and livestock breeding, together with extensive advice on how to increase yields through modern husbandry, many lands recently thought unsuitable for intensive agricultural production are now being converted to more 'productive' use. However, in many cases this may well be at the expense of the three kinds of sustainable resource-use outlined in Chapter 2, paragraph 7 of this report (see p 180). Growing cereals on drained wetlands, raising stocking densities on upland moors and converting heaths to intensive livestock production are probably neither ecologically nor aesthetically desirable, nor do they keep people on the land. They would almost certainly not be economically justifiable if CAP and its supporting national policies did not exist.

23. Body (1982) has attempted to calculate the total cost of subsidy to UK agriculture. He has the advantage of papers presented to the House of Commons Agriculture Committee of which he is a member. His estimate is £3.35bn annually, composed of £1.5bn in price supports of various kinds, £1.0bn in favourable tax concessions (around £700m on income tax deductions due to investment write-offs, £300m because of VAT relief, plus possibly £23m due to capital transfer tax concessions), savings of £200m because local rates are not levied on agricultural land, and £650m of grants and other incentives from the agricultural ministries and their research and advisory services. This works out at about £13,000 annually per farm, though in practice

the large more capital-intensive landowners on the most productive land gain disproportionately more than small farmers on economically marginal holdings on poor land (much of which may have high aesthetic value nationally). In addition, landowners have benefited from the growth in land values since the war, worth, in Body's view, some £40bn of investment that could have been more productively spent in other parts of the economy. Land value escalation encourages investment in land by wealthy people and financial institutions, and enables landowners to invest in even greater productivity gains simply because of the collateral it provides. Unfortunately, from a conservation viewpoint, all these subsidies are not easily reversed for they have created firm political expectations amongst the influential farming and landowning community (see paragraph 1 in this chapter, p 198). In addition, a sudden drop in price supports or other income supplements would only redouble efforts to improve productivity at the expense of the nation's wildlife and scenic beauty. This is why more fundamental and radical reforms are required. The paragraphs that follow analyse the issues.

Indebtedness

24. A recent study (Centre of Agricultural Strategy, 1978) showed that modern agriculture is a remarkably capital-intensive industry, with total assets per net output increasing at constant prices by 69 per cent between 1953 and 1974. According to latest MAFF figures (Ministry of Agriculture, Fisheries and Food, 1982) estimated total bank advances to UK agriculture average about £3.4bn for 1981, some 20 per cent higher than the figure for 1980, and 50 per cent up on the 1979 figures. About 80 per cent of investment is financed out of farm income, and, as with all business, this is subject to tax relief. In 1974, total assets per worker were 10 times those in 1953, though most of this increase can be accounted for by the fall in labour employed and by the increase in the value of land which, until recently, has risen as fast as, and in most cases faster than, historic rates of inflation. The price of even a modest sized farm is now so high that a young farmer, starting out on his own with privately borrowed capital, would simply not be able to meet his mortgage payments even on profitable land (Northfield, 1979). Even on county council holdings, tenants require £20,000 in capital to get started. So, even if the tax laws are changed, it seems unlikely that much new blood will enter farming as owner-occupiers, while those that do (more often than not, relatives of existing farmers) will be tempted to secure long-term money-making invest-ments. Needless to say, the very high costs of entering farming will deter any innovators who might wish to experiment with more sustainable approaches to land management, particularly where such experiments do not prove cost effective in the short-term (for example, organic farming — see paragraph 14 of this chapter, p 201). In this context, it is sad to see the recent demise of the MAFF-funded Land Settlement Association (LSA) which allowed tenants onto small plots of land up and down the country with generous loans, though there was no assurance that LSA tenants were particularly conservation minded. Reid (1981) foresees a potential

crisis looming as indebtedness rises and farm profitability falls, with young farmers particularly becoming concerned with profit-making more than with the quality of management. In this climate, farmers may become less eager to adopt sustainable land management techniques and increasingly resistant to any new policy measures that could reduce further the profitability of agriculture.

Taxation

25. Three forms of taxation are immediately relevant to the farmer: income tax, capital gains tax and capital transfer tax. As far as income tax is concerned, current tax laws enable farmers (especially high income farmers) to run into periodic revenue debt since business expenditures are tax deductible. This can create an 'investment treadmill' through which profitable farmers capitalise income in new machinery or land purchase. Low income farmers on marginal land are placed in a different position on the indebtedness cycle. Because their incomes are low, any improvement through subsidised inputs of various kinds will be eagerly seized. Generally speaking, however, on the middle to larger farms (measured by turnover) investment is paid from income with only about 20 per cent from MAFF grant aid. This has important implications for any policy which seeks to link grant aid to conservation-orientated management. Also significant is the present arrangement through which expenditure on buildings and improvement works (which may have important conservation implications) can only be written off against income tax on the basis of 30 per cent for the first year and 10 per cent per year thereafter. *This is manifestly too slow: it would be desirable for the whole of the expenditure (on approved investment) to be written off during the year in which it was spent.* This would assist farmers or tenants (at least the wealthier ones) to construct buildings to acceptable design standards (eg by using local materials to suit traditional styles) and in undertaking other conservation expenditures (Stanley, 1982). The Inland Revenue should make clear its policy of allowing income tax deduction on expenditures which do not have a specific agricultural purpose but which are of advantage to conservation — for example, lining barns with local stone or brick. *All expenditures approved by bona fide conservation organisations should be subject to income tax relief.* Equally important is the effect of the charge to VAT on repairs and maintenance expenditures by landlords, but not on demolition or new construction costs. This should automatically be removed to encourage landlord investment in conservation work.

26. Capital Gains Tax (CGT) is normally levied at 30 per cent on the disposal of chargeable deferred assets, but this can be deferred by rolling it over (ie deferring payment) into investment, notably the purchase of additional land (assuming that it is available). Given that agricultural land values have, until recently, been increasing, the burden of this taxation, particularly if the farm is sold into a family trust, can be relatively small. However, investment in conservation work financed from the sale of assets is not subject to CGT deferral.

For example, if a landowner purchased an old wind-pump, the cost of acquisition could not be rolled over. *This should be changed so that bona fide conservation investments permit CGT deferral.*

27. Capital Transfer Tax (CTT) was introduced in 1974 to replace estate duty as a single tax payable by the donor on the transfer of property from one person to another. This tax is not now subject to any upper limit on Agricultural Relief on land and buildings. The Northfield Committee were unable to identify any significant effect on agriculture as a result of CGT and CTT, except to point out that it probably encouraged owner-occupancy at the expense of tenancy (though under the 1981 Finance Act, landlords are now granted 20 per cent CTT relief) and possibly encouraged farm amalgamation and the increase in size of farm holdings.

28. What these statistics mean for conservation and/or amenity is anybody's guess, though the effect of 'locking in' agricultural business within families may not be a good omen. Certainly, there is a tendency for larger holdings to seek high productivity gains and to be more investment orientated, though CLA research rather optimistically suggests (as the sample was very small and not representative) that such owners tend to be more conservation minded. There is some evidence that economies of scale begin to fall for farms in excess of 400 ha (Northfield, 1979) though much will depend upon management skills and attitudes and/or actions toward environmental conservation. Also, more studies will be needed of the possible advantages of CTT relief available to landowners (under Section 34 of the Finance Act 1975) who own land that is, in the opinion of the Treasury, 'of outstanding scenic or historic or scientific interest' (this covers land of recognised nature conservation value, scenic attractiveness and historical/archaeological importance) and who agree to maintain the essential character of the property and permit access to the public (see HM Treasury, 1980). Relief is also available from CGT through a 10 per cent douceur, so long as the vendor sells land of heritage value (as agreed by the Treasury) and the purchaser (which must be a public or quasi public body) agrees to certain conditions over maintenance, preservation and public access. In the light of the comments made above on the temptations for improving productivity, both CTT and CGT relief may not be such an advantage as might at first appear and, if available, may not necessarily reduce the value of land if purchase by a conservation body is contemplated. Stanley (1982) comments that the benefits of these two schemes are eroded by the cumbersome procedures for securing tax designation, uncertainty over the rules, failure by the Treasury to be imaginative in responding to landowners' initiatives and the NCC and the two Countryside Commissions, and the inflexibility of the conditional clauses. He concludes that the system needs to be made simpler, more accessible and more widely known. *The tax designation criteria should match those criteria which support official landscape and/or conservation designations and relief should be available even when immediate disposal is not in prospect. Also, the 10 per cent douceur needs*

to be increased and the definition of an eligible purchaser (currently confined to official agencies and the National Trusts) should be broadened to include all bona fide *voluntary organisations*. Because the taxation arrangements are relatively complicated, Table 8 summarises how these hinder conservation investment and what should be done about it.

Income Tax	
agricultural buildings allowance	Expenditure on buildings and improvements to the land are based on a slow write-off period (30% in the first year and 10% thereafter). This should be changed to allow a 100% write-off in the first year where approved conservation works are intended.
VAT relief on property maintenance and repair	Landlords are not always exempted from VAT on expenditures for the maintenance and repair of their tenanted property. VAT recovery should automatically be granted for such expenditures.
Capital Gains Tax deferral on *bona fide* conservation investment	CGT (normally 30% of sold assets) is not deferrable on investments aimed at maintaining or restoring buildings or land. Where such investments are clearly of conservation value CGT should be deferrable until such assets are finally sold.
Capital Transfer Tax CTT relief on lands of outstanding scientific interest	CTT relief (through deferred liability) is available to owners who agree to maintain and preserve property according to agreed objectives and who allow public access to it. This arrangement should be made more widely known, the conditions of tax designation should be made more flexible and more clearly related to existing and proposed conservation designations and to changes in CGT deferral.
conditions of sale of lands of outstanding scientific interest	A douceur of 10% is available to the owner who sells land to a recognised conservation body. The CTT is lost to the Treasury since the purchasing organisation buys at the tax-deducted price. The douceur needs to be increased and the definition of a recognised conservation body should encompass *bona fide* voluntary conservation organisations.

Table 8. **Present taxation arrangements on agriculture and their effect on conservation investment**

Institutional Land Ownership

29. The Northfield Committee discovered that only about 0.5 per cent of full-time farm businesses were owned by non-agricultural corporations, though many holdings may now be held by family trusts (registered as companies) for tax reasons. The pattern of institutional land ownership varies geographically with large holdings on the richer agricultural lands. In East Anglia, for instance, over 20 per cent of farms exceeding 408 ha (1,000 ac) are owned by companies. Institutional landowners are very capital-intensive, accounting for about 20 per cent of all farm assets, though the major financial companies claim that only 5 per cent of their property holdings are in agricultural land. Nevertheless, this involves purchases of about 20,000 ha annually worth about £1.5bn (Norton-Taylor, 1982). While it is plausible to suppose that institutional control tends to

be associated with higher amounts of risk capital, and hence with farming practices which seek high returns on investment, a recent report by Worthington (1981) suggests that this may not necessarily be true. Regardless of the nature of land ownership, it seems that the attitudes and/or actions of the owner, tenant or manager are far more likely to be a determining factor as to how far conservation/amenity interests are taken into account. Nevertheless, some agents or managers of institutionally owned property did believe that 'non-economic' investment in conservation/amenity would not be in their investors' interests, though some owners are now requiring that up to 10 per cent of land be 'given over' to conservation, primarily as enhancement. This approach should be encouraged. The study also revealed that lack of advice about conservation within a programme of investment was a missed opportunity that should be rectified. 'In general, neither the farmers, agents or owners were aware of special areas of particular wildlife value on their farms, even when these still supported attractive plant species such as orchids or oxslips. Even on the rare occasions when there was some knowledge of the wildlife value of an area, this did not necessarily lead to any degree of protection . . .' (Worthington, 1981).

Price Supports

30. Probably the single most important factor influencing the relationship between agriculture and conservation is the existence of price intervention, or guaranteed minimum prices for certain products. As outlined in paragraphs 5 and 6 of this chapter (see pp 198 - 199) these were introduced to stabilise prices and provide a measure of investment security for farmers. Price intervention is now enshrined in CAP. The objectives of CAP make no specific reference to increasing output *per se* (though this appears to be a consequence of high levels of price support) nor is there any direct remit within CAP to take into account environmental aspects. However, since 1972, it has always been understood that the CAP should recognise the Community's successive environmental policies as enshrined in its Action Plans for the Environment. In addition, the European Parliament passed a resolution on 26 March 1980 requesting the Commission 'to attach greater importance than hitherto to the consequences of further intensification, rationalisation and industrialisation of agriculture for the biological equilibrium in nature and the environment'. This is a notable declaration which has not yet been backed up by any noticeable change in policy or statutory powers.

31. In operational terms, the CAP provides both a guidance and a guarantee element, the former relating to grants to improve productivity, the latter to price supports. In 1981, the CAP absorbed about 66 per cent of the entire Community budget (ie about £7bn of a £100bn budget) of which 90 per cent was spent on price supports. Yet it should not be forgotten that the European Community provides only about 35 per cent of all support to agriculture; the rest comes from national budgets mostly in the form of capital grants. In 1981-82, the UK Government was forecast to spend

£683.6m on price supports of various kinds from which it received relief of £651.5m from the guarantee fund. From Table 9 (see p 208), it will be noted that only about 10 to 16 per cent of all UK spending on agriculture is directed at agricultural improvements through capital investment, though, as noted earlier, there is also indirect financial assistance through favourable tax concessions. One important feature of price intervention is its sweeping influence on the agriculture-conservation connection. A favourable intervention price for a particular commodity can cause many thousands of farmers to alter their cropping practices, possibly with little consideration for sustainable utilisation. In recent years, the shift to cereal production away from livestock, brought about largely because of price intervention, has had significant effect on hedgerow loss and the drainage and ploughing of grazing meadows. The Government believes that this shift has gone too far and should be brought more into balance.

32. Price guarantees also tend to encourage public investment in agricultural improvement schemes. This distorts the real social value of additional output, since part of the gain which justifies improvement investment such as arterial drainage schemes is simply a transfer payment (in the form of a subsidy) from consumers or taxpayers to producers. Thus, the prices against which output benefits are estimated are inflated by public investments. Black and Bowers (1981) calculate that this over-estimation of benefit amounts to 24 per cent for potatoes, 130 to 140 per cent for cereals, 700 per cent for beef, and are so high for dairying and sugar beet that, in their opinion, any increase in output should be counted as a net social loss. They claim that the presence of price guarantees and over-production effectively result in wastage of public money on additional productivity investment, irrespective of any additional environmental/conservation costs due to habitat losses — many of which may be irreplaceable. The official view is that world market prices are also not a fair reflection of 'real' value of output; however, one cannot accept highly inflated non-market prices as a basis for economic accounting according to WCS principles.

Improvement Grants

33. In the public mind, agriculture is the beneficiary of apparently bottomless subsidies, a fact all the more annoying to ratepayers and taxpayers surrounded on all sides by cash limits and pay restraint. MAFF payments through approved grant schemes are normally subject to investment ceilings but not to aggregate cash limits, so long as applications for grant meet certain investment criteria. These are that the proposed investment must be agriculturally productive in the sense that it is technically sound, results in at least the equivalent of one labour unit of employment and that the applicant has an economically viable enterprise normally with an approved development plan. From the point of view of a Conservation and Development Programme for the UK, these arrangements are unsatisfactory because:

(a) Such grants are not subject to proper external cost benefit accounting — for farm level improvement grants, no cost benefit analysis is undertaken at all, though presumably farmers are satisfied that the expected return will repay their investment.

(b) Outside of national parks and SSSIs the implications of proposed improvements for conservation and landscape amenity are not considered by qualified people.

(c) Grants for approved works are awarded in far too blanket a fashion — virtually irrespective of farm income, pattern of investment or nature of landholding. In general, grant aid assists the larger and more capital-intensive operations far more than the smaller, economically more marginal, farms. Indeed, farms in excess of 2,000 Standard Man Days (SMD) receive over six times the grant aid (as a proportion of investment) given to farms of between 275 and 600 SMD (MAFF Farm Management Survey data).

(d) Grants generally tend to be awarded for new investment, not for maintenance of existing investments. (Thus it is cheaper for a farmer to knock down an old drystone wall and replace it with a post and wire fence rather than maintain the existing wall.)

(e) Grants do not discriminate between different approaches to landscape management because they are usually based upon a fixed percentage of input costs. (For example, in less favoured areas, a farmer receiving a 50 per cent grant need pay only £1 per metre for a wire and post fence — total cost £2 per metre — but if he wishes to build a drystone wall costing £20 per metre he still only receives a 50 per cent grant so he must pay £10. There is no additional grant aid incentive for costly but socially valued conservation works.)

(f) Because grants are primarily geared to agricultural productivity, public grants can destroy privately owned public assets (eg grants are available to drain and fertilise old meadows which may be of conservation significance).

34. The major grant aid schemes for UK agriculture are as follows:

(a) The Agriculture and Horticulture Development Scheme (AHDS) replaced the Farm and Horticulture Development Scheme (FHDS) in October 1980 continuing the UK commitment to the EEC Directive on Farm Modernisation (72/159 EEC). Its purpose is to help established agricultural and horticultural businesses, whose incomes are below a certain level, to modernise and so improve their income. All that is required is an acceptable development plan and that sufficient additional work must have been created to occupy one worker full time (though an additional worker need not be employed). Rates of grant range from 5 per cent to 32.5 per cent in standard areas and from 10 per cent to 70 per cent in less favoured areas, depending on the kinds of work undertaken.

	1978/79	1979/80	1980/81	1981/82
			(£ million)	(forecast)
Price guarantees and production grants	50.5	45.7	100.8	99.2
Support for capital and other improvements	109.9	158.4	190.1	167.5
Support for agriculture in special areas	46.3	112.8	118.3	107.0
Market regulation under CAP	330.2	359.9	603.2	665.2
Total	536.9	676.8	1,012.4	1,038.9

Table 9. **Public expenditure on UK agriculture**
Source: Annual Review of Agriculture, 1982, Cmnd 8491, p 41

(b) The Agriculture and Horticulture Grant Scheme (AHGS) replaced by the Farm Capital Grant Scheme (FCGS) in October 1980 and provides grants for capital investment which must remain in agricultural use for at least two years. Businesses which employ at least one worker are eligible. The rate of grant ranges from 22.5 per cent to 37.5 per cent in standard areas, and from 22.5 per cent to 70 per cent in less favoured areas.

(c) Less Favoured Areas (LFAs) are statutorily defined as areas with special problems associated with economics and environment, notably the poor quality of soil, steep slope of the land and the short growing season. Landowners and occupiers in such regions are eligible for higher rates of grant and to special Hill Livestock Compensatory Allowances (HLCAs) designed to compensate farmers for the natural handicaps of soil infertility topography, etc. (More will be said about LFAs in paragraphs 35 of this chapter — see below and 26 to 28 of Chapter 6 of this report — pp 234 - 235.)

In 1981-82, public expenditure in AHDS and AHGS was £85.8m and £76.0m respectively (with other related subsidies amounting to £6.1m plus an additional £107m in special areas (mostly LFAs), of which £36.8m and £50.8m was devoted to HLCAs for cattle and sheep respectively (Ministry of Agriculture, Fisheries and Food, 1982).

Less Favoured Areas
35. Apart from guaranteeing prices and supporting agricultural investments, the CAP contains four major directives aimed at improving the economic and social conditions of agriculture in the more depressed areas of the Community. Of these four directives, the most important from a conservation/development viewpoint is the European Community directive on Mountain and Hill Farming which came into force in 1975 (Directive 75/268/EEC). This directive defines three broad categories of LFAs as eligible for assistance:
(a) mountain areas characterised by high terrain, steep slopes and short growing season (Article 3(3) areas);
(b) LFAs in danger of depopulation characterised by natural handicaps, low agricultural productivity and a low and dwindling population primarily dependent on agricultural activity (Article 3(4) areas);

(c) other LFA affected by special handicaps, such as areas where a certain kind of farming needs to be maintained in order to conserve the countryside, and preserve the tourist potential of the area or protect the coastline (Article 3(5) areas).
Of these three categories, nearly all of the LFAs designated in the UK (see Table 10, p 209) fall into category (b), though the Isles of Scilly (part of the Duchy of Cornwall) have now become the first Article 3(5) LFA in the UK.

36. The Select Committee on Agriculture (1982), which investigated LFAs recently, received much adverse comment from conservation interests regarding the manner in which MAFF chooses to interpret the LFA scheme. At present, about 60 per cent of LFAs in England and Wales fall into national parks or AONBS; indeed, almost all the existing national parks fall within LFAs. The major criticisms are that, by virtually excluding Article 3(5) areas and by concentrating on narrow definitions of agricultural grant aid (namely to improve agricultural productivity), MAFF grant aid policies act contrary to the interests of productive and aesthetic sustainability in the uplands. This is because:
(a) Such policies do not permit MAFF funds to grant aid other income generating activity which is agriculturally related and which could increase employment opportunities (for example, landscape maintenenance work, continuation of traditional labour-intensive practices, tourism and other community enterprise projects).
(b) These policies tend to weaken local economies by reinforcing the economic and technological trends which make agriculture more and more capital-intensive, thus shedding labour.
(c) These policies tend to result in damage to landscape amenity and valued habitats since they can encourage over-grazing. For example, HLCA headage payments normally relate to numbers of stock and not to ecologically suitable numbers of stock (see paragraphs 16 and 17 of this chapter, page 202), though MAFF/WOAD have set a stocking limit of six breeding ewes to each forage hectare, a figure which can be set even lower if the land is not considered suitable for such grazing densities. Recent changes in the variable sheepmeat premium encourage very heavy stocking densities in some areas, leading to further intensification of upland grazing (MacEwen and Sinclair, 1983). As already noted,

	% of total land area by country	million hectares
England	11.6	1.1
Wales	57.0	0.97
Scotland	67.0	5.4
Northern Ireland	40.5	0.45
UK total	42.4	7.92

Table 10. **Area of less favoured areas in the UK**

these policies also tend to favour environmentally damaging agricultural investments such as moorland drainage, fertilisation of pastures, destruction of broadleaved woodland in favour of coniferous forest plantations and conversion of traditional buildings.

Current policies in LFAs also discriminate against the principles of social and economic sustainability for rural communities. To begin with, 'part-time' farmers are not eligible for much LFA aid even when they actually work full-time (because the definition of part-time relates to scale of operation not to source of income). So LFA payments are channelled into the hands of bigger farmers at the expense of smaller, more marginal operators (MacEwen and Sinclair, 1983). One must always bear in mind that such grants are subject to virtually no public scrutiny, no proper cost benefit analysis and, in all cases outside of national parks and SSSIs, are awarded retrospectively, ie after the grant aidable investment is completed and when environmental repair may not be possible. Because the management of LFAs incorporates a number of themes relating to rural management, this matter will be discussed further in paragraphs 26 to 28 of Chapter 6 of this report (see pp 234 - 235).

Cost Benefit Analysis and Environmental Impact Assessment

37. At present major public investments designed to improve agriculture production, such as arterial land drainage schemes and flood protection projects which are financed largely by MAFF money via Internal Drainage Boards (IDBs) or Regional Water Authorities (RWAs) (or their equivalent in Scotland and Northern Ireland), are not in practice subject to publicly accountable cost benefit analyses (CBA) or environmental impact assessments (EIA). It is possible for the Exchequer and Audit Department to scrutinise such assessments and pass them on to the House of Commons Public Accounts Committee, but for the vast majority of proposals this is not done. Although the initiating authorities (the IDBs and RWAs) must prepare CBA, MAFF regards these as fairly rough and ready calculations. Since EIA are not done at all, the CBA are not based on social cost benefit accounts but on a financial analysis of costs against agricultural gains. Because these gains are often inflated (see paragraph 30 of this chapter,

p 206), the CBA are erroneous from the viewpoint of a conservation/development programme and may well result in misallocation of public funds. These conservation-related gains or losses are not properly taken into account in project appraisal. The only means by which these CBA can be scrutinised, it seems, is through a public inquiry, but, where land drainage is involved, such inquiries are held at the discretion of the relevant Agriculture Minister. A number of local authorities are presently trying to uncover the CBA calculations made by certain RWAs regarding flood protection and river improvement proposals as notified to them under guidelines prepared by the Water Space Amenity Commission (1980) but so far neither the RWAs nor MAFF are prepared to make these calculations public. This refusal should not be permitted. The whole issue of river improvement schemes should be examined much more closely. At present, some £80m annually are spent on such works often with associated wildlife and amenity damage. In addition, many schemes encourage unsuitable agricultural and building development in flood plains.

The Wildlife and Countryside Act 1981

38. The Wildlife and Countryside Act of 1981 is vital to the analysis of this report, not only because of the new arrangement it provides for the notification of agricultural changes in SSSIs and National Parks, but also because of the philosophy it enshrines *vis á vis* agriculture and conservation. Before the Act is reviewed, it is worth repeating that, with the exception of SSSIs, all agricultural change where grant aid is not sought is not subject to any form of compulsory notification or planning control, while in National Parks only those changes where grant aid is sought are notifiable to the National Park authority in advance. This means that the ecological and aesthetic qualities of sustainable utilisation of about 85 per cent of the rural landscape of the UK depend upon the trust which, at present, society has to place in landowners and occupiers. The philosophy of the Act is summed up in this statement issued by the Minister for Local Government and Environmental Services in a letter to the Institute of British Geographers (January, 1982). 'Although some people advocate compulsory measures, it is the Government's firm belief that the best approach is to build on the good will of all concerned to achieve voluntary solutions to these problems (of land use conflict in the countryside) . . . I cannot emphasise too much the importance of active management of the countryside as the cornerstone of the Government's strategy towards our rural heritage.'

39. One must place this statement in the context of the protective powers and finances available to the NCC, the two Countryside Commissions and the local authorities seeking to safeguard landscape amenity and habitats of conservation importance. Statutorily, these powers are very weak and the budgets extremely small.

The only compulsory powers are those available to the NCC through sections 17 and 18 of the National Parks and Access to the Countryside Act of 1949. These enable the NCC to buy land compulsorily, only if its offer to establish a Nature Reserve Agreement under Section 16 of the 1949 Act is refused by the landowner and where the NCC believe that it is expedient that the land should be managed as a nature reserve, or where the break of a management agreement could prevent or impair the satisfactory management of a nature reserve. (In practice, the NCC has not specifically used these powers which, in any case, require authorisation by the appropriate Minister.) This interpretation might well exclude lands which are in multiple use (ie where part of the use is not strictly for nature conservation). Otherwise, no compulsory powers of acquisition and/or management agreements are available, although a variety of provisions for voluntary management agreements to further the cause of conservation are in existence (see Feist, 1978), and section 39 of the new Act widens this voluntary arrangement still further. (In practice, however, few local authorities appear willing to spend ratepayers' money on section 39 conservation agreements unless 'forced' to do so through objections to a particular development proposal.) It is possible for local authorities to extend a measure of planning control to agricultural buildings and other 'permitted developments' under the General Development Order through such devices as Article 4 Directions and Landscape Area Special Development Orders, but these provisions do not extend to alterations in land management practices. (For an excellent review, see Feist, 1978.)

40. Under the Wildlife and Countryside Act, new arrangements regarding notification apply to SSSIs and National Parks in England and Wales (though it should be noted that, as from October 1980, applicants for MAFF grant aided schemes must consult the NCC or the relevant National Park authority to ensure that all objections on conservation/amenity grounds are taken into account). The new arrangements, with respect to SSSIs, require the NCC first to renotify all landowners and occupiers on whose land there is already an SSSI that the SSSI does exist, and second to notify them of any operation appearing to the NCC likely to damage flora, fauna or any other feature of a special interest to the site. the NCC must also explain to landowners why their land is of special interest. These new arrangements thus ensure compulsory prior notification of all agricultural change potentially damaging to nature conservation, though such warning will only be assured once the NCC has completed this two stage notification process — and this will take at least a year to accomplish. Meanwhile, landowners not seeking grant aid must act on trust. Already, in Norfolk, Yorkshire and Somerset there is firm evidence that this trust is being abused — a legal defiance which does not augur well for the voluntary cooperation philosophy so central to the success of the Act. Where a proposed action is regarded by the NCC as unfavourable to nature conservation, and where the Minister of Agriculture deems the proposed action as 'agriculturally viable' and hence eligible for grant aid, the Minister must consult with the Secretary of State for the Environment (in Wales both ministers are the Welsh Secretary) before deciding whether or not to award the grant. Should the grant not be awarded, the NCC must seek to enter into a management agreement with the landowner within three months of being notified, the terms of the agreement to be determined by financial guidelines (DOE Circular 3/83, 1983). Should the two parties fail to agree, the Environmental Secretary (or Welsh and Scottish Secretaries) may impose a Nature Conservation Order requiring the applicant to hold back any action for a further period of up to nine months, thereby giving more time for a management agreement to be secured. The Nature Conservation Order is only a delaying power: the voluntary principle holds sway. As a last resort, the NCC may seek powers to purchase compulsorily, though this will depend on the nature of the SSSI and the money available. Figure 3 below portrays these procedures. For 1982-83, the NCC has been given an additional grant of only £600,000 to deal with its new responsibilities under the Act, but much of this is earmarked for administrative costs. The NCC believes that £20m over 10 years is required to safeguard all key nature conservation sites (Seventh Annual Report, 1981) but notes that the Government will look favourably on specific requests for additional funds 'within the economic situation' of the country. It remains to be proved how high on the list of the Government's economic priorities the cost of conservation rates.

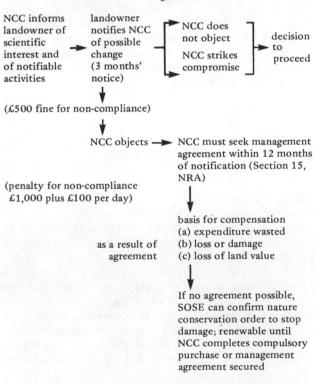

Sections 28 and 29 Agreements (SSSIs)

Figure 3. **The likely pathway of action to safeguard SSSIs under sections 28 and 29 of the Wildlife and Countryside Act 1981**
Note: all proposed land-use changes regarded as notifiable by the NCC must be registered even if grant aid is not sought

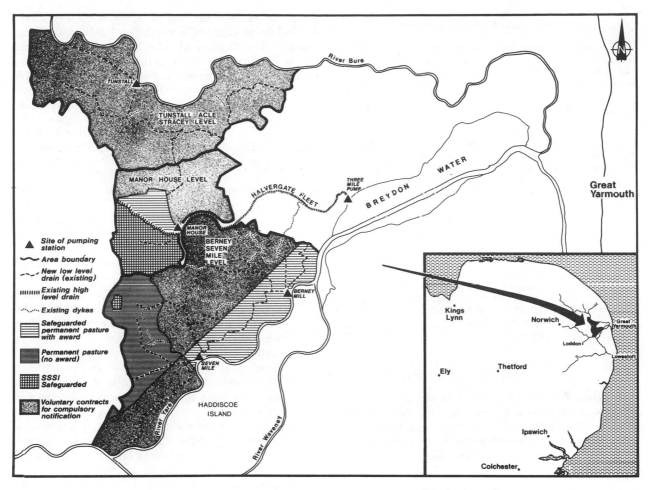

Halvergate Marshes

Halvergate Marshes, Norfolk

In November 1980, the Lower Bure, Halvergate Fleet and Acles Marshes IDB submitted proposals to improve the existing pumps and drains over three drainage levels on the Halvergate Marshes in east Norfolk. Through a voluntary arrangement, the Broads Authority was notified of these proposals and objected to them on the grounds that arable conversion, encouraged by the lower water tables, CAP pricing policies, and increased drainage rates, would unacceptably alter the characteristic marsh landscape. Over the ensuing 20 months, involving 2,000 man hours of professional time, plus equivalent on the part of landowners, a compromise arrangement was arrived at involving the complete safeguarding of 487 ha. However, because arrangements had to be voluntary, because large blocks of land were involved incorporating 17 owners, and because different treatment for compensation for landowners/occupiers in the SSSI increased uncertainty and frustration, a final agreement acceptable to all parties was not possible. In November 1982, the Minister of State for Agriculture announced that he would only accept the IDB's application for grant aid on the new pump at Tunstall but that he would refuse to offer grant aid in new pumps and drainage works on the Seven Mile and Burney levels. (The IDB withdrew the Manor House pump application in February 1982.) Instead he would accept an application for a replacement pump (with no associated

drainage works) for the Seven Mile pump alone. This decision, which involved ministerial intervention in what was officially regarded as a local issue, reinforces the statutory duty imposed on IDBs to further the interests of nature conservation and amenity (Section 48 of the 1981 Act) and establishes official policy that replacement pumps can be grant aided and that economic justification of expensive schemes to produce surplus crops on environmentally sensitive land should be very rigorous. The map above outlines the complicated safeguarding arrangements which were technically abandoned as a result of the decision. The Broads Authority is now seeking voluntary notification agreements with the landowners.

41. With respect to National Parks, compulsory notification of proposed agricultural change legally applies only to applicants seeking grant aid under the farm capital grants scheme. Note that this does not cover all available grants, and may be confined to AHGSs so that national park authorities need not be obliged to offer management agreements. Where grant aid is eligible, but is denied for reasons of furthering conservation interests or landscape amenity, such management agreements will be based on financial guidelines accompanying the legislation (DOE Circular 3/83, 1983) — see Figure 4 (p 212). It is not yet clear whether grant aid would be denied if the agricultural benefits were given equal

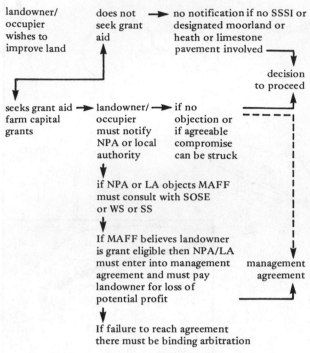

Section 41 Agreements
(National Parks and other designated areas)

Figure 4. **The likely pathway to safeguard parts
of National Parks and other specially defined areas
likely to be subject to official grant aid
but where conservation/amenity interests
are believed to predominate**

Key:
SOSE: Secretary of State for the Environment
WS: Secretary of State for Wales
SS: Secretary of State for Scotland
NPA: National Park Authority

Note:
In both procedures outlined in Figures 3 and 4 (see pp 210
and above) the main objective is not to trigger off statutory
management agreements through objection by conservation/
amenity bodies. Up until now, the indications are that this
approach is working. For example, in Wales since changes to
grant aid notification were announced in October 1980, until
31 July 1982 nearly 2,000 cases have been considered within
SSSIs and National Parks. The majority of those received grant
aid consent and others were subject to modifications. In only
one case did the Welsh Secretary intervene (when the conservation interest was upheld). This kind of experience needs to be
thoroughly investigated by independent research to estimate
the net effects on maintenance of conservation interests and on
the scope for enhancement.

weight to probable amenity losses. All that the Act
says is that the Minister of Agriculture (or the Welsh
Secretary) must 'further' conservation/amenity in so far
as may be consistent with the purpose of the proposal
and with agricultural business, and where that purpose
may be inconsistent with conservation/amenity he must
consult with the environmental interests. The Act says
nothing about any obligation to give way to conserv-
ation/amenity unless the argument is overriding, nor is
the Minister responsible requested to defend his judgement should he side with agriculture. Should the landowner be unwilling to enter into a management agreement, the National Park authority has no compulsory

powers to purchase his land or in any other way secure
the public interest in a particular land management
practice. The Countryside Commission has announced
that it is making £200,000 available in 1982-83 to pay
for management agreements arising out of the Act. This
compares with £4.6m spent by the Commission on all
grant aided schemes. The Government also made
available an additional £125,000 to National Parks
authorities in 1982-83 (via the National Parks
Supplementary Grant) for expenditures incurred in
implementing the Act.

42. These procedures are outlined in some detail because
it is essential to understand why environmental groups
are so frustrated about them and why the Act is so
apparently detrimental to the ethos of a conservation/
development programme for British agriculture (see
Secrett and Rose, 1982). The following points outline
the grounds for concern:

(a) MAFF grant aid for eligible agricultural improve-
    ment appears to be regarded both by Govern-
    ment and farmers as almost a right rather than
    a permissive payment (which is all that it is in
    law).
(b) That right appears somehow sacrosanct even
    when environmental damage is at least as great
    as any private benefit (as narrowly defined and
    valued).
(c) Compensation via management agreements is
    imposed upon the objecting parties out of their
    budgets: they are forced into a costly defence
    often through no fault of their own.
(d) Management agreements are so constructed as to
    place the burden of need for them on the
    objecting conservation authority which must
    make all the running to secure the financial
    agreement. In all cases, except the SSSI where
    a key conservation issue is at stake, the land-
    owner or occupier is free to reject the terms of
    the agreement, and even for SSSIs, only in
    extremely rare cases will he be legally stopped.
(e) Management agreements, sought in such a hostile
    economic environment, are often extremely
    difficult to establish, almost impossible to
    enforce if there is no trust, and make undue
    demands on officials, elected representatives and
    landowners/occupiers.
(f) Where public money, via MAFF, is spent on an
    improvement scheme (notably an arterial
    drainage scheme or flood protection programme)
    more often than not a second payment involving
    public money is required to 'buy out' farmers
    who would not otherwise be in a position to
    improve productivity. Since this second payment
    must come from the hard pressed conservation
    purse this is doubly galling to environmentalists
    and to those who dislike wastage of precious
    public funds.
(g) Under the financial guidelines, the terms for
    compensation may be based on net profits
    foregone assuming the farmer has been eligible to
    deploy his grant and invest his own money. Since
    these profits include price guarantee subsidies

which inflate benefits, again there is a danger of unnecessary public expenditure, irrespective of the conservation importance of protection.

(h) Because grant aid is either available or compensated for (and hence farm income is reasonably guaranteed) land values on protected sites can be unrealistically inflated. In the early stages of preparing a management agreement, however, when the contracting parties are still in negotiation, a variation of planning blight, ie conservation blight, may depress land values and give cause for higher claims to compensation. Both these factors tend to raise the price of a final agreement, and the tempers of the negotiating parties.

(i) Many farmers and landowners willingly forego some 'profit' in order to promote conservation and amenity. This is part of the trust associated with land management that has a deep social history. The new legislation may weaken that resolve as such people see their (possibly unscrupulous) neighbours extracting compensation for foregoing similar 'profit' and being no worse off.

(j) Consequently, the Wildlife and Countryside Act 1981 is in danger of making aesthetic sustainable utilisation of rural resources a purchasable commodity: it could transform what should be a land ethic as first outlined by Leopold (1949) into a money transaction — with all the overtones of what could become dangerously akin to legalised greed. This outcome may not be widespread, but should it come at all, then the Act must be deemed to have failed to assist a new conservation development ethos in the UK (see 'Environmental Ethics and Conservation Action', Part 6).

43. Given these arguments, and bearing in mind the pattern of incentives and subsidies buttressed by a web of expert advice and scientific/technological endeavour, plus the lack of financial/environmental accountability and adequate notification, it is not surprising that there is growing public annoyance over the way in which agricultural activity is so apparently damaging to various aspects of sustainability, and, yet, is so seemingly uncontrolled. Equally relevant is the general ignorance of the forces that shape modern agricultural business. The competing demands for the rural resources of the UK must be accommodated first on the basis of mutual recognition of the various demands made on these resources, second on the basis of trust as mentioned in Chapter 2 of this report and third via new patterns of incentives and penalties as recommended in Chapter 7 of this report.

References

ADAS/NFU. 1981. Energy in agriculture. London, Ministry of Agriculture, Fisheries and Food.

BLACK, C J and BOWERS, J K. 1981. The level of protection of UK agriculture. University of Leeds, School of Economic Studies, Discussion Paper no 99.

BODY, R. 1982. Agriculture: the triumph and the shame, pp 1-25. London, Maurice Temple Smith.

CENTRE OF AGRICULTURAL STRATEGY. 1978. Capital for agriculture. Reading, Centre of Agricultural Strategy.

CORBETT, P S. 1981. Non-entomological impediments to the adoption of integrated past management. Protection Ecology, 3, 183-202.

DOWER, J. 1945. National Parks in England and Wales. Cmnd 6358, paragraph 27. London, HMSO.

ENDS. 1979. The pesticides safety precautions scheme. ENDS, 34 (September), 18-21.

FEIST, M. 1978. A study of management agreements. CCP 114. Cheltenham, The Countryside Commission.

FITTER, A H. 1982. Personal communication, 17 February.

GARDNER, B. 1982. The common agricultural policy and the natural environment, pp 6-7. Brussels, European Environmental Bureau.

GIMINGHAM, C H. (Chairman). 1977. Guide to good muirburn practice. Edinburgh, Department of Agriculture for Scotland.

GRAY, A J. 1979. The ecological implications of estuarine and coastal land reclamation. In Estuarine and coastline land reclamation and storage (editors B Knights and A J Phillips), pp 177-194. Farnborough, Saxon House.

GRIME, J P. 1979. Plant strategies and vegetation processes. Chichester, Wiley.

H M TREASURY. 1980. Capital taxation and the national heritage. London, HMSO.

INSTITUTE OF FISCAL STUDIES. 1982. The distributional effects of the CAP. Working paper no 36. London, Institute of Fiscal Studies.

LEACH, G. 1975. Energy and food production. London, International Institute for Environment and Development.

LEOPOLD, A. 1949. The land ethic in A Sand County almanac, pp 237-263. Oxford, Oxford University Press.

MACEWEN, M and SINCLAIR, G. 1983. New life for the hills. London, Council for National Parks.

MAFF/NFU. 1981. Energy in agriculture. London, MAFF.

MARSH, J S and MACLAREN, D. 1981. Regional impact of the common agricultural policy, UK report. Brussels, Directorate General for Regional Policy, Commission of the European Committees.

MCVEAN, D N and LOCKIE, J D. 1969. Ecology and land use in upland Scotland. Edinburgh, Edinburgh University Press.

MINISTRY OF AGRICULTURE, FISHERIES AND FOOD. 1982. Annual Review of Agriculture. London, HMSO.

NEWBY, H. 1980. Green and pleasant land? Social change in rural England, pp 32, 40. Harmondsworth, Penguin Books.

NORTHFIELD, L. (Chairman). 1979. Report of the committee of inquiry into the acquisition and occupation of agricultural land. Cmnd 7599. London, HMSO.

NORTON-TAYLOR, R. 1982. Whose land is it anyway? How urban greed exploits the land. Wellingborough, Northants, Turnstone Press.

POLLARD, E, HOOPER, M D and MOORE, N W. 1974. Hedges. London, Collins.

POTTS, G R and VICKERMAN, G P. 1975. Arable ecosystems and the use of agrochemicals. In The ecology of resource degradation and renewal (editors M J Chadwick and G T Goodman), pp 17-29. Oxford, Blackwell Scientific Publications.

REID, I G. 1981. Farm finance and farm indebtedness in the EEC. Journal of Agriculture Economics, 32, 265-273.

ROYAL COMMISSION OF ENVIRONMENTAL POLLUTION. 1979. Agriculture and pollution. Cmnd 7644. London, HMSO.

SCOTT COMMITTEE. 1942. Report of the committee on land utilisation in rural areas. Cmnd 6378. London, HMSO.

SECRETT, C and ROSE, C. 1982. Cash or crisis? London, Friends of the Earth.

SELF, P and STORING, H. 1974. The farmers and the state, in Pressure groups in Britain (editors R Kimber and J J Richardson), pp 57-68. London, Dent.

SHOARD, M. 1981. The theft of the countryside. London, Maurice Temple Smith.

STANLEY, O. 1982. Taxation and the conservation of the countryside. Paper available from the Country Landowners Association, London.

STEWART, V I. 1981. Soil drainage and soil moisture. In Amenity grassland on ecological perspective, p 119 (editors I H Rorison and R Hunt). Chichester, Wiley.

STRUTT, N. (Chairman). 1970. Modern farming and the soil. London, HMSO.

TAIT, J. 1980. Treadmills and catastrophies in pest control. New Scientist, 12 June, 254-256.

TAIT, J. 1981. The flow of pesticides: industrial and farming perspectives. In Progress in resource management and environmental planning, vol 3 (editors T O'Riordan and R K Turner), pp 219-250. Chichester, Wiley.

TERRASON, F and TENDRON, G. 1981. The case for hedgerows. The Ecologist, 11 (November), 210-221.

THOMAS, M F and COPPOCK, J T (editors). 1981. Land assessment in Scotland. Aberdeen, Aberdeen University Press.

THURSTON, J M. 1969. The effect of liming and fertilizers on the botanical composition of permanent grassland, and on the yield of hay. In Ecological aspects of the mineral nutrition of plants (editor I H Rorison), pp 3-10. Oxford, Blackwell Scientific Publications.

TOMILINSON, T E. 1972. Nutrient losses from agriculture. Outlook in Agriculture, 6, 272-278.

VINE, A and BATEMAN, D. 1982. Organic farming systems in England and Wales: practice, performance and implications. Aberystwyth, University College of Wales, Department of Agricultural Economics.

WATER SPACE AMENITY COMMISSION. 1980. Conservation and land drainage guidelines. London, Water Space Amenity Commission.

WESTMACOTT, R and WORTHINGTON, T. 1974. New agricultural landscapes. Cheltenham, The Countryside Commission.

WISE, W S and FELL, E. 1978. UK agricultural productivity and the land budget. Journal of Agricultural Economics, 29, 1-7.

WORTHINGTON, T. 1981. The landscapes of institutional landowners. Cheltenham, The Countryside Commission.

CHAPTER 5

A CONSERVATION/ DEVELOPMENT PROGRAMME FOR UK FORESTRY

Introduction

1. Before human settlement became widespread, forest was the natural vegetation of the UK. The fact that only 8.5 per cent of the land surface is now under trees (over half of which has been planted over the past 40 years) can be attributed largely to humans and the grazing of their domesticated animals. In terms of ecological sustainability, forestry science is well equipped to provide the necessary advice as the sustained yield concept is of long standing. Forests cannot be regarded merely as a source of timber. They have vitally important landscape and conservation values which cannot be satisfied by an excessive commitment to wood output. In Chapter 3 of this report, paragraphs 6 to 10 (pp 186 - 187) the basic background to the UK forestry industry was outlined.

Large Scale Coniferous Afforestation and Ecologically Sustainable Utilisation

2. Since its inception in 1919, and especially over the past 40 years, the Forestry Commission has bought land largely with the aim of planting commercial softwood timber. In addition, it has grant aided private landowners seeking a similar objective. The result has been a fairly large increase in even-aged (mostly exotic) coniferous plantations, mostly confined to the poorer upland soils (because the Commission has been unable to buy choicer agricultural lands on the valley sides). This has led to much concern amongst conservation and amenity interests over the possible environmental consequences of coniferous plantations, and to a sensitivity within the Commission as to its public image and wider environmental responsibilities when considering new investment and grant aid.

3. From the perspective of soil management, both the drainage and nutrient rich fertiliser necessary to start a coniferous forest on upland soils have generally improved the soil condition both on peats and mineral soils. However, coniferous trees tend to podsolise (ie change the chemistry and physical structure of the soil profile and remove nutrients) brown earth soils rendering them more acid and reducing ground vegetation browsed upon by ground fauna. Conifers established on heavy textured soils in exposed situations

are prone to windthrow — the blowdown of trees during gales. According to one commentator (Grove, 1982) the standard conifer rotation of 55 years is now being reduced to 30 years to cope with this problem, though the Commission dismisses this as an exaggeration and claims that the timber is still profitable for sawlog and pulp production. Another commentator, whose views are also dismissed by professional foresters (Moore, 1980), argues: 'The national forestry estate is in jeopardy from windblow . . . In the 60 years of the Commission's existence little or no Sitka forest has reached maturity — nor has it shown the profitable timber yield the nation has a right to expect from the orderly conduct of a correctly managed industry . . . Since then (1970) the nation has planted something like a further million Sitka — and I venture to say that none of it will reach maturity'. The Commission believes these views are extreme and the prophesies ill-founded. Nevertheless, the Lords' Select Committee on Science and Technology (1980) received evidence that windthrow could cost the nation £30m in lost timber revenue discounted to 1980 prices and that the old practice of deep ploughing before planting is now to be modified since deep ploughing restricts the growth of lateral roots rendering trees particularly vulnerable. In evidence before the Committee, the Department of Forestry and Natural Resources at the University of Edinburgh argued that far more research was required into the conditions and causes of windthrow before the problem could be overcome. The Department asserted that the Commission 'saw no need' for such research.

4. The Lords' Committee was also very concerned that still far too little is known about the long-term effects of coniferous afforestation on sites which have adapted to suit the climate and vegetation of the alpine tundra. 'Most forest plantations are on sites which, although once covered in woodland, have never had a regular crop harvested from them at present intensities and, in any case, are now covered with species that are not native to the site. Those on deep peat occupy sites, often very poor in nutrients, which have not been under forest for millenia. We do not know what the effect of production forestry will be on the quality of the soil or on future production' (Lords' Select Committee on Science and Technology, 1980). When a soil is drained and supports trees utilising a low nutrient budget (conifers as opposed to hardwoods) it may be difficult to restore its original structure and nutrient status. Certain deciduous trees may find it hard to survive, though professional foresters

argue that hardwoods can come in naturally during second rotation and can become economically viable. With respect to coniferous afforestation of open moorland, as the canopies close, the heath and moorland vegetation that once occupied the ground is killed and replaced by a dense leaf litter with a sparse growth of woodland mosses and scattered vascular plants. This can result in vole plagues, which, in turn, attract owls; of greater significance, plant and animal communities in certain areas, notably various types of valley mire, flush and flush bog, blanket and raised bogs can suffer serious losses. However, as canopies become more open and higher, some of the natural vascular plants return.

5. In evidence before the Lords' Select Committee, the Institute of Biology warned of the ecological dangers inherent in monoculture due to concentrations of pests and pathogens which result from even-aged planting. The Institute stressed that too little is known about the ecology arising from such circumstances or of the effects of widespread spraying of certain chemicals — for example, fenitrothion to control the pine beauty moth caterpillar which damages the introduced lodgepole pine. Widespread pesticide use on conifer plantations is also a matter of concern to the NCC (Ratcliffe, 1980), even though the Commission is cutting down its pesticide applications. The Commission argues that even-aged planting is a temporary though long phase, and that second-generation forests are much more mixed, providing suitable conservation habitats.

6. Afforestation in catchments reduces water yields because it reduces albedo (the reflectivity of the vegetation surface), increases air turbulence in the canopy, traps precipitation by interception and draws moisture from the lower layers through deep roots. It is generally agreed that water flows from coniferous catchments may be as much as 20 per cent lower than from hardwood or unforested catchments with important implications for water supply (Nutter, 1979; Calder and Newson, 1980). However, as always in such studies, there are uncertainties, since the amount of reduction depends on the nature of pre-forest vegetation in the catchment. Nevertheless, it has been calculated that 87 ha of afforestation would cause a loss of 1,000 cubic metres of water per day, the replacement of which would cost £100,000 (Mutch, 1980). Whether this additional cost is more than the import-substituted value of the timber foregone is a matter of much speculation (see Bowers, 1982). The Forestry Commission is aware of this potential conflict and now consults closely with representatives of the water industry before undertaking extensive afforestation in certain catchments. This problem is particularly serious at higher altitudes where rainfall and winds are high. Given that it is also in these areas where conservation and amenity factors may be of the greatest importance, it will be necessary for the Commission to justify more carefully any further large scale plantings in such areas (see also Chapter 4, paragraph 16 of this report, p 202).

7. Recent studies by the Institute of Hydrology suggest that afforestation may also affect the ecology of brown trout. Trout populations in the afforested upper Severn are much lower than in the moor and grass catchments of the upper Wye and Tees. However, as the necessary long-term research has not been completed, these conclusions are largely speculative. Possible causes of trout loss could be lower temperature, lower flows, increase in sediments and chemical residues, all of which may affect the trout directly or indirectly by reducing their food supply. Afforestation (notably coniferous afforestation) also turns drainage water more acid, partly due to chemical releases from the soil and partly because of sulphur dioxide/nitrogen oxide deposition on the leaves (the acid rain effect). Acidity changes can affect the survival of salmon and fish eggs.

8. Coniferous plantations displace the birds associated with the open moor but provide new habitats for other birds. Some of these are common species (chaffinch, wren, woodpigeon) but others are not (goldcrest, crossbill and siskin). Nevertheless, the loss of open moor may have an effect on nationally important populations of specialist breeding birds such as golden eagle, merlin, peregrine, greenshank, golden plover, dunlin and raven. This is the NCC view. Professional foresters believe that more scientific evidence is required, that egg collecting and illegal poisoning are more damaging to raptors and that in Scotland there is sufficient unforested territory to reduce the conflict. However, they do accept that there are problems with merlin, and with golden plover and dunlin in Wales. As for the raven, they argue that improved sheep husbandry which reduces the amount of available carrion is the prime cause of population loss. Currently the Royal Society for the Protection of Birds (RSPB), in conjunction with the NCC, is embarking on a long-term programme of surveys and autecological studies, including a study of the entire British uplands to identify key ornithological sites. Early results indicate a patchy distribution of birds which suggest that forestry operations should be planned with great care. The RSPB is hopeful that the Commission will cooperate closely with them (as well as the NCC which is already consulted) in determining future planting programmes (Broome, 1982), though it is possible that voluntary cooperation may not prove a sufficient safeguard. Some of the open Scottish moor may require tougher protected status, bearing in mind that the north-west Highland region is singled out as an area of global ecological importance in the WCS.

9. In general, however, there is considerable scope for integrating the interests of ornithologists and foresters. Reed (1982) points out how the provision of forest glades, multiple species and different-aged trees can vastly improve the diversity of bird populations, presumably with other conservation gains. But this will require close and effective collaboration between foresters and conservationists, and to date this does not seem to have been the case. A number of members of the BES commented that foresters are still inadequately trained to respond to nature conservation needs, that forestry practices still do not meet minimum conservation objectives, and that, outside of SSSIs, the views of the NCC are far too rarely taken into account. The

Commission counters these accusations by pointing out that it has established conservation plans in a number of forests, with advice and assistance from the NCC and other experts. Admittedly all this is a matter of balance but, in a Conservation and Development Programme for the UK, it seems that the balance should be more evenly weighted. Obviously there will be economic implications, but these must be set in the context of the likely needs for timber products and the considerable conservation (and amenity) gains.

Conservation and Amenity Aspects of Broadleaved Forests

10. Apart from a few upland conifer species (notably in Scotland) the natural tree of the British Isles is the broadleaved hardwood which now constitutes only one quarter of the productive forest area of Britain. Broadleaved woodlands are composed of two kinds: the ancient and semi-natural (composed entirely or mostly of indigenous species) and plantations of introduced species. In its evidence to the Lords' Select Committee (1980), the NCC estimated that 30 to 50 per cent of ancient or semi-natural woodlands was lost between 1947 and 1980 due to changes in agriculture and a switch to conifers (Peterken and Harding, 1975; Rackham, 1976). Since the 1949 Census of Woodlands of Great Britain (conducted by the Forestry Commission) no equivalent data are available, though the Commission is currently undertaking a new survey of trees and woodlands with results due in 1983-84. It has been suggested that there are at least 100,000 owners of small woods (under two ha) in the UK. From a conservation standpoint many of the truly ancient woodlands, ie woods which, in biological terms, have survived essentially unchanged for centuries, even millenia, are of quite unusual significance since many of the rarer vascular plants still found in primary woodlands have virtually no colonising ability. Unless they appeared with the forest they could not have subsequently become established. Similarly a number of insects, notably butterflies, are poor colonisers and so also are uniquely dependent on specific woodlands (Moore, 1976). Smith (1982) describes the biological richness of the ancient wildwood remnants of Snowdonia. In addition, ancient woodlands contain greater biological diversity than newer woodlands especially if they are larger than 10 ha, as seen for birds in Table 11 above. The age and size of the wood are thus vital ecological ingredients: the older and the larger and the more carefully managed, the more their ecological and conservation significance. As Moore (1976) points out, when pressing for the protection of small woods, the emphasis should be upon amenity rather than a conservation. Mabey (1981) believes that woodlands have a 'community' value, not just a scientific one. However, management and commitment are vital ingredients: broadleaved woodlands will have little conservation value if improperly or episodically managed.

11. Trees and woodlands play a vital role in enhancing

Woodland size (ha)	Number of representative species recorded in a typical site	Total number of species recorded in a typical site
0.001 (bush)	0	15
0.01 (corner plantation)	1	28
0.1 (small copse)	8	44
1.0 (wood)	13	51
10.0 (large wood)	33	47
100.0 (very large wood)	37	53

Table 11. Birds and woodland size
Source: Moore, 1976, p 4

the characteristic beauty of the British rural landscape. As the Forestry Commission's principal landscape consultant observed: 'The main elements of the traditional agricultural landscape were functional — hedges were for shelter and confinement of stock, woodlands were for game coverts and timber. To these were added parklands for sheer enjoyment and groups of trees for sheltering buildings. In most parts of lowland Britain, every view was dominated by trees; the land was in tune with human life as well as wildlife. There was visual contrast between horizontal fields and vertical trees, between cultivation and tree growth' (Crowe, 1972). As was indicated in Chapter 2, paragraph 15 of this report (p 182), amenity involves a far more subjective and personal judgement than does conservation. Nevertheless, Helliwell (1976) has sought to produce a scheme for quantifying the amenity value of woodlands, an approach based upon visible area, location in the landscape, viewability, accessibility, condition and other special factors, which he believes should be taken into consideration when grant aided protection policies are formulated. His proposals are outlined in Table 12 (see p 218). Some may quibble that the point spread is too narrow and that other factors should be more prominent, but the principle is a sound one in at least the method focuses the mind on why a woodland should be given special attention.

12. The broadleaved woodland containing exotic species may have less intrinsic scientific value but it certainly does not lack either conservation or amenity interest. What is important here is a management programme which ensures that such woodlands become commercially viable. This is a marketing matter for it will depend upon the demand for coppiced wood and small- to medium-sized trees (to produce cash flow early in the investment cycle) and upon the price available for high quality mature hardwood for veneers (to release cash late in the investment cycle). As with many proposals advanced in this report, a conservation within development approach has to grapple with modern interpretations of economics which are not conducive to implementing the WCS philosophy. Thus, coppicing is not presently an economic proposition in the UK because the demand is small and it is expensive in machinery and labour to deal with the small ancillary wood material. Coppicing

Factor	Points			
	1	2	3	4
Visible area (ha)	0.5 − 1.5	1.5 − 5	5 − 20	20 − 100
Position in landscape	secluded	visible	prominent	very prominent
Number of viewing population	0 − 1	1 − 20	20 − 100	100+
Other trees and woods	densely wooded	some woods	few woods	no woods
Accessibility	no access	access to adjacent land	some access to wood	good access to wood
Condition	poor condition, young plantation	moderate condition, young woodland	good condition, mature woodland	good condition, ancient woodland
Special factors	none	local beauty spot	well known beauty spot	woodland of national importance

Table 12. Method of placing an amenity value on woodlands
Source: Helliwell, 1976, p 29

will only succeed if relative fuel prices change and effective labour costs are very low. Hence it is tempting to visualise an exciting new prospect for British broad-leaved woodland where conservation, amenity and wealth creation intertwine. One should be cautious, however, because from evidence produced for a recent conference (Malcolm *et al*, 1982) the economics of broadleaved forestry are not very promising. To begin with, the home produced component of the British hardwood market is declining and the returns from end use products are failing (see Tables 13 and 14, p 219). Because British hardwoods take a long time to mature, the economic returns are low (with an internal rate of return around 3 per cent and a negative net discounted value even at low rates of discount); hence the need for considerable incentives via grants and tax concessions. Nevertheless, the conservation/amenity aspects of broadleaved woodland are so considerable and the longer-term requirements for home-produced timber sufficiently promising (to offset tropical hardwood imports which add to the destruction of native forests), despite the prospect of timber substitutes, as to suggest that *there should be a much more conscious effort to encourage broadleaved woodland management in the UK*. Steele and Peterken (1982) propose a four fold classification of broadleaved woodland treatment based upon differing priorities over nature conservation and timber production (see Table 15, p 219). It is to be regretted that the Government, in its reply to the request of the Lords' Select Committee on Science and Technology for a long-term policy on broadleaved woodland, noted that: 'the cost of preserving the traditional structure of certain types of broadleaved woodland can be relatively high' (HM Government, 1982). The implication is that such investment must take its place in the (conventionally defined) economic scheme of things.

13. This official response is disappointing to both timber and conservation interests because the fact is that few are prepared to invest the time, effort and money to maintain broadleaved woodland, whether ancient, semi-natural or mostly exotic. Mabey (1981) points out that many of these woodlands are grazed by animals,

and most of those which are not are in need of thinning and replanting and coppicing. (For a good analysis see Smith, 1982, who states that only 700 ha of the 5,400 ha of the Snowdonia wildwood is at present protected.) A recent survey by the Dartington Amenity Research Trust (1980) found that only 20 per cent of farm woodlands were satisfactorily managed from a timber viewpoint, that only another 12 per cent of woods were in a self-regenerating state, and that only about 12 per cent could become favourable for wildlife through suitable management. Another study of small woodland owners in Gwent found that most landowners were not in the right tax bracket to benefit from forestry-related tax relief (see paragraph 17 of this chapter, p 220) and could not reasonably be expected to practise sound management over a 30 year period. It may pay the landowner to grub out the wood and seek grant aid for agricultural improvement. The study indicated that, properly managed, small woodlands have economic potential for sustainable production and marketing. Similar evidence was found from a Norfolk survey, and both reports urged the funding of a woodland officer at county level with wide ranging responsibilities to advise, encourage and initiate woodland management.

The Economics of Modern Forestry

14. Although, as pointed out in Chapter 3 of this report, paragraph 10 (p 187), the present Government has committed itself to an active afforestation policy, there are some who doubt the economic wisdom of massive investments in softwood timber (see especially Ramblers Association, 1981; Bowers, 1982). A Treasury analysis (HM Treasury, 1972) also questioned the net social benefits of forestry, noting that: 'New planting fails to produce a social rate of return, on present forestry practice, and would fail to do so even if regimes were modified as to maximise this rate of return'. Furthermore, the Treasury continued, forestry creates only slightly more jobs than hill farming but at a greater cost,

	1977	1978	1979	1980
Imports				
Temperate origin	221	225	199	179
Tropical origin	416	483	624	402
Total	637	708	823	581
Home produced	735	755	766	519
Actual consumption (minus stock adjustment)	1,200	1,257	1,349	1,084

Table 13. Origin of broadleaved sawnwood
in the UK market, 1977-1980 (1,000m^3)
Source: Elliot, 1982, p 213

	(% end use)	
	home produced (1977)	imported (1973-75)
High value added (furniture, joinery, boat building)	89	28
Utility uses (transport, packages, mining, fencing)	6	66
Miscellaneous	5	6

Table 14. Comparison of end-uses of imported
and home-produced broadleaved woods
Source: Elliot, 1982, p 214

		area involved (ha)
I	Minimal interference maintain or restore ancient and semi-natural woodlands: nature reserve status required	22,000
II	Coppice promote coppice-with-standards on existing ancient woodlands	167,000
III	Restricted high forest plant and maintain species native to the site with preference for selective forest, two-storied high forest and high forest with standards	197,000
IV	Unrestricted high forest manage primarily for timber production with a wider selection of broadleaved species	274,000

Table 15. Suggested management priorities
for broadleaved woodland in the UK
Source: Steele and Peterken, 1982, pp 96-100

ranging from £23,000 per job (in 1972 money, ie £83,000 in 1982 money) in South Scotland to £16,000 (£50,000) in North Wales, compared with £9,500 (£34,000) per job in agriculture in North Wales to £8,000 (£23,000) in North Scotland. In sum, each additional forestry job costs the nation £10,000 (about £36,000 in 1982 money). This study was regarded by the Forestry Committee of Great Britain as misleading and shallow. Accordingly it asked Professor Wolfe to review the evidence. His report (Wolfe, 1973) confirmed their suspicions and concluded that cost per job based on an inappropriate discount rate was an erroneous method for calculating the social and economic advantages of afforestation. Above all, Wolfe recommended that different levels of grant be awarded to meet different objectives, including those of conservation/amenity and recreation. In a policy statement (Forestry Commission, 1972) the Conservative Government of the day argued that forestry investment should be allowed to operate on the basis of a 3 per cent discount rate (compared with 10 per cent for all other public expenditures prevailing at the time) and that such apparently 'uneconomic' expenditure could be justified on the basis of creating employment and stemming rural depopulation. The Forestry Commssion (1977) further justified this investment on the grounds of increasing demand for wood products early in the twenty first century (see Table 3, p 188) but this is based upon crucial assumptions about the state of the world timber market, the conservation-mindedness of existing wood export countries, and the scope for wood product recycling in this country. Price and Dale (1982) argue persuasively that the economics of new upland conifer planting (and hence the implications for upland change) depend critically upon the future trends of timber prices (irrespective of the non-costed disamenity effects). From a study of four forests in North Wales, they estimate that, with no real increase in wood prices, only 23,000 ha (or 19 per cent) of existing rough grazing would be planted, but if stumpage prices rose by 3.5 per cent per year, 95,000 ha (or 85 per cent) of existing rough grazing would be plantable. They conclude that, unless a lot more work is done to improve the modelling of future timber markets and price changes, 'forestry economics will largely be an abstract exercise'.

15. Predicting future timber prices may be difficult enough, but forecasting future timber needs is even more treacherous. Most calculations do not cater for persistent economic recession and inflation and tend to be pessimistic about the possibilities of more efficient use, better harvesting methods and the scope for recycling. At present, only 28 per cent of paper is recovered in the UK, a lower figure than for any other Western economy except for the US where special factors are involved (Turner, 1981). The scope for increased paper recovery is considerable, though this may require price incentives (for example, an environmental depletion tax on virgin timber) together with the breakdown of the quasi-monopoly which presently dominates the secondary paper market in the UK and which determines price, supply and, by inference, demand. Given that a central tenet of the WCS was

increased efficiency in the use of resources, and given the emphasis placed upon this in the companion reports 'Seven Bridges to the Future', Part 1 and 'The Livable City', Part 2, *it is essential that the economics of wood product recovery be reassessed in line with another careful look at the need for new forestry investments, particularly where these are not integrated with other rural land-uses.* These comments refer particularly to the softwood timber market. As regards hardwood timber, Britain should take special care not to demand too much from the tropical forests which are already seriously ravaged (see 'The UK's Overseas Environmental Policy', Part 5). It is in this sector where particular attention should be given to new investment, for the UK imports 60 per cent of its hardwood needs (see Table 13, p 219).

16. The private timber lobby, represented by the Timber Growers England and Wales and Timber Growers Scotland, and by the Ulster Timber Growers Organisation, works very closely with the Forestry Commission consulting jointly through the Timber Growers Great Britain. The lobby is also represented on the Home Grown Timber Advisory Committee, the Forestry Commission's main statutory advisory body. The MacEwens (1982) describe this relationship as 'incestuous', noting that the former Chairman of the Commission became Chairman of the largest private forestry company, the Economic Forestry Group, and Hall (1982) calls it 'a cosy little club'. Certainly the lobby has done well to maintain its level of grant aid funding in these difficult economic times, even though, under the new Forestry Act 1981, the Commission must dispose of some of its holdings (necessarily to private owners) as part of a programme of cost cutting and revenue generation.

17. To understand why commercial forestry is so well protected, one must recognise the psychology of the arguments regarding import substitution — arguments which have been supported by successive Governments. In view of the points raised in paragraphs 14 and 15 of this chapter (see pp 218 - 219) these arguments may be exaggerated, especially in view of the running down of the domestic pulp industry. One must also bear in mind the significant tax advantages available to private landowners. The long interval between planting and felling makes private forestry especially responsive to changes in taxation which affect the net cost of management. Income earners paying at the top end of the scale (60 per cent for earned income and 75 per cent for unearned income) can obtain a tax relief equivalent to 60p (or 75p) in the £ for all funds invested in the early years of a plantation. It also pays for an owner to elect for Schedule D assessment at the beginning (thus no tax is paid at all) so that all early expenditure can be offset against other taxable income derived from elsewhere on the estate, and for his inheritors to elect for Schedule B when thinning and felling takes place. Under Schedule B only a nominal assessment is made resulting in a low tax liability. Thus, timber management can have real economic advantages to high income tax payers long before a tree is cut: the

Treasury estimates it foregoes £10m annually through these factors. CTT is also payable on productive forest land, but unless it is paid at the time of death it may become onerous if the inheritor delays payment until the timber is felled because he would be liable for CTT on the value of the wood cut. This would be considerably more than the value of the timber at the time of death of the original owners. The Economic Forestry Group estimate that a landowner subject to tax at 50 per cent, who invests in 100 ha of upland afforestation, need only pay 41 per cent of a total outlay of £72,550 over 10 years, yet enjoy an asset worth £50,000 excluding the value of the land. Should part of his investment go into agriculture he would be eligible for grant aid subsidy on livestock purchase and management. Private coniferous plantations are subsidised not so much via grants as through tax relief, but because there is no scope for independent assessment of proposals whose economic feasibility in many cases may be questionable (outside SSSIs and national parks) the public interest in the conservation and amenity aspects of private afforestation is not necessarily safeguarded.

18. Private landowners seeking grant aid could previously participate in a Commission-financed dedication scheme of which there have been three kinds: Basis I and II (closed to new applicants in 1972) and Basis III (closed to new applicants in 1981). These schemes were legal covenants with the Commission through which the owner agreed to dedicate his land to productive utilisable timber. The schemes entitle the owner to grants for planting and management. The objectives of the Basis III management plan also included a requirement to promote sound land management and environmental benefits, plus the provision of appropriate opportunities for recreation (including public access). Some 140,000 ha (22 per cent of all dedicated woodland) are currently managed under Basis III. About three-quarters of the land under the dedication schemes consists of new planting (mostly conifers) in contrast to the schemes' original objective of restocking felled woodlands.

19. The conservation and amenity interests remained concerned that these incentives were not sufficient to encourage the planting and management of broadleaved woodlands which were mostly found in small blocks on small estates, but which collectively could be an invaluable asset in any conservation strategy. In 1977, the Commission introduced a small woods scheme to enable landowners with 10 ha or less of woodland to benefit from higher rates of grant. This scheme was administratively simpler to operate involving two payments: a capital sum on initiation of the scheme and a second sum after five years of satisfactory management. There were no legal deeds or contractual obligations thereafter. The Forestry Commission spent £205,000 in 1978-79 on small wood grants, assisting in the planting of 390 ha of broadleaved trees and 294 ha of conifers in the whole of England and Wales.

20. As part of the present Government policy to reduce public sector administrative costs, the Forestry

Commission recently streamlined its administration of private woodlands. The new proposals discontinue the dedication scheme and the small woods scheme to reduce the administrative costs of supervision and of preparing new schemes for successors in title. Existing dedication schemes will continue for present participants but not for new owners. The new scheme is, in effect, an administratively simpler form of Basis III, but covering woods from 0.25 ha upwards (see Table 16). An important feature is the higher rate of grant for planting broadleaved species for small woodlands. It is too early to tell how far this will encourage broadleaved woodland management but it is certainly a step in the right direction (see Table 17). Otherwise, grants will be the same both for replanting and for stocking. Tenants and lessees as well as owners are eligible. Some conservation groups criticise these proposals which appear to remove the long-term advantages of covenanted commitment to sustained management. In fact, the old dedication scheme was largely a negative control ensuring that the land was not used for purposes other than forestry. The new arrangements build in a more positive management approach but may require more supervision and commitment than can reasonably be assumed, given current 'one-off' grant aid. Smith (1982) argues that the Commission should assist a long-term management programme for selected wild-woods with money to pay for stock proof fencing, for the removal of undesirable tree species, and for selective felling to stimulate natural regeneration.

21. All Forestry Commission grants are geared to timber management, though environmental aspects of such management are relevant. The Countryside Commissions also grant aid private owners to plant and manage small woods primarily for amenity purposes. In 1980, the Countryside Commission (England and Wales) was forced to cut off grants to new applicants for wood of less than 0.25 ha (on which expenditure had soared from £122,000 in 1975-6 to £300,000 in 1978-9) because of a reduced budget. In England and Wales, the Countryside Commission spent £1.4m in 1980-1 on existing tree planting schemes, about a third of its total grant aid, yet it is unlikely that new planting is replacing losses of broadleaved trees, especially if the losses due to Dutch elm disease are taken into account.

Safeguarding Conservation-Amenity within Afforestation Practice

22. Forestry operations, like agricultural activities, lie generally outside planning controls, though when processing its planting, grant aiding and felling programmes, the Forestry Commission is expected to undertake a fairly elaborate consultative procedure. The administration of this procedure is currently under review. The reason why environmental interests would like more say in Commission decisions is that a substantial part of the area it recognises as being afforestable lies within areas designated for their scenic

Area of wood	Conifers	Broadleaves
	(per hectare)	
0.25 – 0.99	£600	£850
1.00 – 2.99	£480	£700
3.00 – 9.99	£400	£600
over 10	£230	£450

(Basis III dedication gave grants of £140 per ha for conifers and £315 per ha for broadleaved trees plus an annual management grant of £4.20)

Table 16. **Grants available under the forestry grants scheme from 1 October 1981**
Source: Forestry Commission (personal communication)

	No of applications	Proposed planted area (ha)	Approved planted area (ha)
England	888	8,700	4,340
Scotland	476	42,552	22,194
Wales	126	2,131	1,150
Great Britain	1,490	53,383	27,684

Table 17. **New broadleaved planting for nine months ending 30 June 1982**
Source: Forestry Commission (personal communication)

beauty and/or conservation value. In England and Wales, about 20 per cent of all the Commission's holdings lie in national parks, though about half of the technically plantable area lies within National Parks or AONBs. In Scotland, too, about half the technically plantable area lies in national scenic areas. The Commission's dilemma is that it is generally forced to buy land only as it appears on the market. Hence, neither the shape nor the location of its property may conform to what might be desirable on amenity and conservation grounds.

23. In 1974, the relevant Forestry Ministers directed the Commission to establish new consultative procedures in order that a wider array of interests should be notified before new planting decisions, including private forestry schemes and felling licences, were determined. (For Scotland, see SDD Memorandum No 72/1974; for England and Wales, see DOE Circular 36/78 'Welsh Office' Circular 64/78.) These procedures involve the local planning authorities, and, through them, other interested parties (including conservation and amenity interests) plus agriculture and water supply authorities. Where agreement cannot be reached between these parties and the applicant and/or the Commission, the Commission refers the matter to its relevant Regional Advisory Committee (RAC). These Committees were reconstituted to incorporate representatives of agriculture, planning and environmental interests with terms of reference that included advice on the social effects of the Commission's activities, the scope for development of recreational use and public access, and the continued good relationship between all rural resource-using interests and reconciliation of differences. In considering specific cases referred to it,

*A general view over the Coed-y-Brenin Forest in Merioneth, showing how the new
conifer plantations have been skilfully blended with fields and broadleaved woodlands*
(By courtesy of the Forestry Commission)

the RAC normally sets up a small sub-committee with membership reflecting the interests involved in the dispute. The Commission claims that this sub-committee is 'appropriately balanced' and is not dominated by forestry interests. If the RAC is unable to resolve the dispute, it reports its views on the issue to the Commission. In the case of applications for grant aid or for felling licences, the Commission is required to seek the advice of the appropriate Forestry Minister before reaching a final decision.

24. The conservation/amenity lobby claims that these procedures are inadequate, *ad hoc*, exclusive and unnecessarily secretive (for examples, see the MacEwens, 1982). Currently, the Commission is reviewing the whole consultative mechanism with a view to streamlining it while providing adequate safeguards for taking into account the views of all relevant interests (Forestry Commission, 1980). The Commission is proposing to concentrate its consultation on the more sensitive areas and to extend the method of 'consultation by notification' through which interested parties are given a fixed time in which to comment. The environmental lobby is unhappy about the Commission's use of the local planning authority as the 'representative' local interest for this procedure and remains hostile to the lack of open accountability which appears to permeate the Commission's decision making, no matter how

well-intentioned the aims of reducing unnecessary delays.

25. The Commission's proposals regarding the simplification of felling controls were also controversial. Under the Forestry Act 1967, the Commission formalised its powers over all felling largely in the interests of safeguarding amenity. The only exemptions are in woodlands subject to an approved management plan under a dedication scheme. There is also provision for up to 30 cubic metres of timber to be felled in any quarter without a licence, although not more than 5.5 cubic metres may be sold. Enforcement of such conditions is very difficult. Again, with a view to economising on administration, the Commission proposed to remove felling licence controls for small woodlands of less than 0.25 ha (including hedgerow trees) and to subject any felling proposals to notification to local planning authorities under amendments to the Town and Country Planning Acts. The Commission also proposed that these thinnings and fellings, for 'silvicultural' reasons, would be exempt from notification.

26. Conservation/amenity interests were agitated about these suggestions which, they argued, appeared to rely too much on the trust of the landowners. In May 1982, the Secretary of State for Scotland announced that the Government had decided not to pursue the proposals

*Soudley Ponds, Forest of Dean, Gloucestershire. Conifers planted
well back from the water with a fringe of broadleaved trees retained*
(By courtesy of the Forestry Commission)

relating to the removal of felling licences from detached woodlands of less than 0.25 ha, nor has it changed the existing restriction on the sale of licence-free quotas of timber. The Government has endorsed the proposal to exempt from the felling licence the thinning of trees in woodlands for silvicultural purposes, but the Forestry Commission is to consult with the Environment Departments and the Timber Growers Great Britain to reach a mutually acceptable definition of 'thinning'. While the conservation/amenity interests may doubtless welcome the other proposals, they may not be satisfied with the last decision, since so much will depend upon trust and the nature of advice. In addition, once a felling licence is granted and grant aid for replanting is issued, only one subsequent inspection is to be made to ensure that the job is adequately done.

27. Denial of forestry grants to private landowners on grounds of furthering nature conservation and amenity in national parks and SSSIs is now subject to voluntary compensation arrangements by National Park authorities and the NCC under the Wildlife and Countryside Act 1981. At present, the Forestry Commission is involved in talks with the NCC regarding the financial guidelines relevant to SSSIs. Such an agreement, however, would be non-statutory and would apply to SSSIs only. What happens when eligible grant aid applications are opposed by national park and other local authorities in order to protect landscape amenity remains to be seen.

References

BOWERS, J K. 1982. Is afforestation economic? *ECOS, 3 (1)*, 4-7.

BROOME, C. 1982. The RSPB view. *ECOS, 3 (1)*, 20-21.

CALDER, I R and NEWSON, M D. 1980. The effects of afforestation on water resources in Scotland. In Land assessment in Scotland (editors M F Thomas and J J Coppock), pp 57-59. Edinburgh, Edinburgh University Press.

CROWE, S. 1972. Agriculture and the landscape. *Outlook on agriculture, 6*, 291-296.

DARTINGTON AMENITY RESEARCH TRUST. 1980. Small woods on farms. Shinners Bridge, Devon, Dartington Amenity Research Trust.

ELLIOT, G K. 1982. The British market for broadleaved sawnwood and plywood. In Malcolm *et al.* 1982, pp 211-220.

FORESTRY COMMISSION. 1972. Forestry policy. London, HMSO.

FORESTRY COMMISSION. 1977. The wood production outlook in Great Britain: a review. Edinburgh, The Forestry Commission.

FORESTRY COMMISSION. 1980. Private forestry: a consultative paper on the administration of felling control and grant aid. Edinburgh, The Forestry Commission.

GROVE, R. 1982. The forestry debate. *ECOS, 3 (1)*, 1-2.

HALL, C. 1982. The forestry club. *ECOS, 3 (1)*, 10-12.

HELLIWELL, D R. 1976. The small woodland: social benefits, landscape, amenity and recreation. In The future of the small woodland, pp 23-35. Castleton, Derbyshire, Loosehill Hall.

HM GOVERNMENT. 1982. Scientific aspects of forestry: government response, p 6. London, HMSO.

HM TREASURY. 1972. Forestry in Great Britain: an inter-departmental cost benefit study. London, HMSO.

LORDS SELECT COMMITTEE ON SCIENCE AND TECHNOLOGY. 1980. Scientific aspects of forestry. HL Paper 381 I and II. London, HMSO.

MABEY, R. 1981. The common ground. A place for nature in Britain's future? London, George Allen & Unwin.

MACEWEN, A and MACEWEN, M. 1982. National parks: conservation or cosmetics?, p 212. London, George Allen & Unwin.

MALCOLM, D C, EVANS, J and EDWARDS, P N. (editors). 1982. Broadleaves in Britain, pp 197-232. Edinburgh, Edinburgh University Press.

MOORE, D. 1980. Respacing of sitka spruce. *Quarterly Journal of Forestry, 74*, 63.

MOORE, N. 1976. The scientific, wildlife and education benefits of woods of varying ages and sizes. In The future of the small woodland. Castleton, Derbyshire, Loosehill Hall.

MUTCH, W E S. 1980. Comment on the Calder Newson paper. In Land assessment in Scotland, p 59 (editors M F Thomas and J T Coppock). Edinburgh, Edinburgh University Press.

NUTTER, W L. 1979. Effects of forest plantations on the quantity, quality and timing of water supplies. In The ecology of even aged forest plantations (editors E D Ford, D E Malcolm, J Atterson), pp 357-367. Cambridge, Institute of Terrestrial Ecology.

PETERKEN, G F (editor). 1981. Woodland conservation and management. London, Chapman and Hall.

PETERKEN, G F and HARDING, P T. 1975. Woodland conservation in eastern England: comparing the effects of changes in three study areas since 1964. *Biological Conservation 8*, 279-298.

PRICE, C and DALE, I. 1982. Price predictions and economically afforestable area. *Journal of Agricultural Economics, 33*, 13-21.

RACKHAM, O. 1976. Trees and woods in the British landscape. London, Dent.

RAMBLERS ASSOCIATION. 1981. Afforestation: the case against expansion. London, Ramblers Association (1-5 Wandsworth Road).

RATCLIFFE, D. 1980. Forestry in relation to nature conservation. Evidence before the Lords Select Committee on Science and Technology. HL Paper 381 II, pp 110-144. London, HMSO.

REED, T M. 1982. Birds and afforestation. *ECOS, 3 (1)*, 8-10.

SMITH, M. 1982. How to save the forests of Snowdonia. *New Scientist, 1 July*, 14-17.

STEELE, R C and PETERKEN, G F. 1982. Management objectives for broadleaved woodland conservation. In Malcolm *et al (op cit)*, pp 91-103.

TURNER, R E. 1981. An economic evaluation of recycling schemes. In Progress and resource management and environmental planning, vol 3 (editors T O'Riordan and R K Turner), pp 109-160. Chichester, Wiley.

WOLFE, J N. 1973. Some considerations regarding forestry policy in Great Britain. London, The Forestry Committee of Great Britain.

CHAPTER 6

INTEGRATING RURAL RESOURCE MANAGEMENT

Introduction

1. This chapter seeks to fill the voids not yet covered by the discussion of rural conservation/development relationships of the previous two chapters and to point out the scope for better integration of rural resource-use strategies.

Rural Communities in Transition

2. The pattern and function of rural settlement in Britain are forever changing. The 1981 census returns revealed a continuation in the decline of the older metropolitan centres (see 'The Livable City', Part 2) with growth in the metropolitan peripheries (mainly satellite towns and villages) and in the remoter rural districts (see Figure 5, p 226). However, in recent years, most of the growth was in the regional market towns, not the 'remoter' villages (see Figure 6, p 227). The rising cost of fuel, the decline in services (notably schools, shops, libraries and health care), the escalation in house prices and falling job opportunities have combined to reduce the attractiveness of the remoter village and small town to young, family forming people in particular and to local residents in general. Rural villages and towns remain popular with older and often retired (urban) people with sufficient capital to settle seasonally (in second homes) or permanently (Hodge and Whitby, 1981).

3. The rural community is undergoing a difficult period of transition between a desire to keep up with modern standards of living and a desire to protect a 'traditional' social structure and communal way of life based on viable, locally-provided services. The key to any new balance between the traditional and the modern must lie in better employment opportunities, coupled with the provision of adequate housing and basic social services. At present, unemployment levels in most rural counties are about 50 per cent higher than the national average (though a smaller total is involved); locally, amongst women and young people the rates may be higher still (National Council for Voluntary Organisations, 1980). In Northern Ireland, unemployment levels and general deprivation are worse than in Great Britain. Rural wages are also lower than the national average and opportunities for skill training are limited. Many rural residents live at,

or close to, the 'poverty trap'. Outmigration of young people is partially offset by immigration of the elderly. In most remote rural areas, over 25 per cent of the population is over 60, compared with 16 per cent nationally. Elderly people require special services and tend to be less mobile in a society where personal mobility is the key to access to services (Moseley, 1981). Housing is becoming increasingly difficult to obtain since planning controls reduce the supply of new houses and many local people cannot afford to purchase houses at inflated prices (National Federation of Housing Associations, 1981). Local authorities, squeezed by reductions in the rate support grant and unwilling to raise local rates, are not investing in public housing at a rate sufficient to meet demand. Shortage of people and money result in fewer patrons and customers in local shops, pubs, post offices and cinemas, all of which cannot survive the competition from the larger and more efficient service providers (often backed up by non-local money) in nearby towns. This tends to result in differential deprivation of services affecting those without a car, on low fixed incomes and in need of special care and attention. Limited opportunities for leisure and cultural activities are particularly felt by young people. Those who are short of time as well as cash are especially hard hit, so many under-utilise what services are available.

4. Overcoming all these problems will not be easy; indeed the difficulties may be insurmountable. A Treasury report on rural depopulation (HM Treasury, 1976) concluded that, on purely economic grounds, the arguments for spending a lot of money on job creation were not at all strong, but the authors conceded that on social grounds the effort should be made. Despite their good work, the various national Development Commissions' agencies and boards are all underfunded in relation to the task demanded of them, and, at present, at least, job losses far outstrip job gains. The establishment of a focused rural lobby, Rural Voice, composed of agricultural, voluntary service and environmental interests may help to stimulate action, but, unless there is fairly radical rethinking of existing policies and departmental responsibilities, it seems unlikely that widespread success in terms of retaining a mosaic of viable rural communities will be achieved. It is already apparent that neither agriculture nor forestry as currently operated can provide an adequate employment base; indeed, a recent survey by the Country Landowners Association (1980) found that,

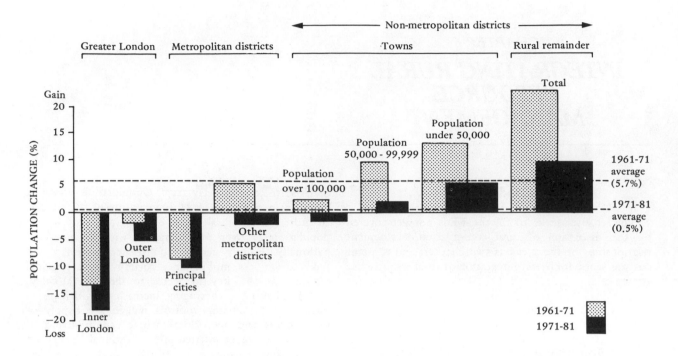

Figure 5. Percentage population change 1961-71 and 1971-81 in urban and rural areas
Source: Craig, 1982, p 15

over a representative sample of areas, employment in farming, forestry and estate management had dropped by 40 per cent between 1960 and 1979. *New job opportunities will have to be found in small industry, craftwork, game management, landscape care and tourism.* It is also likely that job sharing and seasonal complementarity of employment (tourist service in summer; care of land, craftwork in winter) will become more common. *Also, the scope for exchange of services involving an extension of the 'informal economy' should be thoroughly explored.* (See Turning Point, 1981; Woollett, 1981). (The importance of the informal economy for a Conservation and Development Programme for the UK is explored in 'Seven Bridges to the Future', Part 1 and 'The Livable City', Part 2.)

5. One limited success story is the Small Business Divisions of the Welsh and Scottish Development Agencies and their English equivalent, the Council for Small Industries in Rural Areas (CoSIRA), the main agent of the Development Commission. CoSIRA is wholly funded by the Development Commission and provides technical and management advice, training facilities and loans to small firms. Its work is guided by voluntary Small Industries Committees (SICs) in the counties, who are geared to understand local problems and the needs and abilities of local people. Priority is given to firms in Assisted Areas, Special Investment Areas and pockets of need identified by the SIC. Since March 1982, the Development Commission has been offering grant aid for the conversion of redundant farm buildings for workshop or light industrial use. The scheme was extended in October 1982 to cover all LFAs and eligibility widened to potential users of the buildings. The various national Development

Commissions are now working more closely with local authorities, sharing projects, cooperating on planning proposals (eg by allowing for the suitable conversion .of old buildings) and seeking agreement over new housing policies. The rural housing shortage is one of the most serious stumbling blocks to community development — an impediment that can only be overcome with new attitudes, new approaches, new financial and taxing arrangements and a lot of community help (National Federation of Housing Associations, 1981).

6. Over the past 10 years there have been significant changes in most of the factors that affect people's leisure, namely the disposable (free) time available, disposable income and mobility. Add to this the greater interest in the countryside, and the increase generally of recreational opportunities now provided in rural areas, and it is hardly surprising that trips to the countryside have increased dramatically (see Chapter 3, paragraph 11, pp 187 - 188 of this report).

7. It is likely that open air activities, based on small capital expenditure such as walking and picnicking and even driving for pleasure, will not diminish in the foreseeable future, though the growth in more expensive recreational pursuits may slow down from the rather high growth rates of the early 1970s (Countryside Commission, 1979; Blacksell and Gilg, 1981). Locally, there will be problems of congestion, leading in some instances to erosion (popular mountain and moorland walks; coastal dunes) and heightened tension between those who try to use the same recreational space for incompatible pursuits (eg ramblers vs trailbike users; sailors vs motor cruiser users; anglers vs boat users). In general, however, these problems can be handled by

Towns' population change

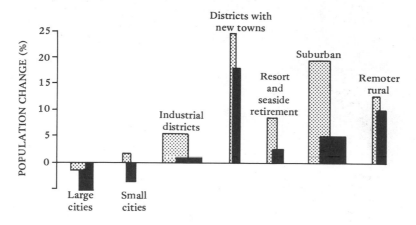

Rural population change

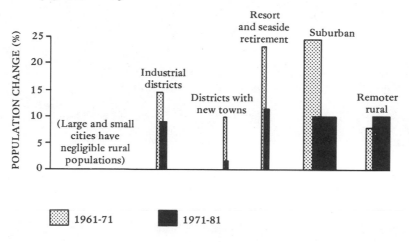

▨ 1961-71   ■ 1971-81

Figure 6. **Percentage population change 1961-71 and 1971-81 by size of town and category of rural area**
Source: Craig, 1982, p 17

considerate management, improved understanding and, on occasion, special restrictive measures. As is so often the case, it is all a matter of priority of public expenditure backed up by management commitment (see, for example, Smith, 1982, who discusses the need to maintain popular walking trails in Snowdonia National Park).

8. Various reports by the Recreation Ecology Research Group confirm these observations: in general, recreation and environmental sustainability can be compatible given appropriate management. For example, a study of moorland erosion in the Peak District (Yalden, 1981) has indicated that moorland damage is due to a variety of causes including acid precipitation, over-grazing, fires (some of which are accidentally started by visitors) and trampling by sheep and walkers. But the last factor is small relative to the other causes. In general, as in most matters covered in this report, coordinated research and monitoring are required. The sensitivity of specific habitat types, the fragility of certain soil/vegetation systems, the disturbance of wildfowl and the

levels of compatibility between recreational use and conservation all need to be better understood. The preparation of management plans based upon land assessment and land capability studies offers tremendous scope here, assuming that trained people are available (and are employed) to do the job properly.

9. One reason why recreational pressures can result in environmental damage is that people tend to concentrate on a relatively small number of well known sites or paths. This is partly a matter of popularity (eg the Snowdonia trails and certain RSPB sites), partly a result of limited information about what alternatives are available (a problem now being tackled through the publication of interpretative trails by the Countryside Commission and local authorities) and partly because of lack of access. The access issue is by no means solved, which was so clearly evident in the arguments over the footpath provisions of the Wildlife and Countryside Bill. In Scotland the problem is less acute at present, though a number of 'hot spots' are causing some difficulties. *More needs to be done to coordinate the work*

A 3,500 square foot advance factory designed and built by CoSIRA at Kingston in the North Herefordshire/
South Shropshire Investment Area. Careful design and landscaping ensure that factories fit into the local scene
(By courtesy of the Development Commission)

of the ad hoc *Spicer Committee* (as discussed in Mattingly, 1982) *at the local level by introducing locally organised access committees operating along the lines of the successful Small Industries Committees. Also, more attention must be given to the matter of publicity, to the provision of footpath networks, and to the safe-guarding of landowners who, through no fault of their own, should be protected against liability in case of accident caused to visitors.* Certainly the time has come for a thorough review of the nature of access rights and the workings of access agreements which are nothing like as ubiquitous as should be the case (Ramblers Association, 1982). Indeed, there is a *prima facie* case for encouraging landowners, especially in the uplands, to improve and extend footpath access through appropriate management agreements, and to work with the Farming and Wildlife Advisory Group (FWAG) and similar organisations to maintain and extend existing footpath access in lowland areas. Westmacott and Worthington (1974) found that landowners were by no means opposed to public access, so long as the footpath network could be reorganised to lessen unnecessary conflict with agriculture. Ramblers' interests fear that 'reorganisation' can lead to closure and increased problems of access.

10. Rights of access onto common land in England and Wales also need to be re-examined. There are approximately 600,000 ha of common lands described by the Royal Commission on Common Land (1958) as 'the last reserve of uncommitted land in England and Wales'. The Commons Registration Act of 1965 was passed in response to a recommendation from the Royal Commission, but the process of registration apparently has opened up a number of loopholes which allow some lands to be taken off the register. This assertion should be investigated and, if proven, appropriate amending legislation prepared. Also, the recommendation from the Commission that all commons should be open to the public on foot as of right should be put into effect.

11. Tourism and recreation have been suggested as having the potential to help rural economies by promoting employment, generating income and improving the viability of local enterprises. This view is supported by the Department of the Environment (1979) and by the Heads of Agreement between the Countryside Commission and the English and Welsh Tourist Boards concluded in 1978. However, ill-planned tourist schemes can impair the quality of outdoor experience and landscape amenity and can destroy the character of local settlements. Nevertheless, amenity interests are less hostile to the tourist industry nowadays, for they see in community enterprise tourism

An electrical switchgear manufacturer installed in one of the Development Commission's advance factories
at Bampton in Devon provides welcome jobs
(By courtesy of the Development Commission)

some scope for rural renaissance.

12. The precise economic effect of tourism in remote rural areas is not well understood because only a small number of research studies has been published and there may well be considerable differences between one locality and another. From the evidence available it seems that tourism does little to boost a local economy, but the fault lies not so much in the tourist industry as in the structural weakness of the local rural economy itself (Tourism and Recreational Research Unit, 1982). This is because the support services which benefit from tourist income are often not in the local area so that very little money remains where it is spent. The general conclusion is also found when analysis of income multipliers (additional income induced by tourist spending) is undertaken; people who earn their living from tourist related activities in remote rural areas, when spending their money, do not stimulate local industry and services.

13. While the tourist industry may not prove a panacea for providing jobs in remote rural areas, at least it does offer scope for supplementing the income of farms. A study of 14 on-farm tourism facilities in West Herefordshire, for example, revealed an average pre-tax income of £2,000, ranging from £380 to £5,900 for a farm offering accommodation and meals for up to 14 people. These kinds of incomes are especially likely if groups of farms which are willing to accommodate tourists are prepared jointly to publicise their services (as is now being tried in the Peak District, the Lake District and other upland areas). For it is in accommodation and meals that most of the local income gains are made, and, indeed, look quite impressive compared to other economic activities. Table 18 (see p 230) gives an indication of income in relation to the points made above.

A survey of local residents in Wales (Wales Tourist Board, 1981) found that local residents welcomed tourism (about 10 per cent of the workforce in west Wales is dependent upon tourism) and seemed prepared to tolerate much of the noise, congestion and litter that tourism often brings.

Game Management, Conservation and Amenity

14. It is sometimes believed that management of lands for game not only leads to jobs and local income but is also compatible with conservation and amenity interests. Such a generalisation should be avoided. The economic

	Income ratio	Income as proportion of £1 turnover***
Agriculture		
dairying	1.37	0.20
livestock	1.22	0.30
mixed farming	1.46	0.33
Manufacturing		
large scale	1.16	0.20
tourism related	1.13	0.40
other	1.15	0.42
Tourism		
hotel	1.75	0.36
guesthouse	1.55	0.42
bed and breakfast	1.22	0.81
self catering	1.46	0.43
retail	1.95	0.22
restaurant	1.82	0.37

* direct income is the sum of wages, rent and profit paid by
the type of business specified

** direct plus induced income is the sum of direct income
plus all income derived from that income (wages, rent
and profit paid by suppliers of the business specified, and
wages, rent and profit as a result of all income earned).

*** a measure of the extra income induced for every £1 spent
in the business specified.

Table 18. **The ratio between direct income***
and direct plus induced income** in selected industries
in and near National Parks in England and Wales
Source: Tourism and Recreation Research Unit,
1982, p 246

gains from game are modest but not insignificant. An economic analysis of the sale of lands with sporting rights attached indicates that almost all profit is swallowed up in maintaining the game and paying the gamekeepers (who, admittedly, might otherwise be unemployed). A study of 12 estate sales in Scotland (Hanson, 1976) revealed that the capital values of grouse range from £200 to £370 per brace, of stag from £3,000 to £4,000 each, of salmon from £400 to £1,000 per fish, and of sea trout about £110 per fish. The average cost of maintaining pheasant was £4.71 in 1975 (about £10.83 in 1982 prices) while the average rental value for the shoot was only £5 per bird (£13.50). It has been calculated that the gross annual return from the grouse shooting industry in Scotland in 1974 was £4m (about £10m) and that moorland management for grouse can be complementary to wildlife and even sheep grazing interests, but not to forestry (Phillips, 1974). It has already been noted that some grouse management methods (notably moorland burning) are not always compatible with soil sustainability or nature conservation. The Game Conservancy estimates that game shooting contributes £100m annually in taxes, sporting rights, letting, wages and sale of game. The 1980 National Angling Survey showed that in England and Wales 2.7 million anglers spent £420m on coarse and game angling. In March 1983, the Standing Conference on Countryside Sports published a comprehensive study of the economic value of field sports.

15. Deer management is less easy to accommodate with conservation/development principles, for deer compete with domestic livestock for food and, if uncontrolled, can damage young trees. The NCC believes that parts of the Scottish Caledonian pine forest are affected by browsing deer. Yet the deer-stalking industry in Scotland is worth £3m annually, and employs 300 people directly and 400 people indirectly (Jarvie, 1981). Much work has now been done by the Red Deer Commission and the Institute of Terrestrial Ecology to understand how red deer forestry can coexist through careful planting design, good deer control and the planting of more 'deer-resistant species'. However, because the wintering grounds for all deer species are being lost owing to developments in agriculture and forestry, the conflict between deer (both red and roe) and commercial forestry and agriculture is becoming more serious (Lords' Select Committee on Science and Technology, 1980, plus evidence by the Red Deer Commission). If deer are to coexist with forest (depending upon what additional areas are planted) it may be necessary to extend deer culling possibly by opening up short-term licences for forest stalking. This might attract continental Europeans who prefer closed canopy stalking, leaving the open moorland stalking to the dedicated traditionalists. Such an operation would have to be supervised according to strict codes of practice, suitably enforced, though in some areas more intensive culling may be required.

16. In lowland Britain, game management is also not very profitable (Westmacott and Worthington, 1974), rarely generating as much revenue as alternative land-uses might provide. However, shooting game is a tradition with important social connotations in many rural areas, and it may well be that many small woodlands and hedgerows are looked after because of the cover they provide, when otherwise they might be neglected. In strict conservation terms, game-managed small woodlands may have little value and public access may be severely restricted, but in amenity terms such woodlands can be of considerable local importance. As a side issue, however, loss of young game due to pesticides has caused some farmers to rethink their spraying policies (Cox, 1981; see Chapter 4 of this report, paragraph 11, pp 200 - 201).

Fitting the Rural Resource Jigsaw Together

17. Most of the discussion in this report has concentrated on resource-uses almost in isolation. This has been deliberate, partly to simplify the analysis, but, sadly, also because most management agencies are so structured in aim and budget that they tend to compartmentalise their expertise and resources into economically wasteful and environmentally counterproductive sectoral investment. This is a highly unsatisfactory state of affairs, yet surprisingly little is done to allow grants in aid and other incentives to flow across the boundaries that separate Departmental responsibilities. Indeed, the difficulties of achieving

effective and sustained cooperation can be quite considerable as the following discussion illustrates.

Forestry and Agriculture

18. A small number of studies backed by many exhortatory reports — for a good bibliography see Stewart (1978) presented as evidence of the Lords' Select Committee on Science and Technology (1980) — showed that, where agriculture and forestry are specifically designed to dovetail into one another, total productivity of the land is increased by at least 30 per cent and more jobs are created. Much of this success can be put down to good local knowledge and careful attention to management detail. No general solution can be imposed nor any standardised approach followed — the need is for local partnership based on practical experience. But too little attention has been given to these possibilities because there is no suitable lead agency, though the Agricultural Development and Advisory Service (ADAS) and the Scottish Agricultural Colleges, given the proper encouragement, could be ideally suited for the task. Another stumbling block is that of obtaining the cooperation from the landowner or occupier. This is possible on some of the larger Scottish estates, though tenants are not always so enthusiastic and the landlord has little scope for forcing them to cooperate. Most suitable catchment areas, however, are managed by a number of owners or occupiers who may not agree on a suitable management plan — unless such a plan has various financial strings attached. The practical problems of achieving a fully integrated management plan must not be underestimated — not least because of objections by conservation/amenity interests to certain afforestation proposals. This is certainly an area which requires more attention. The policy statement by the NFUS (1980) on this problem is an important contribution and its recommendations should be examined carefully.

Upland Management Experiments

19. In 1968, the Countryside Commission began discussions with a view to coordinating the interests of agriculture, landscape management and recreational access in certain upland areas through a series of upland management experiments (UMEX 1-3). Initially, two projects (UMEX 1) were undertaken, one in the Lake District — begun in 1969 — (Countryside Commission, 1976) and one in Snowdonia — begun in 1970 — (Countryside Commission, 1979). To begin with these schemes were very experimental and were looked at cautiously by local organisations. The aims of both projects were:

(a) to test a method of reconciling the interests of farmers, landowners and visitors in the uplands by offering financial encouragement to farmers (and others) to carry out small schemes which improve the appearance of the landscape and enhance the recreational opportunities of the area; and

(b) to assess what effect, if any, this method will have on farmers' attitudes towards recreation and landscape.

Both schemes developed into a second stage (UMEX 2),

involving the appointment of a full-time project officer whose job was to facilitate these objectives in cooperation with local authorities and with officers from MAFF. In Snowdonia, despite the enormous personal talents of the project officer (known as the Agricultural Liaison Officer), and given a genuine willingness amongst landowners to cooperate, the problems of finding suitable labour and of organising work priorities were considerable. Lack of access to the land to implement development work was a major issue, as was the shortage of funds to encourage farmers to maintain important landscape features. Nevertheless, the Agricultural Liaison Officer did much to improve relations between the National Park Authority and landowners and to stimulate flexible solutions for particular local problems. In the Lake District, too, the qualities of the Project Officer, coupled with a reasonable degree of give and take at the local level, contributed much to the success of the scheme.

20. By the late 1970s, it had become apparent that these experiments could be more successful if the programme was extended to encourage development of non-farm enterprises so as to benefit both the local community and landscape amenity. In 1978, the Lake District Special Planning Board launched UMEX 3, with provisions for promoting self-catering accommodation through the conversion of redundant farm buildings close to the steading. The MacEwens (1982) observed a lack of enthusiasm within MAFF for this scheme (which was supported by the NFU) aimed at overcoming some of the inherent conflicts between hill farming grant aid policies and landscape management. While one of the architects of the Scheme (Dunning, 1982) believes that it has demonstrated the complementarity of agricultural, national park and rural community survival objectives, he also confesses to administrative problems, a product of inherently conflicting national policies. He notes: 'Its large steering committee served by officers of the different agencies each with specific duties, was not always able to cut through to the essentials in a way which could meet the requirements on the ground'. He also noted that despite the support of the English Tourist Board, the recession, coupled with high interest rates plus lack of experience, have combined to make farmers reluctant to invest in tourist-related enterprises.

The East Fellside Project

21. This Project came into being in the East Fellside of Cumbria, following the hostile reaction of the farming community and among local people generally to the Countryside Commission's proposal to designate an AONB in the north Pennines. The local view was that the area was desperately in need of new enterprise initiative and investment, not further deprivation as a derelict landscape museum. Led by the Cumbrian branches of the NFU and the CLA, various agencies, including MAFF, the Development Commission, the English Tourist Board and the Countryside Commission, agreed with the Eden District Council to fund a full-time Project Officer with the aim of liaising between the needs of the people on the ground and the relevant

agencies. The Officer has sought to encourage new small scale enterprises by providing advice and facilitating the processes of bureaucracy, particularly in relation to obtaining planning consent. Once again, however, progress has been slow and early achievements modest. The log jam of bureaucratic isolationism remains to be broken. To quote Dunning (1982), also an iniator of this Project: 'Encouragement of new enterprise has been confined to initiatives in a field of craft enterprise or other small scale activity. The initiative has provided a great deal of information on how interest can be stimulated within local communities. However, it also has its shortcomings. It has not touched those potentials with the rural economy which could have made the greatest contribution to the well-being of the area, nor has it been successful in bringing together entrepreneurship, capital and expertise where there was real and obvious scope. However, the greatest difficulty may have been that like UMEX 3 the project has not as yet been entirely successful in drawing the various agencies away from their deep-rooted sectional approach to rural problems'.

The Western Isles Integrated Development Programme

22. This is one of three recently announced initiatives sponsored by the EEC (the others are in Lozere in France and the province of Luxembourg in Belgium) with the aim of linking agricultural improvement to rural economic renaissance. Since the scheme began in late 1982, only a general outline is provided here. Basically, the Programme involves a commitment by the UK Government to finance a development plan worth about £56m over five years, which, if approved by the Commission, will receive about £20m of grant aid through the guidance fund of the CAP. This money will be confined to agriculturally-related projects (though some fishery and forestry schemes may be incorporated) but will only be available if UK regional development funds (financed mainly through the local authority who will attract a 40 per cent rate of grant) are forthcoming. These funds will be used to finance tourism, craft industries and a number of small industrial schemes such as grain or grass drying plant, storage sheds and a slaughterhouse. The Integrated Development Programme (IDP) will be guided by a small project team operating in the locality and reporting to an *ad hoc* steering committee chaired by DAFS. DAFS will administer land improvement projects, while the Highlands and Islands Development Board (HIDB) will handle schemes for livestock marketing and fisheries. Caufield (1982) reports that there are considerable misgivings amongst conservation interests over the scheme because some of the agricultural and fishery improvements may have important effects on the internationally significant bird populations, the botanically rich grazing meadows and other features of the ecology of the 'wet' machair. Critics claim that there is neither overall responsibility nor an adequate budget for environmental protection and compensation arrangements, that DAFS is not prepared to put any money into agriculture where specific conservation gains are likely, and that generally there is little understanding of the need to link the three kinds of sustainable utilisation outlined in Chapter 2 of

this report, paragraph 7 (p 180). These assertions are developed further by Rose and Bradley (1982) who argue that the Programme as proposed will not only be ecologically damaging but wasteful of public money (see also the three hour debate in the House of Lords, 1982). However, there is considerable sensitivity in Scotland over such claims made in advance of implementation. At the very least, the IDP should be monitored by an independent study team. Even the proposed assessment service by the NCC may not be sufficient. One issue that must be examined is how 'integrated' this project will be. Another is how to guarantee local crofters a livelihood off the 'dry' machair, one of the few productive agricultural zones in the region.

The Highlands and Islands Community Co-operative Scheme

23. This scheme was launched by the HIDB in 1977 to promote community initiative in the outer Scottish islands and to maintain local community spirit (Hetherington, 1981). (A similar scheme now operates in Wales.) The HIDB grant aid a wide variety of local projects by providing matching funds to any money raised by a community group to start up a scheme, a training grant sufficient to pay all the wages of a manager for the first three years (when, it is to be hoped, financial self-sufficiency should have been established), plus the normal 50 per cent for specific projects. Much emphasis is placed on community initiative and upon support for the local councils (usually in the form of leasing disused buildings, facilitating planning permission and tendering contracts which might otherwise have gone to non-local firms). The Senior Social Development Officer of the HIDB (Storey, 1978) sees great promise in this programme, especially in promoting a sense of community confidence, though there are still many teething problems relating to financial control, marketing and inter-cooperative liaison. Nevertheless, there is a chance here to link local economic enterprise, tourism and land management which are common to all the schemes outlined in this section, so long as there are no unnecessary impediments.

The Peak District Experiment

24. The European Commission have granted a research contract to the Peak Park Joint Planning Board to help it institute an experimental 'bottom up' approach to integrated rural development. In 1974, a coordinating group — the Rural Land Management Executive Group — was established, consisting of the executive officers of the NFU, the Forestry Commission, the NCC, CLA and the Planning Board. Its aim was to coordinate policies to link land management to conservation and economic development. For the reasons referred to in paragraphs 22 and 23 of this chapter, above and which are developed in paragraph 25 below, this Group failed to achieve satisfactory harmonisation of policies. Hence the formation of a new steering group to operate an experimental alternative package of public supports in three parishes. Its principal feature is the abandonment of the existing grants as determined by the various

The Somerset levels and moors
The Somerset levels and moors comprise a number of poorly-drained basins which provide
an important habitat for ground nesting birds in the spring and summer
and over-wintering birds during the winter floods. Many of the non- or low-fertilised meadows are rich in plants
and the rhynes (drainage ditches) contain a great variety of aquatic vegetation and invertebrate life.
Improved drainage schemes and higher fertilisation, coupled with more productive varieties of grass,
are changing the nature conservation and landscape beauty of the moors which are features which can
only be preserved through expensive purchase or complicated management agreements.
The photos illustrate the high water table grazing marsh of the Somerset moors (above) and West Sedgemore (below).
Candidates for heritage sites and conservation zone status.
(By courtesy of the Somerset County Council)

'development' and 'preservation' agencies, in favour of a single 'Trial Alternative Grant' scheme. These grants will be available for agriculture, conservation, recreation, tourism and community enterprise, but welded into an integrated package to match the needs and opportunities of each of the three experimental areas. The Peak District Scheme is based on the principle that public funds should be directed at 'rewards achieved' in relation to agreed objectives. For instance, money is available to finance the maintenance of dry stone walls, where their presence is identified as a key landscape feature, on the basis of cost per mile; similarly, where the floristic diversity of a field or group of fields is to be retained, grants will be paid according to agreed criteria (number and variety of plants per unit area), not on the amount of fertilisers added or livestock units grazed. Such grants will require on-site inspection with the farmer so that both he and the management team can agree on what has been achieved in relation to set aims (bearing in mind that ecosystems do not always behave as expected). Indeed, this is a key point about the Peak District experiment; where a farmer is contributing to specific multiple objectives he will be paid from the supporting fund in accordance with the extent to which his activities fulfil these objectives. In sum, public money is spent on promoting a wide public purpose. The Peak District scheme is designed to show how alternative allocations of grants can achieve a mutually compatible mix of objectives, linking land care to employment possibilities (for there are many jobs to be formed in caring for the land) and community enterprise. While the scheme is specifically geared to local circumstances, it is purely voluntary and because MAFF grants are not altered the results may not be as satisfactory as intended. Pilot experiments of this kind should be studied with care.

The Somerset Levels and Moors

25. Somerset County Council is preparing a Local Plan for the 56,000 ha of the low-lying land adjoining the Bristol Channel known as the Somerset Levels and Moors. A Report of the Survey was published in April 1981 and the Local Plan policies and proposals will be published in early 1983. The main benefit of this approach is seen to be the use of the formal plan-making procedures rather than any planning powers of responsibilities. The aim is to produce a local solution through the locally elected authority with full public participation. It is hoped that the voluntary procedures of the Wildlife and Countryside Act can successfully accommodate the different countryside interests. The Local Plan, though primarily designed to safeguard the total landscape amenity of the area, includes proposals for recreation, protection of archaeological features and control over peat extraction as well as land drainage, agricultural improvement and nature conservation. Its preparation is guided by a Panel of County and District Councillors and a Liaison Group of over 30 organisations and authorities. The rural land-use strategy will only be implemented by the agreement of the relevant bodies, though this may prove impossible to achieve if current procedures remain. There is much unhappiness amongst the farming community of West Sedgemoor

regarding the precise terms of compensation which the NCC may offer following the designation of an SSSI in that area, yet more SSSIs are likely to be proposed. The dispute over the boundaries of the SSSI embroiled the NCC in a bitter struggle with local landowners and politicians and ecologists employed by MAFF and retained by the CLA. Eventually, the NCC insisted on the area originally considered for the SSSI, but feelings still run high locally and this rather unpleasant experience suggests that, even with much goodwill, it will be very difficult to reach the 'right balance' amicably as outlined in Chapter 2, paragraph 9 of this report (see p 181). That is why this report argues strongly for a new look at the existing pattern of incentives and controls.

Interpreting Properly the Less Favoured Areas Directive

26. A common theme running through these examples is the difficulty facing those in charge of making public money work for the public good. One common impediment is the failure of the Agriculture Departments to apply a broader definition to the term 'agricultural business' which would allow agricultural monies to be spent on husbandry with a conservation/amenity benefit. Even in the innovative, yet experimental, Peak District scheme, MAFF are apparently unwilling to invest any new money in the trial alternative grant scheme and will not change their grant aid policies in the three parishes involved. However, another general problem is that, even if local officials are willing to 'bend the rules', their hands are tied when they seek authority from their headquarters where predetermined, nationally-based policies are adhered to. It is evident that there will be strong opposition to any body which seeks to impose its will on integrated rural development (one reason for the failure of the Northern Pennines Rural Development Board — Childs and Minay, 1979).

27. The issue of Departmental demarcation, which is antithetical to the objectives of the WCS, is most clearly seen in the UK treatment of less favoured areas. As was discussed in paragraphs 35 and 36 of Chapter 4 of this report, pp 208 - 209, the LFA Directive is too narrowly interpreted by MAFF. This results not just in a failure to incorporate widely the aims of linking economic viability to land care identified in Article 3 (5) of the Directive (the experience of designating the Isles of Scilly under this Article remains to be examined) but to a host of activities which are actually detrimental to these wider objectives. While LFA are normally associated with uplands, they can include any area where agriculture faces special difficulties and where 'uneconomic' farming may have to be maintained for the purpose of conserving the countryside, or where farming is necessary to maintain the economic and social viability of the area and its population (see evidence by Lord Melchett to the Select Committee on Agriculture). In short, the LFA Directive has a social

as well as an agricultural economic purpose. Yet MAFF, by avoiding this part of the Directive, has chosen to implement it almost exclusively in terms of aid to support food production. No current MAFF policy or grant aid scheme positively promotes agricultural systems which encourage the maintenance of a landscape consistent with wider conservation objectives. Furthermore, because MAFF grants are not available to 'part-time farmers' (as officially defined), this group may not benefit from funds which might otherwise keep them viable and assist them in maintaining traditional countryside features. Article 10 (2) of the Directive allows funds to be spent on promoting part-time, non-farming activities, particularly tourism and craft industry. Yet, in the UK, such activities have to be funded by the hard pressed development agencies, and tourist boards. Furthermore, such grants are generally offered to farmers who can show they have a financial need and who require fairly sizeable grants (small grant requests involve costly administration). *The scope for automatic entitlement of tourism-related grants should be reviewed.* In any case, the budget of the tourist boards is small (£4m for all schemes in 1981-82) even though their scope has been recently extended to cover the whole of the country and not just the assisted areas.

28. The time has come for a radical rethink of LFA policy, but this must be set in the context of a more comprehensive reassessment of Britain's whole rural development strategy. In this context, it is gratifying to report that the Commons' Agricultural Committee recommended that allowance for hill livestock units should be graduated to take account of the number of livestock units (an important matter for marginal farmers), and supported the principle of deficiency payments or management incentives to reflect efforts to match husbandry to conservation/amenity requirements.

Environmental Assessment of Rural Development Projects

29. It is not uncommon for the major national conservation and amenity agencies (and their non-governmental companions) to appear at public inquiries of various kinds protesting about the environmental implications of a proposed development, be it a reservoir, a quarry, a motorway, a land drainage scheme, an electricity generating station or a site for the disposal of solid or toxic wastes. In almost all of these cases the inquiry is held under the Town and Country Planning Acts which have established procedures for planning permission, and thorough review of decisions. The fact that an inquiry has to be held is either because national issues are involved or because the applicant has been refused planning permission (or has been faced with unacceptable conditions to that permission) and appealed. The public inquiry over 'big' issues is convened in only a relatively small number of instances and is an expensive set-piece which is not ideally suited for questioning either the policy context in which a proposal is advanced or for guaranteeing that a full and proper cost benefit analysis

and environmental appraisal are prepared and justified (O'Riordan and Sewell, 1981). In evidence before the Lords' Select Committee on the European Communities (1981), civil servants in the Scottish and English and Welsh Planning Departments representing the present Government's views complimented the British planning system as being sufficiently flexible to take into account the wider environmental implications of any proposal. This is erroneous: Environmental Impact Assessments (EIAs) are only undertaken when both the developer and the local planning authority see fit, so they are often *ad hoc* and discriminatory (O'Riordan, 1981). The European Commission wishes its Council of Ministers to endorse a Directive on Environmental Impact Assessment which would require thorough appraisals to be made (Article 6) on certain categories of proposals (Annex I proposals) and which would expect national Governments, through the relevant Departments (the competent authorities) to establish guidelines for appraisals, which would not be mandatory, on certain other categories of development (Annex II proposals). Into this second category fall large scale agricultural projects (including land drainage) and afforestation. The UK is opposed to this Directive, and particularly opposed to any formal environmental assessment in agriculture and forestry, on the grounds that the job is already effectively done. The Lords' Select Committee, however, endorsed the Lords' proposed EEC Directive, believing that it would lead to better decisions and would not result in delay or in undue additional costs. Many major industrial corporations now undertake EIAs to expedite their internal management procedures and smooth the path to approval for planning permission.

30. *The proposed EEC Directive on EIAs should be accepted by a Government anxious to implement a Conservation and Development Programme for the UK; the major public investment in agriculture and forestry should also be subject to EIAs.* Only when a systematic environmental appraisal is undertaken, involving sequential discussions by all interested parties who are required to be consulted, can the wider aspects of such schemes be properly taken into account and be seen to be weighed in the political balance. Nevertheless, one must be wary of creating excessive bureaucracy and inflexible administrative procedures when implementing EIAs. They must be tailored to the circumstances of the case a little more than the proposed Directive allows for, but certainly should be less *ad hoc* than they are at present. In addition, careful studies are required of the likely demand for key resources — minerals, aggregates, wood, water, energy, transport — so that the economic justification of major investments is set in the context of national requirements. *The 'need' issue should become a central feature of all future appraisals of major schemes likely to be located in the UK countryside.* Naturally, the final judgement will not be made on environmental grounds alone, and this is necessary for there to be established guidelines and that local and regional forward plans are adequately prepared to provide an appropriate land-use strategy. In this context, the Scottish practice of laying down national planning guidelines is most helpful.

31. *When these procedures come into being, representations should be made at an appropriate time against the use of prime agricultural land for non-agricultural purposes.* At present, at least 15,000 and possibly 20,000 ha of countryside are being lost from agriculture annually, a figure which may arise as proposed relaxations in development control procedures in areas not specially designated are put into effect (Council for the Protection of Rural England, 1981). While there is some doubt as to how serious a problem this is in terms of lost agricultural output (see Centre for Agricultural Strategy, 1976; Best, 1981), nevertheless *there should be a presumption against loss of prime agricultural land in a Conservation and Development Programme for the UK.* This view was taken by the previous administration (Ministry of Agriculture, Fisheries and Food, 1979) which stated: 'Improvements in agricultural productivity cannot be relied upon indefinitely to offset the lost output from irreversible losses of agricultural land to development... The Government intend to pursue vigorously their policy of protecting agricultural land, especially that of better quality, and to bring into use wherever possible derelict and disused urban land'. The present Government should reiterate this view and show in specific instances that it is prepared to act upon it. (Admittedly, it has taken an active interest in promoting the use of derelict and disused land.) Facilitating the procedures for early warning of changes to prime agricultural land should help to remedy this problem. The protection of prime agricultural land must not result in excessive pressure being brought to bear on lands of lower grades but in higher conservation value. This is why a proper EIA is required in advance of any development proposal.

32. The comments made in paragraphs 29 and 30 of this chapter (see page 235) regarding EIA apply to new mineral and aggregate developments as much as they relate to other major construction proposals (roads, reservoirs, power stations and the like). However, a peculiar problem with many mineral developments is that there is little choice in the extraction site. Many of the more economically attractive sites for mineral and hydrocarbon exploitation lie in scenically attractive areas or areas where the resident population is not at all enthusiastic about mining and associated industrial development in their locality (eg the Vale of Belvoir coalfield issue and the Snowdonia copper mining case). Indeed, some groups are so determined to stop such proposals that they use all legal powers in the planning

acts, even objecting to exploration permits (eg the Shell Oil case in the New Forest, and proposals to test drill to discover the qualities of rock for radioactive waste disposal). Determined local opposition cannot lightly be dismissed (as the Government's recent decision to stop the radioactive waste test drilling programme demonstrated). But there has to be a strategic appraisal of the most suitable mineral/aggregates/hydrocarbon sites, coupled to a clear national priority over the best scenic and conservation areas and this relationship should be expressed in ministerial presumptions attached to county level structure plans. In addition, much more needs to be done about the restoration of derelict mine tips. Admittedly some companies have done good work in this connection and the ecology of wasteland restoration is now much better understood. In future, *all major mining proposals should have restoration plans submitted as part of the planning application, coupled to bonds backed by insurance schemes, to ensure that the remedial work is undertaken even if the company involved goes bankrupt.* There are a number of instances where this is already occurring and these should be encouraged. Also, existing derelict areas should be graded in priority for restoration and employment-creation programmes modified to enable these to be made both productive and attractive.

33. The urban fringe is an area of particular problems (Thompson, 1981). It must be managed to reconcile demands for agriculture, small homesteading, horticulture (use of land for horses and ponies, primarily as paddocks), various kinds of outdoor recreation and some development. Often there are particular difficulties of access while vandalism and incompatible neighbouring uses can lead to friction and frustration. Each urban fringe is unique, so it would be unwise to seek generalised policies. However, the role of the urban fringe as a supply of outdoor recreation should be questioned. Recent studies (Elson, 1979) suggest that outdoor recreation sites located in green belts do not attract inner city residents deprived of 'breathing space'. They tend to be used by nearby suburbanites already wealthy in recreational assets. There is scope for improving the recreational opportunities of residents in the mid-to-outer suburbs who presently cannot get to the green belts (too old, too young or lacking transport) and generally for improving the recreational amenities of the major conurbation. (See 'The Livable City', Part 2.)

References

BEST, R H. 1981. Land use and living space. London, Methuen.

BLACKSELL, M and GILG, A. 1981. The countryside: planning and change. London, Allen and Unwin.

CATLOW, J and THRILWALL, G. 1976. Environmental impact assessment. Research report no 11. London, Department of the Environment.

CAUFIELD, C. 1982. Friends of the Hebrides can do without. *New Scientist, 24 June,* 862-863.

CENTRE FOR AGRICULTURAL STRATEGY. 1976. Land for agriculture. Reading Centre for Agricultural Strategy.

CHILDS, G and MINAY, C L W. 1979. The Northern Pennines Rural Development Board. Working paper 30. Oxford, Department of Town Planning, Oxford Polytechnic.

COMMONS SELECT COMMITTEE ON AGRICULTURE. 1982. Financial policy of the EEC in relation to agriculture with special reference to less favoured areas. London, HMSO.

COUNCIL FOR THE PROTECTION OF RURAL ENGLAND. 1981. Planning — friend or foe? London, CPRE.

COUNTRY LANDOWNERS ASSOCIATION. 1980. Report of the Working Party on Employment in Rural Areas, p 9. London, The Country Landowners Association.

COUNTRYSIDE COMMISSION. 1976. The Lake District upland management experiment. CCP 93. Cheltenham, The Countryside Commission.

COUNTRYSIDE COMMISSION. 1979. The Snowdonia upland management experiment. CCP 122. Cheltenham, The Countryside Commission.

COX, G. 1981. Wookey's way without chemicals. The Field, 2 December, 1201-1202.

CRAIG, J. 1982. Town and country: current changes in the distribution of population in England and Wales. In Town and Country: home and work. London, RSA.

DEPARTMENT OF THE ENVIRONMENT. 1979. Local government and the development of tourism. DOE circular 13/79. London, HMSO.

DUNNING, J C. 1982. Personal communication. 3 March.

ELSON, M J. 1979. The leisure use of green belts and urban fringes. London, The Sports Council and the Social Science Research Council.

HANSON, M. 1976. Buyers for Scottish sporting estates: harvesting a secondary crop. Country Life, 29 July, 272.

HETHERINGTON, P. 1981. Uncovering the roots of co-operation. North, 7 (44), 4-6.

HM TREASURY. 1976. Rural depopulation. London, HMSO.

HODGE, I and WHITBY, M. 1981. Rural employment: trends, options and choices. London, Methuen.

HOUSE OF LORDS. 1982. Lords hansard, 345, 20 October, cols 125-168.

JARVIE, E. 1981. The red deer industry: finance and employment. Edinburgh, Scottish Landowners' Federation.

LORDS' SELECT COMMITTEE ON THE EUROPEAN COMMUNITIES. 1981. Environmental assessment of projects. HL paper 69. London, HMSO.

LORDS' SELECT COMMITTEE ON SCIENCE AND TECHNOLOGY. 1980. HMSO.

MACEWEN, A and MACEWEN, M. 1982. National parks: conservation or cosmetics?, p 166. London, George Allen and Unwin.

MATTINGLY, A. 1982. Recreation access to the countryside. London, The Ramblers Association.

MINISTRY OF AGRICULTURE, FISHERIES AND FOOD. 1979. Farming and the nation. Cmnd 7458. London, HMSO.

MOSLEY, M J. 1981. Accessibility: the rural challenge. London, Methuen.

NATIONAL ASSOCIATION OF LOCAL COUNCILS. 1980. Rural Life: change or decay. London, NALC.

NATIONAL COUNCIL FOR VOLUNTARY ORGANISATIONS. 1980. Jobs in the countryside: prospects for rural employment. London, NCVO.

NATIONAL FARMERS' UNION OF SCOTLAND. 1980. Agriculture and forestry: a policy statement. Edinburgh, National Farmers' Union of Scotland.

NATIONAL FEDERATION OF HOUSING ASSOCIATIONS. 1981. Rural housing: hidden problems and possible solutions. London, NFHA.

O'RIORDAN, T. 1981. Beware binding commitments: the British approach to EIA. Environmental Impact Assessment Review, 2 (1), 89-102.

O'RIORDAN, T and SEWELL, W R D. (editors). 1981. Project appraisal and policy review. Chichester, Wiley.

PHILLIPS, J. 1974. The management and economics of grouse species in relation to complementary and competing game interests. Lochwinnoch, Renfrewshire, Calderbank.

RAMBLERS ASSOCIATION. 1982. Open country: public asset or private domain? London, The Ramblers Association.

ROSE, C and BRADLEY, C. 1982. Good news for the crofter is bad for the corncrake. The Guardian, 26 August, 16.

ROYAL COMMISSION ON COMMON LAND. 1958. Cmnd 462. HMSO.

SMITH, M. 1982. The down at heel mountain. The Guardian, 5 August, 17.

STEWART, G G. 1978. Interrelations between agriculture and forestry in Scotland: a forestry view. Scottish Forestry, 153-163.

STOREY, R J. 1978. Community co-operatives — a highlands and islands experiment. Yearbook of Agricultural Cooperation, 89-104.

THOMPSON, K J. 1981. Farming on the fringe. CCP 142. Cheltenham, Countryside Commission.

TOURISM AND RECREATIONAL RESEARCH UNIT. 1982. The economy of rural communities in the national parks of England and Wales, pp 221-80. Edinburgh, TRUU.

TURNING POINT. 1981. The redistribution of work. Ironbridge, Salop, Turning Point (9 New Road).

WALES TOURIST BOARD. 1981. Survey of community attitudes towards tourism in Wales. Cardiff, Wales Tourist Board.

WESTMACOTT, R and WORTHINGTON, T. 1974. New agricultural landscapes, p 70. Cheltenham, The Countryside Commission.

WOOLLETT, S. 1981. Alternative rural services. London, National Council of Voluntary Organisations.

YALDEN, D. 1981. Moorland erosion study. Castleton, Derbyshire, Peak District National Park.

CHAPTER 7

CONCLUSIONS AND PATHWAYS FOR RECONCILIATION

Introduction

1. This report has sought to explore how far the current use of rural resources (defined in paragraph 4 of Chapter 2 of this report, p 179) is compatible with the principles and objectives of the three categories of sustainable utilisation outlined in Chapter 2, paragraph 7, p 180. It will be recalled that these are ecologically sustainable utilisation, aesthetically sustainable utilisation and community social and economic enterprise (see Figure 1, p 180 and Figure 2, p 182). Throughout the discussion in the previous chapters, the aim has been to examine the arguments from a number of points of view, to analyse the sources of trouble where the problems look forbidding, and to investigate how far existing policies and associated economic incentives and administrative guides support or undermine the three sets of objectives embodied in the triple concept of sustainable utilisation.

2. This chapter will draw the threads of these arguments together by cross-referencing to previous chapters, and will explore opportunities for reconciliation. These opportunities lie amongst the themes outlined in Figure 1 (p 180) and discussed at length in Chapters 4, 5 and 6. Any 'ideal' solution will be extremely difficult to implement, because not only is fundamental reform of policy required involving both official and non-official organisations, but also a thorough alteration in outlook is needed as to how resource-users view their responsibilities towards the countryside and towards their fellow rural resource-users. This change in attitude will take time: one must be patient but also firm in purpose. It is in this spirit that this chapter is written. In addition, while, in general, more research is recommended, absence of 'hard' information should not be an excuse for procrastination. The problems and conflicts inherent in the rural resource-use are very real and very pressing; any further delay will only worsen the dilemma and make reasonable solutions even more difficult to achieve.

3. With respect to furthering the principle of ecologically sustainable utilisation, the general conclusion is that there is no firm evidence either way that the long-term health of the land is seriously in jeopardy. What is evident is that there is a serious absence of information concerning what is or could be happening to the ecological fabric of the UK and that urgent steps must be taken to understand and monitor what is occurring (Chapter 3, paragraphs 26 to 27, pp 191 - 192).

Certainly, there can be no sweeping conclusion that ecologically sustainable utilisation of rural resources is taking place in the UK. The following observations can be made:

(a) This lack of comprehensive understanding results from the difficulties in coordinating a systematic monitoring programme amongst a great range of official research establishments and other research institutes (Chapter 3, paragraph 26, p 191), lack of appropriate budgets for financing this work, and problems in establishing modelling techniques that can produce scientifically credible forecasts.

(b) While there is little to suggest that the vast majority of soils in the UK are being structurally or chemically damaged by modern agricultural and forestry practises, structural and chemical changes are taking place in certain soils because of particular land-use activities that should be looked at carefully in order to assess the possible longer-term implications (Chapter 4, paragraphs 7 to 9, pp 199 - 200, and Chapter 5, paragraphs 3 to 5, pp 215 - 216).

(c) The application of chemical pesticides, both in agriculture and forestry, deserves special attention (Chapter 4, paragraphs 10 and 11, pp 200 - 201; Chapter 5, paragraph 5, p 216; Chapter 6, paragraph 16, p 230). It is most unlikely that there are any discernible dangers to human health arising out of the use of these products (with the possible exception of nitrogenous fertiliser) but the use of unsuitable chemicals in an inappropriate manner can lead to unnecessary damage to wildlife and to occupational health risks.

(d) The longer-term effects on plants and animals resulting from chemical substances discharged into the air and water from certain industrial and agricultural processes also need to be examined carefully, despite the good work already achieved by the PSPS with respect to chemical formulations. The deposition of sulphur dioxide and nitrous oxides, both in their wet (acid rain) and dry form, requires more attention (Chapter 3, paragraph 30, p 192; Chapter 6, paragraph 8, p 227) and research budgets should be enlarged, not reduced as is currently being proposed.

4. A large number of research opportunities open up when the relationship between land management and

ecologically sustainable utilisation is fully examined. Research needs that spring to mind arising out of this report include:

(a) better kinds of fertilisers which lock their nutrients into the soil and crops (Chapter 4, paragraphs 12 to 13, page 201);

(b) various approaches to integrated pest management representing different environmental conditions and management practices (Chapter 4, paragraph 11, p 200; Chapter 5, paragraph 5, p 216);

(c) the association between moorland management techniques (on different kinds of moor) and grazing densities, game management and wildlife conservation (Chapter 4, paragraphs 16 and 17, page 202; Chapter 6, paragraph 14, p 229; Chapter 6, paragraph 16, p 230);

(d) the scope for integrating agriculture, forestry, game and wildlife, again in various catchments (Chapter 6, paragraph 18, p 231);

(e) the lesson applicable to conventional farming from the experience of organic farming (Chapter 4, paragraphs 13 and 14, page 201) so that better harmony between these two approaches to husbandry can be attained;

(f) the scope for greater energy use efficiencies in both agriculture and forestry, particularly with respect to the use of more appropriate machinery for certain tasks, and to the opportunities for converting farm waste into usable energy and into organic fertilisers (Chapter 4, paragraph 15, p 201), and low grade forest produce as firewood;

(g) the relationship between the recreational use of certain habitats and their ecological tolerance to withstand that use (Chapter 6, paragraphs 7 and 9, pp 226 and 227);

(h) the relationship between soil, drainage, topography, forest size and tree mix on windthrow (Chapter 5, paragraph 3, p 215).

5. The evidence from this report is that certain rural resource-use practices, together with the policies, administrative guides and economic incentives that lie behind them, are incompatible with the furtherance of the objectives of nature conservation and landscape amenity (aesthetically sustainable utilisation). As indicated in Chapter 2, paragraph 16, p 183 and documented in Chapter 3, paragraphs 24 to 40, pp 191 - 195, the extent and rapidity of habitat loss and landscape change are probably too great for certain ecosystems and species to assimilate or for the informed and concerned public to tolerate. These changes are due to a number of factors, but principally agricultural improvement and cessation of traditional husbandry practices, afforestation with exotic species (especially conifers), thoughtless siting and operation of certain large construction projects (mining developments, motorways, electricity transmission lines and certain housing and industrial developments), pollution of the air and water by chemicals (Chapter 3, paragraphs 30 and 31, pp 192 and 193), and, locally, excessive recreational use (Chapter 6, paragraph 9, p 227).

6. Concern over the incompatibility between some aspects of present rural resource-use and nature conservation and landscape amenity is also caused by what must be seen as a failure in policy. The declaration of intent requesting Government Departments to have regard for landscape beauty and conservation as laid down in various statutes (eg the Countryside Acts, the Water Act and the Land Drainage Act) do not have practical substance. While the Wildlife and Countryside Act lays a more specific duty on Agriculture Departments and land drainage interests to promote conservation (Sections 32 and 48) and landscape beauty (Sections 41 and 48), these duties are ancillary to the primary functions of promoting agricultural and forestry business and land drainage. In any case, these new duties essentially apply only to SSSIs, national parks and other specially designated areas — lands which cover less than 15 per cent of the countryside (see Chapter 3, paragraphs 15 and 20, pp 188 and 190; Chapter 4, paragraphs 32 and 38 to 43, p 207 and pp 209 - 213). Furthermore, previous duties laid on the agricultural advisory services to consider the wider environmental implications of applications for farm capital grant schemes before final determination of grants throughout the wider countryside no longer operate in the 'unprotected' 85 per cent of the countryside (Chapter 4, paragraph 36, p 208). These omissions do not lie within the legal framework of development control (Chapter 4, paragraph 37, p 209), but are dependent upon voluntary consultative arrangements which conservation/amenity interests find quite unsatisfactory and unsuitable for a future conservation/development programme.

7. While the Wildlife and Countryside Act is strongly criticised in this report, because of its procedural inadequacies in protecting the wider countryside and in making formal, legal and economic what really should be a spontaneous conservation ethos (Chapter 4, paragraphs 39 to 42, pp 209 - 213), this legislation is regarded as a transitional stage in the evolution of attitudes and practices which eventually must accompany aesthetically sustainable utilisation. There are many features of the Act with respect to wildlife protection and the control of trade in endangered species which are widely welcomed. And, although the Act has its drawbacks, the long and controversial Parliamentary debate bespattered with amendments showed, both to Parliament and officials, that environmental protection is a matter of great public concern. The Act also establishes a number of important principles:

(a) That all SSSIs (including NNRs) are to be defended by the NCC and that exhaustive justification will be required should their nature conservation value be diminished as a result of failure to invest sufficient public funds in compensation to a landowner for proved income foregone.

(b) That conservation can be expensive, so that where public money threatens conservation values, its purpose should be looked at very carefully.

(c) That landowners should be on trust, ready to display their public obligations to their land: the voluntary principle is on trial.

(d) That officials involved with land management and custody should have a much closer working relationship and respect for each other than was the case prior to the passage of the Act.

8. One reason why the nature conservation/landscape amenity aspects of sustainable utilisation are not adequately incorporated within current rural resource-use in the UK is that there seems to be an imbalance of effective power between those interests responsible for managing the land where wealth and profit are primary objectives, and those who see their role as defending the appreciative qualities of the countryside. This apparent imbalance of power is reflected in the current failure of policies to respond to public concern for the maintenance and enhancement of nature conservation and landscape beauty. This inequality of power also tends to mean that the characteristic British 'compromise' diminishes the conservation/amenity values of the rural scene. Chapter 4, paragraphs 18 to 19, pp 202 - 203, and paragraphs 30 to 32, pp 206 - 207; Chapter 5, paragraph 17, p 220; and paragraph 20, p 220; and the case studies highlighted in Chapter 6, paragraphs 18 to 25, pp 231 - 234 all illustrate this point.

9. This apparent asymmetry of power is also evident in the degree of expertise, the amount of money available to the agencies and their associated lobbies for wealth creating as opposed to the appreciative functions of rural resources (Chapter 2, paragraph 4, p 179). According to official statistics, about £182m is available in 1981-82 for farm capital grants, together with £853m in price supports (to which the CAP contributes £54m and £715m respectively) and £5m is available for timber grants and afforestable land purchases, while the Governmental and non-Governmental conservation/amenity agencies operate on a total budget of about £24m, of which little more than £5m is directly available for protection. (Note that agriculture grants apply to all agricultural land; conservation grants apply to only a tiny fraction of the UK land area.) It would, however, be wrong to infer that these monies are always working at cross purposes; the statistics are merely presented as a guide. In any case, much (but not all) of the agriculture and forestry support funds help to reduce the prices of food, drink and timber for which British consumers are tacitly grateful (Chapter 3, paragraph 5 and Chapter 4, paragraph 6, pp 186 and 199, though such financial assistance can result in surpluses of food and drink which are expensive to store and sell, and which, at the margin, are being produced at the expense of important elements of the nation's scenery and wildlife (Chapter 4, paragraphs 30 and 31, pp 206 and 207). A further problem is that grants and other incentives designed to promote land productivity often conflict with investments aimed at promoting land custody (Chapter 4, paragraphs 30 and 31, pp 206 - 207 in the case of agriculture; Chapter 5, paragraphs 12 and 17, pp 217 and 220 for forestry; and Chapter 4, paragraph 35, p 208, and Chapter 6, paragraphs 26 to 28, pp 234 - 235 for less favoured areas).

10. All this tends to result in a money-wasting compartmentalisation of rural land-use functions. Take the case of planting trees. Agriculture money is available for tree planting for agricultural purposes (eg shelterbelts), forestry money for timber production (but technically also for environmental considerations through the dedication schemes) and Countryside Commission money for amenity. Each of these functions is costly to administer — so much so that, in the present climate of reducing administrative spending, it is becoming more difficult for the modest grant application, which may have considerable local significance in terms of amenity/conservation, to be given proper consideration. Both at the central Governmental and local levels the rural resource-management agencies have little means for formal administrative coordination. Grants and/or advice which specifically integrate forestry, agriculture, tourism, landscape beauty and nature conservation are not available even when heroic efforts are made to overcome this gap (see Chapter 6, paragraphs 18 to 25, pp 231 - 234 for evidence) — unless perchance an individual landowner with a large holding is sufficiently committed to amalgamate the grants himself. This problem is particularly evident in the treatment of the Less Favoured Areas Directive (Chapter 4, paragraph 35, p 208; Chapter 6, paragraphs 26 to 28, pp 234 - 235) where, through Articles 3(5) and 10(2), the opportunity to link land productivity, land care, rural employment and economic revitalisation is there for the taking but, sadly, is missed. *A careful look at the applicability of Articles 3(5) and 10(2) of the LFA Directive in the context of the three fold concept of sustainable utilisation is urgently required.* However, one must be aware that grants are administered by people just as land is also managed by people. Restructuring and linking financial incentives must be coupled to a genuine commitment to manage the countryside in trust (Chapter 2, paragraph 20, pp 183 - 184).

Preparing the Arguments for a System of New Countryside Categories

11. In shaping the recommendations which follow, the basic aim must be to make optimum use of rural resources through the triple strategy of sustainable utilisation outlined in Chapter 2, paragraph 7, p 180. This can be achieved if:

(a) Government policy actively favours the integration of conservation with development;

(b) there is continuing commitment by individual ministers to this principle in policy statements, together with the support of all political parties;

(c) financial incentives, and the economic justification of these incentives, positively encourage such an approach, by rewarding its achievement and, where conservation/amenity is regarded as of high priority, penalising its failure;

(d) there is comprehensive technical advice on how to achieve it;

(e) research evidence indicates that any other way is likely to lead to long-term dangers; and

(f) education, in its most comprehensive meaning, supports this principle.

It is broadly accepted in this report that ethics and attitudes favouring land care follow from the actual execution of custodial management, which is, in turn, shaped by a suitable mixture of incentives and penalties, as much as they emerge through education and advice. A personal commitment to management in trust must be reinforced by a sympathetic climate of policies.

12. There is no single pathway that will lead to a reconciliation of current rural resource-use practices and the three aspects of sustainable utilisation which should form the basis of a conservation/development strategy for the UK countryside. Indeed, there are at least three reasons why it will be so very difficult to strike the twin concept of the 'right balance' introduced in Chapter 2, paragraph 2, p 179 and Chapter 2, paragraph 9, p 181).

(a) The major lobbies representing the wealth creating, appreciative (and, to a lesser extent, community enterprise) aspects of sustainable utilisation do not agree on the nature of the problem, the success or failure of existing policies, or the appropriateness of any proposed remedies.

(b) Resource-users are not separately identifiable: everyone uses the rural resource-mix for a variety of purposes in different roles. Foresters may be ornithologists, farmers can be recreationists and walkers enjoy reasonably priced food and timber products that are readily available in the shops. As individuals we may not be consistent regarding what we want from our rural resources; it is asking a lot for society to act with a single-minded purpose.

(c) Policies must be supported by personal commitment, so personal inclination, social obligation and an appropriate package of incentives and penalties must fit together yet somehow be tolerant to all users in all circumstances. This is unlikely.

13. When approaching the major policy recommendations that follow, the author has accepted the following principles:

(a) *The aesthetic values and development potential of the UK countryside are not equally distributed, so different priorities should apply to different areas.* This is known as the hierarchical or designation principle, but to avoid confusion will be termed 'countryside classification'. Identifying specific areas for particular forms of treatment also enables policies and budgets to be applied selectively and flexibly with little administrative inconvenience.

(b) *Existing land designations (SSSIs, AONBs, National Parks etc), even though they are unnecessarily complicated and inconsistent, should not be altered for the time being.* This is why the system that follows is called classification: it is

to be visualised as a 'veil' placed on top of existing designations (so that their purpose and administration are not obscured) which allows new mixes of incentives and penalties to apply to specific areas according to democratically agreed priorities.

(c) In assembling a package of incentives and controls relating to the appropriate management of each countryside category, no landowner or occupant should be compensated for not producing from his land output which could only be obtained by breaching the three principles of sustainability outlined in Chapter 2, paragraph 7, p 180. *Incentives should be rewarded for attaining these principles.*

(d) *Guidance for the appropriate management of each countryside category should come from the 'bottom up', from a locally-based rural liaison panel (tailored to suit local circumstances) which would advise the relevant local authority over management objectives and conditions of award (compensation) for maintaining the land in national trust.*

(e) *On the ground, rural liaison officers should act as advisers, demonstrators and catalysts in encouraging the practice of management in trust.*

Countryside Classification and the Matter of Planning Controls over Land-Use Change

14. Environmental groups normally dislike hierarchical designations for the simple reason that, in the 'carve up', they fear that some of the choicest areas will be 'lost', and that lower orders of designation imply that conservation values will be given lower priority (Hall, 1981). This was part of the reason why the controversial proposal by the Countryside Review Committee (1979) to redesignate scenically important areas of the UK countryside into two tiers of protection suffered such a hostile reception, as did the recommendation of the National Parks Policies Review Committee (Sandford, 1974) for two tiers of national parks designation. Certainly, the present arrangement of enforcing designations and voluntary codes of practice is unsatisfactory and is proving its failings. An alternative is to dismantle completely the present system of grants and to reassemble in favour of conservation objectives, thereby penalising 'non-sustainable' utilisation, to bring all land use decisions within the rubric of development control, and eventually to alter the pattern of intervention prices of the CAP (Chapter 4, paragraph 30, p 206) so that crop production conforms with conservation objectives (see, for example, Shoard, 1981; Melchett, 1982). This would be a 'conservationists charter', perhaps, but it would not be appropriate for a conservation and development programme for the UK countryside since it would break the 'right balance' sought in Chapter 2, paragraph 2, p 180. It would also have the disadvantages of turning the grant-in-aid system into a

bureaucratic nightmare, would mean an extension of the planning control mechanism beyond the arena for which it was originally designed, and would require a shift in the intervention price policies of the CAP that no Member State has ever contemplated. Nevertheless, reform of the CAP to reflect conservation/development harmony must be sought.

15. Yet, there are a number of reasons why an extension of the planning control system would be attractive in a conservation/development approach:
- (a) Notification by some formal means is essential if landscape change is to be monitored and assessed. No voluntary arrangement can protect all important public interest decisions, nor can it guarantee that the really precious conservation/ amenity sites are adequately safeguarded.
- (b) The local planning authority is geared to development control decisions which involve very sophisticated judgements regarding public and private interests, so it would be administratively convenient to extend its powers.
- (c) The development control apparatus ensures a degree of openness, impartiality and democratic accountability.
- (d) For a majority of land-use decisions it might be assumed that there would be no intervention. All that would be required would be notification, followed by a short delay for consideration. The vast bulk of day to day agricultural and forestry activity would be unaffected. Since compulsory notification of grant aided proposals for land-use change was introduced for national parks in October 1980, for example, about 90 per cent of notifications have been resolved by amicable compromise.

16. However, there are also good reasons why an extension of planning control powers may prove unsatisfactory in respect of countryside care:
- (a) Planning controls really only succeed in stopping 'one off' decisions: to do or not to do something. Such an approach cannot guarantee long-term creative land care tailored to a specific public purpose unless some incentives are available to encourage commitment. Human beings respond to praise and reward more than to punishment, so sustainable rural resource-development is far more likely to occur in a supportive climate of informed advice than in an adversarial atmosphere of scrutiny and negative controls.
- (b) Local planning authorities may not be sensitive either to the specific issues involved in particular land management decisions or to the wider public interest considerations, so local decisions may not necessarily reflect the national purpose.
- (c) Such a system is bound to be bureaucratically cumbersome and administratively expensive to all parties involved, yet, in possibly 70 per cent or more of instances, unnecessary.
- (d) It is far from certain that all planning officers or members of planning committees, unless closely advised by a rural resource-management team,

would appreciate the subtleties of particular cases.
- (e) Enforcement powers are weak and ill suited to insisting that particular land management practices are followed.
- (f) In the majority of cases, the assumption behind development control is that permission will be granted.

17. A 'hybrid' arrangement is proposed here: a simple classification of countryside areas in which notification, coupled to specific packages of incentives and rewards, applies to some of the classified areas (subject to democratic controls), but where in others notification would not be required though management in trust would remain a key concept. It is vital that the management in trust approach be backed by suitable advice and economic incentives to assure conservation interests that the 'lowest order' of countryside classification is to be fully incorporated into the ethos of sustainable utilisation.

A New System of Countryside Categories

18. *The proposal is to establish a three fold classification for the UK countryside:*
- (a) heritage sites
- (b) conservation zones
- (c) agricultural and forestry landscapes.

Note: these do not supersede any existing designations, nor do they alter existing administrative responsibilities. They are merely devices for establishing certain priorities regarding resource-use, for channelling funds, incentives and specialist advice in particular ways, and for prohibiting or penalising certain activities regarded, through democratic decisions, as being incompatible with agreed objectives. However, in the longer-term, should this new arrangement achieve its purpose, it ought to replace the existing array of countryside designations summarised in Table 5 of this report (see p 192). For a summary of the recommendations, see Table 19 (p 243).

Heritage Sites
19. This category should apply to areas with special and irreplaceable nature conservation qualities (of wild or semi-natural vegetation) and/or highly significant landscape beauty. Heritage sites should encompass both conservation and landscape amenity attributes (Chapter 2, paragraph 19, p 183). They should be granted the strongest possible safeguards against undesirable alteration and should be managed so as to conserve for the nation's heritage their geological, biological and scenic qualities. The actual selection of areas for this category would depend upon the appropriate lead agency (NCC, the Countryside Commissions or local authorities — see Chapter 3, paragraphs 15 to 19, pp 188 - 190). These sites would include most, if not all, SSSIs, parts of the national parks and their Scottish equivalents (as determined by the two Countryside Commissions in consultation with local authorities), the heritage coasts,

	Heritage sites	Conservation zones	Agricultural and Forestry landscapes
Approximate percentage of countryside (10% of UK land is urban)	10%	20%	70%
Relevant existing designations	SSSIs: part or all of National Parks and national scenic areas, AONBs plus some other sites.	Probably some SSSIs, some parts of National Parks and national scenic areas, AONBs plus some other sites.	Rest of the countryside except for locally determined Areas of Local Conservation Interest (ALCIs).
How designated	By lead agency (NCCs, CCs, local authorities) subject to ministerial approval with advice from local rural liaison panel.	By lead agency as for heritage sites.	ALCIs established by local authority with advice from local rural liaison panel.
Incentives	Grants geared to particular objectives. Grants not available for 'non-sustainable' utilisation, ie land-use activities not in accord with management objectives. Compensation (reward for managing the land in trust) based on profit foregone (assuming ecologically sustainable utilisation) (similarly for land values) paid by Exchequer through combination of tax relief and direct Departmental payments.	Same as for heritage sites though management objectives should be less demanding in terms of nature conservation/ landscape amenity (but more demanding than present arrangements).	Incentives through grants in aid and tax relief would be available to landowners/occupiers seeking voluntary conservation programmes (notably for landscape enhancement). Comprehensive management advice available. For ALCIs, similar grant, tax and notification arrangements would apply as for heritage sites and conservation zones, except that awards would be paid by local authorities who would also have powers (through ministerial approval) to impose local conservation orders.
Controls	Notification of all potentially inappropriate land-use change, coupled to back up power of countryside conservation order and binding arbitration in case of dispute.	Same as for heritage sites.	No penalties for non-ALCI sites. For ALCIs, similar procedures as for heritage sites and conservation zones would apply except all these would operate through local authority action, subject to ministerial approval.

Note: Throughout all these areas normal development control procedures and structure plan responsibilities as currently exercised by local authorities would still apply.

Table 19. **Summary of the principal features of the proposed countryside categories**

and some AONBs (again as determined by the responsible bodies who may have to manage such sites as joint local committees). There must also be scope for including areas not designated under the existing system. Although the classification would be recommended by the responsible lead agency, the final decision must rest with the appropriate Minister in consultation with his colleagues most directly involved (Agriculture, Treasury). Heritage sites would be owned and managed by private individuals, or privately owned but managed by statutory or voluntary organisations, or owned by Governmental bodies (see paragraph 21 of this chapter, p 244).

20. The lead agency, advised by a local rural liaison panel, should establish management priorities for each heritage site, these priorities to be agreed by the appropriate Minister. All proposed land-use changes, which would in the opinion of the lead agency depart from the agreed management objectives, would be notified to it. (This is similar to the present arrangement applying to SSSIs.) The lead agency should have powers to seek appropriate management agreements or other arrangements (see below) within a specified period and, in the event of disagreement, should be enabled to request

that the appropriate Minister impose a countryside conservation order. This would be a delaying power similar to the present Nature Conservation Order but it should be strengthened by automatic procedures leading to agreement through binding arbitration. (This strengthens the 'back up' powers available to the NCC for most SSSIs, but it is argued that disagreements should be rare because incentives would be specifically geared to sustainable utilisation.) Grants, plus compulsory awards, should be made available in a flexible and integrated manner to meet agreed public objectives (as is presently being tried in the Peak District National Park — see Chapter 6, paragraph 24, p 232 — but in these proposals there would be much greater fluidity of grants and powers straddling departmental budgets and responsibilities). Existing grants for purposes regarded as detrimental to the agreed management objectives should not be payable, but, in order to protect the economic interests of landowners/occupiers, *the new package of grants in aid coupled with management incentives should be equivalent to what would have been earned from the land according to the principles of either aesthetic sustainability or sustained productivity as politically determined.* This is a central feature of these proposals. The incentive/award yardstick for the future must be sustainable management. In simple English, this means management geared to long-term utilisation of soil, water and wildlife so that their productive abilities and their heritage values are not diminished. Which of these two criteria predominates will depend upon the circumstances. Although it was admitted in paragraph 3 of this chapter (p 238) that these criteria may not be known, a commitment to a Conservation and Development Programme for the UK should concentrate minds on this matter, and suitable guidelines should be drawn up. For example, on heritage site moorlands, grants would be available to support traditional grazing practices at densities appropriate to the protection of the existing vegetation, with incentives equivalent to what a landowner would otherwise have earned should he have switched to productively sustainable grazing practices. For heritage woodlands, grants would be payable to manage the woodland so as to maximise natural regeneration and to supply and maintain stock-proof fencing. In general, as is proposed in the Peak District scheme, public money would be invested to reflect the extent to which the public interest is being met.

21. As to taxation (see Table 8, p 206), heritage sites would automatically be subject to CTT relief under the existing Treasury guidelines (Chapter 4, paragraph 27, p 205) but, in addition, the recommendations regarding CGT relief and VAT relief (outlined in Chapter 4, paragraphs 22 and 23, page 204) should also apply. Where a landowner did not wish to continue in private ownership, there would then be far less tax liability should he wish to sell his property to an official or voluntary conservation body. In this context it is hoped that the National Trusts, the Woodland Trust, the RSPB and County Naturalists' Trusts would be able to take full advantage of owning and managing heritage sites in the long-term national interest. *The sale price of the land should reflect its value assuming productively sustainable utilisation* — thereby ensuring that landowners were financially no worse off than they would have been had they continued to manage their property according to the WCS principles. But this should be a once and for all payment as compensation for the loss of future development rights. It would not be sensible to pay annually in perpetuity for the denial of such rights — a permanent restrictive covenant with appropriate legal guarantees would suffice (bearing in mind that the conditions applying to permanent restrictive covenants are challengeable in the courts).

22. Admittedly, private use would be subservient to a public purpose in heritage sites; nevertheless it is vital for landowners/occupiers and their representative lobbies to realise that a combination of grants with a suitable financial reward (for management in trust), or an adequate sale value of the land (bearing in mind approved tax relief) should provide an income that would be at least equivalent to what would have been earned if the land had been managed according to the principles of sustainable utilisation as laid down in Chapter 2, paragraph 7 of this report, p 180, and, where necessary, as politically decided.

Conservation Zones
23. This category should apply to larger areas of important nature conservation value and landscape amenity (which may incorporate or link heritage sites) but where these qualities would be less important than in heritage sites. Again, the precise classification would be determined by the appropriate lead agency (subject to ministerial approval backed by suitable consultation), and, again, similar arrangements for notification backed up by a countryside conservation order and binding arbitration would apply. These zones would possibly encompass the remaining parts of National Parks, non-heritage site AONBs, some areas of great landscape value, including important coastlines and other suitable areas. Similar arrangements regarding grant aid, terms of award (compensation) and taxation/covenant/sale price equivalent and advice from a rural land-use liaison panel would apply as for heritage sites, though the scope linking landscape custody with local employment and rural community economic renaissance should be given the highest priority. The difference between the two categories would lie in the extent to which management incentives and penalties applied to particular land-use priorities and to the level of economic and social regeneration. In the conservation zones, landscape management and community maintenance would predominate, but the objectives of conservation and amenity *should be as high or higher than most lead agencies set for such areas at present.*

24. In general, however, for both conservation zones and heritage sites, grant aid should also be available to stimulate suitable community enterprise, whether it be off-farm economic activity, landscape maintenance work, seasonal employment in a nearby town or participation in the local informal economy operated by service sharing and gift work (see Ecology Party, 1981; Turning Point, 1981). Such areas must not be turned into landscape museums devoid of settlement and social vitality: on the contrary, they must be kept socially and economically buoyant if they are to survive. This is one reason why local control through local authorities, backed by a locally administered steering group is so essential, and why a number of locally employed project officers should be active on the ground. Grant aid and other incentives would be nationally determined (for the sake of comparability and fairness) but locally administered. Sensitive deployment of Articles 3(5) and 10(2) funds of the LFA Directive would be an important step forward in this respect (Chapter 6, paragraph 28, p 235).

Agricultural and Forestry Landscapes
25. These would cover most of the rest of the countryside. Within them, notification of land-use change should not normally be required but conservation investment should be encouraged according to the principles of sustainable utilisation, and, particularly, landscape enhancement through appropriate incentives including management agreements operating on the

basis of trust (Chapter 2, paragraph 19, p 183). There must be a conservation ethos and practice in these areas if the WCS principles are to be upheld. These would also be buttressed by comprehensive advice provided by professionals trained in the multidisciplinary aspects of sustainable land management. In general, the scope for conservation and amenity landscape enhancement, supported by a new breed of advisers and extended incentives, and coupled to voluntary agencies, would be enormous. Note, too, that various tax incentives should encourage such investments.

Areas of Local Conservation Importance

26. As an additional safeguard to ensure the conservation/community enterprise link in agricultural and forestry landscapes, *local authorities should be given a duty to identify, within structure and local plans areas of local conservation interest (ALCIs)*. These might include specific features (such as individual hedgerows or copses of local landscape value) or small areas or linking routeways and would be selected upon the advice of the local steering group. In ALCIs, powers of notification, total safeguarding (through local conservation orders), fluid grants in aid, compensation and taxation arrangements as already suggested for heritage sites and conservation zones should also apply, though the compensation funds would be provided through local rates coupled with national grant in aid. The local authority would thus be responsible for selection and safeguarding of all ALCIs. An important reason for the ALCI category is to enable local people, through democratic procedures, to protect and manage the locally important landscape features — features that are loved by local people because of their intrinsic wildlife interest, heritage value or community associations. Some of these features would be suggested for selection by landowners/occupiers, some by county naturalist trusts and other local voluntary organisations. Some ALCIs may be sold or leased to these organisations or to community groups. The scope for community partnership in landscape care is enormous; what is most urgently required are the proper incentives.

27. These proposals appear cumbersome, but when their main features are outlined (see Table 19, p 243) they need not involve undue additional administration. The main problem is to ensure that the new public interest in sustainable rural development is adhered to. The current arrangements applying to SSSIs need only be extended (with few modifications, though the more flexible grant in aid arrangements would require some attention). All local authorities operate special 'trigger' planning powers for designated areas, so the extension here would not be new. The major point of contention would be the loss of the superiority of private rights over the public interest in certain areas.

28. For major public investments in agriculture and forestry (ie arterial drainage schemes, flood control works, river improvement proposals and major planting programmes) full public accountability, via published cost benefit analyses and environmental appraisals, must be made available to the relevant authorities (Chapter 4, paragraph 37, p 209; Chapter 6, paragraph 30, p 235). Cost benefit analyses should be adjusted to take into account the gains and losses attributed to conservation/amenity and to avoid the errors of incorporating subsidised outputs (Chapter 4, paragraph 32, p 207). When there is serious disagreement between the proponents and those officially representing conservation/amenity interests (disagreements should be less likely if grant aid is made more flexible), a public inquiry should be mandatory. However, if the new countryside classification proposals are implemented, public investment proposals which contradict management objectives would be far less likely to occur.

Expenditure of Public Money and Returns on Investment

29. It may be argued that these proposals will result in a smaller amount of food and timber production, which might bring about food and timber price rises and adverse consumer reaction (Chapter 4, paragraph 6, p 199). This need not be the case, for what is advocated here is a redeployment of public money so that it is more properly applied to wider public interests. The case has already been made (Chapter 4, paragraphs 18, 19, 33 and 39, pp 202, 203, 207 and 209; Chapter 5, paragraphs 17 and 20, pp 220 and 221; Chapter 6, paragraphs 18 to 25, pp 231 - 234) that, under current arrangements, there is wastage of public money leading to environmental damage and unnecessary surpluses. The new arrangements need not use up any more public money and it is doubtful if agriculture or forestry output in the vast bulk of the countryside would be demonstrably affected. Many of the key heritage sites are in upland areas where net agricultural production is a small part of total UK agricultural output. For the majority of the 'unprotected' agricultural landscapes, the emphasis would be upon landscape enhancement, not negative controls. It should also be stressed that the whole point of the WCS is to demonstrate that economics encompass care as well as production and that, if these proposals are pursued, jobs could be created, tourist income increased and viable rural communities preserved through the stimulation of compatible local industry. Indeed, this new package should result in more revenue per £1 of investment and should certainly benefit rural communities as a whole.

Landscape Enhancement

30. There has been a long tradition of creative landscape design in the UK, a practice which notably flourished in the late eighteenth and early nineteenth centuries. The middle of the twentieth century brought drastic changes for the worse. Many great landscapes became over-mature or simply decayed. Much of the specialised expertise was lost. The modern dilemmas are how to

re-establish this profession, preferably through a national lead agency (the Countryside Commissions are presently not equipped to do this) and what styles to follow. What is required is a Landscape Study Centre which would liaise with the design professions (landscape architecture), the applied environmental science professions (forestry, soil science, hydrology and ecology) and the land management professions (planning, surveying and accountancy) to establish a new and exciting set of guidelines and practical hints. Such a centre could be jointly funded by public and private money and should form a focus for the science and practice of landscape enhancement and habitat creation that should provide the heritage of the twenty first and twenty second centuries.

A Land Care Coordinating Group

31. If the land-care aspects of rural resource-management are to be properly integrated with the land-use elements, then a closer integration of the official organisations responsible for nature conservation and landscape beauty is necessary (Chapter 2, paragraph 19, p 183). The objectives and philosophies of these bodies are close enough to deserve better coordination; moreover, there would be more managerial and political 'clout' in coordination because, if left as they are, these bodies could be in danger of working at cross purposes and thus vitiating their efforts. Recent examples of policy inconsistency between the Countryside Commission and the NCC include the dispute over the official designation of the Berwyn Mountains and the differences of view about whether or not to oppose the application by Shell Ltd to explore for oil in the New Forest. A strengthened link should give these two official agencies a more powerful sense of leadership which is urgently required and which would have the support of the voluntary conservation groups. Admittedly, administrative coordination within the Countryside Commission and the NCC does take place both at Chairman and Chief Officer levels, and many proposals for better administrative coordination have been advanced over the years (see especially the Strutt Committee, 1978). So in many ways this recommendation is neither new nor unexpected. However, in view of the proposals for new countryside categories an even closer coordination between these agencies is required, certainly for each country within the UK (as appropriate), coupled to regional or local rural liaison panels for 'ground level' collaboration.

Job Creation

32. It is now officially conceded that high unemployment will be a permanent feature in the UK. The rural economy has suffered from the current recession as much as the urban economy, though the consequences

of widespread rural unemployment, particularly amongst women and young people, are perhaps less well publicised. Central Government should give rural areas equal priority in job creation investment, and encourage a closer link between the Development Commissions, the tourist boards, manpower training schemes and the official and non-Governmental conservation organisations. Wherever possible, inter-agency coordination should be streamlined and at county level rural employment task forces should be given more financial backing and should link with the rural liaison panels, possibly through one or two individuals acting as catalysts. Those with small business experience, assisted perhaps by those with a background in business management who have retired early (an important resource in many rural areas) should be encouraged to form local enterprise trusts to assist others to develop businesses and associated services, thereby avoiding the 'leakage' of locally produced money to nearby towns. Where family incomes are low, part-time and home-based work should be encouraged. Local education curricula should provide special training for rural-based employment, notably in maintenance of machinery, in landscape care and design, in conservation remedial work, in building and repairing houses, in food production, in crafts and other creative skills, and in the management of small businesses. Relaxation of the Employment Protection Act for small businesses, employing at least 20 but less than 50 people, should also be considered as an incentive for rural small businesses to take on labour.

33. The adequate provision of local services, in remote rural areas, in transport, health, education and social care is a very vexing question. It is unlikely that a satisfactory level of service can be provided through the formal cash economy, except by means of mobile facilities. Even this compromise arrangement may not work well in the longer-term. It will therefore be necessary to look at the voluntary, informal, sector of the economy to meet these needs, partly through job creation programmes and partly through official support of the voluntary element in economic activity. Local groups should be encouraged to make village/town appraisals to assess the economic and social strengths and weaknesses of their communities and to propose ways of meeting felt needs. Given flexible planning controls, many disused buildings could be converted into housing, industry, small businesses or locales for various local services.

34. As hinted in Chapter 6, paragraphs 4 and 5, pp 225 - 226, all this will mean that present perceptions of 'work', 'housework', 'leisure' and 'income', plus 'voluntary' and 'alternative', will have to be changed. Cash income, as presently visualised, need no longer be the only criterion of 'wealth'; people may have less but need not be poorer. When social attitudes alter to accept this then it should be possible for the Treasury to consider changing the tax and supplementary benefit rules to suit. This may mean providing tax credits for employing labour, for enabling people to share jobs or take on two or more jobs throughout the year while being guaranteed a minimum income through social

security payments. Clearly, such proposals are subject to abuse, so once again the concept of trust, so central to this report, must apply. Given the appropriate incentives, community and landscape care could be merged with a flowering of local economic enterprise.

Implications for Other Reports

35. The proposals advanced in this report have wide ranging implications for the companion reports in this book.

Coastal Management: 'Conservation and Development of Marine and Coastal Resources', Part 4
It will be necessary to designate key coastal sites, to protect important coastline habitats through the proposed new procedures and to establish within the local liaison groups special mechanisms for dealing with estuaries. The British public loves the accessible open coast: this must be given high priority protection by placing an onus on any developer to prove that there are no viable alternative locations for any proposed schemes.

Urban Areas: 'The Livable City', Part 2
It will be necessary to look hard at existing land-uses and opportunities for multiple land management on the urban fringe (Chapter 6, paragraph 32, p 236) and to examine the policies relating to planning controls on important agricultural areas nearby settlements (Chapter 6, paragraph 31, p 236). There should be a presumption in all structure plans against development on prime agricultural land (some of which may be protected through ALCI status). This report is designed to be complementary to the proposals advanced in 'The Livable City'. The 'greening' of the cities, wider use of environmental interpretation and innovative education schemes, coupled to an extension of community enterprise, all mirror the philosophy of the proposals advanced here.

Industry: 'Seven Bridges to the Future', Part 1
Industry needs to examine the environmental aspects of its products where these potentially damage land-use sustainability. This particularly refers to the agrochemical manufacturers but also to those industries involved in recycling and energy conservation. Also environmental assessment for all industrial proposals in heritage sites, conservation zones and ALCIs should be mandatory and be made public. The issue of landscape restoration and enhancement of derelict land requires closer investigation and there should be insurance bonds to guarantee restoration and enhancement of all new mineral developments. Industry should also be encouraged to 'sponsor' heritage sites and ALCIs, possibly in cooperation with the voluntary conservation movement.

International Considerations: 'The UK's Overseas Environmental Policy', Part 5
The proposals for grant aid/tax reform and the crossing of existing administrative boundaries need to be conveyed to Brussels, not just to Whitehall. Also, environmental assessments of all European Community projects and policies should be undertaken by the Community itself. This must particularly apply to the CAP and especially to the sustainability implications of the guarantee and guidance funds. At the very least, the wider implications of price supports must be examined on an international basis to assess how this policy affects various aspects of sustainability in different environmental and socio-economic conditions. Also, the whole of the less favoured area policy and grant aid programme need to be examined in the light of their effects of productive and aesthetic sustainability and rural socio-economic viability. Cost benefit analysis and environmental assessments must also be re-examined to ensure that 'non-monetary' aspects of project appraisals are given full consideration. It can be argued that only when the UK itself adopts a proper conservation and development programme will it be in a position through its aid budget and through education to influence developing countries in adopting conservation/development practices. In this context, the goal of 'agricultural self-sufficiency' may have to be set against the advantages of international trade in food and related products. Price protection of agricultural products within the EEC may not be in the best interests of a global conservation strategy.

Education: 'Education for Commitment: Building Support in Society for Conservation and Development', Part 7
Education is really improved communication leading to new understanding and a new ethos. There will be a need to widen the element of stewardship in professional training in agricultural and forestry colleges and in schools and universities. The local liaison officers will certainly require this training but will also need to be familiar with the practices of agriculture, forestry, the water industry and tourism. Communication through education must be mutual. But education is equally about citizenship — about preparing people to help and to care for each other and for the land upon which their livelihood depends. The future rural community will require this sense of mutual aid via the sharing of skills (Chapter 6, paragraphs 2 to 7, pp 225 - 227). This will also mean preparing young and old for the twenty first century economy, based upon a mixture of the formal and informal sectors where job training and re-training is shared and where flexibility in occupational skills is encouraged. This will also involve exploiting the revolution in computer and information transfer technology so that unnecessary travel is reduced and that more time is devoted to personal leisure and community interests.

Ethics: 'Environmental Ethics and Conservation Action', Part 6
Ecological humanism is an emerging philosophy which bridges the principles of ecology with the limitless creativeness of humanism (see Skolimowsky, 1981 for a comprehensive discussion). It involves extending society's rights over the land so that the land becomes

even more part of the social fabric. This can only be achieved in harmony with new patterns of incentives and penalties. These should help to overcome the resistance of environmental schizophrenia, which enables people to act in one way but believe that another way, entailing some different behaviour patterns, is morally right. This is an age-old dilemma in human behaviour.

References

COUNTRYSIDE REVIEW COMMITTEE. 1979. Conservation and the countryside heritage. Topic paper 4. London, HMSO.

ECOLOGY PARTY. 1981. Working for a future: an ecological approach to unemployment. London, Ecology Party (36-38 Clapham Road).

HALL, C. 1981. Who needs a national land use strategy? *New Scientist, 2 April*, 10-12.

MELCHETT, P. 1982. Following a hard act. *The Countryman, 87 (1)*, 27-38.

SANDFORD, LORD. 1974. Report of the National Parks Policy Review Committee. London, HMSO.

SHOARD, M. 1981. The theft of the countryside. London, Maurice Temple Smith.

SKOLIMOWSKY, H. 1981. Eco-philosophy: designing new tactics for living. London, Marion Boyars.

STRUTT, N. (Chairman). 1978. Agriculture and the countryside. Report of the Advisory Committee on Agriculture and Horticulture in England and Wales. London, HMSO.

TURNING POINT. 1981. The redistribution of work. Ironbridge, Turning Point (Spring Cottage, 9 New Road).

CHAPTER 8

SUMMARY OF RECOMMENDATIONS

Introduction

The recommendations that follow are presented in a summary form, and will appear more assertive than the supporting arguments in the text would justify. The reader is encouraged to read all of the preceding chapter before considering them, and to dip into the text at the paragraphs indicated. (All chapters and paragraph references relate to this report only.) It is recognised that, in some cases and in some parts of the UK, certain of the recommendations that follow are already being implemented.

Maintaining Sustainable Utilisation

Recommendation Group 1

(a) A systematic programme of ecologically effective monitoring, taking into account the effects of soil, water and wildlife of a wide range of agricultural and forestry practices, should be established immediately (Chapter 3, paragraphs 26 and 27, pp 191 - 192). The lead institutions should be the National Environmental Research Council (NERC) and the NCC.

(b) Before any major new programme of ecological modelling is contemplated, a lead institution or institutions should establish priorities for investigation and comparable methodological approaches (Chapter 3, paragraph 27, p 192).

(c) A comprehensive monitoring programme of all nationally significant habitats should be put into effect immediately (Chapter 3, paragraph 29, p 192). This should make use of satellite data and should be stored in a computer. This programme should be led by the NCC, suitably financed to do the job, plus the Macaulay Institute.

(d) Every major agency responsible for both the development and care of rural resources (the Agriculture Departments, the Forestry Commission, the Countryside Commissions and the NCC) should establish a conservation/development advisory committee with a remit to promote the practice of ecologically sustainable utilisation. Such committees should have a wide representation. (Note that the Farming and Wildlife Advisory Groups should be given further encouragement and assistance, as should other voluntary groups anxious and able to cooperate constructively in this endeavour. There is considerable scope for the formation of small, job creating consultancies, linked through ADAS and the Scottish Agricultural Colleges to FWAG and the farming community.

(e) Every major agency (as identified in (c) above) should include in its Annual Report a section outlining the research, research findings and the practical measures it has implemented to pursue sustainable utilisation in its work (as outlined in Figure 1, p 180).

(f) The various advisory committees (see (c) above) should work systematically towards describing what constitutes ecologically sustainable practice, both in terms of productive sustainability and heritage value (aesthetic sustainability) in each of the major rural resource-use sectors. These guidelines should form the future yardstick for wise resource-use and should provide the basis for determining awards (compensation) and packages of grant aid in areas where the land is managed specifically to promote the national heritage (Chapter 7, paragraphs 20 and 22, pp 243 - 244). This analysis should encompass radical approaches using energy and biological cycles to investigate a new form of environmental accounting (Research Councils).

(g) Grant aid should never be given by any public authority for any rural resource-use that is not ecologically sustainable.

Research Needs

Recommendation Group 2

Research institute and other grant aiding bodies should give serious consideration to financing a variety of research programmes geared to improve knowledge of the relationship between land management practices and ecologically sustainable utilisation. Soil surveys and land suitability classifications should be related more to the concepts of productive and aesthetic sustainability, providing clearer advice for land management (Soil Survey, ADAS).

The major resource-management and research institutions should list priority areas for extended research.

Some of the suggestions listed below are already in hand either in this country or abroad. Possibilities include:

(a) Fertilisers which lock their nutrients into the soil and crops (Chapter 4, paragraphs 12 and 13, page 201), and the effects on wildlife of current fertilisation practices (Chapter 4, paragraph 12, p 201) (agrochemical industry, NCC, voluntary bodies, universities).

(b) Various approaches to integrated pest management, covering different environmental conditions and management practices, economic, legal, psychological and practical barriers to the widespread use of integrated pest management, and an analysis of how current policy could encourage a transition toward integrated pest management (Chapter 4, paragraph 11, p 200; Chapter 5, paragraph 5, p 216) (agriculture research stations, agrochemical industry, universities).

(c) The association between various moorland management techniques (on different kinds of moor) and grazing densities, game management and wildlife conservation (Chapter 3, paragraph 38, p 195; Chapter 4, paragraph 16, p 202; Chapter 6, paragraphs 11 and 16, pp 228 and 230) (ITE, NCC, universities).

(d) The relationship between different tree planting practices and soil structure (Chapter 5, paragraphs 3 and 4, pp 215 - 216), windthrow (Chapter 5, paragraph 3, p 215), wildlife and amenity (Chapter 5, paragraphs 8 and 9, pp 216 - 217), pest management and water availability and quality (Chapter 5, paragraphs 5 to 7, page 216) (agriculture and forestry research stations, universities).

(e) Practical, economic and legal barriers to the better integration of agriculture and forestry on upland slopes and whole catchments (Chapter 6, paragraph 18, p 231), possibly through the establishment of a number of pilot schemes in different parts of the country (universities).

(f) The analysis of how red and roe deer can coexist with forest by opening up short-term licences for stalking (Chapter 6, paragraph 15, p 230) (forestry and hill farming research stations, game conservancy, Red Deer Commission).

(g) The contribution which organic farming can make to the UK agriculture (Chapter 4, paragraphs 13 and 14, page 201) and mixed organic-chemical farming (Chapter 4, paragraph 13, p 201) so that better harmony between these two approaches to husbandry can be obtained. Also, the economic and management factors that affect the profitability of organic farming, combined with an investigation of what policy measures should be put into effect to encourage greater use of organic manures (Chapter 4, paragraph 14, p 201). Also, the transfer of toxic substances from sewage sludge and chemical pesticides and fertilisers into food (Chapter 4, paragraph 14, p 201) (agricultural research institutions and organic research stations).

(h) The scope for greater energy use efficiencies in both agriculture and forestry (Chapter 4, paragraph 13, p 201) (agriculture research stations and institutions coupled with organic growers associations).

(i) The relationship between the recreational use of certain habitats and the ecological tolerance to withstand that use (Chapter 6, paragraphs 8 and 9, pp 227 - 228) (Countryside Commissions, universities).

(j) The relationship between chemical insecticide use (particularly methods of application) and effects on wildlife (Chapter 4, paragraph 11, p 200; Chapter 7, paragraph 3, p 238) and the long-term effects of all kinds of chemical pollutants on wildlife, including industrial pollutants (Chapter 7, paragraph 3, point (d), p 238), the former case extending the work currently undertaken by the PSPS. There is also a case for examining the implications of placing the burden of proof upon agrochemical manufacturers to show more securely that their products are not harmful (Chapter 4, paragraph 11, p 200) (universities, ITE, NCC).

(k) The economic effects of 'conservation blight' should be thoroughly investigated to discover implications for land values, land-use management and attitudes to conservation and development (Research Councils, universities, agricultural interests, RICS).

(l) The implications of reducing the number of crop species for commercial agriculture and forestry, the need for suitable gene-banks and the implications of the European Commission's seeds directives (which make it illegal to buy or sell many of the older varieties of crop seeds) should be closely examined (specialised research institutes).

(m) Bright minds should be freed to devote their attention to a new ecological economic theory to provide a basis for ecological energy audits and accountancy (research institutes).

Integrating Conservation Values with Resource-Use

Recommendation Group 3

Landscape enhancement and ecological variety should be encouraged by conscious measures to manage rural resources in 'degraded' sites so that novel approaches to landscape amenity and nature conservation can be developed. Many agricultural and forestry landscapes could be made visually more pleasing with a little thought, encouragement, advice and economic incentive.

(a) A Landscape Study Centre should be established with public and private funds linked to the design, environmental science and land management professions (Chapter 7, paragraph 30, p 246) (Countryside Commissions, Landscape Institute, universities).

(b) The Countryside Commission, in association with the FWAG and similar organisations, should give landscape enhancement more priority in their financial assistance and advice (Chapter 3, paragraph 31, p 193; Chapter 3, paragraph 41, p 195; Chapter 7, paragraph 25, p 244).

(c) The NCC should cooperate with voluntary agencies in developing nature conservation sites in cities, on derelict land and on restored land.

(d) Local authorities, in conjunction with manpower training programmes together with other job creation schemes, should be further encouraged to prepare schemes for the creative restoration of derelict land, old mine workings and disused land (Chapter 3, paragraph 31, p 193).

(e) All major mining proposals should have restoration plans submitted as part of the planning application coupled to bonds backed by insurance schemes to ensure that remedial work is undertaken even if the company goes bankrupt (Chapter 6, paragraph 32, p 236) (local authorities, Environment Departments).

(f) As a means of ensuring that landscape care is incorporated into all development proposals for rural (and indeed urban) areas, the proposed EEC Directive on EIA should be introduced with appropriate amendments to permit flexibility and documentation tailored to the circumstances as part of existing UK planning procedures, and major public investment in agriculture and forestry should also be subject to EIA. Such EIA should contain sections dealing with landscape enhancement (Chapter 6, paragraphs 29 and 30, pp 235 - 236) (local authorities, Environment Departments).

(g) A major re-think of the cost benefit analyses that are used by the Agriculture and Forestry Ministries to justify major public investments in agriculture and forestry should be undertaken (Chapter 4, paragraph 37, p 209; Chapter 6, paragraph 30, p 235; Chapter 7, paragraph 28, p 245). Cost benefit analyses should be adjusted to take into account the gains and losses attributed to conservation/amenity and to avoid the errors of incorporating subsidised outputs (Chapter 4, paragraph 32, p 207). When there is disagreement between the scheme proponents and official bodies and local government bodies representing conservation/amenity interests, a public inquiry should be mandatory (Agriculture Departments, Treasury, universities, Research Councils).

(h) There should be a presumption in all structure plans or their equivalent against loss of prime agricultural land (Chapter 3, paragraph 30, p 192; Chapter 6, paragraphs 30 and 31, pp 235 - 236). Independent research should be undertaken to discover how far the new planning procedures as laid down in DOE circulars encourage the loss of such land. Care must be taken, however, to ensure that proposed developments on lower quality lands do not endanger conservation/amenity values (local authorities, Environment Departments).

(i) Special attention should be given to enable the urban fringe to cater for a great variety of users (Chapter 6, paragraph 33, p 236). The potential for interpretation programmes in the urban fringe to display how a Conservation and Development Programme for the UK can be put into effect should also be examined (local authorities, Environment Departments, Countryside Commissions).

(j) A determined effort must be made to improve public access to the uplands and lowlands, to encourage landowners even more to make access agreements and to improve public access to common lands (Chapter 6, paragraphs 9 and 10, pp 227 - 228).

(k) The Forestry Commission, other conservation bodies and local authorities should be financially encouraged to create new ecological mixes in relation both to agriculture and forestry. The skills and the basic knowledge are available. A variety of schemes should be encouraged for demonstration purposes. Examples include saltmarsh reclamation and pasture management (Chapter 4, paragraph 16, p 202). Official agencies should sponsor imaginative demonstration programmes coupled to better facilities for providing continuous management advice (Chapter 5, paragraph 20, p 221). These programmes should extend the good work already undertaken by voluntary groups, non-governmental bodies and the various advisory organisations.

Reconciling Productive Sustainability with the Protection of Heritage Values

Recommendation Group 4

A major objective of a UK conservation/development strategy must be to reconcile the growing differences of view between those whose priorities favour ecologically sustainable utilisation and aesthetically sustainable utilisation respectively (Chapter 2, paragraphs 7 and 16, pp 180 and 183; Chapter 3, paragraph 41, p 195; Chapter 7, paragraph 5, p 239). This will not be easy to achieve (Chapter 7, paragraphs 2 and 12, pp 238 and 241) and any worthwhile solution will require changes in policy, taxation, economic incentives and administrative arrangements. The full arguments are outlined in Chapter 7, paragraphs 6 to 17 (pp 239 - 242).

(a) A three fold classification of the UK countryside should be established which does not interfere with existing landscape designations, but which allows management objectives to be clarified, priorities established and appropriate incentives and penalties channelled (Chapter 7, paragraph 18, p 242). These categories are heritage sites, conservation zones and agricultural and forestry landscapes.

(b) For heritage sites the recommendations are (Chapter 7, paragraphs 19 to 22, pp 242 - 244; Table 19, p 243: (i) classification by appropriate lead agency (NCC, Countryside Commissions, local authorities) with appropriate ministerial approval; (ii) management priorities established by lead agency in consultation with local rural liaison panel; (iii) all land-use proposals contrary to agreed management plan notifiable to lead agency: a three month period for settlement plus a further nine months if disagreement, backed up by a ministerially-opposed countryside conservation order and binding arbitration; (iv) fluidity of grants to enable approved agriculture/forestry (and other developments) to be supported by responsible ministries. Public money paid out in relation to agreed public interest priorities; (v) provision for sale or lease or convenanting of land to official or non-Governmental bodies for long-term management with appropriate tax concessions (Table 8, p 206); (vi) terms of award (compensation) and land sale to be based on lost profitability assuming sustainable utilisation, as appropriate for the area; (vii) where possible, development rights in key areas bought out in a single compensatory payment and legally binding restrictive covenants imposed; (viii) further detailed analysis of the distributional aspects of existing agricultural forestry and conservation grants taking into account on what and where such grants are paid and what would be the effects for public expenditure and land management if various lower ceilings were to be imposed on single grant aid payments, and grants were channelled specifically to attain aesthetically sustainable production in key conservation/amenity areas (Agriculture Departments, Forestry Commission, research institutes).

(c) For conservation zones the same arrangements should apply except that agreed management priorities regarding heritage protection would be less stringent and more attention would be given to linking land care with local employment opportunities. However, standards of conservation should be as high or higher than is the case in such areas at present (Chapter 7, paragraph 23, p 244).

(d) For agricultural and forestry landscapes no notification procedures should normally exist, but positive programmes outlined in Recommendation 3 (h) should be in place, coupled with supporting advice from local agricultural/forestry liaison officers.

(e) Within the agricultural and forestry landscapes category provision would exist for local planning authorities to establish a local countryside heritage category, namely areas of local conservation interest (ALCIs) (Chapter 7, paragraph 26, p 245). These would be protected by a similar package of incentives and penalties, as would heritage sites and conservation zones, but would be locally determined and award payments (compensation) would come from local as well as national funding. Again, the local rural liaison panel should provide advice as should the local

voluntary conservation organisations and other voluntary bodies: similar tax arrangements as proposed in Table 8, p 206, should apply.

(f) Agricultural, land management and forestry liaison officers should be appointed at county level to act as advisers and instigators of conservation within development. They will require suitable interdisciplinary training.

(g) A stronger policy coordinating mechanism than exists at present should be established between the Countryside Commissions and the NCC, both at headquarter and regional levels (Chapter 2, paragraph 16, p 183; Chapter 7, paragraph 30, p 246) and locally within rural liaison groups.

Incorporating Community Enterprise

Recommendation Group 5

As outlined in Figure 2 (see p 182) a conservation/development strategy for the UK countryside cannot be divorced from the social and economic vitality of rural settlement. Nor can it be taken for granted that either supporting small farms, or providing new jobs in landscape conservation and off-farm economic enterprise, will be sufficient to maintain employment and rural communities no matter how flexible a grant aid policy.

(a) Ecologically and aesthetically sustainable utilisation of agricultural and forestry practices should be subject to grant aid provisions from the Agriculture Departments irrespective of landscape designation or countryside category.

(b) Artices 3(5) and 10(2) of the EEC Less Favoured Areas Directive should much further be brought into effect by the Agriculture Departments in liaison with the Tourist Boards and Development Commissions.

(c) The Tourist Boards should be allowed to provide grant aid to on-farm tourist enterprises in all heritage sites and conservation zones (Chapter 6, paragraphs 26 to 28, pp 234 - 235).

(d) Jobs for farmers and the land managers should be promoted through encouragement of suitable business initiatives in rural communities. This will involve investment in small business training schemes and a package of preferential loans (Chapter 7, paragraphs 32 to 34, pp 246 - 247).

(e) Provisions of housing for the rural labour force is a key priority. This will require harmonisation of landscape protection and planning policies, imaginative developments in communal self help and cooperative ventures in construction and ownership (Chapter 6, paragraph 5, p 226; Chapter 7, paragraphs 32 to 34, pp 246 - 247).

(f) With the assistance of the Small Farmers Association and Crofters Association there should be a study of the economic viability of the small farm enterprise in different parts of the UK. This investigation should cover the economic and social aspects of maintaining traditional forms of husbandry in heritage sites, conservation zones and ALCIs, the scope for new employment opportunities given alterations in grant aid policies and the meshing of on-farm, off-farm enterprise. The study should also examine the possible effects of new countryside classifications and grant aid structure land values, productivity and commitment to certain land-use practices (Agriculture Departments, universities). In addition it should look at the possibilities of labour intensive agro-forestry operations employing imaginative light industrial techniques.

(g) Official encouragement should be given to rural economic and social enterprise initiatives (Chapter 7, paragraphs 32 to 34, pp 246 - 247) including the establishment or development of county level employment task forces, new incentives for small businesses and the provision of local services, support for the informal sector and better training programmes in community and landscape maintenance (Development Commissions, Employment Departments, Industry Departments).

(h) The recommendations with regard to VAT, income tax, CGT and CTT (as outlined in Table 8, p 206, and as discussed in Chapter 4, paragraphs 25 to 28, pp 205 - 206) should be implemented, namely: (i) income tax relief on approved conservation investment should be written off during the year in which it was spent (Chapter 4, paragraph 25, p 205), and the Inland Revenue should clarify that *bona-fide* investment in conservation work which is not strictly agricultural business should be tax exempt; (ii) *bona-fide* conservation investments should be available for deferral of capital gains tax (Chapter 4, paragraph 26, p 205; (iii) the provisions for deferral of capital transfer tax should be more widely available in heritage sites, conservation zones and ALCIs, with the tax designation criteria matching the countryside classification criteria; (iv) the 10 per cent douceur available to landowners selling their land to approved conservation bodies should be increased, and sale should be possible to any *bona-fide* conservation organisation (Chapter 4, paragraph 28, p 205); and (v) property maintenance and repair by landlords for recognised conservation and landscape enhancement purposes should automatically be subject to VAT redemption (Chapter 4, paragraph 25, p 205).

Education for Countryside Care

Recommendation Group 6
The skills necessary to maintain and enhance the nation's conservation and scenic heritage are already available. They need to be transferred to all resource-users (Chapter 2, paragraph 4, p 179; Chapter 3, paragraph 41, point (a), p 196).

(a) The curricula in agricultural, forestry and other land management courses should further be broadened and more focused to improve both the understanding of basic ecological concepts and the practices of conservation.

(b) The custodial agencies (the NCC and the Countryside Commissions) need to train their officers with the principles and economics that lie behind agriculture, forestry, and the water and mining industries.

(c) Local liaison officers employed to encourage practical conservation with rural development (notably water, agriculture and woodland management) should have special training.

(d) Interpretation and demonstration should be fully integrated into as many aspects as possible of the future conservation/development operations in rural UK. The wider public should benefit much from first hand experience of the Conservation and Development Programme for the UK.

Doing in the Present and Preparing for the Future

Not all of these recommendations can be put into effect immediately. It will take time to alter the outlook of all those directly involved in rural resource-management, and differences in viewpoint are strongly influenced by agency responsibilities and policies plus expectations shaped by grant aid, price subsidies, planning controls and general economic developments, most of which do not recognise the inherent links between conservation and development. In the immediate future, the task is to prepare minds for new ways of thinking and to encourage all aspiring political parties to justify how present or proposed policies fit into a conservation/development ethos. The task is a formidable one: it can take many years simply to produce mutually acceptable management agreements (eg on Exmoor, the Norfolk Marshes, the Somerset Levels) and even management and financial guidelines (which, by definition, are not specific) involve numerous man years of highly paid professional time (eg the Conservation and Land Drainage Guidelines prepared by the Water Space Amenity Commission). Yet it is not unusual to find that these hard fought over documents are almost ignored when 'real world' agreements have to be reached.

If progress is to be made, there must be agreement about facts and trends (even if all the necessary research is not complete); there must be management skills available in the landowner, the professional adviser and the community generally; and there must be a sense of partnership in the care of rural resources, a partnership between the landowner/occupier and the local community. To achieve this, all the recommendations outlined above should be put into effect. Those relating to research (Recommendation Group 2, see pp 249 - 250), must continue for some time whilst more specific actions can be taken immediately.

Attention now should be given to:

(a) The establishment of conservation/development advisory committees in every rural resource-use agency.

(b) The inclusion in annual reports of work done towards implementing a rural conservation/development plan.

(c) Preparation of guidelines as to what constitutes ecologically sustainable utilisation for representation, types of rural resource-use.

(d) Specific initiatives to encourage landscape enhancement by all rural agencies.

(e) Establishment of guarantees for the post-working reconstruction of all new mineral extraction proposals.

(f) Introduction of environmental assessments for all major planning applications.

(g) New guidelines for all cost benefit analyses used by all official agencies, to include environmental appraisal and 'real world' benefit calculations.

(h) A ministerially imposed presumption against any further development of prime agricultural land.

(i) Official endorsement, through further implementation, of Articles 3(5) and 10(2) of the Less Favoured Areas Directive.

(j) Official support for uniting conservation with development within the Western Isles Integrated Development Programme.

(k) Extension of tourist board grants to all less favoured areas.

(l) Extension of grant aid eligibility to all 'part-time' farmers, but only for sustainable practices.

(m) Introduction of conservation/development principles into all professional training programmes for rural resource-practitioners and advisers.

(n) Introduction of community service, maintenance and small business skills in school and college curricula.

(o) Official support for county-level rural management liaison officers and encouragement for county-level FWAG to extend their existing employment of liaison officers, and to spawn local land care consultancies.

(p) Official support for county-level rural employment task forces with officers to act as catalysts.

(q) Official support for county naturalists trusts and other voluntary groups to monitor post-planting care of young trees, and to survey local resources for possible identification as ALCIs.

(r) Official support for community groups and parish councils to survey villages/towns to assess need and potential for community enterprise initiatives.

(s) Establishment of county-level rural liaison groups with a remit to review the scope for heritage sites and conservation zones and to examine the scope for improving public access to rural land.

All these tasks can be completed within a period of three to five years. During that time, attention should be turned on the more administratively complex recommendations, notably those relating to the integration of grant aid incentives and extension of planning controls for certain countryside categories, to reform in the tax arrangements and in job creation and social security conditions. At the very least, a Government committed to a rural conservation/development plan should be prepared to experiment with various alternative mixes of incentives and penalties, through a representative group of pilot schemes in each nation of the UK, but pilot schemes can never be an adequate substitute for the necessary reforms which this report advocates.

In the longer term:

(a) There should be a reconsideration of the demand forecasts of all major rural resource-requirements every five years. This review should include energy, minerals, aggregates, water, timber and recreation needs. The results should be incorporated into strategic planning and should be part of all major EIA (Chapter 6, paragraph 30, p 235).

(b) The proposed countryside classifications should replace designations and should provide the basis for future countryside management in the UK.

(c) This quinquennial reconsideration of the rural resource-requirements should be undertaken in the light of progress made on resource-use conservation as outlined in the companion reports and in the light of the trading obligations of the UK, given that all countries should not make requirements on other countries to the point where the resources and peoples of trading partners are exploited beyond the limits of ecologically sustainable utilisation. It is in this spirit that a fundamental review of the price support policies of the CAP should be made. This should begin now, because the present economic policies enshrined in the CAP are probably the single most important factor influencing the current incompatibilities between the demands for agricultural productivity and aesthetic and socio-economic sustainability.

(d) Rural economic activity (agriculture, forestry, tourism, business, service provision) may well have to accommodate to an entirely new set of conditions regarding energy availability in the early twenty first century. Scenarios should be developed to analyse what actions should be taken to provide adequate preparation. These scenarios should be prepared by the resource-use sector and for the rural economy as a whole. One of these scenarios should examine a UK that is highly self-sufficient in energy and material needs and in resource-consumption. To reach this may well require a radical re-appraisal of pricing policies and units of currency (away from money towards energy and chemical cycles). This is why imaginative minds should be encouraged now to produce new forms of environmental and social accounting.

CHAPTER 9

THE PRACTITIONERS' DEBATE

Introduction

1. Two thousand copies of this report were printed at the end of September 1982. Within three months, over 1,200 copies had been distributed and it is probably reasonable to guess that at least 750 of these had been read by at least one individual. A straight reading takes about four hours, but, from the detailed comments made by many of the correspondents, it is plausible to estimate that the average reading and considering time per reader was seven hours. This adds up to a conservative estimate of at least 5,000 person hours of response. Mere quantification of time means very little but it suggests that many people have volunteered a considerable amount of intellectual effort in considering this document. Their commitment and concern for the objectives and success of the Conservation and Development Programme for the UK is most impressive and enormously gratifying. To everyone who has read and responded to the original draft I am deeply grateful. The Appendix at the end of this report (p 260) lists the names of organisations and individuals from whom I have received comment and states the meetings and themes which were held in various parts of the UK. Reading and listening to their reactions has been very stimulating and exciting, though inevitably not all points can be accommodated.

2. The previous chapters were impersonal but this must be personal. When the Programme Organising Committee asked me to take on the task of preparing this document I had only a vague idea of the scale and complexity of the subject matter and arguments involved. I was aware of the strong views held by different interests, and conscious of the need to find some sort of balance in the analysis and recommendations that would inevitably dissatisfy those at the various extremes of the arguments, including those who were hoping for a much more radical and unorthodox analysis to break the recommendations which do more than merely tamper with the *status quo*. This important group of critics not only included those who sought a major shift in power away from what they saw as entrenched and established interests towards a more ecologically and socially caring community ethos based upon action by people. It also represents those who believe passionately that a conservation with development approach can only be successful if current approaches to economic appraisal are transformed into more ecologically-based accounting, incorporating energy and nutrient cycles. The problem I faced when confronted with such

arguments is that I accepted many of the principles upon which they were based, but I had to judge what would be acceptable to carry conviction with those who must implement my proposals (or modifications of them) sooner or later. However, I have added a recommendation that more practical development of this approach and its implications, especially for economic theory, should be sponsored by relevant research councils. Nevertheless, the proponents of these views will rightly cry out that a golden opportunity has been missed and that any other approaches will merely be an exercise in fudging. To these individuals, for whom I have considerable sympathy, my response is first to encourage them to present their own case in parallel with mine, and second to emphasise that my job was in part that of a rapporteur who must in all conscience shape arguments to reflect genuinely felt views and political realities.

3. My remit was to produce a final report, await response and add a final chapter summarising the views submitted, commenting upon them and revising recommendations where appropriate. The original text was only to be amended for factual errors. However, I believe that this is not a sensible way of dealing with the response to my report because I received so many points of amplification that to do them justice required amending the text. So I have corrected all errors of fact in this published report and elaborated major differences in interpretation. This means that this particular chapter will deal largely with the wider, more philosophical and practical points raised in the response.

4. A report like this should ideally have been written by two authors, one an academic (providing a reasonably 'objective' yet analytical viewpoint), the other a practising rural resource-manager with at least 10 years of experience, preferably in two countries within the UK. This combined authorship should have produced a more readable, more concise document with recommendations shaped by a clear sense of what was practicable, who should be responsible for doing something about them and how precisely they could be reached. Originally, I was expected both to set priorities and a time scale for each recommendation and to estimate costs of implementing them. These were unrealistic requirements. The other major problem facing an individual author is the enormous range and complexity of the many detailed scientific and

political arguments connected with each of the many themes covered in this analysis. This inevitably leads specialists to complain that an unrepresentative selection of references, or an incomplete summary of major research findings, has produced an unacceptable bias that may, in their view, invalidate other arguments in the report about which they have little first hand knowledge. The problem of maintaining credibility, both in analysis and recommendation, proved to be a major headache.

Response to the Report as a Whole

5. As a very broad generalisation I observed that most academics and researchers involved in countryside problems praised the report for the comprehensiveness of its coverage and the depth of its analysis, and most representatives of conservation organisations accepted the philosophy and recommendations. The more practical people (planners, resource-managers, landowners and those responsible for rural resource-policy formulation and action) were less enthusiastic about the analysis, more critical of the arguments in their areas of specialisation and interest, and more hostile to the recommendations which they saw as potentially threatening, and/or unnecessarily cumbersome or already in hand. To the former group I am grateful for their support, and I must emphasise that throughout the preparation of this report I received an enormous amount of documentary help and editorial assistance. To the latter group I can only listen carefully, alter the factual errors and try to balance their views in the light of other options and perspectives, and my own convictions.

6. The other major general criticism related to the length and readability of the report. Some readers found it difficult to grasp the report as a whole, and to cross-reference to related points. This meant that some readers did not realise that a key point relating to a particular discussion had been made elsewhere in the text, and so they misinterpreted the logic of the argument. The fault must be mine. The report grew and grew as more information became available, especially the results of very recent research documents. Also, I like to feel the roundness of an argument before presenting a recommendation, and by 'roundness' I mean collating the different viewpoints so as to shape properly the final analysis.

7. In response to these criticisms I have:
    (a) inserted more cross-references in the text; and
    (b) provided a concise summary of the whole report at the beginning drawing the reader's attention to the Recommendations in Chapter 8.
However, there is a need for a more readable, and more concise version of this report to be available to the more general reader and to the practising farmer, planner, forester and rural and urban resident. As it stands, the report is written for the experienced and knowledgeable practitioner, the kind of person who has already responded to it. Another writer should tackle its translation for the more general reader and person on the ground — otherwise this exercise will not carry to the many millions of people who really must be convinced if it is to achieve its aims.

Defining and Implementing Sustainable Utilisation

8. As I was writing and rewriting this report over the period September 1981 to September 1982, I became increasingly aware that the definition of sustainable utilisation of renewable resources as outlined in the WCS was too narrow for the UK. Hence, the triple definition of sustainability outlined in Chapter 2, paragraph 5 of the draft report and reworded in Chapter 2, paragraph 7, p 180 of this report. I have rewritten the Introduction (Chapter 2, paragraphs 5 to 7, pp 179 - 180) to show why the WCS is so important and, in particular, why it is so crucial to get the response right in the UK. This, in turn, has meant that I have used different labels to describe the three interpretations of sustainable utilisation and have stressed the ecological linkage between sustained productivity and protecting and enhancing heritage values and a sense of personal and community attachment to the land. This has enabled me to clarify the boundaries to the earlier notion of 'ecological sustainability' by stressing the important relationships between inputs and outputs for national and international resource-use. This, in turn, has permitted me to differentiate between the earlier notions of ecological and aesthetic sustainability when discussing the management priorities for the various classifications of land, and the principles on which management incentives and compensation should be paid (Chapter 7, paragraph 19, p 242). This has rid me of a major fault in my previous argument, namely that the level of management grants or the purchase price for land within heritage sites and conservation zones (plus ALCIs) should be based on ecological sustainability. Now these factors can be determined by reference to heritage value alone or to sustained productivity (as deemed appropriate) which means that heritage value in itself becomes a basis for 'economic' assessment.

The Countryside Classifications

9. The three fold countryside classification proposal outlined in Chapter 7 created a lot of controversy. The most widespread criticisms were:
    (a) that they did not logically emerge from the analysis of Chapters 2 to 6 of this report, but seemed to come as an 'afterthought' not in keeping with the philosophy of the report;
    (b) that they confused policy (ie practical implementation), a combination not normally found in planning and management of land in the UK;

(c) that they sat uneasily in the present somewhat chaotic picture of landscape designations, many of which work well (at least in the view of most planning authorities) and hence would give rise to enormous confusion and wasteful bureaucracy;

(d) that it was by no means clear how these classifications would be operated: the 'veil' concept was too vague;

(e) that 'lead agencies' should be more precisely defined, and in general should be local authorities rather than the official or voluntary bodies;

(f) that they appeared alarmingly similar to the 'two tier' recommendations of the notorious Countryside Review Committee Topic Paper No 4, with the implication that the agricultural and forestry landscapes would be thrown to the wolves as far as conservation/amenity protection were concerned; and

(g) that in general they were academic (and by definition impractical) and unnecessary because the present arrangements with minor modifications were perfectly satisfactory.

10. These were powerful criticisms though I should admit to reservations about the immediate practicability of these proposals. However, upon reflection I stick to the arguments, outlined in Chapter 7, which justify this particular recommendation and I am pleased to receive support from a number of thoroughly practical people with long experience in rural resource-management. The main point to clarify is that this new classification, in the first instance, is primarily a mechanism for focusing resource-use priorities, for channelling funds as appropriate to meeting these objectives and for enabling local liaison groups to organise their efforts and funds flexibility so as to get on with the job. One must see this as a long-term objective which should be tried out in stages. At the outset, this approach should be tackled through a number of carefully monitored experiments in different parts of the UK. I believe it to be a logical outcome of all the points raised in the substance of the report. I believe it to be an acceptable means of getting formal notification of intended land-use change into the democratic process without burdening local planning authorities. I believe it to be a sensible means of enabling many departments and agencies to coordinate policies and delimit public spending for socially justifiable purposes in defined localities. I believe it allows for inevitable scientific and technical development in agriculture, forestry, industry and service provision. I believe it provides a magnificent opportunity for the voluntary agencies and other consultative mechanisms to become constructively involved in rural management. Finally, I believe it to be a sensible basis for linking practices of maintenances and enhancement (including the creation of new habitats and landscapes) which must be central to a report of this kind. So I do not share the fear that the 'third tier' will become the cinderella of the countryside, whose conservation values are abused and neglected. On the contrary, I am certain that this arrangement permits the twin objectives of development with conservation (preserving the old and creating the new) in a variety of very exciting ways at the local level.

11. Some critics have argued that an 'integrated' approach is an impossible objective because of the division of responsibilities and interests in the management of rural resources. Others believe that there is no point in trying to control agricultural and forestry land-use practices and new technological developments unless enormous amounts of money or very cumbersome administration is involved. They press for a system of 'countryside apartheid' or separate development between conservation/amenity and agriculture/forestry/planned development. Apart from the fact that this approach would be quite contrary to WCS principles, elements of it are available in the heritage site classification. Hence, in my view, the robustness and flexibility of the triple classification.

12. Other correspondents feel that the administration of the UK countryside should be tackled quite differently. One proposal is for a new Department of Rural Affairs, another for expanded Agriculture Departments to bring in conservation/amenity and the development agencies, a third for all rural grants and administration to be placed in the hands of the county authorities. In every case there would be criticism for one or other vested interest, criticism at least as powerful, if not more so, than that levelled at my proposals. A major new department of state would not be popular, the Agricultural Departments are not keen to expand too far beyond their existing commitments and in any case the loose ends could never be gathered up, and conservation interests would never allow national conservation matters to be handled by country authorities.

13. The other possibility is to tinker with the *status quo*; I hope that this revised report indicates why this would not work.

Shaping the Recommendations

14. Another major criticism was that there were too many recommendations, that many were already being implemented to varying degrees (a view particularly expressed by a number of research institutes and local authorities), and that in many cases it was not clear who should be doing what. I respond by noting that the recommendations were packaged in groups to show up their linkages (so that sheer numbers of recommendations are less important than the connections between them), and that, where possible, I have identified a target group at whom the recommendations are specifically set.

15. I have also altered both the text and the recommendations in the light of comments received. The major changes are:

Chapter 3
More stress has been placed upon the need to speed up the assessment of heritage habitats and to establish an

agency and a set of priorities to encourage landscape enhancement and creative landscape design. The NCC, coupled with the voluntary conservation agencies, are urged to look hard at the possibilities for habitat creation especially in cities, on derelict lands and waters, and on restored land.

Chapter 4

The recent studies of the range and extent of subsidies in agriculture are outlined, coupled with more information on price support policies and expenditures through the CAP. This has led to a call for a greater examination of the relationships between price support and conservation/enhancement, with better meshing of policies and expenditures. Also, the inequitable distribution of agriculture grants in favour of the larger farmers at the expense of small, often low income holdings, is revealed, with a call for a rechannelling of grant aid in favour of lower income farmers and conservation/enhancement practices. The merits of organic farming within a mixed farming enterprise are developed, as is the criticism that fertilisers can be an important source of environmental pollution and a danger to human health. The Agricultural Departments should be given a specific remit to support agricultural husbandry that promotes aesthetically sustainable utilisation.

Chapter 5

No substantial changes have been made here except to add a variety of views expressed by professional forestry organisations and to call for a careful re-examination of the economics of broadleaved forestry. This economic appraisal must not be confined to a bias towards short-term accounting and commercial timber prices.

Chapter 6

No major changes have been made here except to reinforce the call for better public access to the countryside, especially common land and uplands, to ensure that lowland rights of way are protected and that more generous incentives are provided to establish new rights of way. The potential dangers of a too formal requirement for environmental impact assessment are stressed and the recommendation altered to allow for greater flexibility in EIA work, coupled to a general requirement to see that it is done. The view that prime agricultural land must be given the utmost protection is linked to a recommendation that the existing and potential conservation of all land likely to be taken up by large development schemes should be assessed and publicised before final decisions are taken.

Chapter 7

This chapter remains broadly intact primarily for the reasons outlined in paragraphs 9 to 13 in this chapter (pp 256 - 257). A number of detailed comments are made to the text to reflect remarks made by correspondents.

Scotland, Northern Ireland and Wales

16. I thoroughly enjoyed my visits to Belfast and Edinburgh to flavour the response from Northern Ireland and Scotland. Sadly, I was unable to go to Wales or to participate in the most impressive Cynefin exercise. As outlined in the prefatory material, conditions vary greatly in all four countries of the UK, so it would be wise to avoid generalisation. The Northern Irish representatives were particularly concerned that not enough Northern Irish material was provided in the text. I have therefore attempted to meet this point by outlining their detailed comments below. The Scottish view was that resource-management priorities are very different north of the border and that it would be inappropriate to apply some of the arguments in Scotland. For example, it was put to me that moorland protection and landscape amenity generally were less important in Scotland than in England and that the scope for forestry generally, but especially for connecting forestry to agriculture and conservation (including game management), was very great indeed.

17. In detail, the Northern Irish response wished to stress:

(a) That agriculture is a more important contributor to the local economy than it is in Great Britain.

(b) That there are few privately owned large estates in Northern Ireland, so the notion of 'trust' as outlined in the report should be more applicable.

(c) That there are no Province-wide organisations or regional authorities responsible for ecological monitoring, landscape assessment or soil survey. This means that a basic structure for countryside data collection and assessment should have top priority. A soil survey and land capability classification scheme should also be introduced.

(d) That the Northern Ireland coastline should be given special attention to collate strategies for coastal protection, public access, conservation and tourism. There should be a coastal development authority with appropriate powers to coordinate resource-development and planning.

(e) That more attention should be given to the problem of slurry and silage effluent abatement, since slurry discharge is a major cause of river pollution.

(f) That about 60 per cent of Northern Ireland's agriculture takes place in very adverse circumstances with poor soils and/or drainage; that average farm size is only 16 ha (compare 47 ha for England and 54 ha for Scotland) and that on marginal hill land farm size can fall to 10 ha with average field size of 1 to 3 ha. Consequently, the reforms of the LFA Directive must be applied carefully in Northern Ireland with much emphasis on upgrading farm income and diversifying employment opportunities. Also, hedgerow diversity in Northern Ireland is almost three times as high as it is in Great Britain, but most hedgerows are overgrown and badly managed. Hedgerow removal is not such a serious problem but hedgerow management incentives could provide employment and conservation advantages.

(g) That, insofar as landscape protection is concerned, strict planning controls only appear to Areas of Special Control. However, the criteria for establishing ASC varies from one Planning Division to another. There seems to be no consistent policy for landscape protection and enhancement in Northern Ireland. This is an omission which should be rectified by establishing an official agency, coupled with assistance for voluntary organisations linked into the proposed landscale classification. These are welcomed by Northern Irish observers.

18. The Scottish reaction was much more detailed, almost paragraph by paragraph. Most of this response has been incorporated in the final text but a number of more general points are worth mentioning.

(a) Scotland's economy is suffering from recession far more seriously than in England, especially in the Highlands. The need for development projects which create employment is very great indeed and both the Scottish Development Agency and the HIDB have special funds and powers for this purpose. The advisory planning guidelines which help steer development into certain areas are an important stage in conservation/development planning and are particularly appropriate for Scotland. The Scottish Forum for the Environment is also an important venture. It brings together representatives from a wide range of voluntary bodies concerned with conservation and amenity, from the national agencies and from the relevant administrative and technical departments from within the Scottish Office. All these organisations have an interest in oil development impact on Scotland's landscape and ecology. This approach might profitably be extended to other resource-areas in Scotland, and perhaps copied in other UK countries. The prime requirement is to establish priority areas for certain kinds of development (eg forestry or tourism) which relate to conservation and landscape amenity. This task is now being undertaken.

(b) Scotland's agriculture is far more dependent on livestock rearing, and Scotland has many more farms in LFA. The recommendations relating to LFA must be shaped to reflect the size and scale of upland agriculture in Scotland, the lower priority given to moorland protection and the scope for increasing stocking densities. However, this does not deny the arguments about sustained productivity.

(c) Tourism is a major source of potential income for Scotland. Funds for the promotion of tourism are more available countrywide than in England and Wales, so a more holistic approach to tourist planning and the possibilities for on-farm tourist spending is possible in Scotland.

(d) The need to protect the language and way of life of Gaelic-speaking peoples is a matter of especial concern. This can best be achieved by promoting traditional agriculture, fishing and craft activities, opening up the potential for tourism and creating a variety of full- and part-time jobs relating to land care.

19. Although I did not visit Wales I have seen the proposals of the Town and Country Research Groups of Cynefin. Many of their observations and recommendations conform with mine. I was impressed with the proposals for land-use mosaics, based upon the use of satellite data and computer models of land capability and believe that this approach should be encouraged. This would allow for a variety of land-uses to be suited to the local conditions of productivity site, access and settlement. I have presented a recommendation to reflect these views.

A Concluding Observation

20. Almost everyone who corresponded on the report admitted that it will take time to change attitudes and expectations, to encourage a more integrated approach to rural resource-management, and to enable many of the recommendations to be adopted with enthusiasm and commitment. This report in itself cannot do this: indeed, it could become one of many that languishes in libraries and filing cabinets. Its success depends ultimately on a powerful sense of public concern for the future of the UK countryside and a willingness on the part of all rural resource-users and managers to enter into a longish period of give and take, coupled with a preparedness to experiment in good faith. The long-term productivity, old and new heritage, economic likelihood and social well-being of the resources and people of rural UK are at stake.

APPENDIX

CONSULTATIONS ARISING FROM THE REPORT

Meetings

15 October 1982
Representatives of conservation interests, UCL

26 October 1982
Representatives of rural use interests, UCL

29 October 1982
Representatives of Northern Irish interests, Belfast

15 November 1982
Representatives of Midlands community councils, Leamington Spa

16 November 1982
Talk to National Agricultural College, Stoneleigh
Review by Countryside Commission, UCL

22 November 1982
Representatives of Scottish interests, Edinburgh

Comments Received

Institutions

Scotland
Countryside Commission for Scotland
Crofters Commission
Department of Agriculture and Forestry for Scotland
National Farmers Union of Scotland
North-east River Purification Board
Scottish Development Agency
Scottish Landowners Federation
Scottish Tourist Board

Northern Ireland
Northern Ireland Nature Reserves Committee

Wales
Cynefin
Welsh Office

England (plus Wales)
Association of County Councils
Association of District Councils
Council for the Protection of Rural England — Lancashire Branch
Country Landowners Federation
Countryside Commission (unofficial views)
Department of the Environment
Development Commission

Devon Conservation Forum
Ministry of Agriculture, Fisheries and Food
Nature Conservancy Council (unofficial views)
National Farmers Union
Soil Survey of England and Wales
The Exmoor Society

National
British Association for Shooting and Conservation
British Tourist Authority
Council for Environmental Conservation
Ecology Party's Agriculture and Food Working Party
Farm and Food Society
Institute of Biology
Institute for Terrestrial Ecology
Royal Forestry Society
Royal Institute of Chartered Surveyors — Countryside Policies Working Party
Universities Federation for Animal Welfare

Local authority planning departments
Buckinghamshire
Dorset
Gloucestershire
Hampshire
Humberside
Huntingdon
Mid Glamorgan
Somerset
Surrey
Warwickshire

National Park authorities
Lake District National Park
Peak District National Park

Individuals

David Andrews
Mark Blacksell
Allan Blenkharn
P C Coggins
James Cruickshank
John Foster
Paul Ganderton
Andrew Gilg
Bryn Green
W W Gould
A J Hooper
Philip Lowe
John Marsh
Alan Mowle
Paul Munton
Max Nicholson
Jonathan O'Riordan
Ken Parker
Brian Parnell
Joan Margaret Pick
Ian Simmons
Mike Usher
Andrew Warren
Arthur Wigens
Peter Woolley

PART 4
MARINE AND COASTAL

Conservation and Development of Marine and Coastal Resources

A report by D F Shaw

Acknowledgements

The preparation of this report would have been quite impossible in the time available but for the very great help provided by Mr S A Sewell who acted as Research Assistant for the six months available. He spent much time travelling to carry out interviews with various interested parties, collected relevant information from a very wide variety of sources, and checked the whole report meticulously. His contributions permeate the whole report.

Appreciation of the help given by a wide range of individuals from Government bodies, local authorities, water authorities recreational and conservation organisations and universities must also be acknowledged. They are too numerous to list, but together they provided many useful comments and relevant articles. Particular mention should be made of the help given by staff associated with the University of Liverpool Centre for Marine and Coastal Studies who provided expert help on the full range of topics covered by what has proved to be a very wide ranging subject.

Finally, the contribution of the Review Group itself must be mentioned. Members took considerable trouble attending meetings, writing comments on the various drafts, and providing personal advice. The final list of recommendations owes a lot to their efforts. The Review Group Chairman requires special acknowledgement for his helpful advice, and his control of Review Group meetings which ensured they were of the maximum value to the author of this report.

Chairman's Introduction

Among developed countries, Britain is especially maritime: nowhere in the United Kingdom can a person be more than 70 miles (115 km) from tidal waters. Yet because of the density and local concentration of its people, the management of the coastline and the waters that lap it present challenges of frightening complexity. For instance, our shallow seas are expected, on the one hand, to cope with formidable quantities of waste, yet, on the other hand, to be pure enough for healthy recreation; they must also be rich enough to support a variety of fisheries. The task of our Review Group has been to take a broad view of the conflicting needs and make suggestions for the positive utilisation of this immeasurably valuable national asset of marine and coastal resources.

The Review Group was wide enough in its expertise to keep in mind the governance of pure marine science and the administrative problems of conservation, while affirming the applied aspects of fisheries and offshore oil exploration and production; we had in our number a planner from an industrial local authority with port and estuary management within its purview, a lawyer familiar with maritime planning law, and an administrator with experience of coping with the problems of pollution, in particular those of compensation, as much day to day as from spectacular incidents.

During our discussions we were concerned to identify areas in which there was surprising lack of long-term aims and 'anticipatory' environmental management. In common with other Review Groups, we were all too conscious that a fundamental cause of major problems in this direction has been the failure of economic systems to incorporate an adequate qualitative dimension: to advance, we must integrate environmental values with our economic concepts of growth and development, so that conservation and economic policies become complementary for our coasts and the waters within our national control. For instance, so far as fisheries policy is concerned — and this is of course an area where the problems are enormous — our aim should be the establishment of a fleet only large enough to ensure the optimum sustainable yield, and hence a sustainable future for those in the industry. In this, as with all other aspects of conservation and development of marine resources, there is an urgent need for increased scientific work, to strengthen the factual basis from which sound policies can stem.

The recommendations for action contained in this report include far-reaching proposals, not only to strengthen the hands of controlling bodies, but also to simplify that control and make it more effective. The demand of industrial, recreational and fishery activity on the one hand and the need for sensible conservation on the other require to be met by a simplified pathway through the present plethora of overseeing bodies. We hope that our efforts will lead to action that directly reflects the principal aims of the World Conservation Strategy in making wise provision for coastal activity, it is to be hoped in a way that will be copied by other countries faced with similar pressures. These pressures are powerful and certain to increase, and this Review Group is confident that the report's arguments have a sound basis, and is equally convinced that its recommendations for action must be heeded.

D Nichols
February, 1983

CHAPTER 1
INTRODUCTION

World Conservation Strategy

1. In March 1980, the International Union for Conservation of Nature and Natural Resources published, simultaneously throughout the world, its document entitled World Conservation Strategy (WCS). That document outlines a strategy for the conservation of the world's living resources so as to ensure sustainable development. Development is defined as the modification of the biosphere and the application of human, financial, living and non-living resources to satisfy human needs and improve the quality of human life (IUCN, 1980). Sustainable development means that not only should the benefits resulting from a particular development be permanently available, but the potential for further beneficial developments should not be diminished. To be sustainable, developments must be largely dependent on renewable resources, and since most of these are derived from living organisms the conservation of living resources is of great importance.

2. To achieve living resource conservation WCS has identified three requirements which developments must satisfy (IUCN, 1980). These are:
   (a) Essential ecological processes and life support systems must be maintained.
   (b) Genetic diversity must be preserved.
   (c) The sustainable utilisation of species and ecosystems must be ensured.

3. WCS recommends that every country should prepare a review of the extent to which it is achieving conservation, and that the review should form the basis of a national strategy, the aim of which is to see that the requirements for conservation of living resources are met (IUCN, 1980).

4. Acceptance by the United Kingdom (UK) Government of the objectives of WCS places on the Government an obligation to prepare its own conservation strategy to further these objectives. This report on conservation and development of UK marine and coastal resources stands within a wider report which is intended to help with the preparation of a programme to implement the World Conservation Strategy in the UK.

5. The goal of a national conservation strategy is to see that national policies for development conform with the three requirements for living resource conservation.

However, these are just three of many requirements for human survival and well being (IUCN, 1980). WCS recognises this by listing other strategies which are needed — a strategy for peace; a strategy for a new international economic order; a strategy for human rights; a strategy for overcoming poverty; a world food strategy, and a population strategy (IUCN, 1980). In addition to these, and surprisingly omitted from WCS, there is a need for a strategy for the utilisation of non-renewable resources. Since it is not the role of WCS to encompass the requirements of these other strategies, this report will confine itself strictly to determining, as objectively as possible, the changes in policy which are needed to conserve living resources in the UK marine and coastal zone. Matters of ethics, amenity and personal preferences concerning the structure of society will not be considered since these are subjective matters which should be properly determined by the democratic process.

6. A further point which should be constantly borne in mind when reading this report is that the word 'conservation' is not used in the sense of keeping things as they are; it is always used with the meaning intended in WCS, which states that 'conservation is positive, embracing preservation, maintenance, sustainable utilisation, restoration, and enhancement of the natural environment, (IUCN, 1980).

7. It is recommended in WCS that each national strategy should start with a review of developments in relation to the three requirements for conservation set out in WCS (IUCN, 1980), in order to determine the extent to which the developments are in conflict with these requirements. But conflicts can arise from activities which cannot be called developments in the normal sense of the word. Coastal erosion is an example, since this, and other natural processes can destroy an ecosystem just as effectively as developments initiated by man.

8. To start the report with a list of developments would therefore risk missing many conflicts with conservation which arise from natural causes, or from long standing traditional human activities. An alternative would be to list resources and consider conflicts which arise from exploitation of these, but such an approach would also overlook conflicts due to natural processes. Furthermore, there is as much of a problem defining a resource as there is in defining a development.

9. For these reasons, the starting point for this report will be the 'activities' which occur in the marine and coastal zone. This term will include modern developments as well as long standing activities which are involved with resource exploitation. It will also include natural processes and activities where no resource is consumed, both of which can threaten an ecosystem or a species. It will also be sensible to include future activities where these can be anticipated with some certainty.

10. From this starting point the report has been developed by the following steps:

(a) Listing the activities occurring the UK domestic marine and coastal zone, and the ecosystems and key species associated with these activities.

(b) Assessing the effects of each activity against the background of natural change to identify any significant conflicts with the three requirements for living resource conservation. Some activities, far from having an adverse effect on conservation, are beneficial. These have also been identified.

(c) Drawing attention to ecosystems or species threatened by any of these activities.

(d) Assessing the urgency of action needed in each case.

(e) Identifying the fundamental reasons for the conflicts with living resource conservation.

(f) Considering the measures currently in use for mitigating the conflicts, and their effectiveness.

(g) Proposing alternative measures where existing measures are inadequate. This includes measures to encourage those activities identified in (b) as being beneficial.

Reference

IUCN. 1980. World Conservation Strategy. Living resource conservation for sustainable development. International Union for Conservation of Nature and Natural Resources, Gland.

CHAPTER 2
ACTIVITIES IN THE UK MARINE AND COASTAL ENVIRONMENT AND THEIR EFFECTS

Introduction

1. In Appendix A an attempt has been made to list all the activities which may be relevant to this report. In many cases brief examination will indicate that the effect on the environment of some of these is negligible. They have, however, been left in because a full list could form a useful starting point for any future investigations, by which time the situation may have changed, and previously negligible effects may have increased. The activities have been classified according to the resource exploited where possible. Some activities could be included under more than one heading, eg spear fishing could come under the exploitation of fish resources or the recreational use of coastal waters.

2. An activity does not necessarily conflict with the needs of conservation but can do so when associated with a particular habitat and when conducted on a sufficient scale. It is therefore necessary to consider the effect of each activity on the various habitats and their associated communities. Appendix B lists the habitats in the UK marine and coastal environment which can be recognised as being distinct.

3. Because an activity can threaten an individual species without substantially affecting the ecosystem as a whole (for example, when a species is commercially valuable and can be caught without damage to its habitat or to other species) it is necessary to consider each activity in relation to the species present. However, in contrast to the limited number of ecosystems, the number of species is too large to attempt to list. The list of species given in Appendix C is therefore limited to those which are commercially significant, and those non-commercial species which are specially protected because they are thought to be vulnerable and strongly dependent on coastal habitats.

4. Appendix D forms a large part of this report and considers each activity listed in Appendix A in turn. In each case an indication is given of the extent to which the activity is carried out in the UK marine and coastal zone, and then the major effects of the activity on the ecosystem are considered. Finally, the current legislation and other means for controlling the activity are mentioned.

5. The information given in Appendix D indicates that many of the effects of the various activities in the marine and coastal zone are of minor importance, consisting of slight damage to the habitat or a small reduction in the numbers of living organisms. Frequently these effects quickly disappear when the activity ceases. Even after serious damage, marine communities quickly re-establish themselves although it may take several years for the new community to come to equilibrium (Royal Commission of Environmental Pollution, 1981).

6. The small effect of many human activities on the marine environment is due to a number of factors:
   (a) Compared to the terrestrial environment the marine environment is less accessible to humans.
   (b) The physical impacts of human beings on the marine environment are (with the exception of shallow, sheltered areas) small compared with natural processes such as waves, storms, tides and currents.
   (c) the sea has a high ability to disperse, dilute and degrade many materials discharged into it.
   (d) Marine organisms often have a very high fecundity and their eggs and larvae are widely dispersed by the sea. This helps to repair any local damage done to a community.

Harmful Activities

7. However, in spite of the general robustness of the marine environment, a number of activities crop up repeatedly in Appendix D as causing serious and often irreversible damage to living resource-conservation in the marine and coastal zone. These are:
   (a) Developments permanently affecting sensitive habitats, in particular: estuaries and associated wetlands; coastal lagoons; sand dune areas and other 'soft' coastlines.
   (b) Disposal of persistent toxic wastes into the sea. These wastes include organohalogen compounds and heavy metals. Radioactive materials will also be considered since these are potentially harmful and there is a continued need for the existing stringent controls.
   (c) Over-exploitation of fish and shellfish. Most commercial species are subject to this. Pelagic (surface feeding) species are mainly at risk.
   (d) Discharge of biodegradable or non-persistent wastes into estuaries, bays, or other areas where water exchange is slow.

8. The developments referred to in paragraphs 7(a), (b) and (c) above are discussed in detail in Chapters 3, 4 and 5 of this report respectively, where recommendations are made to reduce their adverse effects on living resources.

9. Paragraph 7(d) refers to the effects of discharging biodegradable wastes into areas where water exchange is slow. The most common situation where this occurs is in estuaries where the discharges are from domestic sewers and the oil and food industries. These discharges have been going on for many years, but a type of discharge which has increased recently is oil from tankers and offshore platforms. Usually the effects of oil are unpleasant, as when beaches are polluted or large numbers of birds are killed, but these effects are usually short lived on account of the dispersing and degrading powers of the sea. In some circumstances, oil released in relatively open waters can have longer-term effects as for example when chronic release of small amounts of oil occurs from many relatively closely spaced oil platforms. Although the concentration of oil in production water (water which is present in the reservoir together with oil and gas) discharged from platforms is low, the quantities of water involved are such that the total amount of oil is significant. The particular constituents of the oil of concern here are the most water soluble which are also the most toxic. When these discharges occur in an area where water movements follow a circular pattern, as is the case in some North Sea areas, there is evidence that living organisms are adversely affected (Wilkinson, 1982). Nevertheless the release of hydrocarbons from oil or gas is not regarded as a long-term threat to marine species (Royal Commission on Environmental Pollution, 1981).

10. More serious is the situation in estuaries where the very low water exchange does not result in efficient dispersal of the wastes, and oxygen depletion in the water can occur. It is known, however, from experience in the river Thames that these effects can be reversed, as this once heavily polluted river is now capable of supporting salmon. The problems of biodegradable wastes in estuaries are well recognised and the legislation to solve them is available in Part II of the Control of Pollution Act (1974) which the Government has announced is to be implemented over a four year period to 1986. Implementation of this Act will not only bring long standing discharges of pollutants to estuaries in England and Wales under control (most discharges in Scotland are already under control) but should also make available to the public information on the contents of discharges and the conditions attached to discharge licences. This greater freedom of access to information is regarded as an important contribution to long-term protection of the environment, and hence of living resources in the UK. The rehabilitation of estuaries will then be limited mainly by the availability of capital funds for new trunk sewers and treatment plants. Although progress with this problem will be slow, improvements are being made and only one recommendation will be made on this matter in this report.

Initial Recommendation
11. The government should proceed with its plans to implement Part II of the Control of Pollution Act (1974) more quickly than is planned at present, and should ensure that information on all discharges licensed under the Act and the results of monitoring these discharges and their effects are made readily available to the public. (This recommendation has been withdrawn. See Chapter 8, p 287).

12. An additional problem which emerges from Appendix D but which is not mentioned in paragraph 7 above is the manner in which statutory responsibilities for marine and coastal matters in the UK are widely distributed over many quite different organisations. This is discussed in Chapter 6 of this report.

References

ROYAL COMMISSION ON ENVIRONMENTAL POLLUTION. 1981. 8th Report. London, HMSO.

WILKINSON, T G. 1982. Chemistry and Industry, 115-123.

CHAPTER 3
RECLAMATION OF ESTUARIES AND WETLAND, AND DEVELOPMENT OF SOFT COASTLINES

Estuaries

1. The reasons for reclamation of the sea originate in the demand for land for agriculture, towns, industry and commerce. More recently, the need for space for fresh water storage has been added to this list. Estuaries come under special pressure from these demands as compared with the open coast or deep bays, because their shallow sheltered nature makes the process of reclamation easier.

2. The reclamation of the wetlands fringing estuaries has been practicable for centuries because these lands are only covered by unusually high tides, so quite low embankments are sufficient to prevent flooding. The shelter from wave action provided by the estuary enabled simple earth structures to survive. Although this process resulted in the loss of wetlands around the edges of estuaries, major reduction of the estuarine habitat was not possible using these simple methods.

3. In contrast to methods of traditional reclamation, modern engineering techniques enable high embankments to be constructed in deeper and more exposed areas. Using these techniques the Dutch have enclosed huge areas of the sea converting the enclosed areas partly into a freshwater habitat and partly into agricultural land. In the UK in the 1960s and 1970s large scale schemes for enclosing estuaries for fresh water storage were investigated, and if they are ever implemented there would be a considerable loss of estuarine habitat from some of the largest and most natural estuaries which remain.

4. The demand for estuarine space, already high for the reasons mentioned above, is accentuated by the presence of ports, towns and industry. Ports were attracted to estuaries by the shelter they offered from storms, and towns grew up round them. More recently, industries have developed to take advantage of the easy access to sea transport provided by the ports, and to draw their work force from the towns' population. All three of these — ports, towns and industry — have created demands for space. Ports have caused enclosure for non-tidal docks and reclamation of adjacent land for warehouses and other dockside facilities. As towns have expanded more building land has been needed, and it has sometimes been found convenient to obtain this by filling in the wetlands which fringe estuaries with domestic refuse or with dredging spoil from navigation channels.

Industry has also been the cause of land reclamation since it often prefers sites close to docks for discharge or loading of bulk materials such as iron ore and oil. Access to large quantities of cooling water is another reason for industry seeking waterside sites.

5. For all these reasons, many estuaries have been extensively altered in the past, for example, Southampton Water, the Tyne and the Mersey. In extreme cases the original estuarine habitat has been completely destroyed. The process is still in progress and over the last 20 years much of the inter-tidal area of the Tees estuary has been reclaimed for industrial use. Of the 2,400 ha of inter-tidal flats in the Tees estuary in 1852 only 175 ha remained in 1975 (Mitchell, 1978).

6. A subsidiary reason for the pressure on estuaries arises from the demand for efficient land communications. Estuaries often extend deep inland, so long detours by roads are necessary to get round them. In the past, towns have grown up, often for military reasons initially, at the heads of estuaries where the lowest river crossings frequently occur. These towns have then created the same pressures for reclamation as towns which developed round ports. In more recent years, improved communications across smaller estuaries have been achieved by building roads or railways on embankments which almost completely cut off the estuary from the sea. Part of the argument for estuarine fresh water storage schemes has been based on improving communication by building roads on the tops of the enclosing embankments (Ministry of Housing and Local Government, 1967; Water Resources Board, 1966 and 1972). The demand for better facilities for air travel can also put pressure on estuaries since the noise and large areas of land needed has resulted in resistance to inland sites for new airports. The proposals to build the third London airport on the Maplin sands would have resulted in the reclamation of large areas of the Thames Estuary.

7. It can be seen from the points made above that estuaries are particularly threatened by demands for their enclosure and reclamation. This was recognised in a joint report by the Nature Conservancy Council (NCC) and the Natural Environment Research Council (NERC) on Nature Conservation in the Marine Environment (NCC and NERC, 1979). It is necessary, before deciding whether these demands should be resisted, to assess the ecological value of estuaries.

The Importance of Estuaries

8. The importance of estuaries to living resources arises from the high density of the invertebrate population which provides food for wildfowl and young fish. The high density of invertebrates arises from the way estuaries act as traps for large quantities of plant material carried in by tidal action from the sea and, to a lesser extent, brought down by rivers. This imported plant material is supplemented by additional organic material produced within the estuary, on salt marshes, and by micro-algae on the mud surface when the tide is out.

9. Of the large numbers of invertebrates supported by this abundance of food, the most directly significant to man are mussels, cockles, shrimps and oysters. These species and others are also important as the main food for very large numbers of wildfowl and waders which inhabit estuaries. Some birds such as geese feed directly on the salt marsh vegetation round the edges of estuaries. Following the large scale enclosures of the Zuider Zee undertaken by the Dutch, a number of commercially valuable mussel beds were lost and one race of herring which spawned in the enclosed area has been entirely eliminated (De Groot, 1980).

10. Many other invertebrates which feed on the decaying plant material in estuaries but which are not eaten directly by man (eg worms and various molluscs) have considerable importance as food for fish. It has been estimated on a world-wide basis that three-quarters of marine species of fish spend a critical part of their lives in estuarine or similar habitats (Borgese and Ginsburg, 1978). These include commercially important species which inhabit the mouths of estuaries when young, moving offshore as they get larger.

11. From the above comments it is clear that large numbers of wildfowl, geese, mussels, oysters, cockles and commercially important fish depend on the ecological processes which occur in estuaries. In addition, estuaries provide a gradual transition from seawater to fresh water which is essential for migratory fish such as salmon, sea trout and eels. The importance of estuaries has been acknowledged in the USA by the New York State Tidal Wetland Act of 1973 which requires approval to be given for developments which may affect wetlands or adjacent areas (NCC and NERC, 1979).

12. In view of the ecological importance of estuaries, the extent to which they have been reclaimed or enclosed in the past, and the pressure to continue this process, it is necessary to have clear and effective legislation to protect them. Unfortunately the legislation is complex and unsystematic (NCC and NERC, 1979). Above Low Water Mean Ordinary Spring Tides (LWMOST) development needs planning consent from the local planning authority. But this does not apply to engineering operations in connection with agriculture which are given general approval under the Town and Country General Development Order (1977). Some of these operations, such as land drainage, are encouraged by grants from the Ministry of Agriculture, Fisheries and Food (MAFF). In addition, certain developments by statutory bodies, such as port authorities and regional water authorities, are also approved by the same order.

13. Below LWMOST many different organisations have power to control activities, including:

    Department of the Environment
    Scottish Development Department
    Ministry of Agriculture, Fisheries and Food
        and Department of Agriculture and Fisheries
        for Scotland
    Ministry of Defence
    Department of Trade
    Department of Transport
    Planning Authorities and Coastal Protection
        Authorities
    Regional Water Authorities and River Purification
        Boards
    Crown Estate Commissioners
    Harbour Authorities and Dock Boards
    Sea Fisheries Committees

None of these organisations has a special responsibility to safeguard the estuarine ecosystem and adjacent wetlands, although they are required to have regard to the desirability of conserving the natural beauty and amenity of the countryside. This requirement is strengthened in the case of the Secretary of State for the Environment, MAFF Ministers, Water Authorities and Internal Drainage Boards by the Wildlife and Countryside Act 1981 which imposes a duty to further the conservation and enhancement of natural beauty and the conservation of flora, fauna, geological or physiographical features of special interest. However, the major interests of some of these organisations often conflict directly with the need to preserve the ecology of estuaries. In these circumstances they cannot be expected to balance the conflicting interests in a way which satisfies the community as a whole, and some form of control by a democratically accountable body should be available.

Public Attitudes

14. A factor which may contribute to the lack of protection offered to estuaries may be the attitude of the general public. To many, the upper reaches of large estuaries are wastelands surrounded by marsh which cannot be crossed due to the presence of deep muddy creeks. They are seen as dangerous due to the rapid inflow of tides, strong currents and the alleged presence of quicksand. This is in contrast to the public's attitude to the accessible open coast with sandy amenity beaches, where there is considerable support for the control of commercial and industrial activity. Only two sectors of the public regard the marshy edges of estuaries as an asset: wildfowlers and bird watchers. The public at large is not likely to press strongly for the protection of estuaries unless a convincing educational effort is mounted.

15. The concern over the reclamation of estuaries expressed above should not be taken as meaning that no estuarine land should ever be reclaimed. The economic benefits to the country of industrial and port development are too great for this to be acceptable. However, the continuous loss of wetlands in the UK worries many responsible organisations and experts on the subject, and suggests that current legislation and development planning procedures are inadequate. The reclamation of estuaries is almost always irreversible, and the hazards of this activity are greater because the ecological effects are unlikely to be noticed immediately, particularly as far as fish are concerned. Consequently, remedial action to overcome deleterious effects after they appear is often impossible. It is, therefore, necessary for development planning to ensure a gradual and carefully monitored approach to any further schemes for the reclamation of estuaries.

16. The value of a particular estuary will be determined by its size, position relative to bird migration routes, other estuaries in the vicinity, remoteness from disturbances and pollution, and its importance to young fish. Estuaries are part of a national and international network of wetlands which must be preserved as a whole to provide feeding and roosting grounds for birds along their migration routes between summer breeding sites and over wintering areas. They must also provide well distributed suitable nursery grounds for young fish round the whole of the UK coast so that the commercial fisheries, often situated in quite different areas, are maintained by an adequate supply of young adults. It is clear that decisions which result in the reclamation of estuaries should not be taken entirely on the basis of local interests. Progress has been made by the Nature Conservancy Council, the Scottish Marine Biological Association and the Marine Biological Association with the identification of intertidal sites of importance, and this work should clearly be taken into account when planning decisions are taken which affect estuaries.

17. In attempting to ensure that living resources which depend on estuaries are properly protected, it must be recognised that any organisation which is made responsible for this will inevitably have wider responsibilities. It will also be expected to deal with the protection of amenity and other interests where appropriate. On land, this function is performed by local planning authorities whilst appeals against the planning decisions they make can be made by aggrieved applicants to the Department of the Environment or the Scottish Development Department. Where appropriate, the Minister can institute a public inquiry to assess all the relevant arguments and evidence.

18. At present various organisations can carry out works in estuaries and the sea without needing any form of approval. These include harbour boards, port authorities, water authorities and the Ministry of Defence. To ensure that estuaries are protected, and that where necessary a national view can be injected, it is important to establish some form of independent control, and an appeals mechanism which can apply to developments and activities in the marine environment and on the coast.

Planning Controls

19. One way of controlling marine and coastal developments would be to extend planning authority control to, say, three miles out to sea to cover all development, including new activities or major extensions of existing activities. This change should also be accompanied by a critical review of exemptions from planning control given to a number of statutory organisations. This would give greater control of developments on land and out to three miles by the locally responsible authority. An important function of this procedure would be to ensure that the details of any proposal would be made public. In the Shetland Islands, the Zetland County Council Act 1974 already, in effect, gives planning control to the three mile limit, to the Council. This covers such matters as effluent outfalls, dredging, moorings, and the construction of piers and jetties.

Initial Recommendation

20. Planning control of all developments, new activities or major extensions of existing activities should be extended three miles out to sea, and the exemptions to planning control at present given to various statutory organisations should be critically reviewed. (This recommendation has been retained. See Chapter 9, p 290.)

21. This procedure would ensure that local interests are fully taken into account, even when organisations with national responsibilities are making the proposals. However, some matters are of national significance and there is a danger that local interests would always take precedence. It will therefore be necessary to retain the right of appeal to the Department of the Environment against refusals of planning permission by planning authorities. It will also be necessary, in order to ensure that national interests are protected, to allow certain organisations the right of appeal to the Department of the Environment against a successful planning application. At present this does not exist and once planning permission has been granted by the planning authority there is no formal mechanism for objection. It is suggested that the right of appeal should be restricted to organisations which are required to be consulted on planning applications, together with certain national conservation bodies such as the NCC, the National Trusts and the Countryside Commissions. These bodies have national responsibilities, and it is reasonable that they should be given power to appeal to the Department of the Environment when they feel a development is against the national interest.

Initial Recommendation

22. The right of appeal to the Department of the Environment against refusal of planning consent by a planning authority should be retained, and a new right of appeal, restricted to specified organisations with national responsibilities, should be introduced to enable those organisations to appeal to the Department of the Environment against a planning application which has been successful. (This recommendation has been withdrawn. See Chapter 8, p 287.)

23. With these arrangements, an attempt to reach agreement at local level, which is always desirable for administrative and other reasons, could be followed through without fear of losing the ultimate right to go to the Secretary of State. Without this right of appeal there will be a temptation to play safe and take any planning application with national conservation implications direct to the Secretary of State, so by passing the local planning procedures.

24. Although many wetland habitats occur round the coast and are often associated with estuaries, similar types of habitat also occur inland. Therefore arrangements established to protect these habitats need to be designed with the terrestrial environment in mind to avoid complexities and ambiguities which would arise from having coastal wetlands subject to different legislation from similar habitats inland.

25. Many activities on land are already subject to control by planning authorities, particularly if change of land use is involved. The main exceptions are where exemption from planning controls has been given to certain statutory organisations such as port authorities, water authorities etc, and where changes relate to the use of land for agriculture. It has been recommended in paragraph 20 above that the exemptions given to statutory organisations should be reviewed, but valuable habitats can be lost as a result of their conversion to farm land. This is not strictly a marine or coastal problem, but a number of such habitats exist in coastal areas. For example, salt marshes which are only rarely covered by tides can be enclosed and converted to arable land. Coastal lagoons can support communities which sometimes include rare species which need a saline environment but they are easily filled in and the habitat lost. These habitats are important areas of genetic diversity and some of them need to be preserved.

26. Major developments are probably not the main threat since these are usually the subject of public inquiry. The real problems arise from large numbers of minor changes not subject to planning control such as filling in lagoons, enclosing parts of salt marshes and draining wetlands. Each of these changes may be small but together they can cause significant changes to the environment. It would be very cumbersome to use the procedure, involving national bodies, for designating Sites of Special Scientific Interest (SSSIs) or National Nature Reserves (NNRs) for protecting the large number of these small habitats.

Planning and Agriculture

27. One method of providing some of the protection needed would be to require planning approval for engineering operations associated with agriculture. At present these are exempt from planning control under the current Town and Country General Development Orders so that embankments, drainage operations and infilling to raise the level of farming land do not require permission from the local planning authority.

Initial Recommendation

28. The Town and Country General Development Orders should be amended to remove the exemption from planning control given to engineering operations associated with agriculture. (This recommendation has been retained. See Chapter 9, p 290.)

29. It will be argued that restrictions of the kind proposed will prevent farmers from exploiting their land to the maximum commercial extent. This, however, is already the case for many other land owners who are prevented from undertaking profitable developments, in the interest of the general good. Extensions to factories, hotels and houses are all subject to planning control, and this is often refused if there is conflict with other interests. Owners of listed buildings are not allowed to destroy them and are restricted in the ways they are allowed to modify them, and as a result may forego financial gain. They do not receive compensation for these restrictions which are imposed for the public good, and it is not unreasonable for similar restrictions to apply, without compensation, in order to protect features of the countryside. However, the Wildlife and Countryside Act 1981 specifically requires the NCC to pay compensation when restrictions are placed on agricultural developments in the interests of conservation.

Initial Recommendation

30. The payment of compensation by the Nature Conservancy Council under section 30 of the Wildlife and Countryside Act 1981 when agricultural developments are restricted in order to protect wildlife habitats should cease. (This recommendation has been withdrawn. See Chapter 8, p 287.)

31. Many small features of the coastline and countryside provide valuable habitats for wildlife and help to maintain genetic diversity. Often these may be lost as a result of action by the land owner, farmer or developer in situations where planning permission is not at present required or where the law is unclear. All forms of legislation suffer from this problem and it is probably worth while considering whether small scale features can be protected by introducing arrangements similar to tree or building preservation orders. For example, the local community may wish to ask for a preservation order on a small pond or coastal lagoon. Obviously the land owner would need the right to ask for the order to be repealed in appropriate circumstances. To avoid abuse, any arrangement of this sort should require the support of a minimum number of people, say 50, and a fee of, say, £50 would prevent trivial applications.

Initial Recommendation

32. Consideration should be given to the establishment of procedures, analogous to tree preservation orders or listed building applications, for the preservation of small scale features of the coastlines or countryside on application by the local community

to the planning authority. (This recommendation has been retained. See Chapter 9, p 290.)

33. Other coastal habitats, besides estuaries and wetlands, are also subject to special threats. Most important of these are 'soft' coastlines such as sand dunes, shingle spits, and machair in Scotland. The pressures on the coastlines can arise from industrial and recreational activities.

34. The industrial activities which have caused most concern recently are associated with the exploitation of offshore oil and gas, and apply particularly round the east coast of Scotland. Sandy coasts are very attractive to constructors of offshore platforms because the shore can be profiled and excavated easily to facilitate the construction and launching of these very large structures. These coasts also provide convenient points for bringing ashore gas and oil pipelines since they can be cheaply buried for protection from waves in the shallow inshore waters.

35. The decline in the rate of construction of offshore platforms has removed much of the concern caused by this activity, and it seems unlikely that further serious problems will arise from this in the future. Pipelines once buried have little ecological impact and any local damage done at the time is quickly repaired.

36. However, this does not mean that threats to soft coastlines have disappeared. It is possible that the successful solution of problems associated with the extraction of wave energy will result in the need to construct, store and maintain large numbers of concrete structures such as Salter Ducks and related devices. These activities will be done most easily in sheltered bays with sandy beaches. Local supplies of shingle, gravel and sand will be needed for the construction of concrete structures and this could also create pressure to destroy a number of sensitive habitats. It is likely that

these activities, if they occur, will also take place on the Scottish coast where wave energy is high.

37. Further pressures on sandy coastlines arise from recreational activities and the demand for holiday homes. Whilst the buildings themselves need not be a threat to these habitats, the trampling of vegetation by large numbers of visitors heading for the beaches can de-stabilise sand dunes which can then be eroded by the wind.

38. The recommendations made earlier in this chapter which would bring all marine developments under planning control, and which would make it easier for the Nature Conservancy Council to protect sensitive habitats, should also serve to protect the soft coastlines mentioned here. However, the recent introduction of procedures which make the NCC responsible for advising on the designation and management of marine nature reserves, and the importance of coastal habitats mentioned earlier in this chapter, places a much increased load on the NCC with regard to the marine environment.

Initial Recommendation
39. The NCC should be given the resources needed to increase its level of expertise in the marine and coastal environment to take proper account of its greater responsibilities in this area. (This recommendation has been retained. See Chapter 9, p 290.)

40. It is hoped that, given these resources, the NCC would be successful in designating a series of Marine Nature Reserves round the UK coast to protect sensitive and interesting habitats from damaging activities. The main value of such reserves would be the preservation of diverse marine communities in accessible areas, where their contribution to educational recreation would help mould public opinion towards supporting conservation of living resources as a worthwhile objective.

References

BORGESE, E A and GINSBURG, N. (editors). 1978. Ocean year book 1, 437. University of Chicago Press.

DE GROOT, S J. 1980. *J Fish Biol. 16*, 605.

MINISTRY OF HOUSING AND LOCAL GOVERNMENT. 1967. The Dee Barrage scheme. HMSO.

MITCHELL, R. 1978. Nature conservation implication of hydraulic engineering schemes affecting British estuaries. *Hydrobiol Bul, 12*, 333.

NATURE CONSERVANCY COUNCIL and NATURAL ENVIRONMENT RESEARCH COUNCIL. 1979. Nature conservation in the marine environment.

TOWN AND COUNTRY GENERAL DEVELOPMENT ORDER. 1977. Schedule 1.

WATER RESOURCES BOARD. 1966. The Solway Barrage. *Publication no 3*. HMSO.

WATER RESOURCES BOARD. 1972. Morcambe Bay estuary storage. *Publication no 13*. HMSO.

CHAPTER 4
DISPOSAL OF PERSISTENT TOXIC WASTES

Introduction

1. All materials discharged into the sea will be dispersed to some extent and many will be degraded to harmless substances at the same time. A few, however, are undegradable or degrade only slowly so that, although they are dispersed, the total amount present in the environment gradually increases. When dispersed throughout the oceans as a whole the concentrations will usually build up so slowly that there is no cause for concern. However, where the materials are discharged into shallow enclosed seas the build up will be much more rapid and damage to habitats can occur. Estuaries are an extreme example of shallow enclosed areas and suffer from the further disadvantage that some waste materials are trapped in the muddy sediments occurring there, which can be remobilised years later by salinity changes, storms, erosion or dredging.

2. The Irish Sea, North Sea and English Channel are sea areas which are relatively enclosed so that water exchange with the oceans is slow and dispersal of discharged materials may be insufficient to avoid harmful effects. Even so, the absolute concentrations of discharged materials will usually be very low except in the immediate vicinity of outfalls.

3. The property which can make persistent toxic materials hazardous, even when present in low concentrations, is their liability to be concentrated as they pass along the food chain. In this way, the concentration of a material present in a predator can be many times that present in its food. When there are several species in a food chain, each using the previous one as food, the concentrations of toxic materials in animals at the end of the series can be orders of magnitude greater than that present in the environment. The concentrations of toxic materials which can build up in this way are high enough to affect the health of animals, especially if they are under stress for other reasons.

4. The substances which exhibit the three critical properties (toxicity, persistence and accumulation) are the heavy metals (including cadmium, copper, lead and mercury), certain radioactive materials with a moderate to long half-life, and organohalogen compounds (PCBs, DDT etc). These three groups of materials have quite different origins, properties and effects and will be treated separately below.

Heavy Metals

5. Small concentrations of many heavy metals occur in the environment naturally, and some of these are essential to life as constituents of co-enzymes. If concentrations of these metals rise to higher levels, which may still be quite low in absolute terms, a variety of harmful effects may result.

6. The metals of most concern are cadmium, copper, mercury and lead. Abnormally high concentrations of these can occur by natural leaching from minerals, by rainwater run-off from mine waste heaps and by mine dredgings. However, the most important sources are manufacturing industry and car exhaust fumes. Cadmium is used extensively in the metal plating industry and in the manufacture of pigments. Copper is consumed in large quantities by the electrical industry, and is used as a fungicide and as a constituent of marine antifouling paints. Mercury has been used as a fungicide in the paper industry and in the electrolytic cells of chloralkali plants, although its consumption for these purposes has been reduced. It is also used as a catalyst in the manufacture of a number of important chemicals such as acetaldehyde and vinyl chloride. Lead, in the past, was used extensively in paints and for domestic water pipes, but its most significant use at present is as an additive to petrol in the form of tetraethyl lead.

7. These metals enter the marine environment by a variety of routes. Industry discharges them into rivers which then flow into the sea. Metals discharged into sewers from industry can reach the seas directly, or as constituents of sewage sludge from treatment plants. Sewage sludge which is heavily contaminated with metals is dumped daily in the Thames Estuary, the Severn Estuary, Liverpool Bay and the Firth of Clyde. Toxic materials, including a number of heavy metals, can be dumped at sea from ships, under licence. Finally, large quantities of lead from the combustion of petrol finds its way into the atmosphere and into street dust. From there it is washed into the sea by rainwater.

8. At high concentration, near outlets, heavy metals can result in the complete destruction of life. Lower concentrations kill sensitive species but not others, so resulting in a much reduced genetic diversity. At low concentrations molluscs and seaweeds can accumulate heavy metals without themselves being harmed. Unfortunately vertebrate predators which eat contaminated

invertebrates are poisoned since they do not possess a mechanism which protects them from these substances. These effects have resulted, on occasions, in fish and shellfish being declared unfit for human consumption, usually on account of high mercury or lead content. The sustainable utilisation of such fish as a source of human food is clearly impossible in these circumstances. An extreme example of this effect was the human deaths at Minamata in Japan which resulted from eating fish heavily contaminated with mercury from an industrial discharge. Lead is also known to be toxic particularly to children and can become incorporated in the diet by a variety of routes, one of which is through eating contaminated fish or shellfish. Although this route is normally of small significance it could become important to local fisherman on contaminated estuaries who consume their own catch.

Disposal of Radioactive Materials

9. The low level of radioactivity which exists naturally in the marine environment is increased as a result of a number of man's activities. These include the disposal of small quantities of radioactive materials from a variety of industrial sources, and further quantities from scientific research. However, by far the largest quantities discharged into coastal waters are derived from the nuclear power industry. Some radioactive materials enter the environment from the nuclear power plants themselves but most of the material which enters the coastal marine environment comes from the nuclear fuel reprocessing plants. The radioactive wastes from two such plants affect United Kingdom waters. One is the French reprocessing plant at La Hague on the Channel coast. The other is the United Kingdom plant at Windscale in Cumbria. The most significant radioactive isotopes discharged from the Windscale plant are strontium 90, caesium 137, and smaller quantities of plutonium 239. The strontium and caesium isotopes are carried by currents round the north coast of Scotland into the North Sea and then along the west coast of Norway. On the other hand, the plutonium accumulates in the sediments at the bottom of the sea in the vicinity of Windscale.

10. The quantities of these isotopes present in the environment, and in fish and other living organisms, are carefully monitored, and at present the concentrations are not thought by the authorities to give cause for concern (Royal Commission on Environmental Pollution, 1976). However, a rapid increase in the use of nuclear power and the reprocessing of spent fuel is likely to lead to pressure to license an increase in the quantities discharged. Caesium 137 could be a hazard with an increased nuclear power programme since, although it would be well dispersed in the sea, it can accumulate in the flesh of some fish, including plaice (Royal Commission on Environmental Pollution, 1976). Its half-life of approximately 30 years, however, ensures that it will not pose a very long-term threat to future generations. Strontium 90 will also be well

dispersed and has approximately the same half-life as caesium 137. It poses a special threat because it has a tendency to accumulate in bones of animals. High concentration of caesium and strontium would render fish unsuitable for human consumption on account of the increased risk of cancer.

11. In contrast to the other two metals mentioned above, plutonium is not well dispersed by the sea water but accumulates in the sediments. It also has an extremely long half-life of about 25,000 years, so for practical purposes it does not diminish in quantity even over many generations. Sediments in the vicinity of estuaries commonly drift towards the shore, and accumulate in the estuaries themselves. An accumulation of radioactivity from Windscale has been detected in the sediments of the Ravenglass Estuary, where it can be ingested by the invertebrates which form an important food for young fish and birds. Evidence presented at the Windscale Inquiry in 1980 suggested that plutonium could spread onto the land surrounding local estuaries as a result of wind action on contaminated sediments but more recent evidence indicates that plutonium reaches the terrestrial environment via wind blown sea spray. The importance of these processes is disputed but this controversy cannot be resolved here. However, if there is uncertainty on a matter of this sort it would be wise for the UK to play safe and reduce its discharges. The technology is available to do this and its use is unlikely to affect significantly the overall cost of nuclear electricity. At present the UK discharges more transuranic radioactive materials than any other country into the marine environment, and does it into a relatively enclosed shallow sea area where dispersion is poor.

Initial Recommendation

12. The amount of radioactive materials, particularly plutonium, discharged annually by nuclear fuel reprocessing plant should be reduced to the levels currently regarded as acceptable in other countries involved in reprocessing nuclear fuel. (This recommendation has been revised. See Chapter 9, p 290.)

13. The actual quantities of radioactive isotopes discharged into the sea are very small, so the chemical effects of these can be ignored. The hazard to the environment arises entirely from the ionising radiation which is emitted when the radioactive nuclei disintegrate. The biological effects of radioactivity vary according to the dose.
   (a) High doses cause the death of all organisms.
   (b) Lower doses can cause tumours and leukaemia which are likely to prove fatal in the longer-term.
   (c) Very low doses cause mutations which can result in abnormalities in succeeding generations.

14. The levels of radioactivity in waste materials which are being discussed here are too low to cause immediate death. They are, however, likely to cause the other effects mentioned above — points (b) and (c) — if concentrated significantly along the food chain. The slightly higher mortality and mutation rate amongst marine organisms which may result from the release of

radioactive waste is not in itself likely to be serious. However, fish, shellfish, and wildfowl intended for human consumption, which are found to contain significant quantities of radioactive materials, are likely to be regarded as unfit for this purpose. Therefore, as far as conservation is concerned, the main threat of the discharge of radioactive waste arises from the effect on sustainable utilisation of living resources as a food source for man.

Discharge of Persistent Organohalogen Compounds

15. These substances include the polychlorinated biphenyls used in the electrical and paint industry, and a number of insecticides such as DDT, Dieldrin and Aldrin. They are entirely foreign to the natural environment and are degraded to harmless substances only very slowly.

16. Polychlorinated biphenyls (PCBs) have in the past entered the environment in wastes discharged from the industrial plants which manufacture them. They can also leak from the electrical equipment, such as large transformers, in which they are used as a coolant. They may be discharged directly into rivers and estuaries or may be dumped from ships into the sea along with other industrial wastes. Although not now manufactured in the UK, disposal of materials already in use is a problem. The persistent insecticide group of compounds enters the sea partly by the same routes as PCBs, but also by being washed by rain from agricultural land or forests, where they have found extensive use in the past for controlling pests.

17. Both of these groups of compounds are widely distributed in the environment but they can become concentrated on account of their affinity for the fatty tissue of animals. Further concentration can occur if these animals are eaten by others further along the food chain. It is known that the health of animals can be affected by eating fish contaminated with organochlorine compounds. An example is the great reduction in numbers of the Brown Pelican in southern California where it was shown that lack of breeding success could be directly attributed to eating fish contaminated with DDT discharged from a factory near the coast. The Irish Sea Bird Wreck of 1969 has been associated with the presence of PBC residues in the fatty tissue of the birds. It is thought that the utilisation of the birds' reserves of fat during a food shortage released the PCBs into the blood stream at a time when the birds were already under stress. However, the link between this wreck and PCBs is not established beyond doubt and large scale bird deaths have occurred in the past. Although there is no direct evidence that organochlorine compounds have caused harm to humans, the harm caused to other animals clearly makes it inadvisable for humans to eat food contaminated with these substances.

18. The danger of organochlorine compounds has been much reduced in recent years as a result of a recognition of their effects. It has also been realised that the large scale indiscriminate use of insecticides in agriculture is counter productive, since it can lead to the appearance of resistant strains of pests. In spite of the greater control of the use and discharge of organochlorine compounds, the dumping of industrial wastes containing them into the relatively enclosed waters of the North Sea still takes place. There is no need for this method of disposal since, unlike heavy metals and radioactive isotopes, these compounds can be destroyed by efficient high temperature incineration.

Conventions on Dumping

19. In the past, the dumping of wastes into the sea was regarded as an acceptable activity, because it was assumed that the sea would be able to disperse and dilute the wastes to a level at which they would be harmless. The harmful nature of some of the substances dumped was also not appreciated. In north-western European countries the hazards of dumping wastes into the sea are now much more widely recognised. A number of international conventions to cover these activities have been drawn up and widely ratified. The most important of these are the Paris Convention of 1974 which covers pollution of the sea from land-based sources, the London Convention of 1972 which covers world-wide dumping at sea, and the Oslo Convention of 1972 which is concerned with marine pollution by dumping in the north-east Atlantic.

20. In spite of the fact that these conventions have been ratified by the major industrial nations of northwest Europe, the discharge and dumping of hazardous persistent materials into the sea still continues. The major sources are rivers which bring industrial effluents from inland to the sea, the dumping of sewage sludge contaminated by heavy metals into coastal waters and the dumping of industrial wastes from ships into the North Sea and the Irish Sea. This dumping has to be licensed by a national authority (MAFF in the case of England and Wales; DAFS in Scotland), but very little inspection of cargoes to be dumped takes place, so it is likely that dumping which infringes the conditions of licences would go undiscovered.

21. Control of discharges to rivers and estuaries in England and Wales was made the responsibility of the water authorities by the Control of Pollution Act 1974. As a result of the failure of governments to fully implement this Act, any discharges into rivers or the sea which were taking place prior to 1960 are not regulated. In Scotland, River Purification Boards already have control of most discharges. It is considered that the full implementation of the 1974 Act should be a high priority and it has been recommended (Chapter 2 paragraph 11 p 268) that this should be done as soon as possible.

An important feature of the Control of Pollution Act 1974 is the requirement for the constituents of wastes discharged to the environment to be made available to the public. Although it is sometimes argued that this would result in the release of information of value to competitors, it is considered to be a weak argument and is contrary to the current trend towards giving more information to the public about matters which concern them.

22. Once the discharge of all wastes, into rivers and the sea, has been brought within the scope of legislation the problem remains of how best to use the legislation to control the extent of waste discharge. In the Third Report of the Royal Commission on Environmental Pollution (Royal Commission on Environmental Pollution, 1972) consideration was given to a policy of charging the polluter for discharges to the environment. Although a minority report recommended this procedure it was not considered by the Commission as a whole that there was sufficient evidence available at the time to support this view. During the past years, however, a policy of 'the polluter pays' has been implemented successfully in a number of other countries and is a policy favoured by the European Economic Community (EEC). The other common method of control is by licensing discharges, and imposing sanctions if the conditions of the licence are infringed.

23. As well as there being two common methods of controlling pollution there are two objectives of control which are commonly cited. One is to achieve a particular emission standard and the other is to achieve a satisfactory water quality downstream from the emission. The former objective is favoured by some EEC countries and is justified on the grounds that uniform emission standards ensure fair commercial competition. It is argued that it is unfair for a factory on an open coast to gain a commercial advantage by disposing of its waste with little treatment, whilst an inland factory needs to install expensive treatment plant. However, waste disposal is only one of many factors related to a factory's location which affects its cost. For example, distance from raw materials and markets affects transport costs, and the local climate affects heating costs. No attempt is likely to be made to even out these variables and there is no logic in selecting waste disposal for special attention on the grounds of achieving fair competition. The only criterion for control of wastes, apart from conservation of the waste material itself, should be the protection of the environment.

24. The method of control needed to protect the environment depends on the nature of the pollutants. Two main types are recognised here. Degradable pollutants affect the local environment, usually on account of their Biological Oxygen Demand (BOD), but at a distance from the emission little adverse effect occurs. The open seas are not harmed by these types of discharges to a significant extent, and the control objective should be satisfactory water quality near the point of discharge. This can be achieved either by licensing, so that the waste absorbing abilities of the local environment are not exceeded, or by setting a level of charge to achieve the same result. No recommendations are made here since there is no serious long-term threat to living resources, and, as it is a local problem, it can be solved best by local action, or by water authorities and river purification boards, with the public being given full access to information.

25. The other types of pollutant, and the ones which are of concern here, are persistent materials such as heavy metals, long-lived radioactive materials and organohalogen compounds. These pollutants end up in the sea wherever they are discharged or dumped and gradually accumulate. Both water quality and emission standard at the point of discharge are irrelevant to the interests of other countries bordering these seas. The total amount discharged is what matters. However, the long-term effects of persistent materials discharged to the sea are not known with any certainty. It is possible in principle for the levels of toxic materials to build up slowly to hazardous levels which could not then be quickly reduced by stopping discharges. Some heavy metals are known to collect in sediments and having accumulated over many years they could be released over a short period by changes in erosion patterns or by a severe storm.

26. So far, known adverse effects have been confined to the locality of the discharges or the dumping ground, and have not affected the seas as a whole. Nevertheless, concern over the possible effects of continued disposal of wastes into the seas has led to the Paris, London, and Oslo Conventions aimed at controlling this activity. Although these conventions aim to control all types of pollutants, their special benefit is the medium- to long-term protection of the communal seas against persistent pollutants.

Control of Pollution

27. Control of pollution of the sea by the UK is seen as a two tier operation:
   (a) Local water quality is covered by existing procedures operated by regional water authorities and river purification boards. These will be effective over the whole country when the Control of Pollution Act 1974 is fully implemented.
   (b) The communal seas are protected against persistent pollutants in the medium- to long-term by the three international conventions.

28. The longer-term nature of (b), and the difficulty of reversing any adverse effects which arise, require that the conventions should be effective. At present there are a number of deficiencies which need to be corrected. For example, there is disagreement on the list of substances which may not be dumped. Also, trace amounts of hazardous substances may be dumped but there is no definition of what constitutes a 'trace amount', and,

as a result, the intentions of the conventions are partly frustrated. These points should be clarified and it is gratifying that the administrative bodies for the London and Paris Conventions are attempting to do this (Norton, 1981).

29. These problems must be solved internationally but there are some opportunities for the UK itself to make the conventions more effective. At present, only 0.5 per cent of the loads of waste dumped from ships under MAFF licence are monitored, and this is much too low to ensure that the conditions of the licences are complied with (House of Lords, 1981). Effective long-term assessment of the environmental effects of dumped materials is also important. Carrying out these measures is expensive and it seems reasonable that the costs should fall on the licensee rather than the licensing authority. At present, MAFF and DAFS charge a licence fee which varies between £45 and £550, but this is obviously too low to enable enough monitoring to be done (House of Lords, 1981).

Initial Recommendation
30. The licence fee charged for issuing a dumping licence should be raised to cover the full costs of an increased level of inspection of materials to be dumped, and to cover the cost of monitoring the long-term effects of these materials on the environment. (This

recommendation has been revised. See Chapter 9, p 290.)

31. There is evidence that dumping does not always take place in licensed areas, owing to ships dropping their loads short of the approved positions to save time (Eagle *et al*, 1979).

Initial Recommendation
32. The use of automatic position recorders should be required on dumping vessels to enable their position to be checked when their loads are dumped. (This recommendation has been retained. See Chapter 9, p 290.)

33. An important safeguard against dangerous practices is public access to knowledge of licensed activities, so that individuals and organisations with interests can make their views known.

Initial Recommendation
34. Information on licence applications should be published in advance of consideration, to enable interested bodies to comment, and the results of all inspections of dumped materials and environmental monitoring should be made widely available. (This recommendation has been revised. See Chapter 9, p 290.)

References

EAGLE, R A, HARDIMAN, P A, NORTON, M G, NUNNY, R S and ROLFE, M S. 1979. Fisheries research technical report no 51. MAFF.

HOUSE OF LORDS. 1981. Select Committee on Science and Technology, sub-committee on hazardous waste. 9 April.

NORTON, M G. 1981. The Oslo and London dumping conventions. *Marine Pollution Bulletin, 12*, 145.

ROYAL COMMISSION ON ENVIRONMENTAL POLLUTION. 1972. 3rd report, pollution of some British estuaries. HMSO.

ROYAL COMMISSION ON ENVIRONMENTAL POLLUTION. 1976. 8th report, nuclear power and the environment, p 135. HMSO.

CHAPTER 5
OVER-EXPLOITATION OF FISHERIES

Over-Fishing in the North-East Atlantic

1. Over-fishing in the north-east Atlantic has been recognised since about 1890 when increased effort put into the North Sea plaice fishery failed to increase the yield. Since then, other fisheries in the North Sea and north-east Atlantic have suffered the same fate. The most recent example of over-fishing resulted in a complete ban on herring fishing in the North Sea in 1977.

2. The reduced catch, which results from over-fishing, conflicts directly with one of the aims of conservation which is the sustainable utilisation of living resources. A further disadvantage of over-fishing is the increased fishing effort which goes into landing this lower catch. It has been estimated that, if properly managed, the world yield from fisheries could be increased by a factor of between two and four (Cushing, 1980). However, it needs to be recognised that falls in fish stocks can be brought about by a variety of natural causes. In these cases fishery management cannot prevent a fall in commercial yield, but if the fall in stock is recognised in advance steps can be taken to protect the future of the fishery by reducing the short-term take.

3. Over-fishing can take two basic forms, which can occur together or separately. Growth over-fishing results when fishing causes too large a proportion of each year-class to be caught before it has realised its natural potential for growth. This causes the stock to be reduced and the sustainable catch to fall below what it would have been with less intense fishing. Growth over-fishing is liable to be most pronounced in long-lived species with a large growth potential, and is typical of what has happened in the flatfish fisheries of the North Sea. If the spawning stock is reduced to the point at which it can no longer sustain the previous level of recruitments, then the more serious and dramatic 'recruitment' over-fishing occurs. Unless drastic measures are taken, this form of over-fishing is likely to lead to a rapid collapse of the fishery within a few years, as has happened in the North Sea and Norwegian herring fisheries.

4. The basic cause of over-fishing is that fish are common property, and are there for the taking. In these circumstances it is in an individual fisherman's interest to take as large a catch as possible. The only way this tendency can be overcome is by persuading all fishermen to reduce their catch so that stocks can increase and provide larger catches in future. They will not do this voluntarily since they do not have confidence that other fishermen, particularly those from other nations, will also reduce their catch. Fisheries regulation will only work if there are effective means of monitoring catches and enforcing the rules. This problem is increased by the international nature of many fisheries, which makes it difficult to reach agreement on the regulations. There is also a suspicion that national enforcement bodies take a sympathetic view to infringement of the regulations by their own nationals. The protection of a fishery may need rapid action where recruitment over-fishing is the problem, and here again the time taken to reach international agreement can prevent action being taken until it is too late. Sometimes the young fish which should provide future recruits to one nation's fishery are caught as a by-catch of another nation's fishery for a different species. For example, the Danish industrial fishery has, in the past, caught large numbers of young herring and may have contributed to the decline of the North Sea herring fishery (Cushing, 1980).

5. Economic factors can also add to the pressure to over-fish. Recent restrictions on foreign fishing fleets operating in Icelandic waters have forced these fleets to move elsewhere so increasing the pressure on other fisheries. The increased number of ships involved and the higher costs of operating ships, which has resulted from the increase in oil prices, have both contributed to the pressure for each ship to catch more fish. More efficient methods of fishing have enabled this to be done in the short-term, but the long-term result is an over-exploitation of almost all commercial species of fish.

6. Although a variety of international agreements, such as restrictions on the design of fishing gear used, minimum marketable size for fish, closed areas, closed seasons and total catch quotas have been reached, all these methods result in less effective use of the capital invested in fishing fleets. The problem of conserving fish stocks in international fisheries is only likely to be solved by a permanent reduction in the size of the fishing fleet. Although this was suggested in 1946 by the UK government and not accepted, it is considered that further efforts should be made in this direction.

Initial Recommendation

7. Steps should be taken to reduce the size of the fishing fleets in the NE Atlantic to a level which can operate efficiently without danger of over-fishing. (This recommendation has been revised and amalgamated with the initial recommendation in paragraph 10 below. See Chapter 9, p 290.)

8. It is not likely that this step alone will completely safeguard a fishery, and occasionally natural fluctuations in fish stocks will result in a need to operate additional restrictions for a limited period. With a smaller fishing fleet operating more efficiently, such restrictions would have less economic effect, and would therefore be more acceptable.

Inshore Fisheries

9. A number of small local fishing vessels operate in inshore waters and support small communities round the coast. These fishing vessels find it difficult to compete with the large capital-intensive international fishing fleets. This point has been made by the Food and Agriculture Organisation of the United Nations, and although it was made with reference to the problems of developing countries it is also true of a number of situations in the UK, particularly the west coast of Scotland, Wales and south-west England. In these areas there is often little alternative employment available and the viability of the community depends on the exploitation of the local fishery. Local exploitation of a resource is also easier to control and more likely to be carried out in a responsible manner since the local fishermen cannot move onto new grounds if they destroy the local resource. For these reasons it is considered desirable to provide an exclusive inshore fishing zone accessible only to locally-based fishermen.

Initial Recommendation

10. A means should be found to protect the fishing resources of small communities, whose economic well-being depends on continued exploitation of a local fishery, from the effects of remotely-based fishing vessels with less interest in conserving local stocks. (This recommendation has been revised and amalgamated with the initial recommendation in paragraph 7 above. See Chapter 9, p 290.)

11. In order to obtain the maximum sustainable yield from fisheries as a whole, it is necessary to exploit all commercially viable fishing grounds to the optimal extent. Some of these will be more economic to exploit than others due to a number of factors such as their size, depth of water, closeness to the shore, freedom from obstructions, or better food supply for the fish. If the resulting catches are all sold on the same market, one of two situations can arise. The price will be set by the easy to exploit fishery so that the hard to exploit fishery will not be economic, or if the price is high enough to sustain the difficult to exploit fishery, the overall price to the consumer will be too high and the easy to exploit fishery will make excessive profits. The likely result will be that the difficult fisheries will not be exploited and the easy ones will be over-exploited, so sustainable yield will be reduced.

12. This situation does not arise in agriculture, since land which is hard to cultivate is used for some other purpose such as forestry, or subsidies can be paid to artificially raise its profitability. Neither does the problem arise with the exploitation of non-renewable resources, because in these cases, easily worked deposits of, say, minerals, are worked out first, and then shortage causes prices to rise so that poorer deposits become economic. Only in the case of renewable resources where there is no alternative use of the ecosystem do rich and poor resources need to be exploited together.

13. A way of overcoming this problem might be to auction licences to exploit particular fisheries. Higher prices would result from licences for rich fishing grounds and lower prices for poor grounds. It may be possible for the licence fee from the rich grounds to subsidise the exploitation of poorer grounds, or to support the fishing fleets when fishing is temporarily suspended for management reasons. The number of licences for each area would need to limit the amount of fishing effort to that needed to exploit the fishery, so removing one of the major pressures for over-fishing and implementing the recommendation in paragraph 7 above. Thus, the auction of licences would reduce the fishing power of the fleets, would distribute the fishing effort to correspond to the distribution of fish and, not least, would be largely self-policing, making enforcement easier. International auction between the north-western European or EEC nations would also avoid the problem of setting national quotas. Moving from the present free-for-all situation to a licensed one would clearly cause some transitional problems, but various devices could be used to overcome these. For example, the need for capital resources to purchase a licence could be avoided by collecting the price of the licence annually in arrears. Special financial help may be given to those fishermen who fail to obtain a licence. The auction could be national rather than international, and so be confined to selling a previously agreed national quota. There are many variations of detail possible but the essential requirements are that the number of licences should limit the power of the fishing fleet, and should ensure that its distribution corresponds to the distribution of fish.

Initial Recommendation

14. The auction amongst north-western European or EEC nations of licences to fish specific areas by specific methods should be investigated as a means of regulating the amount of fishing in those countries' sea areas. (This recommendation has been revised. See Chapter 9, p 290.)

15. The recommendation in paragraph 10 above stresses the need to protect local fishing communities, where there are often few alternative forms of employment, against large scale fleets from elsewhere. The use of

licences to fish in specific areas recommended in paragraph 7 above can be used to provide this protection by giving priority for inshore licences to locally-based vessels if they wish to take them up. It needs to be understood that this arrangement is not proposed as a means of reserving the inshore area for one nation, but is intended to protect the local fishing community against any large scale fishing fleets, whether from the same country or other countries.

Initial Recommendation
16. In order to give protection to local communities whose economy depends on exploring inshore fisheries, priority should be given to vessels from those communities in the auction of licences for the inshore areas out to, say, six or 12 miles. (This recommendation has been revised. See Chapter 9, pp 290 - 291.)

17. If found to be practical the implementation of the recommendations in paragraphs 14 and 16 above would be an effective way of bringing about the more general recommendations in paragraphs 7 and 10 above. It would also be necessary in the early stages to find some way of compensating or buying out fishing vessels in excess of the number which could be licensed. Although expensive initially, the long-term benefits to the economy of the fisheries would make it worth while.

18. The emergence of the EEC as an important political force in the exploitation of European fisheries makes it necessary for the EEC to receive advice from an experienced and knowledgeable body of fisheries experts in order to decide on its fisheries policy. The implementation of the recommendations to auction licences for fishing in the EEC or north-east Atlantic waters would also require expert advice on the amount of each type of fishing which should be licensed in each area. In addition, short-term restrictions may need to be enforced from time to time. The International Council for the Exploration of the Seas (ICES) is a regional body which has been concerned with the management of fish stocks in the north-east Atlantic for many years. No other comparable body exists within the EEC which could give the kind of advice required.

Initial Recommendation
19. The International Council for the Exploration of the Sea should be formally regarded as the official advisory body to the EEC on fisheries management. (This recommendation has been retained. See Chapter 9, p 291.)

20. In recent years, the practice of catching enormous quantities of small fish for conversion into cattle-feed or fertiliser has grown considerably. In some cases, where the fish caught has little value as human food, this activity is probably acceptable, although if extended too far the food supply of young birds such as puffins can be threatened. Increasingly, however, the young fish caught in industrial fisheries are the young of fish which form a valuable source of food for direct human consumption. Young herring caught for their own sake or as a by-catch of the sprat fishery are a case in point, which has contributed to the decline of the North Sea herring fishery. The practice of using a resource to provide low value products instead of high value human food must be regarded as highly inefficient and should be discouraged.

Initial Recommendation
21. Industrial fishing should only be allowed by the controlling authorities when there is no risk of conflict with fishing for direct human consumption. (This recommendation has been retained. See Chapter 9, p 291.)

Reference

CUSHING, D H. 1980. European fisheries. *Marine Pollution Bulletin, 11,* 311.

CHAPTER 6
MANAGEMENT OF MARINE RESOURCES IN THE UK

1. Throughout Appendix D, reference is made to the complex legislation and variety of statutory bodies which control activities in the marine and coastal zone. The problems which arise from this have also been noted elsewhere (NCC and NERC, 1979). Many of the organisations concerned with marine resource management were established at a time when the needs of society were quite different from those of the present, and when the need for conservation and development to be closely integrated was not appreciated. The uses of different marine resources conflict with each other, so efficient use of these resources requires a careful assessment of the value of each resource in relation to society's needs. Regulations surrounding the use of one resource must take account of the need to conserve the others. This is difficult to achieve when responsibility for each resource rests with a different organisation. For example, MAFF and DAFS are responsible for exploitation of fish resources; regional water authorities and river purification boards are responsible for control of pollution of rivers, estuaries and the adjacent coastline; sea fisheries committees are concerned with monitoring the discharge of wastes within three miles of the coast within their districts; MAFF and DAFS licence dumping of waste from ships. The Crown Estate Commissioners control the extraction of all mineral resources from the marine environment except oil and gas, which is the responsibility of the Department of Energy. The exploitation of the facilities for transportation offered by the sea rests with the Department of Trade and the harbour authorities.

2. Various measures are taken to ensure collaboration between all these organisations but these never work perfectly, and no one department or organisation has a general remit to ensure that the best balance between the use of marine resources is achieved.

3. In most countries, the absence of specific government departments to deal with marine resources — Canada is unusual in having a Department of Oceans and Fisheries — may be a result of the tradition that the high seas belong to all nations, and that the States' jurisdiction only covers the narrow inshore strip out to three miles. However, this has changed in recent years with the extension of fishing limits up to 200 miles in some cases, the greater importance of seabed mineral resources, and the need to control pollution of the seas more closely than in the past. The exclusion of British fishing vessels from some of their traditional fishing areas has made the waters close to the UK much more important as a national resource. What was a suitable arrangement in the past is not necessarily the best in the quite different situation which exists now. Furthermore, matters of marine policy almost always involve international negotiations and there would seem to be many advantages for these negotiations to be carried out by a minister and a department whose sole responsibility is with marine resources.

4. The World Conservation Strategy recommends that national management organisations for conservation and development should be based on the ecosystem. In the UK, it seems that many organisations have responsibilities for parts of widely different ecosystems which have little in common, eg hill farms and fishing grounds which are both the responsibility of MAFF; marine gravel deposits and the management of Windsor Great Park which are both the concern of the Crown Estate Commissioners. It might be more effective to have fisheries and marine gravel deposits formally under the control of the same ministry so that the correct balance between their exploitation can be achieved.

5. The idea of a Department of Maritime Affairs is not a new one. It has been discussed on a number of occasions (Young and Fricke, 1975) and changes in the management of marine matters was apparently considered by the Government in 1976 (Department of Trade, 1977).

6. Changes to the organisation of Government Departments is not something which should be undertaken lightly, and in a short report it is not possible to assess fully the problems which might arise. However, the arguments set out above suggest that in the UK the responsibilities for marine matters are too widely dispersed amongst Departments with other major responsibilities.

Initial Recommendation
7. Serious consideration should be given to the formation of a Department of Maritime Affairs which would take over responsibilities for marine resources and activities from other Departments. (This recommendation has been retained. See Chapter 9, p 291.)

8. A change of this magnitude would be most economically brought about by phasing it in over a number of years, gradually transferring responsibilities,

staff and resources as suitable opportunities arose. An alternative, but probably less effective, approach would be to establish a Standing Committee on Marine Affairs at high level in the Government. Such a committee would be best regarded as an interim arrangement to cover the period required to set up a new Marine Department, and to coordinate and foster its establishment, rather than to be seen as a permanent solution to the problem.

References

DEPARTMENT OF TRADE. 1977. Marine activities, guide to the responsibilities of government departments and agencies. HMSO.

NATURE CONSERVANCY COUNCIL and NATURAL ENVIRONMENT RESEARCH COUNCIL. 1979. Nature conservation in the marine environment.

YOUNG, E and FRICKE, P. (eds). 1975. Sea use planning. *Fabian Tract 437.*

CHAPTER 7

SUMMARY

1. The approach to conservation set out in the World Conservation Strategy (WCS) is particularly appropriate to developing countries. In those countries, the pattern of use of living and non-living resources is changing rapidly, and it makes sense to carry out ecosystem evaluations to ensure the most effective use of the resources available. Frequently, the organisational framework and the skilled personnel needed to carry out these evaluations do not exist and there is no effective method whereby the public can influence development policy. Consequently, developments tend to be determined by short-term economic considerations.

2. To avoid these problems it is clearly necessary to follow the systematic approach to conservation which is recommended in the World Conservation Strategy. This approach involves the setting up of government organisations which are able to carry out environmental planning for the rational use of resources, and the passing of legislation designed to ensure that policy decisions are implemented (IUCN, 1980). In addition, developing countries will need to improve their capacity to manage the environment by establishing training and research programmes to provide the skilled personnel and knowledge needed for rational resource-planning (IUCN, 1980). It is also necessary to ensure that adequate support for conservation is forthcoming from the public. WCS recommends that this be achieved by a programme of participation and education covering all sectors of society (IUCN, 1980).

3. In developed countries the situation is quite different. There is already a well established pattern of resource-use which has evolved over many years, and which is often in equilibrium with the environment. Much legislation exists to protect sensitive habitats and species, and regulate harmful activities. There are often well staffed specialist government and regional organisations with statutory responsibilities for various aspects of the environment. Public opinion is also able to be expressed through the democratic process, through voluntary bodies concerned with the environment, and through informal pressure groups.

4. In the UK, much has been done to meet the needs of living resource-conservation, as would be expected in a developed country. Many minor adverse impacts on the marine and coastal environment, mostly reversible, remain but it seems unlikely that these can ever be eliminated entirely since the situation is changing continuously. Existing organisations and procedures deal effectively with many problems. Serious conflicts with the requirements of conservation should not arise in developed countries as a result of major developments, because in these cases widespread consultation takes place, pressure groups and voluntary organisations get interested and frequently public inquiries are held. In the UK these processes are usually effective but are sometimes inhibited by failure to disclose the full information on the basis of which decisions are made. A number of the recommendations made in this report relate to greater access to information.

5. The main conservation problems in the UK are likely to arise from a series of minor projects which go unnoticed or which slip through loop-holes in legislation, but which in total have an important effect. Where failures occur they seem to be for one of three reasons:
   (a) Inappropriate and often dispersed allocation of responsibilities between various statutory organisations.
   (b) Faults in legislation which become apparent after the legislation has been in use for some time. These are almost inevitable, but steps need to be taken to rectify the faults as soon as possible.
   (c) Conflict between measures which need to be taken to conserve living resources and other interests, usually of an economic nature. Frequently the conflict is clear and recommendations have been made, but the government in exercising its judgement of priorities prefers, for economic or political reasons, to take a short-term view rather than a more expensive or unpopular long-term view.

In the preceding chapters recommendations have been made which relate to all three of these reasons for failure to take steps to conserve living resources.

6. Conservation in the marine environment is dependent on international agreements to a much greater extent than on land. In Western Europe a number of international conventions controlling pollution of the seas have been evolved. Although these suffer from a number of problems they are having an important effect and their requirements have been widely incorporated into national legislation. Conservation of fish resources has been greatly helped by the work of the International Committee for the Exploration of the Sea. The main difficulty in this area is that fisheries policy is just one of

many political bargaining points between the various countries bordering the north-east Atlantic, and particularly between member countries of the EEC.

7. International pressure to protect coastal habitats is less intense than for the protection of the seas because each nation can itself take effective action to protect its own coastal environment without needing concerted action by other nations. It is perhaps for this reason that the Ramsar Convention on the protection of wetlands has been less strongly supported than other conventions. However, this lack of effective international pressure makes it more important for the UK to take the initiative to protect its own estuaries and other sensitive habitats.

Reference

IUCN. 1980. World conservation strategy. Living resource conservation for sustainable development. International Union for Conservation of Nature and Natural Resources.

CHAPTER 8
THE PRACTITIONERS' DEBATE

1. About 550 copies of the original report, consisting of the previous chapters with Acknowledgements and Appendices A to D, were circulated to 120 individuals or organisations concerned with the protection or exploitation of marine and coastal resources, or having statutory responsibilities in that area. Thirty six responses were received in writing, some of which represented the views of several individuals within the same organisation. A full list of written responses is given in Appendix E. In addition, informal comments were received from several individuals and, in particular, valuable points were made at a seminar on fisheries policy held at the Royal Society of Arts in November 1982.

2. Of the written responses, 14 were neutral in their reaction, 20 were in general agreement with the report and two were generally critical of its approach and contents. Most of the responses, whether supportive, neutral or critical, included useful comments and corrections. The respondents frequently went to considerable trouble to suggest detailed improvements and these have been incorporated wherever appropriate.

3. One area of concern to some respondents, which is not covered by the report, is the enhancement of natural beauty and amenity. This was omitted deliberately to ensure that the report remained closely relevant to living resource-conservation. Conservation bodies commonly link matters of natural beauty and amenity closely to those of conservation of species and habitats, and in many cases this is justified. Often the protection of a beauty spot for its visual appeal will also protect a valuable habitat and the communities which live there. There is therefore an indirect contribution to the aims of WCS. However, beauty and amenity are subjective matters and it is very easy to get drawn into other problems such as plastic debris on beaches, and the conservation of geological features and buildings, which would widen the scope of the report to such an extent that its concern for living resources would be much diluted. Organisations such as the Countryside Commissions, the National Trust and many voluntary bodies will be particularly concerned with this limitation of the scope of the report and will wish to stress the importance of amenity. The author would agree that these matters are important, but measures aimed specifically at protecting amenity and scenic beauty have to be justified on grounds other than the conservation of living resources.

4. A number of respondents were concerned that particular activities have not been dealt with more fully, and that the contributions to conservation made by bodies such as local authorities and voluntary bodies have not been acknowledged. This report could not hope, in the space available, to carry out a comprehensive review of all marine and coastal activities or refer to all sources of information. With such a wide range of activities to cover it has been necessary to concentrate on identifying those activities which threaten the three principles of conservation set out in WCS. Other more benign activities have had to be dealt with very briefly in order to keep the report down to the required length. A reference book of considerable length would be needed to cover all topics in sufficient details to satisfy all readers.

5. It has also not been possible to give credit to the many examples of habitat and species conservation which have been undertaken by voluntary and statutory bodies. These omissions might give the impression that there is nothing good in our legislation or planning procedures. Paragraph 4 of Chapter 7, p 284, attempted to avoid this impression but obviously did not do this effectively enough. It therefore needs to be said again that much has already been done to safeguard living resources in the UK. This report aims to cover only the major remaining weaknesses in the hope that these can be removed or reduced.

Recommendations for the Protection of Coastal Habitats

6. Nine respondents specifically referred to the recommendation to extend planning control to three miles offshore and to review exemptions from planning control enjoyed by certain organisations (Chapter 3 paragraph 20, p 271). Five of these supported the recommendation, one supported the removal of exemptions but had reservations about the extension of planning control, and three did not feel change was needed. One of the arguments against change was that the ownership of the foreshore is vested in the Crown, and therefore Government approval by one route or other would be needed for development. This, however, is incorrect since, particularly in estuaries, the ownership of the foreshore and sea bed has frequently passed

to industry, harbour boards and other statutory bodies, some of which have exemptions from planning control even so far as their land-based operations are concerned. If sensitive habitats are to be protected, both parts of the recommendation need some action. Clearly, the three mile limit is arbitrary and less would be adequate in many areas, but there are areas where a three mile limit is necessary. It is considered that the confused state of legislation in the coastal area, and the pressure on estuaries habitats, does require that steps very similar to those in Recommendation 1 (Chapter 9, p 290) be taken. It is worth pointing out that in the Shetland Islands planning control does, in fact, extend to three miles offshore. It is probably also advisable to require environmental impact assessments to be carried out for any major proposals, prior to consideration of the planning application, as was suggested by two respondents. Once planning authorities had control of developments it would be open to them to insist on environmental impact assessments in appropriate cases.

7. Generally speaking, the recommendation for a new appeals procedure against a successful planning application (Chapter 3, paragraph 22, p 271) was not supported. Out of seven comments, four were against, two were uncertain and one was in favour. This recommendation has therefore been withdrawn. Most respondents considered that most situations are adequately covered by the present arrangements, under which representations can be made to the Secretary of State to call in a particular planning application where it appears that the local authority intends to give approval. It needs to be remembered, however, that the Secretary of State in 1977 refused initially to call in the planning application which eventually became the subject of the Windscale inquiry. Only after an accident had received much press publicity did he reverse the decision. However, a procedure for injecting a national dimension into major proposals for development does exist and it may be as well to leave legislation as it stands at present but keep the way it works under review.

8. Out of six comments on the recommendation to bring engineering operations related to agriculture under planning control (Chapter 3, paragraph 28, p 272), four were in favour, one thought it unlikely to succeed and one thought it too contentious. This activity is one which is frequently responsible for the irreversible destruction of wetland habitats by draining, empounding or infilling. Since it is universally accepted that these habitats are amongst the most seriously threatened, this recommendation has been retained and has been given high priority (See Chapter 9, Recommendation 2, p 290).

9. Of the six comments on the recommendation to protect small habitats using procedures similar to tree preservation orders or listed building applications (Chapter 3, paragraph 32, p 272), three agreed with the suggestion, one disagreed on the grounds that the main problem in this area is provision of finance, and two thought existing procedures were adequate. One of the latter considered that procedures used for creating SSSIs and NNRs could be used in these cases. It would seem, however, to be cumbersome to use national procedures, designed with really important sites in mind, to protect the very many small areas of only local significance. The proven usefulness of the arrangements for protecting trees and buildings, by purely local action, make it worthwhile keeping the recommendation, and considering in detail whether they can be usefully adapted for the purpose in mind here (see Recommendation 3, Chapter 9, p 290).

10. Six respondents commented on the recommendation to abandon the arrangements under which compensation is paid when agricultural activities are restricted to protect wildlife habitats (Chapter 3, paragraph 30, p 272). One was decidedly against the recommendation on the grounds that the public should pay if it wanted a site protected. The other four considered that it was too soon to change the arrangements made in the Wildlife and Countryside Act 1981, and that the best approach to the restrictions on normal agricultural activities for conservation reasons is through management agreements with the owner. One thought a change of legislation might be appropriate. Whilst it is doubtful whether voluntary agreements will be reached in all cases, and whether sufficient money will be made available to finance all the successful ones, the author has withdrawn this recommendation. It is in any case peripheral to coastal conservation, and it is also desirable to adopt procedures on the coast which are compatible with those recommended in the rural report 'Putting Trust in the Countryside', Part 3. The acceptance of procedures, based on voluntary management agreements when normal agricultural activities are restricted, should not be taken as acceptance of the same procedures for engineering operations related to agriculture, such as draining, empounding and infilling. In these cases it is considered that planning permission should be required and compensation should not be paid if permission is refused.

11. There was no disagreement with the recommendation that the NCC should be given more resources to cover its new marine responsibilities (Chapter 3, paragraph 39, p 273) and this recommendation has been retained (see Recommendation 4, Chapter 9, p 290).
One of the supporters, however, suggested that the NCC needed a more positive commitment to the marine environment, and in the past had failed to use the powers it had.

Reduction of Pollution by Persistent Toxic Materials

12. Since this report was started, the government announced plans to implement Part II of the Control of Pollution Act 1974 over a four year period. The recommendation in Chapter 2 (paragraph 11, p 268) suggested that this was too slow. However, as almost half of the four year period will have passed before any

action on this report could conceivably be taken, there seems little point in retaining this recommendation, which has therefore been withdrawn. Furthermore, several respondents stated that more rapid implementation would disrupt long-term plans already being phased in by water authorities. The second part of this recommendation concerning publication of information on discharges, should stand, and has been incorporated in a modification of the recommendation in Chapter 4, (paragraph 34, p 278) which deals with essentially the same problem (see Recommendation 8, Chapter 9, p 290).

13. The main point made in comments on the recommendation concerning the reduction of radioactive discharges from the reprocessing of nuclear fuel (Chapter 4, paragraph 12, p 275), was that all the discharges conform to the recommendations of the International Commission for Radiological Protection and can therefore be regarded as satisfactory. This is certainly true where the pathways by which the radioactive materials enter, and pass along the food chain, are understood. In the case of actinides such as plutonium these processes are still under investigation and there seem to be two routes along which they can migrate from the sea to the terrestrial environment. One is through absorption on the sea-bed sediments which can then move shorewards, and the other is in wind-blown sea spray. The quantitative aspects of these processes are unknown and it cannot be reliably predicted how they will change in the future. The reservoir of silt containing these materials offshore and in the estuaries around Sellafield is large, so there will be a long time lag after stopping discharges before these materials stop coming ashore. This recommendation required modification to make it clear that it referred to the actinide elements only and not to strontium and caesium whose movements are better understood. The real point here is that, in an uncertain situation where there is a large time lag between an action and its consequences, it is better to be cautious. (See Recommendation 5, Chapter 9, p 290.)

14. It is claimed that shortage of finance is not relevant to the level of monitoring of offshore waste dumping grounds or the level of inspection of cargoes to be dumped. Nevertheless, the level of licence fees was a cause of concern to the House of Lords Select Committee on Finance and Technology and it seems entirely reasonable that polluters should pay a larger proportion of the costs incurred by the regulating body, than they do at present. MAFF publishes regular reports on dumping sites in use in England and Wales, so it would be more accurate if the recommendation in Chapter 4 (paragraph 30, p 278) were modified to refer to the need for more inspection of cargoes before they are dumped, and this has now been done (see Recommendation 6, Chapter 9, p 290). Three out of the four respondents agreed that a higher level of inspection is required.

15. There was no dissent from the recommendation that dumping vessels should be equipped with automatic position recorders (Chapter 4, paragraph 32, p 278), although one respondent wondered whether this formed an essential element of marine conservation. Since the validity of the whole programme of dumping-site-monitoring depends on the assumption that waste is dumped on the site, and nowhere else, it was considered that this recommendation should stand (see Recommendation 7, Chapter 9, p 290).

16. Only two comments were received on the recommendation concerning the availability to the public of information on dumping at sea (Chapter 4, paragraph 34, p 278), which has been revised (see Recommendation 8, Chapter 9, p 290). One suggested that improved public awareness would not remedy defects. However, there are plenty of examples of public awareness resulting in the authorities taking action, and some of these relate to dumping of pollutants (drums of cyanide dumped on waste land in the Midlands recently produced very hurried legislation to prevent this practice). The other comment correctly pointed out that MAFF does produce regular reports on its monitoring of dumping sites, but went on to state that information from the inspection of cargoes might be used in subsequent prosecutions and so could not be published. There must be many examples of information, which is available publicly, being used successfully in legal proceedings. However, if this point has validity, the spirit of this recommendation could be met if MAFF or DAFS took a decision quickly on whether or not to prosecute an offender, and published those results not needed for legal action. Results used in prosecutions could be published when the proceedings are complete.

Avoidance of Over-Fishing

17. Since this report was prepared, the EEC has produced draft proposals for its Common Fisheries Policy. Clearly, any UK plan to conserve fisheries will have to conform to this plan and in the following paragraphs an attempt is made to indicate where this might be done. In many areas the UK will no longer have the ability to act alone to conserve its fisheries.

18. Recommendations concerning the control of the size of the fishing fleet, and the protection of communities dependent on fishing (Chapter 5, paragraphs 7 and 10, page 280), received general support and, in fact, are an integral part of a Fisheries Management Scheme for the Orkney and Shetland Islands provided by one respondent. They have been amalgamated into Recommendation 9 (see Chapter 9, p 290). It is particularly disappointing that the EEC seems to have made no attempt to devise a scheme to control the overall size of the fleet fishing in EEC waters.

19. The recommendation that licences should be auctioned at EEC level (Chapter 5, paragraph 14, p 280) is no longer valid since national quotas have now been set. It has therefore been revised (see Recommendation 10,

Chapter 9, p 290). With this approach to fisheries management it will be very necessary to monitor these quotas and the author has little confidence in this being effective. Reduction in the power of the fishing fleet is essential, and the UK should press such a move on the EEC.

20. One feature of the EEC arrangements is that the UK has an exclusive six to 12 mile inshore zone. Within this zone there is scope for action to reduce the fishing effort by the UK alone. Generally speaking, auctioning of available licences recommended in Chapter 5 (paragraph 16, p 281) was not favoured, although licensing is an indispensable part of any realistic attempt at management which hopes to ensure an economically viable fishery. It has therefore been revised (see Recommendation 11, Chapter 9, p 290). No alternative to auctioning, which will both limit the fishing fleet and allow for the variable richness of different fishing grounds, has been suggested. It is therefore considered that when the UK decides how to regulate its inshore fishery the method of distributing licences by auction should be considered alongside other methods, and priority should be given to local vessels.

21. The EEC is proposing to set up a Standing Scientific and Technical Committee to advise on fisheries management. It seems wasteful to duplicate what already exists in ICES, but if such a Committee is established it is important that the scientific basis of its advice be openly published. The recommendation in Chapter 5 (paragraph 19, p 281) has been left unchanged (see Recommendation 12, Chapter 9, p 291).

22. The recommendation which states that industrial fishing should not conflict with fishing for human consumption (Chapter 5, paragraph 21, p 281) was fully accepted and left unchanged (see Recommendation 13, Chapter 9, p 291).

Management of Marine Resources

23. Five out of nine respondents supported the idea of better coordination of marine affairs by a Department of Maritime Affairs (Chapter 6, paragraph 7, p 282). One thought a Standing Committee to coordinate action of various departments would be better, and one suggested a minister responsible for marine affairs is needed, but not a department. The recommendation that this should be seriously investigated stands (see Recommendation 14, Chapter 9, p 291).

Revised List of Recommendations with Priority

24. A revised list of recommendations, which takes account of the points outlined above, is given in Chapter 9. In that list, high priority has been given to those measures which are aimed at preventing irreversible changes. Recommendations with lower priority are not regarded as less important; they are simply less urgent.

Action Programme

25. In the case of almost all of the above recommendations, much detail would need to be settled before they could be implemented, and many minor alternatives would emerge during this process. Very detailed discussions would be needed to make all the necessary decisions, but every attempt should be made whilst doing this to keep in mind the overall objectives of conservation for developing the long-term sustainable utilisation of living resources. There will be conflicts between interested but opposed parties to resolve, but the temptation to accept the kind of compromise which generates no opposition but fails to face up to the real problems, must be avoided.

26. In order that this next step can be embarked on, each recommendation or group of related recommendations needs to be referred to a small group of experts in the appropriate field. These groups will need to include representatives of the appropriate Government Departments, since in many cases amendments to existing legislation would be involved. Other members of the groups should have a direct interest in making the changes. Even in cases where legislation is not required, Government bodies are likely to be affected by the recommendations, or their help will be needed in influencing other, perhaps international bodies. These groups should regularly report progress to an overseeing group with an overall interest in implementing a UK Conservation Strategy.

CHAPTER 9
REVISED RECOMMENDATIONS

Protection of Coastal Habitats

HIGH PRIORITY

Recommendation 1
Planning control of all developments, new activities or major extensions of existing activities should be extended three miles out to sea, and the exemptions to planning control at present given to various statutory organisations should be critically reviewed. (Chapter 3, paragraph 20, p 271 and Chapter 8, paragraph 6, p 286.)

Recommendation 2
The Town and Country General Development Orders should be amended to remove the exemption from planning control given to engineering operations associated with agriculture. (Chapter 3, paragraph 28, p 272 and Chapter 8, paragraph 8, p 287.)

LOWER PRIORITY

Recommendation 3
Consideration should be given to the establishment of procedures, analogous to tree preservation orders or listed building applications, for the preservation of small scale features of the coastlines or countryside on application by the local community to the planning authority. (Chapter 3, paragraph 32, p 272 and Chapter 8, paragraph 9, p 287.)

Recommendation 4
The NCC should be given the resources needed to increase its level of expertise in the marine and coastal environment to take proper account of its greater responsibilities in this area. (Chapter 3, paragraph 39, p 273 and Chapter 8, paragraph 11, p 287.)

Reduction of Pollution by Persistent Toxic Materials

HIGH PRIORITY

Recommendation 5
The amount of plutonium, and other transuranic elements discharged into the sea from the reprocessing of nuclear fuel should be significantly reduced. (Chapter 4, paragraph 12, p 275 and Chapter 8, paragraph 13, p 288.)

Recommendation 6
The fee charged for issuing a licence to dump waste in the sea should be raised to cover the full costs of an increased level of inspection of materials to be dumped, and to make a larger contribution to the cost of monitoring the long-term effects of these materials on the environment. (Chapter 4, paragraph 30, p 278 and Chapter 8, paragraph 14, p 288.)

LOWER PRIORITY

Recommendation 7
The use of automatic position recorders should be required on dumping vessels to enable their position to be checked when their loads are dumped. (Chapter 4, paragraph 32, p 278 and Chapter 8, paragraph 15, p 288.)

Recommendation 8
Information on applications for licences to dump and discharge wastes in the seas or tidal waters should be made available publicly in advance of consideration of the application, and the results of routine inspections of discharges, and of cargoes to be dumped, should be published immediately, unless a positive decision to prosecute has been made. (Chapter 4, paragraph 34, p 278; Chapter 8, paragraph 12, p 287 and paragraph 16, p 288.)

Avoidance of Over-Fishing

HIGH PRIORITY

Recommendation 9
The UK should adopt a procedure of licensing fishing vessels in order to control the power and distribution of the fishing fleet in its exclusive zone. (Chapter 5, paragraphs 7 and 10, page 280, and Chapter 8, paragraph 18, p 288.)

Recommendation 10
The UK should urge the EEC to adopt procedures similar to those in Recommendation 9 above in order to control fishing in EEC waters. (Chapter 5, paragraph 14, p 280 and Chapter 8, paragraph 19, p 288.)

Recommendation 11
Within its exclusive zone the UK should allocate licences

in a way which gives priority to local communities dependent on fishing for their economic viability, and should investigate the possibilities of using auctions as a means of allocating the licences amongst applicants. (Chapter 5, paragraph 16, p 281 and Chapter 8, paragraph 20, p 289.)

LOWER PRIORITY

Recommendation 12
The International Council for the Exploration of the Sea should be formally regarded as the official advisory body to the EEC on fisheries management. (Chapter 5, paragraph 19, p 281 and Chapter 8, paragraph 21, p 289.)

Recommendation 13
Industrial fishing should only be allowed by the controlling authorities when there is no risk of conflict with fishing for direct human consumption. (Chapter 5, paragraph 21, p 281 and Chapter 8, paragraph 22, p 289.)

Management of Marine Resources

Recommendation 14
Serious consideration should be given to the formation of a Department of Maritime Affairs which would take over responsibilities for marine resources and activities from other departments. (Chapter 6, paragraph 7, p 282 and Chapter 8, paragraph 23, p 289.)

MARINE AND COASTAL ACTIVITIES

Harvesting Naturally Occurring Living Resources

Mammals Fish
Seals

Fish
Seine netting
(eg plaice)
Purse seining (eg herring,
mackerel)
Long line fishing
(eg halibut)
Trawling for demersal
fish (eg plaice, cod,
skate)
Drifting (eg salmon)
Trapping with fixed
devices or nets (eg
salmon, eels, flounder)

Crustaceans
Lobster and crab potting
Scuba diving (crawfish
and lobster)
Tangle-netting for lobster
and crawfish
Trawling for shrimps,
Norway lobster and
prawns

Molluscs
Hand gathering
(eg mussels, ormers)
Dredging (scallops and
oysters)

Digging (eg clams, cockles)
Hydraulic dredging
(cockles)
Trawling (queen scallops,
squid)

Other invertebrates
Worms for bait
Sea fans
Sea urchins

Birds
Wildfowling
Egg collecting

Algae
Gathering from the
littoral zone
Cutting from the
sub-littoral zone
Gathering algae washed
ashore
Consumption by sheep
(eg in Shetlands)

Other Plants
Reeds for roofing
Plants for food (cattle,
sheep and horse grazing
on marshes)

Crustaceans
Lobster

Molluscs
Oysters
Clams
Mussels

Queens

Algae
for biomass
for food
for chemicals (eg alginates,
agar)

Extraction of Non-Living Resources

Sand and gravel
from the sub-littoral
from the beaches

Calcareous material
Shell sand
Maerl

Metalliferous sediments

Oil and gas

Coastal mines

Water and its contents
Desalination
Extraction of chemicals

Energy (excluding oil and
gas)
Wind energy
Tidal energy
Wave energy

Marine archaeology

Waste Disposal

Sewage

Domestic refuse

Refuse and oil from ships

*Biodegradable industrial
waste*
*Inorganic and persistent
organic industrial waste*
Colliery waste
China clay waste
Heavy metals
Fly ash

Acid, alkalis, phenols etc
PCBs, DDT etc

Thermal discharge

Dredging spoil

Radioactive waste
Strontium
Plutonium
Caesium

Incineration at sea

Cultivation of Living Resources

Fish
Trout
Turbot
Lemon sole
Brill

Eels
Salmon
Sole
Plaice
Cod

Use of Coastal Land

*Coastal industrialisation
    and urbanisation*
Manufacturing industry
Ship and oil rig
    construction
Housing
Dock side facilities, ware-
    houses, container parks

Car parks
Rock climbing
Sand yachting
Camping and caravanning
Collecting
Bird watching
Access (by car or
    pedestrian)

Recreation
Holiday camps

Military activities on land
Firing ranges

Use of Water Space

Enclosure of estuaries
for fish farming
for docks and marinas
for fresh water storage
by causeways for roads
    or railways

for ports
for waste disposal

Reclamation
for agriculture
for airports
for port installations
for industry
for housing

Recreation
Sailing
Bathing
Scuba diving and
    snorkelling
Sea angling
Power boating
Surfing
Collecting
Bird watching

Artificial island construction
for industry
for airports

Transportation
Spillage from ships
Collisions

Refuse disposal
Tank cleaning
Dredging to improve
    navigation

*Military activities affecting
    water space*

Miscellaneous

*Introduction of alien
    species*
for coastal stabilisation
    (spartina grass)
by accident (eg slipper
    limpet, oyster tingle,
    Japanese seaweed)
for cultivation (eg Pacific
    oyster)

Reintroduction of species

*Control of predatory
    species*
Seals
Salmon eating birds
Shellfish eating birds

Natural processes
Erosion
Siltation of estuaries
Waves
Tides
Accretion
Storms

Currents
Immigration of new species

*Coastal defence and
    maintenance*
Breakwaters and seawalls
Stabilisation of river
    mouths
Dredging
Groynes
Stabilisation of shingle
    banks

Scientific studies
Collecting samples
Incidental damage (eg
    access by vehicles)
Experimental
    manipulation

Education
Collecting samples
Incidental damage (eg
    trampling, noise)
Experimental
    manipulation

MARINE AND COASTAL HABITATS

Offshore and Sub-littoral

Mud
Shell gravel
Stones and unstable
　boulders
Pelagic zone
Sea lochs

Sand
Maerl
Stable boulders and
　bedrock
Artificial structures

Estuarine
(ie brackish water)

Mud
Sand
Piers and pilings
Pelagic zone

Saltmarsh
Stones, boulders and
　bedrock

Littoral

Mud
Shell gravel and shingle
Stable boulders and
　bedrock (of various
　exposures)

Sand
Stones and unstable
　boulders
Tidal rapids
Piers and pilings

Coastal

Lagoons
Sand dunes
Sand spits
Machair

Wet slacks
Cliffs
Shingle spits and
　ridges

MARINE AND COASTAL PLANTS AND ANIMALS: PROTECTED OR OF COMMERCIAL VALUE

'Protected' means protected by the Wildlife and Countryside Act 1981

* Indicates those species of commercial value

Mammals

Dolphin, Bottle-nosed	*Tursiops truncatus*
Dolphin, Common	*Delphinus delphis*
Otter, Common	*Lutra lutra*
Porpoise, Harbour	*Phocaena phocaena*
*Seal, Common	*Phoca vitulina*
*Seal, Grey	*Halichoerus grypus*

Birds

Avocet	*Recurvirostra avosetta*
Bunting, Lapland	*Calcarius lapponicus*
Bunting, Snow	*Plectrophenax nivalis*
Chough	*Pyrrhocorax pyrrhocorax*
Curlew, Stone	*Burhinus oedicnemus*
Divers (all species)	*Gavia*
Duck, Long-tailed	*Clangula hyemalis*
*Duck, Tufted	*Aythya fuligula*
Eagle, White-tailed	*Haliaetus albicilla*
Garganey	*Anas querquedula*
Godwit, Black-tailed	*Limosa limosa*
Grebe, Black-necked	*Podiceps nigricollis*
Grebe, Slavonian	*Podiceps auritus*
Greenshank	*Tringa nebularia*
Gull, Little	*Larus minutus*
Gull, Mediterranean	*Larus melanocephalus*
*Mallard	*Anas platyrhynchos*
Osprey	*Pandion haliaetus*
Peregrine	*Falco peregrinus*
Petrel, Leach's	*Oceanodroma leucorhoa*
Phalarope, Red-necked	*Phalaropus lobatus*
*Pintail	*Anas acuta*
*Plover, Golden	*Pluvialis apricaria*
Plover, Kentish	*Charadrius alexandrinus*
*Pochard	*Aythya ferina*
Ruff	*Philomachus pugnax*
Sandpiper, Purple	*Calidris maritima*
Scaup	*Aythya marila*
Scoter, Common	*Melanitta nigra*
Scoter, Velvet	*Melannitta fusca*
Shorelark	*Eremophila alpestris*
*Shoveler	*Anas clypeata*
Sandpiper, Wood	*Tringa glareola*
Swan, Bewick's	*Cygnus bewickii*
Swan, Whooper	*Cygnus cygnus*
*Teal	*Anas crecca*
Tern, Black	*Chlidonias niger*
Tern, Little	*Sterna albifrons*
Tern, Roseate	*Sterna dougalli*
Whimbrel	*Numenius phaeopus*
*Wigeon	*Anas penelope*

Reptiles and Amphibians

Lizard, Sand	*Lacerta agilis*
Toad, Natterjack	*Bufo calamita*

Fish

Pelagic

*Herring	*Clupea harengus*
*Horse mackerel	*Trachurus trachurus*
*Mackerel	*Scomber scombrus*
*Pilchard	*Sardina pilchardus*
*Sprat	*Sprattus sprattus*

Demersal

*Brill	*Scophthalmus rhombus*
*Catfish	*Anarhichas minor*
*Catfish (Wolf-fish)	*Anarhichas lupus*
*Cod	*Gadus morhua*
*Conger eel	*Conger conger*
*Dab	*Limanda limanda*
*Dogfish	*Scyliorhinus canicula*
*Flounder	*Platichthys flesus*
*Gurnards (various species)	*Triglidae*

Fish (continued)

*Haddock	*Malanogrammus aeglefinus*
*Halibut	*Hippoglossus hippoglossus*
*Halibut, Greenland	*Reinhardtius hippoglossoides*
*Lemon Sole	*Microstomus kitt*
*Ling	*Molva molva*
*Megrim	*Lepidorhumbus whiffiagonis*
*Monkfish	*Lophius piscatorius*
*Norway Pout	*Trisopterus esmarkii*
*Plaice	*Pleuronectes platessa*
*Pollack	*Pollachius pollachius*
*Redfish	*Sebastes marinus*
*Saithe	*Pollachius virens*
*Sandeel	*Ammodytes marinus*
*Skates and Rays (various species)	*Rajidae*
*Sole	*Solea solea*
*Spurdog	*Squalus acanthias*
*Torsk	*Brosme brosme*
*Turbot	*Scophthalmus maximus*
*Whiting	*Merlangius merlangus*
*Whiting, Blue	*Micromesistius pouttassou*
*Witch	*Glyptocephalus cynoglossus*

Molluscs

*Clam	*Mercenaria mercenaria*
*Cockle	*Cardium edule*
*Escallop	*Pecten maximus*
*Mussel	*Mytilus edulis*
*Oyster, European	*Ostrea edulis*
*Oyster, Pacific	*Crassostrea gigas*
*Periwinkle	*Littorina littorea*
*Queen Scallop	*Chlamys opercularis*
Snail, Sandbowl	*Catinella arenaria*
*Squid	*Alloteuthis subulata*
	Loligo forbesi
*Whelk	*Buccinum undatum*

Other Invertebrates

*Lugworm	*Arenicola marina*
Moth, Essex Emerald	*Thetidia smaragdaria*
*Ragworm	*Nereis diversicolor*
	Nereis virens
*Sea Fan	*Eunicella verrucosa*
*Sea Urchin	*Echinus esculentus*

Migratory

*Salmon	*Salmo salmo*
*Seatrout	*Salmo trutta*
*Eel	*Anguilla anguilla*

Algae

*Kelp (various species)	*Laminariaceae*
*Laver	*Porphyra laciniata*
*Wrack (various species)	*Ascophyllum nodosum*
	Fucus sp

Crustaceans

*Crab	*Cancer pagurus*
*Crawfish	*Palinurus elephas*
*Lobster	*Homarus vulgaris*
*Norway Lobster	*Nephrops norvegicus*
*Prawn	*Palaemon serratus*
*Shrimp, Brown	*Crangon crangon*
*Shrimp, Deep-water	*Pandalus borealis*
*Shrimp, Pink	*Pandalus montagui*

Other Plants

Clubrush, Triangular	*Scirpus Triquestris*
Fern, Dickie's Bladder	*Cystopteris dickieana*
Hare's ear, Small	*Bupleurum baldense*
Knotgrass, Sea	*Polygonum maritimum*
Lavender, Sea	*Limonium paradoxum*
	Limonium recurvum
Lettuce, Least	*Lactuca saligna*
Orchid, Fen	*Liparis loeselii*
Spurge, Purple	*Euphorbia peplis*

ASSESSMENT OF EFFECTS

This Appendix covers in a systematic way the activities in Appendix A, and attempts to identify significant effects on the habitats and species in Appendices B and C. It is impossible to define exactly what is meant by 'a significant effect' since this is a subjective matter which depends on personal interests and experience. However, evidence that an activity changes a habitat or reduces the number of a species is not in itself taken in this report as evidence that the effect is significant. For example, the harvesting of any resource, such as a fishery, reduces the number of individuals of the species concerned, but provided the resource is not over-exploited this reduction is usually acceptable. Likewise, a change which reduces the number of birds on an estuary is not taken here as a conflict with conservation, provided the number left is large enough to ensure sufficient genetic diversity for continued viability of the species. This number will usually also be large enough to satisfy the needs of bird watchers and wildfowlers for whom the birds form an exploitable resource.

Harvesting

Mammals

In the UK the only sea mammals utilised as a resource are seal pups which are killed for their skins (see Miscellaneous section, control of predatory species, p 310, for seal culling to protect fisheries). This is done whilst the pups are very young, in order to obtain the white juvenile fur, and takes place on the breeding grounds where they are very accessible and vulnerable to man. Only two species of seals are normally seen in UK waters: the common seal (*Phoca vitulina*) and the grey seal (*Halichoerus grypus*).

Under the Conservation of Seals Act 1970, seals are protected during the calving season, so the killing of seal pups requires a licence which gives exemption from the protective legislation. Existing legislation and strong public concern seem adequate to protect seal species at present.

Fish

Since the sea is an environment which is relatively inaccessible to humans, fish are less likely to be made extinct by their activities than terrestrial animals. The high fecundity of some species also helps to ensure their survival even when fished intensively. Nevertheless, there are risks to the existence of a few species and the sustainable yield of others is well below the optimum level as a direct result of commercial over-exploitation. A brief account of the current state of the major stocks of sea fish around the UK is given in the MAFF publication 'Fishing Prospects', which is produced annually.

(a) Modern fishing methods such as purse seining are so efficient that very large proportions of shoals of pelagic (surface feeding) fish such as herring or mackerel can be caught. Although the very high fecundity of these species means that the escape of only a few individuals should in principle ensure the survival of the species, it is not known whether there is a minimum size for a shoal to spawn or survive predation. If this is the case, the danger of eliminating a whole stock is real and the time taken for its niche in the ecosystem to be filled by immigrants from another stock of the same species is not known. There is also the possibility that the niche would be filled by another species of less value as a resource, but the evidence that this happens in practice is inconclusive (Daan, 1980). Even if none of these threats cause the elimination of a species in its entirety there is ample evidence that modern fishing methods for pelagic gregarious fish and the intensity of their use do lead to over-exploitation, with a serious drop in the sustainable yield (Cushing, 1980).

(b) Demersal (bottom feeding) fish are in general less threatened by current fishing methods (Cushing, 1980). The common skate is however in danger of elimination at least in the Irish Sea (Brander, 1981). This threat arises from its high age of maturity (11 years) and because at birth it is large enough to be caught in trawls used for other demersal fish. There would appear to be little chance of saving this species from local extinction, and this could also apply to other large rays. Although few species other than the common skate are threatened with elimination many demersal fish are over-exploited and yields are below the maximum sustainable level (Cushing, 1980). A further problem with demersal fishing is the damage done to the habitat by the methods used. Large bottom trawls cause particularly serious damage (NCC and NERC, 1979). Commercial long-line fishing is not regarded as a threat to conservation.

(c) Migratory fish are subject to the special risk of being caught in large numbers on their migration routes. The important UK species (salmon, eels, and sea trout) migrate through estuaries where they can be trapped in fixed nets. Existing protective measures need to be maintained if yields are to be sustained. A threat to salmon fisheries which cannot be guarded against by national measures stems from the recent large scale salmon catches in the Denmark Straits west of Greenland. A catch quota has now been agreed for this fishery but a similar, as yet uncontrolled, fishery has started off the Faeroes (Mills, 1982). The latter fishing is currently being investigated by ICES, and recommendations for its management are likely to emerge.

Non-commercial fishing involving long line fishing, rod fishing and spear fishing is not seen as threatening either individual species or the sustainable yield. Local depletion is possible but conservation of living resources is not at risk.

Crustaceans

These species are usually considered as luxury foods in the UK and are not harvested on a sufficiently large scale to form an important food supply. They are, however, of importance to local communities in areas where other forms of employment are often scarce such as Scotland, Wales and south-west England. The case for maintaining a sustainable yield from these resources is therefore still a real one.

(a) The traditional grounds for lobster and crab potting were near the shore. Lobster fishing is still restricted to inshore areas but the fishery for crabs now extends up to 60 km offshore (Brown and Bennett, 1981). The fisheries are most unlikely to threaten the species but over-exploitation is occurring in some areas. Management of the lobster and crab stocks is mainly by regulation of minimum landing size by Orders made under the Sea Fish (Conservation) Act 1967. In addition, the Sea Fisheries (Shellfish) Acts 1967 and 1973 prohibit the landing of lobsters carrying spawn attached to the tail as well as egg-carrying and recently moulted crabs.

(b) Scuba diving can seriously deplete the numbers of lobsters and crabs in areas where diving is popular but at depths beyond 50m they are safe from this activity. The crawfish or spiny lobster (*Palinurus elephas*) occurs in the south-west of England and is probably more seriously threatened than other species.

(c) Trawling for shrimps and prawns in shallow coastal waters is not regarded as a threat. Even though many young fish which feed in these areas are taken in the trawl nets the high natural mortality of these fish means that this activity probably makes little difference to the numbers which survive to maturity. There is, however, concern about the large numbers of small fish killed in the small-meshed nets used in the Norway lobster (*Nephrops*) fishery. Legislation is now being introduced to increase the minimum mesh size of *Nephrops* trawls to reduce this mortality.

Molluscs

The largest molluscan fishery in the UK is that for the cockle (*Cardium edule*). This is carried out mainly in the Wash, Burry Inlet (South Wales) and the Thames estuary, with several smaller areas of local importance (Franklin, 1972). Virtually all commercially exploited beds are intertidal and the cockles are collected by hand. The exception to this is in the Thames estuary where the introduction of hydraulic dredging has enabled the exploitation of subtidal beds. Hydraulic dredging removes the surface layer of the sediment but detrimental effects are only thought to occur in sheltered areas where the sediment is not rapidly replaced (Pickett, 1973). Over-exploitation of oysters in the Solent has led to the extinguishing of the public right of fishing in certain areas in order that stocks can be conserved and developed. Similar arrangements to enhance stocks by private leasing have been made in the case of mussels in the Wash. The heavy, toothed dredges used in the fishery for scallops (*Pecten maximus* and *Chlamys opercularis*) appear to be particularly damaging to the sea bed. They dig out and kill other bottom living invertebrates including the colonial bryozoans on which the larvae of the scallops settle and spend the first six months of their lives. This, and over-exploitation of the stocks, is a cause for concern in some areas. However, the high fecundity of molluscs makes the actual loss of a species as a result of harvesting unlikely. The exception is the ormer (*Haliotus tuberculata*) which is at the northern limit of its geographical distribution in the Channel Isles, and is under threat due to its attractiveness as a souvenir. This species is protected (Russell and Yonge, 1975).

Other Invertebrates

Local depletion of some species of worms such as the ragworm (*Nereis virens*), and damage to shore habitats as a result of bait digging are thought to occur (NCC and NERC, 1979). This seems unlikely to pose any real threat to the species but the damage to the habitat could need regulation if its cumulative effect is large. In some areas bait-digging is already controlled by local bye-laws. Collecting of sea urchins (*Echinus*) for the souvenir trade is carried out commercially by scuba divers and may in the future be carried out for their food value. These species have a wide distribution which extends to depths which cannot readily be reached by divers so their survival is not in question at present. Sea fans (*Eunicella verrucosa*) are also collected for the souvenir trade and their very slow rate of growth makes local depletion a possibility. Protection to ensure the future of this trade is probably not justified and the species is not threatened with extinction other than locally.

Birds

Since seabirds nest and often feed on land they are vulnerable to human activities but they are only harvested for food in a very few localities. Wildfowl are likely to need protection but shooting on the coast is generally closely controlled by sporting organisations. The Wildlife and Countryside Act 1981 retains close seasons for wildfowl and reduces the number of species which may be sold commercially. Egg collecting is generally illegal, but collecting eggs of some species is permitted under the Wildlife and Countryside Act. It is only carried out in a few localities and is not likely to pose a threat since many nesting sites are protected in nature reserves.

Algae and Other Plants

Living algae are harvested for the commercially valuable alginates, and on a smaller scale for fertiliser, fodder and human food (Chapman and Chapman, 1980). The extraction of agar from seaweeds is no longer undertaken in the UK and the use of seaweed as a source of potash and iodine is also no longer economic. In the future it may become worthwhile to use seaweed as a source of biomass for energy production in remote areas. The process of harvesting UK species of seaweed from the littoral and inshore sub-littoral is laborious and is unlikely to become widespread. It is therefore not seen as a direct threat to any algal species nor to the communities associated with them. Indirect threats to habitats may arise from the importation of alien species for cultivation. These aspects are covered later.

The use of other plants such as reeds for thatching, or samphire for human food are very minor activities. Cattle grazing on salt marshes is not in itself a threat to the habitat, provided it is not used as a justification for enclosure and reclamation, which does sometimes happen, and provided the stocking density is not too high. Light grazing may actually increase the diversity of the plant community but heavy grazing leads to a poor, short turf with few species. Some development plans, as for example in the Outer Hebrides, involve seeding, fertilising and drainage and could result in the destruction of the nature conservation interest of large areas of machair without significant benefit to agriculture.

Cultivation

Fish

Fish farming in the marine environment is almost entirely currently restricted to salmonid species (principally salmon and rainbow trout), although there are a few examples of farming turbot, lemon sole and cod. These are farmed in floating cages in estuaries, sea lochs and small bays on the coast. The flow of water through the cages renews the supply of oxygen and removes waste products. The fish have to be fed intensively with artificial foods and there is a risk of eutrophication in the local area due to escape of nutrients into the surrounding water. The intensive farming carried out in the UK means that it will remain a net user of protein rather than a producer of protein and the costs of artificial foods are likely to ensure that farming is limited to prime species for the luxury market.

Farming may be economically feasible for a few species of strictly marine fish and research is currently directed towards the farming of turbot and sole (Purdom, 1979), both of which are landed in only small quantities by the UK fishing fleet. The areas suitable for fish farming close inshore are liable to be affected by pollution and other marine developments, but there is some potential for utilising offshore platforms and vessels (Reay, 1979). Fish farms are unlikely to threaten living resource-conservation provided that they are kept out of sensitive and rare habitats and are limited in size. Selection of particular strains of fish suitable for farming will not affect the overall genetic diversity as most of the total stock of species will continue to be wild. Pacific salmon may offer a greater farming potential than Atlantic salmon (Purdom, 1979) but non-indigenous species such as this may be a threat to natural species and careful thought should be given to their introduction.

Crustaceans

Lobsters are the most likely crustaceans to be farmed and this can be done in artificial reefs and submerged cages. An example of this method of farming which has been attempted was their cultivation inside the hollow breakwaters surrounding Brighton marina (Harvey, 1979). Artificial structures of this sort can provide habitats for diverse communities and so benefit living resource-conservation. The construction of extensive artificial habitats for this purpose would, unless carefully sited, interfere with other marine activities such as trawling, dredging and in shallow waters with navigation. A subsidiary benefit which should not be ignored is the educational opportunities provided by diverse artificial habitats which could be made readily accessible to the public. This activity will be subject to the agreement of the Crown Estate Commissioners, who own the sea bed, and is unlikely to need planning consent from local authorities. The Department of Trade would also have to be consulted with respect to possible interference with navigation.

Molluscs

Cultivation of oysters has been common round the UK coast for centuries and does not appear to conflict with conservation at the present scale of activity. This may change with the recent development of mussel and scallop farming on the west coast. Oyster beds tend to be monocultures and other species which are predators on oysters or may compete for food and space are kept clear of the beds so diversity is low. However, oyster beds usually occupy only small parts of estuaries so the overall diversity in the habitat is not seriously affected. One way of keeping shellfish clear of predators is to grow them on ropes hanging from frames so that they are clear of the sea bed (Reay, 1979). This method is currently being used in the cultivation of mussels in a disused Liverpool dock. Similar methods are being used in a recent development of mussel and scallop farming on the west coast of Scotland. In these situations the benthic communities need not be affected. The presence of oyster beds conflicts to a limited extent with some other, mainly recreational, uses of the estuary.

Algae

Cultivation of seaweeds for food or other products such as carrageenan is not practised in the UK. Trials have, however, been carried out into the growing of the large brown algae *Macrocystis pyrifera* in European waters as a source of material for the alginate industry (Chapman and Chapman, 1980). The introduction of alien species such as *Macrocystis* could pose a threat to native species which could be shaded out under the dense floating canopy of the introduced species. The floating fronds of these species could also be a nuisance to small boats. Concern has already arisen over the possible effects of the accidental introduction of the Japanese seaweed (*Sargassum muticum*) which has become established on the south coast (NCC and NERC, 1979). The deliberate growing or distribution of these two species in the UK is banned under the Wildlife and Countryside Act 1981.

Extraction of Non-Living Resources

Sand and Gravel

Sand and gravel are extracted on a large scale from UK coastal waters to meet the needs of the construction industry. This activity is unlikely to diminish in importance owing to increasing problems surrounding extraction from terrestrial sites. Most sites are seven to 20 miles offshore and consist of deposits with a very low silt content, but when these become worked out, inshore sites and those with higher silt content may be used (NCC and NERC, 1979). If this occurs, ecological impacts will increase.

The most significant ecological effect of dredging for sand and gravel would occur if it took place on herring spawning grounds whilst the eggs were hatching. Complete destruction of the eggs would occur. Dredging in nearby areas would also be detrimental at such a time, since silt could drift onto the spawning ground, settle on the eggs, and inhibit hatching by depriving them of oxygen. The settlement of this silt is not likely to affect the sites permanently, since herring spawning grounds consist of gravel beds where the hydraulic energy is high. Fine silt will not remain in such areas (De Groot, 1980). Complete extraction of a gravel bed will permanently destroy it as a spawning ground, but it is not known whether partial extraction would change the characteristics of the site to such an extent that herring would be driven to use other sites (De Groot, 1980).

The effect of offshore dredging for sand and gravel on demersal fisheries is unlikely to be serious since the fish will usually be able to swim clear of the area. However, some damage will be done by destruction of benthic communities, which will affect the food supplies of demersal fish, and alterations to the topography of the sea bed, especially by anchor dredging, will disrupt trawling. Dredging would seriously affect any scallop fisheries present in the area. It has been suggested that damage could be minimised by dredging from areas of high turbulence or mobile sand waves where the benthos is sparse. If it becomes necessary to exploit inshore sites, which may be important fish nursery areas, a large number of young fish would be killed, since, unlike adults, they would not be able to escape. However, the natural mortality of these young fish is very high so it is difficult to assess whether this effect would be significant. A further consequence of inshore extraction could be depletion of beaches, possibly at some distance from the extraction site, with consequent problems for sea defences, although in areas of sand accretion removal need not be harmful.

A side effect of dredging for sand and gravel is an increase in turbidity. It has been shown that long-term increased turbidity can cause higher mortality in fish (Cronin, 1975). However, most species of fish would be able to avoid turbid areas, and immobile benthic animals can probably tolerate some turbidity since they are affected naturally by the turbid conditions created by storms, waves and currents. Turbidity from dredging falls to normal levels within a few hours of the dredging ceasing (Cronin, 1975).

Sand and gravel dredging is licensed by the Crown Estate Commissioners. In practice, the Nature Conservancy Council (NCC), the Department of the Environment (DOE), and the Ministry of Agriculture, Fisheries and Food (MAFF) are consulted before licences are issued. Removal of material from the foreshore is covered by more complex legislation (Wisdom, 1979) but in general it may not be done in a way which exposes land to the inroads of the sea. Under the Coast Protection Act 1949 a coast protection authority may prohibit the excavation or removal of materials from the foreshore.

Calcareous Material

Shell sand and maerl are sources of calcium carbonate which can be used in cement manufacture or as a fertiliser. Of these, only maerl is extracted in UK waters and this to a small extent. The origin of these maerl beds is the calcareous lithothamnium species of algae and some of the beds are still associated with living lithothamnium. Exploiting maerl deposits is unlikely to conflict with the principles of conservation of living resources since the species are widespread. However, there are no great economic benefits since maerl is no better as a fertiliser than ground limestone. Maerl beds can also be damaged incidentally by trawling and dredging. Regulation of the dredging of these materials is carried out by the Crown Estate Commissioners.

Metalliferous Sediments

Cassiterite deposits resulting from the erosion of old tin mine spoil heaps, or the weathering of mineralised rocks in earlier times, occur in estuaries and drowned river valleys around Cornwall. Some extraction took place off St Ives for a short period in the 1960s (Cronan, 1980). More recently extraction from Cornish estuaries has been considered.

Offshore, effects of this activity will be similar to dredging for sand and gravel, but in estuaries the whole habitat would be destroyed. Nearby areas would suffer long-term increased turbidity, and settlement of toxic materials. Complete elimination of the ecosystem would be certain. By returning the processed waste to the estuary it might be possible to restore and re-colonise the habitat, but the need for this, and compensation for losses to local shell fisheries and the tourist industry, could make the operation uneconomic.

Regulation of offshore extraction would be by the Crown Estate Commissioners but in estuaries the approval of the local authority and the water authority or river purification board would also be necessary.

Oil and Gas Extraction

Oil is now extracted on a large scale from the UK sea areas, particularly off north-east England and east and north-east Scotland. Gas is produced from the southern North Sea (MAFF, 1981). Other areas are being explored and new developments include drilling near shore blocks, for example, in the Channel and in the Moray Firth.

The most obvious effects of offshore extraction arise from the accidental release of oil. Small scale releases are unlikely to be significant since they are no worse than natural oil seepage for which no ecological damage has been observed (Gerlach, 1981). Large scale release of oil resulting from oil well blow-outs, collisions between ships and oil platforms or other accidents can be expected to have a serious effect on birds such as auks and seaducks which react to oil by diving (NCC and NERC, 1979; Cramp, Bourne and Saunders, 1974) and on plankton (Gerlach, 1981). Long-term effects of even quite large oil spills in the open seas seem surprisingly small, but when the oil reaches the coast it can cause damage to commercial shellfish beds, sea birds and other organisms. This damage can take several years to clear up, but, although it is undesirable, it cannot be claimed that the existence of any species is threatened or that long-term sustainable utilisation is at risk. Damage to sea bed pipelines by trawlers could also cause large spills (Royal Commission on Environmental Pollution, 1981) and restriction of fishing areas may be necessary to avoid this.

In addition to accidental releases, oil enters the sea from offshore installations through the discharge of oil contaminated water. Oily water is discharged for operational reasons and the major source is production water (water that is present in the reservoir, together with the oil and gas). This is low in volume at the start of extraction, but gradually increases both as water from the surrounding rocks invades the reservoir and as water is injected to maintain reservoir pressure. Oil is separated from the water before discharge but this mainly removes the insoluble fractions and does not remove water soluble hydrocarbons. Research is currently being carried out to determine the toxicity and rate of degradation of the water soluble components, both before and after they have been degraded microbiologically (Wilkinson, 1982). A large number of other chemicals are discharged from offshore operations and their effects on the environment will depend on their particular chemical properties, their toxicity and the quantities in which they are discharged. Careful evaluation of all chemicals used including drilling muds (many of which are toxic) is required so that environmental effects can be minimised. Damage to the sea bed around installations has been shown to occur through the dumping of oil contaminated drilling mud and cuttings (Royal Commission on Environmental Pollution, 1981). During drilling, the bit is lubricated by pumping down drilling fluid (drilling mud) which also carries rock cuttings to the surface. If the drilling mud is oil-based the cuttings are contaminated with oil. However, very little oil is released from the cuttings into the water, and the major adverse effect on the sea bed is caused by bacterial growth which leads to anaerobic sediments and sulphide production. The ecological impact of the dumping is very localised and there appears to be little reason to change from the existing oil-based mud system (Wilkinson, 1982). The environmental effects of any discharge of oily water or chemicals from oil and gas extraction will often depend on the water movements in the area which determine the rate of dilution. Studies have shown that some areas of the North Sea have relatively restricted water movements and effluent disposal rates should be adjusted to take into account these differences (Wilkinson, 1982).

Beneficial effects of oil extraction can result from the increased diversity of life around offshore structures, which rapidly become colonised by attached organisms and behave like artificial reefs in attracting fish and fish eating birds (NCC and NERC, 1979). This attraction of oil platforms for birds would increase the seriousness of an oil spill.

Oil and gas extraction is licensed by the Department of Energy which is also responsible for safety and pollution standards (Daintith and Willoughby, 1977).

Coastal Mining

Although mining in coastal areas is essentially a terrestrial activity, run-off from spoil heaps can carry toxic heavy metals into the marine environment. The discharge will often be into estuaries the high productivity of which will be affected. Most of the areas affected in the UK by this problem are situated around the Welsh and Cornish coast, where spoil heaps from disused tin, copper and lead mines continue to release toxic material into the sea. The effect of this can be to destroy completely the ecosystem in the immediate vicinity of the discharge and to reduce diversity seriously over a wider area. There is evidence that many estuarine invertebrates can encapsulate excess toxic metals in vesicles, so rendering the excess harmless. Although this mechanism may ensure the survival of the particular invertebrate, a predator (human, fish or bird) which will not have this detoxification mechanism is likely to be poisoned by accumulation of the metal.

Frequently, the mining operations which cause these problems have long since ceased so there are no regulations which can be used to prevent the problem.

CONSERVATION AND DEVELOPMENT OF MARINE AND COASTAL RESOURCES

Usually responsibility for curing the problem will rest with the water authority or local authority. New mines will be covered by the Control of Pollution Act 1974, which, when it comes fully into effect, will regulate release of land-based pollution into waters within the three mile limit. There may however, be exceptions to the effects of this Act under private Acts or the Prescription Act of 1832 (NCC and NERC, 1979).

The only area where substantial quantities of mining waste are actually dumped at sea is off the north-east coast of England. The waste is essentially inert and its main effect is to smother the sea bed. Where it has been dumped on the foreshore, long stretches of sandy beaches have been severely damaged partly by the dumping itself and partly by operators who recover the sea-coal from the beaches. At the sites off the coast where it is dumped, the inshore fisheries have been affected (Eagle *et al*, 1979). However, compared to the total area of the inshore fisheries the area affected by the dumping is small. Dumping of the waste is controlled by MAFF under the Dumping at Sea Act 1974.

Extraction of Fresh Water and Chemicals
The extraction of fresh water from sea water by one of the various desalination processes is unlikely to become of major importance in the UK, although it could be of use for small isolated island communities.

Recovery of other chemicals from sea water is confined to salt, magnesium, magnesium compounds, deuterium oxide and bromine, plus small quantities of calcium and potassium compounds. Chemicals are extracted from sea water at only a few sites on the UK coast (Sibthorp, 1975). The environmental effects of these activities if carried out in future would be similar to or less severe than that of other chemical industries and their significance would be most important in estuaries.

Regulation would be by local authorities which would need to give planning permission, and by water authorities or river purification boards which would need to approve discharges.

Energy Extraction
Extraction of energy from wind, waves, or tides is not at present carried out commercially in UK waters but several experimental wave energy devices are being evaluated, and proposals for wind energy extraction in shallow offshore areas have been looked at (Clark and Dennis, 1981; Grove-Palmer, 1981). The only tidal energy project which has been evaluated seriously is the Severn Barrage scheme but others are likely to be considered in the future.

The ecological impact of wave energy devices has been assessed in some detail for sites off the Hebrides and the Moray Firth (Probert and Mitchell, 1979). While there will be some changes in the local habitats due to such devices, particularly the inshore sea-bed devices, these changes are unlikely to threaten species or reduce diversity of communities. They may, in fact, increase diversity by providing artificial reefs which can be expected to become colonised by invertebrates and hence be attractive to fish and birds. Some adverse effects from the large scale use of anti-fouling paints is possible and changes in wave energy reaching the shore may effect sedimentation. Offshore devices may interfere with the operation of trawlers but by so doing could provide sanctuaries for threatened species of fish such as skate.

Arrays of wind power generators in areas such as the shallow parts of the North Sea would behave like artificial reefs and increase diversity. Harmful effects would be limited to some interference with fishing.

Tidal energy schemes will have considerable ecological effects, but whether these will be overall beneficial or the reverse is not clear (Mitchell, 1978; Mitchell *et al*, 1981; Mitchell and Probert, 1981). The environment above a tidal barrage will continue to be estuarine in nature although the tidal range will be reduced to about half. The reduced range will, in turn, reduce the area of tidal flats which is likely to reduce the number of waders and wildfowl which feed on these. This reduction, however, need not be important provided the reduced number is still viable. Other effects include increased problems of drainage for adjoining agriculture land, interference with migratory fish and increased residence time for pollutants discharged above the barrage. The detrimental impact of these may be reduced by careful design or ancillary works and some benefits may arise from reduced turbidity of water above the barrage with consequential increased productivity. The increased difficulty of draining adjacent areas would help to conserve wetland habitats. The overall effect is difficult to assess in general and may vary from place to place but it seems unlikely that tidal barrages would reduce diversity or threaten the existence of any species.

All the energy extraction schemes discussed above will be very large scale and funding by central government is almost certain to be required. Special Acts of Parliament would probably be needed, so it is likely that all interested organisations such as the Crown Estate Commissioners, water authorities, local authorities, the NCC and other conservation organisations etc would be consulted.

Marine Archaeology
There are sites throughout the UK shallow seas where recovery of materials from historic wrecks is in progress. In a few of these complete recovery of a wreck is attempted, and this will result in the loss of a valuable local habitat. Overall, however, apart from a local increase in turbidity due to removal of silt the effects of marine archaeology will be negligible.

Wrecks of historical or archaeological importance in UK waters are protected from unauthorised interference by the Protection of Wrecks Act 1973.

Waste Disposal

Sewage

Discharge of sewage and sewage sludge into the sea and estuaries is widespread round the UK coast. This material constitutes the largest volume of waste discharged into the sea and much is untreated beyond screening or maceration (NCC and NERC, 1979). On the open coast the discharge is usually onto the beach or into shallow water just below low water mark. In 1970, the Working Party on Sewage Disposal (Department of the Environment and Welsh Office, 1970) recommended that crude sewage should only be discharged through long outfalls, but few have been built. The improvements in sewage treatment which have been made have led to the dumping of large and increasing quantities of sewage sludge at sea. The most important sludge dumping areas are off the Thames Estuary, in Liverpool Bay, and in the Firth of Clyde (Portmann and Norton, 1981).

The ecological impact of sewage arises largely from its high biological oxygen demand (BOD) so when it is discharged into enclosed waters such as bays and estuaries the oxygen levels in the water can be reduced until animal life can no longer exist. In extreme circumstances, only anaerobic bacteria occur with the result that toxic and malodorous substances are produced. The BOD of the large quantities of sewage discharged from the cities which commonly occur on estuaries, is added to by discharges of biodegradable industrial waste, and by detritus brought in from the sea by salinity currents which occur along the bed of most estuaries (Gerlach, 1981). In addition to a large BOD, sewage can introduce pathogenic organisms into the water. These could pose health hazards on nearby beaches (Gerlach, 1981) and can contaminate filter feeding shellfish (NCC and NERC, 1979). The dumping of sewage sludge or the degradation of untreated sewage in enclosed waters can increase the amount of nutrients available in the water. These nutrients can give rise to blooms of microalgae and excessive growth of macroalgae such as *Enteromorpha* and *Ulva* species (NCC and NERC, 1979), which can reduce diversity by inhibiting the growth of other organisms.

Most of the problems which arise from sewage disposal can be avoided by discharge in deep water with strong tidal currents where rapid dilution takes place (Gerlach, 1981). In this way, deoxygenation is avoided, nutrients are diluted, and pathogenic organisms are killed by the action of the sea water (Gerlach, 1981). There is some evidence that under these conditions there is an increase in productivity (NCC and NERC, 1979; Round, 1965).

Unfortunately, sewage and sewage sludge are often contaminated with persistent toxic materials from industrial processes, such as heavy metals and chlorinated organic compounds. Discharge of such material into estuaries is particularly harmful and can cause long-term damage to the ecosystem. Even when discharged offshore, fish and shellfish, especially those which are high up the food chain, may be contaminated making them unfit for consumption.

Disposal of sewage is the responsibility of water authorities in England and Wales, the river purification boards in Scotland, and the Department of the Environment in Northern Ireland. Water authorities license their own discharges to estuaries and adjacent coasts. In Scotland the situation is different and whereas sewage treatment is the responsibility of the Regional Councils, pollution control and the setting of discharge standards are carried out by the river purification boards. This is except for the three Island Councils which have full water responsibilities. When the Control of Pollution Act 1974 is fully implemented all discharge standards will need approval from the Secretary of State for the Environment. In addition, the Minister for Agriculture, Fisheries and Food will be consulted for a view on any likely impact on fisheries, and both ministers are required by the Wildlife and Countryside Act 1981 and the Countryside Act 1968 to have regard to conservation matters. European legislation also has implications for UK sewage discharges through the European Community in 1975 setting standards of water quality for bathing beaches which have applied to all Community members since 1978 (Gerlach, 1981). The dumping of sewage sludge at sea is covered by the Dumping at Sea Act 1974 under which control is exercised by MAFF and DAFS.

Domestic Refuse

Low lying swamps and mudflats bordering estuaries and coastal lagoons are attractive sites for the dumping of household refuse. Such sites appear to many people to be unused wasteland which, after filling in, can be covered over and used for agriculture, housing, industrial sites or dock buildings.

This activity completely eliminates an increasingly scarce habitat and the communities associated with it. The change is irreversible.

Filling of swamps and wetlands will normally require local authority planning permission, but where it is for the improvement of agricultural land the situation is more complex and the tipping of waste materials may or may not require planning permission (Heap, 1981).

Refuse and Oil from Ships

It has been estimated that six million tonnes of refuse are dumped in the sea annually from ships (Gerlach, 1981). Some of this will be dumped in the North Sea, the Irish Sea and the English Channel which are busy shipping areas. In the past, oil from cleaning out tanks of ships or contaminated ballast water was commonly pumped out by oil tankers as they left or approached ports. This practice is now banned but still occurs with old ships and is difficult to detect.

Much of the refuse discharged from ships will degrade or sink, but some will be washed up on the shores causing offence on amenity beaches. Plastic, rope and twine can foul propellors and fishing nets, and cause some injury to fish but they cannot be claimed to be a threat to the conservation of living resources. Nevertheless, these materials should not be discarded into the sea and pressure should be exerted on governments to ratify the IMCO Marine Pollution Convention which aims to control the disposal of waste from ships. Oil discharged from ships makes only a small contribution to the total input of oil into the sea but its harmful effects arise from the short time over which it is discharged and its proximity to land. Before it becomes dispersed it can cause the death of large numbers of seabirds and can be washed up ashore. The conflict with the needs for living resource-conservation comes from the effect on seabirds and the contamination of shellfish beds if the oil is washed into estuaries.

There are no regulations governing the disposal of refuse overboard from shipping, nor the disposal of sewage from the crew or passengers. Discharges of oil are controlled under the Prevention of Oil Pollution Act 1971 which prohibits the discharge of oil of any kind into UK territorial waters by any ship. The Act also makes it an offence for a UK registered vessel to discharge persistent oil into any part of the sea outside UK waters, except in accordance with certain conditions defined in the Oil in Navigable Waters (Exceptions) Regulations 1972.

Biodegradable Industrial Waste

These materials consist of hydrocarbons from the petrochemical industry, fats and carbohydrates from food processing and brewing industries, cellulose from paper mills, and various materials from the manufacture of synthetic fibres and pharmaceuticals.

The ecological impact of these wastes is very similar to that of sewage, and frequently they are discharged into estuaries either with, or alongside, sewage thus increasing the BOD which the receiving waters must satisfy. The high solid content of some of these discharges (eg cellulose fibres from the wood processing and paper industries) can smother benthic organisms. Some biodegradable industrial waste is toxic (eg petroleum refinery waste) and can cause local death of organisms in areas near outfalls.

Discharge is controlled by water authorities and sea fisheries committees in England and Wales, but at present the law allows long-standing discharges to continue. In Scotland control is by the river purification boards and all discharges to the major estuaries and coastal waters are regulated.

Inorganic and Persistent Organic Industrial Waste

Inert solids such as colliery waste and pulverised fly-ash from coastal electricity generating stations are dumped into the inshore sea off Durham, and china clay waste has in the past been deposited into estuaries in Cornwall. A variety of short-lived wastes such as acids, alkalis, phenols etc are discharged from industrial plants into estuaries and some dumping at sea also takes place. Heavy metals are not generally discharged deliberately into estuaries but some find their way there as part of other wastes from which it is expensive to separate them. Mercury in particular has been discharged from chemical plant producing chlorine, vinyl chloride, and

acetaldehyde and from paper mills where it was used as a fungicide (Gerlach, 1981). These discharges have been reduced considerably in recent years as a result of concern over their toxic effects but much mercury still remains trapped in estuarine sediments. Lead is discharged from plant manufacturing organo-lead compounds as petroleum additives, but most lead enters the sea from the air or rain water run-off from cities. Other metals introduced into the sea by industrial processes include copper, cadmium, zinc and chromium. Persistent organohalogen compounds such as polychlorinated biphenyls, and insecticides such as DDT, also find their way into the sea from manufacturing plant.

The environmental effects of these materials vary considerably. Coarse material such as some colliery waste can interfere with trawling operations. Fine inert solids increase turbidity and, if discharged continuously into enclosed water, will decrease light penetration, drive away fish, and smother benthic communities. Discharge into offshore areas where it can be dispersed more widely will probably have less of an environmental effect but may still cause problems (see Extraction of Non-Living Resources section, coastal mining, p 301). Short-lived materials such as acids etc although highly toxic will be rapidly rendered innocuous by dilution or neutralised by the buffering capacity of sea water, if discharged in deep water. Provided these materials are not discharged into confined waters no harmful ecological results should occur. However, heavy metals and organohalogen compounds cannot be satisfactorily disposed of by dilution. They are taken in by algae and shellfish, become more concentrated in animals which eat these, and eventually reach toxic levels in animals near the top of the food chain. Some species of birds have been threatened and fish have been rendered unfit for human consumption by this process (Gerlach, 1981). The only completely satisfactory method of dealing with these materials is by recovery, or, in the case of organohalogen compounds, by incineration. Dumping in the deep oceans is controversial and is not within the scope of this report.

Discharges of industrial waste into estuaries and the sea are controlled by water authorities and sea fisheries committees in England and Wales, river purification boards in Scotland, and the Department of the Environment in Northern Ireland. Until the Control of Pollution Act 1974 is fully implemented, however, there is no general statutory control over pre-1960 discharges in England and Wales. At an international level, the 1974 Paris Convention for the Prevention of Marine Pollution from Land Based Sources and the 1976 EEC Council Directive on Pollution Caused by Certain Dangerous Substances Discharged into the Aquatic Environment, are concerned with reducing discharges of persistent and toxic wastes into waters around the UK (Portmann and Norton, 1981). The dumping of substances at sea is controlled by the Dumping at Sea Act 1974. Except under licence, and in accordance with the conditions in the licence, it is an offence to dump any material into the sea. The relevant licensing authorities are MAFF,

DAFS and the Department of the Environment, Northern Ireland. The Dumping at Sea Act gives effect to the Oslo and London Conventions 1972 on dumping.

Thermal Discharge from Power Stations

Electricity generating stations are commonly situated on the coast or on estuaries, partly to take advantage of the ready supply of cooling water. When discharged this water can be as much as 12°C above the ambient water temperature (NCC and NERC, 1979). Such temperature rises in summer can easily kill all life in the vicinity of the discharge but, provided mixing is adequate, the lethal effects are very local. Outside the lethal zone effects which have been observed include the attraction of fish causing a local shortage of food and reduced health, increased growth rate, high egg mortality (Willemsen, 1979) and the existence of alien warm water species (Gerlach, 1981). Where the warm water is confined by docks, whole new communities can exist (NCC and NERC, 1979). Other effects which have been suggested are interference with fish migration (NCC and NERC, 1979), increased danger of oxygen depletion due to higher activity of bacteria, and reduced solubility of oxygen (Gerlach, 1981). It has also been reported that plankton can be killed by passage through the water pumps (Gerlach, 1981).

There is no doubt that thermal pollution does change communities over a limited area and can be lethal near the discharge, but overall there is no evidence of serious threat. The existence of unusual communities could have scientific and eductional advantages. The main hazards which should be avoided are discharge into water with a high load of biodegradable organic material since oxygen depletion will be made more likely, and discharge into migration routes of salmon, eels and sea trout with inadequate mixing.

Dredging Spoil

The dumping of dredging spoil takes place in the vicinity of most harbours. The spoil can be used as infill behind bunds constructed as a first step in the reclamation of marsh land.

The ecological effects of dumping dredging spoil in the sea will generally be minor provided it is dispersed and care is taken not to dump on sensitive habitats such as herring spawning grounds or shellfish beds. The turbidity associated with spoil dumping will quickly disappear and, although it has been shown that fish can be adversely affected, these effects are relatively short-term (Cronin, 1975) and fish can be expected to avoid the turbid areas. Most bottom living organisms will be able to tolerate some turbidity and the settlement of solid material, since they will encounter these as a natural consequence of storms, waves and currents. Another effect of the dumping of dredging spoil from estuaries, which usually has a high organic content, is the release of ammonia; this increases productivity. The effect of dumping metal containing spoil on the metal content of the water is complex (Cronin, 1975) but this activity has been in progress for many years and no direct harm seems to have occurred.

The ecological effects of using dredging spoil for infill of tidal marshes will result in a complete change in the habitat and is dealt with below in Use of Water Space section, reclamation of land, p 308.

The dumping of dredging spoil at sea is controlled under the Dumping at Sea Act 1974 and may only take place at specified sites. However, there is no control over the dumping of dredging spoil onto tidal marshes, and under the Town and Country General Development Order 1977 it does not require local authority planning permission.

Radioactive Waste

The largest quantities of radioactivity introduced into the marine environment stem from nuclear weapons and the propulsion units in nuclear submarines. While these are undesirable, and every effort should be made to reduce them, they are very diffuse in the environment, and are less likely to be concentrated in living resources used for food than radioactivity from point sources on the coast.

The main source of radioactive material discharged into coastal waters comes from the reprocessing of fuel used in nuclear power plants. Smaller quantities from other sources such as the power plants themselves, medical, scientific and industrial uses of radioactive materials, and nuclear powered ships, can probably be ignored by comparison. Windscale in Cumbria is the only UK reprocessing plant although radioactivity is released into the English Channel from the French reprocessing plant at Cap de la Hague.

A large number of radionucleide species are discharged into the Irish Sea from Windscale. The most important are caesium 137, strontium 90 and various isotopes of plutonium. Their half lives range from less than a year to 30 years for caesium 137 and 25,000 years for plutonium 239.

The actual quantities of these materials released are very small so their chemical effects are negligible. The hazards to the environment come from the ionising radiation they produce on disintegration. The effects of low levels of ionising radiation are a higher incidence of malignancies and genetic damage causing an increased mutation rate. At higher levels the effects can be lethal. The levels of discharge into the sea are such that only sub-lethal effects need be considered. This being the case it is unlikely that any species will be threatened by radioactive discharge, but shellfish accumulate a wide range of radionucleides in their tissues (Hunt, 1980) and in the case of caesium 137 there is a clear increase in concentration along the food chain, with highest levels in fish (Blaxter, 1980). Consequently, unless the discharges are carefully controlled the levels of radioactivity in fish and shellfish may build up and render them unsuitable for human consumption and threaten sustainable utilisation. Isotopes such as caesium 137 and strontium 90 are relatively conserved in seawater and they are carried by the currents round the north coast of Scotland into the North Sea. In contrast, the plutonium isotopes are rapidly absorbed onto sediments and concern has arisen over the build up of contaminated sediments on the coast surrounding Windscale, and their subsequent transport inland by the wind (Taylor, 1982). Although plutonium levels in sheep and cattle grazing on coastal marshes are well below those considered to be hazardous, they are greatly elevated above normal (Taylor, 1982).

In addition to discharges of radioactive effluents, low specific activity packaged solid waste is dumped in the Atlantic Ocean 700km south-west of Ireland in a depth of approximately 4000m. This dumping is a particularly controversial subject (Taylor, 1982) but is not discussed in this report since it takes place well outside UK waters. Medium and high level wastes are not dumped at sea but it has been suggested that in future they may be buried in the deep sea bed.

Discharges are governed by national regulations which are based on recommendations of the International Commission for Radiological Protection (Department of the Environment, 1977) and levels of radioactivity in the sea and in marine organisms are closely monitored. Present levels are well below the limits acceptable, but, since reprocessing of nuclear fuel is likely to increase in importance, it will be necessary to maintain a close watch on levels in the future.

Incineration at Sea
Disposal of certain wastes, particularly persistent organo-halogen compounds, by high temperature incineration is sometimes necessary since other methods of disposal are ineffective. A number of sea going vessels have been equipped with the necessary incinerating furnaces and operate from European ports, incinerating their wastes in the North Sea. The waste gases from this process are normally discharged to the atmosphere but they could with advantage be absorbed by the sea. The hydrogen chloride and carbon dioxide, which are the final products of efficient combustion, would have no effect, other than a small increase in acidity, which would easily be absorbed by the buffering capacity of the sea water. There is some opposition to incineration at sea, but this is difficult to understand. Provided care is taken to ensure that the standards of the equipment are maintained to a high level, and materials with solid toxic residues are not incinerated, this method of disposal is probably less harmful than disposal or incineration on land.

Incinerator vessels are licensed by national authorities which are responsible for seeing that the vessel's equipment is in an efficient condition.

Use of Coastal Land

Coastal Industrialisation and Urbanisation
Many estuaries round the UK coast are associated with large industrialised cities (eg Southampton, Liverpool,

and Newcastle). This association arose because heavy industry and commerce needed access to large ports. Estuaries provided the sheltered waters necessary for the development of these ports. These industrial towns have a serious adverse effect on the estuarine ecosystem and much of it is irreversible. Enclosure for docks, reclamation for industry, port installations, or housing are irreversible and make the habitat quite unrecognisable compared with a natural estuary. Dredging, and discharge of sewage and industrial waste, have impacts which are probably irreversible although in many cases reversal would take many years. It is unfortunate that towns which have such a great impact should so frequently be associated with the sensitive estuarine ecosystem.

Large cities, whether on estuaries or not, have indirectly caused a further impact on the coast by creating a social need to escape from the industrial environment for recreation and relaxation. As a result, towns without significant industry have grown up on the open coast (eg Brighton and Blackpool) or have developed round small fishing harbours (eg Whitby and Yarmouth). The impact of this form of urbanisation is much less than that of industrial towns. These towns, however, are usually on the relatively unspoilt part of the coast where it is particularly important to preserve the more natural and diverse habitats which occur there. The main impacts of coastal resorts are covered in Use of Water Space section, recreation, p 308.

Control of the development of towns and industry is carried out by local authorities which are required to give planning permission for buildings and change of use of existing buildings. Local authorities are preparing, or have already prepared, structure plans which restrict industrial and urban development to predetermined areas. The objective of these plans is usually to encourage developments whilst preserving recreational and residential amenities. Areas of particular conservation interest are included on these plans, and public participation is required in their preparation.

Recreation on Coastal Land
Many recreations take place on the coast and, although some of these are water-based, many are land-based. The activities based on open sandy beaches such as sun bathing, sand yachting, motor and motor cycle racing have little impact on the ecosystem. Coastal rock climbing is usually confined to hard rock cliffs, so little impact would be expected from this activity, although cliff nesting birds may be disturbed. Bird watching is a common recreation associated with estuaries on account of the variety and number of ducks and waders to be found. This must be regarded as a beneficial activity because bird watchers themselves have little impact, but will generate an interest in, and a sense of responsibility towards, the environment. The ornithological societies are also influential in helping to preserve natural habitats. An activity which is stimulated by an interest in natural history is the collecting of living specimens. This can cause a local depletion of coastal plants, so, although the interest is to be encouraged, the practice of

collecting needs to be stopped, especially as it is the rarer specimens which are most sought after.

Overall, coastal land-based recreations themselves have few effects but problems frequently arise due to the numbers of people involved and the ancillary facilities which they need. Often these facilities are situated close to attractive natural habitats and the access to the recreational areas by cars and pedestrians causes considerable damage. Destruction of vegetation on sand dunes by trampling is a particular problem in some areas, since it can be followed by wind erosion and movement of the dunes.

Regulation of recreational activities is partly by local authority bye-laws and partly by the voluntary codes of practice of the national recreational organisations. Control is also provided by the establishment of nature reserves within which certain activities are controlled, and by legislation such as the Wildlife and Countryside Act 1981 which prohibits the collecting of rare species.

Military Activities on Land

At a number of sites round the UK coast, usually in relatively remote unspoilt areas, the Ministry of Defence has established firing ranges and exercise grounds for the armed forces (eg Lulworth Cove and South Pembrokeshire). In addition, naval dockyards have existed for many years on a number of estuaries but the impact of these will be no different from that of any industrial town and its associated port, which were previously covered in this section under coastal industrialisation and urbanisation, p 306.

The noise and effects of gunfire and explosions on firing ranges will tend to frighten away larger animals and birds, but even these are likely to adapt to the conditions. More significant will be the damage to vegetation and soil structure by heavy vehicles on armoured vehicle exercise grounds. The habitats in these areas will be badly damaged. Apart from this latter effect the peacetime activities of the armed forces are not seen as being a threat to living resources in coastal areas, although they undoubtedly conflict with many other human interests such as recreation and farming. The isolation of firing ranges from many human influences results in the development of a natural succession of plants and animals which could provide a useful subject for scientific study.

Ministry of Defence activities are exempt from normal planning controls but public opinion and pressure groups have some effect in preventing some of the damaging activities. Conservation committees have been set up at Ministry of Defence sites for liaison with local naturalists.

Use of Water Space

Enclosure of Estuaries

At present salmonid fish species are farmed in floating cages moored in estuaries, lochs and bays at a number of sites around the UK, particularly on the coast of Scotland. Since the cages enclose only the upper water layers, and there is a free flow of water through them, they do not affect water movements at the site. The areas enclosed are small in extent and the environmental impact is normally limited to the effects of the large amount of fish food which is put into the cages. Some of this inevitably escapes into the surrounding habitat and carries with it a risk of eutrophication. However, if fish farming develops in such a way as to involve the enclosure of large parts of estuaries by solid barriers there would be a much more serious effect, since the environment would be completely changed and would no longer be classed as an estuarine habitat. This method of fish farming has already been attempted on a small scale in a Scottish sea loch (Gross, 1947). Effects of fish farming other than the effects of enclosure were previously covered in the section on Cultivation, fish, p 299.

During the 1960s a number of schemes for enclosing estuaries for fresh water storage were considered. The schemes given serious attention concerned Morecambe Bay, the Solway Firth, the Wash, and the Welsh Dee (Water Resources Board, 1966; 1972; Ministry of Housing and Local Government, 1967; NERC, 1976). None of these schemes is being implemented at present since demand for water has not increased as much as expected. The environmental impact of a fresh water storage scheme would depend very much on the way it was carried out. Complete enclosure by a barrage across the mouth would change the whole habitat from a brackish estuary into a fresh water lake. The large intertidal flats would be lost as bird feeding grounds and special steps would be needed to enable migratory fish to pass the barrage (Corlett, 1979). Most schemes would avoid complete enclosure on account of the expense of the final closing of the barrage (Volker, 1974). Instead, bunds would be constructed to form freshwater lakes along the sides of the estuary (Water Resources Board, 1966; 1972). Whilst such a scheme has a less damaging effect on the habitat, extensive bird feeding grounds would be lost. In some cases, however, continued accretion would result in the formation of new intertidal flats to seaward of the enclosure (Volker, 1974; Corlett, 1979). Where it is clear that such a process would occur it is unlikely that fresh water storage schemes would pose a threat to living resource-conservation.

In the past, many estuaries have been partly enclosed to provide docks. The current trend in commercial docks is towards deeper water which can accommodate very large vessels. Dock construction has, therefore, tended to move from shallow estuaries to the open coast. An example is the new container ship berth on the Mersey. The rapid turn round needed for the economical operation of modern ships has also reduced the size of modern dock systems. As a result of these two effects, the impact on the environment of enclosure for dock construction should be less than in the past. A more common activity at present, which encloses parts of the smaller estuaries, is the construction of yacht marinas at many sites round the coast, particularly in tourist centres such as on the south-west coast of England. The natural state of some of these estuaries makes it particularly important to preserve their communities. Yacht marinas of modest size should not threaten these communities but large marinas could change a substantial part of the habitat and could cause pollution by the metals contained in anti-fouling paints (Gerlach, 1981).

Estuaries and bays are sometimes enclosed by embankments to carry roads or railways. These completely change the habitat converting the estuary into a fresh water lake, or, where a short bridge is incorporated to allow river water to escape, the salinity regime and the extent of intertidal land is much reduced. Although new railways are not at present being constructed, road construction often forms part of enclosure schemes for fresh water storage, land reclamation or tidal energy (Ministry of Housing and Local Government, 1967; Water Resources Board, 1972).

Enclosure schemes such as those for freshwater storage would be major developments, and subject to full discussion between all organisations with a vested interest. Smaller schemes would require consultation and agreement with bodies such as the Crown Estate Commissioners who usually own the bed of an estuary, the Department of Trade on interference with navigation, and the local authority concerning both planning permission and possible effects on coast protection.

Reclamation
The intertidal areas of estuaries and other areas of brackish water such as coastal lagoons are frequently regarded as though they are unproductive waste lands. As a result, these areas have been extensively converted to other uses. Reclamation for agricultural use has been going on for centuries, and during the past hundred years reclamation for docks, industry, and housing has become common and still continues. A preliminary step in this process is often the filling in of the low lying areas with domestic refuse. Southampton Water, the Mersey and the Welsh Dee are amongst the many estuaries which have been significantly altered in this way. On the Firth of Forth waste ash from coal fired power stations has been used to fill in intertidal mud flats. Large areas of the tidal sands at the mouth of the Tees have been reclaimed for industry and port activities, and even the last remaining and ecologically important Seal Sands are expected to be reclaimed in due course (Mitchell, 1978). A more recent use for reclaimed estuarine land is airport construction which needs extensive areas of land away from major towns. The Maplin Sands site for the third London Airport would have required reclamation of a large site in the outer Thames Estuary.

The changes brought about by reclamation result in the complete and irreversible loss of the estuarine eco-system. In general, the reclamation of coastal wetlands with their great importance to wildfowl, young fish, shrimps and shellfish, should be avoided. The exception might be those estuaries which are still being extended seaward by accretion. In such cases, reclamation may simply speed up the processes which result in conversion of intertidal areas into salt marsh and then dry land.

The reclamation and development of intertidal land will usually require local authority planning permission. However, reclamation for agricultural use does not generally require planning permission, and large areas of coastal wetlands have been converted to farmland. The building of embankments for the reclamation and flood protection of agricultural land is no longer grant aided by MAFF, but subsequent drainage operations are grant aided.

Artificial Island Construction
This activity has not been undertaken to any significant extent in the UK. However, it has been suggested as a possible means of providing sites for industry, ports, refuse disposal and airports. It has a number of advantages for these purposes. For example, no agricultural land is consumed, and the pollution (including noise) which inevitably accompanies these activities, is removed from centres of population. Artificial islands would need to be constructed in shallow, reasonably sheltered waters for engineering reasons. This means that the sites would be in or close to estuaries. Unlike most schemes for the reclamation of land from estuaries this need not result in the loss of intertidal wetlands. Depending on the exact design it is possible for a more complex and extended estuarine habitat to be created, particularly if accretion of sandbanks is in progress and seems likely to continue to seaward of the artificial island. The construction of an island could therefore benefit living resource conservation by removing pressure to reclaim wetlands, and in favourable circumstances, creating more wetlands. However, the overall effect would depend on the impact of the activities carried out on the island. Careful control of pollution would be necessary to avoid adverse effects.

Permission of the Crown Estate Commissioners would be needed, since it is likely that the sea bed off the mouths of estuaries would be Crown land. Local authority planning permission would also be needed for the activity on the island, although problems might arise as to which local authority should be involved. Most schemes of this type are likely to lead to public inquiries.

Recreation
Water-based recreations are widespread in UK coastal waters. They include sailing, power boating, water skiing, bathing, surfing, scuba diving and snorkelling. The direct physical impact of these will be small compared with natural processes such as waves, tides and currents. Some pollution will result from power boat engines, discharge of sewage and from anti-fouling paints. These could be significant in small enclosed marinas, but, in general, will not pose a threat to living resource-conservation.

Scuba divers, snorkellers and collectors could cause local depletion of some species by collecting, and may need to be controlled to avoid the loss of amenity which results from a diverse range of organisms. Bird watching is an activity which can have a beneficial effect from an educational and scientific point of view. Wildfowling and angling were previously covered in the Harvesting section above (see p 297), although the motives for these activities are largely recreational.

Control of recreational activities often rests with the voluntary national bodies which organise the activity, such as the British Sub-Aqua Club and the Royal Yachting Association. These organisations usually take a responsible attitude to the environment and encourage good practices. There are also national regulations governing other recreations such as wildfowling and some forms of angling.

The creation of marine nature reserves may be the best way of reducing the adverse effects of water-based recreations, whilst placing the minimum of restrictions on harmless activities.

Transportation

The seas round the UK, particularly the English Channel and southern North Sea, are the busiest shipping areas in the world. In addition, there is a considerable amount of ferry traffic between Europe and the UK which cuts directly across the main shipping lanes. The hazards associated with this high concentration of shipping include deliberate discharge of waste (which has been dealt with previously in the Waste Disposal section, refuse and oil from ships, p 303), collisions, accidental spillage and loss of cargo overboard, stranding and sinking. Examples of all these have occurred and some, such as the Torrey Canyon and Amoco Cadiz strandings, have had extensive environmental effects.

The most serious ecological impacts so far have been the pollution of shores by major oil spills from stranded oil tankers. It seems that the effects of these are not long-term (Royal Commission on Environmental Pollution, 1981) but in the short- and medium-term there can be considerable damage to littoral communities and shellfish beds. Large numbers of seabirds can also be killed. Apart from oil there are examples of loss of toxic chemicals overboard which will eventually be released into the sea as their containers corrode. There does not appear to be any evidence at present to suggest that these incidents damage the environment, presumably because the diluting and dispersing powers of the sea reduce the concentrations of the pollutants to harmless levels. However, some local damage would be expected if containers break open after being washed ashore.

No legislation can prevent these accidents completely, although the introduction of separation lanes for ships in congested areas, and the increasing efforts to enforce their use, has reduced the risk. Arrangements to compensate for damage by oil spills are also in existence and are administered by the International Oil Pollution Compensation Fund, but these arrangements cannot reduce the impact on the coastal habitats. Local and national authorities have emergency plans for dealing with major oil spills which threaten the coast, but these plans leave much to be desired (Royal Commission on Environmental Pollution, 1981). Part of the problem arises from the responsibility for dealing with oil spills being divided between too many different organisations.

Dredging to improve navigation is a direct consequence of sea transport and is almost always associated with shallow estuaries. It is a long-term activity so there will be permanent destruction of the ecosystem in the limited area of the dredged channels. More widespread effects will arise from the increased turbidity due to the dredging and disposal of the spoil. Generally estuaries have high levels of natural turbidity due to strong tidal currents in the shallow water, and the precipitation of silt brought down by rivers. Consequently, the species present will have a natural tolerance of turbid conditions and will not be affected by the occasional increases due to dredging. Of more significance may be the release of hydrogen sulphide, and organic material with a high BOD. The release of ammonia which occurs has been shown to increase productivity, but whether heavy metals in the sediments will be released is not clear (Cronin, 1975). The dumping of dredging spoil sometimes takes place on adjacent marsh land and this will destroy an important part of the estuarine ecosystem.

Military Activities affecting Water Space

Military activities which use water space include seaward oriented firing ranges, torpedo ranges, and exercise areas for ships and submarines. Although these activities will conflict with many other uses of water space, particularly recreation and fishing, little impact other than the local effects of underwater explosions will occur. The operation of submarines is incompatible with commercial fishing so some effect on the sustainable yield from fish resources may be felt. The isolation of an area by the military from commercial exploitation and recreational pressures can provide a haven for seriously threatened species and a useful area for scientific study.

The Ministry of Defence is not subject to control by planning authorities but public pressure and the influence of recreational organisations can modify its operations.

Miscellaneous

Introduction of Alien Species

There are a number of examples of the successful introduction of alien species for commercial cultivation into UK waters. The Pacific oyster (*Crassostrea gigas*) is widely cultivated in estuaries round the coast. The American hard-shell clam (*Mercenaria mercenaria*) has been introduced in Southampton Water where it now forms a useful addition to the range of edible shellfish. The possibility of introducing a species of Pacific salmon has also been considered but it is thought that it may be a competitor to the Atlantic salmon.

New plant species have also been introduced to stabilise coastlines. An example of this is the planting of the infertile hybrid *Spartina X townsendii*, which unfortunately underwent spontaneous polyploidy to become fertile. From then on it was able to disperse fertile seeds, whereas previously it could only spread by the relatively slow and easily controlled vegetative process. It has become a nuisance on a number of estuaries (eg Welsh Dee) where it enhances siltation.

One of the hazards connected with the introduction of an alien species is that it is not known to what extent it will displace and elminate the native species. Another is the danger of introducing pests and diseases at the same time, to which native species may have no resistance. A third hazard is the accidental introduction of a competitor not present in the original environment. When attempts were made to introduce the American oyster (*Crassostrea virginica*) into Britain at the end of the last century, both the oyster drill (*Urosalpinx cinerea*) and the slipper limpet (*Crepidula fornicata*) were also accidentally introduced (Perkins, 1974). The oyster drill is a predator on shellfish and the slipper limpet competes with oysters both for food and space.

Concern has recently been expressed at suggestions that the giant kelp (*Macrocystis pyrifera*) from California could be usefully grown in European waters as a source of material for the alginate industry. The Japanese seaweed (*Sargassum muticum*) has already arrived by accident in the English Channel (NCC and NERC, 1979) and it is feared that it may displace indigenous algal species.

Introduction of alien animal species is banned under the Wildlife and Countryside Act 1981. The Act also bans the deliberate distribution of the two seaweeds mentioned above.

Reintroduction of Species

In general, the reintroduction of a species to an area from which it has been eliminated would not be a threat to living resources since it should increase diversity. However, it can in some cases be a futile occupation since the loss of the species in the first place may have been the result of change of climate or some other natural change to the habitat. Sometimes, reintroduction is carried out as part of a process of re-establishing an ecosystem which has been destroyed by man. Even here there are problems because it is necessary to reintroduce the whole community, otherwise one species may come to dominate the ecosystem due to the absence of its predators or competitors. In the long-term, however, the original community will probably be re-established although there may be more than one distinct but stable community possible in a given habitat. If this is the case the original community may not be re-established and the new one may have less commercial value.

Control of Predatory Species

The culling of seals is carried out in UK waters as a means of reducing their numbers, since it is known that they are predators on the commercially valuable salmon. Grey seals (*Halichoerus grypus*) are host to the adult stage of the parasitic codworm (*Terranova decipiens*), serious infestations of which can affect the value of fish catches. The methods which may be used for killing seals are strictly controlled by the Conservation of Seals Act 1970, which also establishes a close season for the killing of common (*Phoca vitulina*) and grey seals during which they may only be killed under licence from the Home Office, or DAFS in Scotland. Under this Act, NERC has a statutory responsibility to provide scientific advice to the Secretary of State on the management of seal populations.

Predators such as dolphins or porpoises are not common enough to be thought of as a threat to commercial fisheries in the UK.

Amongst waders only the oystercatcher (*Haematopus ostralegus*) has been regarded as a pest and although the scientific evidence for this was doubtful, 7,000 birds were killed in 1973 and 3,000 in 1974, in order to protect the cockle fishery in Burry Inlet, South Wales (Hale, 1980).

The otter does inhabit the shore line to some extent, and has been hunted partly on account of its consumption of salmon. This species is now protected under the Wildlife and Countryside Act 1981.

Natural Processes

These processes are continuously changing habitats and the communities associated with them. They include storms, waves, currents, and tides, changes in climate and in sea level, and evolution itself. The more obvious changes brought about by these processes are coastal accretion and erosion, and the siltation of estuaries. Winds can also cause sand dune movement on some coasts, which can threaten to overwhelm nearby habitats.

In many cases it is not possible to prevent these changes, but this need not necessarily matter from the point of view of living resource-conservation, since, on balance, there is a dynamic equilibrium in which loss of a habitat in one region is compensated by the appearance of a similar one elsewhere. In some circumstances, however, a particularly rare ecosystem may be threatened and its rarity means that there is only a small chance of a replacement appearing. An example might be the inundation of coastal lagoons or wet slacks by unstable sand dunes lying between them and the sea. Ainsdale Nature Reserve on the Lancashire coast is such a situation. Efforts to stabilise the habitat can also be justified in order to maintain local diversity for educational reasons and because, in the case of rare and isolated habitats, the species present may be genetically distinct. There is evidence that in estuaries, which are often isolated from each other by long stretches of non-brackish water, organisms which appear to be the same species are sufficiently different genetically to be incapable of inter-breeding.

Positive action by government bodies or local authorities is needed to protect rare habitats from man's activities, and occasionally these habitats need protection from natural processes. Often there is very little incentive to do this unless there is a direct threat to an economically valued resource such as housing or agricultural land.

Immigration of new species is also a natural process which may result in increased diversity. Where the new species arrives as a result of a marginal extension of its range, perhaps due to a change of climate, it is unlikely that other species will be completely overwhelmed. The previous species present will probably narrow their range slightly, and may re-establish themselves if the original conditions return. It is to be expected that the distribution of species will fluctuate naturally and too much concern should not be shown towards minor changes in geographical distribution.

Coastal Defence and Maintenance

Natural changes which threaten economically valuable resources are frequently countered by construction of breakwaters, sea walls and groynes. These are used to prevent inundation of low lying and subsiding land, and to stabilise river mouths where these provide the entrance to ports. Dredging is a counter to the natural siltation of harbours. Vegetation can sometimes be planted as an alternative to engineering works to stabilise sand dunes and mobile spits. Since the purpose behind these activities is the maintenance of the existing state no living resources will be threatened unless major construction works are undertaken, or part of the defensive scheme involves separation of intertidal areas from the sea by sea walls. Frequently, engineering works constructed to stabilise a coastline or habour can create a new artificial environment which increases local diversity.

Coastal defence operations are carried out by local authorities who are responsible for the protection from erosion of land above sea level, and water authorities who are responsible for sea defence. In addition, various dock, port, harbour and navigation authorities possess statutory powers in relation to sea defence within their particular areas.

Scientific Studies

Organisations involved with specific studies of the sea include universities, polytechnics, government funded bodies such as MAFF, NERC and its associated laboratories, water authorities and independent organisations.

These activities can have a number of minor adverse impacts on the environment due to the need to gain access with equipment and set up experiments, and the need to take samples. However, the increased understanding of the marine environment which results is a major contribution to living resource-conservation. This activity needs to be encouraged.

Educational Activities

Universities, polytechnics and schools are involved in marine environmental education, and field centres exist at a number of coastal sites in order to cover the practical aspects of the subject. Habitats round these field centres are under pressure due to the increased access and collecting, although attempts to limit the impact of the latter are made.

Education on environmental problems is of great importance and needs to be encouraged in order to increase the understanding of ecological problems by all groups of society. The desirable effects include a reduction of damage by individuals, a greater acceptability of legislation to protect the environment, and early attention being drawn to damaging activities. If environmental education can get through to decision makers it should result in more balanced decisions on matters affecting living resources.

References

BLAXTER, K. 1981. Food chains in human nutrition. Essex, Applied-Science.

BRANDER, K. 1981. The disappearance of the common skate *raia batis* from the Irish Sea. *Nature, 290*, 48.

BROWN, C G and BENNETT, D B. 1981. *J Cons int Explor, Ner, 39*, 88.

CHAPMAN, V J and CHAPMAN, D J. 1980. Seaweeds and their uses. London, Chapman and Hall.

CLARK, P J and DENNIS, J A N. 1980. Report on the wave energy programme of the UK ECOR Conference. London, Institution of Civil Engineers. April.

CORLETT, J. 1979. The likely consequences of barrages on estuarine biology. *In Tidal power and estuarine management, Scientechnica.* Bristol.

CRAMP, S, BOURNE, W R P and SAUNDERS, D. 1974. The threats to seabirds. *The seabirds of Britain and Ireland.* London, Collins.

CRONAN, D S. 1980. Underwater minerals. London, Academic Press.

CRONIN L E. (editor). 1975. Estuarine research. Vol. II. New York, Academic Press.

CUSHING, D H. 1980. European fisheries. *Marine Poll Bull, 11*, 311.

DAAN, N. 1980. A review of replacement of depleted stocks by other species and the mechanism underlying such replacement. *Rapp P-v Reun Cons int Explor Mer, 177*, 405.

DAINTITH, T and WILLOUGHY, G D M. 1977. United Kingdom oil and gas law. London, Oyez.

DE GROOT, S J. 1980. The consequences of marine gravel extraction on the spawning of herring *clupea harengus. J Fish Biol, 16,* 605.

DEPARTMENT OF THE ENVIRONMENT and WELSH OFFICE. 1970. Taken for granted. Report of the Working Party on Sewage Disposal. London, HMSO.

DEPARTMENT OF ENVIRONMENT. 1977. Environmental standards — a description of United Kingdom practice. *Pollution paper no 11.* HMSO.

EAGLE, R A, HARIMAN, P A, NORTON, M G, NUNNY, R S and ROLFT, M S. 1979. Fisheries research technical report no 51. MAFF.

FRANKLIN, A. 1972. Laboratory leaflet no 26. MAFF.

GERLACH, S A. 1981. Marine Pollution. Berlin, Springer-Verlag.

GROSS, F. 1947. Proceedings of the Royal Society of Edinburgh B. *63,* 1.

GROVE-PALMER, C O J. 1980. Ocean energy resources — winds tides waves. A review of UK programmes. ECOR Conference. London, Institution of Civil Engineers. April.

HALE, W G. 1980. Waders, 259. London, Collins.

HARVEY, G. 1979. Fish farmer. *3,* 8.

HEAP, D. 1981. Encyclopaedia of planning law and practice. *2.* London, Sweet and Maxwell.

HUNT, G J. 1980. Aquatic environment monitoring report no *4.* MAFF.

MILLS, S. 1982. New Scientist, *11 Feb,* 364.

MINISTRY OF AGRICULTURE, FISHERIES AND FOOD (MAFF). 1981. Atlas of the seas round the British Isles.

MINISTRY OF HOUSING AND LOCAL GOVERNMENT. 1967. Dee crossing study, phase 1. HMSO.

MITCHELL, R. 1978. Naure conservation implications of hydraulic engineering schemes affecting British estuaries. *Hydrobiol bull, 12,* 333.

MITCHELL, R, PROBERT, P K. 1981. Severn tidal power — the natural environment. NCC.

MITCHELL, R, PROBERT, P K, MCKIRDY, A P and DOODY, J P. 1981. Severn tidal power — nature conservation. NCC.

NATURE CONSERVANCY COUNCIL (NCC) and NATURAL ENVIRONMENT RESEARCH COUNCIL (NERC). 1979. Nature conservation in the marine environment.

NATURAL ENVIRONMENT RESEARCH COUNCIL (NERC). 1976. The Wash water storage scheme feasibility study: a report on the ecological studies. *Publication series C, no 15.*

PERKINS, E J. 1974. The biology of estuaries and coastal waters, 409. London and New York, Academic Press.

PICKETT, G D. 1973. Laboratory leaflet no 29. MAFF.

PORTMANN, J E and NORTON, M G. 1981. Chemistry and industry. 285.

PROBERT, P K and MITCHELL, R. 1979. Nature conservation implications of siting wave energy extractors off the Outer Hebrides. NCC.

PURDOM. C E. 1979. Fish farming in the UK — a view from the government. *Biologist, 26,* 153-157.

REAY, P J. 1979. Aquaculture. *Institute of Biology Studies in Biology 106.* London, Edward Arnold.

ROUND, F E. 1965. The biology of algae. London, Edward Arnold.

ROYAL COMMISSION ON ENVIRONMENTAL POLLUTION. 1981. 8th report, oil pollution of the seas. HMSO.

RUSSELL, F S and YONGE, C M. 1975. The seas. London, Warne.

SIBTHORPE, M M. (editor). 1975. The North Sea — challenge and opportunity, 18. London, Europa.

TAYLOR, P J. 1982. The impact of nuclear water disposals to the marine environment. *Political Ecology Research Group report Rb-8.*

VOLKER, A. 1974. In Funnel and Hey (editors). The management of water resources in England and Wales. Saxon House.

WATER RESOURCES BOARD. 1966. Morcambe Bay Barrage. *Publication no 2.* HMSO.

WATER RESOURCES BOARD. 1972. Morcambe Bay Estuary Storage. *Publication no 13.* HMSO.

WILKINSON, T G. 1982. Chemistry and industry, 115-123.

WILLEMSEN, J. 1979. The influence of cooling water discharge on fish. *Hydrobiol Bull, 13,* 94.

WISDOM, A S. 1979. The law of rivers and watercourses. London, Shaw and Sons Ltd.

APPENDIX E
WRITTEN RESPONSES

Written responses were received from the following:

J A Allen *Marine Biological Station, Millport*
M V Angel *Institute of Oceanographic Sciences, Wormley*
J M Baker *Field Studies Council*
D J Bays *Association of County Councils*
G H Bielly *South West Water Authority*
D Buckanan *Highland River Purification Board*
G K Burgess *Cornwall County Council*
R B Clark *The University, Newcastle upon Tyne*
J J Connell *Torry Research Station, Aberdeen*
J Corlett *Ambleside, Cumbria*
Council for Environmental Conservation
Lord Cranbrook *Saxmundham, Suffolk*
D H Durbin *Chichester Harbour Conservancy*
G E Eden *The Institute of Water Pollution Control*
B Furniss *Gloucester County Council*
P S Ganderton *Queen Mary's College, Basingstoke, Hampshire*
J C Goldsmith *Department of the Environment, Tollgate House, Bristol*
K Hiscock *Oil Pollution Research Unit, Pembroke*

C P James *Solway River Purification Board*
R C Kenyon *North Yorkshire County Council*
A J Lebrecht *MAFF, Horseferry Road, London*
G L Mann *Shetlands Islands Council*
B W Oakley *Science and Engineering Research Council*
J Phillips *Crown Estate Commissioners*
D N Potter *Huntingdon District Council*
A Preston *MAFF, Horseferry Road, London*
M J Rogers *The National Trust*
I G Simmons *The University, Durham*
A J Smith *Bristol Ports Association*
H D Smith *University of Wales Institute of Science and Technology*
J K Smith *ICI Petrochemicals and Plastics Division*
E H Staite *Institute of Fisheries Management*
J Swift *The British Association for Shooting and Conservation*
D L Walker *National Water Council*
B C Wallace *Fife Regional Council*
E Young, Lady Kennet *Bayswater Road, London.*

PART 5
INTERNATIONAL

The UK's Overseas Environmental Policy

A report by J R Sandbrook

Acknowledgements

This report was made possible by way of considerable assistance from others.

Dr Ian Barrett acted as a tireless research assistant in the early stages; my colleagues in the International Institute for Environment and Development provided much of the background material and advice on the structure; the study conducted by the University of East Anglia's Overseas Development Group underpins the section on British aid; and Jim MacNeill and the OECD Environment Secretariat provided much of the inspiration for the overall approach taken. The Review Group called together to help draft this report provided a valuable sense of perspective and detailed criticisms of the drafts. In the production of the report, the secretarial staff, namely Annie and Sue at IIED, and Margaret and Colleen at NCC, deserve real thanks for they have coped with frequent amendments to draft upon draft. Finally, a vote of thanks to my wife who put up with a winter of silent evenings when much of the work was done.

Chairman's Introduction

The Review Group met early in 1982 to consider a substantial draft of the report concerned with international issues relating to conservation and development. The group as a whole was impressed by the general direction proposed by the author, and there was strong endorsement for the overall framework and approach. Subsequently the members made many specific suggestions which were incorporated.

The Group particularly supported the thesis that the United Kingdom is in a strong position to respond positively to issues raised in the World Conservation Strategy. It strongly supports the practical proposals that are contained in the recommendations.

I would like to express the personal hope that the report will stimulate the UK to take a much more active part in the international debate. Conservation views which are expressed so vigorously in the national setting need to be broadened and refined and then applied to the cultural problems that exist in the rest of the world. This report should be seen as part of that process.

James Porter
February, 1983

CHAPTER 1

INTRODUCTION

Why Should we Bother?

1. This report is one of a group of seven (Parts 1 to 7 of this book) arising from the requirement to work out the implications for the United Kingdom of the World Conservation Strategy.[1] The Strategy was generally welcomed by the British Government after its launch in 1981, but no formal analysis of its implications has followed. Full compliance with the Strategy involves the formulation, at least in outline, of an overseas environmental policy for the UK, bringing together the many domestic policies, programmes and public interests which affect environmental or conservation problems overseas.

2. Such a policy is made necessary by the plain facts of global interdependence. The United Kingdom is in part reliant upon the rest of the world about it for food, energy and industrial raw materials. In turn, it requires markets for its output of finished goods and services. It is a part of interdependent natural and economic systems; it can not ignore the condition of each of these. Appendix A sets out the trends in the natural system. It clearly shows that there is a marked deterioration in the physical, biological and human conditions of the planet.

3. Framing an overseas environmental policy to address this deterioration involves setting out the full rationale for it; defining the potential for action; putting the policy into context; reviewing the components of our current national effort and making recommendations for improvement. All of this is done, in this report, in relation to the objectives of the World Conservation Strategy.

4. The report by no means completes the tasks but it does show that a UK overseas environmental policy is already taking shape, however unconsciously, partly in response to international institutions and conventions, partly in response to requests for development assistance and partly in the course of internal coordination. Only, however, when the parts are brought into open relationship are we able to gain the advantages of having a coherent policy as opposed to one that is *ad hoc*. Only by grouping the parts can we assess consistencies and inconsistencies, correct anomalies, monitor progress, measure costs and benefits, and detect gaps which need filling, duplications which can be corrected and adaptations or expansions which may prove justified.

5. The condition of the world's natural resources, both biological and non-renewable, is of fundamental concern to us all. Consideration of our national responsibility for their custody cannot be avoided. It is necessary to have a policy for carrying out that responsibility and it needs to be open. In particular, public understanding can be improved, uninformed criticism dealt with, and due credit taken for what is being done, if necessary, through the issue of a Green or White Paper.

6. In such ways, Ministers can be better served and progress made towards the integration of environmental policy and organisation within the overall framework of Government. The contents of this report are marshalled to exhibit this process; in order to keep it concise and easy to follow, much relevant detail is presented separately in a series of Appendices.

Economic and Ecological Interdependence

7. The World Conservation Strategy sets out the broad global objectives of:
   □ Maintaining essential ecological processes and life support systems (agricultural systems, forests, coastal, freshwater systems, the oceans and the atmosphere).
   □ The preservation of genetic diversity.
   □ The sustainable use by humans of species and ecosystems.
It assumes that it is in the interests of all peoples to pursue these objectives, not least because the condition of the earth is ultimately of concern to all of us.

8. Two other recent reports, the Brandt report 'North-South: a programme for Survival' (1980)[2] and the 'Global 2000' report to the President of USA (1980),[3] also promote the interdependence line of argument, and all three, taken together, add up to a powerful statement on the matter. Yet we are living in a time when many nation states are becoming demonstrably less concerned about what is going on outside their own borders or, at least, are more keen to orientate their overseas policy to enhance domestic economic and military security rather than anything else. The response to an increasingly difficult world, consisting of more and more people and fewer and fewer resources *per capita*, is often one of retrenchment. Understandably, when one is in economic difficulty at home the political priority is the home front.

9. This is despite the fact that the current world order, a consequence of growing not declining interdependence, is now under serious strain and there is little evidence to suggest that matters are going to get easier. One suggested solution is to isolate ourselves from the poor world: to delink. But if the British nation decided to isolate itself, perhaps together with its partners in Europe or in the Organisation for Economic Co-operation and Development (OECD), in terms of financial flows, energy supply, food and other renewable and non-renewable resources, such a future would be both bleak, unstable and morally unacceptable. OECD States rely upon the developing countries for 29 per cent (1980) of their primary product imports, excluding fuels, and for 26 per cent of their manufactured exports. In the case of Britain we export some 30 per cent (1979) of our visible exports to the Third World. Of our total foreign investment, excluding oil and insurance sectors, some 25 per cent is based outside the OECD and Warsaw Pact area. In short, our economy is closely linked to the rest of the world, both rich and poor, and there is no sign of a divorce.

10. Economic interdependence cannot be isolated from the moral argument for the global approach. No one better expresses the point than Barbara Ward writing in the foreword to *Down to Earth* by Erik Eckholm (1982): 'No matter how much we try to think of ourselves as separate sovereign entities, nature itself reminds us of humanity's basic unity. The vision of unity shared by so many of the great philosophers and so central to all the great religions is recognised now as an inescapable scientific fact'.[4]

11. The strategic case for global interdependence is becoming increasingly powerful too. The Brandt Commission stated that: 'few threats to peace and survival of the human community are greater than those posed by the prospects of cumulative and irreversible degradation of the biosphere on which human life depends', and, later in the book, 'our survival depends not only on military balance, but on global cooperation to ensure a sustainable biological environment, and sustainable prosperity based on equitably shared resources'.[5]

12. Clearly by no means all adverse environmental (or economic) changes are of direct strategic risk to us in the UK. The condition of the air we breathe (by way of pollutants and the consequences of war) and the security of our sources of food, energy and raw materials are of primary concern. But even remote local environmental damage is of some concern. Local problems all too easily ripple towards us in the longer-term. (See Appendix A and Chapter 3 Section 2, pp 328-330 of this report for a further elaboration of the point.)

13. The strategic risk of global environmental damage is growing but, as yet, is hardly articulated. We are all increasingly vulnerable, in some degree, to the rising world population, the possible threats to the condition of our atmosphere, to disputes over resources and their supply and the massive and often irreversible environmental damage that goes relentlessly on day by day.

14. In a short report prepared in Japan under the chairmanship of Okita, its former Finance Minister, the conclusion was as follows: 'It is an extremely difficult task to secure, for the increasing numbers of people, sufficient resources to maintain peaceful and decent human lives for the future. Under increasing pressures of population, it is probable that further deterioration of the human environment will take place on a global scale. There is concern that once such deterioration progresses beyond certain limits, recovery will become extremely difficult and the earth's life-support capacity will be reduced. Steps must be taken to counter this deterioration before it is too late. It will require the combined efforts and wisdom of every nation on the basis of a recognition that preserving the global environment is in the interest of all' (The Okita Report, 1980).[6]

The Need for Action

15. However, as the World Conservation Strategy points out, it is not the recognition of such a complex set of interrelated problems that provides a solution.

16. We are all in great danger of becoming bored with the restatement of the problems on a global scale. The slogans, catch words and metaphors are beginning to lose their attraction and effectiveness. How small is beautiful? What future shock and when? Limits to whose growth and of what kind? 'As the cliches become media events in themselves, perhaps unwittingly we have obscured the pluralism and the complexity of the real issues of population growth, resource-management and the inequitable division of wealth' (Harland Cleveland, 1981).[7] Many have come to see that it is time to start work energetically on some of the components of the solution, rather than merely to talk of the problems.

17. But there are still plenty who ignore the problems overall or find excuses to do nothing dramatic or comprehensive. Again, Harland Cleveland has said: 'Governments, as we all know, are too responsible to take the responsibility for change'.[8] This seems to be particularly so in the UK where it is a tradition of our establishment to react quietly to problems rather than to charge ahead with highly publicised new initiatives. Thus, our civil servants, politicians and academics have not been notable for leading the crusade of global environmental concern. It may well turn out to be a case of the tortoise and the hare, for once the nation is mobilised in a particular direction it is enormously resourceful, consistent and practical. But even so, it does seem to take an inordinately long time to first convince UK Governments and commercial interests of many of the trends and, second, to act. To take contemporary examples: the condition of the ozone layer, acid rain in Europe and the lead in the atmosphere from vehicle exhausts. In each case the UK has been reticent and accordingly misunderstood by its neighbours.

18. When the issues relate to more distant lands the

arguments needed to justify action and expenditure become all the more difficult to muster. Why, for example, should the UK Government care about the destruction of the rain forests? After all, the erosion of the world's genetic stock has little direct impact on the UK's economy. Why should the tax payer be asked to pay for clean water supply in the Third World when there is a clear reluctance to invest in our own municipal system?

19. It is too easy to blame the politicians and their civil servants. Democratically elected politicans respond to expressed political pressure and, while there is some public concern for the plight of the world's poor — and probably far more for the plight of the world's flora and fauna — there is hardly an overriding clamour for political and administrative change on either ground. Even the environmentalists traditionally have been far more concerned about domestic issues (for example, the health risks of nuclear power as opposed to the millions who already die of water-borne diseases). The chosen environmental *cause célèbre* is rarely, if ever, global and seldom based on a rational analysis of environmental, economic or strategic risks.

Down to Earth

20. Part of the difficulty is that it is impossible to assess the risks that some of us fear. Our understanding of the state of the environment, most particularly in the developing countries, is very scant indeed. In the expert assessment of the state of the world's environment in 1982, performed for the United Nations Environment Programme (UNEP) by Dr Martin Holdgate (UK), Professor Mohamed Kassas (Egypt) and Professor Gilbert White (USA)[9] the conclusion is blunt. They suggest that, on a world scale, we know much about atmospheric trends (CO_2, ozone, turbidity and precipitation chemistry), of food contamination trends (heavy metals, organochlorines) and that we are reasonably informed about the distribution and flow of fresh water. The state of forest cover is becoming better known (but is still an area of some dispute); regionally, we have a good idea of the condition of certain seas, of atmospheric pollutants and their movement and of land-use patterns. But there are vast areas of ignorance. For example, there is little reliable data on the pollution of the oceans, and on the condition of ground waters. Our understanding of desertification rates, the condition of rangelands, farmlands, and other major land-use categories is patchy and incomplete.

21. In contrast, information on human activities, including those that affect the environment, is better. Information on food production, fishery statistics, trade statistics, and information on energy production and use are extensive. Demographic data are quite good, but disease data are often poor. At a national level, and perhaps even more importantly at a local level, our understanding of environmental change and the rate at which it is occurring is very poor indeed.

22. The obvious conclusion is that too little is being done to establish the hard facts and then to bring the issues onto the political agenda in a form that is not just a meaningless restatement of 'global this and that'. Issues, trends, policies and actions now have to be defined in a disaggregated form and in a way that does not result in helplessness and despair. A concerted effort at public education is needed if sacrifices are to be made by this nation on behalf of others. Strident idealism and exaggeration are of little use once the work has begun.

It is Up to Us

23. At the special session of UNEP in 1982, 10 years after the Stockholm conference on the Human environment, Tom King, MP, the then Minister for Local Government and Environment Services, stated: 'The vision at Stockholm was that once problems were identified, they would be solved, that the power of the world's institutions would meet the challenges of the environment. Ten years later, much buffeted by economic and energy crises, we need to restore that vision'.

24. Tom King went on to ask: 'Do we need new principles? Are not the Stockholm principles as valid now as when first decided? Do we need a new action plan? I think not. The truth is that it is not more words we need but more action in carrying them out'.

25. In the decade after the Stockholm conference, it is true that much talking has followed, accompanied by *some* action. However, new insights and attitudes have emerged since the Stockholm conference that could make a great difference to our future, and events have not been insignificant either. For example, during the decade the number of States with governmental institutions dealing with environmental management has grown from 15 to 115 countries (1980). Much domestic environmental legislation has followed. At an international level, the UNEP has been established and it has tried, and to an extent succeeded, in carrying forward a range of substantive environmental reforms. The EEC has recently agreed its Third Environmental Action Programme which includes radical proposals for environmental coordination in Europe and an important chapter on environmental policy outside the Ten. The OECD has begun to debate many of the issues at a ministerial level. The nine leading multilateral lending banks have signed a declaration on the environment (see Appendix F of this report). Many, if not all, of the bilateral aid agencies are trying to integrate environmental considerations into their procedures. The world has seen a series of high level UN conferences all relevant to the issues: for example the Population Conference, the Food Conference, the Human Settlements Conference, the Water Conference, the Tropical Rain Forest Conference, and the New and Renewable Energy Conference. All were pregnant with

worthy environmental recommendations. But, most significantly, there is beginning to be a fundamental shift in political attitudes.

26. In 1972, many influential people in the developing world considered that the environment issue was, amongst other things, yet another attempt by the North to impose trade barriers, by way of expensive pollution controls, on the South. Indeed many in the North did regard environment as being synonymous with pollution. But gradually these two attitudes have shifted.

27. In Nairobi at the tenth anniversary session of Stockholm in 1982 not one developing country raised the pollution issues in these terms. Without exception, Governments expressed concern at the damage being done to their countries' environments which adversely affect their development and the condition of many of their peoples' lives. They called for help.

28. The North has also been jolted into considering the longer-term by the publicity given to, for example, the outer limit theories of the computer modellers — in particular by *Limits to Growth* (1973).[10] The 1972 Organisation of Petroleum Exporting Countries (OPEC) action caused many to consider our economic dependence on raw material suppliers. The sub-Sahelian drought vividly brought the plight of destitute people to our television screens. The rising carbon dioxide levels and the condition of the ozone layer have caused much comment about climate trends and artificial changes to the biosphere.

29. Many Governments and many more people have come to realise that we can not isolate ourselves from the widespread destruction of humanity's resource-base that continues largely unabated.

The New Consensus?

30. As a result there is perhaps more of a consensus on how to proceed into the last few years of this century than 10 years ago. The following points have emerged from Stockholm and after:

(a) Slowing down the rate of the world population growth is an essential goal to solving so many of the problems of developing countries and regions. It is difficult if not impossible to achieve this without an improvement in the wealth and welfare of the world's poorest peoples. Development is the priority for them.

(b) Sound development is not necessarily slowed down by environmental concern but it is demonstrably made more lasting and durable by way of it.

(c) The consideration and integration of natural constraints within economic plans for development is not easy, but is an essential step in the longer-term. Short-term economic benefits have to be weighted with longer-term environmental costs.

(d) The unacceptable position of the world's poor is amongst the most serious global environmental problems we face. Poverty (particularly amongst the rural poor) is a powerful agent of environmental destruction.

(e) The developed world must adjust its economy to much less wasteful, resource-intensive and damaging activity whilst the developing world must respect the carrying capacity of its natural systems.

(f) The world now desperately needs skilled manpower, and money to move the ideas of sustainable development forward into substantive action.

31. The environment is not the only concern. Central to this paper is the concept of sustainable development underpinned by 'sound natural resource-management'. The two are mutually dependent. The UK is, and should be, concerned with both. The rationale for the UK's concern with both is based on the concept of global interdependence: moral/economic/strategic. Our involvement with both sustainable development and natural resource-management should be manifested in terms of our domestic policies and by how we interact with the world around us, as expressed in our overseas environmental policy.

Notes and References

1 The World Conservation Strategy was prepared and published by the International Union for the Conservation of Nature and Natural Resources in cooperation with the World Wildlife Fund and the United Nations Environment Programme.

2 BRANDT COMMISSION. 1980. North-South, a programme for survival. Pan Books.

3 US DEPARTMENT OF STATE AND COUNCIL ON ENVIRONMENTAL QUALITY. 1980. The Global 2000 report to the President: entering the twenty-first century. US Government Printing Office, ref no 0-274-484. Also published as a Penguin paperback, London 1981.

4 ECKHOLM, E. 1982. Down to earth. Pluto Press.

5 Down to earth, *ibid*.

6 OKITA, S. 1980. The Okita report — basic directions in coping with global environmental issues. Japan, Department of Environment.

7 CLEVELAND, H. 1981. A review of the Global 2000 report. Hubert Humphrey Institute of Public Affairs.

8 A review of the Global 2000 report, *ibid*.

9 HOLDGATE, M W *et al*. (editors). 1982. The world environment 1972-1982: a report by the United Nations Environment Programme. Tycooly Int Pub Ltd.

10 MEADOWS, D *et al*. 1973. Limits to growth. Earth Island Ltd.

CHAPTER 2
THE FOREIGN POLICY APPROACH

Introduction

1. The general deterioration of the world's environment is of concern to much of the UK public and, no doubt, to the Government. But how can the UK do more; indeed, how is it already involved?

2. There are two ways of addressing the question. The first is to reduce the impact the UK has on foreign environments, albeit of a secondary nature, by way of its domestic policies. The second is to enhance the direct and highly beneficial impact we might have by way of various components of our foreign policy.

3. The most obvious adverse effects in the former category arise as a result of our population density (one of the highest in the world) and our advanced stage of industrial development. To survive, the UK has to import. Thus we are a net importer of food, of raw materials (mineral and renewable) and, before the end of the decade, of hydrocarbon fuels (see 'Resourceful Britain'). To pay for our food and raw materials we need to export finished goods and services. It would be quite wrong to suggest that this trade is environmentally bad *per se*. But we should be aware that our imported gain in, say, tropical hardwoods, may be some remote forest's loss. Or our need for exotic out-of-season vegetables may be one less area of tropical land put over to food self-reliance.

4. The overseas impacts of our trade and investments are beyond the scope of this account, although the environmental performance of UK domiciled industry is briefly enlarged upon in Chapter 5 of this report. The essential point for the purposes of this report is that the UK needs a stable and growing world economy if it is to survive. The fundamental purpose of our foreign policy is to secure such stability. Stability is based upon the creation of, and the support by others for, political and economic regimes that are based on democracy and sustainable (and hence environmentally sensitive) development policies. For this reason, the ideas and methods set out in the World Conservation Strategy (WCS) to these very ends are also central to our foreign policy.

5. Our environmental performance at home is not without significance in the equation. We can hardly object to resource-destruction and waste abroad if we are profligate at home. We cannot expect to control harmful pollutants for our own people, yet export the same chemicals for use elsewhere. However, such domestic policy questions are the subject of other reports in this book.

Our Responsibilities

6. There are five basic areas of positive action within our foreign policy which require consideration. These can be viewed as the UK's responsibilities to the world community in furtherance of environmentally sound development. They are as follows:
   (a) To ensure that development takes place in the poorer countries and, so far as we have any influence, that this be along sustainable lines.
   (b) To work consistently within international bodies so that the theme of the WCS is pursued.
   (c) To advise and guide dependent territories so that they develop without destruction.
   (d) To encourage the many overseas environmental activities of the UK non-Governmental organisations and institutions.
   (e) To work with UK Industry so that it operates at a high environmental standard in developing countries.

Each of these responsibilities will be dealt with in later chapters. But first it is necessary to set out the principles and constraints that apply.

Basic Considerations

7. In considering our relations with overseas States, there is only one practical position to take, namely: that the UK shall do all it can to enhance the capacity of overseas Governments and peoples to manage their environments better and to plan development within natural resource constraints for themselves.

8. The WCS addresses many global environmental issues within a global development context (see Appendix B of this report for the principal issues raised) but it does not address specific national environmental policies in a domestic or overseas development context. It calls on others to do so.

9. One suspects that if the authors had attempted to reconcile national development aspirations and national environmental practice with global conservation goals, then the document would have been far more controversial. For such a reconciliation would be impossible without addressing difficult questions and making choices on how to answer them. Four are given as examples:

(a) At what point does an environmental problem cease to be only a concern of the nation-state which claims or exercises jurisdiction over the affected resources? To take a case in point. The UK may object very strongly to the way in which Brazil treats its tropical rain forests, but, at the end of the day, current law and practice indicates that the forests are under Brazil's jurisdiction, no matter what the UK may think or say.

(b) To what extent is bad environmental practice and resource-destruction merely a reflection of the underlying economic position of nation-states? The strategy only goes to the point of saying long-term sustainable development is better than the short-term 'go for growth' approach, and that we should focus on the ingredients of the Third UN Development Decade. But any useful analysis of the reasons for natural resource-destruction would have to include questions of wealth distribution *within* and *between* nations. In turn, this implies an examination of the terms of trade between nations, not only to isolate direct environmental effects (for example, the clearing of rain forests to make way for export-led stock rearing), but also indirect effects (for example, a poor balance of payments position that arguably leads to over-use of wood as fuel with great consequential environmental damage). Or, alternatively, the falling price (in relative terms) of key commodity crops arguably increases the use of land for these rather than food crops which in turn increases food imports into countries that should be self-sufficient. The interactions are endless.

(c) How capable are many nation-states of managing their environments even if they wanted to? Do they have the necessary laws? Are the laws enforced or does corruption or simple neglect make them valueless? Does the country have the technical 'infrastructure' to monitor, assess and control problems?

(d) Finally, do people place the same value on environmental goods and hence make the same choices about environmental policy as the authors of the Strategy? What of different creeds, political ideologies and priorities? The Soviet Union, for example, does not appear to have the same attitude to the exploitation of fish stocks as ourselves; nor the Japanese to the exploitation of the great whales.

10. Answers to these questions were avoided in the Strategy in the interest of presenting global conservation issues in a crisp, engaging and non-controversial manner.

This was both sensible and defensible, but when it comes to the foreign environmental policy of a specific country, such as the UK, we cannot ignore them. It is not enough to say what is happening but why it is happening.

11. A further difficulty is the very diversity of the planet. The real world is not a homogeneous place divided into two halves: the North and South. Apart from the obvious physical and biological diversity, the politics, economics and sociology of regions, nations, countries, cities, and even neighbouring villages, vary. Concepts such as 'North' and 'South', and rich and poor are convenient as shorthand, and as a way of making points. But they are redundant, even misleading, when trying to organise a workable approach. Policies have to be flexible to meet different physical, biological, social, economic and political conditions. There is no one way, no universal approach.

12. Furthermore, the approach cannot be fixed in time. We are dealing with dynamic processes. Physical processes have long timescales; biological processes involve constantly shifting equilibria, or points of balance, but change slowly overall. Artificial processes change more rapidly but not nearly as rapidly as many would like to suppose. The approach must recognise how long changes take to come about or to achieve. The direction or trends in the world are the immediate concerns.

A Case in Point and Constraints

13. In development questions, the gulf that lies between the ideal and the politically acceptable is often very wide. A recent example that illustrates this is the commentary that has followed the Brandt report. Amongst other things the report was a bold attempt to restate the imperative for development assistance and to renew concern for the position of the world's poor. Its impact was dramatic in comparison to any recent issue-raising exercise. To have a summit conference called in response to a report of an independent, albeit notable, group of persons is not something that advocates of any cause often achieve.

14. The major critics of Brandt belonged to the 'monetarist school' of economic thought. Some in the development community had their doubts, though few expressed them forcefully. An exception was Dudley Seers,[1] a 'devoted developmentalist' from the Institute of Development Studies (IDS) in Sussex. His basic criticisms, apart from those that can broadly be described as economic, remind us of the real world and fall into four categories:

(a) There is no reason, if one is interested in the plight of the poor, to put all the blame for the current state of affairs on the peoples of the North. The South has more than its fair share of very rich, very corrupt, undemocratic people (and rulers) who do much to prevent the relief of poverty at home. Ignoring the unpleasant realities of the South will not help.

(b) The difficulty we all face is the reconciliation of divergent interests. For the North there is the risk of 'matters getting out of hand'. Retaining control on substantive interests (such as the massive debts from South to North) is the motivation that will perhaps move the North to make real concessions; arguments of mutual interest muddled with morality will not.

(c) The interests (and hence conflicts) of the South *and* the North have to be understood to be accommodated. Many of these are divergent within the North and South. They are very heterogeneous. All are in need of a down to earth and balanced assessment in terms of economic, social and political realities. This work has hardly begun.

(d) The unrealistic targets of the 1960s and 1970s need to be abandoned. Targets for aid, (which Her Majesty's Government accepts at 0.7 per cent of GNP by an unspecified date), Lima Resolutions and the New International Economic Order do not mean anything any more to any significant political force in the North. Reprehensible though this attitude may be, it is clearly the dominant view. To ignore it is to be unrealistic. Idealised demands divert attention from creating an international order that is at least viable. Attention should now be focused on the emergency programme of Brandt and separated from targets for massive transfers.

15. In effect, the overall, foreign policy approach to be taken can not be ideological. There are four challenges to be faced in framing the approach. First, it must be sufficiently down to earth and practical to be politically realistic. Second, it must be honest, and recognise the world as it is and not as armchair critics or idealists imagine it to be. Third, it must be motivated. At every turn the basis for acting at all must be explained to those overseas and to the taxpayers at home. Fourth, it must be comprehensive so that the many points of interaction and impact are encompassed.

What in this Context does the Environment and Sustainable Development Encompass?

16. The student of international environmental affairs is faced with an alarming array of institutions, conventions, treaties and pathways dealing with environmental questions. The very word 'environment' has become an all-encompassing term, used by advertising executives, heating engineers and research ecologists alike.

17. One reason for the apparent lack of interest of Governments in the WCS relates to this question of definition. To many, the matters that the WCS is trying to address are not clear. One commentator put it rather more cynically: 'what exactly is it *not* trying to correct?' It is true that, at first sight, the text encompasses so

many disciplines, issues and concerns (for example, planning as we know it in the UK, ecological science, agricultural science, water management, fisheries policy, rural development policy, and even industrial and energy policy questions) that the reader is left bemused.

18. In order to achieve some sense of order this report assumes the scope of the WCS as being on three distinct levels. First, there are the environmental objectives which are a part of 'sustainable development'. (This term is vague but generally implies development that includes the rational use of resources, that does not erode the natural resource-base on which it is founded and on which life ultimately depends.)

19. The environmental objectives are three in number:

(a) to maintain essential ecological processes and life-support systems (Section 2 of the WCS);

(b) to preserve genetic diversity (Section 3 of the WCS); and

(c) to ensure the sustainable use of species and ecosystems (Section 4 of the WCS).

The arguments in favour of these priorities are not repeated here as the WCS itself sets them out very adequately.

20. The second level of objectives is concerned with the complementary concern for development policies that reduce the current plight of the very poor: we need development policies that reach the poor for it is they who are eroding their natural resource-base simply because they have no other option. They are forced to live off the Earth's 'capital stock' rather than its 'interest' or 'recurrent income'. For them, sustainable development implies development that meets their basic human needs and lifts them out of the resource-destroying trap that they are in (see Appendix C of this report for a summary of the basic human needs approach).

21. The third objective is concerned with the means. We need an organised and cooperative approach to the environment and development in order to carry out a whole series of rather mundane and practical tasks. They are the 'sound environmental practices' the WCS talks of. These are the mechanisms for change.

22. In Section 20 of the WCS, these tasks are listed in a somewhat random order as 'priority requirements — national and international actions'. Appendix B to this report sets them out again in tabular form indicating which might be priorities for our foreign environmental policy and the technical disciplines involved in their execution. The one-line descriptions of the task are necessarily bland, but a reference back to the WCS (the section and paragraph number is given) will clarify what is implied.

Notes and References

1 SEERS, D. 1980. North-South: muddling morality and mutuality. *Third World Quarterly, October, 11 (4).*

CHAPTER 3

THE COMPONENTS OF THE POLICY

The Need for Integration

1. If we assume that this country has a basic interest in forwarding the type of objectives set out in the previous chapter, the next step is to take stock of the relevant current policies and define where they need to change. There are six areas of analysis that follow:

☐ **Section 1**: The UK's Aid and Development Assistance Posture — the current approach.

☐ **Section 2**: The UK as a member of OECD — where a change can be usefully defined.

☐ **Section 3**: The UK as a member of the EEC — a major focus for action?

☐ **Section 4**: The UK and the UN family of agencies — the dialogue between rich and poor and direct action.

☐ **Section 5**: The UK as a member of the Commonwealth — refining the dialogue and targeting the action.

☐ **Section 6**: The UK's direct overseas responsibilities — leading by example.

This leaves out consideration of the UK as a trading nation, the private sector's responsibilities and the links to our domestic policies. This is briefly covered in 'Resourceful Britain' on the UK's conservation strategy taken as a whole, and in Chapter 5 of this report.

Section 1:
The UK's Aid and Development Assistance Posture
The current justification for development assistance overall

2. The rationale of the UK's overseas development assistance (oda), the priorities for assistance and the manner in which it is organised are not well documented so far as the public is concerned. Writing in the Overseas Development Institute Review[1] (in a personal capacity) two members of the Foreign and Commonwealth Office set out a clear analysis of the traditional moral and economic rationales for overseas development assistance in the UK. Three points from their paper are highlighted below:

(a) British aid is, in general, attempting to speed up or accelerate the process of 'development'. In general, aid goes to those countries and those sectors within the developing country economies where the private investor would not tread. Aid is intended to supplement the recipients' limited ability to provide both capital and skills for development priorities, for example, in providing for the basic infrastructure development (water supply, transport, ports, education, health and in key sectors for providing basic needs such as subsistence agriculture).

(b) It is also recognised that, for many, the development process is a first time experience. People are learning by doing, often in unison with the donor Government. Priorities and needs are constantly shifting and some freedom to learn is provided by concessional aid flows (that is, finance at a very low interest rate and with generous repayment terms).

(c) Overall aid is justified on moral grounds: namely the transfer of resources from richer people to help the development of poorer people.

The authors of the paper candidly admit that other motivations such as the promotion of trade, or foreign policy objectives as well as the improvement of the recipient's economy, often apply.

3. In fact, the cost of the aid programme to the Exchequer is of primary concern, to the Treasury if no one else. Securing the direct procurement of British goods and services to reduce the net cost and to enhance the indirect benefit in terms of future trade determines many aspects of our aid policy. Reg Prentice, speaking in the House of Commons debate (11 February, 1982) clearly set out the wider national rationale: 'There are three classic sets of argument. There is the moral argument. There is the argument in terms of the interdependence of our domestic economic problems and those of the developing world. There are the arguments that can be grouped under the headings of foreign policy or strategic consideration'. On strategic questions, he added: '. . . some of my Hon friends are keen on defence, but some may be sceptical about the need for the aid programme. I suggest to them that the two sets of arguments overlap . . . It is probably still true today, as it was when I sat at the Cabinet table, that in public expenditure discussions the defence budget is discussed completely separately from the aid budget. I do not believe that they should so be discussed. In many ways they are related. They have the same purpose — to preserve peace. The need for a strong defence posture and for a growing aid programme are relevant to the preservation of peace'. The report returns to the strategic

theme below, when the work of the OECD is discussed (see p 328). However, the balance of the aid programme, its environmental attributes, the priorities and its size are first considered.

The Current Environmental Policy of UK Overseas Development Assistance (oda)
4. Examining the environmental impact of UK oda is not easily done without an exhaustive study of each budget line within the development assistance programme spread over a number of years. While the tables in Appendix D of this report show the breakdown of the aid budget into crude sectors, each one hides a complex of projects and programmes: some of which are short-term, others long-term; some involve co-financing with other agencies, others not, and so on. In addition, there is the UK's contribution to the UN family of agencies, to the World Bank International Development Agency (IDA) and to the European Development Fund, many of which include an environmental component. In effect, an audit of the historical picture overall, and of the current policy against the priorities set out in the WCS, has not been done — although it could be, given time and Government information. This is a clear weakness in this report and is admitted as such.

5. The most recent study, by the International Institute for Environment and Development (IIED) and the University of East Anglia Overseas Development Group, of the overall environmental emphasis and procedures of the UK aid programme was conducted in 1978-79 when the then Overseas Development Ministry (ODM) was still very much under the influence of the Labour administration, and Dame Judith Hart in particular. An undated ODM memorandum presented to the study team entitled 'Environmental Factors in Third World Development' illustrates the policy as it was at the time of the review. This is shown in Appendix E of this report, p 381. The details of the study's finding are unfortunately not public but many of the recommendations are no longer relevant in any event. Those that are are summarised below. It should be emphasised that the conclusion of the University of East Anglia (UEA) report was positive overall but asked for more emphasis on sound environmental planning so as to make the UK's aid projects more effective and durable.

Summary of Recommendations from the UEA/IIED Study 1978-79
- A highly-placed administrator in the Bilateral Co-ordination Department should assume responsibility for environmental matters.
- Training on the environmental consequences of development should be given to all staff, particularly desk officers.
- The post of Environmental Education Adviser should be established and training of staff of recipient governments promoted.
- Environmental research should be strengthened.
- All administrators and professionals should be made responsible for the detection of environmental problems.
- A Policy Guidance Note (see Appendix E, Section 2

of this report, p 381) and working guidelines on the environment should be issued.
- Projects Committee submissions (the key hurdle for the selection of projects) should incorporate statements on the environmental implications of projects and project evaluation should include environmental considerations.
- The section on the environment in the 'Guide to Economic Appraisal' should be rewritten and a longer-term change to Social and Environmental Impact Analysis considered.

6. Since the study was conducted, there has been a change in government and a change in emphasis for the aid programme as a whole. This has not changed the procedures of the now titled Overseas Development Administration (ODA) significantly except insofar as the manpower budget of ODA has been reduced. This has sadly resulted in the break up of the Natural Resources Advisory Group (NRAG) into geographical desks, a reduction in key professional advisors (for water, land tenure and human settlements) and a degree of contraction in certain key ODA-sponsored institutions (such as the Centre for Overseas Pest Research, see Chapter 4, p 345). A more recent statement of the policy was published in August 1981 (Appendix E, of this report, p 381). This apparently incorporates many of the recommendations of the 1978-79 study, but without a detailed review of how things are in fact, rather than in theory, it is difficult to say more. For example, a major point in the study was that the designated environmental advisor was being asked to fill an impossibly wide brief. Almost alone he was responsible for watching the environmental components of all aid projects, attending key international meetings and interacting with his professional colleagues spread across the geographical desks. In the August 1981 memorandum it is clear that much of the environmental appraisal work has been reallocated to the Geographical Department or to the Development Division responsible for the project (as was suggested). But the advisor continues to have the same title and role and he now also serves in connection with the environmental priorities of the Foreign Office. If he is involved, in practice, with each aid project, one can only think that this is far too wide a job for one person no matter how able and willing; particularly if the approach of the UK aid programme is to involve positive environmental projects (such as institutional support — see Chapter 5 of this report) as well as sound environmental planning and evaluation procedures.

7. However it is the change of emphasis within the aid package that is of greater significance and concern.

Changing Aid Priorities and Budgets
8. In June 1975, the Labour Government published a White Paper advocating a change in British aid policies that might be broadly described by the phrase: 'More help for the poorest'.[2] In addition to targeting aid on the poorest countries, there was to be a shift in emphasis from urban to rural development, small instead of large projects, and from capital- to labour-intensive projects

(see Appendix D of this report). All of these changes took the total UK aid package a step nearer the needs identified in the WCS.

9. It is not within the scope of this report to assess the degree to which this shift in priorities actually occurred, but there was undoubtedly some real change during the period before the 1979 General Election. But from the limited evidence available in the form of various Select Committee reports and Government position papers, the emphasis has now changed. Small scale rural development in the poorest countries, backed up by a real commitment to improve the lot of the average Third World citizen has been replaced by a seemingly more negative attitude to a whole range of North-South issues, and greater concentration of the use of aid to promote and sustain British exports and industrial activity is now a declared policy objective.

10. In addition, the aid budget has fallen recently in real terms (but see Chapter 5 of this report). As some 60 per cent of the total programme is locked into long-term multilateral commitments in the short-term (for example the commitment to Lomé II and the European Development Fund for the period 1981-85) the effect of past cuts falls hardest on the remaining 40 per cent of the programme, which is precisely where the aid to the poorest countries is most concentrated. Given the shift in emphasis towards 'political, industrial and commercial considerations' the emphasis on 'aid to the poorest' appears to be waning. Sadly, many would argue (including the current Foreign Secretary Mr Pym) that our approach of using aid as a form of export credit is precisely the same as that of our OECD partners and that we have no alternative but to follow suit.

11. Tying aid to the procurement of British goods and services is not new or particular to this Government. What is different is the emphasis upon it. The more aid flows towards those sectors favoured by political, industrial and commercial criteria the less likely they are to arrest such environmental damage as is occurring. This is because the greatest environmental damage, and needs, tend to occur in the rural areas and amongst the urban poor of the least developed countries (with the obvious exception of industrial pollution which is not insignificant in some developing countries). The poor require very special assistance programmes designed to work in an economic environment of little or almost no purchasing power and minimal natural resource-potential. Such technology as is required is bound to be 'intermediate' or 'soft' to be appropriate. In short, what is good for UK exports is neither good for basic needs nor for sustainable development.[3]

The Current Challenge

12. The shifts in the emphasis of the UK's aid package (towards more commercial criteria, and away from basic needs strategies) are hard to evaluate in terms of the WCS without detailed study. A negative impact is certainly suspected. But there are other fundamental concerns in 1983.

13. In these hard economic times, and despite such statements as the Brandt report, a new and more worrying chorus has begun, typified by the sentiment represented in the statement that 'we really must get our own economy in order before considering the plight of the poor'.

14. Advocates and administrators of aid now face a common challenge: not only must they cope with the key operational tasks that face them in an ever more difficult development environment, but they must also set about repairing the political mandate that underpins the aid programme in the first place. Linking aid to sustainable development objectives is one way forward.

Section 2:
The UK as a Member of OECD
The renewal of the aid mandate and consistency at home

15. The rationale for overseas development assistance, (oda) in all its forms and for support of the many international agencies concerned directly or indirectly with development, has come increasingly to rest on two of the three arguments for it: economic self-interest and humanitarian concern. The third rationale should now be emphasised — namely the maintenance of a viable, increasingly interdependent, productive, but also valuable global system — the strategic imperative.

16. This is not to suggest that national economic and political considerations should not continue to apply. Nor that the moral argument for aid, particularly to relieve abject poverty and the consequences of natural disasters, is invalid. But the viability of the planet as a place to live is also a compelling rationale for the transfer of resources from rich to poor. It is one of the central arguments of the World Conservation Strategy. It could be an attractive argument for renewing the aid mandate.

17. The 1981 Development Assistance Review by OECD[4] recognises that the rationale for aid and its effectiveness are under serious question (even if certain Governments avoid saying so in as many words), not least because so many problems associated with aid have been glossed over in the past, only to be rediscovered in these times of world recession. Many attempts at development assistance have patently failed. Massive expenditure on arms and overt corruption by a few have not helped the Northern public to open their cheque books either. But OECD continues by reminding us of the greater mutual interests expressed so powerfully in Brandt: namely that, despite all the unpleasant realities, we all live on this fragile and vulnerable globe and we should all cast a long-term eye on its condition. We are commonly affected by certain global problems. In response to them OECD provide a useful list of five common goals we should now consider:

☐ to halt and, where possible, reverse environmental degradation;

☐ to halt the growth of global population, sooner

rather than later, and by humane means;

☐ to achieve a secure balance between world food needs and supplies;

☐ to reduce the rates at which non-renewable natural resources are being exhausted, by means of conservation and the development of renewable natural substitutes — in particular, to bring energy demand and supply into sustainable balance; and

☐ to render and keep the world's training, financial, and monetary systems efficient and viable.

It should be added that each of these goals, (apart from the last, which is more of a means than an end), is an identified priority of the World Conservation Strategy. In short, the current OECD approach set out in the Development Assistance Committee (DAC) report complements the Strategy.

18. The rationale for considering these system-maintenance tasks is clearly set out in the same report (here presented in summary form):

☐ The pursuit of these goals is not altruistic — all are matters of keen self-interest.

☐ Success in any of them is global in effect — no one country can be considered to benefit alone — all would benefit.

☐ The goals represent common ground between those who wish to *maintain* the global system (the North) and those who wish to *change* it (the South). Argument over maintenance and change is now little more than semantic.

☐ Finally, the comprehensive objective of sustaining a viable global system is broadly served by the promotion of developing country development.[5]

19. There are four compelling reasons why the UK should actively pursue a debate within OECD, and beyond, on these themes.

☐ This country's people, in keeping with many of its OECD partners, put a high value on each of the goals separately stated.

☐ This country has a truly remarkable set of resources (apart from money) to offer in pursuit of each of the goals (see Chapter 4 of this report, p 341).

☐ This country is, in the long term, vulnerable to a deterioration in any one of the global sub-systems — with the possible exception of energy in the short term. We are, as yet, a net importer of food and non-renewable resources, and derive enormous benefit from world trading, financial and monetary systems.

☐ The risks of doing nothing are growing year by year. First there are the direct risks of environmental disruption (for example, a change or damage to the atmosphere). Second there are secondary risks where local environmental damage stimulates economic decline which, in turn, results in political instability, the loss of investment and suffering for millions of human beings. Third there is the risk of resource-centred disputes caused by the increasing pressure that is put on shared or scarce resources.

An assessment of these four arguments is required in depth, either by Government or by an independent institution so as to properly underpin the UK's strategic interest in the sustainable development process.

Down to Work

20. No one country can act alone in these matters. It is only by comparing strategies and priorities that any new rationale can be positively articulated, presented and used to tackle the goals and to renew the rationale for development assistance. Within the North, the OECD provides a unique forum for such discussion and clarification.

21. The recent work of the OECD Environment Committee on anticipatory environmental management and its current work are all relevant to the theme. It includes discussion on resource-issues (maintaining biological diversity and the loss of cropland and soil degradation), on environmental management issues (environmental aspects of bilateral development cooperation and on environmental aspects of multinational investment). (See Appendix A, Section 1 of this report.) Similarly, the work on the sustainable development debate within the OECD Development Assistance Committee (DAC) is gaining momentum. As a recent study of the environmental performance of six bilateral aid agencies clearly demonstrated (IIED, 1979-80),[6] there is much going on in the various agencies that amounts to good environmental practice (and the UK is no exception). But it is also true that *each* has particular experiences and approaches to the task that are more forward-thinking and effective than the next, and these experiences have not been adequately shared or explored.

22. The DAC (including the UK) discussed a joint approach to Environment and Development Assistance in April 1982 and agreed the following major points:

☐ That within one year DAC would compile from all Member States a complete set of procedural guidelines and practices for dealing with possible adverse environmental effects of development projects. (This has now been extended to 1984.)

☐ That members should consider extending their technical assistance services to prevent environmental damage in their projects.

☐ That members should evaluate the environmental effects of past projects and make the results available to other members.

☐ That DAC will include environmental issues in its future programme of 'sector' meetings (for example, agriculture and water management).

☐ The DAC noted that more could and should be done to encourage sound environmental practices amongst the private sector operating in the Third World.

☐ The DAC stressed the importance of strengthening the capacity of developing nations to determine their own environmental policies and priorities and to administer them.

☐ As developing nations give increasing attention to threats to their development posed by environmental degradation, opportunities for incorporating environmental considerations in development policy will increase. The committee expects to examine in 1983 positive programmes to improve the environment, achieve better management of natural resources, and preserve the resource-base for sustained development. (This has now been extended to 1984.)

Summary
23. Whilst OECD has no power to regulate (in contrast with the EEC), it does have a clear advantage over any other inter-Governmental forum for providing the Western donor countries with an opportunity to coordinate and consolidate the objectives and procedures in their aid programmes. The opportunities do not only involve policy-making or political dialogue but also many practical and down-to-earth points of detail and coordination (see Chapter 4 of this report, p 341).

24. The work of the OECD secretariat and Member States on the sustainable development theme is highly relevant to the thrust of this report and should become a priority concern of the UK Government. However, the fundamental problems raised, such as the balance of the aid programme by sector and the degree to which it is tied to the export of goods and services can not be avoided either. Ways should be discussed with our OECD partners by which the tax-paying public can be made more aware of the long-term risks we face if we continue to turn inward in our relations with the developing world. In the pursuit of the five identified system-maintenance tasks it is the author's belief that, if the environmental goal can be positively linked to the more development orientated goals (food, population, energy and trade), all could be used to rekindle the political mandate for development assistance. A change in the attitude of the electorate away from aid as charity (the moral argument) and aid as good business (the self-interest argument) towards the long-term strategic approach can serve Britain's overseas foreign environmental policy. It is the responsibility of Government to take the lead.

Section 3:
The UK as a Member of the EEC
A major focus for action?

25. OECD has no powers to put worthy ideas into statutory effect. It has no legislature and no power of directive. It is, however, the most representative 'club' of the Western industrialised powers.

26. In contrast, the EEC[7] and its institutions have their own legislative machine; provided the matter in question falls within the scope of the Treaty of Rome. It also raises revenue for its own purposes from the Community members and thus has the ability to put financial muscle behind its projects and programmes.

27. Within the Commission of the European Community (CEC) there are a series of directorates — Directorates-General, and a number of them have an undoubted impact on overseas environmental policy; in particular,

DG 11 (Environment, Consumer Protection and Nuclear Safety) and DG 8 (Development).[8] In addition, the European Investment Bank is becoming a major multi-lateral lending agency and the European Parliament a major focus for coordinating and generating political opinion in the Community.

28. The CEC has the power to initiate proposals for directives and to plan its budget. But it is ultimately the relevant Council of Ministers who hold the power on behalf of their own sovereign Governments. They agree or do not agree to proposals and the European Parliament has the final say on the budget.

29. As the Community offers an opportunity for coordinated political and economic power in the global context, the UK should take a close interest in it in furthering the World Conservation Strategy. The relevant areas of EEC activity are as follows:

(a) The action programme(s) of the European Communities on the environment within Europe and overseas (under DG 11).

(b) The assistance priorities and environmental procedures of the European Development Fund (EDF) (under DG 8), and the negotiation of Lomé III.[8]

(c) The coordination of foreign policy between the Community States; this is a relatively new development and, although outside the Treaty, has been an area of substantial recent progress.

(d) The environmental aspects of the Community's overseas trade policies, with particular emphasis on food commodities and energy.

(e) The Research Directorate-General (DG 12) in so far as it encourages environmentally sensitive development, energy options, environmental management options and fundamental environmental research.

(It is not the intention of the author to elaborate further on items (d) and (e), but with respect to (d) the reader's attention is drawn to the recent Overseas Development Institute (ODI) publication *The EEC and the Third World: a survey. Hunger in the World*[9] where the significant impact of the EEC's needs and food aid policies are discussed.)

30. The authority of the Community to act at all in matters of environmental concern flow from a Declaration of the Heads of State and Governments in October 1972. Following this Declaration, three action programmes have now been published covering the periods 1973-77, 1977-81 and 1982-86. The third programme presented to the Council during the British Presidency in November 1981, was agreed on 7 February 1983, and it is the third programme which reflects more than its two predecessors the rising tide of international concern over the global issues. Perhaps somewhat ambitiously the draft programme includes the following aim: 'The Community will continue to speak (on environmental matters) in various international organisations with a single voice using to advantage the influence it has acquired in other areas of international cooperation . . . More specifically it will use this influence to ensure that

plans drawn up at international level such as those of the UN Environment Programme and the World Conservation Strategy of IUCN are actually implemented'.

31. But more significantly (for the purposes of this report) the programme sets out a full commitment to the ideas of the WCS.

'The Community should . . . henceforth regard environmental protection as an integral part of its aid to development policy . . . the seriousness of the environmental position in developing countries stems from the pressure of population, often increasing, on the surroundings in the poorest countries as well as from unwise use of resources. In addition, the creation of modern industries or agricultural developments can result in new threats to the environment resembling those found in industrialised countries.'

'To contribute to resolving these problems, the Community, in cooperation with developing countries, should promote conditions for lasting economic development which respects the interdependence of development, environment, population and resources. The Community will have regard to environmental problems both in drawing up its development policies and in implementing the Lomé Convention and other cooperation agreements. Under the provisions of these agreements, the Community will help these countries to tackle the environmental problems with which they are faced and to rectify existing damage, as well as to manage efficiently the resources for technical assistance in training environmental specialists.'

'The priority aims will be the conservation of tropical forests, the fight against the spread of deserts, water management, and the introduction of agricultural systems and forms of energy use which are compatible with the environment.'

'Particular attention will be given to education and information activities so that developing countries will become able to undertake these tasks by themselves in future.'

In effect, the Commission has put forward a set of radical proposals that, if fully carried forward, would have a profound effect on the total spectrum of the Community activities, (including its aid programme and its work on industry policy, agriculture policy and energy policy) consistent with the objectives of the WCS.

32. But matters are most unlikely to be so straightforward. There are four distinct problems.
   (a) First and foremost, the action programme, even if adopted, has no binding effect on the Member States. Member States may well adopt it somewhat cynically for this reason alone. Good environmental rhetoric has no political costs. Nevertheless for the Commission it is a 'mandate to forward specific proposals' that have yet to be defined but that fall within the programme.
   (b) Second, the staffing of the Commission is such —

only three people are involved in the international environmental section of DG 11, and DG 8 (Development) has no full-time environmental staff — as to limit seriously the subsequent output in terms of effectively framed and then negotiated measures. (It is impossible to say what financial resources are available for the task.)
   (c) Third, there is no guarantee that, even if the Council of Environment Ministers agree to the programme, the Council of Energy Ministers or Development Assistance Ministers, etc will subsequently carry the 'Community policy' forward. Similarly, the enthusiasm within DG 11 of the Commission is not necessarily reflected in DG 8 or DG 1 (External Relations), etc.
   (d) Fourth, even if everyone in Europe is enthusiastic, there is no guarantee that the concerns as perceived by Europeans will be welcomed by the recipients of Community aid: the African, Caribbean, Pacific and associated areas (the ACP states).[10]

33. Given that there is not much by way of improvement that the author can suggest for the draft action programme, attention is focused on four ways of advancing it.

34. First, the implications of the foreign environmental approach should be fully understood within the Commission itself. The contact between different Directorates-General must be clearly established and the sentiments of the environment programme integrated into the EDF's policy and procedures. To this end, there is a need for the Commission to include the approach in its own training activities and in its internal coordination system.

35. Second, the Commission should examine closely its environmental policy and procedures for the operation of the EDF.

36. EDF has been provided with a preliminary study of its environmental procedures on which to base change[11] (see Appendix G of this report for the summary recommendations), and with a further set of recommendations framed in a European Environment Bureau/World Wildlife Fund sponsored meeting in Brussels in October 1981.[12] A critical point in the latter recommendations is that the Lomé III negotiations beginning in 1983 should involve extensive discussions with the ACP States and other countries (EDF's clients) as to what sustainable development priorities they have and what particular assistance they require in the resource-management area (see also Chapter 4 of this report, p 341). To date, the EDF has talked at length about improving its environmental record, but many allege that it still has one of the worst performances.

37. A catalyst is provided by an initiative taken by a number of the multilateral lending agencies, including EDF, in 1980, when they signed the Declaration of Environmental Policies and Procedures relating to Economic Development (see Appendix F of this report).

This sets out, in general terms, the policy that should be followed.

38. Subsequent to this declaration, each of the signatories agreed to meet regularly to review progress. They formed a liaison committee with the title The Committee of International Development Institutions for the Environment (CIDIE) and appointed permanent environmental specialists as staff to carry the Declaration forward. (Some development institutions, such as the World Bank, already had environmental departments.) The EDF has participated actively in this process.

39. It has to be recognised that the EDF is constrained in its activities by the Lomé conventions which set out the relationship between the Fund and its ACP clients for five year periods.

40. Work is now beginning (January, 1983) on the renegotiation of Lomé and in this regard it is worth noting that Pisanni, the Commissioner for Development, has prepared a memorandum for Parliamentary and Government review. This includes sustainable development, in the sense implied throughout this report, as one of its key points. The memorandum has yet to be approved by the Council of Ministers.

41. In addition, as a result of the CIDIE process the CEC has now undertaken two studies for the multilateral 'club' on environmental guidelines and on environmental training, and within the CEC there is a growing sympathy for improvements in the environmental procedures for projects and for more environmentally sensitive project alternatives. The critical link is to encourage the ACP States to come forward with requests.

42. Third, there is a need for political coordination. It is suggested that the Environment Ministers (DG 11) of the ten Member States of the EEC meet with the Development Assistance Ministers (DG 8), or Foreign Ministers[13] with the staff of DG 11 and DG 8. Such a meeting would have to be suggested by the Presidency of the EEC and this would be a difficult meeting to justify without a clear agenda provided by the CEC. But the scope for progress is significant on three separate grounds.

(a) The agreed text of the third action programme relating to the environment without the ten Member States should be discussed in Council by both sets of Ministers, given that the literal implications of it are so significant. Whilst UK Government Ministers may argue that they operate under the notion of 'collective cabinet decision making' and therefore that a meeting is unnecessary, the very act of bringing two sets of bureaucracies (aid and environment) together to prepare for such a meeting would be extremely beneficial.

(b) A meeting could be used to focus and advance the environment/development policy of DG 8 by bringing together in position papers the work of: (i) the OECD DAC Committee and the approach of the European bilateral agencies on environment/development questions; (ii) the resolutions of the UNEP Session of Special Character held in May 1982 and their follow up; (iii) the work now beginning to arise as a result of CIDIE; (iv) the overall objectives, for the Community, of the Lomé III renegotiation in the area of sustainable development.

(c) The Commission could set out, in advance, those areas where the Community should properly act, and those areas where it clearly should not act but be in an informed position, (eg in the area of bilateral relations and programmes).

An important justification for the joint meeting is the recurring difficulty of coordination. Those parts of Government that are concerned with European or domestic environmental issues are not necessarily those which know about the multilateral lending programme, or the work of the executing agencies of the UN (and this applies within the OECD context as well). This problem appears to be more acute with some of our European partners than it is in the UK, but, as later sections of this report suggest, the coordination in Whitehall may not be all that it could be, either.

43. The fourth area concerns the commitment of Governments. Will they support the European Parliament in its demands and give the Commission the means to act positively in this area at all? At the end of the day, this is a matter of budgetary allocation within the relevant parts of DG 8 and DG 11, in terms of workforce and spending power. For example, it is possible to imagine a situation where DG 11 has an agreed Third Action Programme, including the current draft text, but with no significant budget or workforce to do anything about it. The allocation of funds and workers within the EDF is more complex but still slender. Also, according to certain personnel, until there is an earmarked budget line for environmental priorities ACP countries will not request assistance in this area, not least for fear of losing out on more prestigious and capital-intensive projects.

44. The Community can move very fast on environmental issues (as is shown by the speed with which it introduced a ban on whale products), but frequently it is a slow and somewhat cumbersome animal. Every little step has to be agreed by ten Governments, with a review by the European Parliament and the Economic and Social Committee. Inadequate staffing brings this process to a halt. Thus, if initiatives to follow up on the full implications of the draft environmental action programme were to occur — such as a combined approach to environmental training or a combined approach to environmental technical assistance — and carried through to substantive action, additional resources would have to be provided.

45. However, the Commission does start out with some of the necessary tools for the job. For example, DG 8 deploys a diplomatic team in the ACP countries. The members of this team — if properly engaged in the policy outlined in the draft programme — could be of significant value in identifying priorities and

opportunities in pursuit of the Strategy in each of the ACP developing countries.

46. The extent to which the EEC Member States act in concert (by way of the Commission or otherwise) on domestic or foreign environmental matters is a political decision. It is possible to have an improvement in environmental procedures in EDF and even a commitment of funds to a range of developing country natural resource-management needs and projects without a parallel change in the Member States' priorities. However, while the Commission can accelerate change alone if Member States have a neutral or positive view, it is equally the case that any Member State can obstruct and prevent progress alone should it want to.

47. The British Government could act positively to ensure that a sensible proportion of the annual expenditure by the EDF went on projects and programmes specifically designed to advance the natural resource-management capability of ACP countries. It could act to improve EDF's environmental procedures and it could inject a new and more vigorous approach to overseas development assistance along the lines of this report and the WCS. It is clear that within parts of the present Commission there is a very willing and ready team of support (see the Recommendations in Chapter 5 of this report).

Section 4:
The UK and The UN Family of
Specialised Agencies
The dialogue between rich and poor and
direct action

48. The World Conservation Strategy was drafted principally by the International Union for the Conservation of Nature and Natural Resources (IUCN), but various UN agencies also had a significant part to play in its preparation (and sponsorship). Foremost in this was UNEP, which not only provided a significant part of the cost but also had, in a late stage of the drafting, a radical effect on its final shape and balance. The other sponsoring partners were the Food and Agriculture Organisation (FAO) and United Nations' Educational Scientific and Cultural Organisation (UNESCO). The contribution of these three agencies (and, less directly, a number of others) to the aims of the Strategy must be considered, together with our national posture toward them. However, of all the UN specialised agencies it is our attitude to UNEP that is most critical for reasons that will become apparent.

This section is thus organised into three parts:
  ☐ The UNEP, its mandate, record to date and future plans.
  ☐ The other relevant agencies.
  ☐ The UK posture toward them.

The United Nations Environment Programme
(See also Appendix H)
49. UNEP was created as a result of the Stockholm Conference in 1972. Ever since, its role has been widely misunderstood. It is not a UN executive agency, empowered to carry out its own programmes in the member states (like FAO or UNESCO). It is not a sprawling UN organisation with a huge staff and massive budget. And it is not responsible for the world's environment, most of which lies within the boundaries of sovereign nations who, in turn, stand for no interference from UN bodies in their internal affairs.

50. However, UNEP's job is to coordinate the environmental activities of the UN agencies and other international organisations, and to promote national activities. UNEP is 'the environment conscience of the UN system'. Its role is catalytic: it is meant to spark off activities and programmes that might otherwise not occur. Thus far, its resources for the task have amounted to a professional staff of 100 to 150 people and an annual budget of about £20 million.

51. In fact, UNEP's resources are smaller than those of many local government departments. By way of comparison, the Greater London Council's Architects Department has a professional staff of 1,660 people. And, as a matter of record and perspective, the Governments of the UN will spend more money in the next six hours on military budgets than they have spent on the combined resources of UNEP in the decade since Stockholm.

52. Because UNEP has little money and few staff, its job is to persuade others to do the work. However, it has few incentives to offer and no means of enforcing its wishes. Again, by comparison, it is a little like creating the UK's Natural Environment Research Council (NERC) without pooling the financial resources of its constituent member organisations and without coordinating their management structure.

53. In the early 1970s, relationships between UNEP and other UN agencies were difficult. Some agencies saw UNEP simply as a source of some additional money for their work. Others complained that UNEP interfered on tiresome environmental matters when they had more important things to do. But the view of UNEP's current Executive Director was (and is) quite clear. In 1975, he said: 'We will never stop interfering in everyone else's business so long as it involves the environment. That is our mandate'.[14]

54. But the arguments over what is UNEP's business and what is not continue. Hours of debate took place at the special tenth anniversary session with very little change. UNEP remains an agency with no significant executive powers, surrounded by apparent distrust within the UN system.

55. Partially as a result of its somewhat unhappy past with the other agencies it is now involved in a major planning exercise called the System Wide Medium Term Environmental Plan (SWMTEP), which should clarify which agency does what environmentally during the years 1984-89. This, in theory, should allow UNEP to

plan its programme in advance, instead of tacking environmental considerations onto the already existing programmes of other UN bodies. The resultant programme should complement those of the specialised agencies rather than duplicate or compete. Its suggestions for the period 1984-89 were presented in a preliminary form to its Governing Council at its tenth session (1982) and will be finalised during the eleventh session (1983).

56. In effect, UNEP has not yet become the 'environmental focal point of the UN system', as was intended. It has had great difficulty in establishing itself, and many UN agencies appear to continue to see it as having a marginal impact upon them and on the problems of the environment.

57. But blame for this state of affairs certainly does not rest only with the Secretariat but also with its Member States and the Governing Council which represents them. When their immediate economic and political interests have been affected, national Governments have proved unwilling to grant significant powers to any international authority, let alone UNEP. This is a general problem for the UN, but there is another problem that is more specific to the Agency.

58. When the Stockholm Conference[15] created the Governing Council of UNEP, it gave it seven jobs to do. Briefly summarised, these were to:
☐ promote international environmental cooperation;
☐ promote policy guidance for the UN environmental programme throughout the UN system;
☐ review progress in the UN environmental programme;
☐ review the world environmental situation so that Governments could be alerted to emerging problems;
☐ promote international activity which could aid the UN environmental programme;
☐ review the impact of environmental policies (International Treaties, Conventions and regulations) on developing countries to ensure that development was not hampered;
☐ approve the spending of the Environment Fund.
In fact, the Governing Council spends well over half of its time on the last of these tasks and as a result it is arguable that the UN does not actually have an environment programme at all — merely a programme on how a tiny secretariat should spend a tiny voluntary fund of some £20 millions a year.

The Future
59. In this tenth year of its existence, the agency has been busy seeking a new mandate and renewed confidence from Governments.

60. Because ideas about what is encompassed by the term 'environment' are different from 1972, it has planned its future actions around three concepts:
(a) The relationships between people, resources, the environment and development.
(b) The rational use of natural resources.
(c) New patterns of development and lifestyle.

61. UNEP also makes two important points about priorities for the coming decade:
(a) Few of UNEP's programmes can be carried out unless there is adequate background knowledge about each problem. 'For the next decade, a colossal effort is needed to strengthen the Environmental data component of the work of UNEP'[16] (See Appendix H, Section 2 of this report, p 388.)
(b) Many world conferences during the past decade produced action plans. While funds were available to develop these plans, there were insufficient national and international resources to carry them out. UNEP says: 'without such resources, action plans will become academic exercises that gather dust on bookshelves. This trend needs to be reversed'.[17]

62. But one suspects that such conceptualisation as 'new patterns of development and lifestyles' will remain somewhat theoretical from UNEP's point of view unless a few practical matters are looked after first. The UNEP Secretariat clearly needs to:
(a) Re-establish some confidence, most particularly with the donor Governments and institutions, so as to rebuild its declining reputation, budget and programme support.
(b) Continue to strengthen the professional capabilities of its staff, (as it has so clearly done for staff who work on the regional scale), again to win confidence and cooperation from Governments and the UN's specialised agencies.
(c) Re-establish the original concept of an environment programme for the whole UN system in order to be able to act positively in dealings with the UN Agencies.

63. At the UNEP tenth anniversary session (1982) the UK made a move in the right direction by increasing its contribution from £600,000 to £750,000 per annum. However, if the United Kingdom Government chose, together with its 'Western European and other Groups' 'WEOG' (industrial) partners, to grasp the initiative, the following practical priorities could be made to bear fruit.

64. First, financial and institutional back-up should be given to UNEP's own recommendation concerning Earthwatch. The Agency needs to pay far more attention to the environmental data-gathering job that it is engaged in. At Stockholm, Governments agreed that the world needed a reference system for sound environmental information so as to provide useful baseline data on specific environmental trends. This does not amount to a vast computerised system located in Nairobi — but a series of identified centres for monitoring key environmental variables, assessing the data that are gathered and drawing conclusions from them (see Appendix H, Section 2, of this report, p 388 for a more comprehensive analysis).

65. Sadly, such information as there is is not published regularly in a comprehensive yet concise form. The annual UNEP State of the Environment Report[18] is not

too impressive and is certainly not widely read. *Unless Governments and people know what is occurring to the environment internationally they can hardly be expected to do much about it.*

66. Second, Governments should take the proposed 'System Wide Medium Term Planning exercise' (SWMTEP) seriously. The plan should, above all, indicate which UN agencies are best suited to take a lead in the environmental management arena. It presents a golden opportunity for consolidating resources and effort. But this does not mean, or should not mean, that UNEP should try to tell existing centres of excellence how to work. Rather, it should reinforce the coordination and interrelationships within the UN family. The FAO fisheries division, for example, knows more about fisheries than the one or two experts in Nairobi. UNEP should show how such recognised centres of excellence fit into the overall resource-management scheme of the UN family, what the priorities are, what they intend doing about them, and, most importantly, what financial and technical help is needed.

67. SWMTEP is only a potential device for introducing a measure of coordination and effectiveness into the UN family. It will come to nothing unless *all* Governments participate in the process fully. They, and only they, can ensure that what is agreed under UNEP auspices is carried over to the other agencies. The Governing Council of UNEP is the place to start; the remaining governing councils of the UN the places to continue.

68. The SWMTEP approach could also be dovetailed into the coordination activities of OECD in order that the many national, bilateral and non-UN multilateral activities of the OECD states are at least recognised and, so far as possible, coordinated with those of the UN family.

69. Third, UNEP should continue to catalyse initiatives within and without the UN family by using its Environment Fund. It would be a great mistake if the Fund started to be used for direct environmental management purposes as has been suggested. The technical assistance budgets, for example, of the existing multilateral and bilateral agencies are far larger and more effectively deployed to these ends. However, within the UN family, there is a clear need for position research, coordination, and seed funding of initiatives. For example, technical assistance in many areas (see Chapter 4 of this report, pp 343-344) requires a framework of priorities with a theoretical underpinning.

70. An analysis of the existing Fund budget lines, and the scope of them, is beyond this report. Figure 15 in Appendix H of this report (see p 390) gives a ranking of the subject areas and the amount allocated to them.

Summary
71. At the end of the day, the unavoidable truth is that the combined resources of the Governments who came together at Stockholm to create the UN Environment Programme have simply not:
☐ funded the Programme adequately;
☐ cooperated with it adequately;
☐ intervened with sufficient vigour to improve its performance;
☐ taken much notice of it (as Governments) save when it suited their short-term ends.
This is not a criticism of the UK alone but a comment related to all the Governments who came together at Stockholm.

72. The many national and international civil servants who have worked hard to develop UNEP have not been adequately supported. Just as important, many of the non-Governmental organisations (NGOs) and individuals who created the impetus for the agency in the first place, frustrated, have long since departed to do their own thing outside the system. This is one more area where the UK, if it chose to act with more conviction than it has shown at times in the last 10 years, could make a significant impact within UNEP, and thereby make an impression on the global problem.

73. Given that this report lays much emphasis on the UN's own planning exercise as a mechanism for bringing the best of the UN to address the demands of the WCS, little further analysis follows. This is, the purpose of the planning mechanism itself.

The Rest of the UN Agencies
74. Four other UN agencies are of particular importance to the WCS: FAO, UNESCO, the World Health Organisation (WHO), and the regional economic groupings, such as ECE. There are also others such as the World Meteorological Organisation (WMO), and the International Maritime Organisation (IMO) that are certainly relevant.

75. In Appendix I of this report there is a brief description of certain activities of UNESCO not only to illustrate how diverse and involved the agency is in the concerns expressed in the WCS (something that is not widely appreciated) but also because, as far as the environment is concerned, it is the most relevant of all the UN agencies other than UNEP.

76. FAO houses relevant 'centres of excellence' concerned with fishery management, forestry management, pest control, arid land management, agricultural development, but no detailed work on the agency has been done for this report. This should follow if the overseas policy is to be comprehensive.

77. Also of particular note is the Economic Commission for Europe (ECE) and its *ad hoc* programme to protect flora and fauna and habitats in the ECE region. This programme was designed in part to be a supporting effort for the WCS. Again, no work has been done on this programme for this report but it has clear relevance in such critical areas as atmospheric pollution (acid rain, carbon dioxide build up etc) as it is the only forum where environmental discussion takes place between East and West Europe.

78. For an account of the UN Development Programme's (UNDP) environmental performance and those of a

number of other multilateral funding agencies the reader is referred to *Banking on the Biosphere* by Johnson and Stein, IIED.[19]

The UK's Posture in the UN

79. No one can give an objective view of how the UK Government regards the UN, or more particularly those parts of it that relate to sustainable development as described in the WCS. It is also naive to believe there is any one view; there are many factors and views that determine our foreign policy as has been stated before.

80. However, to judge from people working within the UN (including UK nationals), from indiscreet diplomats in Europe, the USA, Canada and many Third World countries, and from some UK civil servants and practitioners, the UK's stance in the relevant agencies has often been:

☐ apparently negative or at least a little condescending;

☐ somewhat pedantic often to the point of being a trifle annoying;

☐ late in making commitments clear. Enthusiasm is rarely expressed.

81. In short, the UK does not seem to like the UN and its agencies very much. It appears impatient with its increasing politicisation, the obvious inefficiency, its unrealistic approach, and the expense involved. The UK appears to be much happier with bilateral links to the Third World, and with the regional groupings provided by OECD, the EEC and ECE as places and routes for doing international business. On any objective analysis of the UN, one would be bound to find much to merit this stance. The UN has recently been castigated by the United States, the Soviet Union and Britain — an unlikely alliance — for its alleged extravagant spending and flaccid bureaucracy, which is plagued by staff discontent (see Pysariwsky in *The Times*, 26 November, 1982). The organisation which was established in 1945 with a mandate to prevent war, establish international justice and respect, reaffirm faith in fundamental human rights, and promote better standards of life in larger freedom, is in difficulty.

82. Should the UK do more? Where appearances count for much, is it really in our long-term strategic interest to be quite so unambitious? Somehow, countries comparable to our own manage to do better at being seen to care, even if at the end of the day they do not give, in relative terms, significantly more than ourselves. The obvious examples are Sweden, the Netherlands, Canada and Norway.

83. Why is it, for example, necessary for us to be quite so crisp about personalities in the Councils of UNESCO? — which means that we get pushed off the relevant councils and committees. But if this is part of a UK 'grand design', then this approach is not consistent. For example, the links of our meteorological office to the WMO are, by all accounts, exemplary.

84. One suspects that our posture, case by case, is not

one of commission, but of omission, and very dependent on personalities. But given that we make a fair, at times even generous, contribution in financial terms to most of the agencies, there seems to be no logic in being negative and impatient thereafter. Enthusiasm, tolerance and professionalism would go further. These criticisms will be denied, and will not change as a result of the WCS. Another formula has to be found. Thus, the recommendations of this report, regarding the UN, are limited to four simple points:

(a) To ensure that SWMTEP is considered seriously and acted upon.

(b) To back all efforts within OECD, EEC and the Commonwealth that support Earthwatch and SWMTEP.

(c) To continue to support such centres of excellence for environmental purposes as there are in the UN agencies and regional commissions.

(d) To positively help in the field of information, education and training in environmental matters via the UN system.

Section 5:
The UK as a Member of the Commonwealth
Refining the dialogue and targeting the action

85. Relations with the Commonwealth are an important component of our foreign policy. No Foreign Secretary would wish nor could afford to ignore it. It is an institutionalised network of 44 Member States, representing a quarter of the world's population, tied to one another by historical links and common traditions. As an interactive group of nations, it is unique and potentially extremely important, not only to the members themselves but to the regions in which they exist.

86. As one member of the Secretariat put it, 'The Commonwealth is not a power block, it is not even a club but it is a first rate vehicle for the protection and development of intangibles. It is a morality, a conscience, for both sides of the so-called North and South debate. It is an institution that allows for give and take among a collection of heterogeneous countries'.

87. An important function of the Commonwealth, apart from its small but highly significant technical assistance activity (see Chapter 4 of this report p 343), is that it can change the field of play in international relations. It can 'leap over the rhetoric, the entrenched positions, into new areas of common cause'. This function becomes more important as the 'UN system falters or is bypassed'. (See the previous section in this chapter.)

88. For example, the only concrete progress made to date in the North-South dialogue is on the Common Fund, and deadlock in its negotiation was broken via the Commonwealth Trade Ministers agreeing on the recommendations of a Commonwealth Expert Group report. The settlement of the Zimbabwe crisis owes much to Commonwealth institutions.

89. However, political advances are not the substance of this report. As has been pointed out in previous sections, it is not the grand design that changes the *status quo* in environmental affairs, but the persistent application of small but targeted initiatives. The Commonwealth is particularly well placed to translate the notion of sustainable development into an array of many such small scale initiatives and to then regroup them through its unique consultative processes so as to demonstrate their collective worth. In short, the Commonwealth can and should become a major focus for the technical assistance effort called for by the Strategy, solidly backed by the UK Government. This is not to suggest that the Commonwealth should try to become a mini UN with a series of duplicate agencies (although some would argue why not). Rather, that use should be made of the Commonwealth Secretariat and its existing structures to advance the key issues identified in previous sections of this chapter and Appendix B (see pp 326-336 and 372), via a purpose-built technical assistance programme. Fundamental to the argument is the Commonwealth's demonstrated ability rapidly to mount truly expert multinational groups to advise on particularly urgent problems and their sustained ability to transfer expertise within a framework of 'informality, frankness and trust'.

90. The Commonwealth Secretariat is already dedicated to upgrading the skills required for development in many areas relevant to the WCS, and with institution-building at a national and regional level. This effort could be substantially increased in the field of natural resource-management and in the field of human settlements. As it is as much engaged in technical cooperation between developing countries and with transfers from the industrialised Members to the disadvantaged the learning process is self-reinforcing and mutually beneficial.

91. Appendix J of this report outlines the overall structure of the Commonwealth Secretariat including that of the Commonwealth Fund for Technical Cooperation (CFTC). However, what does not come out of that institutional profile is its style and sense of priority. From reading the material, including the criteria used to select projects, and in discussing its work (and, in the author's case, in being involved in CFTC-sponsored work) it is clear that the Commonwealth Secretariat overall is concerned with developing human resources to the full. It is not involved in prestige or grandiose schemes, it is very much concerned with the small scale, labour-intensive and appropriate approach to development problems. It recognises the need to develop administrative competence solidly over a number of years. Thus, the CFTC is assisting Member States in:

(a) discovering and exploiting indigenous energy resources;

(b) negotiating exploitation and production agreements for natural resources (fish, forestry, energy, minerals);

(c) preparing agricultural projects for third party funding;

(d) managing development projects in the food sector;

(e) stimulating research into appropriate technologies in renewable energy and rural technologies;

(f) water management projects;

(g) natural disaster relief through low cost housing;

(h) special assistance in small island states (22 Member States have populations of less than one million);

(i) various training schemes and applied studies of government.

92. It is suggested that the Commonwealth Secretariat could provide a standing technical assistance function in natural resource-management in the sense outlined in the WCS. It would be highly significant if, for as little as 10 years, the Secretariat and CFTC, together with the many institutions associated with the Commonwealth (see Appendix J of this report), built up an intensive programme for developing indigenous environmental management capability. But this will not happen without the full financial support and backing of the UK Government and other donor countries and the mustering of those countries' undoubted expertise. It *will* cost money.

93. However, in so far as there is one central recommendation of this report, it is that the British Government materially assist in designing and funding a 10 year programme of such assistance. The working title should, in effect, be 'A decade for the development of indigenous environment management capability in Commonwealth countries' (see Chapter 5, Recommendation 6, p 351).

Section 6:
The UK's Direct Overseas Responsibilities

94. This report would not be complete without reference to a number of direct responsibilities we have toward implementing the WCS Strategy internationally. These come in four categories:

(a) Our treaty and convention obligations — intended, signed and ratified.

(b) Our colonies, dependent territories and areas within our (claimed) jurisdiction.

(c) Our obligations to the convention programmes of Europe — both within and without the Community.

(d) Our obligations to the authors of the strategy itself — namely the IUCN. The various other relevant international organisations such as the International Council of Scientific Unions (ICSU) and the International Council for the Exploration of the Seas are not considered.

Each of these categories deserves more consideration than this paper will provide.

The UK's Position toward International (Environmental) Conventions

95. For example, ideally under the first category the following should be given consideration:

☐ The various conventions arising under the auspices of the IMO such as the Convention for the

Prevention of Marine Pollution (MARPOL) (1973 and 1978), and the (Ocean) Dumping Convention (1972).

☐ The World Heritage Convention (unratified by the UK) (1974).

☐ The Convention on International Trade in Endangered Species of Wild Flora and Fauna (1973).

☐ The Bonn Convention on Migratory Species of Wild Animals (1979) (unratified by the UK).

☐ The Ramsar Convention on Wetlands of International Importance (1971).

☐ The Berne Convention on the Conservation of European Wildlife and Natural Habitats (1979).

☐ The environmental articles in the Law of the Sea Treaty, (the final draft of which attracted an abstention from the UK in 1982).

☐ The Antarctic Treaty and the related conventions and measures, such as the agreed measures for the Conservation of Antarctic Fauna and Flora (1964); the Convention for the Conservation of Antarctic Seals (1972); and the Convention on the Conservation of Antarctic Marine Living Resources (1981).

☐ The International Convention for the Regulation of Whaling (Washington, 1946).

☐ Our various fishery obligations in the North Atlantic.

☐ The International Convention for the Protection of Birds (Paris, 1950).

☐ The Convention of Long-range Transboundary Air Pollution (1979).

96. The UK has always taken its treaty and convention obligations very seriously. It does not ratify until it is certain that it can live within the terms that are laid out. Thereafter, it tends to take its responsibilities as seriously as any other nation-state.

97. There is no point in describing the various obligations we have under each legal instrument mentioned above. Such an account would run to many pages and can be found in many reference texts.[20] But three particular points are discussed as they underpin problems common to all.

98. The first point concerns the finance that is required to carry forward conservation internationally via the various legal instruments. If the UK ratifies a 'conserving' convention, it must thereafter be prepared to put some research money behind its signature. Take the Southern Oceans as a case in point. The Conservation Convention for Antarctic Marine Living Resources (CCAMLR) was drawn up against the possibility of a large Southern Ocean fishery for krill (shrimps) and fish. We, as a nation, do not at present run a fishery in the area but we had much to do with the fact that the convention is as scientifically far-sighted as it is. We were a leading conservation-minded state throughout the negotiation. Now the convention is in force it is essential that some fundamental scientific work is done on the implications of the key management articles. This can not be done out of the regular budget of, say, the British Antarctic Survey (BAS) (the obvious NERC institution) because

that is not what BAS is financed to do; it is unlikely to be done out of the regular university research budgets; and the Nature Conservancy Council (NCC) has no pot of gold. Apparently, there is no Government money and it is likely that the voluntary organisations will have to foot the bill for such research as is vital for the smooth running of the Convention.

99. The same broad position applies for the International Whaling Commission (IWC), the Council of Europe, much work arising under the Convention on International Trade in Endangered Species (CITES), the Ramsar Convention and, no doubt, the Berne Convention. A small fund is required (presumably under the control of the Department of the Environment or an appropriate lead agency) specifically to finance research work necessary to the successful working of international environmental conventions and treaties.

100. The second point concerns the identification of what is or what is not in our national interest. If the only criterion for the ratification of international conventions is 'what is in it for us?' then, by definition, we will only sign where there is an identified advantage to us. But many conventions are of no immediate UK concern. This is not to create 'straw men', as the UK has acted in an altruistic way on a number of occasions (Antarctica being a case in point) but there are instances that seem to go the other way. For example, we should, if only for the sake of other countries, join the Convention for the Protection of the World Cultural and Natural Heritage and contribute to the World Heritage Fund. Our resistance has been financial[21] (based on the view that we will derive no benefit, so why spend the money? — circa $85,000). It is the case that we are unlikely to derive as many domestic conservation benefits as some other countries, but the fund, in particular, is an important adjunct to the World Conservation effort.

101. The third point concerns the participation of the voluntary sector in the drafting and implementation phases of international agreements. The non-Governmental sector has contributed significantly on a technical level to CITES, Ramsar, the IWC, Antarctica, the Bonn Convention and so on. It is right and proper that they should, for it is precisely what many were established to do. By and large, the access that NGOs have to this process has been open and cooperative. But the Government does not carry this process through to its logical conclusion. They should invite NGOs to join many more delegations (in the way that now occurs for the IWC). NGOs would contribute to the effectiveness of the delegation, by way of expertise, and understanding between the UK position and the public. They should be paid their expenses by the UK Government. Many other countries have now instituted this procedure for their delegations at UNEP, UNESCO and IMO and for meetings arising under the Antarctic Treaty, CITES, Berne, Bonn, etc (eg the USA, Canada, Sweden, the Netherlands, Germany and, on occasions, France).

Overseas Territories

102. Under this category there are a number of territories

that fall within our jurisdiction, but most particularly:
☐ Hong Kong.
☐ The Turks and Caicos Islands.
☐ The Falkland Islands, and those sub-Antarctic islands north of 60°S (the Skag rocks, South Georgia and the South Sandwich Islands).
☐ The British claim on the Antarctic continent and the South Shetlands and the South Orkneys.

103. What is the UK environmental policy for each of these? This report makes no attempt to answer the question. It has only one point to make. In the Falkland Islands, South Georgia and the South Sandwich Islands, the UK should insist on environmental standards that are consistent with those that it eventually wishes to achieve for the Southern Ocean and Antarctica. The two Shackleton reports provide an excellent basis for this approach as both have carefully considered the sensitivity of the area to artificially created perturbations.

104. The standards the UK has proposed for the exploitation of the Southern Ocean, and now successfully has included in the new Convention, are revolutionary in their scope. For the first time in fisheries law, the concept of multispecies management is introduced. In effect, no one species should be exploited, either to its detriment or to that of any other species. The opportunity for the UK to lead by example in the waters of the Falkland Islands is clear. We should manage those waters as we expect the Southern Ocean (and, in time, all other oceans) to be managed.

105. Similarly, in the case of minerals, oil and gas in Antarctica, one suspects that the UK will go for the very highest of standards for environmental control without going quite to the point of saying no to exploration and exploitation altogether. The regime (environmental or otherwise) for such exploitation in Antarctica cannot be separated from the problem of jurisdiction in the area and may as a result take years to negotiate. However, exploitation of oil and gas is more likely in the Exclusive Economic Zones (EEZs) off the sub-Antarctic islands, and the environmental risks are no less significant. The weather is not so inclement but the flora and fauna are richer than in Antarctica itself. What is allowed and not allowed in such waters could be an important precedent for further south. The UK should insist on, and achieve, the most vigorous of environmental controls and procedures in the whole of the South Atlantic.

Our Wider European Obligations
106. Within this category we should consider the UK's attitude to the Community's various proposed environmental directives, not in terms of their effect on our domestic environment but on the environment within the nine remaining States.

107. To take a contemporary example: if we continue to oppose the proposed directive introducing an environmental impact assessment procedure in the EEC, what are the environmental disbenefits for the remaining Member States? No matter what the domestic arguments are, we must at some point consider the wider implications for others. It is argued that some Member States look to the Community to do their legislative work for them. The concept of Community concern should certainly stretch to environmental benefits for Europe as a whole and not just for us, but using the Commission as a way round domestic difficulties seems very short-sighted.

108. The EEC works for the benefit of the UK because there are certainly instances where our policy has been advanced by its work (for example the sixth amendment on the control of toxic chemicals). If, on balance, we need the Commission to act in this area at all we should be prepared to compromise on certain directives that, *prima facie*, do not seem to be necessary for us.

109. In addition there is the Council of Europe. This body is highly regarded by many who seek to protect the flora and fauna of Europe. It has no legislative powers of its own but does create strong moral pressures on the Governments that take part in its proceedings. For instance, it has developed Conventions for European States to ratify (for example the Berne Convention on the Conservation of European Wildlife and Natural Habitats 1979). Its Secretariat successfully promotes a range of educational, research and species and habitat protection schemes in Europe beyond the Common Market States. The UK's contribution, coordinated by the Department of the Environment and the Nature Conservancy Council, has been, from all accounts, positive and thorough. (However, the participation within the voluntary sector has not always been all that it could have been.)

International Organisations Outside the UN[22]
110. With respect to the various international organisations outside the UN, IUCN is in a special category. It not only acts as a coalition of non-Governmental organisations but also of state members, including the UK. Its role as a broker between the two groups is of prime importance. But it also has many key functions and responsibilities in the international system of environmental institutions beyond this. It now houses the Survival Service Commission for endangered species, a number of other standing commissions that are internationally drawn, and the Secretariat for the CITES. It is also running (with the International Institute for Environment and Development) a limited service of environmental technical assistance under the title of the Joint Environmental Service. In short, it is, apart from UNEP, the only organisation with the full scope of the WCS on its agenda.

111. IUCN has all the advantages and disadvantages of being a membership organisation. Its assembly, every three years, is a political occasion and is therefore somewhat unpredictable in terms of results; its members do not always support it as they could and its priorities are necessarily coloured and spread by its financial sponsors, including the WWF. However, the organisation has a highly competent, but small, staff capable of doing far more than an equivalent number in the UN system. Via its member Governments and organisations it is

possibly the most important world-wide force for coordinating and pursuing the objectives of the Strategy.

112. However, in the interests of promoting the science that underpins the Strategy's case, it is vital that IUCN remains as politically neutral as possible. This is because the real value of IUCN is to marshal the best of science internationally behind the concerns of the WCS, not to act as yet another political talk shop. The UK does and should continue to make a significant contribution to IUCN. If it so chose, any number of routes could be found for sponsoring our scientists into opportunities created by the organisation. (This is also suggested in this report in the Commonwealth Section of this chapter and technical assistance Section of Chapter 4 of this report (see pp 336-337 and 343-344.) Such sponsorship could include money, sponsored sabbaticals and leave of absence, research funds in UK institutions and a strongly supported national committee for IUCN (already organised by the NCC).

Notes and References

1 HEALEY, J AND CLIFT, C. 1980. The developmental rationale for aid re-examined. *ODI Review, 2.*

2 More help for the poorest. 1975. White Paper (Cmnd 6370). HMSO.

3 A recent study by the 'Independent Group on British Aid' under the Chairmanship of Professor Charles Elliot, 'Real Aid: A Strategy for Britain', brings out many of these points. As a source of information on how ODA works, how aid is spent and how the policy has shifted under various administrations it is an excellent paper. Many of its conclusions are consistent with the recommendations of this report (in particular, those relating to the tying of aid to the procurement of British goods, greater help for the very poor, and the importance of professional advisors in the aid process). Other conclusions go much further than this report could, for reasons of scope; concentrating on the weak position of the Aid Minister, on food aid and other aid policies. Distributed by Oxfam, 274 Banbury Road, Oxford.

4 OECD. 1981. *Development Co-operation 1981 Review, November.* Paris, OECD.

5 For example, in the matter of population growth, 'the linkage between development and diminished fertility is now established beyond reasonable doubt: it is not an instant or inflexible linkage; it is lagged; it can be accelerated by positive population restraint policies and apparently by tilting the pattern of development in favour of such specific dimensions of welfare as lowered infant mortality and increased female literacy. But lowering birth rates is an uphill task in the absence of improvements in economic welfare'.

6 IIED. 1980. The environment and bilateral development aid. IIED.

7 For a fuller review of the European Communities' environmental programme see *Environmental Policy and Law, 7 (1), February 1981.* This sets out at length the advantages (and disadvantages) of working through the Community for each of the Member States.

8 For a fuller review of DG 8 and the workings of the European Development Fund see the House of Lords report from the Select Committee on the European Community's 'Development Aid Policy' Paper 146, 1980-81 Session. The Lomé Convention runs for five years, and is the agreed basis for development assistance and cooperation between the European States and the African, Caribbean, Pacific and other 'client' states.

9 STEVENS, C. 1982. The EEC and the third world: a survey. 2. Hunger in the world. Hodder & Stoughton.

10 The Programme is also ambitious in its aims for the *internal* environmental affairs of the community in so far as it calls for: 'help in creating new jobs (in) . . . key industries with regard to products, equipment and processes that are either less polluting or use fewer non-renewable resources; a reduction of any form of pollution or nuisance, or of interference with spatial features, the environment or resources which creates waste at unacceptable cost for the Community; economy (in the use) of certain raw materials that are non-renewable, or of which supplies can be obtained only with difficulty, and to encourage the recycling of waste and the search for less polluting alternatives; prevention or reduction of the possible negative effects of using energy resources other than oil, such as coal or nuclear power, and promotion of energy saving and the use of less polluting energy resources'.

It is as well to remember that the community institutions are a useful route for many Member States to improve their internal environmental policies. The UK should therefore hesitate before blocking proposals on the grounds that we have a different approach or already have adequate provisions. The consequence of a little inconvenience for us may result in a major improvement elsewhere.

11 IIED. 1980. The European Development Fund and the environment. IIED.

12 EUROPEAN ENVIRONMENT BUREAU. 1981. The world conservation strategy in Europe. Brussels, EEB.

13 Recognising that the 'Council of Ministers' is *de jure* the meeting of the Foreign Ministers.

14 EARTHSCAN. 1982. Stockholm plus ten. IIED.

15 The United Nations Conference on the Human Environment. Stockholm, 1972.

16 Stockholm plus ten, *op cit.*

17 Stockholm plus ten, *op cit.*

18 UNEP. 1982. Annual state of the environment report.

19 JOHNSON, B AND STEIN, R. 1979. Banking on the biosphere. Levington Books.

20 The reader is referred to the IUCN Law Centre, Bonn, for such information.

21 Although the position of the dependent territories may now be impeding progress on this and the Bonn Convention (Migratory Species).

22 For an excellent review of all the international organisations concerned in the conservation of nature see: BOARDMAN, R. 1981. International organisation and the conservation of nature. Macmillan Press.

CHAPTER 4

MECHANISMS FOR CHANGE

Introduction

1. In the preceding sections the report has drafted a rationale for a positive UK approach to sustainable development — both as outlined in the WCS and as encompassed by the basic needs development approach. The rationale has been argued at a strategic level although, as subsequent sections show, there is also potentially a strong element of national self-interest involved. The moral arguments have not been explored.

2. But the arguments are worthless if they fail to stimulate action. The report has argued for a shift in emphasis in our aid policy and for continued vigilance on environmental procedures; for a new era of coordination of ideas and the building of a new mandate for aid within OECD; for specific action from the community institutions; for a major coordinating role for UNEP within the UN system and, finally, for an ambitious technical assistance initiative by way of the Commonwealth. The trade/environment arguments stand apart and have not been considered.

3. What follows is a brief, and very preliminary, review of the national assets (other than money) that can be mustered behind these different areas of suggested activity. But before that is done the report reviews the mechanisms that must be brought into action. There are two components to consider:
   (a) Marshalled voluntary pressure organised to: provide greater public awareness of the issues; provide defined political objectives, both short- and long-term; and work, by way of the Parliamentary process, to see them achieved.
   (b) The bureaucracy that determines what happens in detail.

The New Political Alliance?

4. Within the UK (and throughout Europe) there are two powerful groups of organisations that could work together in furtherance of the WCS: the environment lobby and the development lobby. At present, they barely talk to each other (but see the Practitioners' Debate, Chapter 6 of this report).

5. This is sad for there is much they could talk about.

Few UK NGOs campaign, research or promote public education of the international environment/development issues.[1] The overriding reason for this apparent lack of concern is the difficulty the organisations have in defining campaigns that have a focus and a realistic result in terms of their own supporters. The agenda is so enormous that they turn to smaller, more achievable goals at home. As a result, there is little or no pressure for political change, few calls for public accountability from our civil servants and a superficial public understanding and knowledge of the issues (apart from that provided by certain exemplary media programmes).

6. There are, of course, many different types of development NGOs that could be involved — for example those:
   (a) directly involved in development assistance (such as Oxfam, Christian Aid); often supported by the ODA via the pound for pound scheme of the volunteer programme;
   (b) concerned with new approaches to development (the Intermediate Technology Development Group — ITDG);
   (c) raising political pressures for development objectives (the World Development Group);
   (d) underpinning the development lobby with research (Development Studies Units);
   (e) concerned with development education (the Council for World Development Education) — sadly an area where the Government is now withdrawing support (see the Real Aid document referred to in Chapter 3 Section 1, p 327).

7. Similarly, the environment NGO topography is varied — there are those concerned with:
   (a) environmental education (CEE);
   (b) environmental research (ecological and environmental science groups);
   (c) wide environmental issues — 'the rational use of the Earth' (FOE);
   (d) new environmental approaches (the Green Alliance);
   (e) species and habitat protection (Flora and Fauna Preservation Society);
   (f) and those concerned directly with environmental protection overseas (WWF/IUCN).

8. But of the three million people who belong to conservation-based organisations and of the many millions more who give money in the cause of development, only

a tiny minority have the first idea of the environment/development issues that the WCS attempts to address. No one so far has linked the two bodies of concern into a coherent alliance. This could surely happen.

9. A basic requirement is more public education regarding the issues involved. There is now an enormous new opportunity for this to occur via the TV Channel 4 (and then there are all the existing channels and propaganda methods). This could perhaps be a priority for all the individual organisations to follow immediately.

10. But it is well known to those in the world of pressure groups that 'turning the public on' is not enough. Ideas, issues and reforms must be provided for the interested public to follow. At some point, environment/development organisations should meet to thrash out such an agenda together. (See Recommendation 12, Chapter 5 of this report, p 352.)

11. It is not the brief of this report to define such a campaign; suffice it to say that, with a little imagination and knowledge, the complementary concerns of the 'furry animal brigade' and the 'do-gooding public' could be fused to powerful effect. What is required is leadership.

The Bureaucracy

12. For the layman, understanding Whitehall's organisation poses very real difficulties. Making suggestions for change is more difficult. Figure 1 draws the crude structure that appears to be involved in administering the UK's overseas environmental policy, but it gives no insight as to where the components of the policy are coordinated. Nor does it give any indication of the internal structure of each ministry when it comes to execution.

13. For example, how or where policy is coordinated within the Foreign and Commonwealth Office (FCO) is unclear. The office with the most relevant name is the Maritime, Aviation and Environment Department. But, to judge from the Civil Service Book, this is most concerned with environmental matters that are only secondarily linked to development (eg the Law of the Seas negotiation, ocean dumping, fisheries enforcement etc). Other relevant desks must include the UN Department, the European Community Department (external), the Aid Policy Department (joint with ODA) and the various regional desks. No doubt all have a role to play but it seems fairly clear that there is no one place in Whitehall where the concerns of the WCS overseas are the single priority. Sadly, the subject is not quite in anyone's bailiwick.

14. Before suggesting that more positive progress would be made if there was one responsible unit of Government to design and then enact a 'UK Overseas Environmental Policy', it is necessary to demonstrate that the current disaggregated structure does not work effectively. For example, does the Department of Education and Science (DES) regard its responsibilities as in any way linked to the technical assistance programme of ODA or *vice versa*?

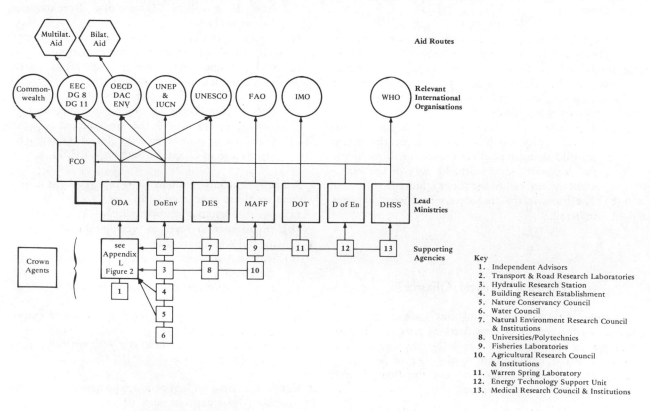

Figure 1. **A simplified diagram of the UK institutions involved in the overseas environmental scene**

Does it see any point in the link? How exactly does the Royal Society fit into the picture when it comes to determining our policy for UNESCO? Does the permanent representative in Brussels responsible for DG 8 know that NERC (DES) is trying to win relevant technical assistance and research contracts from the EEC? Does it help NERC in this endeavour? Is its role to help? Is the policy of the Ministry of Agriculture, Fisheries and Food (MAFF) at FAO to support SWMTEP in UNEP? Who knows what SWMTEP is? What links does MAFF have to ODA? Questions of this sort can only be answered by the bureaucracy itself. However, as no lobby or interest group is calling for answers or for a coordinated sustainable development policy, it is very unlikely that there is the mechanism to produce one. Coordination for coordination's sake is not a hallmark of any efficient management machine, Whitehall included.

15. The acid test of this report's worth is whether or not it stimulates such a coordinated response. The WCS on its own has singularly failed to do this; no Whitehall Department could see anything 'in it for Britain' beyond a general welcome, although one hopes that the enormous amount of work carried out for the Conservation and Development Programme, as presented in this book, now stimulates a response. Clearly, the thrust of much of this report is that a coordinated effort is justified and logically an interdepartmental review is required to achieve it. How else is the work of several Departments going to be fused into a sustainable development posture for overseas purposes?

16. The work and the Departments who, *prima facie*, should be involved are:
  (a) in DOE, the international work of the Central Directorate on Environmental Pollution (UNEP, EEC, ECE, OECD); the Directorate of Rural Affairs (Wildlife and Nature Conservation Treaties and agreements, see Chapter 3, paragraph 42 of this report, p 322);
  (b) the NCC International Branch;
  (c) the international work of MAFF in fisheries and FAO;
  (d) the international work of ODA and DES(?) relating to UNESCO and its policy for promoting our universities and research councils abroad;
  (e) the work of the Bilateral Coordination Department and the Natural Resources, Engineering, Education, Health and Population Division of ODA;
  (f) the Foreign and Commonwealth Office.
Just as an interdepartmental response is indicated to draw up the policy, so too is a unit indicated to coordinate the delivery of the policy abroad throughout our foreign service (bilaterally, at the UN, in various Treaty and Convention forums, in the EEC, in the OECD and the Commonwealth). This was, in part, the original role of the Central Unit on Environmental Pollution when situated in the cabinet office, and to an extent it still retains this role. Perhaps it should change its name and move from the DOE to whence it came! Certainly, the overall issues involved are of sufficient importance that they require an occasional review by the appropriate Cabinet Committee dealing with foreign policy questions.

Components of the National Effort

Technical Assistance and Fundamental Research

17. An overriding conclusion of a comparative study of the environmental procedures of six bilateral aid programmes carried out by the IIED in 1979-80, and its subsequent study of the environmental management needs of four developing countries (Sudan, Malaysia, Ghana and Venezuela) is the need for environmental technical assistance. (See the Practitioners' Debate, Chapter 6 of this report.) Developing countries usually lack the necessary institutional and human infrastructure that is required to put good natural resource-management into effect. Until the technical means is in place, efforts to introduce further sustainable development planning will remain a dream.

18. However, raising the level of expertise is going to take time. It is now recognised that inputs of 'know-how' from outside in the form of foreign experts are not enough. What the poor countries need is a capacity of their own: in a trained workforce under institutional arrangements that ensure that raising the level of expertise is self-renewing. 'Self-reliant and sustainable development will be inhibited until the poorer countries and regions have built a "critical mass" of expertise in key fields, and until more of the sources from which they derive technical sophistication have been brought closer to home' (OECD-DAC, 1981).[2]

19. Even the smallest and poorest nation-state needs a fair amount of sophistication in the scientific and other relevant development disciplines to begin the process. It needs to choose intelligently from the world-wide knowledge emporium of the mass of foreign experts seeking opportunities for work. But it is better appreciated now than it was 20 years ago that delivered assistance, information and advice must be selected and adapted; it must be married with local preferences and cultural factors and supplemented, as far as possible, by indigenous research and training. The short-term, often commercially minded approach, of parachuting in experts for three or four weeks at a time is perhaps on the decline.

20. Nevertheless, according to OECD, the way in which donors organise their technical assistance is, by now, grievously outmoded. Technical assistance, in general, remains the most fragmented form of aid. It is haphazard and organised in a second rate fashion. In the bilateral case it is tied overwhelmingly to the individual donor country. Experts typically must come from the funding country. There is little collective willingness to finance specialists from other developing countries, nor to fund training in third countries (although the UK does do this on a limited scale). Technical assistance is often doubly tied: being limited to national expertise and to uses that are defined by and bound to particular projects the donor has taken up in its larger aid programme. Is the UK the exception?

21. OECD also reports that, in their chosen specialised fields and even when they break out into the more general infrastructure area, concerned donors are not content to fill gaps. They tend to want to transfer whole systems or sub-systems of structured institutions and expertise — namely, their own.

22. The OECD goes on to suggest a new and radical scenario. This, in summary form, involves:

(a) donor and recipient countries agreeing to pool their contribution of expertise in defined areas of need;

(b) donor and recipient countries agreeing to undertake joint programming of needs perhaps in concert with the appropriate UN agencies; (in the UK's case via the Commonwealth);

(c) the donors agreeing, within reason and once the programme is settled, to pull back and behave more like a 'stock-room' rather than a 'pundit' in responding to specific requests.

23. Such an approach would raise the level of developing countries' environmental management capacities as set out in the WCS. In theory, all the mechanisms are there: the UN is about to begin its SWMTEP exercise; OECD is to explore its constituent members' expertise and approach; and the unilateral funding agencies have established a mechanism for coordinating their environmental policies and practices. But perhaps most important of all in the matter of management and natural resources, we are dealing with a politically neutral subject at least in so far as it involves the transfer of technical information and expertise.

The Expertise and Information available in the UK

THE UNIVERSITIES

24. Before any grand design can be established, it is necessary to identify which natural resource-management disciplines are required and then to advance mechanisms to deliver them. As part of the research for this report, the author and Dr Ian Barratt set about assessing the expertise needed for meeting the demands of the WCS internationally. A rough checklist of the indicated expertise for each separate recommendation in the Strategy was constructed (see Appendix B of this report). Then some 50 separate UK academic departments, together with some 20 specialised institutions, were selected and circularised. An analysis of the results follows.

25. The first stage surveyed all the institutions of higher and further education in the UK, together with some 30 Government-run research institutions, revealing a large body of expertise in all areas of environmental science and related disciplines.

26. In order to find out the extent to which these resources were already deployed in technical assistance programmes, the availability of researchers for overseas work, and the attitude of these experts to the WCS, we circularised 50 of them. All were sent copies of the Strategy, the 'checklist' which links priority requirements with academic disciplines, and a questionnaire.

27. The questionnaire asked each respondent to provide information on the following: what expertise is available in the department; the extent of awareness of the mechanisms for generating work overseas; whether the Government should do more to facilitate it; the degree to which overseas students from outside the OECD countries were catered for; and finally, each respondent's views on the Strategy itself.

28. All of the respondents felt that their departments had something to offer and, although more than three-quarters were already doing some form of research overseas, they all felt that more could and should be done.

29. Knowledge of the ways and means of obtaining such work was patchy, with about half of the departments admitting to little or no knowledge, while a few had extensive contacts. Only six departments had individual members registered as consultants with ODA, and representation on other agencies' registers was equally limited.

30. In general, overseas work developed out of the researchers' own interest or via informal contacts with officials and researchers in the countries concerned (many of whom were past students). A few departments had long-standing and formal associations with particular institutions in particular countries, and a small number were specifically set up to work in this area.

31. Almost without exception, the respondents thought that the Government, and in some cases their own university, should be doing more to facilitate overseas technical assistance and various comments were made in support of this assertion. For example, that: 'the total cost of such programmes is very small indeed compared to the goodwill which can be won, the scientific experience gained, and the benefit received by the host country', and that: 'those of us who take part in overseas programmes realise how very small the existing contribution is and how much ground in terms of social and political influence we have lost to other countries'. There was also a strong feeling that, as one Department of Geography put it: 'This country has a great deal of value to offer and is failing to use its intellectual resources adequately in contributing to development programmes'.

32. Most departments tried to encourage students from developing countries to take both ordinary and higher degrees, and a few ran special short courses specifically aimed at this market. The numbers were usually small and in many cases had fallen since the increases in fees. Data collected on the subsequent careers of overseas students show that many have moved into positions of responsibility in their own countries, and most of the respondents had reason to believe that their courses had been of value to these students. Some suggested that they should be doing far more to design courses for overseas needs.

33. The vast majority of those surveyed supported the overall approach of the WCS, in particular the merging of development and environment. Although some expressed reservations on points of detail or were pessimistic about the possibilities for its implementation, most were evidently eager to meet the challenges it poses.

34. In Appendix K of this report, Figure 16 shows the universities and the departments within them that had replied when the survey closed (subsequently 12 more replied) and Figure 17 gives a simplified analysis of the questionnaire.

THE INSTITUTIONS

35. As Figure 1 in this chapter on p 342 indicated, there are many institutions within the UK specifically designed to contribute overseas in the general area of rational resource-management. There are many more not designed for overseas operations, but which nevertheless contain highly relevant expertise. The ODA itself has traditionally put great emphasis on its own in-house professional expertise (see Chapter 6 of this report).

36. This report does not present a critique of the work of these institutions, nor a detailed explanation of how they relate to the concerns expressed in the Strategy. Appendix L of this report lists the institutions, with a brief description of their work. Section 2 of Appendix L (see p 403) presents a diagram of how many of these relate to the ODA and Section 3 (see p 404), for the purposes of comparison, sets out how one long-established institution, the Institute of Geological Sciences (IGS) is organised to provide technical assistance. It should be noted that there is no comparable structure for applied biology, or environmental science, *per se*.

37. Without exception, those agencies contacted and/or visited in the course of preparing this report expressed a positive response to the Strategy. This was based on the arguments presented by the WCS, both in terms of specific topics (such as soil erosion, pest management, genetic loss, river basin management) and overall in terms of the linkage between conservation and development. It was not hard to arrive at the conclusion that once the senior staff in these institutions were made aware of the Strategy, they wished to see it acted upon.[3]

38. Particular agencies, such as the Centre for Overseas Pest Research and the NERC, were quick to point out that they already did much in support of the WCS recommendations — but with improved finance, access to problems and some coordination of direction, they could do far more. To take a case in point, NERC and its constituent agencies were held out to be a significant potential national asset to any UK overseas sustainable development strategy. But reservations were expressed as to whether any Department fully recognised this as being the case. NERC is a grant-aided institution within the domain of the DES (although its Council is widely drawn), but no one in the DES can help it to obtain contracts in, say, Europe for no one is apparently skilled in the processes involved. ODA consults some NERC agencies as a matter of routine within the context of its work. But does this mechanism provide NERC with a regular intelligence service of technical assistance work 'out for contract' in the multilateral agencies? More to the point, does the ODA pay sufficient regard to *all* the NERC institutions as a potential resource in furthering its aid policy in the environmental field beyond the Institute of Geological Sciences and the Institute of Hydrology? (See Appendix L, Section 3 of this report, p 404.) Sir Hermann Bondi, writing in NERC's Annual Report, 1980-81, regards this as important when he states: 'Our work overseas has in the past been largely through and for the Overseas Development Administration. It is a great source of satisfaction that other demands for expertise — some of them of long standing — have grown (recently) in number and value, both scientific and financial. The variety of work that comes to us as sub-contractors to consulting and construction engineering houses, to overseas or British-based development organisations, through foreign Governments and their agencies, is of the utmost importance in giving satisfaction to our scientists. Through this work we get opportunities to do science of a kind we would not otherwise have, and they are warmly to be welcomed. But, at the same time, it must be appreciated that obtaining contracts of this kind involves a great deal of preparatory work. Most of these contracts are open to international competition. Our competitors are neither lazy nor incompetent, nor unduly expensive . . . It is inevitably a major effort to make new customers, and potential new customers, aware of our existence, aware of our expertise and aware of what we can deliver for how much money in what time'.[4]

39. Integrating Western-based research institutions into the development process is not easy. The business of identifying projects that relate to an overall development strategy in a particular country, executing them with staff briefed and able to operate in overseas conditions, giving attention simultaneously to building local institutions and expertise, and then following up to ensure that good work initiated is carried through to a long-term result, requires a deal of patience, expertise and money. As one senior member of an ODA institution put it: 'there is nothing very romantic about working overseas once you have done it once or twice'. It would be quite wrong to gloss over the very real difficulties involved. A particular attitude is required of the expert, far removed from concepts of academic excellence. A degree of personal sacrifice in terms of home comforts, security and family conveniences is inevitable. However, if the UK is concerned about the long-term implications of the WCS, mechanisms, facilities, back-up and money will have to be provided to help overcome these difficulties. It is sad that many qualified people appear to want to take on such engagements but complain that the opportunities are not open to them. An initial and, perhaps, naive conclusion is that the UK has barely begun to realise the extent and richness of its own human resources in the field of environmental management.

Summary

40. The traditional applied science disciplines of land-use and urban planning, geological and hydrological surveys, agricultural science and forestry, pest management, engineering and health sciences have featured strongly in the ODA's research and development programme. They are included in the UK technical assistance programme. In addition, the ODA has supported four special units: the Centre for Overseas Pest Research, the Tropical Products Institute, the Land Resources Development Centre, and the Directorate of Overseas Surveys. At the time of writing (January, 1983) the future strength of these units is in considerable doubt. The operations of two of them, the Tropical Products Institute and the Centre for Overseas Pest Research, are to be merged and the Land Resources Development Centre is to be closed down. Overall, there is talk of up to 40 redundancies. Also relevant are the ODA-sponsored units in eight other Government Departments ranging from the Transport and Road Research Laboratory to the Energy Technology Support Unit at Harwell and the occasional support for NERC- or NCC-based research and studies. One sincerely hopes that this substantial body of experience and expertise will not be abandoned or weakened in the interests of short-term economic considerations. It takes literally years to develop but days to destroy. ODA cannot address the needs of the developing world in the natural resource-area without using its existing body of knowledge to design, plan and execute relevant projects to the full. But, in addition, the ODA should consider how it could improve its access to multi-disciplinary environmental or natural resource-management expertise. This applies to the general discipline of development and to those specialising in environmental aspects of particular sectors of development concern (such as rural development or energy supply). The emphasis the ODA puts upon work is weak in comparison to that of other disciplines (eg economic advice).

41. This is not the place for suggesting bold new institutions or mechanisms (for this, see the Recommendations in Chapter 5 of this report), but suffice to say:
(a) the UK should consider how it could better focus the natural resource/environment expertise it has available for technical assistance in pursuit of WCS objectives and for the purposes of improving the quality of its aid. (Perhaps it could be focused around one chosen institution as is the case for the Agricultural Extension and Rural Development at Reading, Development Studies at Sussex, or Hygiene and Tropical Medicine in London.)
(b) the Crown Agents could also consider how natural resource/environmental management services could be included in the technical assistance offered by them (although not at the expense of ODA expertise).
(c) the ODA's research and development boards and committee could include a body concerned with natural resource/environmental management research.
(d) the UK could look to the Commonwealth Secretariat as a vehicle in which to coordinate assistance, develop priorities and needs, and target its delivery.
(e) a unit in the Department of Trade (DOT), or in the Crown Agents, could be established to give advice to grant-aided institutions on contracts and legal provisions.
(f) a briefing service (such as exists at Farnham Castle) could be used to appraise UK exporters of the conditions, culture, economy etc of countries they were visiting for the first time.
(g) special attention should be given to the terms of service so that no disadvantage accrues to the individual who goes overseas on two to three years contract, secondment or project.

Environmental Training
42. This section does not cover degree courses, many of which contribute significantly to overseas needs, as has been noted in previous sections.

43. The WCS lays great emphasis on training. What can the UK do overseas with regard to this? From the outset, a distinction has to be made between those people who deal with an aspect of environmental management as their profession and those who need to consider the environment in the context of their job, whether as an economist, engineer or civil servant. For the latter, short course training in environmental questions is required, not a degree. This section addresses the problem the latter have, internationally, in gaining access to such post-experience training. Three themes for the UK are considered:
(a) Target groups for environmental training.
(b) The outcome of UNEP's Review of Environmental Training in 1979.
(c) The existing UK structure for environmental training.

Target Groups for Training

44. Target groups for environmental training have been defined by an *ad hoc* group interested in the question.[5] Two groups were identified:

THOSE IN AID-RECEIVING COUNTRIES

(a) Top level civil servants, who, it is assumed, need a very general orientation to environmental and resource-management questions. In effect: What is the environment? Why should Governments care about it? What general approaches and methods can be used by Governments to manage it?
(b) Middle level civil servants, who need all of the above plus some experience of impact assessment techniques, the various pollution control methods and options, and the general financial and staffing implications of sound Governmental practice in environmental management.
(c) Practitioners, who, we assume, need different skills depending on what they do. Thus water engineers need different skills from local health

officials; road builders from harbour constructors, and so on. But all need some perception of environmental questions.

THOSE IN DONOR COUNTRIES

(a) The bilateral studies performed in the late 1970s all indicated that far greater emphasis should be put on training desk personnel in the aid agencies themselves. The UK does not in general provide such training.

(b) The same applies to the multilateral aid agencies. Although the possibility of a cooperative enterprise providing environmental expertise and training should not be ruled out, much could be done in the UK to help the multilateral agencies.

The Outcome of UNEP's Review of Environmental Training in 1979

45. UNEP's review of environmental training[6] is an extremely useful starting point if the UK decided that it wanted to contribute in this area overseas (not least because the inputs were broad and in some cases well prepared). It sets out target groups, current facilities for training in the UN system, a very strong political justification for an accelerated programme (based on past UN decisions and recommendations) and a classification of needs and the scope of an idealised system.

46. On target groups, the overriding conclusion is that in too many cases courses have been begun without being preceded by a proper survey of needs.

47. In considering the UN system of training, it is clear that the presently committed UN resources are woefully inadequate world-wide. From 1977 to 1981, the total was less than $9.5m dollars in any one year. These totals include training for technicians in a host of specialised fields such as sanitary engineering, soil ecology, air pollution monitoring, etc. In fact, it would be very surprising if the total for these target categories exceeded $500,000. Much more work is needed to update figures and to separate out real (as opposed to planned) deeds.

48. The work needed to fill gaps in environmental management competence are listed in the UNEP report (but not repeated here). As can be imagined, they range from intensive courses to field courses, manuals, text books and lecture notes.

49. However, in general, the UNEP review is unconvincing on what should follow. It identifies gaps in the current system and makes a general case for more training, but does not go on to propose anything very concrete for Governments to do.

50. It should also be noted that the EEC (DG 8) is now conducting a similar survey of training in environmental management for developing countries.

The Existing UK Structure for Environmental Training

51. The survey carried out for this report of UK universities served to show how rich and diverse the UK faculty skills are for teaching the broad gamut of environmental topics to a first or post-graduate degree level. However, it also revealed that no UK university, apart from Aberdeen, is now running short post-experience courses on environmental management specifically aimed at the overseas client. The Monitoring and Assessment Research Centre (MARC, Chelsea) used to do this, but it has temporarily retired from the race owing to lack of finance. Post-experience environmental training for the UK, let alone for overseas personnel, is apparently not widely available. However, there is training at Loughborough, Aberdeen and Bristol (School for Advanced Urban Studies) and various polytechnics. (Nevertheless, the author admits that more research is needed on this point.)

52. This situation is surely because, in general, post-experience training is based on the existing UK bureaucratic structure for environmental management and pollution control, which itself is highly compartmentalised and professionally bound. Thus, the Royal Commission on Environmental Pollution noted in its Fourth Report (1974)[7] that: 'There were some grounds for thinking that current concern with environmental problems might have led to a proliferation of broadly-based environmental science courses, designed to give an understanding of the range and multi-disciplinary nature of these problems. While fully accepting that such courses make a valuable contribution to general understanding, the Commission's view is that they do not provide a suitable foundation for people who are to be employed on scientific and technical work in the field of pollution control. We consider that the best basis for this work is a specialist degree in a relevant basic discipline; this will provide the theoretical background to which further knowledge, acquired by practical experience and from post-experience courses, may best be added. Our views on this matter were supported by nearly all the professional institutions which commented on it in their evidence'.[8]

53. In effect, the general tone and style of the UK post-experience training sector is geared to the existing base of UK legislation and bureaucratic responsibilities. It would have little application across the Channel, let alone across the Mediterranean Sea. If this is so, nothing very beneficial would follow if we simply opened our doors to the world outside. However, as we have such a considerable body of relevant expertise and experience in the UK can we do more?

54. Internationally, there is a clear need for leadership and for centres of excellence in post-experience environmental training for the following reasons:

(a) Development strategies that incorporate notions of sustainability, conservation, environment et al, imply a basic knowledge of natural systems and stocks, an assessment of the possible environmental effects that arise from development, monitoring of environment change, and environmental control. Each need requires trained people who do not exist in sufficient numbers in the agencies, Governments or private sector concerns that are involved.

(b) There is as yet no clear strategy for environmental training in the UN system.

(c) There is apparently no clear strategy for environmental training in donor (Western) Governments (save possibly in the US where the African scheme is now under a budgetary threat) for overseas development assistance or for aid agency competence.

(d) There is no clear strategy for environmental training in the multilateral agencies.

55. But no one Government or national organisation can possibly tackle all subjects, all target groups and all nationalities at once. To try to do so is clearly absurd. Therefore, in an international context, there is a need for a series of centres of excellence by region, by target group and by subject (see the Practitioners' Debate, Chapter 6 of this report).

56. The UK (along with most OECD states) is very rich in environmental science, and in having an academic and educational system containing all the elements needed to provide good short training courses at home or, much more appropriately, abroad. However there is no available or earmarked money for this need, no system of student recruitment to call upon, no framework within which initiatives can be taken either domestically, regionally or internationally, and no clear source of experience or coordination (scope and needs) and follow-up to call upon. From the author's limited experience, those that run courses do so in a vacuum.

57. If all OECD Governments attempt to promote individual approaches, then there is going to be conflict and confusion in those countries that receive assistance from many sources. Some international coordination is needed on organisation and curricula design, as different Western countries employ very different environmental tools (for example, compare our planning procedure with the National Environmental Policy Act — NEPA).

58. Therefore, there are a number of useful jobs to be done (within and outside the UK). (See Recommendations, Chapter 5 of this report.)

☐ Someone in the UK should prepare a report on 'The case for short post-experience training courses in environmental management overseas needs in a selected number of countries'. This would set out to define the target groups more systematically, together with their needs, and establish who in Europe and North America is doing what to meet them. (A useful starting point would be the study commissioned on training by EDF in 1982.)[9]

☐ This might lead on to a possible design for a series of UK- (or European-) based courses, to include scope, topics, faculty, facilities, or to an experimental series of courses to improve curricula design, to develop course material, and to establish a network of past students to call upon. The priority could well be the training of trainers.

☐ However, optimistically, this might lead to the reinforcement of existing centres overseas or to new ones in the developing world. No one doubts that the most economical long-term approach is to train via local centres where knowledge is applied.

☐ Failing a comprehensive approach, the ODA should, if possible, identify environmental courses run by other agencies (such as the US in Africa) and establish a partnership with them for faculty and financial purposes.

The rationale for this is not simply altruistic. Much of our ability to make UK environmental competence available to overseas needs will rely upon the exposure of overseas personnel to our experience and expertise and *vice versa*. Short post-experience courses would provide the impetus for this interaction.

Conclusion

59. The foundation stone of Britain's overseas environmental posture is to materially assist in raising the level of environmental management competence overseas, by way of university education, training and technical assistance. In all these the UK is capable of doing far more.

Notes and References

1 There are exceptions, such as Oxfam's exemplary work on pesticides and fuelwood problems in the Third World, the International Coalition for Development Action's work on the patenting of genetic resources and Friends of the Earth's emerging interest in the fate of the moist tropical rainforests. Then there is the very creditable record of WWF (UK) and the UK IUCN activities.

2 THE ORGANISATION FOR ECONOMIC CO-OPERATION AND DEVELOPMENT. 1981. *Development Co-operation 1981 Review. November*. Paris, OECD.

3. The agencies visited by the author or B Johnson included NERC headquarters, Swindon, the Centre for Overseas Pest Research, the NCC, the Countryside Commission, the Commonwelath Forestry Institute, the Tropical Products Institute, the British Council and the ITDG. The agencies circularised included all of the above bar the NCC and the Countryside Commission. In addition, views were sought from the Tropical Products Institute, the National Vegetable Research Station, Department of Trade (Shipping), the Water Council, the Institute of Geological Sciences, the Institute for Marine Environmental Research, the Weed Research Organis-

ation, the Grassland Research Institute, and the Forestry Commission.

4 BONDI, SIR H. 1981. Annual report. National Environmental Research Council.

5 In 1978-79 the following convened an *ad hoc* group on 'UK Environmental training for overseas clients': Dr Sors (MARC), Professor Brian Clark (Aberdeen), Professor Gordon Goodman (Bieyer Institute), Dr Pauline Marstrand (SPRU), Richard Sandbrook (IIED). Whilst many of the points in this section arise from their work, the group has now disbanded and in no way should they be held responsible for the points set out.

6 UNITED NATIONS ENVIRONMENT PROGRAMME. 1980. Environmental training. UNEP report no 9.

7 ROYAL COMMISSION ON ENVIRONMENTAL POLLUTION. 1974. Fourth report. HMSO.

8 The 'professional institutions' referred to include, *inter alia*, The Royal Society of Health — Diploma in air pollution control; The Environmental Health Officers Education Board — Diploma in environmental health; The Institute of Water Pollution Control — Diploma in water pollution control.

9 European Development Fund Study on Environmental Training. To be completed in Spring 1983.

CHAPTER 5

SUMMARY AND RECOMMENDATIONS

Chapter 1

In Chapter 1, the case for an open, coordinated and deliberate UK response to the WCS overseas is set out. It begins by drawing together the common themes of the WCS, the Global 2000 report to the President of the USA (1980) on global trends and the Brandt report — namely that we live in an interdependent world and we should all have an eye to its worsening economic and ecological condition. The rationale for economic and ecological interdependence is built up by way of moral, economic and strategic arguments. The facts which justify the approach are not set out at length in the text, but in Appendix A of this report. Chapter 1 includes a brief resumé of progress made toward better global management of the environment in the past decade, and ends with a description of the new consensus that has emerged. This, it is argued, *should now underpin the UK's foreign environmental policy*.

No recommendations are made in this chapter.

Chapter 2

In Chapter 2 a response to the WCS overseas is set out in terms of UK foreign policy. First, the responsibilities of the UK are set out. The principle objective is defined: to raise the self-reliance of overseas states so that they can better manage their natural resources. In so doing, the UK must respect sovereignty; the UK cannot ignore the economic relationships within and between nations, and the UK cannot avoid the harsh political realities of those of other countries.

Other practical constraints are set out and the response to the Brandt report is used to illustrate their importance. The approach is summarised as 'down to earth' and practical, motivated and comprehensive. The chapter finishes with a definition of the environmental scope of the report. Conservation is defined as in the WCS: to maintain ecological processes and genetic diversity and to ensure the sustainable use of natural resources. Sustainable development is also defined as the process by which the living conditions of the poorer majority of the human race are improved, whilst avoiding the destruction of natural and living resources. Both conservation and sustainable development are linked; both seek

to increase production and exchange and to create better conditions for humanity, but in a manner that can be sustained in the long term. The report adopts the basic needs approach to development as the route most likely to achieve the desired results. Appendix B of this report sets out the conservation tasks that need to be considered (taken from the WCS) and Appendix C of this report outlines the basic needs approach and its relationship to the WCS.

No recommendations are made in this chapter.

Chapter 3

The components of the UK's overseas environmental policy are listed as: our aid programme and its environmental effects, our participation in the environment/development work of OECD and the EEC, our contribution to the relevant parts of the UN, our relationships with the Commonwealth on these questions and finally our direct responsibilities arising by way of Conventions, Treaties and UK overseas jurisdiction. The important missing components, trade and investment links, are not considered at length in the report for the reasons set out in the Practitioners' Debate.

With respect to the UK aid policy, much reliance is placed on the study of the ODA's environmental procedures carried out by an independent group in 1978-79. Not all of its conclusions are now relevant but some of the recommendations on training, staffing and ODA processes stand as additions to this report.

However, the major concern is that the UK aid policy has moved away from the basic needs approach and the overall financial commitment is in decline. Both are bad in terms of our commitment to the WCS overseas. The conclusion drawn is that the political mandate for aid is under strain and now needs to be renewed. Another trend that is highlighted is the apparent decline in the relevant professional advice within ODA that is so vital to an environmentally sensitive aid programme.

The section on OECD refers to work attempting to re-establish the political momentum behind by linking the traditional moral and self-interest arguements for it with the new strategic imperative. A series of 'system maintenance' goals or tasks are outlined, including those relating to environmental quality as the strategic issues to be faced. An argument is put forward for the UK's close involvement with the international coordination and effort to achieve these goals. The OECD section concludes by reviewing the recent positive work of the OECD environment and development committees, and urges that the UK gives close support.

However, the major conclusion and recommendation is that Government, or an independent institution on behalf of Government, should set out as a public document an assessment of the UK's proper response to long-term environmental degradation on an international scale. There are four areas that deserve close public scrutiny:

(a) The risk to the UK, in the long term, of a gradual international deterioration in environmental quality, leading to food insecurity and natural resource-scarcity, both renewable and non-renewable.

(b) The emphasis the UK now places on solving these questions in cooperation with other States.

(c) The resources the UK can deploy to offset or reverse the undesirable trends, in terms of people and money.

(d) The risks to the UK of doing nothing.

Whilst the report sets out many ideas on these points, it is by no means as complete or as informed as an equivalent Government Paper would be. Such a document would do much to bring the public into the debate and rekindle our national drive to face the world as it is.

Section 3 of Chapter 3, (see p 330) relates to the EEC's international environmental posture. In general, the plans of the Commission, the CEC, in furtherance of the Strategy are positive and welcomed and four recommendations are made for advancing them.

Recommendation 1

The positive views of the Environment Directorate should be promoted throughout all other directorates of the CEC.

Recommendation 2

The environmental procedures of the EDF should be overhauled (see the detailed suggestions in Appendix G of this report).

Recommendation 3

A degree of political coordination should be established between the Environmental Ministers and the Foreign and/or Overseas Development Ministers of the ten Member States; to be achieved by way of a joint Special Council meeting on the theme.

Recommendation 4

The UK Government should act positively to advance the international side of the Environmental Directorate's agenda by way of full cooperation and leadership.

The UN and its various agencies are considered in Section 4 of Chapter 3, pp 333-336. The recommendations are broad and reflect the limited scope that there is for any one Member State to make significant inroads into UN policy and performance. Thus:

Recommendation 5

The UK should:

(a) ensure that the UN's System Wide Medium Term Environmental Planning Exercise (SWMTEP) is seriously considered and acted upon;

(b) back all efforts within OECD, EEC and the Commonwealth that support the United Nations Environment Programme but particularly Earthwatch and SWMTEP;

(c) continue to support such centres of excellence for environmental purposes as there are elsewhere in the UN;

(d) positively help in the field of information, education and training in environmental matters via the UN system.

In Appendix H of this report there is a more detailed analysis of Earthwatch and the UN Environment Programme with recommendations that are particular to it. Appendix I of this report considers UNESCO in more depth.

In Section 5 of Chapter 3, page 336, the Commonwealth is singled out in the report as a target for UK technical assistance and action for it offers a series of advantages over the UN for political dialogue, cooperation and resolve. As a result:

Recommendation 6

The British Government should materially assist in designing and funding a 10 year Commonwealth programme of environmental management technical assistance. The working title should, in effect, be 'A decade for the development of the indigenous environmental management capability of Commonwealth countries'. (The components and priorities of the decade are picked up in the recommendations from Chapter 4, see p 341.)

In Section 6 of Chapter 3, page 337, Britain's direct responsibilities overseas are considered. The various conventions and treaties we have signed or ratified are not dealt with in any depth; only three points are made, each accompanied by a recommendation:

Recommendation 7

The UK should create a fund for such scientific research and coordination as is required to fulfil 'environmental' Treaty and Convention obligations (eg CITES, Antarctic Conventions, the IWC, etc).

Recommendation 8

The UK should set about joining the Convention for the Protection of World Cultural and Natural Heritage.

Recommendation 9

UK voluntary organisations (NGOs) should be considered for membership, as official observers, on many more Government delegations to international meetings.

With respect to our overseas territories, the report is also very brief, and recommends that:

Recommendation 10
The environmental standards we set for the Falklands and the other British sub-Antarctic islands should be consistent with those we wish to achieve for Antarctica as a whole.

Finally from Chapter 3 it is recommended that:

Recommendation 11
The UK should continue to give positive assistance to IUCN — as the 'umbrella' organisation charged with the international promotion of the WCS.

Chapter 4

Chapter 4 is divided into four sections. The first considers the voluntary sector that is involved in overseas aspects of the WCS, and then the Whitehall Departments that are concerned. These two sections set the scene for consideration of scientific and technical assistance in the fields of environmental management and environmental training for overseas personnel.

The technical assistance section starts with a broad comment on how poorly it is organised internationally; and without further comment on the UK's record the report goes on to assess our national assets for doing more. The universities are the first component; the grant aided institutions the second. In the case of the former, a survey of them was conducted as part of the research for the paper, and the results are given. In the case of the latter, visits were made to a number and an analysis follows. Finally, there is a section on the international scene for environmental management training and the UK's relationship with it. The following recommendations are made:

Recommendation 12
The Voluntary Sector should convene a meeting of the relevant environment and development organisations to discuss a combined follow-up agenda to the WCS overseas.

Recommendation 13
An interdepartmental policy for the overseas implications of the WCS should be prepared. The work and the departments who, *prima facie*, are involved are:
(a) the Central Directorate on Environmental Pollution in DOE (UNEP, EEC, ECE, OECD), the Directorate of Rural Affairs and the international section of the NCC;
(b) the international work of MAFF in respect of fisheries and FAO;
(c) the international work of ODA and DES (?) relating to UNESCO and the policy for promoting our universities and research institutions abroad;

(d) the work of the Bilateral Coordination Department and the Natural Resources, Engineering, Education, Health and Population division of ODA; linked to the delivery of financial aid and of technical assistance in the aid programme;
(e) the Foreign and Commonwealth office for the policy overall.

Recommendation 14
A unit to coordinate the delivery of the policy abroad throughout our foreign service (bilaterally, at the UN, in various Treaty forums, in the EEC, in the OECD and the Commonwealth). (Note: this recommendation *excludes* the UK's trading policy and its effect on the environment internationally.)

Recommendation 15
The UK should consider how it could better focus the natural resource/environmental expertise it has available for technical assistance in pursuit of the WCS objectives and for the purposes of improving the quality of its aid (perhaps around one chosen grant-aided institution).

Recommendation 16
The Crown Agents could consider how natural resource/environmental management services could be included in the technical assistance offered by them (although not at the expense of ODA expertise).

Recommendation 17
The ODA's research and development boards and committees could include a body concerned with natural resource/environmental management research.

Recommendation 18
The UK should look to the Commonwealth Secretariat as a vehicle in which to coordinate assistance, develop priorities and needs and target its delivery.

Recommendation 19
A unit in the Department of Trade (DOT) (or in the Crown Agents) could be established to give advice to grant aided institutions on contracts and legal provisions overseas.

Recommendation 20
Briefing services (such as exists at the Centre for International Briefing at Farnham Castle) could be better used to appraise UK environmental experts of the conditions, culture, economy etc of countries they were visiting for the first time.

Recommendation 21
The terms of service for UK Government employees working for limited periods overseas (on short-term secondments, aid missions or under contract) should not be such as to detract from their career advancement or pension rights.

Recommendation 22
The UK should prepare a paper on 'The case for short post-experience training courses in Environmental Management overseas'. This would set out to define the

target groups systematically, together with their needs, and establish who in Europe and North America is doing what to meet them. This might lead on to a possible design for a series of UK- (or European-) based courses — to include scope, topics, faculty, facilities. (International collaboration should be included.) Or this might lead to an experimental series of courses to improve curricula design, to develop course material and to establish a network of past students to call upon. The priority could well be the training of trainers. However, optimistically, such an approach would lead to the reinforcement of existing centres overseas and to new ones in the developing world. *The most economical long-term approach is to train via local centres in the place where knowledge is applied.*

Recommendation 23

Failing a comprehensive approach, the ODA should identify environmental courses run by other agencies (such as the US in Africa) and establish a partnership with them for faculty and financial purposes.

The conclusion of the report is that while the UK may well be vulnerable to a world-wide decline in environmental quality, many others are more so. This being said, the most significant contribution that Britain has to make in furtherance of the WCS overseas is to raise, world-wide, the manpower capability for meeting the natural resource-management crisis we all face. But improving the environmental technical ability of nations will solve nothing if the long-term security of the very poor nations is not improved also. Environmental quality is linked to population pressures which in turn are linked to the health, wealth and welfare of *all* humanity.

CHAPTER 6
THE PRACTITIONERS'
DEBATE

Introduction

1. Between July 1982 and January 1983, some 900 copies of this report were circulated for comments. It was sent to a wide range of civil servants, academics, professionals, non-Governmental organisations, international agencies and European Governments. There was a considerable response, both in terms of bulk and of quality. In addition, three meetings were held to discuss the report: a well-attended session at the Royal Society of Arts to discuss the technical assistance proposals; a special session of the UK IUCN committee at the NCC and a meeting of some NGOs drawn from the Environment and Development camps.

Again the response was constructive and enthusiastic. Very few concrete objections to the report, other than points of detail, were received although, by and large, the civil servants and many academics remained silent. The report has been considerably revised in the light of comments received, both to condense it in length and to correct factual errors. Additionally, many aspects of it have been expanded, and, in particular, three have been developed: the strategic rationale for the UK supporting the WCS overseas, the impact of our trade and investment, and the contribution we could and should be making in terms of technical assistance. The International Review Group had a final meeting, and blessed the approach to the revisions.

Basic Considerations

2. Most of the comments received were very supportive of the integrative nature of the piece. When all the components of the UK's overseas activities in the environmental sphere are collected together, they amount to a considerable body of work. As Max Nicholson suggests, once it is realised that we have many of the components of a coherent overseas environmental strategy already in place (albeit on an *ad hoc* basis), it is but a small step to coordinate the parts together, find gaps in the strategy and promote the end result. Omissions in the policy were pointed out in the report and these, and more, were emphasised in the response. Others agree with the author that we do not properly inform the UK public of the interrelated trends in overseas environment and development; we do not make our expertise as available

as we should; and our image is poor, not least because our pragmatism and the quest for value for money frequently comes across in a negative way in important international forums. In effect, we need far more hard-headed enthusiasm from those in Government and in key institutions in the framing and execution of our contribution to sustainable development overseas.

What About the Money?

3. Of course, the report attracted the expected criticism on the financial front. Who is going to pay? What will all the idealised suggestions cost? The lazy response is to suggest that only Government can work up a price tag for itself and then weigh the costs against the tangible and intangible gains. Only Government can judge the risk of doing nothing more. But an alternative and more constructive response was emphasised in the debate. If we already have the civil servants, the experts, the institutions and the processes in place in many instances, we are talking of redeployment rather than new costs; changing priorities rather than new commitments. There is bound to be some extra finance required to put the recommendations of this report into effect, but many resources are already in place. Make our universities more applied in the problems of natural resource-management, make our Ministries more supportive of our overseas environmental agencies, help to make our tax-paying public more aware of the urgency of the issues and make our enormous contribution of over £200m per year to the UN specialised agencies and multilateral aid agencies and the £800m we spend in direct aid more telling in terms of result.

Real Aid

4. One very significant event in the debate period was the publication of 'Real Aid' by the Independent Group on British Aid. They reinforce the conclusion of this report that development assistance (aid) really can have a significant beneficial impact on the lives of the very poor overseas, provided its direction is to that end. What matters at all times is the quality of our aid, not just the quantity. How should the £20 per head of the UK

population be spent? The Group make suggestions for improving the quality that are consistent with this report: less emphasis on export, the abolition of the aid-trade provision or at least a move to put export 'guarantees' into the trade budget, less food aid except in very special circumstances, better programming and project evaluation, more public scrutiny, a stronger position for the Ministry, fewer target countries, a standing body of professional advice, more international coordination, and more use of the non-Governmental agencies as routes for spending.

Strategic Considerations

5. Such considerations revolve around the perceived purpose of our aid programme as a part of our foreign policy. Is aid for us or for the poor? Mr Francis Pym addressed the question in December 1982 when he spoke at the Royal Commonwealth Society. Announcing a small but significant increase in the aid budget (£85m or 9 per cent), he stated: 'Our foremost aim must be to encourage faster economic growth in the poorest countries . . . The moral and humanitarian case . . . is overwhelming'. He went on to address the strategic imperative, a recurring theme of this paper. 'Prosperity helps to create political stability and that is the basic objective of foreign policy. A more stable world fosters and encourages trade and this benefits everybody.'

6. Putting the trade benefits aside for a moment, all that needs to be added to Mr Pym's speech in this context is a sad tale. When a representative of the Foreign Office was faced with this report, he said that the case for improving our foreign environmental posture had not been made by the author in *strategic* terms. This is by far the most damning comment (to date) of the report.

7. The basic argument for conserving our planet is to provide future generations with the same substrate of material existence as we enjoy. This is surely of fundamental strategic, moral and humanitarian concern to this country and to all others. A development process that leaves out the poor so that they continue to multiply and to live ruinously on (and off) the margin of material existence is not sustainable. A development process that encourages a waste of resources and irreversible pollution of the biosphere is not sustainable. A development process that encourages short-term economic gain at the all-time expense of forests, fish stocks, water tables, mineral reserves, fertile soils and clean water is not sustainable. Such development cannot lead to political stability or durable economic growth. Strategically, development without destruction is as important as peace without war.

Trade Considerations

8. The missing component of this report that has attracted most criticism is that relating to trade and investment flows. The UK aid flow of £1,000m per annum is insignificant in money terms compared with the external debts (*circa* £50,000m in Mexico alone) and net foreign direct investments in Third World countries (£1,300m in Brazil in one year — 1979). The impact of this trade and investment should have been addressed in the report. However, there is no point in approaching the subject in a lazy way. It is a research job that still needs to be done.

9. The statement made by Mr Pym that 'trade benefits everyone' is probably not quite correct. The determinants of much short-term environmental expediency are unquestionably trade and investment linked. René Dumont pointed out some years ago that Africa could either develop its agriculture for export or for itself, and he demonstrated that the results, in terms of environment, are quite different.[1] 'Export or die' is as much a slogan of the poor countries as of the rich. They have the enormous debt burden (all too readily permitted by the rich) and they have a need for imported oil and manufactured goods. It has certainly occurred to the author that 'the shackles' of world trade may well force us toward an environmental desert, rather than the gardens of Eden. But what is the alternative? The response involves a genuine sense of uncertainty: namely that if a country has chosen to develop then it needs the ability to anticipate environmental change, a level of economic activity sufficient to improve the lot of its poor and the institutions to manage that economy sustainably (and that may or may not involve a high level of commodity export). Only if a country is self-reliant in these matters will the pace of environmental destruction abate. Helping countries to achieve such independence seems to be a more realistic and humanitarian response than advocating a break in the trading links between the peoples of the world. Thus, there should be economic and ecological interdependence but with management self-reliance.

Our Traders

10. An aspect of trade that could and should have been addressed is the way in which the UK-domiciled private sector behaves (and those parts of the multinational club that we can influence). Mr Tom King, Secretary of State for the Environment, pointed out in a speech in November 1982 that great opportunities lie ahead for our pollution control industry in the rich and poor worlds. How true, but the words of Dr Martin Holdgate[2] (Chief Scientist at the Department of the Environment) must also apply to all industry and not just to the pollution control sector: '. . . the challenge of the next decade is to promote environmentally sound development in the Third World and it is in the interests of British firms to set a high standard there'. Increasingly, countries are setting higher environmental standards for themselves, but there are still pollution havens for the industrialised world to run to. In environmental terms,

this is not an insignificant risk. During the last decade, 60 per cent of all investment in Third World countries originated from outside those countries and much of it was made by overseas companies. A large proportion of the investment went into natural resource-exploitation (minerals, fuels, timber, fish etc) for use in OECD countries and this will no doubt continue. Cheap labour, the absence of environmental and social controls and the proximity of natural resources are temptations to any board room, as are the markets for prohibited pesticides, surplus skimmed milk, patent medicines (pharmaceuticals) and the like. Again, it is nice to be able to wash out one's oil tankers at points where Fleet Street has no correspondent watching. International controls can apply to some of these practices (ranging from product controls to shipping regulations). But by and large there are only two satisfactory answers given the nature of multinational enterprise and free trade: one is restraint on the part of the enterprise and the other local controls promulgated by the local State.

11. The tradition of voluntary controls within certain industries works reasonably well in some domestic circumstances (eg Pesticides) but these (via the OECD) should now be encouraged internationally. Thus the suggestion made that the OECD Guidelines for Multinational Enterprises (1976 and 1979)[3] be revised to include the environment is to be welcomed. Similar work by the UN also goes in the right direction.

12. With little research to back it up, it appears that most of UK industry has a creditable record of good environmental behaviour in developing countries (the Solomon Isles apart) and appears to believe that pollution and short-term resource-exploitation does not pay. 'Invest to stay rather than make hay' is the operating slogan. The UK has also played its part in advancing voluntary guidelines via the International Chamber of Commerce and by other means. Thus one can do no more than endorse the sentiments of the Deputy Director of the CBI when he stated in response to this report that: 'British industry's contribution to all this should be the "export" of appropriate technology and expertise and, in pursuing overseas development projects, ensuring that environmental/conservation considerations are taken into account from the start'.

The Question of Technical Cooperation

13. The area of the report that attracted most comment was that relating to technical cooperation (assistance) and training. The sentiment that we do too little as a nation to make the most of our national skills hit a sympathetic chord with nearly all those who expressed views during the consultation debate.

14. For example, Professor Furtado, Science Advisor to the Commonwealth Secretariat, stated: 'If the United Kingdom Government should wish, the Commonwealth Secretariat could act as a vehicle for its overseas aid relating to environmental and natural resources-management. Such an initiative on the part of the UK Government would enhance its visibility and long-term interests in developing countries, would reinforce the spirit of the Commonwealth, and would help make the Commonwealth an example of development and interdependence in the spirit of the New International Economic Order and the North-South dialogue'.[4]

15. Others commented on this proposal with reservations. The Secretariat has little money to spend (circa £9.3m in 1981 in the technical cooperation fund), is not staffed to do the job and has much else to do already. All this is true, but overall if a new and positive initiative is to follow the Ten Year technical assistance 'push', the Commonwealth seems to be the most popular candidate for the task that this report has suggested.

16. The professional societies also reinforced the point on our record overseas. The Royal Town Planning Institute said: 'What we should be doing is using our universities' research councils, professional institutions and so on to help promote the development of appropriate institutions in the developing world'. And a District Council Director of Planning that: 'The opportunities for fixed-term job swaps between planners in this country and overseas has recently been explored and could be extended . . .'

17. The report also brought welcome comments from the institutions, for example from NERC and those familiar with its workings. Lord Cranbrook stated: 'Not only does UK at present have considerable expertise in the field of good environmental management, but also — because of our methods of training through research and personal supervision — we have the capacity to pass on this expertise and maintain the quality of our personnel from one generation to the next provided that opportunities for overseas experience are fostered. It is thus mutually advantageous to UK and to the developing world to maintain a high level of overseas contract work involving British institutions . . . I suggest that scientific and/or commercial attaches at all UK overseas missions ought to be thoroughly briefed on the nature of expertise available and on appropriate institutional contacts (Government or commercial). British Council information services, too, could be considered useful means of informing potential clients of available expertise'.

18. A representative of NERC made a number of comments, some of which are presented here. 'NERC is of course very well equipped to handle multi-disciplinary problems and . . . our expertise extends far wider than geology and hydrology. Much of what we already do is in effect tackling aspects of the WCS.'

19. 'This research can be turned to overseas benefit in two ways, the first being the development of basic research methodology. The other is involvement in world-wide problems such as acid rain, carbon dioxide build up, multi-species fisheries, and the spread and effects of agricultural chemicals world-wide.'

20. 'I agree with the report, and with many statements made at subsequent meetings, that the UK has not made very good use of its environmental skills overseas. The underlying problem is, as somebody said, "The UK has turned in on itself".'

21. The academic community also added to the already powerful collection of constructive examples given in the survey (see Chapter 4 of this report). Two are picked out as being particularly attractive. The first is a suggestion made by a number of commentators for the twinning of institutions to encourage a regular flow of cooperation and understanding (possibly via the British Council). The other was an emphasis on the decline in post-graduate students coming to Britain owing to the fee position. A number of academics regretted this decline in terms of the WCS overseas, particularly for the units and/or centres specifically designed to help (eg the Commonwealth Forestry Institute and the London School of Hygiene and Tropical Medicine).

22. However, it must be stated that by no means all the responses were critical about our national efforts to date. A number wrote to say that much work of great credit to the UK was being done and we should not forget it. However, sadly, since the report was published, the professional expertise involved in our aid programme seems to have taken a further blow. The ODA professional advisors in the natural resource-area seem to be gradually disappearing and the ODA-sponsored institutions (eg the Centre for Overseas Pest Research, and the Tropical Products Institute) are being merged and are presumably losing staff as well. Appropriate professional skills are essential to an aid programme concerned with the issues that this paper addresses. The private sector consultant has his role in aid but can never replace the public servant, consistently hired, with a lifetime of experience to put to good effect. Sadly, at the very time that we should be building up such expertise to meet the growing world environmental problems, we appear to be losing it.

Training for Sustainable Development

23. The emphasis on developing local skills was supported by all commentators. Thus Professor Conway of Imperial College wrote: 'Whether we are talking about upland denudation, desertification, the consequences of irrigation or agricultural mechanisation, urban sanitation or marine oil pollution, the problems and their solutions are all heavily dependent on site-specific physical and ecological variables (eg temperature, rainfall, soil type). Of equal importance are the economic, social, cultural and historical factors of a local nature. An intimate knowledge of these factors and the experience necessary to weight them in an appropriate fashion is an essential component of any lasting solution. By implication environmental and resource-issues in developing countries cannot be properly resolved by overseas experts, or even teams of experts, however able, nor (and this is

something that is being only slowly recognised) can the problems of outlying provincial regions in the developing countries be solved by experts from their own capitals, however well trained. Indeed I believe that the greatest development challenge of the next two decades is the necessity to establish, man and institutionalise centres of excellence in development and environment expertise in the provinces of the developing countries (in particular in countries such as Indonesia, Nigeria, Sudan, Brazil and China which encompass vast and varied topographies and environmental conditions)'.

24. This local approach was carried across in comments on training: 'Encourage local centres of training, not expensive courses in remote places'. But there is undoubtedly a place for UK-based training as well (for example, the three week Environmental Assessment Course at Aberdeen now attracts some 90 excellent students per year). Conway suggested that the best innovations in this regard have come from 'independent or semi-independent foundations or agencies' (such as the International Development Research Centre (IDRC) in Canada and the Rockefeller Ford and Inter-American Foundations). He thus would welcome a semi-independent Commonwealth initiative underpinned by Governmental finance.

25. Professor Poore of the Commonwealth Forestry Institute (CFI), in a paper on the report, added the final say: 'I maintain that with a little constructive planning, ingenuity and positive Government initiative it would be possible to realise a 10 year programme for the development of indigenous management capability in Commonwealth countries based on existing institutions (such as CFI) and elements in UK universities where allied interests are found'.

The Voluntary Sector

26. In the report it was suggested that the two voluntary sectors representing environment and development concern should get together. A meeting to this end was arranged and from small beginnings some enthusiasm is now building up. The links will be on specific topics, such as pesticide use abroad, rain forests and energy resources, but will, one hopes, lead on to a far deeper public awareness of the inter-linkages between the two approaches. In Southern terms the separation of environment and development is absurd, as some Southern organisations pointed out in response.

27. Some non-Governmental organisations (NGOs) pointed out how much more they were doing than the report gave credit for. Thus, the Commonwealth Human Ecology Council pointed to its efforts, over many years, to achieve the sort of cooperation the report wanted. The Royal Geographical Society highlighted its 400 annual expeditions and the wealth of cooperation, understanding and real help they brought in their wake. The Voluntary Service Overseas gave a similar response in terms of tangible results.

THE UK'S OVERSEAS ENVIRONMENTAL POLICY

28. The 'development' voluntary sector is already supported by our aid programme on a pound for pound basis. In time, one hopes that this will spread to environmental organisations capable of delivering real help to 'those parts of countries and groups of people which official aid (through government channels) cannot reach' (Pym, December 1982).[5]

Conclusion

29. We are by now far along the road in describing what is happening to the world's environment. We have yet to face up to the unpleasant realities of why it is happening. Only when that is done, and the political will to stop it is generated, can we get down to the job of putting things to right. It is in all our interests to try a bit harder.

Notes and References

1 See also: DINHAM AND HINES. 1983. Agribusiness in Africa. London, ERR. (28 Pentonville Road, N1) which is an excellent analysis of the point.

2 Martin Holdgate to the CBI, November 1982. 'Industry and environment, a view from Government'.

3 ORGANISATION FOR ECONOMIC CO-OPERATION AND DEVELOPMENT. 1976 and 1979. Guidelines for multinational enterprises. OECD.

4 Professor Furtado in a speech to the Royal Society of Arts, November 1982, entitled 'Technical assistance and the environment'.

5 Speech to the Royal Commonwealth Society, December 1982.

THE ISSUES AT STAKE

Section 1:
Global Economic and Ecological Interdependence
(Extracted from the OECD publication of the same name April, 1982)

The growing interdependence of the international economic and political system has become a central question for Governments and international organisations as they examine the critical issues likely to dominate the world scene to and beyond the turn of this decade and century. This interdependence is seen to cover not only population, migration, energy, food, financial transfers and technology, but also the environment and, increasingly, the ecological basis for development: renewable and non-renewable resources, the oceans, the atmosphere and climate, land, space and mankind's genetic resources and heritage. Understanding of this interdependence and its implications can lead to hope or despair, depending on one's view of the will and capacity of Governments to make necessary adjustments within and among their countries.

The Issues Considered in the Report

CO₂ AND CLIMATIC CHANGE

Increasing concentrations of CO_2 in the atmosphere, due mainly to the burning of fossil fuels, might cause a warming trend, leading to climatic changes in the next century of sufficient magnitude to produce major physical, economic and social dislocations on a global scale. Significant uncertainties persist, however, as to causes and effects.

A team of NASA atmospheric scientists recently predicted that there is a high probability of warming in the 1980s and that the mean global temperature will increase by 1 degree to 4.5 degrees centigrade by the year 2100. (See *Science*, 28 August 1981, vol 213).

Temperature increases of this magnitude could, for example, produce changes in rainfall patterns, geographical shifts in areas suitable for food production and areas sensitive to desertification, higher sea levels due to the melting of polar ice, and changes in fish stocks, forests, and water supplies. Depending on their magnitude and timing, these changes could have profound social, economic and political impacts. Some changes might be beneficial to the region concerned, others deleterious,

and differences in impacts, of course, could have repercussions on a global scale.

Any action to establish more precisely the nature of the risk and, if necessary, action to avoid or mitigate the future effects, would have to be initiated mainly by OECD Member countries, (ie the Western industrialised world).

A major constraint may stem from the early lack of evidence of any significant temperature and climatic effects associated with an increase in atmospheric CO_2. Even if CO_2 emissions were to increase at a constant rate, temperature might not, since the oceans can absorb both heat and CO_2 from the atmosphere up to a certain point. Hence, a low rate of temperature increase in the near term could mask the full extent of the problem in the longer run. In other words, evidence of climatic change may be both delayed and difficult to detect until CO_2 loading is such that appreciable climatic change becomes inevitable. Consequently, action adequate to understand and anticipate such changes is necessary.

THE OZONE LAYER

The ozone layer plays an important role in protecting the earth from damaging ultraviolet radiation, and research indicates that continued emissions of chlorofluorocarbons (particularly CFC-11 and CFC-12) and certain other substances could lead to depletion of the ozone layer. Significant uncertainties concerning these phenomena persist, however. Chlorofluorocarbons (CFCs) are used as propellants in aerosol cans, in foam production, and as solvents and refrigerants.

CFCs are not the only chemicals thought to affect the ozone layer. There is an array of man-made chlorinated compounds which are also thought to have an impact. The same is true of emissions of nitrogen oxides (NOx) from aircraft and nitrous oxide (N_2O) from the burning of fossil fuels and from the nitrification and denitrification of both organic and inorganic nitrogen fertilisers. Increasing concentrations of CO_2 in the atmosphere, through its effect on temperatures, could also affect the ozone layer by ameliorating to some extent the effects of ozone depleting substances.

One of the principal concerns about increased ultraviolet radiation resulting from any depletion of the ozone layer is an increase in skin cancer. Laboratory studies indicate that an increase in ultraviolet radiation might cause damaging effects on animal and plant life (certain crop species and marine organisms).

A range of views exists concerning the degree of confidence which can be attached to calculations of ozone depletion, given present uncertainties in model formulation, chemical reaction rates, atmospheric and trend analysis parameters.

The uncertainties relate to:
  (a) long-term effects of emissions of CFCs and other man-made chlorinated compounds as well as CO_x, N_2O and NO_x;
  (b) long-term effects of ozone depletion on health and the environment; and
  (c) whether to take further control measures at this time, with attendant economic and social dislocations, or to wait for more research and monitoring data.
As a result of these considerations a number of countries are reluctant to take action to halt the increase in CFC emissions.

ACID PRECIPITATION (ACID RAIN)

Sulphur and nitrogen oxides (SO_x and NO_x) and other acid precursors emitted by natural and man-made sources can travel long distances in the atmosphere, undergoing chemical transformations, and returning to earth as acid precipitation. In sensitive areas, this increases the acidity of water bodies and the soil, and can damage aquatic ecosystems, crops and forests. Any satisfactory solution requires increased knowledge and a shared perception of the nature and extent of actual and future damage caused by acid precipitation and of the costs and benefits of counter-measures, so that appropriate strategies can be developed at both national and international levels.

Acid rain has been linked to emissions of sulphur and nitrogen oxides produced mostly by fossil fuel combustion in power plants, by smelting industries and from motor vehicle exhausts. Converted by chemical reactions in atmosphere to sulphates and nitrates, the emissions return to the earth in rain or as dry deposition. Their effects are felt not only in the neighbourhood of the sources, but also at distances of hundreds of kilometres. Acid rain has been observed throughout the world, particularly in Scandinavia, in parts of the western USA, in the north-eastern USA and over large sections of eastern Canada. Much of it results from pollutants which have travelled distances of over 500 km.

It is now generally accepted that acid deposition can cause impairment of aquatic ecosystems (decrease in fish population of acidified lakes) and corrosion of materials. The potential effects on human health and on yield of forests and crops are under study.

OECD Member countries, because of their high industrial development over limited geographical areas, are large scale producers of man-made SO_x and NO_x. In Europe, however, the contribution of Eastern European countries to acid rain may also be significant.

While some of the consequences of acid precipitation are well established, the mechanisms underlying the chemistry of acid rain formation are complex and are not completely understood.

Nor is it clear how cost effective the available counter-measures would be in avoiding or reducing damage in recipient countries at long distances from the source. The relationship between costs and benefits is less well known with regard to NO_x than it is for SO_x.

Indeed, a major problem stems from the fact that the population in the source jurisdiction may have different priorities than that at a long distance in the affected jurisdiction, and may place quite different values both on the costs of damage and on the costs of various control strategies.

Moreover, the current economic climate tends to reinforce the position of those who prefer to postpone investment in counter-measures, given that the ability to define and to cost the damage is far less developed than the ability to cost available technologies to control emissions.

CHEMICALS

For new chemicals, the issue is to develop and to introduce internationally harmonised schemes for their assessment, prior to their entry into the market; while for chemicals which are already on the market, the issue is rather to establish criteria for their selection for further testing and assessment and for determining how best to harmonise and share the burden internationally.

As modern man's dependence on chemicals for societal benefits has grown, the potential for widespread pollution or contamination has also increased. There are now some 70,000 chemicals on the commercial market, and many of these are currently used and released into the environment with little or no knowledge of their potential long-range effects. It is estimated that 1,000 new chemicals enter the market each year.

Consumption of chemicals in OECD countries amounts to more than $400bn, and more than 80 per cent of the overall world trade in chemicals takes place among OECD Member countries. This means that a high percentage of the problems in production and use of chemicals are first recognised or anticipated and forestalled in OECD countries. Increasing information on the potential long-term effects of some chemicals is revealing the significance of the management problem for chemical-dependent societies. The question can be posed whether the rate of growth of development of understanding and of institutions to deal with the issue is sufficient to address the problem.

Legislation already enacted by a number of (OECD) Member countries gives a clear indication of the scope which exists for policy action. But at the national level there is the difficult task of integrating control strategies across an array of different types of chemicals, some of which have been regulated for many years, eg pharmaceuticals and pesticides, and others, which, like industrial chemicals, have only recently attracted attention in most OECD countries.

At both the national and the international level it is difficult to develop comprehensive strategies which provide a framework within which both new and existing chemicals can be controlled.

A significant obstacle to the effective control and assessment of existing chemicals lies in the lack of knowledge of, and access to data on, any given marketed chemical especially in cases of imported chemicals. The costs of developing data and the confidentiality of some data are further constraining factors.

OECD countries have a major role and responsibility as the primary producers and users of chemicals. Progress in managing contamination of the global commons will depend on the ability of OECD Member countries to develop effective policies concerning the production, use and disposal of chemicals and in so doing to anticipate their potential hazards. Central to effective management of chemicals will be the availability of consistent and adequate information to all countries in order to enable each to take informed decisions.

INTERNATIONAL MOVEMENT OF HAZARDOUS WASTE

The management of hazardous wastes requires an appropriate framework of policies, both for the export and for the import of such wastes between countries.

During recent years thousands of abandoned storage sites for hazardous wastes have been located in North America and in Europe. Events such as those at Love Canal (United States) and Lekkerkerk (Netherlands) have led governments of OECD Member countries to consider new and more effective measures to deal with the registration, movement, treatment and safe long-term disposal and storage of hazardous wastes. These measures normally require the proper siting of treatment and storage facilities, a process that is proving difficult in some Member countries because of public concern and opposition.

The 'not in my backyard' syndrome and the growing cost of treatment, storage and disposal of hazardous wastes, provide strong incentives to 'export' such wastes to other regions or countries for treatment or for temporary or permanent storage.

There are various legitimate reasons for such exports. At the same time, however, under other conditions, the export of hazardous wastes may simply reflect a search for a jurisdiction in which environmental awareness and regulations are weak or non-existent.

Most (approximately 80 per cent) of the world's hazardous waste has accumulated, and is currently produced, in OECD Member countries. The need for comprehensive policies to manage hazardous wastes has therefore arisen in OECD countries, and the benefits of sound management will accrue mostly to them.

The uncontrolled movement of such wastes, however, could result in serious long-term damage to health and property in importing countries and to the global commons.

MAINTAINING BIOLOGICAL DIVERSITY[1]

The genetic base of many of the world's crops and livestock has narrowed, making them more vulnerable to pests and diseases and to changes in soils and climate. At the same time, the world's genetic resources essential for reducing that vulnerability, as well as for producing a great range of pharmaceutical and industrial products, have been depleted, and this trend continues. Some 25,000 plant species and more than 1,000 vertebrate species and sub-species[2] are now known to be threatened with extinction, and as much as 10 per cent or more of all species on earth could be extinguished over the next two decades. Extinction of species on this scale is without precedent in human history.

The most serious threat to species is the destruction of their habitats, such as wetlands and forests. Tropical forests, in particular, harbour over one-third of all species world-wide. In many developing countries the tropical forests are being exploited at a rate which scientists consider ecologically and economically unsustainable. A rapid decline of tropical forests and their genetic resources over the next two decades is likely to have serious environmental, economic and social consequences for developing and developed countries alike. Yet the magnitude of the problem and the likely consequences, and especially of the implications for present national development and aid policies, have only begun to be assessed. Furthermore, the loss of wetlands and forest habitats is endangering food-chains and overall ecological stability, so the problem is more than just a threat to certain genetic resources.

The destruction of species and genetic materials has been, and is, opposed on ethical grounds, but their protection is also a matter of self-interest for all countries.

Genetic materials and biological diversity are foundation stones for global economic development, food security and the supply of fibres and certain drugs. This is particularly true for OECD Member countries.

The breeding of plants for high yields, improved quality and greater resistance to disease and pests has been one of the most spectacular successes of agricultural research. More than 70 per cent of the crop production in the USA, for example, is based on plant species brought in from outside, and, as in other OECD countries, almost all crops contain genetic material from a number of developed and developing countries.

As genetic diversity is reduced, however, so is the capacity of scientists to develop new and improved commercial species; and the genetic base of the world's present and future crops and other living resources is being rapidly reduced. Many wild and domesticated varieties of food plants, such as wheat, rice, millet, beans, yams, tomatoes, potatoes, bananas, limes and oranges, are already extinct, and many more are in danger. Useful breeds of livestock are also at risk: 115 of the 145 indigenous cattle breeds in Europe and the Mediterranean region are threatened with extinction.

Medicines and other pharmaceutical products are heavily dependent on plant and animal species. It is estimated, for example, that more than 40 per cent of the prescriptions written each year in the USA contain a drug of natural origin — from higher plants (25 per cent), microbes (13 per cent), or animals (3 per cent) — as the sole active ingredient or as one of the main ones. It is also noted that the commercial value of all medical preparations in the USA derived from natural origins now surpasses $10bn a year. The most important applications of higher plants and animals in the bio-medical area are as constituents used directly as therapeutic agents, as starting materials for drug synthesis, and as models for drug synthesis, for toxicity testing and for serum preparation.

In addition to containing about one-third of the world's plant and animal species, tropical forests provide a wide variety of goods, useful to affluent industrial and poor rural communities alike, including timber, pulpwood, fuelwood, fodder, fruit, fibres, pharmaceuticals, resins, gums, waxes and oils. Many developing countries are heavily dependent on their tropical forests; eight of them each earn more than $100m a year from exports of forest products.

Tropical forests, however, are being exploited today at an unsustainable rate, with little regard for their global, regional or even local ecological value. They are contracting rapidly as a result of expanding and shifting agriculture, spontaneous settlement, planned colonisation, clearance for plantations and ranching cutting for fuel and logging. In order to protect their usefulness as habitats, scientists estimate that at least 10 per cent, and possibly 20 per cent, of the total area of tropical forests needs to be set aside as protected areas. At present, only 2 per cent of such forests are protected, and many developing countries lack the institutional and financial capacity to protect even this proportion.

Many species that may seem to be of little consequence could in fact have important medical and commercial applications, or be key elements of the major life-support systems and processes on which mankind depends. The accelerating loss of genetic resources is an issue which needs to be addressed now for reasons of ethics for some, and of self-interest for all.

About 70 per cent of the world's genetic resources are located in developing countries, which themselves have little capacity to protect or to exploit them and, for the sake of their own economic development, tend to encourage activities such as the exploitation of forests, which pose the greatest threats to these resources. At the same time, genetic resources, especially in developing countries, are dealt with as 'free-goods' and the host country derives little or no economic benefit from their exploitation. The scientific and technical expertise to exploit species' genetic resources is confined largely to OECD and other developed countries.

It is difficult for most developing countries simply to set aside any sizeable territory in order to preserve forest ecosystems. The short-term opportunity costs can be substantial. In addition, there are the costs of actually managing the protection of designated areas. For many developing countries, and the rural poor constituting the majority of their population, there is simply no choice. Without alternatives, or assistance with management, their short-term requirements for economic development, for fuelwood and for physical survival takes precedence over the need to preserve the tropical forest and its genetic resources.

Environmental policies in OECD countries may also be contributing to the destruction of the tropical forest. In his report to the Japanese Government, Mr Okita[3] observed that 'an action that may be reasonable in terms of protecting one country's environment may not be so in terms of environmental protection on a global scale'. The example he cited was the 'felling of tropical forests overseas because forests in one's own countries are protected'. The example also serves to highlight the complexity of economic and ecological interdependence on a global scale, in that the extension of protected parklands in an OECD Member country might ultimately compromise future agricultural production in that country by contributing to the loss of tropical forests and biological diversity in some distant country.

LOSS OF CROPLAND AND SOIL DEGRADATION

Most of the land in the world that is best suited for crop production is already being farmed. If the current rates of conversion of agricultural land to non-agricultural uses continue in OECD Member countries, and if the current rates of land degradation continue in developing countries, within 20 years more than one-third of the world's arable land could be lost or destroyed.

Only about 11 per cent of the world's land area (excluding Antarctica) offers no serious limitation to agriculture. The rest suffers from drought, mineral stress (nutritional deficiencies or toxicities), shallow soil depth, excessive water or permafrost. The world's cropland currently occupies 14 million km^2 and, even using the most optimistic assumptions, it would appear that croplands world-wide could be no more than doubled.

Within OECD Member countries as a whole, large areas of prime quality land have already been lost permanently for agricultural purposes, primarily through urban and industrial development, recreation development and the construction of transportation infrastructure and reservoirs. At least 5,000 km² of cropland in OECD Member countries is lost each year to urban sprawl.

Erosion is already a serious problem in some OECD Member countries. For example, in the USA and Australia as much as 50 per cent of the cropland is already degraded by wind and water erosion. In the USA, one-third of the cropland is losing topsoil faster than the rate of natural soil generation. For all practical purposes, soil is a non-renewable resource: once it is gone, the loss is permanent. Nature takes from 100 to 400 years, or more, to generate 10mm of top soil.

Currently, such losses are compensated by intensifying production on the remaining land or developing new cropland from existing pastures, forests or wetlands. However, these measures have a number of undesirable environmental consequences. Drainage of wetlands destroys habitats and threatens species and food chains. Much of the new land is more marginal than that which it replaces; hence more fertiliser is required, soil erosion is greater, and loss of nutrients and pesticides to surface and groundwater increases.

Developing countries are also experiencing an increasing loss of arable land, in part because of conversion from agricultural to non-agricultural uses, but largely because of soil degradation. Soil loss has accelerated sharply in most developing countries.

In OECD Member countries which are net exporters of agricultural products and commodities, some analysts argue that the agricultural land-base is adequate to meet domestic food and fibre needs for many generations and, perhaps, indefinitely. However, this perspective does not adequately account for global interdependence in basic commodities and natural resources including, most notably, energy and food. If projected international food needs are taken into account, the future adequacy of the agricultural land resource-base of these countries to satisfy all sources of demand without significantly higher real public and private costs of production, and without seriously degrading agriculture land, polluting ground water and so on, is, at best, uncertain. Those OECD Member countries which are net importers of agricultural products and commodities are even more vulnerable to the combined effects of increasing world demand for food and the increasing loss of arable land through conversion to non-agricultural uses in their own and in other countries.

Growing global interdependence for basic food, energy and other resource-needs will increase the pressure on agricultural lands in all countries. Within OECD countries, the conversion of a small proportion of prime agricultural land to non-agricultural uses may lower current urban development costs and, for some, appear insignificant in contrast to the overall national endowment of agricultural resources. Yet the effects of such conversions are cumulative, and contribute to significant and avoidable reductions in agricultural potential and environmental quality.

For developing countries, any net losses and degradation

of their arable land will, without compensating increases in agricultural productivity, increase their own demands and dependence on other countries (especially OECD Member countries) for additional food and increased financial and technical assistance. Having said this, it should be recognised that certain reductions in arable land are unavoidable and indeed necessary to development. Moreover, the potential for increasing crop yields is great in most developing countries.

The potential inflationary consequences of world food deficits in the international food market were noted in the report of the Brandt Commission,[4] which further pointed out that: 'if additional assistance is not forthcoming, there will also be far more calls for emergency food supplies, which are in the long view an expensive and irrational way of coping with food problems. Food relief programmes often cost more in one year than would the five year local investment programmes which might have made them unnecessary'.

The seriously poor in rural areas of developing countries constitute nearly a third of the world's population and 500 million of these suffer from malnutrition. In their efforts to satisfy their needs for food and fuel, the rural poor disrupt their own life-support systems, impair ecological processes and destroy genetic resources which limits, and sometimes forecloses, future possibilities for agricultural production. It is extraordinarily difficult to deal with these problems because of their huge scale, because there are so many people and production units with which to deal, and because of the pace of change. Because of the lack of economic flexibility among the rural poor, measures for the protection and conservation of agricultural land and soils will need to be complemented by measures that at least maintain and, preferably, improve their standards of living.

Section 2:
A Summary Drawn from Recent Publications

Section 2 of Appendix A draws on the Global 2000 report, the WCS, the Brandt Report and *Building a Sustainable Society*, by Lester Brown.[5]

Man on the Planet
World population currently stands at over 4.4 billion. By the year 2000 it will have risen to around six billion unless drastic action is taken to reduce birth rates. At that time 80 per cent of the population will live in developing countries, while eight countries — China, India, Pakistan, Bangladesh, Indonesia, Nigeria, Brazil, and Mexico — will between them contain more than half of humanity.

Such massive increases must place even heavier burdens on the resources and life-support systems of the planet, many of which are already being depleted or damaged by the present population. Already, production of food, wood and oil is failing to keep pace with population growth (see Figure 2). Our failure to prevent environmental degradation is undermining food production and, if not checked, will prevent the developing countries from maintaining present standards of living, and will certainly not improve the situation.

Energy

World energy consumption will probably rise by between 2.4 and 3.3 per cent per year to the end of this decade — depending on the rate of growth of GNP. It is expected to increase by approximately 40 per cent by the year 2000 from 10.9 billion metric tonnes coal equivalent (mtce) in 1980 to 15.2 billion mtce in 2000. Even if production can be increased to this level, *per capita* consumption will decline slightly from 2.48 mtce to 2.41 mtce. Figure 3 (p 365) shows the relative contribution of different sources.

The greater reliance on coal that must occur if production is to keep pace with demand poses severe environmental threats: acid rain is already causing serious damage to plant and maybe marine life in the Northern hemisphere, and carbon dioxide emissions are expected to double by 2000. Although no firm predictions can be made about the effects of this increase the scientific evidence at present available indicates that large disruptive climatic shifts *could* result in the early part of the twenty first century, but there is no clear argument on this issue.

Oil production is unlikely to grow much over the next 20 years, continuing a trend which began in 1974, and this must affect food production which depends heavily on oil for fuel and fertiliser.

The growing use of alcohol as a replacement for oil also threatens food production. 'Energy crops' compete not only for land, but also for investment and credit, water and fertiliser. In the case of the United States, official programmes to boost ethanol production to two billion gallons a year by the mid-1980s threaten to reduce the exportable surplus of grain significantly.

Increasingly expensive oil will also increase the demand for wood as fuel. In the industrialised countries, the last few years have seen a drastic increase in the use of wood for domestic heating. Firewood cutting in the developing world poses a major threat to forests and woodlands, threatening water supplies and precious oil. Shortages of wood already force large numbers of people to spend long periods of time or considerable parts of their income on obtaining wood, and force rural populations in Africa and Asia alone to burn some 400 million tons of cow dung each year.

Food

World food reserves, including idled US cropland, in 1980 stood at only 151 million tons, representing 40 days' supply. During the period 1950 to 1980, the area planted with cereals rose from 601 million hectares

Year	Forests (wood m³)	Oil (barrels)	Coal (tonnes)*	Fisheries Fish (kgs)	Grain (kgs)	Grasslands Beef (kgs)	Mutton (kgs)	Wool (kgs)
1960	–	2.5	.82*	13.2	285	9.32	1.88	.85
1961	.66	–	–	14.0	–	9.62	1.90	.84
1962	.65	–	.784	14.9	–	9.85	1.89	.85
1963	.66	–	–	14.7	–	10.74	1.88	.83
1964	.67	–	–	16.1	–	10.06	1.84	.80
1965	.66	3.3	.78*	16.0	297(est)	9.92	1.79	.78
1966	.66	–	–	16.8	–	10.20	1.77	.78
1967	.64	–	–	17.4	–	10.38	1.89	.78
1968	.64	–	–	18.0	–	10.67	1.89	.79
1969	.64	–	–	17.4	–	10.70	1.85	.78
1970	.64	4.5	–	18.5	309	10.60	1.87	.75
1971	.64	4.7	–	18.3	330	10.27	1.87	.73
1972	.63	4.9	.78	16.8	314	10.56	1.88	.71
1973	.64	5.3	–	16.8	332	10.46	1.79	.66
1974	.63	5.2	–	17.7	317	10.97	1.73	.64
1975	.61	4.8	–	17.2	316	11.28	1.75	.66
1976	.62	5.1	–	17.7	337	11.58	1.78	.63
1977	.61	5.2	.82*	17.3	330	11.52	1.74	.62
1978	.61	5.2	–	17.3	351	11.36	1.73	.61
1979	.60	5.2	–	16.9	331	10.88	1.72	.60
1980	.60	4.9	.85	16.1	324	10.53	1.74	.62

Notes: peaks are underlined
* indicates estimate including lignite

Figure 2. **World production per capita of basic resources 1960-1980**
Sources: Global 2000 report, 1980; Brown, 1981; Lovins, 1977[6]

Year	Coal %	Petroleum %	Natural gas %	Nuclear electricity %	Total %	Decade %	Rates of growth Annual %	Per capita annual %
1950	63	27	10	—	100	70	5.4	3.7
1960	53	33	14	—	100			
1970	36	44	20	—	100	58	4.7	2.8
1971	34	44	21	1	100			
1972	33	45	21	1	100			
1973	32	46	21	1	100			
1974	32	46	21	1	100			
1975	32	45	21	2	100	36	3.1	1.3
1976	32	45	21	2	100			
1977	32	45	21	2	100			
1978	31	45	21	3	100			
1979	32	44	21	3	100			
1980	33	42	22	3	100			

Figure 3. World commercial energy use: fossil fuels and nuclear power 1950-1980
Source: Brown, R L, 1981.[7]

to 758 million hectares, yields have increased from 1.05 tons ha to 1.89 tons ha, and production has gone up from 631 million tons to 1,432 million tons. *Per capita* consumption of grain increased slowly until 1978, but is now declining. During this period the area of cereal cropland per person had fallen from 0.24 ha to only 0.17 ha.

As Figure 2 shows (see p 364), *per capita* production of fish, beef and mutton has already peaked. The rate of increase in grain production has declined from 3.1 per cent per year in the 1950s to 2.3 per cent per year in the 1970s, and total production has actually fallen for the last two years for which figures are available — 1979 and 1980 (See Figure 4.)

In addition to the political problems this state of affairs may cause in the future, it is bound to reduce both the amount of grain available to the developing countries and force up prices. This trend will be reinforced by two other factors: the increase in energy crops and the recent decline in the terms of trade between grain and oil.

From 1950 to 1973, the prices of oil and wheat remained in rough parity, but the ratio has now widened to 6:1 in favour of oil. Since cereal production in North America is heavily dependent on oil, food prices must, in due course, follow oil prices upwards. In the meantime, the current relative cheapness of food tempts populous, oil exporting countries that are having problems with their agriculture to import more of their food; further reducing the amount available to the poorest developing countries. (See Figure 5, p 366.)

Increasing production sufficiently to maintain even the present inadequate levels of consumption, unless drastic measures were taken to redistribute existing supplies, would be a formidable task under any circumstances. But the difficulty of expanding the cropland base, the effects of soil erosion, loss of productivity, future

Year	Population (billions)	Area of production (m ha)	Yield (t/ha)	Grain production (m tonnes)	Annual rate of increase in production by decade (%)	Grain production per capita (kgs)	Annual rate of increase per capita by decade (%)
1950	2.51	601	1.05	631	3.1	251	1.2
1960	3.03	682	1.26	863		285	
1970	3.68	704	1.62	1,177	2.8	309	0.8
1971	3.75	—	—	1,237		330	
1972	3.82	—	—	1,197		314	
1973	3.88	—	—	1,290		332	
1974	3.96	—	—	1,256		317	
1975	4.03	—	—	1,275	2.3	316	0.5
1976	4.11	—	—	1,385		337	
1977	4.18	—	—	1,378		330	
1978	4.26	—	—	1,494		351	
1979	4.34	—	—	1,437		331	
1980	4.42	758	1.89	1,432		324	

Figure 4. World grain production: total and per capita 1950-1980
Source: Brown, 1971.[8]

Region	(million tonnes) 1934-38	1943-52	1960	1970	1980
North America	+ 5	+23	+39	+56	+131
Latin America	+ 9	+ 1	0	+ 4	− 10
Western Europe	−24	−22	−25	−30	− 16
Eastern Europe and USSR	+ 5	0	0	0	− 46
Africa	+ 1	0	− 2	− 5	− 15
Asia	+ 2	− 6	−17	−37	− 63
Australia and New Zealand	+ 2	+ 3	+ 6	+12	+ 19

Note: The USSR imported 31 million tons in 1980

Figure 5. **The changing pattern of world grain trade**
Source: Brown, 1981.[9]

shortages of water, and diminishing returns on the use of fertilisers in the major producing areas all combine to make a difficult task all but impossible.

Deforestation of river basins increases run-off and soil erosion, which in turn silts up irrigation systems and reservoirs, thereby shortening their lifespan. The likelihood of flooding also increases. India, Pakistan and Bangladesh are all suffering from the effects of the deforestation of the Himalayas; in 1978, in one flood, 65,000 villages were flooded and 2,000 people and 40,000 cattle drowned and crops worth $750m were lost in the states of Uttar Pradesh and West Bengal.

Erosion and overuse of the land is drastically affecting the productivity of large parts of the world's crop and grazing land. More than half of India, for example, suffers from some form of soil degradation: out of 3.3 million km^2, 1.4 million km^2, are subject to erosion, while 270,000 km^2 suffer from floods, waterlogging, excessive salinity or alkalinity. An estimated six million tons of soil are lost each year from only 800,000 km^2 and more nutrients are washed away than the amount of fertiliser used to improve the soil. Soil degradation is not confined to the developing countries. Experiments in the US show that Iowa alone loses 260 million tons of topsoil each year. In Tennessee the average loss was 11.4 tons per acre, in Missouri 11.4, in Mississippi 10.9, and Texas a startling 14.9 tons per acre. Across the USA, sheet and rill erosion remove 1.01 billion tons of topsoil each year, equivalent to 781,000 acres.

Irrigated lands, which produce a disproportionate part of the world's food, are also threatened. A recent UK report (1977) estimated that one-tenth of the total irrigated area is waterlogged; its productivity down by 20 per cent. An equal area is suffering from salination. Other areas face shortages of water as aquifers are 'mined'. The south central region of the USSR and the Great Plains and south-west of the United States are particularly vulnerable as agriculture must compete with domestic and industrial consumers for dwindling supplies.

Valuable cropland, often of the best quality, is also lost

to urban expansion, growing villages, energy production, mining, industry and roads. The US loses one million acres a year of prime cropland in this way. No figures are available for the Third World, but, as the population continues to grow, millions of acres will be lost for good.

Just as environmental degradation adversely affects food production, attempts to increase food production without taking account of environmental conservation can promote further environmental decay. A vicious spiral is created with declining food production and lower standards of living as the inevitable result.

Fisheries, marine and freshwater, are a vital source of protein for millions in both developed and developing countries, but yields of marine fish peaked in 1970 and freshwater fish catches have grown only slowly. Both are threatened by pollution. In the case of sea fish, yields have been maintained only by the development of new species as traditional stocks have been decimated by over-fishing. The management of multi-species fisheries is poorly understood.

Maintaining even present levels of consumption in the developing countries will require wide ranging changes in agricultural practices, much more attention to environmental factors, and ideally a change in the dietary habits of the developed world to allow some redistribution of resources to feed the growing numbers in the Third World.

Water

It is estimated that the world's total annual water use amounts to 3×10^{12} tonnes, or an average of 800 tonnes, per person. Water is needed by domestic consumers, by industry (including mining), for energy production, and to irrigate crops (see Figure 6, p 367).

The global supply of water is, theoretically, extremely large, of the order of 4×10^{13} m^3 per year. Present consumption may rise to 5.4×10^{12} m^3 per year by the end of the century. Most of the water withdrawn from the available resources is returned to the environment in one form or another, and actual consumption may amount to only 3 per cent of the aggregate supply. Even at the levels forecast for the end of the century, withdrawal would account for about half of the aggregate supply and about 15 per cent would actually be consumed.

While these figures suggest that such an increase could easily be sustained, the essentially local nature of the water economies and the uneven distribution of water, both spatially and over time, means that even a doubling of withdrawals by the year 2000 is almost certain to cause major shortages in certain areas. Countries likely to suffer most are those with low *per capita* availability and high population growth — especially parts of Africa, South Asia, the Middle East and Latin America. Areas of the US and USSR that rely heavily on 'fossil' water are already experiencing problems.

	Total use in millions m^3		Projected growth rate	Fraction of total use in %	
	1976	2000	% per year	1976	2000
Agriculture					
Irrigation	1,400,000	2,800,000	2.1	70	51
Livestock	58,800	102,200	1.7	3	2
Rural domestic	19,800	38,200	2.0	1	—
Other					
Urban domestic	73,000	278,900	4.1	4	5
Industry and mining	437,000	2,231,000	5.0	22	41
Total	1,984,300	5,450,400	3.1	100	100

Figure 6. **Estimates of world water use in 1976 and projections to 2000**
Source: Global 2000 report, 1980.[10]

	000s of m^3 per capita per year		% change in population
	1971	2000	1971-2000
Europe			
Great Britain	2.7	2.0	34
Asia			
USSR	17.8	13.6	31
China	3.8	2.7	42
Pakistan	1.1	0.5	125
Bangladesh	1.8	0.9	102
India	2.9	1.5	92
Philippines	10.1	4.2	139
Africa			
Sudan	4.0	1.9	107
Nigeria	4.7	2.4	96
Tanzania	5.7	2.4	142
Kenya	3.4	1.2	191
North America			
USA (48)	8.4	6.6	27
Mexico	5.5	1.9	185
Central America			
Panama	54.8	25.1	118
Jamaica	1.1	0.6	93
Cuba	3.1	1.8	74
South America			
Brazil	59.5	26.0	128
Ecuador	52.2	22.7	130

Figure 7. **Per capita water availability 1971-2000**
Source: Global 2000 report, 1980.[11]

Projections of water availability to the year 2000 show that all of the world's nations will show a decline in *per capita* water availability (Figure 7, p 367, shows figures for selected countries).

In addition to the problem of quantity there are problems of quality. The use of water for waste disposal and irrigation increases the salinity, and erosion caused by deforestation and the cultivation of unsuitable land increases the sediment load, inadequate drainage of irrigated areas promotes waterlogging, while irrigations schemes may spread diseases — notably schistosomiasis and malaria. Pollution may also render water hazardous and all these will adversely affect fish.

Silting of reservoirs threatens both irrigation schemes and supplies of drinking water for growing urban populations.

In Pakistan, 11 million hectares out of 15 million hectares (71 per cent) of irrigated land suffers from waterlogging, salinity, or both. In Iraq, 50 per cent of irrigated land in the Euphrates Valley is seriously affected, while in Egypt 30 per cent of the total is degraded.

The potential for conflict over water resources is considerable, with 148 of the world's major river basins being shared by two countries and another 52 by two to 10 countries. Longstanding quarrels over la Plata (Brazil, Argentina), the Jordan (Israel, Jordan), the Euphrates (Syria, Iraq), the Indus (India, Pakistan), and the Ganges (India, Bangladesh) could easily worsen as populations, and thus the demand for water, rise. By the year 2000 the Ganges basin alone will probably contain more than 500 million people.

Human Settlements
In 1950, 29 per cent of the world's people lived in urban settlements. This share grew to 39 per cent in 1975. If present trends continue, it will approach 50 per cent, or more than three billion people by the year 2000.

UN projections indicate that 59 per cent of the population growth of less developed countries (LDCs) will occur in urban areas: a rise in 1.2 billion people by the year 2000. Figures 8 and 9 show the trends in urban populations in cities of more than 100,000 and in particular cities. Since most of the increase would take place within existing cities, many will become almost unimaginably large. For instance, Mexico City will house (or not house) 32 million people by the year 2000, Sao Paulo would hold more than 26 million, and altogether 400 cities would pass the million mark. Already many urban inhabitants live in uncontrolled settlements and recent studies indicate that populations there double every five to seven years, as against the 10 to 15 for urban areas in the Third World as a whole. In Bombay, where 45 per cent of the six million citizens live in shanty towns, population growth in these areas is about 17.4 per cent per year.

Simply maintaining present living standards over the

	Population (millions)		
	1950	1975	2000
World	392	903	2167
Industrialised countries	262	503	756
Less developed countries	130	480	1411

Figure 8. **Urban population in cities of 100,000 or more**
Source: Global 2000 report, 1980.[12]

	Population (millions)			
	1960	1970	1975	2000
Calcutta	5.5	6.9	8.1	19.7
Mexico City	4.9	8.6	10.9	31.6
Greater Bombay	4.1	5.8	7.1	19.1
Greater Cairo	3.7	5.7	6.9	16.4
Jakarta	2.7	4.3	5.6	16.9
Seoul	2.4	2.4	7.3	12.7
Delhi	2.3	3.5	4.5	13.2
Manila	2.2	3.5	4.4	12.7
Tehran	1.9	3.4	4.4	13.8
Karachi	1.8	3.3	4.5	15.9
Bogota	1.7	2.6	3.4	9.4
Lagos	0.8	1.4	2.1	9.4

Figure 9. **Estimates and rough projections of populations in selected urban areas in developing countries**
Source: Global 2000 report, 1980.[13]

next 20 years will mean a two-third increase in services. And at present at least 25 per cent of city-dwellers in the Third World do not have house water connections or access to standpipes which provide safe drinking water; a similar proportion have no household systems for disposing of human wastes. Totally inadequate sewage systems mean that urban populations live under the constant threat of disease, a threat that often extends over the surrounding countryside as well.

Cooking fires, automobile exhausts and industrial pollution combine to pollute the air of many developing country cities, causing respiratory disease among the inhabitants and affecting crops and forests in the vicinity. Urban demands for fuelwood (often in the form of charcoal) and food increase environmental pressures on the surrounding countryside, exhausting and degrading the land. Many experts believe that the monster cities cannot in fact come about, and that they would simply collapse under the weight of numbers, even if the resources of energy and food and raw materials could be found to support them.

Economic and Resource Factors

GNP

Projections of GNP are notoriously unreliable even in the short term because data is inaccurate, absent, or incompatible. Moreover, where environmental impacts are concerned, GNP figures are somewhat misleading

	1975	1975-1985 Growth Rate %	*billions $ 1975 constant* 1985*	1985-2000 Growth Rate %	2000*
World	6,025	4.1	8,991	3.3	14,677
more developed	4,892	3.9	7,150	3.1	11,224
less developed	1,133	5.0	1,841	4.3	3,452
Major regions:					
Africa	162	5.2	268	4.3	505
Asia and Oceania	697	4.6	1,097	4.2	2,023
Latin America	326	5.6	564	4.5	1,092
USSR and Eastern Europe	996	3.3	1,371	2.8	2,062
North America, Western Europe, Japan, and Australasia	3,844	4.0	5,691	3.1	8,996

Note: * = projection

Figure 10. **GNP estimates and projections* 1975, 1985 and 2000**
Source: Global 2000, 1980. Medium projections.[14]

because they include the cost of, say, cleaning up pollution or reclaiming degraded land as if these things were positive contributions to an economy. The effects of environmental degradation may be slowing down GNP growth rates as renewable resources are undermined and non-renewable resources are depleted but evidence to support this view is not yet clear (see Figure 10).

Despite these caveats, GNP figures can still be used as a rough indicator of the burden natural systems will have to cope with in the future. The 'Global 2000' report projects world GNP to increase from $6 trillion in 1976 to $14.7 trillion in 2000, implying a proportionate increase in pollution and waste generation. Increased industrial production will, unless measures are taken to prevent it, mean increased demand for raw materials (including wood, natural fibres, minerals, and water) and this, in turn, will add to the environmental impact of food and energy production that is already in some instances overstressing the planet's life support systems.

Minerals
Figure 11 (see p 370) gives the projected life expectancies of the existing known reserves of 17 vital mineral commodities. In all cases further resources exist which have yet to be assessed accurately or cannot be extracted at the moment because of economic or technological limitations. It is important to note that, while no immediate shortages are likely, increases in the costs of extraction and processing (caused by increased energy costs, and the need to turn to lower grade ores and more inaccessible deposits) may reverse the historic decline in the price (in real terms) of most mineral commodities. Insofar as it encourages recycling, this would be a good thing.

Mineral production is expected to double by the end of the century directly affecting some 94,000 square miles, an area the size of West Germany. In addition to this

land, mining activities also affect the rest of the environment in a variety of ways.

Six commodities cause most of the environmental damage that results from mining activities: sand/gravel, stone, copper, iron, clays, and phosphates. Approximately nine billion tons of these minerals were produced in 1976, generating 14 billion tons of waste. The projection for 2000 is 18 billion tons of commodities and 34 billion tons of waste. Much of this stays in spoil heaps on site, but large quantities find their way into the air, rivers and seas, where it is joined by pollutants produced during processing. For example, the Cuajone copper mining and smelting project in Peru releases 60,000 tons of sulphur oxides into the air and 30 million tons of tailings into the sea each year. Copper-nickel smelters in Sudbury, Ontario and Canada emit 2.7 million tons of sulphur oxides annually, causing losses of timber with an estimated worth of $117,000 per year in the immediate vicinity and acid rain over a much larger area. The cost of safely disposing of the 140 million tons of uranium tailings currently lying around in the US is conservatively estimated at $1 per ton. Discharges of about 100,000 tons of mine tailings per day into the eight major river systems of the Philippines is affecting the productivity of around 130,000 hectares of good agricultural land. Dumping of 67,000 tons of asbestos wastes into Lake Superior over the past 23 years has polluted the drinking water of nearby Duluth. The courts have now ruled that $270m must be spent on pollution control.

Returning mined land to productive use is extremely expensive. For example, rehabilitating coalfields in western United States can cost between $925 and $2,750 per acre.

Technology
Used in its widest sense, technology is a major, some would argue *the* major, determinant of both the future shape of our society and our long-term impact on the

Mineral	1976 Reserves	1976 Primary demand	Projected demand growth rate (%)	Life expectancy in years at: Static 1976 rate	Life expectancy in years at: Growing projected rate
Fluorine (m short tons)	37	2.1	4.58	18	13
Silver (m troy ounces)	6,100	305.0	2.33	20	17
Zinc (mst)	166	6.4	3.05	26	19
Mercury (thousand flasks)	5,210	239.0	0.50	22	21
Sulphur (m long tons)	1,700	50.0	3.16	34	23
Lead (mst)	136	3.7	3.14	37	25
Tungsten (m pounds)	4,200	81.0	3.26	52	31
Tin (000 tonnes)	10,000	241.0	2.05	41	31
Copper (mst)	503	8.0	2.94	86	43
Nickel (mst)	60	0.7	2.94	86	43
Platinum (m troy ounces)	297	2.7	3.75	110	44
Phosphate rock (m tonnes)	25,732	107.0	5.17	240	51
Manganese (mst)	1,800	11.0	3.36	164	56
Iron ore (mst)	103	0.6	2.95	172	62
Al in bauxite (mst)	5,610	18.0	4.29	312	63
Chromium (mst)	829	2.2	3.27	377	80
Potash (mst)	12,230	26.0	3.27	470	86

Note: m = millions; mst = millions of short tons

Figure 11. Life expectancies of 1976 world reserves of selected minerals
Source: Global 2000, 1980.[15]

Area	% Share
Military	24
Space	8
Energy*	8
Health	7
Information processing	5
Transportation	5
Pollution	5
Agriculture	3
Basic research	15
Other (all sectors under 3%)	20
Total	100

* Fission and fusion research took up over 50 per cent of International Energy Agency members' budgets in 1979, the remainder was largely concerned with oil and coal.

Figure 12. Global R and D budget 1979
Source: Brown, R L, 1981.[16]

environment. The production of new varieties of food crops, the utilisation of new species for food or fuel, the control of pollution, recycling of waste, the more efficient use of energy, etc all depend on advances in technology or the wider application of existing technologies. There is, however, another side to the technological coin. Technology also makes it possible for us to degrade the environment, even to the point of destroying it completely in a nuclear war. Figure 12 gives some idea of which way up the coin is likely to land.

Notes and References

1 The term 'biological diversity' embraces both genetic diversity (the variability in a given species) and ecological diversity (the number of species in a community).

2 These figures are given in The World Conservation Strategy (Chapter 3) and are based on the IUCN Red Data books. The Global 2000 Report estimates that 15 to 20 per cent of all species on earth could be extinguished by the year 2000.

3 OKITA, S. 1980. The Okita report — basic directions in coping with global environmental issues. Japan, Department of Environment.

4 BRANDT COMMISSION. 1980. North-South, a programme for survival. Pan Books.

5 US DEPARTMENT OF STATE AND COUNCIL ON EN-VIRONMENTAL QUALITY. 1980. The global 2000 report to the President: entering the twenty-first century. US Government Printing Office. Also Penguin, London, 1981. The World Conservation Strategy, 1980. IUCN; North-South, a programme for survival, *op cit*; BROWN, L R. 1981. Building a sustainable society. W W Norton. This section was prepared by Dr Ian Barratt from the above sources.

6 Building a sustainable society, *op cit*.

7 The global 2000 report, *op cit*; Building a sustainable society, *op cit*; LOVINS, A B. 1977. Soft energy paths. Pelican Books.

8 Building a sustainable society, *op cit*.

9 Building a sustainable society, *op cit*.

10 The global 2000 report, *op cit*.

11 The global 2000 report, *op cit*.

12 The global 2000 report, *op cit*.

13 The global 2000 report, *op cit*.

14 The global 2000 report, *op cit*.

15 The global 2000 report, *op cit*.

16 Building a sustainable society, *op cit*.

THE OVERSEAS PRIORITIES OF THE WORLD CONSERVATION STRATEGY

Introduction

The list is set out to help the reader understand what the WCS involves. It is important to note the following:

(a) The reference numbers in the first column relate to the paragraph numbers of the WCS.

(b) A list of abbreviations can be found at the end of this book (see pp 494-496).

(c) What this tabulation does not convey is the level of investment or effort that is required to achieve in practice any one of the indicated tasks. For example, to say 'prevent soil degradation' is not particularly helpful if it is not accompanied by a 'where, how, and with what'. But such questions are not within the scope of this report to answer; it is assumed by the author that the UK's contribution is always going to be modest in comparison to the tasks ahead.

The Overseas Priorities of the WCS

Priority requirements (for all countries and regions)	Indicated academic disciplines and UN agencies
(i) Reservation of prime quality croplands for crops (5.1-5.2)	Agricultural Sciences, planning disciplines (including Geographical Sciences) throughout, FAO/UNEP
(ii) Adoption of management practices to maintain the productivity of croplands/ grazing lands/forests (5.3-5.5; 6.9; 11-7.12)	Agricultural Sciences, Ecology, Soil Sciences, Forestry, Microbiology, Agronomy, FAO/UNEP
(iii) Prevention of soil degradation, restoration of degraded lands (5.5)	Agricultural Sciences, Arid Land Management, Microbiology, Soil Sciences, Earth Sciences, FAO/UNEP
(iv) Protection of watersheds, especially upper catchment areas (5.6)	Water Management, Ecology, Forestry Policy, Soil Sciences, Agricultural Sciences, WHO/UNEP
(v) Maintenance of fisheries (5.7)	Ecology, Fishery policy, Marine Biology, FAO/UNEP
(vi) Prevention of species extinction (6.1-6.3)	Ecology, Planning disciplines, Environmental Sciences, UNESCO/UNEP

By way of:	
a. Establishment of protected areas (6.8-6.12)	Applied Botany/Zoology, Ecology, Environmental Sciences, UNESCO/UNEP
b. Preservation of domesticated stocks (6.4-6.7)	Animal Husbandry, plant breeding, FAO/UNEP
c. Regulation of living resource-utilisation (7.1-7.4; 7.6; 7.8; 7.10)	Environmental Law and various Biological Science disciplines, UNEP
d. Maintenance of the habitats of utilised species (7.7)	Ecology, Land Management, Agricultural Sciences, Forestry, Fishery Sciences, FAO/UNESCO/UNEP

Priority requirements (of national Governments overseas)	Indicated academic disciplines
(i) Preparation of national strategies (8.1-8.10)	Various, but mainly Environmental Sciences and Development Studies
(ii) Anticipatory environmental policies (9.6-9.7; 9.13)	Various, but mainly Environmental Sciences and Development Studies
(iii) Cross sectoral conservation policies (9.8-9.12)	Environment and Development Studies
(iv) The inclusion of non-monetary indicators of conservation performance in national planning (9.14)	Social Sciences
(v) Preparation of ecosystem evaluation (10.3-10.5)	Environmental Sciences, Ecology
(vi) Environmental assessment studies of major developments (10.6-10.7)	Environmental Sciences, Planning disciplines
(vii) Land and water use planning (10.8-10.11)	Planning disciplines and various other academic disciplines
(viii) Environmental legislation/enforcement (11.7-11.9)	Environmental Law and various other academic disciplines
(ix) Development of environmental management capability (11.10-11.12)	Public Affairs Administration, Law
(x) Development of soil and water conservation policies (11.13)	Soil Sciences and Agricultural Science, Freshwater Biology, Water Management
(xi) Development of marine living resource policy (11.14)	Fishery Sciences, Ecology

Priority requirements (of national Governments overseas)	Indicated academic disciplines
(xii) Development of a sustainable rural development policy (14.5-14.11)	Environmental Science and Development Studies
(xiii) Environmental management training (12.5-12.8)	Various academic disciplines
(xiv) National environmental research programmes (12.9-12.13)	Various academic disciplines
(xv) Public participation (13.4-13.5)	Not applicable
(xvi) Control of pollution (5.8)	Applied Physical and Chemical Sciences, Environmental Sciences, Biological Sciences
(xvii) Reduction of incidental take (7.5)	Marine Biology, Fisheries Policy
(xviii) Management of timber concessions (7.9)	Forestry
(ixx) Environmental education programmes (13.6-13.14)	Environmental Sciences

Priority requirements (international)	Indicated academic disciplines
(i) International law — development of (15.4-15.9)	Environmental and International Law
(ii) Implementation of conventions (15.5-15.9)	Not applicable

Priority requirements (international)	Indicated academic disciplines
(iii) Assistance programmes — definition of priority areas above (15.11-15.12)	Various academic disciplines
(iv) Cooperative programmes for tropical forests (16.1-16.7)	Forestry Policy
(v) Cooperative programmes for drylands (16.8-16.12)	Arid Land Management
(vi) Site protection for species and critical habitats (17.1-17.5)	Various academic disciplines
(vii) Management of the oceans (18.2-18.7)	Various academic disciplines
(viii) Implementation of certain conventions (18.6-18.10)	Not applicable
(ix) Control of deep sea mining (18.7)	Various academic disciplines
(x) Support of world climate programme	Meteorology
(xi) Antarctic policy (18.11-18.14)	Not applicable
(xii) International river basin's management (19.1-19.6)	Various academic disciplines
(xiii) International seas management (19.1-19.2; 19.7-19.12)	Various academic disciplines

MEETING BASIC HUMAN NEEDS

Introduction

As the text of the report constantly refers to 'basic human needs' this appendix is included to illustrate what is meant.

It is based on the recent book *First Things First* by Paul Streeten with Shahid Javed Burki, Muhbub Ul Haq, Norman Hicks and Frances Stewart,[1] and occasionally on *Basic Human Needs — A Framework for Action* by McHale and McHale.[2]

Why Basic Needs?

The basic needs strategy is concerned with removing mass deprivation, a concern that has always been at the heart of development. The discussion started in the 1950s, strongly influenced by Sir Arthur Lewis and others, who emphasised economic growth as the way to eradicate poverty. At this early stage, sensible economists and planners were quite clear (in spite of what is now often said in a caricature of past thinking) that growth is not an end in itself, but a performance test of development.

There were three justifications for the emphasis on growth as the principal performance test. First, that through market forces economic growth would spread its benefits widely and speedily, and that these benefits could best be achieved through growth. Second, it was assumed that Governments are democratic, or at any rate are concerned with the fate of the poor. Therefore, any Government action would spread the benefits of growth downward. The third justification, more hard headed than the previous two, claimed that the fate of the poor should not be a concern in the early stages of development. It was thought necessary first to build up the capital, infrastructure, and productive capacity of an economy so that it could improve the lot of the poor later.

None of the assumptions underlying these three justifications turned out to be universally true. Except for a very few countries, with special initial conditions and policies, there was no automatic tendency for income to be widely spread. Nor did Governments always take corrective action to reduce poverty; after all,

Governments were themselves often formed by the people who had close psychological, social, economic, and political links with the beneficiaries of the concentrated growth process (even though their motives were often mixed). And it was certainly not the case that a period of enduring poverty was needed to accumulate capital.

It became evident that the Lewis model, which strongly dominated not only academic thought but also political action, did not always work. It did not work for four reasons:

(a) The rural-urban income differentials were much higher than had been assumed, owing to trade union action on wages, minimum wage legislation, differentials inherited from colonial days, and other causes. This produced an excess of migrants and, at the same time, impeded the rapid absorption of the rural labour force.

(b) The rate of growth of the population and the rate of growth of the labour force were much larger than expected.

(c) The technology transferred from the rich countries to the industrial sector was labour-saving and though it raised labour productivity it did not create many jobs.

(d) In many developing countries a productivity-raising revolution in agriculture was a precondition for substantial and widespread progress in industry, and this revolution did not occur.

Thus attention was turned away from GNP and its growth toward employment objectives. Since 1969, the International Labour Organisation (ILO) has attempted to promote jobs. While this was a useful learning exercise, it soon became evident that unemployment is not really the main problem either. In *Asian Drama* Gunnar Myrdal[3] devoted many pages to criticising the concepts of employment, unemployment and under-employment in the context of underdeveloped Asia. Employment and unemployment make sense only in an industrialised society where there are employment exchanges, organised and informed labour markets, and social security benefits for the unemployed. This does not apply to the poorest developing countries.

The root problem is poverty, or low-productivity employment, not unemployment. Indeed, the very poor are not unemployed, but work very hard and long hours in unremunerative, unproductive forms of activity.

Attention is also directed to the women who, in some cultures, perform hard tasks without being counted as members of the labour force because their production is not sold for cash.

These difficulties turned the development debate to the question of income distribution. A landmark was the book published in 1974 for the Development Research Center of the World Bank and the Sussex Institute of Development Studies, entitled *Redistribution and Growth*.[4] It was quite clearly seen that in poor countries growth is a necessary condition for eradicating poverty, but it also seemed that economic growth sometimes reinforced and entrenched inequalities in the distribution of income, assets, and power. In societies with very low levels of living, meeting basic needs is more important than reducing inequality for three reasons. First, equality as such is probably not an objective of great importance to most people other than utilitarian philosophers and idealogues. Second, this lack of concern is justified, because meeting basic human needs is morally a more important objective than reducing inequality. Third, reducing inequality is a highly complex, abstract objective, open to many different interpretations and therefore operationally ambiguous.

After the dead end of 'employment', as interpreted in industrial countries and the limitations and irrelevance of egalitarianism, basic human needs is the next logical step in the path of development thinking. Concentrating on basic needs has at least four fundamental advantages over previous approaches to growth, employment, income redistribution, and poverty eradication.

(a) Most importantly, the basic needs concept is a reminder that the objectives of the development effort is to provide all human beings with the opportunity for a full life. The basic needs approach recalls the fundamental concern of development, which is human beings and their needs.

(b) The approach goes beyond abstractions such as money, income, or employment. To consider basic needs is to move from the abstract to the concrete; from the aggregate to the specific.

(c) The basic needs approach appeals to members of the national and international community and therefore in this case resources are mobilised, unlike vaguer (though important) objectives, such as raising growth rates to 6 per cent, contributing 0.7 per cent of GNP to development assistance, redistributing for greater equality, or narrowing income gaps. People do not normally share lottery prizes or other gains in wealth with their own brothers and sisters, but they do help when their siblings are ill, or their children need education, or some other basic need has to be met. The same is true in the wider human family. The basic needs approach therefore has the power to mobilise support for policies that more abstract notions lack.

(d) The approach has greater organising and integrating power intellectually, as well as politically.

Basic Needs as the Integrating Concept

One merit of the basic needs approach is that it provides a powerful basis for organising analysis and policy-making. Just as it can mobilise political support, it is also capable of integrating thought and action in different fields. This can be illustrated in the areas of energy, environmental pollution, raw material exhaustion, appropriate technology, appropriate consumption patterns, urbanisation, rural-urban migration, international trade, dominance and dependence, and the treatment of transnational corporations. A host of technical and apparently disparate problems are seen to be connected and become amenable to solution, once it is assumed that the ultimate purpose of development is to meet the basic needs of individuals.

A development strategy guided by the goal of meeting the basic needs of the poor, points to a different composition of products and choice of techniques. It is likely to encourage more labour-intensive methods of production and thereby generate jobs and primary sources of income for the poor. It is also likely to reduce the demand that rapid urbanisation makes on scarce capital, scarce skills, and exhaustible natural resources. By redirecting the composition of production towards products consumed by the poor, such a strategy encourages more intra-Third World trade, so that developing countries produce more of what they consume, and consume more of what they produce.

It so happens that for quite different historical reasons, the specialised agencies of the UN are already organised to meet the principal basic needs: WHO for health, UNESCO for basic education, FAO for food and agriculture, ILO for employment, UNICEF for children and their families.

Finally, while it is clear that some political regimes are incapable of meeting basic needs, the basic needs philosophy is not the monopoly of one creed.

What are Basic Human Needs?

It is common to refer to the core basic needs as those for food, health services, education, shelter, and water and sanitation. This classification fits the organisation of Governments into ministries and corresponds to the sector lending programmes of agencies and bilateral donors. But the notion of basic needs presents certain analytical difficulties.

There are two ways of defining a basic needs approach to development. The first sees it as the culmination of 25 years of development thought and experience. According to this definition, the basic needs approach embraces the components of previous strategies and approaches, such as rural development, the alleviation of urban poverty, the creation of employment through small scale industries, redistribution with growth, and other poverty-, employment-, and equity-oriented approaches, especially those aimed at making the poor more productive. The merit of such a definition is that it rallies a wide variety of people, interests, and institutions under the appealing banner of basic needs. The new elements are a shift towards social services and households, and an emphasis on so-called new-style projects in nutrition, health, and education. The fact that the basic needs approach means many things to many peoples is, from this point of view, an advantage.

But there are also drawbacks in elevating the approach to an all-embracing, almost exclusive development strategy.

The second definition of a basic needs approach brings out sharply its distinctive features and describes it as supplementing or complementing existing strategies: a basic needs approach to development attempts to provide the opportunities for the full physical, mental, and social development of the human personality and then derives the ways of achieving this objective. It is the resource of 'people' that is to be developed.

The approach has three objectives:

(a) Raising real incomes to the point where they are adequate to buy necessities such as food, clothing, household goods, transport, fuel, and shelter. This, in turn, implies productive and remunerative livelihoods (employment and self-employment) that give people a primary claim to what they produce and recognition of their contribution.

(b) Access to public services such as education, health care, water, and sanitation. This implies a physical and social infrastructure adequate to provide basic goods and services on a sustained basis and to allow for the growing fulfilment of basic needs.

(c) Participation by the people affected in the formulation and implementation of projects, programmes, and policies by the people affected — the local mobilisation of under-utilised (human) resources.

Why Should we Care?

This approach will tend to make more financial resources available, both domestically and possibly internationally. More resources will be available domestically for three reasons:

First, the composition of output needed to satisfy basic needs is likely to be more labour-intensively produced. In countries with under-employed labour, this will raise not only employment but also production.

Second, an attack on malnutrition, disease, and illiteracy not only lengthens life and improves its quality (desirable goals in their own right) but also improves the quality of the labour force.

Third, a basic needs approach that is based on participation will mobilise local resources in many ways. Paramedical personnel and teachers can be (partly) paid in kind; the local community can support the programmes; local materials can be used for projects. The purpose of such mobilisation is twofold: it harnesses previously under-used resources, and it economises on the use of scarce central resources such as administration, transport, and materials.

A direct attack to reduce infant mortality, to educate women, and to provide for old age, illness, and disability is thought to reduce the desired family size and fertility rates more speedily and at lower cost than raising household incomes, at any rate after a time lag in which the population growth rate may rise. (Family planning needs having been assumed and provided.)

More resources may be available internationally, because meeting the basic needs of the world's poor has stronger moral and political appeal and therefore a higher claim on aid budgets than most other schemes advanced for the promotion of international assistance. Food is an important element in basic needs and, given the distribution of votes in Western democracies, food aid is often politically easier than financial aid. Properly channelled so as not to discourage domestic agriculture, food aid can make an important international contribution to meeting basic needs. The basic needs approach is thrice blessed: it is good in its own right, it raises productivity, and it lowers reproductivity.

Basic Needs and the Environment:

That conservation and sustainable development (for basic needs) are mutually dependent can be illustrated by the plight of the rural poor. The dependence of rural communities on living resources is direct and immediate. For the 500 million people who are malnourished, or the 1,500 million people whose only fuel is wood, dung or crop wastes, or the almost 800 million people with incomes of $50 or less a year — for all these people, conservation of their meagre resource-base is the only means by which they can at best avoid abject misery, and at worst an early death.

Unhappily, people on the margins of survival are compelled by their poverty, and their consequent vulnerability to inflation, to destroy the few resources available to them. In widening circles around their villages they strip trees and shrubs for fuel until the plants wither away and the villagers are forced to burn dung and stubble. The 400 million tonnes of dung and crop wastes that rural people burn annually are badly needed to regenerate soils already highly vulnerable to erosion now that the plants that bind them are disappearing.

It would be wrong, however, to conclude that conservation is a sufficient response to such problems. People whose very survival is precarious and whose prospects of even temporary prosperity are bleak cannot be expected to respond sympathetically to calls to subordinate their acute short-term needs to the possibility of long-term returns. Conservation must therefore be combined with measures to meet short-term economic needs. The vicious circle by which poverty causes ecological degradation, which in turn leads to more poverty, can be broken only by development. But if it is not to be self-defeating, it must be development that is sustainable and reaches the very poor. Hence the attraction of the basic needs approach to those who wish to promote the WCS.

Notes and References

1 STREETEN, P. *et al*. 1981. First things first. Oxford University Press.

2 MCHALE, J AND MCHALE, M C. 1978. Basic human needs — a framework for action. Transaction Books.

3 MYRDAL, G. 1968. Asian drama: an inquiry into the poverty of nations. Penguin Books, Harmonsworth.

4 WORLD BANK. 1974. Redistribution and growth. World Bank Publications.

THE BRITISH AID PROGRAMME: A SUMMARY OF THE POLICY

Extracted from OECD 1981 Development Assistance Report and ODA Sources

In 1980, net oda[1] disbursements from the United Kingdom amounted to $1.71m and represented 0.34 per cent of GNP. Their 23 per cent decline (in national currency) from their 1979 level, when they totalled $2,105m or 0.52 per cent of GNP, was due mainly to two factors:

(a) the sixth replenishment of IDA was not fully ratified during 1980 so that the United Kingdom did not deposit a promissory note in that year; and

(b) drawing of bilateral aid against available resources by certain recipients (eg India) was relatively sluggish in 1980.

Oda disbursements should rise significantly in 1983. IDA promissory notes for 1980 and 1981 have been deposited; some of the backlog in bilateral disbursements was made up in the final quarter of the fiscal year 1980-81.

Longer-term oda volume prospects are affected by the British Government's decision in 1980 to reduce aid appropriations in real terms. This reduction is part of a policy of overall public expenditure restraint, designed to fight inflation and to encourage a shift from public to private sector spending. The most recent Public Expenditure White Paper (CMND 8175 of March 1981) shows a planned reduction in the level of overseas aid of about 15 per cent in real terms over the period 1980-81 to 1983-84. The United Kingdom authorities have also indicated that they intend to give greater weight in the future allocation of oda to political, industrial and commercial considerations, alongside their basic development objectives.

The grant element of total oda commitments was 97 per cent in 1980. Some 95 per cent of oda, including all aid to the least development and low income countries, is now in the form of grants. In general, bilateral aid remains tied to procurement of British goods and services. Where appropriate, however, a limited amount of aid in 1980 was untied, for example to meet local costs associated with aid projects (some $112m in 1980 or 9 per cent of bilateral oda), and in particular cases some third-country procurement was permitted.

As regards the bilateral and multilateral shares of total oda, the Government has made it clear that multilateral contributions will be examined critically because of the need for more room for manoeuvre in bilateral programmes. This policy is reflected in a reduction in the level of contributions to UK programmes from $146m in 1979 to $111m in 1980. In future replenishment negotiations for contributions to IDA and international financial institutions, the Government has also stated that, as a general aim, it will seek a reduction in its share to a level more consistent with the United Kingdom's relative economic strength.[2]

Bilateral oda is extended to some 130 countries. The 10 largest recipients in 1980 (India, Bangladesh, Sri Lanka, Tanzania, Pakistan, Sudan, Kenya, Zambia, Egypt and Malawi) accounted for 61 per cent of the total. About 59 per cent went to countries with a *per capita* GDP in 1978 of $320 or less; the least developed countries received 30 per cent.

While the Government fully recognises the importance of official development assistance, especially of the poorest countries, it also believes that more attention should be given to the role of non-concession flows in the development process. Total net non-oda flows from the United Kingdom to developing countries in 1980 amounted to some $11.0bn ($11.6bn in 1979), and corresponded to 2.09 per cent of GNP (as against 2.82 per cent in 1979) the second highest GNP figure, after Switzerland, among DAC countries. This partly reflects the role of the financial institutions based in the United Kingdom in recycling private funds from British and other sources (eg OPEC) to the developing countries (see Table 1 and Table 2 on p 379).

	(£m)		1980-81	1981-82 (planned)
Multilateral			203	309
Bilateral			700	674
made up of:				
(i) Project aid of which		280		
Infrastructure	101			
Rural development	60			
Industry and mining	67			
Education	15			
Health	24			
Other	13			
Total	280			
(ii) Technical assistance (personnel overseas, students and trainees etc)		201		
(iii) Other non-project aid		219		
Total		700		
Total net official aid			903	983

Table 1. **The structure of the British Aid Programme**
Source: British Aid Statistics, 1981.[3]

	£m and percentages							
	1965	1970	1975	1976	1977	1978	1979	1980
Total bilateral aid £m of which (percentage):	177	198	305	376	388	542	539	604
Project	43	34	39	35	35	35	39	46
Non-project	34	43	29	31	32	37	32	17
Technical cooperation	23	23	32	34	33	28	29	37
Non-project £m of which (percentage):	77	85	89	118	124	202	202	101
Programme (import) finance	50	69	62	62	63	66	78	69
Budgetary support	31	19	10	7	8	7	5	10
Food aid	—	5	12	8	6	7	4	9
Debt refinancing	—	—	11	11	21	3	9	2
Other	19	7	5	12	7	17	4	10
Project £m of which (percentage):	60	68	120	131	137	187	251	280
Transport and communications	15	22	23	23	15	32	27	36
Social and community services	2	30	25	16	14	10	13	14
Energy	5	6	14	12	11	8	14	18
Agriculture and livestock	13	7	11	9	12	8	10	8
Agricultural primary processing	7	9	11	3	6	8	3	4
Other manufacturing			1	6	7	7	6	6
Unallocated and other	58	26	19	31	25	27	27	14
Technical cooperation £m of which (percentage):	40	46	96	127	127	153	185	223
Students and trainees	11	19	16	14	16	16	18	22
Wholly financed personnel	7	10	11	11	12	13	13	11
Partly financed personnel:								
Pensions and compensation to retired officials	22	36	7	10	10	9	7	6
Other (mainly educational)	?	6	26	21	21	19	19	17
British Council	?	8	11	17	14	13	11	11
Other (mainly research and educational)	34	21	28	26	27	30	31	32
Bilateral aid as a percentage of gross aid expenditure	90	90	70	73	66	75	72	70

Table 2. **Functional distribution of UK bilateral aid: gross expenditure**
Source: British Aid Statistics, 1981.[4]

Notes and References

1   oda is overseas development assistance. ODA is The Overseas Development Agency.

2   Since this report was prepared, the 1982 Development Assistance Report of OECD has been published. This updates the statistics. Also many of the relevant details can be found in the publication 'Real Aid' available from Oxfam, 274 Banbury Road, Oxford.

3   BRITISH AID STATISTICS. 1981.

4   BRITISH AID STATISTICS. 1981.

BRITISH AID AND THE ENVIRONMENT

The Policy in 1978-79

The following is an outline of the environmental policy of the Overseas Development Ministry as indicated by UK delegation to UNEP in 1978-79.

In considering the contribution which we can make, the key factor is that it is for the Governments of the developing countries themselves to decide what priority they wish to give environmental factors within their own development programmes. This is a political issue to be considered against the demands for economic and social development in any individual country. The Ministry of Overseas Development is prepared to give, and indeed does give, assistance and advice on environmental matters to developing countries, but strictly on request. In addition, we take into consideration and bring to the attention of recipient Governments the environmental implications of the aid projects we support. With the increased emphasis on aid for the poorest countries, and particularly for the rural poor, many of our projects are in the natural resources field where environmental problems could well arise unless appropriate precautions are taken. In these (and indeed in all relevant) cases we seek to take into account the environmental implications at every stage in the planning and execution of a project and we encourage aid recipients to be aware of them also.

We [the UK] accept that developing countries will regard it as essential to press forward with the economic and social development, but that they should be helped and encouraged to take account of the environmental implication of their actions. We [the UK], other developed countries, and the UN institutions, can help in this by providing advice both generally and in relation to the activities and projects which we [the UK] or they support in the developing countries.

The Government's Current Policy

The following is an ODA policy guidance note on aid projects and the environment, issued in August 1981.

(a) Since the 1972 United Nations Conference on the Human Environment, ODA has been committed to the avoidance of serious and irreversible damage to the environment in its promotion of economic development, and to aiming for the overall improvement of the quality of the atmosphere, of water sources and of life itself. [The UK] is party to a number of international conventions on a range of environmental issues. We are also committed to drawing the environmental implications of development projects, which we were asked to finance to the attention of potential recipients. This Policy Guidace Note (PGN) offers Geographical Departments and Development Divisions guidance on how to apply these principles to development projects.

(b) Development disturbs the environment. That is in part its point to use resources more intensively, or in a different place, or in different combinations, so that people may have more or better food or drink, clothing, shelter, education, health, employment, opportunities for a better life. Few environments are stable anyway; population pressure is one frequent agent of change. But disturbance of the environment has costs as well as benefits. Sometimes ODA may be asked to finance projects whose main purpose is to restore environments disturbed by other processes (eg soil erosion). More often, ODA will be asked to finance projects whose effects on the environment are more complicated than they may at first sight appear. An industrial project may pollute a river with effects on health and agriculture downstream. The removal of forest cover may have environmental effects which are bad: rapid run-off of water, flash floods, soil erosion, silting up of rivers or reservoirs, loss of genetic resources; or which are good: increased water availability for reservoirs or irrigation, removal of insect pests or predators; or mixed. Whenever a project has indirect effects, proper project appraisal requires that they should be taken account of, and quantified when that is possible without inordinate expense. In general, a proper accounting or 'appraisal' to encompass the net long-term change in human well-being resulting from implementing it [is required].

(c) The money and time it is worth devoting to assessing the effect of development projects on the environment depends on how serious, complex and long-lasting those effects are likely to be. Fragile environments and changes difficult to preserve need the most careful consideration. How important the environmental effects of a particular project are likely to be should be considered by the Geographical Department or Development Division responsible, with appropriate professional advice, at an early stage of its appraisal. Where there is doubt, the Environment Adviser should be consulted. Projects which will have major environmental effects which ought to be considered in depth include all projects which involve: (i) substantial changes in land-use (eg the introduction of forestry, arable or bush fallow farming or human settlements where they have not previously been); (ii) substantial changes in water-use (eg irrigation, water supplies); (iii) substantial changes in farming or fishing practice (eg use of pesticides and fertilisers, introduction of new crops, mechanisation); (iv) major infrastructure (eg dams, ports); (v) industrial processes generating toxic waste (eg pulp mills, chemical plants, mining); (vi) changes in fragile environments (small islands, thinly or densely populated areas, arid areas); (vii) resource recycling, energy and nutrient conservation, waste management. The Environment Adviser should be consulted as a matter of course about all projects involving wildlife conservation or nature reserves, whether with or without tourist development. Where appropriate, he in turn will consult the Nature Conservancy Council or other sources of advice available in Britain.

(d) The environmental costs and benefits of a project often do not accrue to the same people. In particular the benefits to the project area or target group may need to be weighed against costs imposed on other areas, groups or even countries. The acquifers which wells tap have a limited capacity to replenish themselves, so if one village starts using ground-water to irrigate its crops another may go short of drinking water. Such questions are often of political importance in the beneficiary country. Clearly ODA cannot compel any potential recipient to accept policies of environmental protection or social equity in environmental costs, or to value them more highly than economic growth over the short-term. But ODA can and should explain the options and their implications, so that at least the choice is a conscious one; and it is of course open to ODA not to support a choice with which it disagrees.

(e) The inclusion of the effects of a project on its environment in the appraisal of that project shows the difference between private or project-related costs and benefits, and costs and benefits to society as a whole. There is also a fundamental question about the *timing* of benefits and costs. Acceptance of the importance of the environment within which all development occurs involves concern for *sustainable* benefits, which may have to be weighed against greater short-term but *unsustainable* benefits.

(f) ODA's professional advisers in all disciplines, including the Scientific Units, will bring knowledge of and concern for the environmental effects of projects to their normal consideration of them. But it is essential that these effects should be explicitly dealt with in the planning and appraisal of any project in which they are likely to be important. In the case of such a project, the Geographical Department or Development Division responsible should: (i) see that appraisal missions or consultancy studies take account of the wider environmental aspects (including the ecology) of the project area and its likely development in the absence of the proposed project. The Environment Adviser should be given a chance as time permits, to comment on terms of reference and composition; (ii) ensure that project submissions describe the environmental consequences of the proposed project (both beneficial and otherwise in the short- and longer-term) and, where necessary, weigh these against other costs or benefits identified by the appraisal. Normally ODA's professional Advisers will be able to do this, but in a few cases it may require a special investigation to be financed to quantify and, so far as possible to cost the environmental consequences; (iii) include the environmental changes resulting from the project among the points to be covered in monitoring the project during its implementation. Those responsible for the monitoring arrangements will need to consider whether this requirement can be adequately covered by a general direction to those monitoring the project to pay attention to its environmental consequences or whether it is appropriate to include, for example, periodic measuring of soil loss, stream flow, chemical changes in air and water systems, vegetation cover, key species of plants and animals, human health; (iv) see that ex-post evaluation covers the environmental effects of the project. The Environment Adivser should be given a chance as time permits, to comment on the terms of reference and composition of the Evaluation Mission.

(g) In general the Environment Adviser should be informed of all significant environmental issues arising in the administration of bilateral and multilateral aid.

(h) Inquiries about this Policy Guidance Note should be addressed to the Bilateral Coordination Department.

DECLARATION OF ENVIRONMENT POLICIES AND PROCEDURES RELATING TO ECONOMIC DEVELOPMENT, FEBRUARY, 1982

RECOGNISING THAT the major environmental problems of the developing countries are not necessarily of the same nature as those of developed countries in that they are problems which often reflect the impacts of poverty which not only affects the quality of life but life itself;

AND WHEREAS economic development is essential to the alleviation of major environmental problems by providing for an integral relationship between societies and their environment;

REALISING also that such economic development should be pursued in such a manner as to avoid or minimise environmental problems peculiar to it;

CONVINCED that in the long run environmental protection and economic development are not only compatible but interdependent and mutually reinforcing;

ACKNOWLEDGING that the need for environmentally sensitive and responsible development has become more important and urgent in the light of increasing population and concomitant pressures on the earth's resources and life-supporting ecological systems in some areas;

ACKNOWLEDGING the sovereign right of governments to determine their own priorities and development patterns;

RECALLING that the States which adopted the Declaration of the United Nations Conference on the Human Environment (Stockholm, 1972) stated their common conviction (principle 25) that they will ensure that the international organisations play a coordinated, efficient and dynamic role in the protection and improvement of the environment;

CONSIDERING furthermore that international development assistance institutions have, along with their Member Governments, a responsibility to ensure the sustainability of the economic development activities financed by them;

THEREFORE the undersigned declare that they:

I

Reaffirm their support for the Principles and Recommendations for action of the United Nations Conference on the Human Environment.

II

Will, to the best of their abilities, endeavour to:

1. institute procedures for systematic examination of all development activities, including policies, programmes and projects under consideration for financing to ensure that appropriate measures are proposed for compliance with Section I above.
2. enter into cooperative negotiations with Governments and with concerned and relevant organisations and agencies to ensure integration of appropriate environmental measures in the design and implementation of economic development activities.
3. provide technical assistance, including training, on environmental matters to developing countries, at their request, thus developing their indigenous capacity and facilitating technical cooperation between developing countries.
4. give active consideration to project proposals that are specially designed to protect, rehabilitate, manage or otherwise enhance the human environment, the quality of life and resources thereto related.
5. initiate and/or otherwise cooperate in research and studies leading to improvement of project appraisal methodologies, including cost benefit analysis of environmental protection measures.
6. support the training and information of operational staff in the environmental dimension of economic development.
7. prepare, publish and disseminate documentation and audio-visual material providing guidance on the environmental dimension of economic development activities.

The declaration was signed by the Presidents of the following institutions:

African Development Bank *Abidjan*
Arab Bank for African Development *Khartoum*
Asian Development Bank *Manila*
Caribbean Development Bank *Bridgetown*
European Community (for the EDF) *Brussels*
Inter-American Development Bank *Washington DC*
Organisation of American States *Washington DC*
United Nations Development Programme *New York*
World Bank *Washington DC*

THE EUROPEAN DEVELOPMENT FUND

(The following has been extracted from the IIED study of EDF 1979-80)[1]

Section 1: Environmental Policy

The Institutional Context for Environmental Procedures: EDF's operation characteristics and project cycle.

EDF operations are controlled by three partners: the EEC countries, the ACP states and the CEC. Any project passes through four main phases: programming, examination, execution and evaluation.

Programming

In EDF's project cycle the programming exercise for the five years of each Convention period takes place at the start of the period — environmental sensitivity to be built into the programme at the earliest stage.

Each ACP country lays down the line of its own development strategy. However, generally the programming phase begins with information and study of each ACP country, inquiry as to the results of former EDF-financed projects, examination of the country's financial position etc.

So far as it is able to ascertain, no part of this process of information collection and study of plans involved a specific focus on environmental issues. It is precisely at this earliest stage in project conception that environmental considerations must be incorporated.

The next stage is for the Fund to get a general view of the project, or proposals for projects, it intends to finance. This is done by use of a high level EDF mission. There is no systematic procedure to ensure that natural scientific, ecological or land-use planning expertise is incorporated in such missions, indeed experience is that such a viewpoint has been missing entirely.

From the standpoint of the ACP country, this programming work provides a clear idea of what aid may be expected and for what purpose.

Project Examination

From the programme stage projects are put forward to the Community by the government concerned in the form of project files or *dossiers de projects*. The country concerned can obtain Community aid for technical assistance in drawing up all or part of the file.

The project is then considered in close cooperation with the government of the country concerned. The Lomé II Convention now explicitly states in Article 112e, that: 'appraisal must take account of the non-quantifiable effects of projects and particular attention shall be paid to the effects of the project on the environment'.

Lomé II has emphasised the need for speeding up financing decisions. This has produced a tendency to see any consideration of projects from an additional point of view as yet another filter being applied to a pipeline already largely clogged by procedural obstructions.

The Financing Proposal

When the examination is over, the EDF and the Government concerned get together to draw up a financing proposal. Subject to a favourable opinion, it goes for decision to the CEC.

In a number of cases, especially in the area of projects designed to check desertification in arid and semi-arid lands, EDF projects are intimately concerned with environmental improvement. In such cases, naturally, environmental effects have been dealt with quite fully in the financing proposal. But in other cases examined environmental considerations were conspicuously absent from documentation or inadequately dealt with.

Project Execution

The execution calls for continuous joint action by the beneficiary country and the CEC. Works and supply contracts are awarded through competitive international tender, open on equal conditions to all persons or bodies corporate in the countries of the ACP.[2]

It should be noted that tendering requirements do offer the possibility that a wider range of environmental as well as specifically developmental expertise may be brought to bear than is often the case with bilateral national aid programmes.

The EEC Commission sets up its own technical and financial supervision through the Commission delegate, its representative on the spot. His job is to keep the Commission informed.

Subsequent Evaluation

Once completed the Commission and the Government concerned carry out regular joint evaluation surveys. This is intended to enable the Commission to inform the Council of the use made of these investments and the conditions in which they operate. It is in the area of project evaluation that the particular environmental responsibilities lie. At present the evaluation bureau of EDF is extremely small and has so far been limited to economic analysis only.

Section 2:
Suggested Environmental Measures for Adoption by EDF[3]

Recommendations[4]

The leadership of EDF should follow up the Community's signature of the Declaration of Environment Policies and Procedures Relating to Economic Development (see Appendix F of this report). With a policy paper on jointly decided guidelines regarding the Fund's commitment to more sustainable, or environmentally positive, development. The policy statement should give instances or examples of problems and also, most important, of solutions to environmental problems with which the Fund was able to help.

GENERAL PROCEDURE

Recommended

1. That the management of EDF introduce a *simple manual* of procedures to ensure that environmental considerations are referred to at each phase of project preparation *including* project identification.
2. That *country background papers* identify the principal environmental and resource-constraints facing the country and assess the priority to be given to them.
3. That environmentally-sensitive *sector papers* be prepared on *all* the major sectors of EDF lending.
4. That the case for 'touring teams' including environmental expertise be examined by EDF's senior management.

SPECIAL AREAS OF FOCUS

Recommended

That critical areas for environmental focus be examined, in particular the case for a special fund for alternative energy — as proposed recently by one ACP country in the course of the Lomé II Convention negotiation.

COUNTRY SURVEYS

Recommended

That specific provision be made for appropriate environmental expertise to be incorporated into each country survey.

PROJECT APPRAISAL

The experience of national aid agencies so far is that environmental appraisal works best when done under existing arrangements with some procedures for screening and identification of projects with particular environmental problems. Provisionally, it may be said here that no major institutional or structural change seems desirable in this area. At the same time, the common experience of other development agencies has been that some established procedure for introducing environmental screening is essential. This should be laid down at the project design stage.

PROJECT MONITORING AND POST-AUDIT

Recommended

That responsibility for an initiative to support developing country institutions capable of environmental assessment, monitoring and post-audit be given to one particular division of EDF in Brussels.

TRAINING AND RESEARCH

Recommended

That the environmental focal point in EDF be given responsibility for preparing a training programme (internal and external) and collection of relevant data for research.

ORGANISATIONAL STRUCTURE

Two general suggestions may be made.

The first is that some high level environmental advice should be made available on a routine basis *to the Director General's office.*

Second, the focal point for environmental activities (or environmental office) should be located in the Projects Division. The main functions of the focal point are going to be the promotion and stimulation of environmental appraisal, monitoring and audit and the training and research functions referred to immediately above. There may be a case for adding some of this expertise to the Evaluation Division.

EXTERNAL RELATIONS AND THE ENVIRONMENT

Following the signature of the Declaration (Appendix F of this report) an EDF representative attended a meeting of signatory agencies. This meeting resolved to form a Committee of International Development Institutions for the Environment (CIDIE).

Recommended

As a signatory of the Declaration, the European Community should attend CIDIE meetings[5] and participate in its activities, including the support and use of any joint facility which the group decides to create or support.

Notes and References

1 INTERNATIONAL INSTITUTE FOR ENVIRONMENT AND DEVELOPMENT. 1980. The European Development Fund and the environment. IIED.

2 Although, as the House of Lords Select Committee on the European Communities 'Development Aid policy' report shows, the UK has traditionally got less than its 'fair' share of the contractual work in the area of consultancies, works and supply. (House of Lords Select Committee on the European Communities, twenty first report, 1980-81.)

3 The EDF and the environment, *op cit.*

4 No other work has been done to review the implementation of these recommendations.

5 In fact, the EDF has attended all meetings of CIDIE and hosted the most recent successful meeting of CIDIE in April 1982.

THE UNITED NATIONS ENVIRONMENT PROGRAMME

Section 1:
The Background

The UN Conference on the Human Environment in Stockholm in 1972 recommended that four institutions be created to carry out the plan of action developed at the event.

(a) A Governing Council for Environmental Programmes;

(b) A small Secretariat, to serve as the 'focal point for environmental action and coordination within the UN system';

(c) A voluntary Environment Fund, to finance environment programmes;

(d) An Environmental Coordination Board (ECB), consisting of members of all relevant UN bodies.

At a meeting of the UN General Assembly later in 1972 these four bodies became known as the UN Environment Programme (UNEP). The General Assembly also voted to site UNEP in Nairobi, despite determined opposition from the developed countries. As a result, UNEP became the first major UN body to be established in a developing country. It was also agreed that the Council and the Secretariat were to be financed from the UN regular budget. But the programmes themselves were to be financed from the Voluntary Fund, augmented by the budgets of the rest of the UN system. The Fund's target for the first five years (1973 to 1977) was $100m.

As a result, UNEP has perhaps one of the most difficult jobs in the entire UN system. What it attempts to do in a wide range of programme areas is to coordinate the work of others, promote policy initiatives with others and provide environmental information to others. And by and large the 'others' are the executing agencies of the UN: UNDP, FAO, UNESCO, WHO, ILO, IMO, etc. In fact, during 1980, UNEP gave funds to 145 projects in other UN agencies (37 per cent of the funds), 23 NGO projects (9.7 per cent of the Fund) spent 33 per cent of the funds on 53 internal projects and 20.3 per cent to 'other Governments and NGOs' for 26 projects. (The total was 269 projects and $32m.) Within the UN category, 20 different organisations were involved, but over half went to three organisations: UNESCO, WHO and FAO. Within the Government category, the lion's share ($3.8m out of $5.5m) went to the USSR in unconvertible currency. Within the NGO category, 70 per cent of the total went to five organisations, including IUCN and IIED.

Over the decade, UNEP has experimented with several ways of cooperating with the UN agencies. It has tried drafting memoranda of understanding with each agency, planning environmental programmes with the agencies, and, more recently, planning whole areas of its programme — such as food or water — with other agencies in an exercise known as thematic programming. Another route has been the creation of Programme Activity Centres (PACs), each with a small UNEP staff to coordinate the work of several agencies. So far, PACs have been created for:

(a) The Global Environmental Monitoring System (GEMS) (see Section 3 of Appendix H, p 392);

(b) industry and trade;

(c) the International Referral System for Sources of Environmental Information (INFOTERRA), UNEP's information system;

(d) The International Register of Potentially Toxic Chemicals (IRPTC);

(e) The Regional Seas Programme.

But none of these PACs has been wholly successful, despite steadily improving relations. (See Chapter 3, Section 4 of this report, pp 333-336, for the report's recommendations on this point.)

Section 2:
Where the Money Comes From and
How it is Spent

The Environment Fund has received money from 96 out of the world's 160 countries. During the past four years (1978-1981), 64 countries have made no contribution.

Over the same period, contributions have ranged from $1,500 (the Bahamas and Sri Lanka) to $15.4m (the Soviet Union) and $40m (the United States). However, money from the USSR, China, Cuba and Eastern Europe is considerably less useful as it is in local currency, and can be spent only in donor countries. Some other nations pay partly in non-convertible currencies.

The United States has been a major funder of UNEP — disproportionately so, even by UN standards. During 1973-81 the US provided 36 per cent of the voluntary fund. The size of the US contribution in the future is now in some doubt due to budget cutting in Washington and disenchantment with the UN system as a whole.

As percentage of GNP in 1978, x one million	
Sweden	88.50
Norway	86.39
Kenya	36.20
Finland	35.54
Kuwait	30.78
Denmark	30.34
Switzerland	28.61
New Zealand	22.09
Austria	20.86
United States	18.79
United Kingdom	17.87
Zaire	17.77
Ghana	17.72
Australia	17.63
Japan	16.64
Canada	16.25
USSR***	15.97
Saudi Arabia	15.86
German Federal Republic	15.50
Netherlands	14.21
Belgium	13.47
Iraq	13.29
France	12.66
Senegal	10.89
Ireland	8.78
Italy	7.33
German Democratic Republic**	7.17
Tunisia	6.88
Jamaica	6.86
Venezuela	6.38
Spain	6.21
Mexico	5.93
Libya	5.36
Iran	5.17
Argentina	5.16
Tanzania	4.42
Israel	4.25
India**	3.46
Nigeria	2.84
Malaysia	2.76
Hungary***	2.67
Yugoslavia**	2.60
Philippines	2.58
Egypt	2.55
Bangladesh**	2.23
China	2.05
Colombia	1.89
Thailand	1.83
Algeria	1.80
Czechoslovakia***	1.53
Poland	1.47
Uganda	1.47
Pakistan	1.12
Republic of Korea	0.94
Greece	0.92
Bulgaria***	0.65
Romania***	0.53
Turkey	0.46
Brazil	0.43

* only those countries contributing $15,000 or more
** partly in non-convertible currency
*** wholly in non-convertible currency

Figure 13. **National Contributions* to UNEP Voluntary Fund 1978 to 1981**
Source: Stockholm Plus Ten, 1982.[1]

The funds donated by nations are shown as a percentage of their GNP in Figure 13. In these terms, the contributions from Europe (particularly Scandinavia) and some developing countries are extremely high. There have been three financing periods so far: a five year (1973 to 1977), a four year (1978 to 1981) and a two year period (1982 to 1983). The target of $100m for the first period was virtually reached, and the target of $150m for the second fell about $25m short. The target for the third period is about $120m; there is no possibility of it being reached.

The fund's annual income has stayed at around $30m over the past five years. Because of inflation, this has meant that UNEP has been able to do less and less.

Income over the past nine years is shown below in Figure 14, both in current value and in the 1973 dollar value. The 1973 figures allow an average of 9.4 per cent inflation a year. This is the average rate of inflation quoted by the World Bank over the period 1970 to 1978 for 18 industrialised countries. Together, these countries provided 82.14 per cent of the UNEP Voluntary Fund during 1973 to 1981. The figures show that in real terms UNEP has less to spend now than it did in 1973. Its real income has progressively decreased over the past four years.

Year	Income (nominal value)	Income (1973 value)
1973	11.92	11.92
1974	21.18	18.58
1975	15.80	13.20
1976	24.80	18.94
1977	30.51	21.30
1978	32.58	20.79
1979	33.76	19.69
1980	34.37	18.33
1982	31.98	15.59

Figure 14. **UNEP income since its inception**
Source: Stockholm Plus Ten, 1982.[2]

Figure 15 (see p 390) shows how it is planned to spend the environment fund in 1982-83.

Section 3:
Earthwatch[3]

The third section of Appendix H is intended to outline and review the environmental assessment activities of UNEP (EARTHWATCH). The recommendations are made in the text of the report (Chapter 3, Section 4, pp 333-336), with particular reference to the requirements of the WCS.

Rank programme area	$m	%
1. Regional seas	9.0	9.7
2. Desertification	9.0	9.7
3. GEMS	6.0	6.5
4. Information	6.0	6.5
5. Technical assistance	5.8	6.2
6. Water	4.6	5.0
7. Wildlife and protected areas	4.2	4.5
8. Pest management systems	4.0	4.3
9. Environmental management and integrated development	3.9	4.2
10. IRPTC	3.3	3.5
11. Research and assessment	3.2	3.5
12. Settlements planning and environment	3.1	3.3
13. Health and the work environment	2.29	3.1
14. Soils	2.9	3.1
15. Industry and environment	2.9	3.1
16. Environmental education	2.8	3.0
17. Environmental training	2.5	2.7
18. INFOTERRA	2.4	2.6
19. Genetic resources	2.3	2.5
20. Tropical forests and woodlands	2.2	2.4
21. Energy	2.1	2.2
22. Outer limits	2.0	2.1
23. Environmental data	1.5	1.6
24. Environmental law	1.0	1.1
25. Marine pollution	0.9	1.0
26. Environmentally sound technology	0.7	0.8
27. Mountain, island and other ecosystems	0.6	0.6
28. Living marine resources	0.6	0.6
29. Natural disasters	0.6	0.6
Totals	93.0	100.0

Figure 15. **Ranking of programme areas according to the proposed resource-allocation for the biennium 1982-1983**
Source: The Environment Programme:
Medium-Term Plan, 1982-1983, UNEP/GC.
9/6. and Corrigenda.

Introduction

The general intent of the Stockholm Action Plan (1972) can be summarised as follows: 'To launch a set of internationally coordinated activities aimed first at increasing knowledge of environmental trends and their effects on man and resources, and secondly, at protecting and improving the quality of the environment and the productivity of resources by integrated planning and management'.

The Action Plan also included three functional tasks:
(a) global environmental assessment (Earthwatch);
(b) environmental management;
(c) supporting measures.

Earthwatch was defined as: 'a dynamic process of integrated environmental assessment, by which relevant environmental issues are identified and necessary data are gathered and evaluated to provide a basis of information and understanding for effective environmental management'. Earthwatch was conceived as a global system composed of national facilities, services and research and the relevant work of other international organisations. The system was to be coordinated and in some cases supported by UNEP.

'Earthwatch' consists of three types of activity: *research* into environmental processes, *monitoring* of environmental variables, and the *evaluation* of environmental trends. It was always intended that these component activities should be closely interlinked.

As the WCS makes clear, the assessment of environmental baseline data and trends is a prerequisite for effective environmental or natural resource-management, and over the years great emphasis has been attached to this fact by the UNEP Governing Council. However, during the Seventh Governing Council (1979), a number of Member States (including the UK) expressed concern about the apparent lack of substantive progress in Earthwatch. As a result, a group of 'Government experts' met in Geneva in November 1979 to consider the further development of the unit. Their recommendations, accompanied by an in-depth review (prepared by UNEP), were submitted to the 1980 Governing Council.

In addition, two of the components, 'monitoring' and 'information exchange' have been separately reviewed by outside experts groups. The monitoring programmes, under the UNEP title of the Global Environmental Monitoring System (GEMS) have been repeatedly reviewed and evaluated over the years.

An Evaluation of Earthwatch Coordination

Although it was put more diplomatically in the various reviews, the main obstacle to the development of Earthwatch as an authoritative unit appears to be a total lack of an adequate organisational structure and the necessary financial resources:
(a) the head of Earthwatch functions as a coordinator rather than as an executive of the programme;
(b) there is no director for Earthwatch research;
(c) there is no director for the Earthwatch information exchange;
(d) there is no director for Earthwatch evaluations;
(e) the director of GEMS reports directly to the Executive Director of UNEP rather than to the director of Earthwatch;
(f) Earthwatch, as distinct from its component parts, has a professional staff of only two to three people.

The budget reflects this state of affairs:

Most of the money under the Earthwatch heading is allocated to the individual components and very little to Earthwatch *per se*.

Furthermore, the total funding allocated to Earthwatch and its four components is far too low in absolute terms and arguably in proportion to the UNEP total (1978-79 $11.00m, or 16.7 per cent of the total; 1982-83 $18.4m, or 19.8 per cent of the total).

Perhaps more fundamentally, the three level programme structure of UNEP, divided into priority subject areas (such as human settlements and health; terrestrial ecosystems; environment and development; oceans; energy and natural disasters), and the parallel functional tasks such as Earthwatch and the supporting measures (education training and environmental law) do not relate sufficiently to each other. In short, there appear to be problems of organisation, budgeting and programme management within UNEP as a whole which detract from Earthwatch. These inter-agency problems in turn reduce the efficacy of the unit to the world outside.

In his statement to the Group of Experts considering Earthwatch (November, 1979) Dr Tolba (the Executive Director) admitted as much when he said, 'up to now environmental assessment has not been systematically identified in the various components of Earthwatch . . . The Environment Programme (as a whole) has, over the years, performed a number of "assessments", perhaps without stressing that what it was producing were in fact "assessments", and all too often without calling enough attention to them'. In the same statement he went on to say that the benefits of such assessments should accrue to national Governments: to that end they must be both understandable and properly disseminated. Conversely, national assessments can, if passed back to Earthwatch, be used internationally.

The above underlines the fact that, even if Earthwatch assessments exist, which in the view of some is highly debatable, they are not used. Is this because there are really no users? — which renders the need for Earthwatch as highly questionable — or is it because the unit is not doing its job adequately? Expertise familiar with the unit highlights three points:

(a) As Dr Tolba admits, Earthwatch has kept a very low profile internationally; no one has had much chance to evaluate its use;

(b) Due to a lack of an effective dialogue between national Governments and Earthwatch, any assessments produced by the latter are not necessarily useful to the former;

(c) In most countries, there is no clear focal point for such a dialogue; no one department of Government who might receive and then use Earthwatch assessments. In fact, there are often several focal points for the various GEMS and information exchange programmes in each nation state.

A further difficulty relates to UNEP's standing in the UN family. As has been repeatedly stressed, Earthwatch and its component parts have intended to be an activity of *all* the relevant UN agencies, but coordinated by UNEP. In this sense, environmental assessments undertaken by WHO, WMO, UNESCO, FAO, the International Atomic Energy Agency (IAEA) etc can be considered as part of Earthwatch, but in the case of GEMS, there is both a UNEP staff and UNEP budget with which to coordinate and, to some extent, direct, environmental monitoring in the rest of the UN. For Earthwatch *per se* there is no significant manpower or budget. As a result, there is virtually no overall environmental assessment activity within the UN, and the relevant activities undertaken by the individual agencies are not properly coordinated, or evaluated.

Evaluation of the Earthwatch Component Parts

Research
It is difficult to undertake any evaluation of Earthwatch research since there is no specific research budget line in UNEP. A number of the GEMS programmes, particularly the pilot projects, have a strong research component.

Information Exchange
The Earthwatch-related information exchange is carried out under the INFOTERRA and IRPTC programmes. INFOTERRA is a decentralised network of environmental information (referral) systems, operating through a grid of national, regional and sectorial focal points. In short, an international 'yellow pages' directory for environmental purposes. The system is operational, with 112 member nations, 8,500 sources of environmental information and with a reported 7,500 plus referrals having been provided. The UK INFOTERRA index lists 270, plus separate 'sources' (see technical assistance, Chapter 4, pp 343-344 of this report). The DOE library is the 'focal point' and they report about two to four referrals per week into the UK.

In 1980, an independent evaluation of INFOTERRA was conducted, under the auspices of UNESCO, which concluded that it had fulfilled its mandate as given in Stockholm. This is a fair conclusion, in so far as the system is firmly established. But the consensus is that it is substantially under-used. It is a potentially useful formal networking tool; rival informal networks working through professional contacts etc, appear to work rather better. Initial hopes that developing countries would become major users of INFOTERRA have not, so far, come to pass (see technical assistance, Chapter 4, pp 343-344 of this report).

In February 1976, the IRPTC, which was recommended at Stockholm, became operational as a UNEP PAC, located in Geneva. This is an ambitious exercise, and against the general trend towards smaller, more specialised data banks. However, with the large number of chemical notification schemes being developed by national and international organisations, the global data bank, *prima facie*, makes good sense.

However, to maximise its utility, a great deal of effort has had to be made to keep up the quality of the data in the register. IRPTC has had to concentrate on certain classes of chemicals to make this practical, and recent studies have been carried out to identify priority chemicals by virtue of their risk to human health and/or flora and fauna at the global level. This paper attempts no evaluation of IRPTC.

Monitoring (GEMS)

Following the recommendations of the Stockholm Conference a GEMS Programme Activity Centre was established in UNEP, Nairobi in 1975. GEMS has five major programme areas:

(a) Health-related monitoring.
(b) Climate-related monitoring.
(c) Renewable resources monitoring.
(d) Monitoring of the long-range transport of air pollutants.
(e) Ocean monitoring (in collaboration with the UNEP Regional Seas PAC).

GEMS activities are mainly carried out by the UN agencies with significant financial support from UNEP. For example, WHO is the main operating agency for health-related monitoring, and WMO for climate-related monitoring.

Although all of the GEMS programmes have some relevance to the WCS, renewable resources monitoring is probably of most direct interest. The necessary techniques for monitoring renewable resources are still under intensive development and, as a result, GEMS, too, is still under development in this field. Two global problems in particular have received much attention: the apparent decrease in the productivity of rangelands and the decrease in tropical forest cover. Both monitoring exercises are described as ecological monitoring as they are an extension of survey methods for wildlife populations based on an understanding of the underlying ecological relationships involved. A combination of ground 'truth' and remote satellite sensing methods are now also used to assess the condition of soil, fresh water courses, vegetation cover, the density and abundance of certain wild and domestic animals, etc. With UNEP help, ecological monitoring is now being tested and developed in some eight African and three South American countries.

Observers have commented that the GEMS programme in the renewable resource-monitoring offers an enormous potential in support of the executive of the WCS, and it is vital that it continues to develop.

However, whilst GEMS has great potential, it has still to be recognised that:

(a) The lack of a strong evaluation/assessment within Earthwatch as a whole, limits its use.
(b) UNEP's non-operational mandate is of some disadvantage in the development of its monitoring work as it has to rely on the cooperation and work of others (particularly that of the US).
(c) GEMS is operating in a general climate of pessimism about the usefulness of global monitoring (for example, see the UK position in the main body of the report).

The post-Stockholm enthusiasm for monitoring virtually everything (or so it seemed) resulted in the development of numerous local, national and regional monitoring systems and programmes. However, in general, many of these have not lived up to expectations: they have not provided any particular clarity over trends or 'hot spot' environmental issues. Any number of reasons can be suggested for this, but three stand out:

(a) Many of the programmes lacked sufficiently defined objectives, not only in terms of measuring biological change but also in terms of purpose. Thus resources were wasted and seen to be wasted.
(b) The practical difficulties involved are still becoming apparent. The where, when, what and how of monitoring are simply not defined.
(c) The evaluation and validation of data (yet another component of Earthwatch) often never occurs.

Relevance of Earthwatch to the WCS

The WCS is based on the belief that many global environmental trends are going in the 'wrong' direction, and that it is now necessary to make a major effort to reverse them. Much of the Strategy is itself based on statements or conclusions drawn from UNEP/Earthwatch projects (eg on tropical forest cover, desertification and wildlife).

The Strategy calls for continued assessment of environmental trends and it is clear that Earthwatch is the logical vehicle for promoting, coordinating and reporting on this task at an international level, in so far as an international level of activity is justified. Nevertheless most valuable work in terms of data collection and analysis is bound to occur at a national or even local level.

Recommendations for Earthwatch

A major deficiency lies in the supervision of Earthwatch via UNEP's annual Governing Councils. The Council occurs too frequently and is too time-consuming for UNEP staff in general, but for a unit that is meant to be staffed by competent people, it is truly absurd.

Earthwatch as a whole should become an inter-agency programme, coordinated by UNEP, in the same manner as GEMS. It should have a Secretariat headed by a Director of sufficient seniority to direct, develop and coordinate the whole inter-agency assessment programme, and, in turn, he or she should be responsible to a small inter-agency management committee composed of representatives of each agency's Governing Council.

Once an agenda has been agreed for Earthwatch on an

inter-agency basis, it should receive a very much larger budget, and of this a substantial proportion should be devoted to the establishment of the Secretariat.

Earthwatch assessments should be published in widely disseminated documents. They should be authoritative and sent for extensive peer review prior to publication. These assessments should contain 'alerts' or 'warnings' addressed to particular national Governments as and when appropriate. They should also point out areas of ignorance. All of this would could be published every two years in the form of a more popular 'State of the World's Environment Report' — an ambition of UNEP's that has not been achieved.

The success of the Regional Seas Programme underlines the advantages of regional groupings. In the longer-term, Earthwatch should establish internationally funded regional assessment centres based on collecting regional research, monitoring and evaluation and assessment work from regional, national and local agencies.

Notes and References

1 EARTHSCAN. 1982. Stockholm plus ten. IIED.

2 Stockholm plus ten, *op cit*.

3 Prepared with assistance from Dr A Sors (DG 12 EEC).

APPENDIX I

UNESCO AND THE MAN AND THE BIOSPHERE PROGRAMME

UNESCO runs the Man and the Biosphere Programme (MAB) — now a part of the UNESCO Natural Resources and Environment Programme (1981-83). It also runs the International Hydrological programme, the International Geological Correlation Programme, and the Intergovernmental Oceanographic Commission (IOC). The broad aims of the MAB are: 'to develop the scientific basis for the rational use and conservation of the biosphere and for the improvement of the global relationship between man and the environment'. In 1980, $7.00m was allocated to UNESCO's ecological science and conservation programme, including MAB. MAB itself is organised on the basis of 14 themes — all highly relevant to the WCS:

☐ Ecological effects of increasing human activities on tropical and sub-tropical forest ecosystems.

☐ Ecological effects of different land-uses and management practices on temperate and Mediterranean forest landscapes.

☐ Impact of human activities and land-use practices on grazing lands: savannah and grassland (from temperate to arid areas).

☐ Impact of human activities on the dynamics of arid and semi-arid zone's ecosystems, with particular attention to the effects of irrigation.

☐ Ecological effects of human activities on the value and resources of lakes, marshes, rivers, deltas, estuaries and coastal zones.

☐ Impact of human activities on mountain and tundra ecosystems.

☐ Ecology and rational use of island ecosystems.

☐ Conservation of natural areas and of the genetic material they contain.

☐ Ecological assessment of pest management and fertilizer use on terrestrial and aquatic ecosystems.

☐ Effects on humans and their environment of major engineering works.

☐ Ecological aspects of urban systems with particular emphasis on energy utilisation.

☐ Interactions between environmental transformations and the adaptive, demographic and genetic structure of human populations.

☐ Perception of environmental quality.

☐ Research on environmental pollution and its effect on the biosphere.

In turn, it currently supports over 1,000 semi-autonomous field projects — under the control of a MAB International Council.

Perhaps the most advanced MAB theme and one of specific relevance to the WCS is theme 8 which has led on to the 'development of the International Network of Biosphere Reserves'. The main aims of this network are as follows:

(a) to promote the conservation of representative ecosystems, with their full array of component species, as a strategy for maintaining genetic diversity;

(b) to provide sites for long-term research on the structure, functioning and dynamics of ecosystems, thus serving as a logistic base for other MAB Project Areas;

(c) to provide sites for monitoring of environmental change;

(d) to make available facilities for education and training.

By the end of 1980, 1,977 biosphere reserves had been designated in 46 countries. However, in practice, only a few of these reserves are being studied and managed, as envisaged in the biosphere reserve concept.

An extract from the recent MAB Council minutes (1980) illustrates the problems:

'Needs for international cooperation'. Delegates, particularly from developing countries, requested the cooperation of UNESCO and of industrialised countries in the implementation and demonstration of the biosphere reserve concept in selected areas. They expressed the hope that cooperative links within MAB would develop further and would assist in acquiring the urgently needed expertise, skilled manpower, and logistic means required for proper multiple purpose management in biosphere reserves . . . The Council was informed about the work of the UNEP/FAO/IUCN Ecosystem Conservation Group, which was concerned with the coordination of the activities of these international organisations in the field of conservation. The Council felt that the idea of joint programming and cooperative activities between these bodies was an attractive one, at least in theory. The test of its practicability lay, however, in the existence of concrete actions jointly sponsored by members of the Group. The Council felt that there were very few indications that the Ecosystem Conservation Group had to date engendered such joint action, at least as regards cooperative activities between UNESCO and UNEP for the development of biosphere reserves. The Council expressed the hope that examples of productive cooperation would be available by its next session and called upon UNEP and UNESCO, in particular, to make renewed and sustained efforts to help countries in their conservation efforts . . . In this respect, the Council recalled debate at its previous sessions about the launching of a UNEP-UNESCO project for helping countries in the establishment of biosphere reserves in arid zones. The Council expressed regret that the project had still not been formally approved and launched, in spite of discussions between UNEP and UNESCO having stretched over at least a four year period. In view of the special need for helping arid zone countries in their conservation efforts, the Council reiterated the plea, made at its fifth session, that this project be approved and carried out with all possible expediency and vigour.'

Sadly, similar tales of disharmony and wasted opportunity are to be found in the history of the UNEP/ UNESCO Environmental Education Conference, in the IOC and in the running of MAB itself.

MAB was always an ambitious international undertaking which has proved extremely difficult to handle in a systematic, well-coordinated manner. However, by international standards, the programme has been successful in bringing together the practitioners in natural resource-conservation. A large number of countries have established MAB committees (including the UK) and some of these are fairly active.

MAB offers a useful framework for maintaining and encouraging research interests in natural resource-conservation.

Strengthening the programme as a whole would require concentration on a few priority areas, such as the proper development of the biosphere reserve concept, and there are signs that this is beginning to happen in practice.

Clearly, the MAB programmes should be more explicitly linked to the WCS, and the data and results of MAB projects should be made available to an expanded Earthwatch as a matter of routine.

As to the UK's contribution to MAB, the reader's attention is drawn to the sections on technical assistance (see Chapter 4 of this report, pp 343-344) and the Recommendations in Chapter 5 (p 351).

THE COMMONWEALTH

Section 1:
The Commonwealth Secretariat

The Commonwealth Secretariat is organised into two major parts: the Secretariat itself and the Commonwealth Fund for Technical Cooperation (CFTC). Each of these is further sub-divided as follows:

Secretary General's Office
Divisions:
Administration
Applied Studies in Government
Economic Affairs
Education
Export Market Development
Food Production and Rural Development
Information
International Affairs
Legal Affairs
Health
Science
Youth
Women

CFTC
The Industrial Development Unit
General Technical Assistance
Education and Personnel Services
Technical Assistance Group (TAG)
Special Advisors

The total staff of the Secretariat, including CFTC, was 394 people from 28 Member Countries in May 1981. The budget in the same year was £3,250,000. CFTC pledged funds amounted to £9,400,000.

The Commonwealth now has 46 members, ranging in size from India's 631 million to Nauru's 7,500. Just over half of the independent countries belonging to the Commonwealth are republics; the rest acknowledge the Queen as Head of State, or have a monarchy of their own. In addition to these countries, there are a number of self-governing and dependent territories associated with member nations. Self-governing states associated with Britain are: Antigua and St Kitts-Nevis-Anguilla. Britain's remaining dependencies include: Bermuda, British Virgin Islands, Cayman Islands, Falkland Islands, Gibraltar, Gilbert Islands, Hong Kong, Monserrat, Pitcairn, St Helena, and the Turks and Caicos Islands.

The Commonwealth acts as a channel for information, technical assistance and financial assistance on a variety of levels. Heads of Government meet every two years in a formal conference and the Secretary-General has access to all Heads of Government at the regional level. There are also meetings of Senior Officials. Meetings may also be held on topics of special concern, such as the Gleneagles Agreement on sporting links with South Africa.

The Secretary-General visits many countries each year, and attends conferences and other functions of international agencies within the UN system, providing many opportunities of formal and informal exchanges of views and information.

The Secretariat (as a whole and by division) coordinates programmes in particular areas, provides in-house expertise, arranges exchanges of experts between Member Countries, funds (in a variety of ways) conferences and professional associations and organisations, promotes cooperation in science, provides scholarships, conferences on particular topics at international and regional level, arranges consultancy services in areas such as health, funds three regional youth centres, brings parliamentarians into contact, and generally acts as a clearing house for a wide variety of information.

In addition to these official channels, there are a considerable number of unofficial associations and organisations of varying size and membership which exist to foster Commonwealth links. Some of these are funded by the Commonwealth Foundation.

Special associations exist in the fields of law, media, science and technology, youth, health and education.

The Secretariat, most of the divisions, the CFTC, and most of the specialist agencies and associations produce various bulletins, newsletters, reports, studies, indexes, and magazines on an occasional or regular basis.

Commonwealth organisations may promote particular ideas and programmes, or offer assistance to Member Countries. More often, they respond to requests for help or advice from individual Governments or groups of Governments, and the provision for tapping expertise outside the organisation seems rather *ad hoc*.

The CFTC is the main channel for transferring funds and expertise between Commonwealth countries. (NB not just from rich to poor). It was created in 1971 on the basis that all members subscribe on a voluntary basis. Nigeria is now the third largest contributor.

In 1978-79 CFTC had more than 300 experts in the field, but this dropped in 1979-80 to 226. 1979-80 expenditure was £9.37m, nearly two million less than in the previous year. In 1980-81 expenditure is expected to be around £10.7m. Half the experts are from the developing countries, and are employed on a long-term basis. More than 2,200 persons benefited from CFTC-supported training in 1978-79. In 1979-80 this dropped to 1,300. Nearly all of the training takes place in developing countries.

As well as supplying its own experts, the CFTC uses consultancy firms to provide advice and undertake particular studies for Governments. The reports of these studies are confidential and are not released to the public or to other researchers.

Money paid to the CFTC is also used to finance the work of TAG — a permanent body of experts plus specialist advisors appointed on a short-term basis — and the Secretariat Divisions concerned with Food Production and Rural Development (FPRD) and Public Administration training. Within the CFTC structure there also are a number of specialist groups and committees which deal with subjects such as alternative energy, mineral resources and mining, and forestry, but none of these groups deals specifically with environmental management *per se*.

The TAG consists of economists, lawyers, fiscal and tax specialists, and although much of their work is concerned with the development of natural resources, they appear to concentrate on technical, legal and economic matters. For instance, they may be asked to advise a Government on negotiating mining concessions with a transnational company. The FPRD division is involved in rural or appropriate technology and alternative energy resources, and it clearly lays emphasis on environmental constraints.

CFTC education and training covers only town planning in the environmental sphere; but not environmental impact assessment, pollution control/monitoring, environmental health or any other ecological speciality.

The overall impression gained from the available information (reports of the Secretary-General, booklets on the structure of the Commonwealth and Secretariat, various pamphlets, and lists of conferences, meetings, seminars, titles or reports) is that few, if any, Commonwealth activities acknowledge in any formal way the environmental dimension of development. However, in the author's experience individuals within the organisation, or who are employed by it, do.

Commonwealth Countries

Australia	Barbados
Bahamas	Botswana
Bangladesh	Britain
Canada	Nigeria
Cyprus	Papua New Guinea
Dominica	St Lucia
Fiji	St Vincent
The Gambia	Seychelles
Grenada	Sierra Leone
Guyana	Solomon Islands
India	Sri Lanka
Jamaica	Swaziland
Kenya	Tanzania
Kiribati	Tonga
Lesotho	Trinidad and Tobago
Malawi	Tuvalu
Malaysia	Uganda
Malta	Vanuatu
Mauritius	Western Samoa
Nauru	Zambia
New Zealand	Zimbabwe

British Self-Governing States

Antigua	St Kitts Nevis-Anguilla

British Dependencies

Belize	Gibraltar
Bermuda	Gilbert Islands
British Virgin Islands	Hong Kong
British Indian Ocean Territory	Montserrat
The British Antarctic Territory	New Hebrides
	Pitcairn Island
Cayman Islands	St Helena
Falkland Islands	The Turks and Caicos Islands

Brunei is associated with the Commonwealth via its treaty with Britain.
Vanuatu is jointly administered by Britain and France.

New Zealand Self-Governing Territories

Cook Islands	Tokelau islands
Niue	

Australian External Territories

Norfolk Island	Cocos (Keeling) Islands
Heard Island	Christmas Island
McDonald Island	

Section 2:
Commonwealth Organisations Relevant to the WCS

Official Organisations

Commonwealth Agricultural Bureaux
Commonwealth Institute of Entomology
Commonwealth Mycological Institute
Commonwealth Institute of Biological Control
Commonwealth Institue of Helminthology
Commonwealth Bureau of Agricultural Economics
Commonwealth Bureau of Animal Breeding and Genetics
Commonwealth Bureau of Animal Health
Commonwealth Bureau of Dairy Science and Technology

Official Organisations (continued)
Commonwealth Bureau of Horticulture and Plantation
    Crops
Commonwealth Bureau of Pastures and Field Crops
Commonwealth Bureau of Plant Breeding and Genetics
Commonwealth Bureau of Soils
Commonwealth Committee on Mineral Resources and
    Geology
Commonwealth Foundation
Commonwealth Forestry Bureau
Commonwealth Scholarship and Fellowship Plan
Commonwealth Science Council

Unofficial Organisations
Agriculture and Forestry
Commonwealth Association of Scientific Agricultural
    Societies
Commonwealth Forestry Association
Commonwealth Forestry Institute
Royal Veterinary Association
Royal Agricultural Society of the Commonwealth
Standing Committee on Commonwealth Forestry

Education and Research
Association of Commonwealth Universities
Commonwealth Geographical Bureau
Commonwealth Institute
Royal Institute of Public Administration

Environment
Caribbean Conservation Association
Commonwealth Association of Architects
Commonwealth Association of Planners

Commonwealth Association of Surveying and Land
    Economy
Commonwealth Human Ecology Council

Law and Parliament
Commonwealth Legal Advisory Service
Commonwealth Legal Bureau
Commonwealth Parliamentary Association

Science and Technology
Commonwealth Engineers Council

Regular Conferences and Meetings
ACU Conference of Executive Heads of Commonwealth
    Universities
Commonwealth Agricultural Bureaux Review
    Conference
Commonwealth Conference on Plant Pathology
Commonwealth Engineer's Council
Commonwealth Entological Conference
Commonwealth Education Conference(s) (various)
Commonwealth Forestry Conference
Commonwealth Law Conference
Commonwealth Science Council Meeting
Commonwealth Senior Officials Meeting
Conference of the Commonwealth Meteorologists
Conference of Commonwealth Surveyors
Conference of the Royal Agricultural Society of the
    Commonwealth
Congress of the Universities of the Commonwealth
General Assembly of the Commonwealth Association of
    Surveying and Land Ecology

A SURVEY OF UNIVERSITIES FOR THIS REPORT

University	Department/Research Unit
Aston	Joint Unit for Research on the Urban Environment
Bath	Centre for Development Studies
Birmingham	Department of Plant Biology
Bristol	Department of Botany
Cambridge	Department of Applied Biology
Durham	Department of Botany and Department of Geography
Imperial College	Centre for Environmental Technology
King's College	Department of Geography
Liverpool	Department of Geography and Department of Zoology
Reading	Agricultural Extension and Rural Development Centre, Department of Botany and Department of Soil Science
St Davids University College	Department of Geography
Sussex	Department of Biological Sciences
East Anglia	Overseas Development Group (comprising staff from the Schools of Environmental Science and Development Studies)
University College London	Department of Botany and Department of Microbiology
University College of North Wales	Department of Marine Biology
University College Swansea	Department of Oceanography
York	Department of Biology
Total 17	22

Figure 16. **Respondents to a questionnaire (received before March 1982)**

Information/opinion requested	Response
1. Any relevant expertise?	Yes: 22 No: 0 No data: 0
2. Would more applied work overseas be welcome?	Yes: 19 Yes, with reservations: 3
3. Does short-term overseas work cause your department problems? If so, what are they?	Yes: 11 No: 10 No data: 1 Financially: 2 Teaching/organisational: 7 Other: 2
4. How good is your awareness of existing means of obtaining overseas work?	Good: 9 Fair: 4 Poor: 6 Non-existent: 3
5. Are any individuals registered with ODA? Or any other agency?	Yes: 8 No: 13 No data: 1 Yes: 11 No: 10 No data: 1
6. Any relevant work overseas? (a) short-term (under one year) (b) long-term	Yes: 17 No: 5 Yes: 13 No: 9

Information/opinion requested	Response
7. Any formal Technical Assistance links with overseas institutes?	Yes: 9 No: 13 No data: 1
8. Is the Government doing enough to promote Technical Assistance?	Yes: 2 No: 16 No date: 4
9. Does your department collect data on its overseas students? Particularly: (a) feedback on usefulness of courses? (b) subsequent careers?	Yes: 17 No: 1 No data: 4 Yes: 10 No: 7 No data: 4 Yes: 14 No: 5 No data: 3
10. Does your institution encourage non-OECD students?	Yes: 11 Not really: 3 No: 3 No data: 5
11. Do you run any environment management courses for overseas students?	Yes: 3 No: 18 No data: 1
12. Do you run any special short courses for overseas students?	Yes: 2 No: 19 No data: 1
13. Do significant numbers of overseas students take ordinary First or Second degree courses?	Yes: 12 Only a few: 4 No: 4 No data: 2
14. What is your department's general opinion of the WCS?	Support: 12 Support with minor reservations: 8 Disagree: 1 No data: 1

Total number of respondents: 22 out of 50 at the time of analysing the data

Figure 17. **Analysis of questionnaire replies**

INSTITUTIONS THAT COULD HELP TO CARRY FORWARD THE WCS OVERSEAS

Section 1:
A Brief Listing

Organisation	Description
Ministry of Agriculture, Fisheries and Food, the Librarian	The Librarian can provide information on all aspects of agriculture, fisheries and food.
Directorate of Fisheries Research (Ministry of Agriculture, Fisheries and Food)	Research into fish stocks, fisheries and their management, fisheries oceanography, and pollution of the aquatic environment.
Royal Botanic Gardens	Plant taxonomy, distribution, utilisation and conservation. Threatened plant committee secretariat.
The UK National Library for Meteorology and Climatology, the Librarian	The Library holds information on hydrology and oceanography.
Department of Energy	Renewable resources, energy conservation, resource-development, resource-appraisal, and resources-management.
Department of Health and Social Security	Information on environmental health, health aspects of chemical contamination of the environment, and food.
Laboratory of the Government Chemist	Advice is given in selected fields, particularly oil pollution, agricultural materials, and water.
Centre for Overseas Pest Research	The Centre aims to develop safe and efficient pest control techniques in mainly tropical areas, concentrating on migratory and endemic pests and providing information on ecological effects of pesticides, their effects on fish and ecosystems in semi-arid regions and insect upsurges.
Land Resources Development Centre	Information in the field of agricultural development in developing countries, natural resources, land development for agriculture and forestry, physical environment, vegetation, agronomy, land-use, earth sciences, atmospheric and water studies.
Head of Library and Information Services, Tropical Products Institute	The aim of the Institute is to help developing countries to make optimum use of renewable natural resources such as plant and animal products, with emphasis on the post-harvest sector.
Agricultural Research Council	The aims are to advance and exploit scientific knowledge to increase the efficiency of the agricultural, horticultural and food industries and to safeguard and improve their products. Information can be given on land-use, erosion, soils, drainage, agrochemicals, farm wastes, and agricultural noise.
Weed Research Organisation Information Department	The Information Department constitutes an authoritative centre for information on weeds, weed control and herbicides.
Macaulay Institute for Soil Research	Soil science topics.
Soil Survey of England and Wales	Methods of identifying and mapping soil; agronomic use of information shown on soil maps; soil surveys of areas of special interest.

Organisation	*Description*
British Antarctic Survey	Multi-disciplinary research in the British Antarctic territory and Falkland Island dependencies.
Natural Environmental Research Council Scientific Services:	
☐ Experimental Cartography Unit	The unit promotes the use of automated cartography techniques within various fields of research in the natural environment.
☐ Freshwater Biological Association	The Association promotes the investigation of the biology (in its widest sense) of plants and animals in fresh and brackish water.
☐ Institute for Marine Environmental Research Library	The Institute studies selected marine ecosystems as entities through the integration of all the necessary scientific disciplines.
☐ Institute of Hydrology	The Unit can supply information on water balance studies, flow estimation techniques, hydrological data analysis, chemistry of natural waters, ground-water movement, and water resources.
☐ Marine Information and Advisory Service	Information and advisory service covering all aspects of oceanography.
☐ Institute of Oceanography Sciences Library	Can supply data on the physics and chemistry of the sea.
☐ Institute of Terrestrial Ecology	The Institute's work (300 to 400 research projects at any one time) concerns most aspects of terrestrial ecology and (in collaboration with sister institutes) fresh-water and marine ecology. It can mount multi-disciplinary research teams and specialises in modelling and systems analysis techniques.
☐ Marine Biological Association of the UK	Can provide information on marine and estuarine biology, ecology and pollution, oceanography, fisheries, marine scientific research and chemical pollution hazard profiles.
☐ Unit of Comparative Plant Ecology	Mechanisms controlling plant distribution, structure of vegetation, responses and tolerance to a range of environments. Projects include: vegetation surveys, screening herbaceous plants of contrasted ecology, plant strategies, and phenology.
☐ Institute of Virology	The Institute studies viruses in the natural environment, specially viruses of insects and wild birds. Other information topics include ecology, forestry and insect pests.
☐ Freshwater Fisheries Laboratory, Pitlochry	Topics include fish biology, physiology, behaviour, management and water chemistry.
Countryside Commission Library	Conserving and enhancing natural beauty and amenity; public recreational access and providing information on environmental planning, protection and ecology.
Nature Conservancy Council	The Council promotes nature conservation, establishes and maintains national nature reserves. Information is available on nature conservation and wildlife management.
National Water Council	Water resources; supply and treatment; sewage treatment and disposal; fisheries; water recreation; land drainage; organisation, management and finance.
Field Studies Council Preston, Montford	The Information Office provides information on field studies of all environmental aspects. Topics include ecology, geography, geology and history.
Institute of Water Pollution Control	The Institute promotes the science and practice of water pollution control. It can advise on sewage and trade waste treatment and disposal and on the prevention of water pollution.
Soil and Water Management Association	Information on all developments in soil and water management: drainage, cultivation of soil, land improvement, irrigation, crop care and development. The Association organises conferences, courses and study visits, tours, forums and workshops.

Section 2

ODA Headquarters

Geographical Desks ◄——— supported by ◄——————— **Advisory Groups**   (☐ Brigaded Geographically)

			Natural Resources (x19)	Agriculture
				Forestry
Development Division	*based in:*	*supported by:*		Fisheries
	Barbados	Natural Resources (x12)		Veterinary
	Kenya	Engineering (x7)		Agricultural Research
	Malawi	Economics+		Engineers
	Thailand	Financial+	Engineering	Architecture
	Fiji	Education (x1)	(x7)	Energy

Special Units

Tropical Development and Research Institute
 (formerly TPI and COPR)
Land Resources Development Centre
Directorate of Overseas Surveys

Education (x5) — Education

Health and Population — Medical
 Nursing
 Health
 Population/Demography
 Nutrition

Economic Service* (x58)+ — Economists
 Statisticians

Overseas Units in Other Departments of Government

Department of Environment
Transport and Roads Laboratory (x40)
Hydraulics Research (x18)
Building Research (x12)

Advisors
Social Development (including role of women) (x2)
Physical planning (x1)
Cooperatives and Institutions (x2)
Environment* (x1)

Research Councils
NERC Institute of Geological Sciences (15 HQ + 60 Field)
Institute of Hydrology (x8)
The Marine Biological Association
ARC National Institute of Agricultural Engineering (x12)
Weed Research Station

Department of Energy
Technology Support Unit, Harwell

Specialised University Departments

Edinburgh — Centre for Tropical Veterinary Medicine
Stirling — Institute of Aquaculture
London — Overseas Spraying Machinery Centre
Bristol — Development Planning Unit
Reading — Agricultural Extension and Rural Development Centre
Bradford — Project Planning Centre
Sussex — Institute of Development Studies
Wales — David Owen Centre for Population Studies (Cardiff)

Independent Specialist Groups

Intermediate Technology Development Group
Overseas Development Institute

Liaison Officers

Plant Pathology (at Commonwealth Mycological Institute)
Statistics (at Rothamsted Research Station)

Numbers in brackets are the approximate professional staff numbers

+   The staff of 58 are spread across headquarters and the overseas development divisions
*   The starred advisor(s) also provide advice to the Foreign and Commonwealth Office
ARC Agricultural Research Centre
TPI   Tropical Products Institute
COPR Centre for Overseas Pest Research

Figure 18. **ODA advisory services relating to environmental factors**

Organisation	*Description*
Professional Institutions Council for Conservation	An interprofessional body which acts as a forum for the exchange of views on conservation topics, publishes reports and newsletters on conservation and environmental issues and encourages professional education on conservation objectives and techniques.

Also of great importance are:

The Zoological Society of London

The Royal Society

The British Museum (Natural History)

The Royal Geographical Society

Section 3:
Overseas Activities of the Institute of Geological Sciences — An Illustration of Potential[1]

From the beginning of this century, the Mineral Resources Division of the former Imperial Institute, London, provided for overseas — mainly Commonwealth — territories a central information and laboratory service for the economic study and commercial appraisal of rocks, ores and minerals, including mining, beneficiation, uses and commercial specifications of economic minerals, and advice on legislation relating to mineral prospecting, mining and taxation.

In 1947, following a reorganisation of geological services overseas, the Directorate of Colonial Geological Surveys assumed responsibility for the Mineral Resources Division, and subsequently Age Determination, Geophysical and Photogeological Units were added. A Special Surveys Unit was set up in 1961 (by which time 'Overseas' had replaced 'Colonial' in the Directorate's title) to meet an increasing number of requests from developing countries for assistance with comprehensive mineral resources surveys in the field and for on-the-job training for local staff.

In 1965, British geological services were reorganised, the Directorate of Overseas Geological Surveys being merged with the Geological Survey of Great Britain and the Geological Museum to form the Institute of Geological Sciences (IGS) under the aegis of NERC. The Special Surveys Unit and Photogeology Unit of the former Overseas Geological Survey (OGS) then became the Overseas Division of IGS.

The Overseas Division, therefore, inherited a reservoir of knowledge and experience of overseas geology gathered together over many years by the earlier organisations. Nearly half the total Divisional strength comprises senior officers with long service in one or other of the less developed countries. Links with the departments concerned with geological mapping and with the evaluation and exploitation of mineral resources in these countries have thus been maintained and new ones have been forged consequent on the expansion of

the Division's work into countries outside the Commonwealth which started in 1962-63. This long association with the developing countries has produced an appreciation of political and social attitudes, as well as a sensitive approach, which is of great value to the Division in its advisory as well as its executive role.

The primary function of the Overseas Division is, therefore, to assist the developing countries, on behalf of the ODA of the Foreign and Commonwealth Office, in assessing and developing their natural resources (including those of the continental shelf) with particular emphasis on minerals, ground-water and energy. This is achieved by integrated surveys involving initial, basic geological mapping, and includes geochemical, geophysical, hydrogeological and engineering geological components. The training of local staff, both in-service and by means of bursaries tenable at British universities, is an important element in this.

The role of the Overseas Division is fulfilled by:

(a) Carrying out specific programmes of geological mapping, mineral prospecting, geothermal and hydrogeological investigations at the request of foreign and Commonwealth Governments under British Technical Cooperation arrangements. In this manner, the dual purpose is achieved of accelerating the assessment of the countries' natural resources and affording their geologists training in modern techniques.

(b) Employing the specialist services of other IGS experts in all branches of geology (eg mineral intelligence, radioactive minerals, coalfield geology) to advise as and when required.

(c) Provision of advice to the ODA and to overseas Governments on geological and related matters by the Director of IGS, as Geological Adviser to ODA, and by senior IGS officers acting on his behalf.

(d) Providing cadres of scientific staff to strengthen geological survey departments in the developing Commonwealth countries until local nationals are fully trained.

(e) Advice to the British Council on the placing of geoscientists from the less developed countries in

British universities and other scientific establishments for practical, in-service training or formal academic, mainly post-graduate, courses.

(f) Undertaking basic research to facilitate an understanding of global geological phenomena.

In the current work programme the IGS staff is divided between Technical Cooperation projects (TC), and residential secondments to Commonwealth Geological Surveys under the Overseas Service Aid Scheme (OSAS).

Technical Cooperation Projects

Technical Cooperation projects staffed by Overseas Division personnel, and supplemented where necessary by specialists from other IGS Divisions, are carried out in cooperation with overseas Government geological surveys which provide counterparts and certain support services. Experience has shown that these projects are most efficient when they are able to function, irrespective of the degree or quality of support provided by the local organisations.

In consequence, they are now supplied, wherever possible, with their own transport, field scientific equipment, camp equipment and in many cases analytical and petrological laboratories. The larger projects are normally organised on a long-term residential basis when the IGS geologists live in the country concerned for tours of up to three years. The smaller, more specialised projects are sometimes undertaken by short-term visits of a few months duration.

The official requests from overseas Governments to which TC projects are the response are invariably drawn up in discussion with senior officers of the Division in the course of liaison visits, and this is a major function of the four Regional Geologists who are responsible to the Assistant Director, Overseas Division. The Regional Geologists, who are each in charge of one of the four global areas: Africa, Asia, Pacific and Latin America, are thus able to ensure that the projects are tailored to the needs of the countries concerned, lie within the scope of IGS to carry out, and are realistically costed. When implemented, these TC projects are largely self-administered by the IGS residential Team Leader but remain under the overall direction of the Regional Geologists. They have sufficient built-in flexibility to allow a degree of re-orientation or the addition of special expertise at any time during the course of the project should this be deemed necessary. A range of specialisations covering practically all of the geosciences is available within IGS giving it a significant advantage over many other similar organisations.

This project-based type of activity is, in the IGS view, the most efficient means of conducting geological aid programmes. There is also merit in fielding teams of six to 10 officers, in contrast to the position formerly obtaining of offering two to three person teams. It has the advantage, particularly in the case of mineral exploration, of allowing the whole range of modern techniques to be deployed by experts in the various fields, with appropriate back up from other IGS specialised units as required. Recent examples are the North Sumatra Project and the Precambrian project in eastern Bolivia. Such teams, including local counterparts, can number up to 40 in total strength.

Secondments under OSAS

The original aim of British geological aid was to provide experienced British geological staff to those geological survey departments in the newly independent countries of the Commonwealth which lacked a full complement of qualified local personnel. This principle is still accepted, and in 1980 81, for example, 16 such officers were in posts which included Director and Deputy Directors of Departments, geochemists, geophysicists, hydrogeologists as well as geologists. Some territories, eg Botswana, which are almost devoid of indigenous scientists, employ the whole range. Elsewhere, with advancing 'location', the need for support from seconded officers of IGS may well decline over the next decade. At present, IGS supplied geological staff under the OSAS scheme to Botswana, Fiji, Malawi, Swaziland, Vanuatu and the Solomon Islands.

The division of responsibility among four Regional Geologists improved the managerial and administrative structure and provides a clearly defined chain of command. It also increases the Division's familiarity with the geological and allied fields in the less developed countries so that the Overseas Division is now in a better position to advise the ODA on technical aid matters, and non-Governmental organisations which frequently seek information on matters within the general geo-sciences ambit. In the course of overseas tours the Regional Geologists familiarise themselves with the geology of the various countries and also with Government Departments and other organisations concerned with geosciences.

The *ad hoc* nature of some requests for IGS services, many of which cannot be anticipated by the Regional Geologists, render forward planning difficult. The unpredictable nature of the demands does therefore produce difficulties particularly in budgeting and staffing arrangements. However, such matters are under constant review with ODA, and problems are generally surmounted by maintaining as flexible an approach as possible.

As the distribution of British bilateral aid depends on a variety of factors, continuing guidance from ODA is also provided about which regions or countries should be assigned priorities in geological technical cooperation. Following the publication in 1975 of the White Paper 'More Help for the Poorest' (CMND 6270) the main emphasis of the aid programme remains the development of rural areas in the poorest countries. This has implications for the role of the Overseas Division. The attention of ODA has been drawn to the contribution which IGS can make in these sectors, in geological mapping which is fundamental to development of all kinds, and in such activities as 'small mining', water resources surveys for agricultural and domestic use.

Specialist Support

Specialist support to teams and individuals, as well as to institutions overseas, is provided by the Geochemistry and Petrology Division particularly where local facilities do not exist, in applied mineralogy and major, minor and trace element analysis of rocks, minerals, steam sediments, soils and water by chemical, spectrographic and X-ray fluorescence methods (Analytical Chemistry Unit). The Petrology Unit continues to provide services in gemmology and specialised petrographic studies. Geochronological surveys have been carried out by the Isotope Geology Unit in Botswana, Burma and Thailand in cooperation with the Geological Surveys of these countries. Geochronology support work for Overseas Division projects in Bolivia and Colombia continues as required. Computer programmes for use overseas are being continually developed and advice and assistance in this field has been given to Indonesia, Botswana, Bolivia, Ecuador, Costa Rica and Malaysia.

The Applied Geophysics Unit has recently undertaken surveys in India, Oman (gravity survey), Lesotho (regional gravity survey), Korea, Indonesia, Sri Lanka, Botswana and Bolivia.

Notes and References

1   Prepared by the Institute and quoted in full.

PART 6
ETHICS

Environmental Ethics and Conservation Action

A report by Professor R J Berry

Acknowledgements

The matters in this Report have been discussed by the Review Group supporting the author, Professor R J Berry. However, the views and omissions are his alone. All members of the Review Group have contributed in their own ways. But by far the greatest input to this report has come from Lord Ashby FRS, both from writings and conversation. Those familiar with Lord Ashby's writings will recognise the dependence of the report on his work and thought in the environmental field.

Other people have contributed ideas and comments. Particular thanks are due to Dr J Morton Boyd, Director Scotland, of the Nature Conservancy Council, the Very Revd Professor John McIntyre of New College, Edinburgh, Professor Aubrey Manning of Edinburgh, Professor T O'Riordan of the University of East Anglia, Mr John Burton of the Fauna and Flora Preservation Society, Mr Max Nicholson CB, of London, Professor I Eibl-Eiblesfeldt of Seewiesen, and Professor Paul Ehrlich of Stanford.

Foreword

William Ophuls dedicated his essay on 'Ecology and the Politics of Scarcity': 'to the posterity that has never done anything for me'. This might well be an appropriate dedication for the seven reports. But I say 'might', for the degree of commitment to altruism in the World Conservation Strategy (WCS) is unclear. As this report asserts, it is 'an extraordinary omission' that the WCS says nothing directly about ethics. Also (I would add), it is surprising that ethics should come sixth and not first in this series of topics. Can one really deduce the ends for a conservation and development programme from the means recommended by the other six reports? I doubt it.

For the ends, as these seven reports show, are anything but clear. Is it really sufficient that environmental education should *convince people that conservation is central to their own interest*? (The italics are mine.) Are we keen to preserve genetic diversity simply because, one day, we might need to use these genes in the breeding of crops? Does our concern for conservation in the Third World rest on unselfishness? Or do we want to make sure the Third World continues to provide us with food, energy, industrial raw materials and markets for our products?

It is encouraging that some recent laws to protect the environment — the Endangered Species Act in the USA and the Wildlife and Countryside Act in the UK — do not have regard to the question 'What's in it for us?' However, they rest on a flimsy ethical foundation, and when nature's interest clashes with humanity's interest, it is commonly humanity's interest that prevails; as

happened when the Alaskan oil pipeline was exempted from the requirements of the National Environmental Policy Act.

This sixth report shows how vulnerable are many of the recommendations made in the other six reports. No doubt, while it benefits (or, at least, does not inconvenience) the UK, its citizens will welcome these recommendations: to upgrade industry's environmental resources ('Seven Bridges to the Future', Part 1), to control the disposal of toxic wastes ('Conservation and Development of Marine and Coastal Resources', Part 4), to reduce SO_2 emissions from power plants ('The Livable City', Part 2), to give aid in developing countries ('The UK's Overseas Environmental Policy', Part 5), to propagate environmental education in schools ('Education for Commitment: Building Support in Society for Conservation and Development', Part 7), and to conserve our rural resources ('Putting Trust in the Countryside', Part 3). On all these issues the politician receives good advice from scientists and economists and sociologists and lawyers, but at a time of stress and austerity these issues are likely to become the first casualties. At such a time, what advice does the politician receive about the ethics for environmental policy? None, except what he assumes from his assessment of public opinion. That is why the recommendations in this report may become necessary for the survival of recommendations in the other six reports. Until we have a strategy for managing the conflict between the homocentric and ecocentric aspirations of humanity, our good resolutions about the survival of the earth will remain precarious.

Eric Ashby
March, 1983

CHAPTER 1

INTRODUCTION

Values and Ethics

1. This report is different from all the other reports in this book. There are two reasons for this:
   (a) People want recipes to solve environmental problems; they are not interested in philosophical or platitudinous moralising over the need for environmental ethics. This report will be read only if it is pertinent and pungent.
   (b) The six reports that accompany this one deal with particular sets of problems (rural and urban, maritime, industrial, international and educational). Environmental ethics takes up the examples used in the sister reports and uses them as the basis for its own argument. However, there has been no attempt to repeat the details (or references) to situations described elsewhere.

2. The World Conservation Strategy (WCS) defines the conditions necessary for the earth to sustain continuing life. It explains the actual and potential consequences of human demands upon finite resources. It says nothing directly about ethics. This is an omission which can only be justified if the rational case that WCS makes for its three specific objectives (to maintain essential ecological processes and life support systems; to preserve genetic diversity; and to ensure the sustainable utilisation of species and ecosystems) produces an inevitable right response. It would be pleasant to think that all we need to do is to increase an awareness of our environmental problems, but bitter experience tells against this. Although reason clarifies alternatives, it cannot lead to someone taking a particular course of action unless he or she wants to. The perception of alternatives, and the decision on which item to take, differs among different groups of people (O'Donovan, 1978). The reason that the UK Government (and many individual citizens) rejected the advice of the Roskill Commission in 1968 to develop Cublington as the third London airport was not because they disbelieved the facts collected by the Commission, but because they came to a different conclusion from them. We shall return to the arguments of the Roskill Commission later in this report (Chapter 5, paragraphs 16 to 19, pp 427 - 428). The important point from which we start is that there is *no inevitable link between knowledge and action* (or in psychological language, between attitude and behaviour). Environmental education by itself does not necessarily produce motivation (see paragraphs 18 to 20 of this chapter below, page 414. In this respect the WCS is flawed because it implicitly assumes that its conclusions are inevitable.

3. This report is concerned to supply the gap missing in WCS. It seeks to answer the question, whether, given the facts of environmental misuse, resource depletion, accelerating population numbers and human self-interest, there is any hope for the world? Because we are concerned here with the situation in the UK, the examples used in seeking the answer are British ones. It can be argued that UK problems are trivial when compared with those of developing countries, and that it is intellectual narcissism to concentrate on matters of the mind when in some countries men, women and children are dying by the thousand through existing environmental mismanagement. The response to this is simple: the underlying problems will not be solved until we start asking the right questions. It matters what the bases of our environmental decisions are; it is proper to ask if there is such a thing as a 'right' approach to the environment.

4. Ethics is a branch of philosophy, but this is not a philosophical report. It stands in the no-man's-land where philosophy, psychology, politics, human biology, and management economics meet; it takes historical examples to illuminate how problems have been faced, rather than as indicators of solutions. Being multi-disciplinary, it lacks the rigour of any one of its contributing components, and is subject to attack from all sides. But that does not necessarily invalidate its arguments. Environmental ethics are crude and immature. This contribution should be seen as a starting-point for experts to work out solutions in their own disciplines.

5. Ethics depends on values. Skolimowski (1981) has claimed that there is an inverse relationship between factual knowledge and intrinsic human values, in that 'as one goes up, the other is pushed down'. He blames for this the deification of nineteenth century Positivism and twentieth century Logical Empricism, following the separation of values from knowledge by Kant and others in the post-Renaissance period. Skolimowski may be historically right but this analysis does not really help in developing an environmental ethic. However, his general conclusion that our problems are due to an over-simplistic reductionism is certainly important, and is considered in Chapter 2 below.

6. The key to this report is an insistence that we are both *apart from* nature and *a part of* nature (see Chapter 2). This sounds trivial but it is the key to understanding and resolving the arguments between industrialists and conservationists which plague the environmental scene and limit effective action on environmental issues. Chapter 2 onwards is devoted to exploring the complications and implications of this apparently simple complementarity: Chapter 3 discusses how population numbers, resource-use, stress, and the perception of risk complicate it; Chapter 4 uses three examples of changing attitudes (towards property, air pollution, and contraception) to emphasise the dynamic nature of the humans/nature relationship; and Chapter 5 shows how religion, law and economics can contribute to, but not in themselves produce, an environmental ethic. Having thus cleared the ground, Chapter 6 lists the four considerations which must be catered for in any viable ethic (self-interest, public interest, posterity's interest, and nature's interest), and links these to the ultimate but shadowy goal of a high quality of life. This leads naturally to the implications of all this for politicians and others who take decisions affecting the quality of life (Chapter 7). The crude and tentative nature of this final section underlines the importance of developing the arguments used in this report. Ethics are implicit in the WCS; unless we can build on the facts and warnings contained within the Strategy and the other reports in this book, we shall never achieve the motivation to implement either a national or international conservation strategy.

7. Before going further, we need to define what we mean by 'ethics' and 'values'. Ethics is the name given to any assertions we make that a statement or behaviour is right or wrong; it is the expression of our moral understanding usually in the form of guidelines or rules of conduct. Ethics are based on values. Much of this report is concerned with how environmental values arise, and we must begin by rescuing the word 'value' from the arrogance of economists, obfuscation of philosophers, and rhetoric of politicians (Ashby, 1978). It has at least four different meanings: cost in the market-place, quantified as cash; usefulness, for persons or society; what Locke called 'intrinsic natural worth', which is the objective quality of the thing itself, in contrast to the market-place cost (which is its value only in relation to the value of other things which can be acquired in its stead); and the meaning attached to symbols or concepts, such as a national flag or liberty. The same object can carry all these values. Thus, a piece of land has a market value; it has value-as-use for a farmer or developer; it may have intrinsic value for its beauty; and it may be valuable as the symbol of homeland, to be defended to the death against enemies. The problem is that these four meanings may change independently for the same thing. For example, water in a river in highland Scotland or in lowland England will be valued by an economist in terms of its usefulness — whether it is drunk, fished or treated as an amenity; it may be an object of beauty or a stinking sewer; and it may represent a boundary between counties or countries

or a barrier to pest spread; and so on. Once we set out to define environmental values we have to be careful about our use of words; if we could be certain of our values, we would be closer to developing a realistic ethic.

8. The link between values, ethics and action can be illustrated by the Cow Green Reservoir saga. In 1964, the Tees Valley and Cleveland Water Board which was responsible for providing an adequate water supply to the industrial area of Teesside, wanted to build a reservoir at Cow Green in a remote and barren valley in upper Teesdale. The reservoir was to meet the needs of expanding industry, especially to enable ICI to build the largest ammonia plant in the world. There was no problem of rehousing people or dispossessing farmers; no one lived around Cow Green, and the place was useless for agriculture. But the site overlapped the sole remaining site in England for a rather dull little plant called the Teesdale Sandwort, along with some other rare plants believed to be survivors of the Ice age in Britain. The area was, therefore, of concern to botanists.

9. Some of the botanists believed the Teesdale Sandwort and its fellow relics would be imperilled if the reservoir were built, and they rallied to protect it. A Teesdale Defence Committee was set up. Letters were written to *The Times* expressing grave anxiety about the fate of the flora. The issue was inflated into a conflict of values: on the one hand an important industry needing water (with a hint that there might be unemployment if the ammonia plant could not be built); on the other hand the 'integrity' — that was one of the emotive words used — of a few acres of natural vegetation in a high and unfrequented stretch of moorland. A generation ago there would have been no discussion: the Teesdale Sandwort would have stood no chance against the ammonia plant. But in the 1960s a botanical David going into battle with an industrial Goliath enlisted massive public support. The affair went to Parliament. A Select Committee of the House of Commons recommended that the reservoir be approved, but when its report came back to the House an amendment was moved, 'That this House declines to consider a Bill which would involve irreparable harm to a unique area of international importance'. The amendment was defeated — but only by 112 votes to 82. The matter then went to the House of Lords, where it was remitted to another Select Committee. This committee met 19 times and even visited the site. During the debate on the Bill, which lasted eight hours, it became clear that the reservoir could be built, if care were taken — without destroying the botanical interest of the area. The botanists lost and the reservoir was built. It occupies only some 6 per cent of the limestone outcrop where the rare plants grow, and the Teesdale Sandwort still flourishes there. The importance of the episode was not the outcome; it was that Parliament concerned itself with what may be termed altruism. The Teesdale Sandwort did not directly affect the well-being of electors, but both Houses spent time and energy in considering its value.

Protecting People as well as the Environment

10. The significance of the WCS is its emphasis that sustainable development depends on positive conservation, ie upon human management of the environment. This is explicit in its definition of development as 'the application of human, financial, living, and non-living resources to satisfy human needs and improve the quality of human life'. The WCS is unapologetically human-centred, and thus differs from the dominant tradition in most conservation writings, which has tended to regard human beings as pests, degrading the long term survival of the world. This view has always been regarded with suspicion by agriculturalists and industrialists alike, and is an important reason why pleas for conservation action have not received as much attention as they might have done.

11. The importance of regarding humans as both a part of nature and also apart from it is the theme of Chapter 2. It is necessary here to examine the WCS intention 'to satisfy human needs and improve the quality of human life'. This is a clear statement of the utilitarian utopia of extracting the greatest good for the greatest number, although it complicates the issue by mixing quantity ('human needs') with quality. This is not the place to comment extensively on the utilitarian ideal, beyond pointing out that it is based on the possibility of arriving at the total happiness in a situation by a cost-benefit analysis of pleasure minus pain. The prime architect of Utilitarianism, Jeremy Bentham, envisaged a sort of hedonistic calculus quantifying all the elements in pleasure and pain. The impropriety of cost-benefit analysis for environmental decision making is discussed in Chapter 5, paragraphs 16 to 22, pp 427 - 428. Here, it is only necessary to note that utilitarian arithmetic has the dilemma that great joy for some (eg a high quality of life or standard of living) has somehow to be matched against a lesser joy for a greater number. Bentham solved this by adding a principle of equity. 'Everybody counts for one, and no one for more than one'. Unfortunately, this destroys the alleged simplicity of the utilitarian calculus. Instead of dealing with the straightforward maximisation of total pleasure minus total pain, it means that two quite different principles are at work, one concerning pleasure, the other concerning justice and equal distribution. It is impossible to claim these are the same; the simple utilitarian premise has to be qualified, probably in a complicated way.

12. The practical difficulties of achieving the greatest environmental good for the greatest number can be illustrated by the state of the Rhine. Industries along its banks use the river to remove their wastes, because they have difficulty in disposing of them elsewhere. Alternative methods of disposal tend to run up against other interests. For example, French potash producers successfully thwarted one proposal for purification, because a side effect would have been the extraction of salt. In 1980, the Rhine carried across the German-Dutch border 16 tons of mercury, 322 tons of lead, 890 tons of copper, 8,900 tons of oil, etc. Water authorities in Switzerland, Germany and the Netherlands have identified about 2,000 different toxic impurities in Rhine water. The river is an important source of drinking water throughout its length.

13. A problem which raises similar ethical problems for Britain is that of acid rain. Between 1956 and 1965, the acidity of rain over parts of Scandinavia doubled owing to the presence of small quantities of sulphuric and nitric acid in the rainfall. This caused concern, particularly in Sweden, because it was feared that the acid rain was damaging crops and fisheries. At the United Nations conference on the environment in Stockholm in 1972, it was claimed that the cause of increased acidity was wind-borne pollutants from the burning of coal and oil in neighbouring countries. The acid rain was blamed for increased corrosion of metals and deterioration of stonework, lower productivity in forests, and hazards to fish. The Swedes estimated they were suffering about £10,000,000 of damage every year.

14. In 1972, the Organisation for Economic Co-operation and Development (OECD, 1977) undertook a study of the long-range transport of air pollutants. Eleven European nations took part. The purpose was to decide how much pollutant from sulphur in the air was generated within the cooperating countries, how much was imported from other nations, and how much was exported. Seventy six sampling stations were set up in rural areas so that the records would not be affected by local emissions. The data collected showed that, in 1973-74, Britain put between five and six million tons of sulphur dioxide into the air. Sixty per cent of this left the country, to be carried several hundreds of miles on the prevailing winds. There is an excess of sulphur in the air over and above the amount generated from fuels burnt in Europe. Some of this comes from natural sources and some may come across the Atlantic from America. Notwithstanding, it is clear that Britain contributes between 11 and 16 per cent of the imported sulphur pollution in Sweden, and between 26 and 47 per cent of that in Norway.

15. It is possible that the Swedish claims of the harm from sulphur pollution are over-estimated. The productivity of forests is affected by other environmental and climatic factors; these effects have not yet been disentangled from the possible effects of acid rain. As for damage to fisheries, the salmon catches in some Swedish rivers were falling long before acid rain became a problem. Acid rain is merely one factor in a complex situation involving land-use practices, epidemic disease and over-fishing. Indeed it seems that the immediate agent of the damage is likely to be the release of aluminium caused by *any* acids in the environment, including run-off from agriculture.

16. Moreover, it is now clear that acid rain falls in the UK, but so far without any apparent devastation. A national policy for the desulphurisation of coal and oil does not have a high priority for us. But should it have a high priority as an international policy? The Scandinavians think it should and they are sharply

critical of British policy. The difficulty from the UK's point of view is that the amount lost to the Swedish economy — even on Sweden's own estimate — is trivial compared with the enormous cost of ridding coal (and to a lesser extent, oil) of sulphur. The Central Electricity Generating Board has estimated that the cost of fitting flue gas desulphurising plant to existing coal-fired power stations alone would be of the order of £2bn, and the running costs £195m to £330m a year to produce a reduction of about a quarter in present levels. *Nature* summed up the position with a headline 'Million dollar problem — billion dollar solution?'

17. It is easy to argue that every polluter should pay the damage he or she produces. This is much easier said than done. The cause of the damage may be debatable; the cost of removing the pollutant disproportionate in technical, employment and sheer economic terms; there may be a clash of interests — who would ban X-rays in the interest of reducing ionising radiation?, or skimp on testing drugs merely to reduce animal experimentation statistics? — and so on. This is not an argument that there is no 'right' answer to environmental problems, but a recognition that the decisions taken by individuals, industries, pressure groups, and Governments often depend on choices and commitments between conflicting 'goods' (eg the convenience and economy of discharging domestic wastes into a river, and the purity of the river water for fish and human consumption). The choices we make are derived from our values, and our values arise from more factors than a simple knowledge of hard facts.

Education

18. This leads us to the final introductory point, that environmental education *per se* is not enough for making moral environmental choices. This does not mean that education can be neglected — far from it. Our decisions must be as informed as it is possible to make them. But decision is based on moral judgement and commitment as well as on knowledge; we must be clear that our environmental morality and action are distinct from the data we may be able to collect about any situation. It is this distinction which makes this report so crucial in any response to the WCS: a defective ethic will lead to environmental disasters.

19. A well-documented example of the differences between knowledge and response is the history of smoke-pollution control in Britain (Ashby and Anderson, 1981). We shall return to this in Chapter 4 below, but it is worth recalling that Britain did not have a comprehensive Clean Air Act until 1956 despite centuries of awareness of some, at least, of the effects of smoke. As long ago as 1662, John Graunt used the weekly Bills of Mortality to establish a correlation between death-rates and the burning of coal; at the same time John Evelyn was complaining about: 'That Hellish and dismall Cloud of Sea-Coale perpetually imminent over London . . . which was so universally mixed with the otherwise wholesome and excellent Aer, that her Inhabitants breathe nothing but an impure and thick Mist, accompanied with a fuliginous and filthy vapour, which renders them obnoxious to a thousand inconveniences, corrupting the Lungs and disordering the entire habit of their Bodies; so that Catharrs, Phthisicks, Coughs, and Consumptions rage more in this one City than in the whole Earth besides'.

20. In the 1880s there was a prolonged campaign to control smoke. Technologically this was becoming possible for industry through better-designed steam furnaces and effective stoking; and it would have been possible to install domestic fires that burned coke or anthracite. But — and this was the crucial factor — such a change had no chance of acceptance. To ask an Englishman to give up his open coal fire in his own home was a threat to liberty. Clean air remained lower in the scale of values than freedom to pollute the air. Only after the London smog in 1952 which killed 4,000 people was it accepted that smoke control from domestic fires must be a priority. The damaging effects of smoke had been known for 300 years, but the commitment to remove the hazard came slowly and gradually.

References

ASHBY, E. 1978. Reconciling man with the environment. London, Oxford University Press.

ASHBY, E and ANDERSON, M. 1981. The politics of clean air. Oxford, Clarendon Press.

O'DONOVAN, O. 1978. The natural ethic. In Essays in evangelical social ethics, 19-35. Wright, D F. (editor). Exeter, Paternoster.

ORGANISATION FOR ECONOMIC CO-OPERATION AND DEVELOPMENT. 1977. OECD programme on long range transport of air pollutants. Paris, OECD.

SKOLIMOWSKI, H. 1981. Eco-Philosophy: designing new tactics for living. London and Salem, New Hampshire, Marion Boyars.

CHAPTER 2
CONFLICT OR COMPLEMENTARITY?

Introduction

1. Conservationists have long been warning of irretrievable damage to the environment and impending catastrophe to the human race, yet they have remained a largely unregarded force. Part of the reason for this is that the cries of 'wolf' have not yet brought doom, but the more important factor is the brute force of human ingenuity in controlling natural obstacles. Technological development has not been straightforward: human history is littered with dust-bowls, broken dams, shifting waste-heaps, failed crops, and the like from at least as far back as the decline of artificial irrigation in Babylonia, centuries before Christ. But we still survive, and still manage to find enough food and fuel to support the world's population (although local or temporary shortages produce recurring tragedies). Conservationists emphasise our ultimate dependence on nature; industrialists and agriculturalists have continually demonstrated our relative independence of it. The result is (in C P Snow's words): 'Two groups — comparable in intelligence, identical in race, not grossly different in social origin, earning about the same incomes who have almost ceased to communicate at all, who in the intellectual, moral and psychological climate have so little in common that instead of going a few hundred yards from South Kensington to Chelsea one might have crossed an ocean' (Snow, 1960).

2. Many people have attempted to establish and maintain dialogue between environmental preservers, managers, and despoilers. The 'Countryside in 1970' conferences and studies were a major endeavour; the WCS is another (Nicholson, 1970; 1973). There is no doubt that goodwill abounds; equally there can be no question that both 'sides' in the environmental debate believe the success of those who disagree with them would be disastrous for the future development and survival of humanity.

Apart From or a Part Of Nature

3. It is the Review Group's conviction that the distinction between the human species as apart from nature or as a part of nature does not exist. This assertion is the most important factor that we want to introduce into the environmental debate. This chapter is devoted to expounding the meaning of this statement; the rest of the report with exploring the implications of it.

4. Stated baldly, the statement that humanity is both apart from and also a part of nature appears trivial. However, the assumption that humanity is one or the other runs right through the environmental debate — it is implicit in some of the accompanying reports to this. It gives rise to contrasting attitudes which may be called respectively:

(a) *technocentric*, which is the application of rational scientific and managerial techniques to an environment which is regarded as a morally neutral resource; and

(b) *ecocentric*, 'resting upon the supposition of a natural order in which all things move according to natural law, and in which the most delicate and perfect balance is maintained up to the point at which man enters with all his ignorance and presumption' (McConnell, 1965).

5. The real difference between these attitudes is that the former is concerned with means while the latter is concerned primarily with ends and only secondarily with means (O'Riordan, 1981). Problems arise, as in so many fields of human endeavour, when means are separated from ends. It is at this point that the danger of over-simplification becomes manifest: reductionism is the strength of science (and therefore of technology) because it enables specific problems to be recognised and attacked; but it is the enemy of management (including that of the environment) because it isolates elements from an interconnected whole and thus too easily warps interpretations.

6. Technocentrism and ecocentrism are understandable polarisations, but it cannot be emphasised too strongly that they are both descriptions of the relation of humanity to the environment which distort and parody the reality. To repeat, humanity is both apart from and a part of nature; it cannot avoid being a manager and also suffering the conseqeuences of its own management. Good management is that which benefits both manager and managed. Or, as the WCS says: 'the concern of environmental management (conservation) is for maintenance and sustainability which is a rational response to the nature of living resources (renewability plus destructability) and also an ethical imperative, expressed in the belief that "we have not inherited the earth from our parents, we have borrowed it from our children" ' (IUCN, 1980).

7. Technocentrists have a dull image They are the

anonymous 'them': the industrial concerns, the men from the ministry, the unrelenting legislators apparently obsessed with sectional interests. Personalised bogeys sometimes appear, but they tend to be no more than convenient targets (Government ministers, multinational companies apparently responsible to no one, nuclear power industry and factory farmers) but the essence of technocentrism is impersonal. In contrast, ecocentrists abound in prophets: Leopold, Roszak, Fraser Darling, the Ehrlichs, and many others. This means that there are many points of view, from the eminently sane to the wild excesses of some ecofreaks.

8. This is not the place to repeat the arguments or pleas of either technocentrists or ecocentrists although this report would become much more readable if some of them were quoted at length (see among many: Carson, 1962; McHarg, 1969; Darling, 1970; Montefiore, 1970; Curry-Lindahl, 1972; Dubos, 1972; Commoner, 1972; Taylor, 1972; Schumacher, 1973; Ward, 1979; Shoard, 1980; Ehrlich and Ehrlich, 1981; Eckholm, 1982). Suffice it to quote the Duke of Edinburgh (1982): 'Detached and analytical intellectuals tend to rationalise the whole thing by saying that someone, or something called "man" is responsible for all the problems. How often one hears enraged conservationists talking about "man" being greedy, irresponsible, self-indulgent or guilty of any other sin they care to mention? I have to admit that I have done it myself. It is easy to pick on "man" as the culprit, it sounds rather grand and impressive, but in reality the expression "man" is a convenient but meaningless generalisation. Lumping the world's four billion people into one category is patently absurd, and if the term is to include all men who have ever lived, it is even more ridiculous . . . In anything to do with conservation, I believe it is particularly important to keep cool, read the World Conservation Strategy, think deeply and be particularly careful to identify the interests of the people and groups most directly involved'.

Complementarity

9. The conservation debate can be easily portrayed as a dilemma or unresolvable *impasse* between opposing attitudes (Berry, 1975; Duke of Edinburgh, 1978). Does it help to assert that it is all a mirage and misunderstanding, and that if we really understood people's relation to their environment, the arguments would disappear? Such a belief sounds perilously like the arrogance of the most hardened technocrat or the naïvety of the most devoted ecofreak. Nevertheless, it is clearly important to explore the grounds for resolving basic disagreements about the environment, because the survival of the world will be sorely hindered if there is a major dissension about how this can be done. The question to be faced is: is it realistic to accept that we are inevitably and irretrievably both apart from and a part of nature? The answer goes behind the specific problem to an argument of far wider implication and again brings in reductionism.

10. Science is concerned with causes. Once the cause of an event is known, we tend to assume that we have a full explanation of the event; we explain the growth of crops as caused by the provision of appropriate fertiliser, a broken limb as caused by an awkward fall, the boiling of water as caused by the increased movement of heated molecules, and so on. Yet these 'causes' are only part of the full explanation: plants are dependent on soil and water for their growth; a fall may follow disease, drunkenness, assault, or an uneven pavement; boiling water must be preceded by putting the kettle on the stove; etc. These are trivial instances, but they emphasise that events may have more than one cause, and that an event may be described adequately but independently in terms of different causes. For example, a picture can be described either in terms of the distribution of molecules that make it up, or in terms of the inventiveness and design of its artist – both explanations are accurate, complete in themselves, and do not overlap. Yet a full description ought to include a recognition of both the chemistry of the pigments and the role of the artist.

11. Aristotle saw this problem. He described material, efficient, formal and final causation; the first two refer to the mechanistic question 'How?'; the latter two to the teleological question 'Why?' (see Arber, 1953). In modern times, Polanyi (1969) has dealt with the same problem as levels of explanation, and more recent discussions are summarised by MacKay (1980) etc. As far as understanding the relationship of people to the environment is concerned, it is important to realise that we are falling into a logical fallacy if we regard humanity only as a manager or only as an element in a complex ecological net. Technocentrists and ecocentrists are both wrong in so far as they each selectively ignore particular aspects of humanity's responses and capabilities; to obtain an undistorted picture of the situation we must accept that humanity is, in the language already used, a part of and apart from nature at the same time. If we fail to accept this, we are immediately open to the accusation of crude brutalism or impotent mysticism which enlivens but not enlightens the environmental debate.

12. The future of the WCS depends on a sensible holism, not a simple reductionism. Fortunately, there is hope in that the message preached by Blake, Wordsworth and Clough in poetry is now being preached by such scientists as Dubos, Schumacher and Thorpe (see Thorpe, 1978). Ashby (1978) explains this as the result of: 'being more and more impressed – awed is perhaps a better word – by the interdependence of things in nature. Animals, green plants, insects, bacteria are partners with man in the same ecosystem. No one can predict the full consequences of tinkering with any part of an ecosystem . . . Hamlet's comment "We fat all creatures else to fat us, and we fat ourselves for maggots" is a curt but accurate summary of man's place in the biosphere . . . New techniques are being worked out for the analysis of complexity: information theory, catastrophe theory, systems analysis. But these techniques cannot yet begin to deal with anything so complex as

an ecosystem, and the techniques of reductionism are irrelevant for this order of complexity. (If this seems to be an exaggeration, consider how little you could learn about the function of a computer if all you were given was a list of the components in it, together with the chemical and physical properties of those components)'.

References

ARBER, A. 1953. The mind and the eye. Cambridge, University Press.

ASHBY, E. 1978. Reconciling man with the environment. London, Oxford University Press.

BERRY, R J. 1975. Ecology and ethics. London, Inter-Varsity.

CARSON, R. 1962. Silent Spring. London, Hamilton.

COMMONER, B. 1972. The closing circle. New York, Knopf.

CURRY-LINDAHL, K. 1972. Conservation for survival. London, Gollancz.

DARLING, F F. 1970. Wilderness and plenty. London, British Broadcasting Corporation.

DUBOS, R. 1972. A god within. Sydney and London, Angus and Robertson.

ECKHOLM, E P. 1982. Down to earth — environmental and human needs. London, Pluto.

EDINBURGH, Duke of. 1978. The environmental revolution. London, Deutsch.

EDINBURGH, Duke of, 1982. A question of balance. Salisbury, Russell.

EHRLICH, P and EHRLICH, A. 1981. Extinction. New York, Random House.

INTERNATIONAL UNION FOR CONSERVATION OF NATURE AND NATURAL RESOURCES. 1980. World Conservation Strategy. Living resource conservation for sustainable development. Gland, IUCN.

MCCONNELL, G. 1965. The conservation movement: past and present. In readings and resource management and conservation, 890-201. Burton, I and Kates, R W. (editors). Chicago, University Press.

MCHARG, I L. 1969. Design with nature. New York, Natural History.

MACKAY, D M. 1980. Brains, machines and persons. London, Collins.

MONTEFIORE, H. 1970. Can mankind survive? London, Fontana.

NICHOLSON, E M. 1970. The environmental revolution. A guide for the new masters of the earth. London, Hodder and Stoughton.

NICHOLSON, E M. 1973. The big change. After the environmental revolution. New York, McGraw-Hill.

O'RIORDAN, T. 1981. Environmentalism, 2nd edition. London, Pion.

POLANYI, M. 1969. Knowing and being. London, Routledge and Kegan Paul.

SCHUMACHER, E F. 1974. The age of plenty. Edinburgh, St Andrew Press.

SHOARD, M. 1980. The theft of the countryside. London, Temple Smith.

SNOW, C P. 1960. The two cultures and the scientific revolution. The Rede lecture for 1959. Cambridge, University Press.

TAYLOR, R. 1972. Rethink: a paraprimitive solution. London, Secker and Warburg.

THORPE, W H. 1978. Purpose in a world of chance. London, Oxford University Press.

WARD, B. 1979. Progress for a small planet. London, Penguin.

CHAPTER 3

COMPLICATING FACTORS

Introduction

1. The simple proposition that humanity is both a part of nature and apart from it are inevitably complicated by factors which act on, and interact with, the simple humans/nature relationship. The four most important factors are: population numbers, resource-use, the effect of stress, and the perception of risk.

Population Numbers

2. The WCS has rightly been criticised for saying nothing about human numbers. The pressure of people is the force above all that makes conservation necessary. The entire population of Britain in the Old Stone Age was probably under 1,000. A rapid increase took place during Neolithic times, when our ancestors learned to domesticate animals and cultivate crops; a small area could support greater numbers than previously. The next major increase was in early modern times when plague and war ceased to kill off a large proportion of every generation, and improved agricultural practices were able to provide for more people. This phase extended through the time of the Industrial Revolution. Better communications allowed increasing urbanisation and the development of economies not directly dependent on the primary producers of the land.

3. At the present day, population increase is for the first time linked to technical expertise (success in controlling communicable disease) and separated from social change. The world's population is now doubling every 35 years. The deaths of babies before their first birthday have fallen in England and Wales from 130 per 1,000 births in 1900 to less than 20 per 1,000 in 1980. In some respects we can accept and contain the population increase in a developed country like Britain where our economy has for long been only secondarily dependent upon food production. Basic difficulties arise where an economy depends primarily on its own agricultural production that barely suffices to meet the needs of the existing population. In countries such as India, a high rate of infant deaths, coupled with periodic epidemics of cholera, plague and the like, was for long sufficient to keep the population roughly in balance with its food supply. Nowadays, the annual rate of increase is 2.5 per cent — or 1,000,000 people a month.

4. The classical response to an increase in population numbers was migration — from tropical to temperate climes; from the Old World to the New; from areas of natural to artificial irrigation. Such possibilities are largely gone as the habitable parts of the world's surface have filled up. The common response is better technology, leading to more efficient animal husbandry, improved strains of crop plants and mechanisation of agriculture; and new sources of food — protein from micro-organisms, fish farming, etc. Unfortunately, this is technological tail-chasing: common sense and economic projection suggest that there must come a point where the increase in population will overtake the highest possible rate of food production. According to the Food and Agriculture Organisation of the United States (FAO), there is enough food currently being produced for more than the world's present population; people are undernourished largely because they cannot afford to buy food. With better means of distribution combined with efficient resource management, it is technically possible to keep production ahead of a population for a few more years, but not indefinitely.

5. Changing attitudes to contraception are discussed in Chapter 4 of this report, paragraphs 17 to 20, page 423. The point here is that in no way can the world sustain indefinite population growth, and a conscious decision must be taken by both Governments and individuals to reduce the reproductive rate. In passing, it should be noted that the official Roman Catholic abhorrence of contraception is based on a strained attitude to natural laws — the biblical command to 'fill the earth' is related to the continuance of God's people, and this became a spiritual rather than a physical matter following Christ's redemptive work.

6. One consequence of reducing population growth will be a high proportion of old people — a heavy burden on the rest of the population. This is a transitory problem which is easily over-dramatised. Children as well as old people have to be supported by people of working age. According to the Registrar General's projection, the numbers of old people in Britain will fall slightly during the next 20 years, and then rise again early next century. Bearing in mind that many retired people can still contribute usefully to society, it seems probable that the burden of a dependent child is overall at least as high as that of a retired person. In a stable, non-growing population, the median age will be about 39 years.

Resource Use

7. If more people have one or two children, instead of the three or four they used to have, but only in order to afford two cars instead of one, the effect on the environment of a decline in population could be entirely wiped out. Paul Ehrlich has expressed the environmental impact of humanity as equal to: population x affluence x technology. Charles Birch has expressed the equation more graphically: 'Originally a unit of population was simply a human being whose needs were met by eating 2,500 calories and 60 gms of protein a day. Man's daily need of energy was equivalent to the continuous burning of a single 100 watt bulb. A unit of population today, in the developed world, consists of a human being wrapped in tons of steel, copper, aluminium, lead, tin, zinc and plastic, gobbling up 60 lbs of raw steel and many pounds of other materials. Far from getting these things in his homeland he ranges abroad much as a hunter and more often than not in the poorer countries. His energy need . . . is equivalent to 10 1,000 watt radiators continuously burning' (Birch, 1972).

8. Two Americans, Ehrlich and Commoner, indulged in a well publicised debate in the early 1970s, as to whether population numbers *per se* or their use of resources was more detrimental. The outcome was an acceptance that the factors in the Ehrlich equation needed modifying because of interactions between them. The details of this do not matter here, although it is worth noting that the differences between Erhlich and Commoner were largely ideological, based on the possibility and extent of coercion in dealing with environmental impacts — Ehrlich called the necessary steps 'life-boat ethics'; Commoner called this approach the 'new barbarism'. This recalls what we have already said about the compound nature of 'values', and the possibility of drawing different conclusions from the same facts. We say nothing here about the continuing arguments about the need and morality of economic growth which is obviously related to both the 'affluence' and the 'technology' elements of the equation. From the point of view of the WCS, it has to be accepted that the impact of an average Briton on the environment is considerably greater than that of an average Third World subsistence farmer.

The Effect of Stress

9. One of the most pervasive influences to intrude in the world in the last few decades is uncertainty about the future: society, religion and Government are all affected; apparently established realities have proved fallible and fickle (Toffler, 1970). David Lodge has brilliantly caught the sense of this in the UK in a chronicle of the spread of uncertainty and anarchy in a group of English Roman Catholics (Lodge, 1980). Rejection of the past has induced failure to cope with the present. Consider communes as a fashionable response to modern problems: 'He could not ignore the fact that many communitarians lacked the discipline to practise what they preached — they denounced the pollution and plastic of the outside world, yet created a junk culture of their own in squalid psychedelic shacks and lofts, over-populated by drifters who were high on dope and low on energy. Everywhere he went, he heard young people learning to live in organic harmony with the earth, to inhabit a peaceful place remote from greed and hostility; but he found communes with hassles and marathon encounter meetings, that couldn't resolve questions like whether to leave the dogs in or out. Everywhere, cars that wouldn't run and pumps that wouldn't pump because everyone knew all about the occult history of tarot and nobody knew anything about mechanics . . .' (Talese, 1980).

10. The experts are no better at discovering where we are going. In 1954, in addressing the British Association Sir Harold Hartley (Ashby, 1975) singled out the three prime factors which determine the destiny of mankind: population, energy and food. By the year 2000, he said, the world's population might rise to 3,500 millions. The present United Nations projection for the year 2000 is 7,000 millions. Hartley predicted that the world's energy consumption, extrapolated to the year 2000, would reach the equivalent of 7.5×10^9 tonnes of coal; by 1972 the figure had already reached the equivalent of 8.8×10^9 tonnes. For cereal production, Hartley made the assumption that yields in developed countries with sophisticated agriculture might double by 2000. In fact, yields of wheat in the United States rose from 2,500 kg/ha in 1954 to over 5,500 kg/ha in 1974. Hartley was probably as accurate as anyone could be in 1954, but the extent of his inaccuracy is such that it inevitably produces unease about the future — and uncertainty leads to stress.

11. In his *Treatise of Government*, John Locke wrote: 'Though the water running in the fountain be everyones, yet who can doubt but that in the pitcher is his only who drew it out? His labour hath taken it out of the hands of nature, where it was common, and belong'd equally to all her children, and hath thereby appropriated it to himself'. Ashby (1979) redraws this moral for the present day: 'If the fountain begins to dry up, if demand for what the economists call a "free good" exceeds supply, then the proposition is insufficient. Either the amount which each can draw has to be rationed by some authority under some principle of fairness and justice, or some of those who use the fountain will begin to show signs of passion; there will be conflict'.

12. Under conditions of life where there is no stress there is a balance among reasonable people between self-interest and concern for others. Under conditions of stress that balance is upset. When a community is threatened from outside, as in time of war, self-interest is put aside and the balance tips towards concern for the common weal. But when a community is threatened from within, the balance may tip towards possessiveness and self-interest. No one doubts that we are now

living in a time of stress, possibly in a climacteric of human history. In affluent countries, the optimism of the post-war 1940s — a prospect of prosperity for everyone and a harvest of the fruits of technology — is being displaced by the pessimism of the 1970s and now the 1980s — a prospect of scarcity, followed by desperate competition to possess the dwindling resources of the planet. It is a time of perplexity. Of course, we do not know what direction history will take, although plenty of people are making predictions, uttering prophecies and trumpeting doom. But two statements about the present can be made with confidence. One is that thoughtful people are deeply apprehensive about the future; the other is that this apprehension is already in some ways (but not in others) changing social values. This apprehension has not, so far, persuaded rich nations to lower their material standard of living, nor has it reconciled poor nations to the prospect that they are likely to remain poor. These are threats which loom like storm clouds ahead of us. But among rich nations, apprehension about the future of the environment has already shifted the attitude of people from indifference to concern.

13. Ashby (1975) in *A Second Look at Doom*, points out that the effect of declining resources and competition for ever-rarer materials will not produce equal misery for all; 'the date when we run out of everything is not what matters. Society is a good deal more likely to be thrown out of gear by the turmoil resulting from people's efforts to avoid the predicted dangers . . . A disastrous oil war could break out long before the wells dry up'. Ashby's recommended reading is not the *Limits of Growth* nor the *Blueprint for Survival*. It is Gibbon's *Decline and Fall of the Roman Empire*.

Perception of Risk

14. The final complication in our consideration of the apparently simple humans/nature relationship is the irrationality of how we actually perceive risk. In a simple, computer-ridden apparently value-free objective world, we should approach risks to health or future in direct relation to their probability of occurrence. However, our attitudes are, in fact, much more complex. Our perception of risk is influenced by scale and rarity almost as much as by the chance of exposing ourselves to hazard; we are much more worried about the dangers from nuclear power than about crossing the road; we are scared about plane accidents, whilst not bothering to keep to the speed limits.

15. A good deal is known about the risks of death from environmental hazards. Thus, the chance of being killed by lightning is about one in a million per year of exposure; the chance of being killed in an industrial accident is about one in 30,000 per year of exposure; the chance of being killed on roads in Britain is about one in 8,000. These statistics are fairly well known. Notwithstanding, public perception of the same risks is very different from their factual nature. For example, when 350 people were lost in a jumbo jet accident in the USA there was a national shock wave — yet 350 people are regularly killed every 55 hours on American roads. A man, who would be outraged if he was exposed to a one in 400 chance of death at work every year, will happily expose himself to the same risk by smoking 25 cigarettes per day.

16. The mean overall risk of death per annum from disease, disregarding the effects of age, is about one in 100. The risk of death through natural disasters (floods, hurricanes, earthquakes and the like) is about one in a million. As a very rough generalisation it can be said that most risks of one in a million are of no concern to the average person. Risks of one in 100,000 may elicit warnings (eg parents tell their children not to go into deep water or play with electric equipment). When the risk rises to one in 10,000 the public is prepared to pay for it to be reduced (eg by the erection of crash barriers on motorways); when it becomes one in 1,000, it becomes unacceptable to the public.

17. All of the complicating factors discussed above influence political decisions about environmental policy: the need to distribute resources fairly in an overcrowded island and to conserve non-renewable ones; the danger of stress and disorder in a society where resources, including opportunities to get a job, are limited; and the mismatch between the statistical assessment of risks to society and the ways these risks are perceived. Correct action needs an understanding which goes beyond a simple knowledge of facts. As Edmund Burke wrote many years ago, 'The public interest requires doing today those things that men of intelligence and goodwill would wish, five or 10 years hence, had been done'. However, there is hope for the future because attitudes to the complicating factors described in this chapter are not fixed; our relationship to nature is fluid.

References

ASHBY, E. 1975. A second look at doom. Twenty-first Fawley Foundation lecture. Southampton, University of Southampton.

ASHBY, E. 1976. Protection of the environment: the human dimension. *Proc R Soc Med, 69,* 721-730.

ASHBY, E. 1978. Reconciling man with the environment: London, Oxford University Press.

BIRCH, L C. 1972. Carrying capacity of the global environment — biological limitations. *Anticipation, 13.*

LODGE, D. 1980. How far can you go? London, Secker and Warburg.

TALESE, G. 1980. Thy neighbour's wife. London, Collins.

TOFFLER, A. 1970. Future shock. London, Bodley Head.

CHAPTER 4

CHANGING ATTITUDES

Introduction

1. Mention has already been made of changing public attitudes towards the environment. These are important, because the Review Group is convinced that the future of the world depends on a widespread public commitment to responsible attitudes to our environment. It is no use a few outstanding figures preaching the virtues of the WCS or any other strategy, unless there is a general preparedness to accept the importance and constraints of responsible behaviour.

2. The formation of attitudes, and the means of changing them, is a major study in its own right. This is not the place to penetrate into social psychology. The most helpful approach would seem to be to present three crisis cases where environmental attitudes have changed radically: the management of property where the change has been a secondary consequence of political and social change; the need for clean air, where political and technological impetus have achieved positive and generally respected legislation; and the moral acceptance of contraception, where technical possibility has been given moral approval. The accounts are drawn from, respectively, Black (1970), Ashby and Anderson (1981) and Morgan (1976).

Property

3. Primitive man depended (indeed depends) upon land to hunt and on which to grow crops. The land was common property, in the sense that no one had any particular right to it. In Western Christendom, the use was regulated by a natural law interpretation of the Bible. For example, St Ambrose wrote in the fourth century AD: 'Our Lord God intended the world to be the common possession of all men, and that it should produce its fruits for all, but covetousness has portioned out individual rights of property. It is just, therefore, that if you claim something for yourself as a private person which was bestowed upon the human race, every living soul of it in common, you should at all events distribute some of it to the poor so that you do not deny food to those to whom you owe a share of your legal rights'.

4. Two hundred years later, Pope Gregory I asserted:

'Our property is ours to distribute, but not ours to keep; to withhold from those who are in need'. The concept of stewardship is clearly here, and the condemnation of waste has a very modern note of sound management. Thomas Aquinas confirmed this position in the thirteenth century, but made important additions: that human law requires that a system of private property be set up for the management of material things, and that the use of property must be limited to that which is reasonable for the individual.

5. Aquinas' influence retarded the development of the modern view, because of his limitation on the ownership of property and associated condemnation of usury; either the rules had to be relaxed or economic development had to languish. It was only with Locke's *Treatises on Government* in 1690, that future advance was possible. Locke founded his theory of property on the argument that a man's labour is his own, to do with as he likes (see above, Chapter 3, paragraph 11, p 419). The importance of this lies in the relation of individuals to the society of which they are members. If their labour is their own, to do with as they please, society is not involved; if the right to unlimited property rests on personal labour, property rights no longer carry social obligations. Thus, the earlier restriction on the unfettered accumulation of property was set aside and the way was clear for the worst excesses of the Industrial Revolution.

6. The emancipation of property rights from religious or social constraints has not gone unchallenged over the last three centuries. For instance, criteria for the limitation of self-sufficiency recurred in the writings of the nineteenth century utilitarians. J S Mill, though satisfied with the concept of private property, held that land ownership should be conditioned by expediency; access and enjoyment should be limited to that which is necessary for efficient exploitation.

7. It seems a far cry today from the belief that people hold the resources of the world on trust, and are accountable to God for the use they make of them. We have become conditioned to the all-pervading influence of central Government over so many aspects of everyday life that we find it difficult to realise to what extent contemporary mythology has allowed the State to usurp many of the functions previously allocated to the Deity (such as permissible land-use). We are now approaching the position where individuals are expected to look on their property as on trust to them for society, to whom

they are responsible for the way they manage it. This is a major change from Locke's argument. He wrote, 'The great and chief end of men's uniting into common wealths, and putting themselves under Government, is the preservation of their property'. The ideal state of humanity was the 'state of nature', in which there would be no restrictions on individual behaviour or freedom of action. Since this was not a workable proposition in the everyday world, a modicum of organised Government was a necessary evil in order that the rightful enjoyment of private property might be preserved. Locke argued that the State could not turn round and separate individuals from their property, since the only justification for the existence of the state was the preservation of private property.

8. The privacy of property rights has increasingly been challenged, even in countries like the USA and Britain where it has the strongest influence, as well as being rejected by countries which have been exploited by political and economic systems arising out of them. Modern political debates on the subject have followed the takeovers of the Suez Canal by Egypt in 1956 and the Falklands by Argentina in 1982. There has been an ever-increasing tempo of change from the Lockean principle of unfettered rights over property, to the modern acceptance of the State as legitimately intervening in the economic and social life of its citizens. In previous centuries, there was a gradual shrinkage in the area of responsibility of the Church, so that matters of economic and commercial signifiance were increasingly excluded from the Church's responsibility; there has now been a contrary movement in which the State, starting with a concern for only these matters, has gradually widened its coverage to include aspects of personal welfare as well. In this way, we have come to accept the State as the ultimate authority to which individuals owe a duty for the management of the natural resources 'entrusted' to their care. This change of attitude has, naturally enough, proceeded at different rates in the various countries of Western civilisation. It has gone much further in some countries (for instance, the Netherlands and Great Britain) than in others (such as the USA), depending on the traditional attitude to centralised Government.

9. As the State has taken over control of the land, so it has also imposed restrictions on the land owners, not only for direct economic purposes, but on behalf of conservation interests, maintenance of scenic beauty, and the protection of wildlife. Such restrictions range from the type of trap or poison permissible for the control of vermin, to the movement of lands between parallel uses, such as between agriculture and forestry. Many of these regulations are both necessary and welcome, and are aimed at preventing the further deterioration of the environment (eg the limitation of persistent chlorinated hydrocarbon insecticides). The point here is that these regulatory powers set firm limits to the authority of the manager, and could not have arisen until the Lockean tradition was replaced by one giving Government the right to control the use of property.

10. The use, control, enclosure, registration and transference of common land is a particular example of the acceptance of central authority over land in Britain. It has been well documented by Hoskins and Stamp (1963).

Clean Air

11. There was a time when people in Britain could burn what they liked when they liked so long as they caused no 'nuisance' to their neighbours. Since 1956, there has been power to control smoke everywhere in the country. One aspect of progress to the necessary legislation has been described in Chapter 1, paragraph 9, p 414 of this report; we describe here in more detail the change in attitudes that were necessary before the Clean Air Act could be accepted.

12. The effective beginning of smoke control in Britain was the Alkali Act of 1863, which set up an Inspectorate with the power to enter factories on behalf of something inanimate — the atmosphere and property damaged by acid fumes. The first Chief Inspector, Angus Smith, set the tone for the subsequent practice of the inspectorate, and with it the overall basis for pollution control in Britain to the present time: 'There are two modes of inspection, one is by a suspicious opponent, desirous of finding evil, and ready to make the most of it. The other is that of a friendly adviser, who treats those whom he visits as gentlemen desirous of doing right . . . The character of the inspection which I have instituted is one caused partly by my own inclination, and partly by the nature of the circumstances'.

13. This trusting approach, coupled with the fact that industrial expansion in the latter half of the nineteenth century cancelled out some of the benefits of the inspectors' efforts, laid the inspectors open to criticism that they were in the pockets of the manufacturers. Prosecutions were rare (there were only nine in the 20 years that Smith was Chief Inspector). In Smith's view, this was a measure of success: a multitude of prosecutions would have been a sign that inspectors were failing in their task of educating manufacturers. Speaking in the House of Lords in 1876, the Duke of Northumberland agreed: 'The inspectors have discharged their duties very fairly on the whole; they have greatly diminished the cause of complaint . . . they wish to lead rather than to drive men, which I believe, where great issues are involved, to be the best and wisest way of proceeding'. Three-quarters of a century later, the inspectors are recorded as following the same pattern: pragmatic, flexible, forbearing in difficult cases, strict where strictness was justified (W A Damon was Chief Inspector from 1930 to 1955; in this time he brought only two prosecutions).

14. There were three keys to the undoubted success of the Alkali inspectors: positive criticism, an insistence that control should be by the 'best practical means',

and a gentle incorporation of other air pollutants other than that given to them by the 1863 Act. The issue of whether control is best exercised by laying down absolute standards or by the 'best practical means' has been debated repeatedly over the past century. It is an issue that divides continental (and EEC) practice from that of Britain. The issue is relevant here because it has a potential influence on the attitude of those controlled by statute: a numerical standard is arbitrary, and a simple aim for manufactures; the 'best practicable means' of control is: 'an elastic band, and may be kept always tight as knowledge of the methods of suppressing the evils complained of increases' (Inspectorate Report for 1878). The inspectors fixed the best practical means only after full consultation with manufacturers. It is intriguing that the elegant Napoleonic prohibition that: 'manufacturers which give out an unwholesome or unpleasant odour will not be allowed to be established without the authority of the Administration' was regarded by the end of the nineteenth century as: 'a failure of the most decided kind'; the edict had been made without preliminary discussions with industry, and was enforced by a specialised inspectorate.

15. The Alkali Inspectorate was established to control the emission of hydrochloric acid from alkali works. In 1863, this was the only practicable smoke control. But the inspectors tended to interpret their duties as covering the reduction of all atmospheric pollution by all industrial processes, and this activity, associated with various pressure groups (both private and the gas and electricity boards with vested interests), resulted in the Clean Air Act of 1956. The Minister responsible for it could justly claim: 'there is no difference of opinion in this House and very little outside'. This was a significant judgement because at least 12 Bills to control smoke had been rejected during the previous century.

16. The change in attitude to clean air came through sociology, not technology. Ashby and Anderson (1981) wrote of the work of the pressure group (the Smoke and Fog Committee) in 1881: 'There were already stoves on the market which would burn coke or smokeless anthracite coal. These coals cost no more than ordinary coal. But the householder, eager enough by now to suppress smoke from the factory chimneys, was unwilling to forego his own cheerful fireplace for the silent and colourless emanations from a closed stove; nor, by all accounts, were servants anxious to exchange the daily chore of brushing up cinders and buying new fires for the cleaner job of tending an anthracite stove. (At one meeting of the Fog and Smoke Committee, Mr Owen Thomas offered 'to send a couple of Welsh maids to town to show London maids how to burn smokeless coal in stoves suitable for dometic purposes'). However, as already recorded, the final straw that led to the Clean Air Act was the 1952 London smog; 160 cattle at the Smithfield show needed veterinary attention, La Traviata had to be abandoned at Sadlers Wells because the audience could not see the stage, and over 4,000 human deaths were attributed to the smog. The smog was the stimulus, but the credit must

go to the Alkali Inspectorate who swam with history for a century and managed not to minimise pollution, but more importantly to optimise it. By 1964, there was virtually no opposition to the statutory control of smoke.

Contraception

17. Contraception was practised at least as early as the second century BC. Early Christian writings took a variety of attitudes towards it. Church attitudes antagonistic to contraception came from Greek and, subsequently, reaction to Manichaean philosophies. These were formalised through the teaching of Augustine and Thomas Aquinas, that the education and upbringing of children was an integral part of marriage, and that the justification for intercourse is procreation. Contraception came to be regarded as a violation of the purpose of marriage. This has remained the view of the Roman Catholic Church, reinforced by the controversial papal proclamation 'Humanae Vitae' in 1968.

18. In 1878, Charles Bradlaugh founded the Malthusian League to spread the knowledge of contraception for demographic reasons. The 1908 Lambeth Conference of Anglican Bishops reacted against the burgeoning practice on traditional grounds: 'the Conference records with alarm the growing practice of artificial restrictions of the family, and earnestly calls upon all Christian peoples to discountenance the use of all artificial means of restriction as demoralising to character and hostile to national welfare'. The 1920 Conference was more concerned to uphold the family as the basic social unit, and regarded the appropriate way of doing this was for all its clergy to be well versed in traditional moral theology.

19. During the next decade there was much discussion about the role of sexual development, and the 1930 Lambeth Conference resolved that: 'where there is a clearly felt moral obligation to limit or avoid parenthood, complete abstinence is the primary and obvious method . . . But that if there was a morally sound reason for avoiding abstinence, the Conference agrees that other methods may be used, provided that this is done in the light of Christian principles'. This decision was taken in recognition of the dangers of high population growth, particularly at a time of economic depression, abhorrence of abortion as a means of contraception; and the changing role of women in society ('facts and conditions of modern civilisation'). These factors were coupled with an examination of the traditional position; it was pointed out that the Roman Catholic Church did in practice allow some exceptions in its apparently absolute prohibition of contraception methods.

20. There is now effectively no debate about contraception in Anglican and other Reformed Churches; the emphasis is wholly on the significance and strengthening of the family unit. The change in attitude in this case and the point of including it here was that it was brought about by authoritarian leaders re-examining

accepted beliefs in the light of new information. Because of the nature of this authority, contraception was rapidly accepted as permissible in English society, and it is not a divisive matter.

Conclusions

21. It is impossible to generalise about how atti-tudes are formed and how they may change. Some attitudes have a rational base; others represent out-dated traditions. The common factor in the three cases described above was a change in the face of new facts, pressures or interpretations. It is obviously im-portant that education about the environment is as effective as possible, but commitment beyond education depends upon leadership which is both honest and practical.

References

ASHBY, E and ANDERSON, M. 1981. The politics of clean air. Oxford, Clarendon Press.

BLACK, J. 1970. The dominion of man. Edinburgh, University Press.

HOSKINS, W G and STAMP, L D. 1963. The common lands of England and Wales. London, Collins New Naturalist.

MORGAN, J L. 1976. A sociological analysis of some develop-ments in the moral theology of the Church of England since 1900. Thesis presented for the D Phil degree in the University of Oxford.

CHAPTER 5

POSSIBLE SOLUTIONS

Introduction

1. To anyone with even a slight acquaintance with environmental issues, it is obvious that a whole range of solutions have been urged with varying degrees of realism. Remembering that the aim of this present exercise is to produce an effective and positive humans/ nature relationship, we discuss here the main approaches under three headings. It will become clear that all three approaches help us in fostering the humans/nature relationship, but none gives us the complete answer.

Religion

2. Religion is both blamed for problems and hailed as the saviour of the environment. The blame is summed up in an article entitled 'The historic roots of our ecologic crisis' by Lynn White, a Californian historian (White, 1967). He starts with the beginning of farming in Neolithic times. Every family unit was independent. Early ploughs did not turn furrows, but merely scratched the surface. Cross-ploughing was needed, and fields were square. This was fine for light soils and the dry climate of the Mediterranean, but ineffective on the wet and often sticky soils of northern Europe. By the seventh century, the modern plough with its attached share had been invented. This needed a team of oxen to pull it, and fields became long and thin to make strip cultivation easier. Now a team of oxen involved the pooling of resources of individual families. Human beings became exploiters of both their fellows and their fields. This is elegantly shown by illustrated calendars which, prior to 830 AD, showed the months as passive events each with its own attributes, but then changed to depict humans as coercing nature — ploughing, harvesting, chopping trees, butchering pigs. Humans and nature were two things, with humans being in control.

3. The explicit justification for this was the dominion over nature that God has given to man at creation (Genesis 1: 28), a command which Christians have accepted as a direct mandate. The Puritan settlers of New England justified their journey as a voyage to the Promised Land — a sanctuary from their Egypt, a testing ground and a meeting place with God. Since Eden was a garden, they assumed that the reduction of wilderness to garden (and, incidentally, the elimination of the native 'Amalekites') was a properly Christian task. To them, wild country was basically immoral, and its cultivation was glorifying God. Any action to control wilderness or exploit natural resources was virtuous (Passmore, 1974). They would have been horrified by the later, romantic wilderness cult of Thoreau and Leopold. It was in terms of this Puritan wilderness-to-garden ethic that the advance of the frontier westward across America took place.

4. A comparable British example was the 'improvements' of the Scottish Highlands in the first half of the nineteenth century, involving the clearance of the inhabitants to the coast or colonies. In almost all cases, this was supported by the local ministers, because they saw this action as being of benefit to their flock, even though it destroyed the local community. To 'conquer' nature in these circumstances was no more than obedience to God's original command to Adam. As a matter of pure theology, the instruction to 'have dominion' over nature is, in the Bible, given in the context of the definition of man 'made in the image of God', implying that human attitudes and behaviour are limited by being based on divine traits. In this context of the definition of man 'made in the image bility (Moule, 1964). The proper Christian approach to the environment is one of responsibility, not rape; pollution is seen as the effect of humanity's estrangement from God (Romans 8: 19-22), and its increase as a measure of a progressive rejection of spiritual values (Peacocke, 1979; Elsdon, 1981; Moss, 1982).

5. The Christian world view is the one that has shaped British thinking. But religion has — or is urged to have — an influence on nature. Frequently, these calls are an element in the despair of practical environmental managers. Francis of Assisi and Teilhard de Chardin are most often cited as examples of people who had a 'proper' attitude to nature. In fact, both blurred the humans/nature relationship (ie they emphasised that humanity is part of nature, but played down the fact that it is also apart from nature), thus leading to the divisiveness we have already described (see Chapter 1 above). Exhortations to espouse eastern religions (especially Buddhism, which is essentially an existentialist approach to life, see Palihawadana, 1980) have the same problem. In effect, the religions make respectable a biocentrist escapism; they legitimise disengagement with the real problems of the environment. This is

a criticism that cannot be levelled against Christianity, *sensu stricto*.

6. However, it would be foolish to assume that religion has nothing to offer to the development of a useful environmental ethic. All religions (including secular humanitarianism) are concerned with the nature of the human race, and its proper approach to human organic, and inorganic, encounters. The relationship of humanity with nature can be described in secular or religious language (Eibl-Eibesfeldt, 1971; Birch and Cobb, 1981), but the language used does not affect the interactions that take place — only their interpretation.

Law

7. It is obvious that statutory control has some part to play in regulating the humans/nature relationship. It is equally clear that law is of little value unless it is accepted and enforced: an act to control smoke in London was effective so long as Palmerston was Home Secretary and concerned to make it work; the Clean Air Act of 1956 could not be universally applied for a number of years because there was not enough smoke-less fuel available. A Royal Commission on Air Pollution which reported in 1878 posed two questions that still trouble those who have to legislate to protect the environment. Firstly, there seemed to be no indisputable evidence that noxious vapours (other than smoke and sulphurous gases) harmed human health. This being so, how far should Parliament go in passing laws merely for the preservation of private property or the protection of nature? Secondly, there are some flagrant nuisances which cannot be abated. Should such nuisances be tolerated or suppressed? Should we, for example, ban aircraft to reduce noise, or (in the words of a recent advertisement) ban television so that more people will buy books?

8. Laws can help in providing a standard which educates people, even if they fail to reach it (or even if they reject it). EEC legislation may be influential here (see Chapter 7, p 436). But the main proponents of stronger environmental legislation in Britain have been fired by a conviction that the law can help citizens assert their rights to a high-quality environment, that individual liberty must be tempered by obligations to others (and to the future), and that Governments secrecy hinders citizens in obtaining the best solutions for individual and environmental good. Unfortunately, all these aims are adversarial. Furthermore, the growth of environmental law has the effect of putting considerable power in the hands of limited groups of people. The clashes at planning inquiries show this only too well. Whilst there can be no argument that law is a guard against environmental damage (and, properly enacted, an 'elastic band' reducing damage — see Chapter 4, paragraphs 14 to 15 of this report, pp 422 - 423), it is much more difficult for it to be a positive force for environmental improvement.

9. It is tempting to think of law as objective and impartial. This is (arguably) true in its application, but not in its formulation. A disconcerting amount of chance occurs in the way Bills are put before parliaments, or are amended during the parliamentary process. The recent Wildlife and Countryside Act 1981 still awaits full testing, but already it is clear that it may be unworkable in parts; we have already described how the Clean Air Act was stimulated by the London smog of 1952; another example was the rash of valuable controls (and other actions) that followed the grounding in 1967 of the tanker Torrey Canyon off Land's End, which in retrospect was a fairly minor environmental incident.

10. The control of poisonous waste is another cautionary tale for those who believe that law ought to be a safety net for environmental protection (Ashby, 1978). The story began in 1963 when some sheep and cattle died on a couple of farms in south-east England. *Post mortems* showed they had been poisoned by fluoroacetamide, which was traced to a field next to a factory that produced pesticides. The factory had dumped drums which had rusted, and their contents drained into ponds from which animals drank. The incident caused no great stir. The main effect was a Technical Committee appointed by the Minister of Housing to advise what changes were desirable to ensure safe disposal of toxic solid wastes. This committee met 20 times over six years, and reported in 1970 that existing legislation on toxic wastes was inadequate. Nothing was done.

11. Meanwhile, a Royal Commission on Environmental Pollution was appointed in 1970 with wide powers of inquiry. Its first task was to survey the state of the environment in Britain. It found evidence of 'fly-tipping', ie illicit dumping of toxic wastes in places not registered to receive them; and it urged the Government to tighten the law. The Government said that it had too heavy a programme for the matter to be dealt with in the coming session; there was to be a reorganisation of local government that would affect the administrative arrangements, and a comprehensive Bill to control pollution would be introduced in 1974. Nothing was done.

12. Then, in January 1972, the Birmingham *Sunday Mercury* published the story of Lonnie Downes, a lorry driver in a Midlands waste-disposal firm. He had discovered that some of his mates were being given a bonus of £28 a week for dumping loads of cyanide, chromic acid, caustic soda, phenol and other noxious substances on delivery tickets that described them as 'suds oil'. Mr Downes complained to his boss, who replied with vague threats of dismissal. A few weeks later Mr Downes was offered promotion, which he declined. Then, so it was reported, he was offered £300 if he would leave the company; again he declined. Instead he reported the whole affair to the Conservation Society, who sent a detailed report to the Secretary of State for the Environment. When he did nothing, the Society, having given due warning of its intention, passed the whole story to the press.

13. Press, radio and television descended on the refuse

dumps of Britain like scavenging gulls. Pictures of alleged toxic waste drums appeared in the newspapers. Parliament was forced to hold a special debate on the issue, but still the Government maintained that their timetable was too full for legislation to be introduced before 1974. On 24 February 1972, 36 one-hundredweight drums were discovered on derelict land near Nuneaton where children played. Attempts had been made to remove the drum labels saying 'sodium cyanide'. Action was finally triggered by the death of a lorry driver whose load reacted with material already in the pit where he was dumping. The Department of the Environment hurriedly drafted a Bill to control the deposit of poisonous waste. It was read for the first time on 8 March, went through its remaining stages on 16 March, and became law on 30 March 1972. *The Times* wrote about all this: 'It is instructive to note what did and what did not prompt the Government to squeeze a Bill as a matter of urgency into an already overcrowded legislative programme. The urgent representations of an official Commission composed of distinguished persons who were moved by "the disturbing cases which have come to our knowledge of local problems and anxieties" did not. Headlines about drums of cyanide waste on derelict land in the Midlands did' (*The Times*, 7 March 1972).

14. It can be argued that legislation about smoke control, oil pollution and toxic wastes would have all reached the statute books in due course, the only factor to be criticised being the speed with which the relevant Bills were introduced. That might have been so, but laws do not emerge of their own volition, however industrious bodies like the Law Commission are in trying to foresee necessary legislation. All the environmental laws in the world amount in the end to regulation of the humans/nature relationship. All a politician can sensibly do is apply judgement to the claim of pressure for legislation. This judgement depends on two factors: an understanding of the issue, and attitudes to the components of the understanding, ie the weight the politician attaches to each of them. The response will be a subjective one, even if many of the elements involved are 'objective facts'. In other words, we are right back to the question of 'values' and how they arise. We shall have to return to this in Chapter 6 of this report.

15. However, before leaving the topic of law, we need to say something about the concept of 'rights'. Increasingly, 'rights' are claimed as absolute and therefore non-negotiable factors in arguments: rights of trespass, hunting (or to stop hunting), grazing, and the right to life itself. Examination of all such claims show that rights do not exist in the abstract. Black (1970) has shown how the notion of 'human rights' grew up to contrast with another absolute that was claimed: 'the good of the State'. The American Constitution and, more recently, various Declarations of the United Nations, enshrine claims to various rights, but virtually always as expressions of dissent from restrictions on political or social freedom. In other words, rights are used in an adversarial as well as an absolute sense. The crucial question we are facing in this report concerns the relationship (between humanity and nature), which is clearly a dynamic process. It is better to avoid 'rights' language in debates about environmental ethics, and use instead language about responsibility and privilege.

Economics

16. The firmer the ground on which decisions are made, the better. No one will dispute that, least of all the politicians whose problems were touched on in paragraph 14 above in this chapter, above. A tendency that must be restricted as firmly as possible is to dress up opinions or prejudices as objective data by giving them numerical values. Environmentalists very properly seek to quantify the cost of their proposals but this can very easily lead to absurd results. An excellent example of the nonsense that comes from spurious objectivity can be drawn from the debates about the need for another airport to serve London. In 1968, the Government of the day appointed the Roskill Commission to carry out as impartial an investigation as possible of the alternatives. It was important that possible alternative sites should be objectively compared, and be seen to be effectively compared. Whilst local opposition to any final decision about the site of a third London airport would be understandable, it would be more easily over-ruled if it could be 'objectively' demonstrated that the benefit to the majority should not be thwarted by the selfish interests of a few.

17. The main task of the Commission was to make as comprehensive a comparison as possible of the costs and benefits to each of four (originally five) possible sites (Cublington, Foulness, Nuthampstead, and Thurleigh). The largest single element of cost for an airport is 'airspace movement' (about 42 per cent of the total). This turned out to be similar for all four possible sites. The next largest amount is 'passenger user' costs (about 38 per cent). This allocates passengers to airports in proportion to the distance to be travelled. The calculation used by the Roskill Commission depended heavily on the assumed capacities of the four airports, and the assumption that the relationship between accessibility and traffic will remain constant (ie that there will be no change in the methods of getting to the airport); the first assumption is arbitrary, and the second is dubious. But the questionable part of the Roskill costings was the attempt to put a monetary value to amenity losses. For example, some ancient churches would have had to be destroyed at three of the four sites. Their 'loss' was calculated on the insurance value of the buildings concerned. It was recognised that this method 'did not fully take into account historic benefits'. The problem is that insurance values must be related to market values or replacement costs; since there is no market for the sale of old churches, their market value is rather low.

18. Adams (1970) repeated the Roskill calculation for an airport centred on Westminster. Such an airport would cut journey time by at least an hour as compared

to an airport outside London. Assuming the average cost per journey in the year 2000 is likely to be £1.50 per journey, the annual savings would be £300m a year or £9,000m over an assumed 30 year life of an airport. There would be a large property cost because of the value of houses in central London, but it seems reasonable to assume that a five square mile central London site could be purchased for around £2,500m and another seven square miles could be insulated against sound and depreciated property values for another £1,000m. Westminster Abbey could be insulated or moved; in any event, it is unlikely to be worth much more than its insured value of £1.5m. The loss of central London parks would be a major amenity loss but this was taken into account in Adam's costing of the site and anyway the airport itself would be a major recreational amenity. The safety of those on the ground would not cost too much: Roskill anticipated an average of one Third Party accident over 30 years, and the costs assumed are only £9,300 for each fatality and £625 for each injury. So in all, there seems to be as 'objective' a case for building the next London Airport in Hyde Park as anywhere.

19. Adams' calculations make a mockery of the solemn cost benefit analysis carried out by the Roskill Commission. He has carried out similar deflating analyses of Department of Transport costings of road schemes. These are based largely on an arbitrary amalgam of four elements: one involves hard cash (construction costs), one is insignificant (vehicle operating costs), one is contentious (time saving), and one is largely meaningless (the cost of accidents). In January 1976, a fatal road traffic accident was valued at £44,000 of which the greatest amount was the value of the average human life — £34,600. (The 'value' of a Canadian at that time was around £70,000 and of a citizen of the USA £90,000. This is roughly equal to the damage awarded at about the same time to an actor in a libel action against a newspaper which accused him of being drunk and forgetting his lines.) Notwithstanding, the Department claims that: 'the probable environmental effects of a new road, both positive and negative, are fully taken into account before any appraisal is completed'.

20. Decisions based on cost benefit analysis use a straightforward application of utilitarian thinking: any development must make one or more people better off while leaving no one worse off, often qualified by an attempt to give most benefit to the most deserving. We have already criticised the utilitarian ethic in its basic form (see Chapter 1, paragraph 11 of this report, p 413), but there is an economists' trick which makes nonsense of its application, and that is so-called 'discount budgeting'. This involves discounting the capital cost of a project over a period of variable length into the future. Depending on the discount rate and the time chosen, actual capital costs can be 'assumed' to be reduced, almost to vanishing point. Thus any benefit from a development can be shown to be overwhelming.

21. Economists argue that their role as policy makers is legitimate because they are neutral about competing values. This takes us straight back to our discussion in Chapter 1, paragraph 7 of this report, p 412, showing how much confusion there is about the word 'value'. The beauty and danger of cost benefit analysis is that, no matter how relevant or irrelevant, wise or stupid, informed or uninformed, responsible or silly, defensible or indefensible a want may be, an economic analysis is able to derive a legitimate policy from cost benefit analysis because all the options are considered to be equally valid and good.

22. The role of the scientists in environmental decision making is still influential because scientists have not tried to include in their advice information that cannot be treated credibly by their techniques. What they quantify obviously lends itself to quantification. In contrast, the economists' contribution to decision making has deservedly lost some of its influence. The search for a 'Solomon Machine' that produces a perfect cost benefit analysis is no longer pursued with as much enthusiasm as it was a few years ago. The assumption that fragile values can always be expressed in financial terms has been proved wrong. The claim that a view, a home or an attribute is 'priceless' has been upheld too often. Cost benefit analysis is unreliable because it is usually based on a wrong premise: on the whole it asks 'What is efficient for society?' instead of 'What is good for society?' For some enterprises, much of industry for example, the aim is to maximise efficiency, and this premise may be acceptable. For the protection of the environment, the premise is not acceptable. By all means let us use the most cost effective ways to achieve our ends, but do not let us use only cost benefit analysis to determine the ends in the first place.

References

ADAMS, J. 1970. Westminster: the fourth London airport? *Area 2*, 1-9.

ADAMS, J. Transport planning. London, Routledge & Kegan Paul.

ASHBY, E. 1978. Reconciling man with the environment. London, Oxford University Press.

BIRCH, L C and COBB, J B. 1981. The liberation of life. Cambridge, University Press.

BLACK, J. 1970. The dominion of man. Edinburgh, University Press.

EIBL-EIBESFELDT, I. 1971. Love and hate: on the natural history of basic behaviour patterns. London, Methuen.

ELSDON, R. 1981. Bent world. Leicester, Inter-Varsity.

MOSS, R. 1982. The earth in our hands. Leicester Inter-Varsity.

MOULE, C F D. 1964. Man and nature in the New Testament. London, Athlone.

PALIHAWADANA, M. 1980. Buddhism and the scientific enterprise. In Faith and Science in an unjust world, vol I, 138-152. Shinn, R L. (editor). Geneva, WCC.

PASSMORE, J. 1974. Man's responsibility for nature. London, Duckworth.

PEACOCKE, A R. 1979. Creation and the world of science. London, Oxford University Press.

WHITE, L. 1967. The historic roots of our ecologic crisis. Science, NY, 155, 1204-1207.

CHAPTER 6

TOWARDS AN ETHIC

Introduction

1. The last three chapters have been concerned with the problems of devising an ethic which adequately reflects the complementary humans/nature relationship, described in Chapter 2 above. We have considered some of the complications and red herrings in the search for this ethic. We have now reached the stage of bringing our discussions towards the point of helping those who have to take decisions about the environment. Especially we are seeking a way forward to resolve the ethical problems encountered in the sister reports, in order to produce an agreed commitment to implement the WCS (not merely an agreement to implement it; that is easy, but weak).

2. However, we must continue critically for a moment in considering previous attempts to construct an environmental ethic. The value of these attempts is that they emphasise the key element to be considered is the relation between humanity and nature (White, 1967; Berry, 1972), but, generally speaking, they are more concerned with philosophical niceties than practical decision making (eg Barbour, 1972; Kozlovsky, 1974; Passmore, 1974; Regan, 1981, etc). The important studies of Ashby (1978; 1979) must be excluded from this criticism, and it is not intended to include such practical approaches as those of Schumacher (1973; 1974, etc), which are concerned with specific levels of action.

3. Ashby (1979) identifies four interests which must be taken into account in formulating an environmental ethic: self-interest, public interest, posterity's interest, nature's interest.

Self-interest

4. As individuals, we are a mixture of selfishness and altruism. Selfishness is well described by Hardin's (1968) 'tragedy of the commons'. Imagine a common which can support 40 beasts with 20 herdsmen entitled to graze their animals. This means two beasts per farmer. But any of the 20 may ask what would be the effect of acquiring a single extra animal? The answer is a spectacular 50 per cent increase in personal output and wealth at the expense of one extra animal on the common. The problem is that all 20 are likely to reason the same way, and 60 animals will appear on land capable of feeding only 40. Result: deterioration of pasture and animals.

5. Hardin applied this parable primarily to the number of children each couple agrees to have, but extended it to the way we treat the environment. For example, discharged waste (sewage, chemical or radioactive effect) costs less if a manufacturer releases it into the common stream, air or sea, and then pays his 'share' of purifying the common. In other words, voluntary cooperation for the group good is largely fictitious. But this is not the whole story: most of us are certainly prepared to sacrifice ourselves for our immediate family, and often for a wider group of our intimates, even if we are not related to them. T H Huxley wrote many years ago that the greatest restrainer of the anti-social tendencies of men is 'fear not of law, but of the opinion of their fellows' (Huxley, 1974).

6. Self-interest gives us three options for our environmental concern: firstly, let everyone cooperate in cleaning up litter, observing the speed limit, giving up using aerosols containing fluorocarbons, except me; in other words, pure selfishness. Secondly, there is pure altruism — to involve myself in these activities, even if no one else does. Thirdly, cooperation — provided everyone does. It is the third option which is the one consistent with down-to-earth practical politics (Hirsch, 1977). But it is usually against human nature to expect a consensus without some intervention by authority. This is where the public interest comes in.

Public Interest

7. The public interest is not a simple extension of individual self-interest: trawlers largely destroyed the North Sea herring stock by pursuing their self-interest, although, if the fishing industry had disciplined itself, a sustainable catch rate could have been achieved; if everyone visits nature reserves, the reserves become largely valueless; if everyone moves out of the city, the suburbs lose the qualities that attracted people in the first place; and so on. Unfortunately, there is no way to deduce the real public interest from the discordant preferences of individuals; the identification of public

interest becomes a matter of political judgement. So a dispute as to what is the public interest about (say) energy policy, or water pollution, or the preservation of wilderness is resolved by bargaining and compromise between adversaries arguing from different sets of values. In fact, decision makers are forced to balance objective fact with public perception of the problem, as suggested at the end of Chapter 3 of this report.

Posterity's Interest

8. Environmental decisions differ from technological decisions in often having permanent effects. Once a species is extinct, no wishful thinking can resurrect it; once a hill is quarried away, cosmetic landscaping can only produce a shadow of the original; once the tropical rain forest is cleared, the ground is an eroding disaster, not a fertile prairie. Some activities are less catastrophic: natural ecosystems have a remarkable resilience for recovery, although the final state is often different from the first. It is sometimes possible to determine the long-term consequences of decision, although it needs remembering that prophets of doom have a better record of being proved right than the Utopian optimists, from Thomas More and Francis Bacon on. In taking decisions we can rarely do more than consider that they may affect many future generations, but it is still important to bear this in mind.

Nature's Interest

9. Finally, we come to the most difficult consideration, the interests of nature itself. This is where ecocentrists concentrate their enthusiasms, but, as we have seen, their arguments are not persuasive to those concerned with humanity's future on the planet: to protect birds and bees seems to contribute little to helping the homeless, the hungry, the under-privileged. Yet it is here that we come full circle in our insistence that humanity is both apart from nature and a part of it, and that these two aspects of humanity's relationship to the world are logically or operationally separated only at the risk of degrading the whole. And it is here that we come back to the WCS, with its emphasis that sustainable human existence and dependence rely on a responsible concern for conservation and the management of the natural world. Nature exists, whether or not humanity is around to wonder at or harm it; clearly we must accept that it has its own interests.

10. In his examination of the way to protect nature's interest, Ashby (1976) suggests that we should seek to value ecological and evolutionary *processes* as distinct from the *ends* of these processes. He thus avoids getting drawn into the preservationist situation of the more extreme biocentrists who are, as we have seen, concerned almost exclusively with ends. He reaches this

conclusion by starting from the premise that we are only too aware that nature is in increasingly short supply, and will have to be rationed unless we are careful. This is exactly the point where the WCS begins. However (Ashby continues), 'man uses the environment not only to satisfy his material needs; he depends upon it for aesthetic satisfaction. Thoreau wanted to preserve the wilderness so that he could have wilderness and tranquillity, not for the sake of the wilderness but for himself . . . [However] any man-centred approach puts the environment at risk, for it is essentially a utilitarian approach. If it suited man to exploit nature for strip mining, deforestation, pollution, recreation, there would be no forbidding ethic to prevent him from doing so. The decision would be solely a matter of expediency, of cost benefit analysis. The argument that to over-exploit the environment is to kill the goose that lays the golden eggs is a sound argument, and in practical politics it is often an effective one to use. But it is not an argument which supports the interests of nature against those of man. And it's a shaky argument for conservationists to use, for they profess to be interested in nature for nature's sake, not for the sake of man; in the goose for its own sake, not just for its golden eggs'.

11. In his search for an ethic of nature which is not human-centred, Ashby compares the process of evolution to the playing of a Beethoven sonata: 'You don't play it toward any goal. What matters, what is intrinsically valuable, is the experience of playing it. Its intrinsic worth does not reside in the printed marks on the page. The printed marks could (as Einstein said) be transformed into a diagram of air pressure curves. This would be a rationally faithful way to express them, but it wouldn't convey what Beethoven intended to convey. Only the process of playing the music can do that . . . [For nature] one practicable rule of thumb would be to apply to the treatment of natural objects criteria similar to those we apply to the treatment of objects created by man. To permit a river to be damaged by pollution would be the same kind of negligence as to permit a Renaissance mural to fall into disrepair. In the course of evolution some species will anyway become extinct; to hasten their extinction by wanton hunting or by unnecessarily depriving them of their natural habitats (as happens when wetlands are drained) would be the same kind of insensitivity as to pull down, without good reason, a mediaeval church. This argument does not rest on such concepts as beauty (that is a man-centred value), nor does it imply a divine immanence pervading nature (that would be a resort to pantheism); though both of these concepts are useful adjuncts to an environmental ethic. In other words, in our examination of the man/nature link, we ought to make sure we respect the "nature" end of it as much as the "man" end of it' (Ashby, 1976).

The Need for Wilderness

12. At this point, we have to digress to consider the concept of wilderness, which is clearly part of 'nature's

interest'. Any disturbance of the environment is likely to be inimical to the animals and plants adapted to it. This is an aspect often ignored by writers who claim that man has a 'need for wilderness'.

13. The problem with wilderness is that the word has changed its meaning and implications several times; perhaps it is simplest to regard it as a term used for the 'purest' form of the environment.

14. Max Nicholson (1981) has traced the development of different words (and hence concepts) that have been used for the environment. At the beginning of the Renaissance, people's eyes opened to their surroundings and conditions of life and the word 'nature' began to be used to distinguish that which people do not create from that which they do, leading to 'natural history' for the study of animals and plants and of what came to be called their 'habitats'. At this time, the Dutch tradition of 'landscape' painting reinforced the Graeco-Roman ideal of order. Mountains and wilderness were no place for ordinary men and women: they were the home of the gods, and of wild beasts; they were dangerous and frightening. Landscape meant a managed countryside, and led great landowners to embark on major projects to make countryside more 'picturesque', another eighteenth century word. This was followed somewhat later by 'scenery' to accommodate the emerging appreciation of such wild and romantic subjects as mountains, hitherto dismissed as 'horrid' since they were a betrayal of such order and harmony as humanity was entitled to expect from God's creation. (The Derbyshire Peak was described by Charles Cotton in 1681 as: 'A country so deformed, the traveller would swear these parts Nature's pudenda were'. Forty years later, Daniel Defoe wrote about the Lake District: 'a country eminent for being the wildest, most barren and frightful of any that I have passed over in England, or even in Wales; the wet west side is hounded by a chain of almost impassable mountains, called Fells'. Huxley (1974) has cut through the jargon and emotion surrounding the idea of wilderness. He affirms that its definition involves a 'human egocentric purpose', although wilderness *per se* is 'a valid objective both for debate and as a tool in land-use'. The irony about wilderness in the UK is that threats to it have a direct relationship to accessibility: UK wilderness is an aesthetic aim, not a real possibility.)

15. In the nineteenth century the word 'ecology' was coined and in 1875 came the first use of the word 'biosphere', in German. So, science met naturistic romanticism, and begat wilderness; for example, Darling (1970) used scientific language to express a biocentric sentiment: 'The ecologist sees the decline of a great natural buffer of wilderness as an element in our danger. Natural wilderness is a factor for world stability, not some remote place inimical to the human being. . . Wilderness is not remote or indifferent, but an active agent in maintaining a half-stable world, though the cooperation is unconscious'.

16. The cult of wilderness is centred in the United States. As the real frontier of civilisation has retreated before easy travel, agricultural technology, and Indian treaties, it has been replaced with a romantic boundary around land where humans are subservient to untamed nature. Such current enthusiasms would have been anathema to the original New England settlers who saw their new country as 'a hideous and desolate wilderness, full of wild beasts and wild men'. Nowadays, the wilderness is a symbol of purity, formally recognised in the Wilderness Act of 1964, defining areas 'where the earth and its community of life are untrammelled by man, where man himself is a visitor who does not remain'.

17. But what does this imply? To quote Darling (1970) again, 'The wilderness does not exist for our recreation or delectation. There is something we gain from the great function of being with the oceans, part of the guardianship of the world in which we have so recently become denizens'. Does this have any meaning? The UK possesses no region which has not been modified by humans; the WCS urges that the Scottish Highlands should be a priority protected area, but even this is an artificially created wet desert.

18. Wilderness has come to be appreciated; the important question in the present context of increasing pressure on land is whether there is any basic psychological need for it. J S Mill believed that: 'it is not good for man to be kept perforce . . . in the presence of his species . . . A world from which solitude is extirpated is a very poor ideal'. More recent interpretations see a much more complicated situation, with a conflict between the acceptance of familiar neighbours (and a fear of strange people) and a need for a private (personal) territory, whilst needing places for communal meeting and play (Eibl-Eiblesfeldt, personal communication). In other words, anonymity is both desired and abhorred; we seek space, but are afraid of what we may meet in it. There has been considerable North American interest in the therapeutic effects of wilderness, and there are many case histories of people who have overcome fears and achieved a feeling of controlling their own destiny through 'wilderness experiences'. As yet, we do not know whether such experiences are necessary for all, or whether they are merely important for some people.

19. Wilderness is a beautiful ideal, but it can be too naïvely rationalised. The experience of Thor Heyerdahl (of *Kon Tiki* and *Ra* fame) is instructive. As a young man he was oppressed by the tensions of city living, and took his bride to find an unpolluted arcadia on a South Pacific island. They lived miserably there for about a year before returning home. Back in Norway, Heyerdahl wrote: 'There is no Paradise to be found on earth today. There are people living in great cities who are far happier than the majority of those in the South Seas. Happiness comes from within: we realise that now . . . It is in his mind and way of life that man may find his Paradise, the ability to perceive the true values of life, which are far removed from property and riches, or from power and renown'. René Dubos expressed a similar sentiment some years later in *Life* magazine:

'The problem of the environment involves the salvation and enhancement of those positive values which man uses to develop his humanness. It involves, ultimately, a social organisation in which each person has much freedom in selecting the stage on which to act his life: a peaceful village green, the banks of a river, the exciting plaza of a great city. Survival is not enough. Seeing the Milky Way, experiencing the fragrance of spring and observing other forms of life continue to play an immense role in the development of humanness. Man can use many different aspects of reality to make his life, not by imposing himself as a conqueror on nature but by participating . . . Otherwise man may be doomed to survive as something less than human'.

The Quality of Life

20. If we accept that 'wilderness' is a human aim rather than an inherent property of nature, it does not help us in understanding the interest we have in nature. Indeed, the above discussion shows that our interest in wilderness is really self-interest — perhaps with a little public interest thrown in for good measure.

21. Can we define the object of the WCS as anything more than human survival? Certainly, the differing aspirations of environmentalists in developed and developing countries are united in wanting more than this. Most commonly, environmental concern is expressed as an aim for a better quality of life. How can we define 'quality of life'? In the UK it is conventionally equated with a raised standard of living and hence with earnings, and this attitude is reflected in international league tables of average income per person, or some such statistic. This is not the place to discuss the relationship between quality of life and quantity of possessions: it is clear that, on the one hand, everyone needs a minimum of food, access to health care, freedom from oppression, etc, but on the other hand, an abundance of TV sets, motor cars, motorways, washing machines, leisure, etc, add little to happiness, or freedom from stress, etc. Too often we assume that our expectations (of bigger houses and meals, etc) are the same thing as quality of life. Advertising — both direct and covert comparison with others — produces a desire for material benefit unrelated to real satisfaction. 'Quality of life' is a notion linked to expectation engendered by social and cultural milieu. Because of its individualistic content, the idea often produces conflict. It seems likely that usefulness to the community and to others (ie sensible employment) may be a more valid indicator of something legitimate called quality of life (McIntyre, personal communication).

22. Is this diagnosis glib? Perhaps. But it is certainly facile to identify quality of life with either material possessions or some measure of environmental purity. Quality of life involves a self-respect which one can justify to oneself, and acceptance (or esteem) by one's peers. It is dependent on neither internal capacity nor external surroundings but on the relationship between them. In other words, we come once again to a need for a full understanding of the humans/nature relationship. It is at this point that the interests of self, public prosperity, and nature meet. Quality of life is something to be desired by and for everyone, but it is to be sought in the dynamic and varying interplay of humanity and nature. Here is the source of any real environmental ethic.

References

ASHBY, E. 1978. Reconciling man with the environment. London, Oxford University Press.

BARBOUR, I G. 1972. Earth might be fair. Englewood Cliffs, NJ, Prentice-Hall.

DARLING, F F. 1970. Wilderness and plenty. London, British Broadcasting Corporation.

HARDIN, G. 1968. The tragedy of the Commons. *Science, NY*, *162*, 1243-1248.

HIRSCH, F. 1977. Social limits to growth. London, Routledge and Kegan Paul.

HUXLEY, T. 1974. Wilderness. In Conservation in practice, 361-374. Warren, A. and Goldsmith, F B. (editors). London, Wiley.

KOZLOVSKY, D G. 1974. An ecological and evolutionary ethic. Englewood Cliffs, NJ, Prentice-Hall.

NICHOLSON, E M. 1981. Whose environment? Address given at the Athenaeum Club, London.

PASSMORE, J. 1974. Man's responsibility for nature. London, Duckworth.

REGAN, T. 1981. The nature and possibility of an environmental ethic. *Environmental Ethics*, *3*, 19-34.

SCHUMACHER, E F. 1973. Small is beautiful. London, Abacus.

SCHUMACHER, E F. 1974. The age of plenty. Edinburgh, St Andrew Press.

White, L. 1967. The historic roots of our ecologic crisis. *Science, NY*, *155*, 1204-1207.

CHAPTER 7

RECOMMENDATIONS

Introduction

It is insufficient merely to know that human activity can cause permanent harm to the environment and thence to humanity (since we are dependent on our environment for both inorganic and organic resources). Knowledge must lead to action; intellectual understanding is useless unless linked to moral commitment. It is this commitment to action which is the only way in which the aims of the WCS can be achieved (Chapter 1, paragraph 2 of this report, p 411). Unless we can achieve a widely accepted environmental ethic, the WCS will be, at best, only partially implemented.

Unfortunately, the utilitarian argument of the WCS (that human survival depends on joining in international cooperation on the environment) is defective: my concern is to do what is best for me, and it takes a great deal to persuade me to be wholly altruistic in my actions (Chapter 1, paragraph 11, p 413). This report is concerned to examine how commitment to the WCS aims can be achieved, and it seems clear that the way forward is to adopt neither the WCS position that humanity is a potentially efficient manager of nature (Chapter 1, paragraphs 8 and 9, page 412), nor the traditional conservationist position that humanity is a disastrous interloper in the world, with its future dependent on minimising its influence. In other words, we must accept that we are both apart from and a part of nature (Chapter 2, paragraph 3, p 415); we cannot afford the lazy way out of a moral dilemma through mystical ecocentricity or reductionist technocracy (Chapter 2, paragraphs 9 to 12, pp 416 - 417). The essential base to an acceptable environmental ethic is a proper understanding of the humans/nature relationship.

In analysing the humans/nature relationship, we are faced with a series of interactions (the most important being with population numbers, use of resources, and how we regard environment risks: Chapter 3 of this report) in a dynamic situation, so that different factors seem to be important at different times (Chapter 4 of this report). It is false to think that we can or will develop an ethic by translating our humans/nature relationship into a mystical, legal or (worse) an economic equation (Chapter 5 of this report). We must take these attempts at solution into consideration, but none of them is sufficient by itself.

Is the search for an environmental ethic anything more than intellectual narcissism? We believe so, and in Chapter 6 of this report we described how politicians and others concerned with environmental decision making must take into account the potential conflict of interest between self, public, posterity, and nature. It is difficult to define nature's interest without lapsing into the argument that nature exists for humanity; the best way of viewing it is simply as one end of the humans/nature link (Chapter 6, paragraphs 9 to 11, page 431). This means that 'humans' and 'nature' almost inevitably exist in tension with one another, with posterity and public interest affecting the way this tension is worked out. For example, industrialists may pour all their wastes into a convenient river and make themselves a public nuisance to others as well as making the river useless for drinking, fishing, or amenity for future generations, but they gain cheap disposal of material they do not want. However, they may be prevailed upon to purify their waste by statutory control, particularly if their competitors are subject to the same constraint, so that the river is not polluted, their firms are not harmed, and both posterity and public benefit. Law in this way has the support of all, and properly applied (as was smoke pollution in Britain by the Alkali Inspectorate, despite criticisms that the Inspectorate was impotent and conniving: Ashby and Anderson, 1981) can lead to a positive and progressive attitude to the environment.

Conflict and Vested Interest

This report affirms that our environment must be a fundamental concern to the present and posterity. It is now the time to spell out some of the presumptions which ought to become part of our way of thinking and hence be expressed in the solutions to our problems. These recommendations can only be tentative at this stage. But they are based on the assumption that:

(a) The WCS cannot be successfully fulfilled unless practical programmes of action in each major relevant field are adequately complemented by drives to transform the outdated beliefs, attitudes and practices which underlie the recent trends giving rise to the urgent need for such a Strategy.

(b) Such drives are timely in view of the growing disillusionment with traditional creeds, political convictions, institutions, policies and methods, and the worldwide reaction towards something more relevant and satisfying.

(c) The devoted adherents of conservation will not be satisfied to maintain their loyalties and efforts unless they are given clear, realistic, constructive guidance on what they themselves can do towards putting things right.

Recommendation 1

There should be a refusal to accept reasoning which leads to conclusions directly hostile to natural processes, in particular: assumptions which view humans as conquerors of nature, or having a divine mission to subjugate nature; programmes overtly or covertly attacking parts of the biosphere in scientifically unsound attempts to redress previous human interferences, eg indiscriminate use of toxic chemicals on land.

Recommendation 2

There should be active discouragement of irresponsible attitudes, which may be directly hostile to nature but assume its expendability or unimportance. In particular:

(a) Pursuing material gain or 'development' at the expense of careless or cynical disregard of the environment by local destruction, damage, pollution or spoliation, or by releasing harmful substances capable of inflicting wider deterioration.

(b) Using vehicles or other equipment which cause excessive or unnecessary damage to soils, vegetation or wildlife.

(c) Misrepresentation of the pleasures of scenery or wildlife to advertise unconnected products such as cigarettes or motor cycles.

(d) The design, manufacture or distribution of products and packaging which add to litter and pollution.

(e) The adoption of technology or other practices incompatible with the best economy of resources and built-in obsolescence or transitory fashion.

Recommendation 3

There should be positive encouragement of values and attitudes which increase respect and consideration for nature, and an appreciation of humanity's role and responsibilities towards it, such as:

(a) Acceptance of recycled materials, and that the durability of goods generally needs to be increased.

(b) An emphasis on teaching which recognises humanity's stewardship towards the natural world.

(c) An emphasis on the value of the individual and posterity; and a responsibility to follow courses to correct the present trend towards feckless multiplication.

(d) Active environmental education.

(e) Steps to secure a prominent role for environmental conservation in the impending expansion of information and entertainment, based on electronic advances.

Recommendation 4

There should be new patterns of employment, possibly involving work-sharing, extended education, creative leisure, etc.

Recommendation 5

There should be reduced centralisation and politicisation of public affairs.

Recommendation 6

There should be abatement of the pressures for rushed change in favour of more gradual and participatory processes, with increased explanation to all concerned.

Recommendation 7

There should be enhanced education for capability and adaptation through life, recognising that human ignorance is a major cause of poverty, injustice and environmental misuse.

Recommendation 8

Our overseas responsibilities require that:

(a) Government and public alike must enforce and monitor trade in all non-domestic species and their products, especially endangered species.

(b) We should not export our pollution or environmentally harmful technologies.

(c) We have a responsibility to developing countries.

Clearly, there are occasions when an industrial or agricultural practice (eg tree-felling or forest planting, reclaiming wetlands, development of nuclear power stations, or industrial emissions) conflict with the interests of individuals or society. We believe that three practical steps are possible:

Recommendation 9

The adversarious element in our conflict should be reduced and be replaced with discussion, or, in modern jargon, 'open-ended dialogue'.

Pressure and vested interest groups are useful in gathering and presenting information, but there is an increasing tendency for such groups to confront rather than talk with each other. Furthermore, confidence in the person or body that has to make the eventual decision about any conflict is weakened if the affair is thought to be determined by industrial bullying or (to a lesser extent) by emotional stridency. There has been an attempt in Britain to reduce this danger by moving towards massive public inquiries (as in the Windscale nuclear processing inquiry of 1977). The formal public posturing in such events is unenlightening; for justice to be done and known to be done it may be better for much of the argument in such cases to be conducted in private. So long as all interested parties were involved, this would enable controversial data to be challenged without embarrassment.

Pressure groups exist to pursue particular points of view and thus tend to be selective in their judgement of relevant data. Most people have difficulty in making informed decisions (which is the subject of this report) because of their lack of education.

Recommendation 10

Independent seminars on major issues (such as motorway proposals, mining applications, nuclear power or forestry developments) could help more of the un-committed. This is a function which could be carried out by institutes of higher education. For example, extra-mural classes held by the Universities of Leicester, Nottingham and Loughborough might have analysed the Vale of Belvoir mining proposal. Perhaps those with class certificates could be given preference in formal inquiries! such initiatives would need ear-marked — presumably government — funds.

Recommendation 11
There should be a requirement for the provision of relevant data and documents, and provision for financial support for non-governmental bodies involved in discussion.

If non-governmental agencies are seen to be more involved in the making of decisions this will increase their status, and hence probably support, and reduce the need to embrace extreme views in order to gain publicity.

Ashby (1980) has described a brave and successful exercise by the Californian San Diego Gas and Electric Company on these lines. They had to decide on a site for a new power station, and began by calling a general meeting of interested parties to involve local people. The company persuaded the latter to set up a committee, which they financed and left to get on with the work of choosing a site. The committee toured the area, held hearings (for which experts were provided), and came up with a recommendation of a site which the company adopted. The Teesdale saga (Chapter 1, paragraph 8 of this report, p 412) also achieved a generally acceptable solution, but this was in spite of adversarial argument, not because of it.

Implicit in the procedure of 'adversaries' talking with each other and revealing data to each other, is that environmental decisions will become micro-decisions rather than mega-decisions. This will not remove the need for decisions about major principles (for example, whether to proceed with the development of a nuclear power industry, and which technology to adopt for this), but it will reduce the likelihood of major conflicts. These hopes may be too sanguine. After all, many government industries have advisory panels with a wide membership which can be totally ineffective. Nevertheless, the need for automatic dialogue rather than automatic dispute comes from first principles and should be encouraged whenever and however possible.

International Considerations

The European Economic Community (EEC) was set up for trading purposes. In 1972, the Heads of States of the Community (before Britain joined) decided that: 'economic expansion is not an end in itself: its first aim should be to enable disparities in living conditions to be reduced ... It should result in an improvement in the quality of life [sic] as well as standards of living. As befits the genius of Europe, particular attention will be given to intangible values and to protecting the environment so that progress may really be put at the service of mankind' (EEC, 1972). This led to a Declaration on the Environment in November 1973, which has been the basis of the EEC's policy ever since. In practice, this has led to a policy of unison, not harmony: an attempt to impose uniformity from the north of Scotland to the south of Greece. It is a policy basically different from British practice where several centuries of evolution have led to impracticable ideas being eliminated, utopian aspirations discarded, and the policies which have survived being those which have been proved to work.

These comments are not intended to assert that the British are environmental paragons or to denigrate the need for a European environmental policy. There are important by-products of EEC policy, such as that under the Lomé II Convention adopted in 1979, whereby environmental needs have to be taken into account in assessing aid projects to some 60 African, Caribbean and Pacific countries (House of Lords, 1980). This is a very practical spur to a reasonable implementation of the WCS. The point to be made is that the EEC's policy is a narrowly legal one. While it is dangerous to suggest that we in the UK have an ideal environmental practice, since there are plenty of evidences that there are many weaknesses in our system, nonetheless, our approach to environmental matters is more closely in accord with the realities of the humans/nature link than more recent and arbitrary practices. Barbara Ward makes the point very clearly in her Progress for a Small Planet (1979), that Britain has been concerned with improving her own environment for a very long time now, and the message for other nations very often should be: 'follow me and try to avoid the mistakes I have made'. Therefore:

Recommendation 12
From every point of view, we urge that British precedent and practice should become generally accepted within EEC policy.

Postscript: A Practical Ethic

The art of political leadership is to make proposals that are ahead, but only just ahead, of public opinion and to time political action in such a way that it makes explicit what is already becoming implicit in the values held by the more articulate members of society. As far as environmental values are concerned, there can be no doubt at all that they have changed for the better in many ways over the past few decades. Much of the credit for this must go to the pressure on Government exerted by both statutory and non-governmental organisations (Nature Conservancy Council; Countryside Commission; Friends of the Earth; World Wildlife Fund; etc), and the fortuitous occurrence of events like the wrecking of the Torrey Canyon which stimulate public opinion. British public opinion is willing to respond to sensible leadership in environmental matters and Parliament is now more ready to pass altruistic legislation than probably ever before.

The worry and danger now is not the assent we give to environmental controls, but the changing standards affecting our own behaviour and that of others: our values have changed in a desirable direction, but the standards by which we translate those values into behaviour have slipped unpleasantly. No longer do we accept a personal responsibility towards society; we are tending towards anarchy under a spurious claim to freedom. The days are long gone when the personal example of an ordinary man and woman could radically affect the environment. My behaviour in leaving litter or speeding or using non-recycled paper may be sad, but it is not disastrous. What is potentially disastrous is when this attitude infects industries or other groups, so they believe that they can get away with anti-social behaviour. Too often they can. This is the problem and the 'tragedy of the commons' all over again (Chapter 6, paragraphs 4 to 6 of this report, page 430). Therein lies the main threat to an ethic which could put life into the WCS, and change the fate of the world.

References

ASHBY, E. 1980. What price the Furbish lousewort? *Environmental Science and Technology, 14*, 1176-1181.

ASHBY, E and ANDERSON, M. 1981. The politics of clean air. Oxford, Clarendon Press.

EUROPEAN ECONOMIC COMMUNITY HEADS OF STATE. 1972. Declaration of the Council of European Communities on the Programme of action of the European Committees on the Environment. *Official Journal, 16, C-112 for 20 December 1973.*

HOUSE OF LORDS. 1980. Select Committee report on EEC environment policy session 1979-80. Fifth report. London, HMSO.

CHAPTER 8

THE PRACTITIONERS' DEBATE

Introduction

1. The practitioners' debate ran from December 1982 to February 1983. During that time, a large number of written commentaries were received and there were a number of seminars at which this report was discussed. All of these were most interesting in their content and, as a result, some minor changes have been made to the recommendations where it seemed appropriate. Many people criticised the report; some looked at it from the human point of view and found it weak; others found it lacking because it regards humanity as a manager of nature. The existence of this disagreement encourages me to think that the argument of the report is on the right lines.

2. The danger of writing about ethics is that those who have to make decisions about conservation do not want to bother about what they regard as ineffectual academic waffle, while philosophers are unimpressed by an ethic unrelated to their academic rigour. Let us be clear that this report is simply about the factors and hindrances to commitment for conservation. To explore this it has been necessary to parody 'technocentrists' and 'ecocentrists'; it has been necessary to touch on economic, philosophical and psychological issues, but there has been no intention to ridicule or trespass on other specialities: the sole aim is to produce intelligent and responsible action. The WCS argues forcefully and cogently that we need to make changes in the way we use resources, but only in terms of enlightened self-interest. This report spells out some of the presumptions which need to become part of our way of thinking when we face up to conservation, and thus be expressed in our solution to environmental problems.

Where Now?

3. This report is addressed to all who have to make decisions about environmental matters. Politicians at both the national and the local level make decisions which may affect many people, but those who advise politicians or who pollute (or not) their own back yard also need to have their thinking moulded by the considerations listed in these pages if our world is to continue in anything approaching a healthy state.

4. The WCS is concerned with continuance and sustainability. Our environmental attitudes and decisions affect the far-distant future as much as next week. In Chapter 6, paragraph 8 of this report, p 431, we spoke of the need to consider 'posterity's interest': if we are going to take the WCS seriously we cannot avoid doing this.

5. Traditionally, the recognition of being part of nature has meant an acceptance that we are unable to control our surroundings; the ability to control our environment has meant a progressive insulation for us and has thus set us apart from nature. However, being part of nature does not imply subservience, nor does being apart from nature necessarily mean unthinking management. Biologically, socially and culturally we are both a part of and apart from nature, and, however difficult we find this idea, we shall never achieve a harmony of the self, public, posterity and nature's interest until we accept it.

6. The way decisions are made is a study for psychologists. All we can set out here are the factors that we should bear in mind in deciding. As far as the environment is concerned, we must remember that we are at the same time both part of nature and apart from it, and that we must temper our judgement with the interest of ourselves, our neighbours, posterity and of nature. If we can do that, we can indeed claim to have an environmental ethic.

7. Human response is at the heart of response to WCS aims. In *The Common Ground*, a book commissioned by the Nature Conservancy Council to review their own practices, Richard Mabey (1980) comments that the WCS: 'is the first major international policy statement to affirm the human importance of conservation . . . On the surface the problems of conservation present themselves as practical ones: how to manage woods so that they produce timber at the same time as sustaining wildlife, which areas of countryside are best used as farmland and which as nature reserves. Yet underneath there are more fundamental and less easily resolved conflicts of values — about who can legitimately be said to 'own' natural resources, about the rights of humans and animals, about the relative importance of present livelihoods and past traditions — conflicts which involve deeply held personal beliefs and meanings'. The WCS will be a dead letter unless these underlying conflicts are faced and solved. This report is about doing this.

Reference

MABEY, R. 1980. The common ground. London, Hutchinson.

PART 7
EDUCATION

Education for Commitment
Building Support in Society for
Conservation and Development

A report by John D Baines

Acknowledgements

As well as the Review Group members, many individuals and groups have contributed their ideas to this paper.

Many are aware of their contribution, because the paper represents an accumulation of ideas, information and experiences relating to the environment acquired over many years. Thanks are due to them all. The following do, however, deserve special acknowledgement.

R Booth; Dr C Gayford, Reading University Department of Education; S Sterling, Council for Environmental Education; R Mabey; members of the CEE Development and Planning Group; members of the CEE Schools Advisory Group for Environmental Education; members of the Scottish Environmental Education Committee; authors of other parts of this book.

Chairman's Introduction

I imagine I was asked to chair the environmental education group as I had served as an education spokesman in the House of Lords and had played a small part in helping Lord Melchett when he was leading for the Opposition during the Wildlife and Countryside Act's long passage through the House of Lords. I was very pleased to extend my own education in this field by listening to the experts from many different disciplines who were good enough to serve on the Education Review Group and share their wide experience and ideas. I should like to thank them all. Even though we never had a full attendance at any of our four meetings, members have been visited by John Baines, the author of this report, and he has had the opportunity to talk with them and make use of their varied gifts and knowledge in a number of fields. We needed advice not only from those in the world of formal education, but also from those with ideas on how to influence and bring about changes in attitudes and make the entire population — young, middle aged, and old — aware of the environment in which they lived, and of the harm they could do to it and to future plant, animal, and even human life, if they were ignorant or careless.

We wanted it to be clear what environmental education was, and were anxious to be able not only to advise on its content but also to make recommendations on how to get the message across. Why, for instance, did some campaigns like Save the Whale — or grey seals — have an impact on the public and others, like Keep Britain Tidy, have only a minimal impact? Those working in journalism, radio and TV were very important to us in suggesting ways of projecting ideas and the best means of expression. The World Conservation Strategy will get nowhere unless the message is sent out in a language that is easy to read and clear for all to understand. I do not think we have solved all the problems but I hope that some of our recommendations, aimed at a wide range of sectors, will be acceptable and may achieve success, some in the short-, and some in the longer-term.

Lady David
February 1983

CHAPTER 1

INTRODUCTION

1. 'A world strategy for the conservation of Earth's living resources is needed now because human activities are progressively reducing the planet's life-supporting capacity. The combined destructive impacts of a poor majority struggling to stay alive and an affluent minority consuming most of the world's resources are undermining the very means by which all people can survive and flourish' (IUCN, 1980).

2. The achievement of the conservation objectives described in the World Conservation Strategy (WCS) is important for everyone, whether they live in developed or developing countries. While the most pressing conservation issues differ from country to country, the need for all citizens to live in harmony with the rest of the natural world is very urgent. The Strategy recognises that, if conservation objectives are to be achieved, entire societies must transform their behaviour towards the biosphere. This requires the adoption of a 'new ethic', one that embraces plants and animals as well as people. It is the task of education to foster or reinforce attitudes and behaviour compatible with this new ethic.

3. The Strategy identifies those obstacles that education is most suited to help overcome, and recommends an education strategy to complement other activities that are considered essential if the conservation objectives are to be achieved. Fundamental requirements include:

   (a) Building support for conservation. Ultimately, the environment is being degraded because people do not recognise that it is in their best interests not to damage it.
   (b) Increasing public participation in conservation/development decisions.
   (c) Substantially expanding environmental education activities at all levels of the formal and non-formal education sectors. These programmes should raise the general level of understanding of the way environmental systems operate, as well as focus on the most urgent environmental issues of individual countries. They should show the importance of linking conservation and development objectives.
   (d) Developing environmental education programmes for specific target groups. The most important ones are: (i) legislators and administrators; (ii) those with responsibilities in development associated with industry, commerce, farming, forestry and fishing; (iii) professional bodies and special interest groups; (iv) communities most affected by conservation and development activities; (v) lecturers, teachers, students and school children.

4. This report is aimed at those with responsibility for education programmes and activities, and those who are able to influence them. It does not restrict its attention to those in the formal educated sector, but includes all those whose activities may, in a wide sense, be regarded as educational, including advertisers, journalists, writers, etc.

5. The report reflects the emphasis of WCS on human use of living resources. However, it recognises that, in the UK, 80 per cent of the population is urban-based and that for the majority of UK citizens environmental education programmes will begin with the urban environment. It also recognises that environmental education relates to the total environment and that it is concerned with more than environmental issues. However, the report has concentrated on those areas of environmental education that are most relevant to achieving the aims of WCS in a UK context.

6. The report has not restricted its recommendations only to schools or the formal education sector as a whole. Education is a lifelong process and there are recommendations addressed to the formal and non-formal education processes, youth and adult education sectors.

7. Education is sometimes equated with the provision of information. While information can be one of the raw materials for an education programme, successful environmental education should provide a wide range of environmental and educational experiences. Information in educational programmes should provide people with the opportunity to understand the social, political, economic and ecological factors involved in human use of the environment. It is hoped that this report will go some way towards bringing together the aims of conservationists, developers, educationists and others in the pursuits of conservation for development.

8. Finally, the report should be seen as suggesting a framework for future action. It suggests a range of opportunities, and it is hoped that people will seize on these and derive support for their educational activities

from the report. However, it does not attempt to dictate precisely the content or methods of an environmental education programme in support of a conservation and development programme for the UK.

References

IUCN. 1980. World conservation strategy. Living resource conservation for sustainable development. Gland.

CHAPTER 2
THE NATURE OF ENVIRONMENTAL EDUCATION

Introduction

1. The International Union for the Conservation of Nature and Natural Resources (IUCN, 1970) and The United Nations Environment Programme (UNEP, 1978) have made a major contribution to the evolution of an internationally accepted conceptual, methodological and information framework for environmental education. Within this framework a great variety of programmes has developed relating to particular needs.

2. A widely accepted definition of environmental education was adopted by IUCN at a conference in Nevada in 1970. It states: 'Environmental Education is the process of recognising values and clarifying concepts in order to develop skills and attitudes necessary to understand and appreciate the interrelatedness among people, their culture and their biophysical surroundings. Environmental Education also entails practice in decision making and self-formation of a code of behaviour about issues concerning environmental quality'. This was presented more neatly in a report by HM Inspectors of Schools for the Scottish Education Department, 1974. 'The ultimate aims of environmental education are the creation of responsible attitudes and the development of an environmental ethic.'

3. The definitions outline the major features of environmental education; it is concerned with the development of caring values and attitudes towards the environment; it promotes understanding of the environment and environmental issues; it relates to the natural and artificial environments, living and non-living resources; it entails participation in decision making processes; and it advocates the acceptance of life styles compatible with environmental conservation.

The Aims of Environmental Education

4. Living resource issues, the main concern of the WCS, clearly fall within the remit of environmental education. It seeks to promote those concepts and values that will assist humans to achieve development and conservation objectives, that is, the maintenance of an environment which is productive and pleasant to live in for present and future generations. It also recognises that the acquired skills, knowledge and attitudes need to be translated into practical activities that will ensure wise management of the living resources. Hence, environmental education's ultimate objective is to develop among humans the will and ability to act as responsible stewards of the environment, be it natural, partly modified or totally artificially created. Environmental educational programmes should have the following aims. They should:

(a) create *sensitivity to* and *awareness of* the total environment;

(b) help develop a basic *understanding* of the total environment and the interrelationships between humans and the environment, so that they may more easily appreciate why conservation is fundamental to human survival and well being;

(c) help develop the *skills* to investigate the environment and to identify and solve actual and potential environmental problems;

(d) promote the acquisition of *strong feelings of concern* for the environment;

(e) help people identify *alternative approaches* and make *informed decisions* about the environment based on all the relevant factors — ecological, political, economic, social and aesthetic;

(f) motivate people to *participate actively* in environmental improvement and protection and provide people with opportunities to be actively involved in working towards the resolution of environmental problems;

(g) help people *appreciate* and *enjoy* their environment.

A Broad Approach

5. Such aims cannot be achieved through any one existing academic discipline or any one area of education. Neither will they be achieved by relying upon the introduction of a new academic discipline. Rather, environmental education seeks to weave its objectives into all educational processes, so that care for the environment becomes as much a part of human life as caring for oneself.

6. The environmental approach to education requires the integration of three basic features:

(a) Education *in* the environment. The environment provides a resource for the acquisition of relevant knowledge and skills, the development of feelings of concern for and appreciation of the environment, and the opportunity to participate in practical activities in the environment.

(b) Education *about* the environment. Knowledge about environmental systems is essential for informed debate about how humans should use the environment. It includes learning about the various social, economic and political factors that influence decisions about its use.

(c) Education *for* the environment. This seeks to develop those values and attitudes that lead to the adoption of a personal code of conduct that ensures that decisions and actions support conservation objectives.

An Issues-Based Approach

7. Environmental education requires the study of real environmental issues. However, the issues highlighted in the WCS are often beyond the immediate experience of people in the UK. Hence, the study of issues should be part of a structured and progressive educational programme, appropriate to the particular age group. They should attempt to widen horizons progressively and increase sensitivity, understanding and depth of knowledge of the environment. For the majority of people in the UK, the immediate environmental issues will be domestic and urban ones, and they will provide the starting point, even though they may seem to have little relevance to living resource issues. Implied in this recommendation for an issue-based approach is the requirement that education programmes should give practice in solving problems and encourage participation in decision making processes. Many of the environmental problems and the methods of either preventing or solving them are highly controversial, and environmental education programmes should help people form their own opinions about the issues.

8. Complementary to the building of general support for conservation is the inclusion of environmental education in the specialist training of those whose work directly affects living resources, including farmers, planners, industrialists, foresters and engineers. They will be referred to as environmental intervenors. Such programmes aim to help intervenors assess the impact of their professional activities on the environment, and assist them to make their activities compatible with the objectives of living resource conservation. They also need access to information and advice from environmental experts when working on specific projects. It is a further aim of environmental education to train these experts.

9. There are also professionals such as politicians and business people, whose work may not be directly concerned with living resources but whose policies and decisions may determine how others use them. They too represent an important target group for environmental education. At worst their policies and decisions should not undermine efforts to link development objectives with conservation. At best they should support and promote them.

References

IUCN. 1970. International working meeting on environmental education and the school curriculum. Nevada, Gland.

SCOTTISH EDUCATION DEPARTMENT. 1974. Environmental education, a report by HM Inspectors of Schools. Edinburgh, HMSO.

UNESCO. 1978. Intergovernmental conference on environmental education, final report. Paris, UNESCO-UNEP.

CHAPTER 3

THE NEED FOR ENVIRONMENTAL EDUCATION

Introduction

1. The WCS identifies a fundamental human dilemma: human survival and well being are dependent upon both using and protecting living resources. The achievement of a proper balance is the aim of the WCS. It must be achieved as a matter of urgency. Environmental education can contribute to the resolution of this dilemma because, by convincing people it is in their own best interests to use resources in a sustainable way, it can generate concern and then support for the implementation of a new environmental order linking conservation and development.

Consensus Not Legislation

2. Legislation has been proposed as the most effective way of ensuring protection of the environment, but as long as it fails to reflect what people consider their main priorities it cannot guarantee success. Legislation for conservation is likely to be resisted by those it seeks to control because it is felt to be either an expensive luxury or inappropriate to their circumstances. Enforcing the rules in an unreceptive atmosphere requires monitoring and control by independent authorities that are expensive and economically unproductive. For conservation legislation to be truly effective, it should be in accord with the prevailing climate of opinion. A commitment to conservation and development objectives is therefore necessary if environmental legislation is to avoid unproductive and costly confrontation between different interest groups. This commitment should be based on a sound understanding of both conservation and development processes. Broad-based environmental education programmes are able to provide the knowledge and experience from which the relevant values and attitudes for developing this commitment are acquired.

3. Legislation is generally limited to particular environmental issues and is reactive. It follows, therefore, that it is concerned with only the most pressing of environmental issues. Sometimes, irreparable damage to living resources will precede the legislation. At this stage one is also faced with overcoming the inertia of an established

practice. If society is environmentally literate and committed to conservation, then all development will be planned in an atmosphere of environmental concern which can ensure that conservation and development objectives are considered concurrently. In this way, possible conflicts can be identified and means of overcoming them included at the planning stage. Environmental education can assist the growth of this 'atmosphere' because it aims to promote an appreciation and awareness of the total environment in which the individual issues are components. This holistic approach to the study of the environment should ensure a more rational response to individual issues that become topical, since they can be understood in relation to broader conservation and development objectives.

A Practical Base

4. These contributions to the achievement of conservation and development objectives appear somewhat intangible. Attitudinal changes are slow and the success of programmes cannot be judged overnight. However, there are practical activities whose benefits are more immediate. Environmental education seeks to achieve its objectives by offering people a wide variety of educational experiences, including practical work leading to environmental improvement. Such practical work also provides a good starting point for understanding the issues of the WCS in a local context. Where communities participate in the planning and development of their local environment, the changes are more likely to be appropriate and therefore accepted. Expensive mistakes are more likely to be avoided and vandalism reduced, thus making maintenance costs lower. For example, an underpass in the centre of Newcastle was painted with local scenes by children from the surrounding schools. In the past three years damage from graffiti has been negligible while adjacent walls continue to be daubed regularly. While such activities may not be directly related to the aims of the WCS, the values and attitudes they promote are wholly compatible with the development of the 'new environmental ethic' demanded by it. The money spent on constant repairs can then be reallocated to something more productive.

Conservation Makes Sense

5. The adoption of a way of life that is compatible with a conservation ethic is an aim of environmental education. The beneficial impact on the environment, both at home and abroad, on the economy and unemployment, could be considerable, and deserves more serious study than it is receiving at the moment. For example, it can generate public support for recycling activities that can reduce imports and the harmful impact on living resources of gathering new materials. The desire to save energy in buildings can increase employment opportunities in insulation work and reduce the need for capital-intensive power stations that create little employment and sterilise large areas of land as well as increasing air pollution. The demands to clean up effluent from factories, reduce the amount of pesticides and fertilisers in agriculture, produce more fuel efficient appliances, etc, create new opportunities for industry to develop the techniques and manufacture the equipment that will be in demand.

6. Education is an important part of the Conservation and Development Programme for the UK because it generates the support for conservation through helping people understand environmental processes, informing them about specific issues, and encouraging participation in decision making.

CHAPTER 4

THE IMPACT OF ENVIRONMENTAL EDUCATION IN THE UK

Introduction

1. The WCS report is a recent addition to the literature advocating a new relationship between humans and their environment. It is therefore too soon to assess objectively what impact it is having on people in Britain. However, outside the conservation movement few know of its existence, and even among those who consider themselves conservationists few are aware of its main messages. The fact that it has received so little publicity and support suggests that people do not recognise that conservation is deeply relevant to their own interests and aspirations.

2. This is perhaps surprising, considering that there is considerable public interest in certain of our living resources and environmental issues. Natural history programmes on television are extremely popular, with the BBC programme 'Wildlife on One' able to attract audiences of about nine million people. Many show their interest in more practical ways by belonging to nature societies. For example, The Royal Society for the Protection of Birds (RSPB) has 352,000 members, and 143,000 people belong to the 43 County Trusts for Nature Conservation. Interest in conservation is sufficient to support the commercial publication of a weekly magazine *The Living Countryside* which has a circulation of approximately 108,000. From time to time, particular environmental issues are able to generate considerable public concern both at local and national levels, and there is evidence that this concern has been able to influence environmental decisions at a high level. The Wildlife and Countryside Act 1981, prior to its becoming an Act, generated more correspondence than any other Parliamentary Bill. However, the debate was largely unproductive since it led to the greater polarisation of the opinions of conservationists and developers. Other issues which generate much debate are energy conservation, urban problems, pollution, landscape change, whaling and seal culling. Global environmental issues also attract interest when they are clearly articulated.

3. Some of the larger industries, whose activities have an impact on the environment in the UK, have recognised the need to take account of public concern. Some, such as Shell UK, British Petroleum and Coca Cola, have set up education departments which produce environmental education materials for use in schools. Some attempt to influence public opinion with television advertisements and free literature describing how their company tries to minimise its impact on the environment, while others involve children and the general public in special schemes such as bottle banks.

A Need for Coordination?

4. A number of curriculum guidelines have been produced for environmental education, but they have found little popularity across the country as a whole. (However, it would be unfair not to recognise that there are some excellent activities taking place locally.) Progress is hindered by a lack of communication between individual establishments, a lack of adequate training for teachers in the environmental approach and inertia in the institutional structures that influence education.

5. There is a lot of information available for use on environmental education activities. It is available in school text books, or on tapes, films and filmstrips, from professional and subject associations, industry, commerce, voluntary organisations and Government. Better use could be made of this information if dissemination mechanisms were improved.

6. In general, there is no shortage of information for use in environmental education programmes, although certain topics are more completely covered than others. There are also curriculum guides and schemes which suggest the methods and subject matter for good environmental education courses in schools. However, these and other initiatives tend to be badly coordinated, and more purposeful planning is imperative to consolidate progress. It is likely that constraints to further progress in environmental education will be found in the many institutional structures which influence education, rather than in the lack of suitable schemes and information.

Interest, but No Commitment

7. While the precise messages of the WCS may not be well known or understood, similar themes have been part of education programmes for a long time and have succeeded in making conservation a popular topic, especially among young people. However, while there may be an increased awareness of some of the problems,

only a small minority are willing to contribute actively to their resolution, either through expressing their opinions, becoming involved in conservation action or changing their own lifestyles to reduce impact on the environment. Further, while many people may privately support and work for conservation, they are either unable or unwilling to show the same commitment in their working lives.

8. There is a dearth of research data by which educators can evaluate the success of environmental educational programmes. Research by Richmond and Morgan (1977) into the environmental knowledge and attitudes of fifth formers revealed that, while many showed concern at environmental degradation, their knowledge of environ-

mental processes was poor. BBC audience research has revealed a similar lack of knowledge. However, Friends of the Earth claim that information and education programmes from many sources about nuclear energy have turned a 2:1 majority in favour of nuclear energy to a 2:1 majority against over the last 10 years. It would be valuable to know if attitudes towards living resource issues have similarly changed in the last 10 years.

9. In the following sections individual areas of the formal and non-formal education sectors will be examined in greater depth and recommendations made that will foster a more rapid growth of support for linked conservation and development.

References

RICHMOND, J M and MORGAN, R F. 1977. A national survey of the environmental knowledge and attitudes of 5th year pupils in England. Columbus, ERIC/SMEAC.

CHAPTER 5

EDUCATION COURSES DESIGNED TO ACHIEVE CONSERVATION OBJECTIVES

Introduction

1. The UK educational system has very little central curriculum control, unlike many countries where both the curriculum and the syllabuses of individual subjects within that curriculum are determined by a Ministry of Education. In the UK, the curriculum and the syllabuses of the individual subjects within it, are largely determined by each institution. In spite of what may appear as curriculum anarchy, there is a great deal of uniformity between establishments. Similar training courses for teachers, strong subject associations, local education authority advisory staff, examination syllabuses and certain Schools Council curriculum projects have all contributed to this. The disappointing progress of environmental education within this system is partly explained by the difficulty of integrating cross curricular approaches within the established structures.

Course Content

2. There has been considerable change in the content of courses and in methods of teaching over the last 20 years, but environmental education has not influenced or benefited from these changes as much as many would wish. Yet the development of environmental knowledge and skills, and the encouragement of caring attitudes to the environment, are proper concerns of formal education. The environmental education movement can turn to rather vague supportive statements from Departments of Education, and can draw attention to particular initiatives from them, such as 'Environmental Education: A review' (DES, 1981), and 'Curriculum 11-16: Environmental education' (1979), but their impact is not very great. Curriculum guidelines and actual teaching schemes for environmental education have been produced by the Schools Council, the Environmental Education Advisers Association, the National Association for Environmental Education and other organisations, but they have not gained the acceptance that their promoters wished. It is for this reason that this report has concentrated its recommendations on the structures that influence education and not on the content of courses designed to achieve conservation objectives. However, it was felt that there was a need to identify those aspects of environmental education which are particularly relevant to the achievement of the conservation and development objectives described in the WCS. The list below is not intended to be used as a syllabus for a separate subject which may be called environmental education, environmental studies or environmental science, but it picks out content that can contribute to WCS aims, and which ideally would be incorporated into the existing formal and non-formal school or college curriculum. It is based on lists published in the document 'Environmental Education: A review'.

(a) knowing of and studying various plants and animals in their natural environment;

(b) recognising interdependences among soil, air, plants, animals and man, and the delicacy of the ecological balance;

(c) recognising the main types of biological communities and the influence of humans upon them, both directly and indirectly;

(d) understanding the main factors affecting the distribution of organisms, including competition;

(e) knowing the major living resources in the sea and the importance of coastal wetlands in life cycles;

(f) understanding how the ecosystem is maintained by a cycling of energy;

(g) knowing the necessity of water for life, its influence on the distribution of biological communities and how the balance can be affected by human activity;

(h) understanding basic air/sea interactions, energy exchanges, the hydrological cycle and thermostatic influence;

(i) understanding soil function and conservation measures;

(j) recognising the limits of planet earth;

(k) understanding human reliance on the stable balance of natural systems;

(l) being aware of endangered species and reasons for their conservation;

(m) observing trends in urbanisation and its impact on living resources;

(n) relating food, clothing and shelter needs to available resources;

(o) recognising the main types of pollution, the principles of conservation, and the wise use of resources;

(p) considering environmental problems in connection with the quality of life;

(q) encouraging constructive action in environmental matters;

(r) applying aesthetic values in relation to other

values in environmental situations;

(s) knowing local legislative controls and understanding the main political and other decision making processes;

(t) contrasting attitudes towards the use of natural resources;

(u) contrasting the resource, social and economic implications of strategies for planned obsolescence and durability in manufactured goods;

(v) considering environmental problems in connection with the quality of life;

(w) encouraging constructive action in environmental matters;

(x) being aware of the strategy of planned obsolescence and its implications for living resources.

3. If such a programme for environmental education can be successfully implemented, it can provide the foundation upon which education programmes relating to specific issues can be built.

4. The role of the conservation movement is to identify the issues and publicise them. It is the role of the environmental education movement to encourage debate and to make sure the debate is supported with appropriate well balanced information. Education will then be able to help people form their own opinions about the issues.

Global Concern in the UK Dimension

5. The WCS identified at a global level the priority issues concerning living resource management. These are:

(a) The maintenance of essential ecological processes.

(b) The preservation of genetic diversity.

(c) The sustainable use of species and ecosystems.

Following on from these three issues is the need to adopt development practices that are sustainable.

6. An education programme must help people understand these three basic concepts, for without that understanding the debate concerning living resource management can have little impact.

7. The Conservation and Development Programme for the UK applies the three concepts to the UK dimension, identifying those activities and pressures that threaten the achievement of conservation objectives. Educators should examine the issues and use them in their education programmes, firstly to contribute to their understanding and secondly to help people form their own opinions about aspects of living resource management. The following priority issues and dilemmas should be part of UK environmental education programmes. It is important that programmes contain practical advice on ways individuals can contribute to the achievement of the three conservation objectives.

8. The following paragraphs identify some of the issues that are raised in other reports in this book, and which

ought to be reflected in educational programmes in an appropriate manner.

9. The rural report 'Putting Trust in the Countryside', Part 3:

(a) WCS advocates sustainable development. This concept needs to be introduced in its widest context, including ecological, aesthetic, social and economic sustainability.

(b) It has been the policy of national governments since the Second World War to encourage and support greater self-sufficiency in agriculture. This has led to far reaching changes in the appearance and ecological structure of the countryside, as well as the social and occupation structures of its residents. People should be made aware of these changes, the financial and administrative structures that support them, and competing interests of different groups. The importance of the resource users to the UK economy must not be omitted. In brief, education should try to improve the communications between the various interested parties.

(c) The current use of rural resources should be examined to see in which ways it supports or undermines the achievement of WCS aims. The needs for, and benefits of, conservation need to be made explicit.

(d) A move to a more sustainable use of rural resources has implications for personal and collective life styles. People need to be aware of these implications and can be helped by education to make adaptations.

(e) Education objectives should be reassessed to take account of future technological developments and social and economic scenarios.

10. The marine and coastal report 'Conservation and Development of Marine and Coastal Resources', Part 4:

(a) The importance of coastal wetlands in the maintenance of a stable maritime ecosystem and the current threats to them.

(b) The impact of over-fishing on fish stocks and the reasons behind the slow progress for a proper European fishing policy.

(c) The use of the sea for the disposal of waste.

(d) The problems associated with reaching international agreement on the use of the seas.

11. The international report 'The UK's Overseas Environmental Policy', Part 5:

(a) The need to recognise the global environmental and development crisis and to raise the workforce capability for meeting the crisis.

(b) The need to show the interrelatedness of environmental and developmental problems.

(c) The effects of population pressure on the health, wealth and welfare of all humanity.

(d) How UK policies affect the ecology of overseas states, eg through its aid programme, and investment.

(e) The impact of a worsening global environment on the supply of food and other resources to the UK.

12. The urban report 'The Livable City', Part 2:
    (a) Much development is initiated and used in towns, yet urban populations remain largely ignorant of the scale, diversity and consequence of that development which impacts on a much wider environment than cities alone.
    (b) The uses of energy, land, building materials, water and other resources by urban populations and the impact of expanding urban areas on surrounding 'natural' systems, including land-take, vandalism and pressure from recreational activities.
    (c) Increasing the provision for people to have more contact with nature within cities, eg ecological parks, city farms, urban parks and gardens, and for community initiatives in conservation.
    (d) Changes in the morphology of cities and reasons for the changes.

13. The industry report 'Seven Bridges to the Future', Part 1:
    (a) The implications for future development of failing to reduce the impact of industry on natural resources, contrasted with the implications of adopting conservation practices on competitiveness, availability of products, employment, etc.
    (b) The importance of industry to the social and economic welfare of the UK.
    (c) Factors affecting the location of industry. How long-term ecological concerns can be integrated with short-term economic and political concerns.
    (d) The potential of industry's processes and products to solve, as well as create, environmental problems.
    (e) The impact on industry's environmental performance of public opinion and legislation.

    (f) The changing industrial structure of the UK and its implications for the social, economic and ecological environment.
    (g) The impact on living resources of various types of pollution.
    (h) The costs and benefits of recycling.

14. The ethics report 'Environmental Ethics and Conservation Action', Part 6:
    (a) The non-sustainable use of the earth's resources is a reflection of the current ethos. Education can help people to examine that ethos, to understand its origins and enable individuals to formulate ethical codes that are more appropriate to sustaining the earth's resources.
    (b) The problems today caused by the historical separation of values from knowledge.
    (c) Providing an ethical base from which to make environmental decisions.

Common Themes

15. Within all the reports there are certain educational themes that are common and should be included in educational programmes:
    (a) The benefits of conservation for people and nature should be promoted.
    (b) People should be made aware of the urgency of the need to introduce conservation measures.
    (c) The skills necessary to support conservation should be developed.
    (d) People should be helped to examine their own values, attitudes and behaviour regarding their use of the environment.

References

DEPARTMENT OF EDUCATION AND SCIENCE. 1979. Curriculum 11-16: supplementary working papers by HM Inspectorate, Environmental Education. London, DES.

DEPARTMENT OF EDUCATION AND SCIENCE. 1981. Environmental education: a review. London, DES.

CHAPTER 6

ENVIRONMENTAL EDUCATION IN SCOTLAND

Introduction

1. In Scotland, most of the government departments, statutory and non-governmental bodies interested in the environment and education are relatively independent of their counterparts elsewhere in the UK. Although there is much cooperation, national differences have led to programmes with different characteristics, notably in the formal sector of education, some of which have affected the development of environmental education.

2. Secondary education starts at age 12, and both upper primary and lower secondary curricula tend to be organised on a subject basis. Pupils taking certificate examinations may first do so in their fourth year (for ordinary grade) and fifth year (for higher grade). These provide the main qualifications for entry into tertiary education. In the sixth year there is also available a Certificate of Sixth Year Studies, which is designed to bridge the gap between secondary and tertiary styles of work. The GCE boards do not operate in Scotland (apart from some independent schools) and there is no Scottish CSE Board (although some Scottish Schools use the Northern CSE Board). Both GCE and CSE are replaced by the Scottish Certificate of Education (SCE) Examination Board, which does not have a Mode 3 type of syllabus. There are no SCE courses designated as environmental science, nor at present is there separate provision for environmental education in the pre-certificate years S1 and 2.

3. It should also be noted that Scotland does not have a Schools Council. Some of its functions are exercised by the Consultative Committee on the Curriculum which operates through curriculum development centres, with full-time staff.

A Central Incentive

4. An early move to develop environmental education in Scotland was the establishment, by the Secretary of State for Scotland, of the Committee on Education and the Countryside, which was set up in 1968 at the same time as the Council for Environmental Education in England and Wales. Then an HMI Report on Environmental Education was published in 1974 by the Scottish Education Department which received a good reception both in Scotalnd and beyond, where, in many respects, it was ahead of the field. In Scotland, however, it coincided with a period of reorganisation of local government and the establishment of committees to study possible changes in the structure of secondary education and examinations. These circumstances probably contributed to a poorer response in schools than had been anticipated.

5. In various ways, however, the interest which was kindled in environmental education has been kept alive. Some courses have been offered in colleges of education: for example a Certificate in Environmental Education course is current in Moray House College of Education, supported by the Outdoor Education Organisation. Lothian Region Youth and Community Development Officers receive training in the use of environmental education programmes. Some schools already offer units of environmental education mainly to non-certificate pupils or as a complementary studies option for a wider ability range. Similar material is being incorporated into new interdisciplinary courses currently under development, although not constituting a full environmental education course in themselves. In the primary sector a recent report on 'Learning and Teaching in Primary 4 and Primary 7' (1980) picked out environmental studies as a problem area, and this may lead to development.

Local Incentives

6. In several parts of Scotland groups of people interested in environmental education have been working towards its further extension. In Tayside, a group produced a guide to facilities for environmental education in the area, and a south-east Scotland group publishes a useful newsletter. The Strathclyde Environmental Education Group organised a series of conferences and workshops which led to a redefinition of the aims and objectives of environmental education, a review of scope and content, and the application of these to a teaching model which is now under trial in several schools. This may also provide a basis for development in other sectors of education.

7. Following publication of the HMI Report and the demise of the Committee on Education and the Countryside, there was clearly a gap to be filled in the provision for continued development of environmental

education. A Scottish Environmental Education Committee (SEEC) was set up in 1977, as a result of initiatives stemming from the Strathclyde Group and the Scottish Civic Trust which provides the secretariat for it, and it now has a membership representing most of the interested parties.

8. It still lacks financial resources, however, and is not yet able to offer the kind of services available in England and Wales from the Council for Environmental Education (CEE) and the Prince of Wales Committee, although there are proposals for close cooperation with the CEE when resources can be found.

9. Useful work continues to be done outside the formal sector. There is a strong educational element to the multi-agency schemes for inner city rehabilitation in Glasgow, and some planning authorities have shown, and others are beginning to show, a willingness to be involved in education. The Countryside Commission for Scotland has had staff committed to promoting environmental education since 1968.

10. The Royal Zoological Society for Scotland's Education Centre runs a well-supported programme for schools, in collaboration with the Royal Botanic Gardens and the Royal Scottish Museum. A valuable connection with IUCN has been maintained through the North West Europe Committee of the Commission on Education, of which one of the Scottish inspectorate has been a member for many years. In Scotland, there is thus a continuing interest and active involvement in environmental education, although, at present, a lack of a coordinated policy. Competing interests for the development of interdisciplinary courses, problems of organisation, and an unfortunate, and unfounded, suspicion that this sort of work is below the ability range of certificate pupils have all to be overcome.

References

HM INSPECTORS OF SCHOOLS. 1980. A report on learning and teaching in Primary 4 and Primary 7. HMSO.

CHAPTER 7

ENVIRONMENTAL EDUCATION IN NORTHERN IRELAND

1. Environmental education in Northern Ireland does not differ markedly from the rest of the UK. The main conservation legislation is the Amenity Lands Act 1965 and although this does not confer educational responsibility on the Nature Reserves Committee or its executive, the Conservation Branch of the Department of the Environment, they have taken on a number of educational functions including two countryside centres and several nature trails. The Field Studies Council (FSC) does not operate in Northern Ireland but there are several Education Board Field Centres and a list has been published (Thomlinson, 1975). The Queens University Marine Laboratory at Portaferry on Strangford Lough and the New University Limnology Laboratory at Traad Point on Lough Neagh are both primarily research laboratories with a subsidiary field centre function.

2. A list of field sites available for educational use has been published (Committee on Field Study and Outdoor Pursuits Centres, 1972). Currently, only one of the six Education and Library Boards has any environmental advisors — in fact, two environmental advisors.

3. The Ulster Trust for Nature Conservation was set up in 1977 and has already assumed an active role. The RSPB and the National Trust are also both active in the education field. There are periodic initiatives designed to infuse more environmental education into the school curricula but they are no more or less successful than comparable initiatives in Britain.

4. The small size and centralised administration of Northern Ireland make for effective personal contacts and liaison. Examples in the educational field might include the short courses run each year on conservation for Agricultural Advisory Officers and for foresters. The latter are organised by the New University at Coleraine and centre on the conservation management of a particular habitat such as bog. The attendance by the foresters, from the Chief Forestry Officer downwards, is very impressive. There has recently been a controversial proposal for a tidal power barrage across the mouth of Stranford Lough, and Queens University Extra-Mural Department are currently organising a series of lectures/discussions involving some of the main proponents and opponents of the scheme.

References

COMMITTEE ON FIELD STUDY AND OUTDOOR PURSUITS CENTRES. 1972. A handbook of centres in N Ireland, Belfast.

THOMLINSON, P M. (editor). 1975. Field study sites in N Ireland, QUB Teachers' Centres. Belfast, Queens University Science Library.

CHAPTER 8

SUMMARY

Introduction

1. The main purpose of this report is to suggest how education in the UK can best contribute to achieving the aims of the WCS. It has been noted that the WCS specifies that environmental education programmes are needed to convince people that conservation is central to their own interests. It considers that there must first be such a conviction to motivate people into wanting to learn how to manage their environment wisely. The WCS recognises that human survival and well being depend upon both developing and conserving the resources of the planet. However, at the moment the balance between them is seriously upset and human exploitation of resources is reducing the capacity of the planet to support life. The Strategy seeks to restore an acceptable balance once again, but, if this is to be achieved, societies will have to adopt new attitudes and values towards the environment, ones that include plants and animals as well as people. It is the task of environmental education to foster or reinforce attitudes and behaviour compatible with what has been described as a 'new ethic'.

The Environment is Everywhere

2. The WCS recommends environmental education programmes rather than ones relating only to conservation or nature education which would be narrower in their approach to the issues. Environmental education is concerned with the total environment, from wilderness to metropolis, and it is maintained that it is important to study the local environment and environmental issues as an introduction to the global issues that are clearly presented in the Strategy. Environmental education also supports the expansion of public participation in the decision making processes affecting human use of the environment, because there is a greater chance of public acceptance of conservation policies and practices if people are fully involved in the creation of their own environment. For 80 per cent of people in the UK, the immediate environment is an urban one and this should be adequately reflected in the education programmes being developed. Our urban way of life is sustained by reliance upon the exploitation of living and non-living resources. When supplies of the finite resources, such as minerals, begin to run out, our urban society will have to look for their replacements to the renewable resources of the natural environment such as wind power and forests. Therefore, it is not in the interests of urban populations to reduce further the capacity of living resources to support them. To achieve responsible public participation, people must be knowledgeable about the issues concerned. This entails taking account of the relevant social, economic and political factors, as well as the ecological ones, relating to human use of the environment.

3. This report has attempted to reflect the straight-forward approach of the WCS which summarises the present state of the environment and identifies priority issues. It examines how far conservation aims and objectives have been achieved, states what still needs to be done and, recognising the constraints, recommends the action needed to ensure the success of the aims and objectives. A fundamental principle upheld by the Strategy is that conservation practices are essential if humans are to achieve sustainable development. In the 'Review of Environmental Education' (Appendix A of this report), the progress to date is briefly described and a few of the excellent education programmes are highlighted. In 'The Impact of Environmental Education in the UK' (Chapter 4 above), the report suggests that, despite the determined efforts of committed individual educators, local authorities and numerous environmental organisations, the success of the education programmes has not been sufficient to match the scale of the environmental problems. Education programmes have succeeded in generating a great interest in nature and a concern for the natural and built environments, but they have not succeeded to persuade people to translate this interest and concern into their own behaviour patterns. They might have been more successful if greater emphasis had been given to explaining and providing the scientific basis of the need for conservation and sustainable development.

Commitment, Not Information

4. The aims and objectives of environmental education, and the means of achieving them, have evolved over the last 15 to 20 years. A summary of the process appears in 'The Development of an Environmental Education Philosophy' (Appendix B of this report). The aims,

objectives and methods of environmental education are stated in 'The Nature of Environmental Education' (Chapter 2 above). While environmental education may not have achieved the degree of success hoped for by the environmental movement, if more vigorously pursued it could contribute more effectively to the achievement of conservation objectives. In the past, conservationists have not given adequate support to environmental education. Such education has been perceived as the provision of information about the environment and environmental issues, in the belief that if only people had the facts they too would become committed conservationists. This policy has not been successful. It is therefore a significant development that environmental education (which argues that commitment to conservation will only come about through exposure to a wide variety of environmental and educational experiences) has been fully integrated with the Conservation and Development Programme for the UK.

Constraints and Recommendations

5. Chapter 9 of this report examines further some of the constraints to progress in environmental education before making recommendations. The recommendations are not intended as an action plan to be implemented immediately in their entirety. They form within an identifiable framework, an action plan from which Government departments, organisations, etc can identify opportunities to take the initiative. (To ensure that inertia is overcome, the task of promoting, coordinating and monitoring progress should be allocated to an appropriate organisation with sufficient resources being made available.) The recommendations cover all areas of the formal and non-formal, youth and adult education sectors, and they are addressed to all the institutions, associations, organisations, etc whose activities may contribute to, or influence, environmental knowledge, skills and attitudes, including those whose activities might actually undermine the achievement of the 'new ethic'. The recommendations are restricted to three priority aims:
  (a) To build support for conservation and development.
  (b) To provide adequate education and training for environmental intervenors and policy makers.
  (c) To provide support for environmental educators.
6. The major constraint to more rapid progress in environmental education is not related to a shortage of appropriate environmental information, or a lack of professionally developed curriculum guidelines and information about methods of environmental education. These all exist, but they are not accepted and used widely because the institutional and administrative structures which influence education do not adapt easily to new topics with unfamiliar approaches. A preliminary step in the education strategy must be to create the conditions in which environmental education can flourish. To exert the pressure needed to bring about and guide the changes, it is essential to have a powerful central organisation.

Concern, Support and Action

7. Environmental education leads naturally from a study of the environment, and the expression of concern about the way humans use the environment, through to the consideration of alternative ways of life, including social and economic strategies. These issues are controversial and therefore it is frequently suggested that they are not proper subject areas for education, especially in schools. Education which aims at the indoctrination of particular views is regarded as propaganda. However, education should help people form their own opinions, by giving them access to a variety of viewpoints and enabling them to assess critically information with which they are presented. It should also show how to use the mechanisms set up for ensuring that people are free to express those opinions. An education which fails to prepare and maintain an individual's ability to participate in a democracy is not an adequate education, and therefore environmental educators cannot and should not ignore controversial environmental issues.

8. Merely feeling concern for human use of environmental resources will not bring about the changes sought by the World Conservation Strategy. The concern must be translated into active support for conservation. The support may be practical in the form of adapting life styles to be less demanding on the environment, participating in environmental protection committees: cleaning up eyesores or simply campaigning for the application or introduction of environmental controls. But, as well as creating an atmosphere in which care for the environment can thrive, environmental education is concerned with offering adequate environmental training for those whose work affects the environment, and with the provision of special training for environmental experts able to identify actual and potential environmental problems and contribute to their satisfactory solution.

9. The report provides further support for environmental education as a means of helping humans to see themselves as stewards of the environment with a responsibility to ensure that it is both productive and pleasant to live in for future generations. Environmental education will be succeeding when care for the environment becomes as much a part of human life as caring for oneself.

CHAPTER 9

RECOMMENDATIONS

An Education Framework for the Conservation and Development Programme for the UK

1. As noticed in Chapter 4 paragraph 1, p 449, most people fail to appreciate the contribution that conservation can make to the achievement of the needs and the solution of the problems which they recognise as their own. This failure is further attested by the progressive deterioration at national and global levels of the living resource-base upon which all humans depend for their survival and well-being. It is education that can help people to this realisation and commitment.

2. These aims may best be achieved within the framework of the environmental education movement whose aims are entirely compatible with those of the WCS and the Conservation and Development Programme for the UK.

3. This chapter will make recommendations that support the above aims and should be read in conjunction with Chapter 10 which highlights the comments made during the Practitioners' Debate on the proposals. For easy reference, they are summarised at the end of this chapter in separate sections as follows:
   (a) Build support for conservation: (i) Schools; (ii) Further and Higher Education Institutions; (iii) Continuing Education (formal sector); (iv) Youth Groups and Youth Training Schemes; (v) Continuing Education (non-formal sector).
   (b) Education for environmental intervenors (vocational training) and policy makers.
   (c) Provide support for environmental educators.

4. The recommendations do not represent an action plan to be undertaken step by step. Rather, they suggest opportunities for developments that will further the conservation objectives of the WCS, in the UK, within an identifiable framework.

5. In schools, building support for conservation will not be achieved through any one academic discipline; the complex nature of environmental systems and problems makes cross-disciplinary reference automatic. Any strategy must also take account of the special contribution of the hidden curriculum. In fact, only if the whole school community generates an atmosphere conducive to the growth of awareness of and concern for its own environment, as well as the total environment, both natural and artificial, will effective environmental education take place. Environmental education is a function of the whole curriculum.

6. Fundamental to building support for conservation is that students should undertake field work in the countryside and the town, both within the locality and beyond. There should also be opportunities for students to become actively involved in environmental projects. Teachers are encouraged to enlist the support of specialists from outside the school, eg planners, farmers, architects and industrialists.

Constraints and Conflicts

7. However, it is important to recognise the constraints to such developments. The curriculum, internal organisations of schools and education support services are designed first to give adequate training in basic skills and secondly to achieve academic excellence in a limited number of subject areas. Topics which require a cross-disciplinary approach are therefore difficult to integrate. In secondary schools especially, the strict demarcation of subject areas is upheld by strong professional associations, teacher training institutions and the internal organisations of schools. Spending cuts in education are reinforcing the demarcation of subject areas, rather than assisting or encouraging the elements of cross-disciplinary teaching needed in environmental education. Exam syllabuses, too, can reinforce the organisation of teaching in the subject divisions. Some exam syllabuses seem primarily designed to equip students for academic courses in higher education institutions and much less to educate them for life. However, it is difficult to assess a student's performance in courses such as environmental education which are designed to promote values and attitudes appropriate to conservation objectives.

8. Teachers are often reluctant to become involved with political issues which may question the established policies of institutions, codes of behaviour and current values, as well as suggest alternatives to current economic strategies. (Political education is concerned with assisting students to make informed decisions, and should not be confused with the indoctrination of particular political philosophies.) Teachers generally lack confidence in using the perceptions and ideas of pupils, especially in areas not directly related to their subject training. They also feel less secure when allowing discussion or when working outside the classroom locally or at field centres.

9. Individual teachers, committed to the principles of environmental education, often have to work in isolation

and without adequate support from their colleagues, parent-teacher associations, school governors and even the local education authority. The present career structure in schools gives insufficient incentive for teachers to qualify in environmental education or environmental science. Departments, where they exist, are small and offer little opportunity for promotion.

10. Recommendations 5 to 8 are designed to bring about: curriculum change, examination change, better teaching of environmental education, better support for teachers, and better training of teachers through pre- and in-service training courses.

11. Institutions of further and higher education run many more courses than schools. Some are vocational, some are academic and some are of general interest. Many of the courses provide opportunities for environmental education, but others are environmentally neutral. There is little to be gained from contriving links between such environmentally neutral courses and environmental education courses. Vocational courses for those whose work has a direct influence on the environment or education should promote support for conservation and development and provide appropriate training.

12. Extra-mural departments at Universities, the Open University and local education authorities (LEAs) provide adult education courses. Many which reflect the growing interest of the public in environmental matters are non-vocational and attract those who are interested but do not necessarily want a qualification at the end of it. Other special interest courses are mounted by voluntary organisations for members of the public. These courses can provide an opportunity for conservation issues to be explored, thus contributing to environmental education.

Formal and Informal Education

13. Education is a life long process. All our activities contribute to the constant development of knowledge, skills and attitudes. The educational processes outside the formal sector of education are thus able to contribute to the achievement of conservation objectives. Educators must consider how best to use these opportunities. (For the purposes of this report, non-formal education refers to the opportunities for environmental education among young people out of school and adults not involved in organised education courses.)

14. Over two million young people belong to youth organisations and clubs, and over half a million young people seek employment and training with Manpower Services Commission programmes. Participants expect something different from their school experiences. The WCS, and its application in the UK, provides scope for new initiatives in education and training. Many organisations and their leaders have already recognised the value of integrating environmental education with their activities.

15. Non-formal education for adults is piecemeal. It happens through watching television, reading newspapers and magazines, chance conversations, travel, recreational activities, etc. Many educational experiences will influence attitudes towards the use of the environment. While programmes and articles highlighting the environment and current environmental issues contribute to building support for conservation, their beneficial impact is offset to some extent by others, as well as advertisements, which undermine the growth of an environmental ethic. Public behaviour and opinion very often reveals that there is insufficient understanding of ecological processes, the need for conservation and the political, social and economic factors affecting human use of the environment. This restricts widespread informed public debate or responsible participation. To achieve wise decisions, democracies must be supported by a strong public education programme.

Specialist Programmes

16. While there is a need for general environmental education programmes to build support for conservation and development, there is also a need for programmes designed specifically for environmental intervenors and policy makers. The activities of farmers, foresters, industrialists, and others who seek to satisfy human demands for precious resources, frequently do not take full account of the need to achieve a satisfactory balance between conservation and development. Education and training programmes tailored for individual groups can contribute to the attainment of this balance but unless the financial and administrative structures, within which the intervenors are forced to operate, support and encourage conservation, the ability to act responsibly may not be a possibility. It is therefore important that policy makers, too, understand the need for conservation and provide supportive structures for it.

17. Progress in environmental education will be hindered unless adequate support is available to environmental educators. Environmental educators are those who develop or use environmental education programmes, or use the environment as a resource within their educational activities. They may include curriculum developers, teachers, lecturers, youth and adult group leaders, publishers, reporters, producers of television and radio programmes and parents. To support their environmental education activities, they need to have easy access to appropriate information, training in the environmental approach to education, and be able to understand how their particular activity relates to the overall aims of environmental education. Environmental educators have not derived sufficient support for their activities in the past, either at policy or at practical levels. The Conservation and Development Programme for the UK is able to provide a focus and a mechanism for this much needed support.

Recommendation 1
(see paragraphs 5 to 10 of this chapter, pp 459-460)

Aim:
For all schools to have a written environmental education policy with specific reference to living resource issues.

Key organisations and agencies:
Departments of Education, Her Majesty's Inspectorate, LEAs, head teachers and directors of studies, the School Curriculum Development Council, and trade unions.

Constraints:
While written and personal advice on how to develop a school policy for environmental education is available through a number of channels, it is not used extensively because there is frequently little demand from parents, governors, employers, and those in charge of education for cross-curricular activities.

PROPOSALS FOR ACTION:

(a) All schools should have a written policy for environmental education within the total curriculum policy of the school and the LEA. This should include environmental education objectives, and guidelines on how the school can achieve these objectives. All teachers should be involved in the formulation and implementation of the policy. Schools would be assisted to make such policies, if there was pressure and support from Government, LEAs, parent-teacher associations, school governors and trade unions.

(b) As well as a curriculum policy, there should be a conservation policy developed and implemented by staff and pupils together. This might include: (i) energy saving schemes; (ii) recycling of waste paper and using recycled paper; (iii) improving the environment of the school and its grounds; (iv) developing an area of the grounds as a nature reserve or ecological park.

Recommendation 2
(see paragraphs 5 to 10 of this chapter, pp 459-460)

Aim:
To assist the growth of environmental education programmes within the existing administrative and curriculum structures.

Key organisations and agencies:
Head teachers, directors of studies, teacher trainers, the School Curriculum Development Council, LEAs, advisors, and environmental organisations.

Constraints:
Present administrative and curriculum structures are not conducive to the inclusion of cross-curricular topics. In the short-term, such activities will have to be designed to operate within the established structures, while continuing to advocate change. Even where individual teachers are keen to include aspects of environmental education in their teaching, support from a senior level is rarely forthcoming.

PROPOSALS FOR ACTION:

(a) Each school should designate responsibility to a member of staff for planning, coordination and oversight of environmental education, perhaps as part of an overall responsibility for introducing related topics such as 'Third World issues', world peace' and 'population' across the curriculum. Without adequate coordination, there is a danger that certain topics and issues covered by more than one teacher will not be complementary.

(b) Ways of adjusting the timetable should be explored to provide opportunities for a measure of cooperative teaching, and to permit a proportion of the student's learning experience to be undertaken out of school.

(c) Syllabuses of individual subjects should be examined to see how they can support environmental education, and also how environmental education can support them.

(d) All teachers should be encouraged and assisted to use environmental information in their teaching.

(e) In the fourth and fifth year, time should be allocated in the common core for environmental, social, political and economic issues. Such teaching is at its best when it draws on the experience of the pupils in the rest of the curriculum.

(f) Schools should invite appropriate professionals from outside the school to share in environmental education programmes.

Recommendation 3
(see paragraphs 5 to 10 of this chapter, pp 459-460)

Aim:
To include an environmental dimension in the examination syllabuses of appropriate subjects.

Key organisations and agencies:
Examination boards and The Examinations Council.

Constraints:
(a) Post third year courses in secondary schools are dominated by the demands of examinations. While a few pupils may benefit from the study of an environmental subject, the majority will study subjects which give little opportunity for the inclusion of an environmental dimension consistent with the aims of WCS.

(b) The proposals for a new examination structure at 16+ provide an excellent opportunity for progress in environmental education. While most of the new examination boards intend to offer an environmental subject for examination (Rural Studies, Environmental Studies, Environmental Science) this is not sufficient to ensure that all students receive an environmental education since it is not a core subject.

PROPOSALS FOR ACTION:

(a) All examination boards should set up a cross-curricular environmental advisory committee to scrutinise syllabuses over a wide range of subjects, and suggest how those subjects can assist or be assisted by the inclusion of environmental education objectives. It would be useful for the boards to study the example of the vocational foundation courses offered by the City and Guilds of London Institute, all of which include a compulsory environmental component.

(b) Wherever possible, syllabuses should provide opportunities for the students to undertake studies outside the classroom, in the school grounds, the local environment and in environments different from the local one.

(c) Syllabuses should provide opportunities for students to study real environmental issues at local, national and global levels.

Recommendation 4
(see paragraphs 5 to 10 of this chapter, pp 459-460)

Aim:
To assist all teachers to adopt an environmental approach in their teaching.

Key organisations and agencies:
Teachers and teacher associations, colleges of education and education departments in universities and polytechnics, and all those providing information or training courses for teachers, including voluntary organisations, Departments of Education, statutory bodies, and LEAs.

Constraints:
Few teachers in schools have received any training in environmental education, either at pre- or in-service levels. Few pre-service training courses for teachers include advice on team teaching methods, issue-based learning, or prepare them for cross-curricular teaching. There are very few opportunities for teachers to train specifically for posts in environmental education because as yet such teachers do not suit the way schools are organised, or fit into established career structures. While there are some opportunities for in-service training, this usually has to be undertaken in a teacher's own time and at the teacher's expense. As a result, only teachers highly motivated in this area benefit from any training. In the absence of adequate training, teachers lack confidence in adopting an environmental approach to their teaching.

PROPOSALS FOR ACTION:

(a) All institutions should have a written policy for environmental education. Training courses at colleges and departments of education should provide an opportunity for students to become familiar with the nature, aims and objectives, and methods of environmental education. A common course for all students may be the most appropriate way of achieving this.

(b) Opportunities for in-service training by LEAs should be increased. While financial restrictions may limit the number of teachers given time off to attend long courses, short courses can be arranged at little cost or inconvenience to the authorities.

(c) Authorities should recognise for promotion purposes the value of training which encourages the introduction of certain topics across the curriculum. (This has already been achieved on the pastoral side.)

(d) Where voluntary environmental organisations provide courses for teachers, conservation should be included. Environmental organisations providing courses for teachers include The Field Studies Council, The Scottish Field Studies Association, The Prince of Wales Committee, The RSPCA and the RSPB.

Recommendation 5
(see paragraph 11 of this chapter, p 460)

Aim:
For further and higher education institutions to show by example that they support conservation objectives.

Key organisations and agencies:
Vice-chancellors of universities, governing bodies, principals and directors of polytechnics.

Constraints:
In further and higher education institutions there are both vocational and academic courses. The former will be covered in a later section. Many academic courses provide opportunities for environmental education, but others are environmentally neutral, and there is little to be gained from contriving links between them and environmental education.

PROPOSALS FOR ACTION:

With professional advice, conservation policies and activities can be implemented and the policies communicated to staff and students. For example: (i) guidelines for the maintenance of the institution's estate, and guidelines for the management of waste-paper, food containers, etc; (ii) guidelines on the use of living resources within the institution; (iii) energy conservation; (iv) conservation and environment groups and societies should be encouraged within the institutions.

Recommendation 6
(see paragraph 12 of this chapter, p 460)

Aim:
To ensure there are environmentally related courses easily accessible for all those who wish to join them and that such courses contribute to building support for conservation.

Key organisations and agencies:
LEAs, workers education associations, environmental organisations, (Youth Hostel Associations, Field Studies Council, Scottish Field Studies Association, RSPB, RSPCA, etc), the Open University, extra-mural departments of universities, extra-mural departments in higher education institutions and the National Institute of Adult Education.

Constraints:
Although organisations mount education programmes, there is little cooperation between them when they draw up programmes or publicise courses. Members of the public are often unaware of the number and variety of courses that are available. The amount of money allocated to adult education is only 0.5 per cent of the total education budget. This compares poorly with, for example, 6 per cent, in Sweden.

PROPOSALS FOR ACTION:

Education and environmental organisations should cooperate at a national and regional level with course providers to promote education programmes that contain courses relating to living resources and their conservation. A list of all the courses should be widely publicised in relevant journals, public libraries, the local press, local radio etc.

Recommendation 7
(see paragraphs 13 to 14 of this chapter, p 460)

Aim:
To make conservation objectives an integral part of the objectives of youth group activities and youth employment training programmes.

Key organisations and agencies:
Youth organisations, youth leaders, Manpower Services Commission (MSC), employment programmes, and further education colleges.

Constraints:
Few leaders and trainers receive any information about how environmental education can contribute to their overall objectives. Examples of good practice exist but information about them is not adequately communicated to other groups. Most national headquarters are not aware of the opportunities for environmental education. To achieve the conservation objectives as outlined in the Conservation and Development Programme for the UK requires a fundamental change in the approach to employment training.

PROPOSALS FOR ACTION:

(a) The Youth Unit of the Council for Environmental Conservation should be strengthened so that it may more effectively support environmental education in the non-formal youth education sector through its coordinating activities. Its activities should supplement those of the Council for Environmental Education.
(b) There should be greater publicity for, and use of examples of, good practice that other leaders and trainers may wish to follow or learn from.
(c) The WCS and the Conservation and Development Programme for the UK should provide an important component when devising policy, activities or courses. The headquarters of organisations should prepare a policy statement on environmental education and also prepare

guidelines for its integration into local schemes.
(d) There should be opportunities for training in skills appropriate to achieving the conjoint objectives of conservation and earning a living, eg installing solar panels for plumbers, insulation of buildings for builders, etc.
(e) In the foreseeable future it is unlikely that the economy will support full employment of the type we have known previously. New training opportunities should recognise this and provide training that will enable people to live purposeful and satisfying lives without necessarily being wholly operative within the formal economic sector. Working towards conservation objectives can create new opportunities, for example encouraging increased self-sufficiency through small scale, labour intensive horticultural and agricultural activities.
(f) Colleges of further education, which will have to cope with the training aspect of current MSC proposals, should explore how environmental education can be integrated into their programmes.

Recommendation 8
(see paragraph 15 of this chapter, p 460)

Aim:
To assist the dissemination of information about the environment, environmental issues, the objectives of conservation and development and personal involvement to the general public.

Key organisations and agencies:
Environmental organisations, local authorities, industrial and commercial organisations, government departments, the media, environmental interpretation centres and museums.

Constraints:
Suitable information is not always available for educators to use. When it is, it may not always be readily accessible, and is therefore not used to best effect in public education activities. Public attitudes often reflect a shallow understanding of environmental issues and misinformation.

PROPOSALS FOR ACTION:

(a) Information prepared for the public needs much greater publicity. Environmental organisations could cut publicity costs by coming together and promoting their information and publications jointly. In particular, there should be publicity for information which explains what the individual can do to support sustainable development.
(b) A national environmental information centre should be set up, so that writers, journalists, programme producers and others involved in public education activities have rapid access to reliable environmental information, the names of environmental experts, and the location of successful projects.

(c) A commercial environmental education unit should be set up to organise the supply of programmes about conservation and conservation issues to television and radio companies. It should also encourage the companies to weave conservation into general programme output.

(d) When attempts are made to secure effective and responsible public participation on important environmental matters, eg the use of energy and nuclear power, wildlife and the countryside and transport decisions, major educational programmes involving radio, television and the press should precede them.

(e) The promotion of an environmental ethic is fundamental to any education programme. The Government should launch a massive and continuing campaign to promote and implement environmental concern.

(f) Environmental interpretation services (which may range, for example, from visitor centres to display boards and publication programmes) should be considered for all sites which attract people to explore or enjoy any aspect of the environment. Such informal public education provision should also be developed as an indispensable part of major programmes of environmental change, particularly those instigated by public environmental planning bodies.

Recommendation 9
(see paragraphs 13 to 17 of this chapter, p 460)

Aim:
To improve the range and quality of public participation in environmental decision making.

Key organisations and agencies:
Local authorities, Government, representatives of ethnic minorities, special interest groups and statutory bodies.

Constraints
In spite of a statutory requirement for public participation in local planning, progress has been disappointing.

PROPOSALS FOR ACTION:

(a) There should be support by local authorities, local industries and commercial organisations, voluntary organisations and the Manpower Services Commission for education centres to act as focal points for public participation in the environmental management of the locality. This will involve the provision of information, facilities for the exchange of ideas and opportunities for participation.

(b) Responsible participation requires educational support and communication between different interest groups. To assist this, lines of communication between schools and colleges, community groups, the local authority and voluntary bodies should be developed. This could be the task of an Environmental Education Liaison Officer, most probably employed by the local authority.

Continuing on from this development, joint working parties should be set up in each local authority area, consisting of educators, planners, architects, local councillors and members of the local community, to collaborate on promoting an inter-sectoral environmental education policy for the locality.

(c) The Commission for Racial Equality should encourage the production of environmental education information in mother tongue languages.

Recommendation 10
(see paragraph 16 of this chapter, p 460)

Aim:
To introduce or strengthen the environmental component in professional and vocational training courses.

Key organisations and agencies:
Institutions of further and higher education, business management schools, colleges and departments of agriculture, civil service colleges, trade unions and military colleges.

Constraints:
Conservation is a component of many training courses, but it may not be set in the wider context of the aims of the WCS. Also, the achievement of conservation objectives may not be perceived as an important component of the course.

PROPOSALS FOR ACTION:

Those who plan professional and vocational courses should recognise their responsibility to provide an appropriate environmental perspective where possible. Courses should build support for conservation, warn students about possible harmful impacts of their activities on the living resource-base, and show ways to overcome or diminish them. They should also introduce the concept of sustainable use of resources. To be taken seriously by the students, environmental aspects must be accorded the highest status by the training body concerned.

Recommendation 11
(see paragraph 16 of this chapter, p 460)

Aim:
To provide appropriate and acceptable advice on conservation to professionals at work.

Key organisations and agencies:
Professional associations, trade unions, Government departments, statutory bodies, environmental organisations and industrial and commercial organisations.

Constraints:
Advice about conservation is available from statutory bodies, voluntary organisations and Government. Because it does not come from within an individual professional's own association or interest area, it may be inappropriate or be seen to be inappropriate.

PROPOSALS FOR ACTION:

(a) Conservation advisory units should be an integral part of the professional advisory services, with a brief to assist professions achieve development and conservation objectives. They should draw on the advice available from the main conservation organisations whose capacity to provide advice should be extended.

(b) Where financial and administration structures do not encourage professionals to achieve conservation objectives, their professional associations should actively campaign for change.

(c) Codes of practice should be available to guide the activities of those making use of living resources, from highest management level to labourers.

(d) Individual industries, whose activities have a major or potentially major harmful impact on the environment, should develop internal advisory services. Environmental interests should be represented at the highest level of decision making.

Recommendation 12
(see paragraph 16 of this chapter, p 460)

Aim:
To assist policy makers to introduce policies that reflect the urgent need to protect living resources.

Key organisations and agencies:
Government and Government departments, local authorities, statutory environmental bodies, industry, trade unions, professional associations and local government associations.

Constraints:
The financial and administrative structures set up to implement policies decided by local and national politicians frequently act as a disincentive to conservation.

PROPOSALS FOR ACTION:

(a) All policy statements, and the legislation required to implement them, should be scrutinised by the conservation advisers. Their advice should have a very high priority in the issues considered when decisions eventually come to be made.

(b) The findings of the WCS, and in particular its educational implications, should be considered by the Parliamentary Select Committee for Education and Science with a view to addressing Parliament on how to include the environmental education dimensions in its deliberations.

Recommendation 13
(see paragraph 17 of this chapter, p 460)

Aim:
To ensure as far as possible the implementation of the education strategy.

Key organisations and agencies:
Government, IUCN UK Committee, consortium of environmental organisations, Council for Environmental Education and statutory environmental organisations.

Constraints:
No single organisation has the resources to oversee the implementation of the strategy.

PROPOSALS FOR ACTION:

Responsibility for promoting, coordinating and maintaining the education strategy should be allocated to an appropriate organisation, and adequate resources made available. It should also monitor educational changes and advise on their implications for environmental education.

Recommendation 14 (see Chapter 6 of this report)

Aim:
To set up in Scotland a viable national environmental education centre to provide a focal point for the environmental education movement.

Key organisations and agencies:
Scottish Environmental Education Committee (SEEC), Scottish Civic Trust, Scottish Education Department, Countryside Commission for Scotland, National Trust for Scotland and the Nature Conservancy Council.

Constraints:
While SEEC has the representative structure and brief to provide such a centre it does not have the resources available.

PROPOSAL FOR ACTION:

As a major priority, resources should be made available for SEEC to develop into a viable national centre. (SEEC would need only modest resources if it benefited from the systems and structures already developed by the Council for Environmental Education based in England.) The national centre should coordinate environmental education activities in Scotland, and widen its horizons to include the non-formal as well as the formal education sector.

Recommendation 15
(see paragraph 17 of this chapter, p 460)

Aim:
To provide an academic power base for the environmental education movement.

Key organisations and agencies:
University or polytechnic departments of education and colleges of education.

Constraints:
Environmental education lacks a power base within the educational establishment from which teachers, lecturers, educational administrators, local education authority advisers and Her Majesty's Inspectorate can derive support for their efforts.

PROPOSALS FOR ACTION:

A centre should be established in a university or polytechnic department of education to:

(a) promote the study of the history, philosophy and methodology of environmental education and its implementation into formal and non-formal education programmes.

(b) It should carry out research and advanced training and assist the progress of an interdisciplinary approach to environmental education.

(c) It would ideally be located in a university or polytechnic where a number of key departments support the aims of environmental education in a practical manner. (The importance of such a base can be demonstrated by the way in which geographical education progressed rapidly once a university chair was established.)

(d) It would also provide the academic complement for the information/coordinating services of CEE.

Recommendation 16
(see paragraph 17 of this chapter, p 460)

Aim:
To improve the information services available to educators.

Key organisations and agencies:
CEE, Conservation Trust, Curriculum Development Council and those organisations producing or exhibiting education materials, Microelectronics Programme, CET and colleges of education.

Constraints:
Environmental information and specially produced teaching materials are available from many sources: Government Departments, voluntary organisations, industrial and commercial organisations, educational bodies and publishers, — but it is difficult and time consuming for individuals to identify all the sources and materials. They need to know about the range of information available if their courses are to be comprehensive and well-balanced.

PROPOSALS FOR ACTION:

The CEE has developed a system for classifying information and retrieving it simply. It is used mainly to compile resource sheets on environmental topics and issues. The information services of the Council should be expanded to provide a focal point for all educators seeking environmental information or details about environmental education materials. As it is unlikely that one information centre will have the expertise or capacity to cope with all the available information, specialist information centres will be needed. They should adopt a common system that will allow all the centres to be part of a national environmental education information network.

Recommendation 17
(see paragraph 17 of this chapter, p 460)

Aim:
To extend facilities for educators to evaluate environmental educational materials, exchange ideas, find out about the local environment and be aware of opportunities for participation.

Key organisations and agencies:
Teachers' centres, libraries, field and urban studies centres, and their managing authorities and The Conservation Trust.

Constraints:
Centres are threatened by cuts to the education budgets of local authorities. Therefore, it is difficult to attract funds for new activities. However, opportunities should be available where several centres in an area are replaced by one as a contribution to the cuts in the budget.

PROPOSALS FOR ACTION:

It is valuable for educators to be able to see materials that they may wish to use as part of their education programmes. Collections of materials should be available at local centres and accessible at convenient times for inspection. Centres should also provide information about local organisations, events and opportunities to involve students in practical activities. They should encourage meetings or workshops at which educators can exchange information and ideas relating to environmental education. There should be at least one centre in each LEA area with special responsibility for environmental education.

Recommendation 18
(see paragraph 17 of this chapter, p 460)

Aim:
To provide educators with information and ideas to help them prepare or improve educational programmes about the WCS and its relevance to the UK.

Key organisations and agencies:
The School Curriculum Development Council, publishers, environmental organisations and curriculum developers, including LEA advisers.

Constraints:
There are many educational resources that contain information which can be used in environmental education programmes. However, it is difficult for teachers and others to have sufficient access to the materials so that they can extract what they need and prepare coherent education programmes. Further, examples of good practice are not sufficiently publicised, and there has been little guidance on how to implement environmental education programmes in schools, colleges or other centres.

PROPOSALS FOR ACTION:

For school teachers and college lecturers, information packages relating to the themes of the WCS and the issues identified in the Conservation and Development Programme for the UK should be prepared. They should be appropriate for inserting in existing subject syllabuses so that they are not rejected as 'foreign bodies'. These packages should be prepared jointly by appropriate organisations with assistance from teachers. Their availability should be widely publicised, and workshops organised where teachers can work together to suggest how the packs may best be used. If this activity was coordinated by a national body, valuable guidelines for introducing environmental education across the curriculum could be produced.

Summary of the Recommendations

Build Support for Conservation

Schools
All schools should have an environmental education policy, and this should include how the school intends to deal with the pressing living resource issues. The activities and the whole atmosphere of the school should be seen to support this policy. (See paragraphs 5 to 10 of this chapter, pp 459-460)

Each school should designate a senior member of staff to have responsibility for the planning, coordination and oversight of environmental education as a function of the whole curriculum. (See paragraphs 5 to 10 of this chapter, pp 459-460)

All examination boards and the Examinations Council should set up a cross-curricular environmental advisory committee to scrutinise syllabuses over a wide range of subjects. (See paragraphs 5 to 10 of this chapter, pp 459-460)

All teachers should have the opportunity to receive training in the adoption of an environmental approach to their teaching. (See paragraphs 5 to 10 of this chapter, pp 459-460)

Further and higher education
Institutions should act in an environmentally responsible way and should show by example that they support conservation objectives. (See paragraph 11 of this chapter, p 460)

Continuing education (formal sector)
There should be short and long non-vocational courses for adults on conservation matters. They should be well publicised and easily accessible, either through the media or local schools, libraries, etc. (See paragraph 12 of this chapter, p 460)

Youth groups and youth training schemes
Adequate advice and support should be available to leaders and trainers so that they can include conservation objectives in their education and training programmes. In particular, courses should promote environmentally related skills. (See paragraphs 13 to 14 of this chapter, p 460)

Continuing education (non-formal sector)
All organisations, especially those interested in the environment and education, should link with the media in an unprecedented publicity and education (not propaganda) campaign about conservation. The campaign should aim to stimulate discussion and action on a scale adequate enough to help to achieve understanding of current environment issues. (See paragraph 15 of this chapter, p 460)

Government and local authorities should help to open lines of communication between schools, the community, the local authority, voluntary organisations and local business and industrial concerns, to promote fuller participation in local environmental management. (See paragraphs 13 to 15 of this chapter, p 460)

Education for Environmental Intervenors and Policy Makers
All vocational courses should contain a common core module designed to build support for conservation. This should be supplemented with specific material relevant to the target group to assist them to support conservation objectives in their daily work. These aspects of courses must be accorded a high status. (See paragraph 16 of this chapter, p 460)

Advice on how to achieve conservation objectives should be available to intervenors through their own professional advisory services, as well as to Government Departments, local authorities and the statutory environmental bodies. (See paragraph 16 of this chapter, p 460)

All policy statements from Government, local authorities, industry, etc should be scrutinised by conservation advisors to ensure they are compatible with conservation objectives. (See paragraph 16 of this chapter, p 460)

Provide Support for Environmental Educators
Allocate responsibility for promoting this education action plan to an appropriate organisation and make adequate resources available. That organisation should also monitor educational changes. (See paragraph 17 of this chapter, p 460)

(Scotland) Resources should be made available urgently for the SEEC to become a viable national centre for environmental education. (See Chapter 6 of this report)

Set up an academic power base for environmental education from which teachers, lecturers, educational administrators, advisers and Her Majesty's Inspectors can derive support. (See paragraph 17 of this chapter, p 460)

Adopt for educational purposes a common system for classifying information about the environment, environmental issues and learning materials in order to facilitate the expansion of a national environmental education information network. (See paragraph 17 of this chapter, p 460)

Provide regional centres for environmental education at which educators can examine educational materials, find out about relevant events and opportunities, and attend training courses. (See paragraph 17 of this chapter, p 460)

Produce information packages relating to themes from the World Conservation Strategy and the Conservation and Development Programme for the UK which can be easily and relevantly inserted into existing subject curricula. (See paragraph 17 of this chapter, p 460)

Recommendations by Target Audience

Government Departments, local authorities and statutory bodies
1, 4, 5, 6, 7, 9, 12, 15, 17.

Voluntary organisations, non-government organisations
4, 6, 7, 8, 13, 15, 16, 17, 18.

Professional associations
4, 7, 8, 9, 10, 11, 12.

The media
8, 9.

Schools, examination boards, teacher trainers
1, 2, 3, 4, 7, 9, 17.

Further and higher education establishments
4, 5, 6, 8, 9, 10, 13, 15, 17, 18.

Industry, commerce, trade unions
7, 8, 9, 10, 11, 12.

CHAPTER 10

THE PRACTITIONERS' DEBATE

Introduction

1. This report was circulated in June 1982, allowing for six months' debate by practitioners in the field before the writing of this chapter. Over 40 individuals and organisations submitted substantive comments which are reflected throughout the report.

2. When analysing the comments, the responses divided into the following categories:
   (a) UK Government departments (England, Wales, Scotland and Northern Ireland)
   (b) Local government (mainly local education authorities)
   (c) Further and higher educational institutions
   (d) Non-government organisations
   (e) Schools examination boards
   (f) Miscellaneous (comprising a number of individuals and organisations with an interest in environmental education).

3. Although a special debate was held in Scotland, the comments were not sufficiently different from those originating elsewhere in the UK to warrant a separate category. However, there are a few comments that relate particularly to Scotland and these will be presented. Those from Northern Ireland and Wales are all included within the main categories already listed.

4. The Programme Secretariat circulated over 1,000 copies of the report. The debates were organised by the author and individuals within the various organisations that have responded. The Countryside Commission for Scotland undertook arranging the national response from Scotland and the Institution of Environmental Sciences organised a major conference in England. To all those who have given so generously of their time and thought to read and make comments, both critical and flattering, the author is extremely grateful.

The Reception of the Report

5. The report elicited a variety of responses, ranging from great enthusiasm to outright rejection. Those who welcomed it did so for similar reasons: it presented a strong case for the support of environmental education as a means of assisting the achievement of joint conservation and development aims; the language was clear; the recommendations realistic and practical; and, above all, it was possible to use the document immediately to press for change. For example, one LEA has already extracted paragraphs and recommendations it felt to be particularly relevant, and they are being used in debates on educational policy. Others have welcomed it as a document bringing together the sometimes seemingly disparate elements of environmental education, and providing a cogent framework for educators to use when developing new initiatives. There was also praise for the format in which the recommendations were presented.

6. Criticism was most frequently expressed as a reservation for a particular part, rather than the whole, of the report. For example, the proposal to set up an academic power base received a very mixed reception. Others felt the recommendations were too bland and that there should have been more precise suggestions on how they could be implemented and what the implications would be for those involved. There was a general feeling that the main part of the report was too long and that there were too many recommendations. It would have been better to have identified priorities and then to have suggested practical ways of achieving success in these limited areas.

7. Other criticisms have shown that certain issues have not been adequately explored or that the author has not made his intentions clear enough. The following section attempts to identify the gaps, to comment on them, and to clarify the author's views.

Filling the Gaps and Identifying Main Issues

Curriculum Change

8. There was no intention to infer that central curriculum control was favoured. However, it is important for there to be effective mechanisms to promote and assist curriculum change. The author accepts the advice received from some LEA advisers that nationally-based curriculum projects, such as Art and the Built Environment, Geography for the Young School Leaver and Keep Britain Tidy and working with locally-based teacher groups, already provide an example to be followed in other areas of environmental education. Also, the

professional teacher associations frequently work in a similar way, and the changes in Geography teaching over the last 20 years have been largely achieved through this mechanism.

Environmental Education — A Separate Subject?

9. There was criticism that the report, by emphasising the cross-curricular approach, was undermining the efforts of those seeking to promote the study of a separate environmental subject at school and university and to have it examined at all levels. This was not the intention. There should be an opportunity to study an environmental subject within the school curriculum, but this should complement environmental education across the curriculum, not replace it.

Built or Natural Environment

10. The World Conservation Strategy (WCS), on which this book is based, is concerned predominantly with living resource issues. This report reflects this emphasis. However, within the UK, the most pressing environmental problems are perceived as urban ones, and for the majority of people the most familiar environment is an urban one. In reality, there is only one environment, encompassing everything from wilderness to metropolis. The environmental education movement should not attempt to impose artificial distinctions between the study of urban and rural environments and should recognise that for the majority of environmental education programmes the starting point will be the urban environment.

The Ethical Environment

11. Some educators were profoundly disappointed that the report did not tackle the unreceptive ethical environment in which environmental education takes place. As long as children and adults are immersed in an environment where consumption is the major goal, the pleas of those concerned for the environment will make little progress. The author was very much aware of the need for a fundamental change of attitude, but has left this issue to the report which deals specifically with ethics 'Environmental Ethics and Conservation Action', Part 6 of this book.

Purpose of the Report

12. As mentioned in paragraph 6 of this chapter (p 469), many thought the report too long, with too many recommendations and proposals for action. However, these should be seen as a framework within which educators can operate. Individuals and organisations will be able to derive support from this for those projects that they can realistically undertake. The recommendations should not be taken as an action plan to be implemented in its entirety or not at all. One suggestion made was that short separate documents should be produced for individual target groups. The author endorses this suggestion.

Priorities

13. Some critics felt that the report had failed to confront the real issues of environmental education and, as a result, is shallow and unlikely to be effective. The following appeared in one or more sets of comments:
   (a) The need for education programmes to address population issues.
   (b) The need to come to terms with the politics of scarcity.
   (c) The need to consider the contribution of environmental education to future social and economic scenarios.

Comments Relating to the Recommendations

Schools

14. There was strong support for most of the proposals, and particularly that schools should develop environmental education and conservation policies (preferably in consultation with the LEA) and that a member of staff should be made responsible for coordinating their implementation. Similarly, the proposal for there to be centres at which teachers could examine teaching materials, exchange ideas and information, and attend courses, was endorsed. It would be necessary to set up new centres only rarely, since there are already well-established teachers' field study and urban studies centres which could provide this service. (Some areas already have centres providing these facilities.)

15. The major criticisms were as follows. The recommendations do not give adequate recognition of the contribution of the voluntary sector, which has provided the majority of the support for environmental education in schools. However, it has become clear that it can no longer afford to do this at an effective level. It would be hypocritical to talk of a national environmental education strategy if such groups were forced to cease to exist through a lack of funds. However, environmental education frequently has a low priority in the eyes of employers, parents and school governors, and critics felt that the situation would not improve until the Government had made a firm commitment to environmental education, perhaps in a similar manner to the way it has committed itself to health education and information technology.

16. From professional geographers there was the criticism that the report had failed to recognise Geography's contribution. There were many recommending that Geography should become the focus in the school for environmental education. While recognising the invaluable contribution of Geography to the progress of environmental education in schools, geographers usually lack the knowledge and expertise in Ecology which is fundamental to sustaining resource use. It is important for environmental education to use existing subject structures in school, but it is unwise to put any one subject area at the heart of it.

17. There was the suggestion that, because environmental issues are so complex, it is easy to take extreme positions on the basis of little knowledge. As a result, it was suggested that environmental education should restrict its aims to increasing environmental awareness, understanding and powers of observation. These are important aims, but unless students are given practice in assessing information, and are provided with opportunities to solve the problems and state opinions, they will not be developing the skills necessary to participate in the democratic process. Environmental education should not avoid the consideration of controversial issues, but should avoid presenting them in a doctrinaire way.

18. Some felt that the value of outdoor work was not given sufficient emphasis. This was not intended. Outdoor work should be part of every child's curriculum at least once a term. Although most of it will have to be undertaken in the local environment, all children should have the opportunity to study an unfamiliar environment at least once in their school career. Outdoor work should involve the study of 'natural' and built environments. Children should have an opportunity to have direct contact with plants and animals and should also be able to study them in their natural environment. The author deplores the closure of field centres which have provided expert courses for children and teachers alike. All teachers should receive some training to allow them to feel confident when working with students outside the classroom.

19. The report has not given adequate recognition to the opportunities offered to schools by the education departments of zoos, museums, historic houses, etc.

Examinations

20. While examination boards sympathised with the proposal to include an environmental dimension in examination syllabuses, responsibility for this was passed to the individual subject panels. They also suggested it was not practical to recommend that field work be examined, because schools may experience financial and administrative difficulties. However, examples show that where a school believes in outdoor studies the problems can be overcome.

Teacher Training

21. Most of the recommendations addressed to schools were equally important for institutions providing teacher training. In particular, the need for environmental education and conservation policies. It was also stressed that all teachers should be aware of environmental problems, so that their teaching has the potential to contribute to the aims and objectives of environmental education. Colleges which already provide courses on environmental education, for example, Avery Hill, welcomed the report as it gave support for their courses which have been frequently threatened as they are considered 'fringe activities'.

22. There was very strong support for the recommendation advocating the improvement of in-service training facilities for teachers. Although pre-service training is now obligatory, many teachers have received no training in the environmental approach, and there is no obligation to undertake any further professional training. In-service training should be mandatory, and although funding will be required, teacher unions, professional associations and LEAs should continue to work together to increase training facilities. Within the schemes there should be provision for training in the approach, methods and content of environmental education.

Further and Higher Education

23. This section was perhaps the most disappointing part of the report. It failed to give sufficient recognition to the role of the Institution of Environmental Sciences. As an association of educators in further and higher education establishments, it has promoted influential national and international conferences and has been active in promoting environmental courses. Considering that more than 75 per cent of people at some stage in their career receive education or training in the further education sector, the value of including environmental education is clear. One particular recommendation was to establish full-time training schemes to produce scientific monitoring technicians. This step would facilitate the creation of effective environmental monitoring systems by the Government and help to meet the related manpower needs within industry.

24. New training initiatives by the MSC will rely very much on the further education sector. The opportunity to include environmental education should not be lost, and it is to be hoped that the Institution of Environmental Sciences will take full advantage of these opportunities.

25. The proposal for an academic power base for environmental education to be set up in a further or higher educational establishment proved to be very controversial. The main criticism was that this would be creating a new body which could easily become divorced from the main initiators of curriculum change in LEAs.

However, these critics supported the proposal for local centres. In Northern Ireland and Scotland there was strong support for the foundation of effective national centres. There was also support for a centre which could provide a focus for research activity which was regrettably absent in the environmental education movement.

Non-Formal Education

26. The response to this section of the report was very disappointing. Although people recognised the importance of non-formal education programmes for adults — and there were a few exhortations to the media to improve their coverage of environmental issues — there were few specific endorsements or criticism of the recommendations. Some of the individual comments deserve mention:

(a) People are confused by the inability of the conservationists to agree on how best to solve environmental problems. This failure perhaps reflects the inadequacy of the scientific method in solving problems which also have a moral dimension.

(b) People do not yet understand why conservation is so important. In comparison with unemployment, inner city problems and threats to world peace, conservation is perceived as trivial.

(c) Conservationists do not recognise the constraints imposed upon those using the environment, such as farmers, foresters, industrialists. Financial and administrative controls may make conservation practices impossible, and conservationists have a duty to learn about these constraints if they expect to enter into a meaningful dialogue with the developers.

(d) Some research is needed to find out if environmental education programmes lead to changes in attitudes and, if so, whether the change is reflected in behaviour patterns.

(e) Greater encouragement should be given to non-environmental organisations. For example, the National Federation of Womens Institutes has supported a very successful education programme on WCS.

(f) Local politicians have been largely ignored by the report, and it was suggested that the National Association of Local Councils be used as a vehicle for the exchange of ideas and information relating to the environment and environmental education.

(g) Educators should take a cue from television companies who have realised that the public is fascinated by the natural world of plants and animals. They should extend the range of opportunities to study nature where it is — outside the home and the classroom.

(h) Planners and architects, especially in local planning departments, have shown a commitment to environmental education and public participation over the last few years. Educators should be made more aware of the contribution they can make and be encouraged to use these professionals in their education programmes. Contact should be made with planning departments.

Looking to the Future

Setting a Good Example

27. In the debate, most people restricted their comments and criticisms to the formal education sector, and in particular schools. There was almost an assumption by some critics that if only there was good environmental education in schools then the UK environmental problems would be resolved. This may overstate the case, but it serves to illustrate that we expect too much of schools. School education is only a short part of an educational process. It lays foundations of knowledge, skills and values which can be built on throughout life.

28. Children learn by example, yet the example set by their peers in the way they use the environment often conflicts with what they are learning. When commenting on schools, one person recounted how she had seen a young pupil throwing stones at some ducks while the teacher looked on. The audience was horrified, but is the action and attitude behind it any different from that of the adult who shoots ducks out of the sky? Is the child who breaks down a newly planted tree any more of a vandal than the farmer who rips up trees on his farm? Such contradictions are not lost on children, especially the older ones.

29. The poor opinion of school education that some people held was largely based on ignorance of what was happening in schools. Here the education professions must accept much of the blame for not communicating sufficiently with those outside the profession. Many schools have excellent environmental programmes, and some have been referred to in the report, but information about them is not widely known.

30. In fact, environmental education has failed to sell itself to the conservation movement, parents, school governors and others. Until this is rectified, it is not likely to get the support it deserves. A main priority of the environmental education movement should be to increase public awareness of what environmental education is, what it is doing and what it wants to achieve. When it is seen as something interesting, exciting and, above all, relevant and useful, it will gain greater acceptance.

How Effective is Environmental Education?

31. In the comments received from non-educationists, impatience with environmental education for not getting results fast enough was detected. It is difficult to refute this criticism because of the difficulty of assessing performance in non-cognitive or non-skill areas. However, there is clearly a need to undertake research

into the effectiveness of environmental education programmes.

Preparing Materials

32. There is a good deal of material available for environmental education programmes, but, following this book, more will be needed to:

(a) help people understand why conservation is essential.

(b) allow education programmes to be developed on the main themes and topics identified in the other reports.

(c) make practical suggestions as to how individuals can support conservation.

Using the Report

33. Specific target groups should be identified, and those sections and recommendations relevant to them should be extracted from this report and made available in separate documents. Documents are proposed for:

(a) those concerned with school education, including teacher training.

(b) those in further and higher education, working in both vocational and non-vocational courses.

(c) those working in public information or education.

(d) those professionals whose decisions or activities have a direct impact on the environment.

Priorities

34. This report presents a framework to guide future activity in environmental education. It is more concerned with identifying opportunities than priorities. However, certain prerequisites have become apparent in addition to those listed above.

(a) The voluntary sector has provided the habitat for environmental education. However, in the present economic climate that habitat has shrunk, and some species of environmental education are threatened with extinction. Further success will depend to a considerable extent on a strong verbal, financial, and practical commitment to environmental education by Government.

(b) The environmental education movement has failed to make a great enough impact on those outside its circle. To achieve the progress it seeks, the movement must popularise its image, expose itself to public criticism and obtain publicity. In achieving these ends, it must retain its high ideals and maintain its high standards of practice.

A REVIEW OF ENVIRONMENTAL EDUCATION

Introduction

The purpose of this brief review of environmental education is to provide a background from which to develop a strategy. It will describe general trends in a number of target areas in the formal and non-formal education sectors, illustrating them on occasion with examples. There is no shortage of examples of the best practice in all the sectors and many have had to be omitted. However, because of the lack of data, it has proved impossible to gauge the extent to which environmental education has been introduced within each sector, and how effective they have been.

It would be comforting to conclude that if the examples of good practice were the rule rather than the exception, then the aims and objectives of environmental education would be achieved. Such a conclusion would be presumptuous, since there has been little evaluation of environmental education programmes. In reality, it might prove impossible to isolate the effects of environmental education on an individual's values and attitudes from all the other influences.

While a review is essential to assist and guide the development of an environmental education strategy, because of other limitations it would be unwise to over-emphasise its importance. Hence the review has not attempted to be comprehensive. Also, it is important to remember that some of the excellent programmes referred to may only benefit a handful of people.

The DES has produced a review of environmental education which complements this Appendix.

The Impact of Environmental Education

The term environmental education is only 15 years old. It was coined, very informally, to reflect both a dimension of concern for the environment that was growing within the established environmental studies courses, and a recognition of the contribution that education could make in the solution of environmental problems. It was born at a time when the greatest concern was for the rural environments, but today the concept relates to the quality of all environments. It is concerned with issues, the successful resolution of actual and potential conflicts between human activities and the environment, and public participation in environmental management.

In its short history, environmental education has made a tremendous impact. It aims to change attitudes and behaviour patterns through education, a process that has been proved to be slow. Yet, in spite of few resources being available, the tremendous counteracting forces of vested interests, and its early lukewarm reception by some environmentalists, progress has been comparable with the anti-smoking movements and the drive to wear seat belts in cars, both of which have received much more Governmental financial support and public attention.

Such rapid progress would normally attract congratulations, but, as the environmental problems that surround us have grown at a rapid pace, it might appear that environmental education has been ineffectual. To create the will to solve environmental problems requires educational programmes. This review gives a glimpse of what has already been achieved.

Increased exposures to the public of information about the environment and environmental issues have created a more aware and knowledgeable electorate which increasingly demands its views to be taken into account at local and national levels. Pressure groups are flourishing. While environmental issues have always been political, the increased pressure from public opinion is forcing politicians to take greater account of the views of the public when developing policy.

However complacency is ill-placed. There is still a parochial attitude towards environmental issues, and environmental education should strive to increase an awareness of global issues and a desire to contribute to their solution. Although it is now acceptable to be an environmentalist, the movement has not successfully erased the image that it is anti-development and naïve. On the other hand, it has not overcome its own prejudice that all developers are irresponsible and cavalier in their use of the environment. Such polarisation of views is not beneficial to anyone, and in the years to come endeavours must be made to bring both sides together in a spirit of cooperation rather than confrontation. The publication of the WCS gives support to this effort.

Environmental Education in Schools

Curriculum development

The curriculum is the responsibility of the school in partnership with the LEA and central Government. The burden of that responsibility falls on the head teacher and staff. In junior schools, environmental education is well-established as the school organisation favours the use of an interdisciplinary approach. It is in secondary schools that the inadequacy of environmental education is most apparent. Local education authorities can promote curriculum development in certain areas through the allocation of resources, for example, in those authorities where environmental education advisers have been appointed there is more and better environmental education taking place. Field work activities can be greatly encouraged by the payment of travel and accommodation grants, and by the financing of LEA field centres both within and outside the authority's area. Curriculum development is also brought about through continuing professional training provided by LEAs, DES, voluntary organisation, professional associations, and educational institutions. There are very few courses on environmental education as such, but many on environmentally related topics sometimes related to specific subject areas. They tend to be evening, one day, or weekend courses. Professional courses in environmental education for teachers lasting one term or longer (full- or part-time) involve only six institutions and less than 50 people a year. Part-time courses can only attract local teachers, and full-time courses require secondment which is at the discretion of the LEA. The number of teachers able to benefit from such courses is therefore limited.

In 15 years the Schools Council produced over 160 projects, a number of which have relevance for environmental education, eg Project Environment, (1974) Environmental Studies 5-13, Geography for the Young School Leaver, Geography 16-19 and Art and the Built Environment. While the content of the environmental projects is excellent, the take-up by schools has been very low. Currently, the Council is embarked on programmes of new work which place teachers at the centre of curriculum research and development and puts emphasis on collaborative working with national and local statutory and voluntary organisations. Within this framework an attempt is being made to develop a policy and an approach to environmental education for the Schools Council. This is being pursued through consultation with other interested and concerned persons, agencies and organisations at national and local levels.

The Department of Education and Science traditionally has left the management of the school curriculum to LEAs. However, in the late 1970s it initiated the 'Great Debate' about what should be taught in schools, particularly secondary schools, and published in 'A Framework for the School Curriculum' (1980) components of a 'good' school curriculum. A revised version, 'The School Curriculum' was produced in 1981. There has also been passing mention of environmental education in documents such as the primary and secondary surveys. Following the environmental education seminar at Tbilisi, DES produced two major publications about environmental education: 'Environmental Education: a review' (1981) and 'Environmental Education: Sources of Information 1981'. (In Scotland, education is the responsibility of the Scottish Education Department, in Wales the Welsh Education Department, and in Northern Ireland the Department of Education for Northern Ireland.)

Her Majesty's Inspectorate (HMI) contributed to the 'Great Debate' with the discussion document 'Curriculum 11-16'. It was supported by a number of subject papers, one of which was 'Curriculum 11-16: Environmental Education', DES, 1979. This document stresses that environmental education is a function of the whole curriculum. It represents a valuable contribution to the literature about environmental education in schools and has been circulated to every secondary school in the UK. It has formed the basis of three regional seminars for head teachers and curriculum.

Voluntary organisations play a very important part in the promotion of environmental education. Their contributions are too many and varied for this Appendix. There are organisations that relate to most areas of environmental interest (a useful list is included in the DES book *Environmental Education: Sources of Information 1981*, (DES 1981)) and professional associations for teachers and others interested in environmental education. Some organisations, for example the RSPB, and the Town and Country Planning Association, have set up education units which produce materials, liaise with schools and run courses for students and teachers. In 1980, 2,500 teachers attended training courses organised by the Royal Society for the Protection of Birds. While some organisations concentrate on the provision of information, others such as the British Trust for Conservation Volunteers (BTCV) encourage involvement in environmental improvement projects.

In 1980, 1,500 volunteers completed 79,000 days work through BTCV. A number of teacher professional associations have environmental education sections, for example the environmental education working group of the Geographical Association. An important professional association is the National Association of Environmental Education which comprises teachers from all subject areas. Through one of its publications, 'Environmental education: a statement of aims' (1976) it encourages all schools to adopt an environmental education policy and offers guidelines. Within the charitable environmental organisations there is sometimes a debate as to whether funds raised ostensibly for conservation projects should be used for education.

Field Work

Field work is a term used to include all studies that take place outside the classroom, whether in the school grounds, the immediate locality, either urban or rural, or more distant areas. Education in the environment is not new — it has been a feature of the rural studies curriculum since the turn of the century — but the movement was boosted by the formation in 1943 of the Council for the Promotion of Field Studies, now the Field Studies Council (FSC). In 1981, the *Directory of Outdoor Studies Centres in England and Wales*, listed over 500 day and residential centres for field studies. They are managed in a number of ways through a number of organisations, including FSC, LEAs, the Youth Hostels Association, and charitable and private organisations.

Since the production of the Skeffington Report in 1969, which advocated education for children and adults about the urban environment and urban issues, about 15 urban studies centres have been set up. As well as the study of towns, they encourage community involvement and action in environmental management, and they are linked by the Council for Urban Studies Centre.

Certain subject associations, such as the Institute of Biology, the Geographical Association and the National Association for Environmental Education, fully endorse the value of field work in the schools curriculum. Some examination boards allow students' field work to be examined at A level, and the majority of CSE (England and Wales only) exam syllabuses in environmentally related subjects make field work compulsory. Traditionally, field work concentrates on the development of environmental skills and knowledge.

Education cuts and rising costs are reducing the opportunities for teachers to take children to residential centres, especially outside their home area. Several centres have been closed, and the National Association of Field Studies Officers is conducting a survey to find out how cuts are affecting field study provision.

Resources

There is a very wide choice of environmental education teaching and learning materials. They are available from commercial publishers, industry, business, charitable organisations, Government Departments and environmental pressure groups. Some materials are concerned predominantly with environmental topics such as weather studies or the ecology of a pond, and others with environmental issues such as the use of energy, use of farmland, or pollution. Some materials are available free of charge. However, teachers have been handicapped by not knowing what information is available.

The establishment of an information centre in 1980 at the Council for Environmental Education has enabled annotated bibliographies to be produced on over 20 environmental topics and issues. These bibliographies enable teachers to make a balanced selection of resources for teaching. Many of the materials listed are available on postal loan from the Resource Centre of the Conservation Trust.

The major curriculum projects in environmental education have been very impressive. They have identified the important areas of knowledge, skills and concepts and have linked them to the age and ability of children. They have been cross-curricular but have not shown

adequately how they can be adapted to suit a traditional subject approach. As a result, the specially prepared resource packs, etc have limited use in schools.

Examinations

During the 1970s, exam syllabuses at 16+ and 18+ were developed in environmental studies and environmental science with the idea of making the topics academically respectable. They have not achieved the popularity the originators hoped for because most students still opt for the traditional subjects. However, examination boards have been willing to retain these minority subjects even though they are uneconomical.

There has been much debate among environmental educationalists about the value of having a separate subject called environmental education, but this has been largely resolved. Environmental education integrated into the whole curriculum is an ideal, but in practical terms, less than the ideal has often to be accepted. Examinations considerably affect the curriculum of secondary schools, and, with the possible change to the new 16+ examination in England and Wales, there is now an opportunity to discuss how best to include environmental education.

The traditional subject areas, even though they may have a strong base in the environment, have not always developed a strong environmental education component. For example, biology exam courses require students to learn a lot about plants and animals, but comparatively little of the course is devoted to a study of ecology. Environmental issues are rarely studied.

Where separate environmental studies courses have been introduced by examination boards, the similarities between them are few. This is one reason why they have limited acceptance as a qualification for further study or employment.

Teacher Training

'Environmental education demands a reasonably sophisticated level of understanding of the process of education — probably a level beyond that generally achieved by graduates . . . doing the post-graduate Certificate of Education' (Carson, 1978). As a result, after initial training few teachers have the competence or confidence to become involved in effective environmental education teaching schemes.

Prior to colleges of education which trained teachers mainly for primary and middle schools being hit by cuts, about 2,500 teachers a year enjoyed a course which included guidance on teaching in an environmental manner.

Now that these colleges have either disappeared or have been absorbed into institutions of further and higher education, there has been a trend towards more academic courses being organised on a subject basis. As yet they do not appear to meet the needs of environmental education as well as the previous course.

There are facilities for teachers to receive in-service training in aspects of environmental education. Long courses of one term or more probably involve less than 50 teachers a year, but a greater number attend courses and conferences organised by Government Education Departments, the LEAS and the professional and voluntary organisations. They often take place in the evenings, or at weekends, and attendance is purely voluntary and usually at the teachers' own expense. As the majority of such courses are organised on a local basis, it is impossible to be certain how many teachers participate in them. However, as attendance is voluntary, only those teachers with the necessary motivation are likely to attend. Courses which are concerned with specialist subjects, or particular environmental topics or issues, do not usually reflect the holistic approach sought by environmental educators.

Environmental Education in Further and Higher Education Establishments

Environmental education in technical and vocational training in further and higher education falls into two main categories:
  (a) Courses devoted almost entirely to environmental sciences;
  (b) Environmental options, which can be studies within the more traditional subjects.

In higher education there has been a proliferation of new degree courses in the environmental field. About 90 are listed by the National Association for Environmental Education (NAEE) in a document which is regularly updated. These are of a specialised and vocational nature, with four main bases:
  (a) environmental health within the medical and health professions;
  (b) environmental design within the general area of planning, landscaping and architecture;
  (c) resource-conservation within the natural sciences, often with a base in geography and biology, and including aspects of management, eg forestry, agriculture;
  (d) social science/human ecology approach to the human environment and community.

Because of the specialised nature of most of these courses, the holistic view of the environment advocated by environmental education is rarely achieved. Also, they rarely emphasise the positive contribution the courses could make to the development of a personal environmental ethic.

It has been suggested that students with post-graduate qualifications in environmental sciences have found it more difficult than other graduates to obtain employment which uses their special talents. This has led some people to suggest that students wishing to study environmental science would be better off studying a main-line science subject, such as physics, chemistry or biology, and choosing the environmental options offered within it.

However, research by the Institution of Environmental Sciences (1979) has shown that the proportion of students finding employment in areas related to their studied subject is the same as those finding employment in other areas. *An Introduction to Careers in the Environmental Sphere* is published jointly by CEE and CoEnCo Youth Division.

Environmental education is sadly lacking in business management schools, both in the initial training and in-service courses. Many of the middle management in larger industries have not had the benefit of school-based environmental education programmes, and without suitable programmes for use in in-services training they are not able to consider the environmental impact of their decisions responsibly. At a time of recession, it is likely that conservation will have a low priority because it will be thought to be of secondary importance. *Ends*, a magazine published by Environmental Data Service, helps to keep decision makers in touch with environmental legislation and promotes concern for the environment.

The Professional Institutions Council for Conservation (PICC) was founded in 1972 to provide a forum for inter-professional discussion and action on environmental issues. Presently, it consists of some 16 professional institutions, and many other organisations with conservation interests. The Council holds regular meetings and seminars and, through its newsletter and other publications, seeks to disseminate information and advice. From time to time it appoints working parties to consider particular issues of environmental concern.

At a lower level of training, the City and Guilds of London Institute offers examinations for young people seeking jobs in industry, agriculture, the public services, etc. A most encouraging development is that an environmental component has been made compulsory in all the Foundation courses. This unit relates mainly to the area in which they are seeking employment, but it also promotes the concept of interdependence in their view of the environment.

Environmental Education and Environmental Information

Youth and community organisations have become more aware of the wider implications of environmental issues, and environmental groups have recognised that their aims are parallel to those of the youth and community movement. Projects involving environmental improvement have proved very popular among young people and have been able to attract a lot of support, both moral and financial, from Government, charitable and commercial organisations. It has been suggested that such activities could provide useful employment for school leavers without jobs, but the voluntary organisations have rejected the suggestion that such activities be made compulsory.

Television, radio, newspapers and magazines are the major sources of information on environmental topics and issues and formers of public opinion. How far they are able to achieve fundamental changes to environmental values and attitudes is debatable. However, it is significant that, in totalitarian states, control of the media is seen to be essential in the moulding of public attitudes, and, even in the democratic states, various interest groups seek to influence the public sources of information.

Comparing today with 10 years ago, the general public shows a much greater awareness of, and interest in, the environment. Natural history programmes on television, such as 'Life on Earth' and 'Botanic Man', have attracted large audiences, and environmental issues are debated regularly in current affairs programmes. About seven million people watched a special 'Wildlife on One' programme (BBC 1) about the Wildlife and Countryside Bill in 1981 which itself has generated more discussion than any other Parliamentary Bill. The quality newspapers, too, devote space regularly to environmental issues at local, national and international levels and the *Guardian* has a regular feature called 'Alternatives' which from time to time deals with environmental matters. There are now also a number of 'environmental' magazines for the public and professionals, produced by both commercial publishers and environmental and professional organisations. Some are specifically concerned with environmental education, including *Review of Environmental Education Developments* (REED), produced by the Council for Environmental Education, *Environmental Education*, produced by the National Association for Environmental Education, *Bulletin of Environmental Education* (BEE), produced by Town and Country Planning Association and two new international journals launched in 1981. Circulation is small, about 4,000 altogether. However, since the demise of *Vole* in 1981, there is no magazine on bookstalls dealing predominantly with ecological and environmental issues.

Environmental information is available through a number of channels:

(a) the Government Departments and Statutory Bodies
(b) various non-government organisations
(c) pressure groups
(d) industry and commerce
(e) the media, including commercial publishers.

Information about the environment that has reached the public has four main purposes:

(a) To increase the general level of awareness and appreciation of the environment and to under-stand the interrelatedness of its systems. There is little public information available on this. The WCS has provided a convenient vehicle for developing such information and WWF-UK has produced a film for hire and a short publicity leaflet on the issues dealt with by the WCS. Use of these resources is being encouraged. In 1981, a weekly magazine *The Living Countryside* was launched.

(b) To increase awareness of specific issues of topics. Over the last three years, for example, the Department of Energy has developed a comprehensive education programme which uses advertising, information packs, public lectures, etc, as part of its 'Save It' campaign. Most organisations produce educational information relating to their area of concern and organise activities, although many are primarily of a recreational nature.

(c) To change or reinforce attitudes and modes of behaviour, and involve people more directly in the decision making process. Certain environmental issues are very controversial, and 'educational' materials are produced by the different factions to try and attract the allegiance of members of the public.

(d) To reassure the public that environmental difficulties are being adequately taken care of.

Earthscan acts as an agent for development and environment news material, supplying it to the press, radio and television. This organisation is threatened with closure, and, if this happens, there will then be no systematic way of channelling information about environmental topics to the media except for the press releases issued by individual organisations.

There is no mechanism comparable to the Development Journalists Group, which brings together journalists interested in furthering the theme of conservation.

Most education takes place on an informal basis, but there are formal courses in adult education relating to various environmental topics and activities organised by LEAs, the Workers Educational Association and various statutory and voluntary organisations. For example, the Countryside Commission, in association with the Association of Agriculture, has developed a programme of Farm Open Days. On these days, certain farms are open to the public and an education programme is arranged. The residential study centres in the national parks arrange regular courses, which, as well as becoming more popular with home audiences, are attracting participants from overseas. However, these formal courses reach only a minority of the public and are usually attended by people who already sympathise with the aims of the environmental movement.

Some industries, particularly the largest ones, have become concerned with the hostility of environmental groups to the impact of industrial processes on the environment. Some have set up educational units to produce educational materials to counteract these views, and devote resources to building up a 'good neighbour' image. Industry is now aware that it cannot afford to ignore the criticisms levelled at it by environmentalists, that it must provide answers to their questions and, in certain cases, change its policies.

There has also been a growing interest in environmental interpretation which contributes so much to the education of the public. In 1980, the Carnegie Trust provided funds for the institution of a national Centre for Environmental Interpretation which is housed at Manchester Polytechnic. It aims to encourage and support environmental interpretation in the UK.

One aim of environmental education is to encourage public participation in environmental decision making. This approach has been eagerly developed by planners, and, based on over 10 years of experience, the Royal Town Planning Institute has published 'Public participation: an issues report' (1980). It identifies 24 primary issues which raise fundamental questions about the conduct of public participation at all tiers of government. In spite of attempts to involve the public more in the decisions affecting their local environment, progress has been disappointingly slow.

A valuable initiative has been made by the National Federation of Womens Institutes. In cooperation with CEE, a leaflet about the WCS has been circulated to every group, and a support programme encouraged.

The response has been excellent and could serve as an example to other organisations.

Promotion of Regional Cooperation in Environment Education

Since the introduction of the term environmental education in the 1960s, the movement has been characterised by considerable international and regional cooperation which has enabled environmental education to assume an accepted identity throughout the world. The UK has made a major contribution to the international acceptance of environmental education, and is supporting a number of regional activities, involving both government and non-government organisations.

The Institution of Environmental Sciences and the World Environment and Resources Council organised the second European Seminar on Environmental Education in Bern, Easter 1980. It was attended by more than 100 participants. It has organised a number of other international conferences and was instrumental in the introduction of two international environmental education journals in 1981.

The UK Government is a member of IUCN and several non-government organisations are also members. The UK has eight members on the Commission on Education. The Commission on Education NW European Committee meets annually to exchange ideas and information and develop projects. In 1980, it produced the leaflet 'Care for the Coast'. The UK sends three representatives.

Environmental Education Network is a project initiated in 1977 for junior schools by the European Commission. It aims to encourage the development of environmental education materials and programmes. The UK is participating in the programme. Through the Council for Environmental Education, the UK is contributing to the environmental education research project based at the Institute for Science Education at Kiel University on materials for environmental education.

The UK is also closely involved with Council of Europe programmes for environmental education.

The strengthening of the Council for Environmental Education as the national centre has enabled information about regional and international activities to be exchanged more effectively. The advice of the Council on the development of environmental education is frequently sought by individuals and organisations from overseas. An important medium for the dissemination of information on these and other environmental education issues is the Council's journal *Review of Environmental Education Developments* (REED).

The Government and Environmental Education

Environmental education predominantly concerns two Government Departments: the Department of Education and Science and the Department of the Environment. Other departments also have an interest in particular aspects of environmental education, eg the Department of Energy and the Ministry of Agriculture, Fisheries and Food. Most financial support for the environmental education movement has come through the Department of the Environment's 'Small Grants'. Recipients of grants include the Keep Britain Tidy Group, the British Trust for Conservation Volunteers and the Council for Environmental Education. Funding is for one year, and must normally be matched by equal funds from non-government sources. The Department has announced more secure funding arrangements for the Council for Environmental Education.

The Department of the Environment is particularly interested in projects that relate to inner city areas. It has given support to a number of urban studies centres, and commissioned the Environmental Board's report 'Environmental Education in Urban Areas' (1979). (The Environmental Board was disbanded in 1980.)

The activities of the Department of Education are more related to formal education, but it has little power to influence the curriculum in schools or colleges of further and higher education. In response to the Tbilisi recommendations (1977) two booklets have been produced 'Environmental Education: a review' (1981) and 'Environmental Education Sources of Information for Teachers' (1981). These received a considerable input from HMI which also produced 'Curriculum 11-16: Environmental Education' (1979). HMI has given considerable encouragement to the environmental education movement, but it has not funds to support initiatives. The English Department of Education and Science makes only a small financial contribution to environmental education activities.

Statutory Bodies and Environmental Education

The Countryside Commission's education work covers a very broad area. It is involved in promoting conservation awareness among adults, such as farmers, councillors and professional advisers, whose actions have a direct influence upon the way the countryside is used and managed. Also, educational materials which deal with landscape conservation and access issues have been developed for schools. Future work will probably include the promotion of worthwhile new educational initiatives in the voluntary sector. In its reorganisation, the Countryside Commission has closed its education department.

The Nature Conservancy Council was established 'for the purpose of nature conservation and fostering the understanding thereof', and the development of responsible attitudes towards the environment is fundamental to its work. Through the experience of its widely dispersed staff in conserving flora, fauna and geological and physiographic features, and the specialist service provided by its Training and Education Advisory Section, it seeks to assist professional educationists.

References

CARSON, S McB. (editor). 1978. Environmental education: principles and practice. London, Edward Arnold.

DEPARTMENT OF EDUCATION AND SCIENCE AND WELSH OFFICE. 1980. A framework for the school curriculum. London, HMSO.

DEPARTMENT OF EDUCATION AND SCIENCE. 1979. Curriculum 11-16: supplementary working papers by HM Inspectorate. Environmental Education, London, DES.

DEPARTMENT OF EDUCATION AND SCIENCE. 1981. Environmental education: a review. London, DES.

DEPARTMENT OF EDUCATION AND SCIENCE. 1981. Environmental education: sources of information for teachers 1981. London, DES.

ENVIRONMENTAL BOARD, DEPARTMENT OF THE ENVIRONMENT. 1979. Environmental Education in Urban Areas. London, HMSO.

NATIONAL ASSOCIATION FOR ENVIRONMENTAL EDUCATION. 1976. Environmental education: a statement of aims. Birmingham, NAEE.

ROYAL TOWN PLANNING INSTITUTE. 1980. Public participation: an issues report. RTPI.

SCHOOLS COUNCIL. 1974. Project environment. Harlow, Longmans.

THE DEVELOPMENT OF AN ENVIRONMENTAL EDUCATION PHILOSOPHY

Introduction

In the UK there has been a long tradition of interest in natural history. In the last century some of our most prestigious environmental organisations were founded, including the Zoological Society of London and the Royal Entomological Society. Concern for nature was reflected in the foundation of such organisations as the Commons, Open Spaces and Footpaths Preservation Society, the RSPB and RSPCA.

During the early part of this century, rural studies formed an important part of the curriculum in schools in the rural areas, and it is on this rural/nature interest that environmental education laid its foundations. However, environmental education recognises that the environment is one — a continuum from wilderness to metropolis — and advocates the introduction of educational programmes designed to help solve environmental problems.

By describing a few landmarks, this brief survey traces the evolution of an environmental education philosophy which has received international acceptance.

Countryside in 1970, Second Conference Held at University of Keele, March 1965

Seventeen recommendations were made and the majority referred to the use of the natural environment as an educational resource (field studies). However, they also included recommendations for the training of specialists and the provision of information services for teachers and others.

Field studies were already a component of environmental education, but this recommendation gave a further stimulus to its use. Today, there are few schools which do not take their students out to learn from their environment. Facilities for outdoor education have been much improved, with the provision of centres run by LEAs, the Field Studies Council, the YHA, other organisations, and private individuals.

Recommendations relating to the role of Field Work in environmental education are being achieved and in some cases have gone further than at first envisaged, since field work also takes place in urban areas and includes studying the built as well as the 'natural' environment.

Less successful have been the recommendations that refer to the changes in the school curriculum. The 'out-dated barriers between many school subjects' are becoming more rather than less entrenched in spite of repeated exhortations to consider the school's curriculum as one unit rather than a collection of pieces. There have been other very positive achievements based on the recommendations: the development of a national centre for environmental education in 1968 and the introduction in 1980 of an environmental education centre which provides a nationwide information service.

Skeffington Report UK 1969

The report was concerned mainly with planning and the built environment, but included a section on the need for education and public participation in decision making. This added a new dimension to environmental education in the UK, which has now spread, through UK attendance at regional meetings, to other European countries. Environmental education developed from a concern for the natural environment, and it reflected the content and methodology of rural studies courses. This 'rural' approach has contributed to environmental education:

(a) the use of the environment as an educational resource;
(b) an appreciation and concern for environmental quality;
(c) techniques and skills for studying the natural environment;
(d) a body of knowledge.

The inclusion of the urban dimension has contributed to a more active, and political, environmental education movement, eg:

(a) public participation in environmental issues;
(b) the problem solving approach;
(c) community action;
(d) techniques, skills, and a body of knowledge relating to the urban environment.

International Working Meeting on Environmental Education and the School Curriculum, IUCN, Nevada 1970

The first generally accepted definition of environmental education was produced at this meeting: 'Environmental education is the process of recognising values and clarifying concepts in order to develop skills and attitudes necessary to understand and appreciate the interrelatedness among man, his culture and his biophysical surroundings. Environmental education also entails practice in decision making and self-formation of a code of behaviour about issues concerning environmental quality'.

It has guided the development of environmental education from that date. However, like most definitions it is very wide ranging and needs further explanation. Hence, while accepted by environmental education experts, it has had little impact on people in other fields and there is still much confusion as to what environmental education is all about.

Further suggestions that came out of the meeting included making environmental education obligatory in school, teacher training and other courses. While compulsion is not an appropriate way in the UK for influencing curricula, the Department of Education recently initiated a debate about what should be taught in schools, contributing curriculum recommendations in 1980 and 1981. Although environmental education was recommended there was no detail provided as there was for traditional subject areas.

Conference on the Human Environment, UN, Stockholm 1972
This conference considered the global issues that required men and women's urgent attention: limits to economic growth, world poverty, environmental degradation and the nuclear threat. Although there was already a degree of 'internationalism' in school courses, in newspapers, on the radio and television, and in the literature of many organisations, the conference gave much support and respectability to discussion of these issues. It recommended a new effort in international environmental education and set up UNESCO-UNEP, the United Nations Environmental Programme.

The International Workshop on Environmental Education, UNESCO-UNEP, Belgrade 1975
This conference produced the first major intergovernmental statement on environmental education. Recognising that the global problems highlighted at Stockholm required nothing short of a new global ethic if they were to be solved, the conference produced goals, objectives, guiding principles and recommendations for environmental education. The statement, which has become better known as the Belgrade Charter, is a very clear statement of what environmental education is and what it is attempting to do. It has therefore given a very firm foundation for the environmental education movement to build on, and its importance is reflected in the high degree of agreement internationally on the aims and objectives of environmental education and the means of achieving them.

Environmental Education — A Report by HM Inspectors of Schools, Scottish Education Department 1974
The report recommendations showed that the messages of previous environmental education meetings had reached those people with a closer responsibility for the education of children. The report also gave more practical advice on the introduction of environmental education in schools. It is still valid today.

Regional Meeting of Experts on Environmental Education in Europe, UNESCO-UNEP, Helsinki 1977
There are few new recommendations in evidence, but the key features of environmental education are repeated, ie involvement with issues, fostering of values and attitudes, its interdisciplinary nature, and a desire to influence personal behaviour. However, there were recommendations concerning the criteria for the development of environmental education materials that they should be multi-media, interdisciplinary, cheap, adaptable and stress various teaching and learning processes and techniques. In the UK there were already a number of environmental education resources available to teachers from Government Departments, statutory bodies, commercial organisations, publishers and voluntary organisations. Many reflect a particular view point and need careful use as educational resources.

Intergovernmental Conference on Environmental Education, UNESCO-UNEP, Tbilisi 1977
The first intergovernmental conference was able to draw together the many threads of environmental education that had developed over the past 15 to 20 years in a common statement. Such consolidation was necessary before announcing any recommendations for future action. The 41 recommendations are comprehensive and over the last four years have provided a focus for individuals, organisations and Government Departments.

The benefits are now being seen, eg joint activities between planners and schools, environmental education programmes for adults, a discussion document on environmental education in the school curriculum 11-16 by HM Inspectors, a DES Review of environmental education, further financial support for a national centre for environmental education, etc. Tbilisi has been a major stimulus to the environmental education movement in the UK.

Environmental Education in Urban Areas, Environmental Board, Department of the Environment 1979
Originally, environmental education evolved from a concern for the natural environment and many people still regard environmental education as a form of nature studies. Stockholm gave full recognition to the total human environment, including the built environment, although in the UK, urban environmental education has been a growing part of environmental education since the Skeffington Report. The report repeats many previous recommendations from UK conferences; the highest priority is in secondary schools, the need to develop an interdisciplinary approach and use of the local environment as an educational resource, but it also recommends making available support for Urban Studies Centres, involving the professions and trades in education activities, and giving financial support to 'enabling' agencies.

The World Conservation Strategy, IUCN, UNESCO-UNEP, WWF 1980
Although the Strategy says nothing new, it brings together all aspects of conservation for the benefit of

politicians, environmental managers (planners, farmers, foresters, etc) industrialists and other developers and educationalists. It provides another opportunity for mankind to work out a more sensible relationship with the environment. One chapter of the report concentrates on the role of education. Following closely on from the Tbilisi recommendations, it is helping to maintain the momentum of new activities. The WCS has caught the imagination of the environmental education movement and is the cause of many initiatives which will encourage better knowledge and understanding of its main themes:

(a) The maintenance of essential ecological processes.
(b) The preservation of the diversity of earth's species.
(c) The careful and sustainable use of the earth's resources.
(d) Conservation and development are mutually dependent.

References

IUCN. 1970. International working meeting on environmental education and the school curriculum. Nevada.

IUCN. 1980. World conservation strategy. Living resource-conservation for sustainable development. Gland.

SCOTTISH EDUCATION DEPARTMENT. 1974. Environmental education. A report by HM Inspectors of Schools. Edinburgh, HMSO.

UNESCO-UNEP. 1975. Belgrade workshop on environmental education. Paris, UNESCO-UNEP.

CONTRIBUTORS TO THE PRACTITIONERS' DEBATE

UK Government and Statutory Bodies
Education Department of England, Scotland and Northern Ireland.
Welsh Office.
Ministry of Agriculture, Fisheries and Food.
Cynefin Organising Committee.

Local Authorities
Avon, Staffordshire, Lincolnshire, Huntingdon, East Sussex.
Association of County Councils.

Further and Higher Education
Through the Royal Geographical Society, the universities of: Hull, Exeter, Durham.
Universities of Manchester, Edinburgh, Bristol, East Anglia.
Colleges: Avery Hill, St Mary's Strawberry Hill, Crewe and Alsager, Queen Mary's Basingstoke.

Non-Government Organisations
Council for Environmental Education, National Association of Environmental Education, Youth Hostels Association, Museums Association, Royal Society for the Protection of Birds, Keep Britain Tidy Group, National Federation of Women's Institutes, Association of British Zoo Educators, Conservation Society, Institution of Environmental Sciences, Green Alliance, Scout Association, National Trust, British Trust for Conservation Volunteers, Council for Environmental Conservation, Ecology Party, The Royal Town Planning Institute, The Design Council, Institute of Biology.

Examination Boards
The following Regional Examination Boards: South-East, West Midlands, North-West, London.

Scotland
Fife Education Authority, The Fife Regional Council, Central Regional Council, Lothian Regional Council, Countryside Commission for Scotland.

Others
Very many individuals commented on the Report and to all those thanks are also due.

USEFUL READING LIST

Chapter 2
CARSON, S McB. (editor). 1978. Environmental education: principles and practice. London, Edward Arnold.

CURRICULUM DEVELOPMENT CENTRE. 1981. Environmental education: a source book for primary education. Canberra, CDC.

MARTIN, G C AND WHEELER, K. (editors). 1975. Insights into environmental education. Edinburgh, Oliver and Boyd.

NATIONAL ASSOCIATION FOR ENVIRONMENTAL EDUCATION. 1976. Environmental education: a statement of aims. Birmingham, NAEE.

SCHOOLS COUNCIL. 1974. Project environment. Harlow, Longman.

Chapter 3
CARSON, S McB. (editor). 1978. Environmental education: principles and practice. London, Edward Arnold.

DEPARTMENT OF EDUCATION AND SCIENCE. 1979. Curriculum 11-16: supplementary working papers by HM Inspectorate, Environmental Education. London, DES.

MARTIN, G C AND WHEELER, K. (editors). 1975. Insights into environmental education. Edinburgh, Oliver and Boyd.

Chapter 4
DEPARTMENT OF EDUCATION AND SCIENCE. 1981. Environmental education: a review. London, DES.

Chapter 5
CARSON, S McB. (editor). 1978. Environmental education: principles and practice. London, Edward Arnold.

DEPARTMENT OF EDUCATION AND SCIENCE, WELSH OFFICE. 1980. A framework for the school curriculum. London, HMSO.

ENVIRONMENTAL EDUCATION ADVISERS' ASSOCIATION. 1981. Environmental education in the curriculum: the role of some major contributory subjects and areas. Manchester, EEAA.

NATIONAL ASSOCIATION FOR ENVIRONMENTAL EDUCATION. 1976. Environmental education: a statement of aims. Birmingham, NAEE.

Chapter 9
CARSON, S McB. (editor). 1978. Environmental education: principles and practice. London, Edward Arnold.

DEPARTMENT OF EDUCATION AND SCIENCE. 1979. Curriculum 11-16: supplementary working papers by HM Inspectorate, Environmental Education. London, DES.

DEPARTMENT OF EDUCATION AND SCIENCE. 1981. Environmental education: sources of information 1981. London, DES.

ENVIRONMENTAL BOARD, DEPARTMENT OF THE ENVIRONMENT. 1979. Environmental education in urban areas. London, HMSO.

MARTIN, G C AND WHEELER, K. (editors). 1975. Insights into environmental education. Edinburgh, Oliver and Boyd.

NATIONAL ASSOCIATION FOR ENVIRONMENTAL EDUCATION. 1976. Environmental education: a statement of aims. Birmingham, NAEE.

SMEAC. 1978. From ought to action: a report of the National Leadership Conference on environmental education. Washington DC, SMEAC.

UNESCO. 1978. Intergovernmental conference on environmental education, final report. Paris, UNESCO-UNEP.

MEMBERSHIP OF
THE PROGRAMME STANDING COMMITTEE

Chairman:

E M Nicholson CB CVO LLD
President, RSPB; Vice President RSA and WWF UK;
Chairman Land Use Consultants

Members:

The Viscount of Arbuthnott DSC
Deputy Chairman, Nature Conservancy Council,
representing Scottish interests

The Lord Ashby FRS
The Royal Society

D Barber
Chairman, Countryside Commission

Dr Jean Balfour CBE FRSE
Former Chairman, Countryside Commission for
Scotland

Sir Terence Beckett CBE
Director General, Confederation of British Industry

R E Boote CVO
Formerly a Vice President of IUCN

W D Clark
President, International Institute for Environment and
Development

K D Collins MEP
Chairman, European Parliament Environment
Committee

The Rt Hon Lord Craigton CBE
Chairman, CoEnCo and All-Party Parliamentary
Conservation Committee

The Earl of Cranbrook
House of Lords Select Committee on the European
Communities Sub-Committee G (Environment)

R N Crawford CBE
Chairman, Nature Reserves Committee Northern Ireland

The Rt Hon Lord Duncan-Sandys CH
President, Civic Trust

G England FEng JP
Former Chairman, Central Electricity Generating Board

P Hardy MP
All-Party Parliamentary Conservation Committee

J E Hooson JE
Chairman, Parliamentary Committee National
Farmers' Union

C Jenkins
General Secretary, ASTMS

The Lord Kearton OBE FRS
Former Chairman, British National Oil Corporation

The Lord Kennet
Author

Sir Robert Marshall KCB MBE
Former Chairman, National Water Council

The Lord Melchett
Chairman, Wildlife Link Committee of CoEnCo

The Lord Middleton MC DL
President, Country Landowners' Association

The Lord Nathan
Former Chairman, Committee for the Environment,
Royal Society of Arts

D Nickson
Chairman, Countryside Commission for Scotland

Sir Arthur Norman KBE DFC
Chairman, World Wildlife Fund UK; Chairman, The
De La Rue Company

Dr F B O'Connor FIBiol
Chairman, Programme Organising Committee

Sir Peter Parker MVO
Chairman, British Railways Board

The Viscount Ridley TD
Chairman, National Trust's Conservation Panel

486

The Rt Hon Geoffrey Rippon QC MP
A former Secretary of State for the Environment

Sir Denis Rooke CBE FRS FEng
Chairman, British Gas Corporation

S Ross FRICS MP
Liberal Parliamentary Spokesman on the Environment

The Rev and Lord Sandford DSC
President, Council for Environmental Education

Sir Ralph Verney Bt KBE DL JP
Chairman, Nature Conservancy Council

R H Wade CBE
Former Chairman, Council for the Protection of Rural England

The Baroness White
President, Council for the Protection of Rural Wales

Sir Geoffrey Wilson KCB CMG
Chairman, Oxfam

Professor M J Wise CBE MC
President, Royal Geographical Society

Mrs E A O'Sullivan
Programme Secretary

C J Robertson
Programme Secretariat

Miss E M Duncan
Programme Secretariat

Miss G Holmes
Programme Secretariat

MEMBERSHIP OF
THE PROGRAMME ORGANISING COMMITTEE

Chairman:

Dr F B O'Connor FIBiol
Deputy Director General, Nature Conservancy Council

Members:

R E Boote CVO
Formerly a Vice-President of IUCN

Dr J Morton Boyd
Director for Scotland Nature Conservancy Council

V Cable
Overseas Development Institute

T Cantell
Assistant Secretary (Environment), Royal Society of Arts

R N Crawford
Chairman, Nature Reserves Committee Northern Ireland

R Dafter
Energy Editor, Financial Times

J Davidson
IUCN Commission on Environmental Planning

E Dawson
Secretary, Council for Environmental Conservation

J Foster
Director, Countryside Commission for Scotland

B Lymbery
Director, Prince of Wales' Committee

G J Medley
Director, World Wildlife Fund UK

The Lord Melchett
Chairman, Wildlife Link Committee of CoEnCo

E M Nicholson CB CVO LLD
President RSPB; Vice President RSA and WWF UK; Chairman Land Use Consultants

A Phillips
Director, Countryside Commission

Dr D A Ratcliffe
Chief Scientist, Nature Conservancy Council

B D G Johnson
Vice President, International Institute for Environment and Development; Environmental Consultant; author of 'Resourceful Britain'

S Johnson MEP
Member for Wight and Hants East, European Parliament, Chairman of the Industry Review Group

J Elkington
Managing Director, Environmental Data Services; author of the industry report

Miss A Lees
Controller of Transport and Development, Greater London Council; Chairman of the Urban Review Group

Mrs J Davidson
Honorary Research Fellow, University College London; co-author of the urban report

Mrs A MacEwen
Honorary Research Fellow, University College London; co-author of the urban report

M Schreiber
Of the Economist and the Countryside Commission; Chairman of the Rural Review Group

T O'Riordan
Professor of Environmental Sciences, University of East Anglia; author of the rural report

D Nichols
Professor of Biological Sciences, University of Exeter; Chairman of the Marine and Coastal Review Group

Dr D Shaw
Director, Centre for Marine and Coastal Studies, University of Liverpool; author of the marine report

J E Porter
Director, Commonwealth Institute; Chairman of the International Review Group

R Sandbrook
International Institute for Environment and Development; author of the international report

R J Berry
Professor of Genetics, University College London;
author of the ethics report

Lady Nora David
Opposition Whip and Spokesman for Education;
Chairman of the Education Review Group

J Baines
Director, Council for Environmental Education; author
of the education report

Mrs E A O'Sullivan
Programme Secretary

C J Robertson
Programme Secretariat

Miss E M Duncan
Programme Secretariat

Miss G Holmes
Programme Secretariat

MEMBERSHIP OF
THE SECTOR REVIEW GROUPS

Part 1. Industry:
'Seven Bridges to the Future'

Stanley Johnson MEP (*Chairman*)
Member for Wight and Hants East, European Parliament

John Elkington (*Author*)
Managing Director, Environmental Data Services Ltd

Mr C M Barnett
TUC North West Regional Council

Mr D Boatfield
Engineering Services Manager, 3M (UK) Ltd

Mr D Broadbent
National Coal Board and Business and Industry Panel for the Environment

Mrs D Bruce
Environmental Section, Central Electricity Generating Board

Mr T Burke
Friends of the Earth International and the European Environmental Bureau

Mr A J Clarke
Head, Environmental Section, Central Electricity Generating Board

Dr M Cooley
Open University, Technical University of West Berlin and the Centre for Alternative Industrial and Technological Systems

Mr F Dean
Chief Environmental Planning Officer, British Gas Corporation

Mr M Flux
Group Environment Adviser, ICI Ltd

Mr J Garbutt
General Manager, Environmental Affairs Office, Blue Circle Technical Ltd

Mr P Hamilton
Director, Good Relations (Corporate Affairs) Ltd

Dr H Holden
Medical Officer, BICC Ltd

Mr G Larminie
General Manager, Environmental Control Centre, BP Ltd

Dr J Lawrence
Director, Brixham Laboratory, ICI Ltd

Mr F Lester
Director, Scientific Services, Severn-Trent Water Authority

Professor K MacMillan
The Management College, Henley-on-Thames

Mr G Medley
Director, World Wildlife Fund, UK

Mr M J Shanks
Chairman, National Consumer Council

Professor J Stopford
London Business School

Ms M Sykes
Industrial Common Ownership Movement

Mr R Waller
Director, Environmental Consultancy, W S Atkins Group

The report draws heavily on work carried out by a very wide range of individuals and organisations, some being listed in the Acknowledgements in this report (see p 36) — and some remain anonymous, either intentionally or through oversight. Our thanks to them all.

Part 2. Urban:
'The Livable City'

Audrey Lees (*Chairman*)
Controller of Transportation and Development, Greater London Council

Joan Davidson and Ann MacEwen (*Authors*)
Honorary Research Fellows, University College London

Chris Baines
Landscape Consultant, West Midlands Urban Wildlife Group

Professor David Cadman
Department of Land Economy and Wolfson College Cambridge

Ian Dair
Nature Conservancy Council

John Davidson
Countryside Commission, Groundwork Northwest

Robert Davies
National Council for Voluntary Organisations

David Hall
Town and Country Planning Association

Dr John Handley
Groundwork Trust (formerly Merseyside County Planning Department)

Simon Jenkins
The *Economist*

Gerald Leach
International Institute for Environment and Development

David Lock
Conran-Roche and Partners

Brian Lymbery
Prince of Wales' Committee

Professor Alan Proudlove
Department of Civic Design, University of Liverpool

Harford Thomas
The *Guardian*

Alan Turner
Alan Turner and Associates

Neil Wates
Bore Place, Edenbridge

David Wilcox
David Wilcox Associates

Part 3. Rural:
'Putting Trust in the Countryside'

Mark Schreiber (*Chairman*)
Journalist for The *Economist* and Member of the Countryside Commission

Timothy O'Riordan (*Author*)
Professor of Environmental Sciences, University of East Anglia

Allan Blenkharn
Director, Water Space Amenity Commission

Jack Boddy
National Secretary, Agricultural and Allied Workers National Trade Group — TGWU

Lester Borley
Chief Executive, English Tourist Board

Eric Carter
Advisor to the Farming and Wildlife Advisory Group, and formerly Deputy Director General, Agricultural Development and Advisory Service, Ministry of Agriculture, Fisheries and Food

Ian Cunningham
Professor of Agriculture at the University of Glasgow and Principal of the West of Scotland College of Agriculture

William de Salis
Chief Economic Adviser, Country Landowners Association

Robin Grove White
Director, Council for the Protection of Rural England

Christopher Hall
Editor, *The Countryman*

George Holmes
Director General, The Forestry Commission

Paul Howell MEP
Member of the European Parliament

Patrick Leonard
Assistant Director, Countryside Commission

Richard MacDonald
Parliamentary and Land Use Adviser, National Farmers Union

Lord Melchett
Chairman, Wildlife Link Committee of CoEnCo

Derek Ratcliffe
Chief Scientist, Nature Conservancy Council

Part 4. Marine and Coastal:
'Conservation and Development of Marine and Coastal Resources'

Professor D Nichols (*Chairman*)
Department of Biological Sciences, The University, Exeter

Dr D F Shaw (*Author*)
Director, Centre for Marine and Coastal Studies, The University, Liverpool

Mr S A Sewell (*Research Assistant*)
Department of Zoology, Liverpool University

Lt Cmdr A Bax
Fort Bovisand Diving Centre, Plymouth

Mr R J H Beverton
Secretary (Retired), Natural Environment Research
Council

Dr P Boaden
Director, Portaferry Marine Laboratory, Queen's
University, Belfast

Mr C R B Brown
County Planning Officer for Hampshire

Mr R H Ganten
Director, International Oil Pollution Compensation
Fund

Professor J F Garner
Planning Lawyer (Retired), Nottingham University

Mr C Lucas
Association of Sea Fisheries Committees

Dr R Mitchell
Nature Conservancy Council

Dr J Morton Boyd
Director (Scotland) NCC

Dr C Tydeman
World Wildlife Fund

Dr T G Wilkinson
Shell UK Exploration and Production

Part 5. International:
'The UK's Overseas Environmental Policy'

James Porter (*Chairman*)
Director, The Commonwealth Institute

Richard Sandbrook (*Author*)
International Institute for Environment and
Development

Dame Diana Reader Harris
Vice-President, Royal Society of Arts

Dr Peter Gay
The Nature Conservancy Council

Alistair Gammell
The Royal Society for the Protection of Birds

Jack Thornton
Retired, ex-Overseas Development Administration

Richard Bourne
Freelance Journalist

Pauline Marstrand
Formerly of the Science Policy Research Council Sussex
and now of the Primary Communications Research
Centre, Leicester

Grenville Lucas
Conservation Department, Kew Gardens

Adrian Phillips
Director, Countryside Commission

Guy Barnett MP
Member of Parliament for Greenwich

James Pickett
Director, David Livingston Institute of Overseas
Development

Jimoh Omo-Fadaka
Environmental Consultant – Nigeria

Part 6. Ethics:
'Environmental Ethics and Conservation Action'

The Lord Ashby FRS
Corresponding Member

Professor R J Berry (*Author*)
Department of Zoology, University College of London

Dr E D Cook
Westminster College, Oxford

Dr R Gambell
International Whaling Commission

Dr B Green
Department of Environmental Studies, Wye College

Professor B Griffiths
Centre for Banking and International Finance, City
University

Ms P Johnson
Formerly of Green Alliance, London

Dr U Loening
Centre for Human Biology, Edinburgh University

Mr G McRobie
Intermediate Technology Group, London

Professor R Moss
Professor of Geography, Salford University

Ms B Mostyn
Consultant Social Psychologist

Mr W Patterson
Freelance Journalist

Mr J Robertson
Turning Point, Telford

Part 7. Education:
'Education for Commitment'

Lady David (*Chairman*)
Opposition Whip and Spokesperson for Education

J D Baines (*Author*)
Director, Council for Environmental Education

E Dawson
CoEnCo

Professor P J Newbould
New University of Ulster

A Tucker
Freelance Journalist

Professor J Smyth
Paisley College of Technology

K Wheeler
Leicester Polytechnic (retired) and Leicester Urban
Studies Centre

A Fyson
Centre for Environmental Interpretation

H Elliott
National Farmers Union

K Marks MP
Member of Parliament for Gorton

R Williams
Schools Council Field Officer

J Cousins
John Brown and Co Ltd

P Townsend
Peak National Park Study Centre

R Jeffries
Workers Educational Association

C Conroy
Friends of the Earth

C Sinker
Field Studies Council

J Craven
BBC Newsround

J Wray
Inner London Education Authority

ABBREVIATIONS

ACARD	Advisory Council for Applied Research and Development
ACE	Association for the Conservation of Energy
ACP	African Caribbean and Pacific (States)
ADAS	Agricultural Development and Advisory Service
AEUW	Amalgamated Engineering Union of Workers
AHDS	Agriculture and Horticulture Development Scheme
AHGS	Agriculture and Horticulture Grant Scheme
ALCI	Area of Local Conservation Interest
AMA	Association of Metropolitan Authorities
AONB	Area of Outstanding Natural Beauty
ARC	Agricultural Research Council
ASA	Advertising Standards Authority
ASTMS	Association of Scientific, Technical and Managerial Staffs
BAS	British Antarctic Survey
BEE	Bulletin of Environmental Education
BES	British Ecological Society
BIM	British Institute of Management
BOD	Biological Oxygen Demand
BRIC	British Reclamation Industries Confederation
BSBI	Botanical Society of the British Isles
BTCV	British Trust for Conservation Volunteers
CAITS	Centre for Alternative Industrial and Technological Systems
CAP	Common Agricultural Policy
CBA	Cost Benefit Analysis
CBI	Confederation of British Industry
CCAMLR	Conservation Convention for Antarctic Marine Living Resources
CEC	Commission of the European Communities
CEE	Council for Environmental Education
CEGB	Central Electricity Generating Board
CENE	Commission on Energy and the Environment
CEP	Community Enterprise Programme
CET	Council for Educational Technology
CFI	Commonwealth Forestry Institute
CFTC	Commonwealth Fund for Technical Cooperation
CGT	Capital Gains Tax
CHP	Combined Heat and Power
CIBS	Chartered Institution of Building Services
CIDIE	Committee of International Development Institutions for the Environment
CITES	Convention on International Trade in Endangered Species (Washington Convention)

CLA	Country Landowners Association
CO_2	Carbon Dioxide
CoEnCo	Council for Environmental Conservation
CoSIRA	Council for Small Industries in Rural Areas
COPR	Centre for Overseas Pest Research
CP	Community Programme
CPH	Combined Heat and Power
CPRE	Council for the Protection of Rural England
CRE	Commission for Racial Equality
CSE	Certificate of Secondary Education
CTT	Capital Transfer Tax
DAC	Development Assistance Committee
DAFS	Department of Agriculture and Fisheries for Scotland
DANI	Department of Agriculture for Northern Ireland
DC	Development Commission
DDT	A common insecticide
D/En	Department of Energy
DES	Department of Education and Science
DG	Directorate General
DHSS	Department of Health and Social Security
DIY	Do It Yourself
DOE	Department of the Environment
DOT	Department of Trade
DPU	Development Planning Unit
EAG	Economists Advisory Group
ECB	Environment Coordination Board
ECE	Economic Commission for Europe
EDF	European Development Fund
EEB	European Environmental Bureau
EEC	European Economic Community
EEZ	Exclusive Economic Zone
EIA	Environmental Impact Assessment
ENDS	Environmental Data Services Limited
EPA	Environmental Protection Agency (United States)
ERL	Environmental Resources Limited
ETSU	Energy Technology Support Unit
FAO	Food and Agricultural Organisation of the United Nations
FBC	Fluidised Bed Combustion
FCGS	Farm Capital Grant Scheme
FCO	Foreign and Commonwealth Office
FGD	Flue Gas Desulphurisation
FHDS	Farm and Horticulture Development Scheme
FIG	Financial Institutions in Government Group

FOE	Friends of the Earth	MAFF	Ministry of Agriculture, Fisheries and Food
FPRD	Food Production and Rural Development		
FSC	Field Studies Council	MARC	Monitoring and Assessment Research Centre
FWAG	Farming and Wildlife Advisory Group		
		MARPOL	Convention for the Prevention of Marine Pollution
GB	Great Britain		
GCE	General Certificate of Education	MSC	Manpower Services Commission
GDP	Gross Domestic Product		
GEMS	Global Environmental Monitoring System	NAEE	National Association for Environmental Education
GLC	Greater London Council		
GNP	Gross National Product	NCC	Nature Conservancy Council
		NCVO	National Council for Voluntary Organisations
HIDB	Highlands and Islands Development Board		
HLCA	Hill Livestock Compensatory Allowance	NEDO	National Economic Development Office
HMI	Her Majesty's Inspectorate	NEPA	National Environmental Policy Act
		NERC	Natural Environment Research Council
IAEA	International Atomic Energy Agency	NFU	National Farmers Union
ICC	International Chamber of Commerce	NFUS	National Farmers Union of Scotland
ICES	International Council for the Exploration of the Seas	NGO	Non-Governmental Organisation
		NNR	National Nature Reserve
ICSU	International Council of Scientific Unions	N_2O	Nitrous Oxide
IDA	International Development Agency	NO_x	Oxides of Nitrogen
IDB	Internal Drainage Board	NPA	National Park Authority
IDP	Integrated Development Programme	NRAG	Natural Resource Advisory Group
IDRC	International Development Research Centre	NSA	National Scenic Area (Scotland)
		NT	National Trust
IDS	Institute of Development Studies (University of Sussex)	NTS	National Trust for Scotland
IEA	International Energy Agency	ODA	Overseas Development Administration
IGS	Institute of Geological Sciences	oda	overseas development assistance
IIED	International Institute for Environment and Development	ODI	Overseas Development Institute
		ODM	Overseas Development Ministry
ILO	International Labour Organisation	OECD	Organisation for Economic Co-operation and Development
IMCO	International Maritime Consultative Organisation		
		OGS	Overseas Geological Survey
IMO	International Maritime Organisation	OPEC	Organisation of Petroleum Exporting Countries
INFOTERRA	International Referral System for Sources of Environmental Information		
		OSAS	Overseas Service Aid Scheme
IOC	International Oceanographic Commission	OTA	Office of Technology Assessment (United States)
IRPTC	International Register of Potentially Toxic Chemicals		
		OTEC	Ocean Thermal Energy Conversion
ITDG	Intermediate Technology Development Group	OU	Open University
ITE	Institute of Terrestrial Ecology	PAC	Programmed Activity Centre
IUCN	International Union for Conservation of Nature and Natural Resources	PCBs	Polychlorinated Biphenyl Compounds
		PEP	Political and Economic Planning
IWC	International Whaling Commission	PGN	Policy Guidance Note
		PICC	Professional Institutions Council for Conservation
JURUE	Joint Unit for Research on the Urban Environment		
		PRU	Pollution Research Unit
		PSPS	Pesticide Safety Precautions Scheme
LA	Local Authority		
LAMSAC	Local Authority Management Services and Computing Committee	RAC	Regional Advisory Committee
		R and D	Research and Development
LDC	Less Developed Country	REED	Review of Environmental Education Developments
LEA	Local Education Authority		
LFA	Less Favoured Area	RGF	Real Growth Farmers
LNR	Local Nature Reserve	RIBA	Royal Institute of British Architects
LSA	Land Settlement Association	RICS	Royal Institution of Chartered Surveyors
LWMOST	Low Water Mean Ordinary Spring Tides	RPA	Rural Preservation Association
		RSA	Royal Society of Arts
		RSNC	Royal Society for Nature Conservation
MAB	Man and the Biosphere Programme		

RSPB	Royal Society for the Protection of Birds	UCBT	Union pour le Commerce des Bois Tropicaux dans la CEE (France)
RSPCA	Royal Society for the Prevention of Cruelty to Animals	UDAP	Unit for the Development of Appropriate Products
RTPI	Royal Town Planning Institute	UEA	University of East Anglia
RWA	Regional Water Authority	UK	United Kingdom
		UMEX	Upland Management Experiment
SCE	Scottish Certificate of Education	UMIST	University of Manchester Institute of Science and Technology
SCOPE	Scientific Committee on Problems of the Environment	UN	United Nations
SEEC	Scottish Environmental Education Committee	UNDP	United Nations Development Programme
		UNEP	United Nations Environment Programme
SERC	Science and Engineering Research Council	UNESCO	United Nations Educational, Scientific and Cultural Organisation
SIC	Small Industries Committee	UNICEF	United Nations Childrens Fund
SMD	Standard Man Day	US(A)	United States of America
SO_2	Sulphur Dioxide	USSR	Union of Soviet Socialist Republics
SO_x	Sulphur Oxides		
SOS	Secretary of State	VAT	Value Added Tax
SPRU	Science Policy Research Unit		
SOSE	Secretary of State for the Environment	WCS	World Conservation Strategy
SS	Secretary of State for Scotland	WDA	Waste Disposal Authority
SSRC	Social Science Research Council	WEA	Workers Education Association
SSSI	Site of Special Scientific Interest	WEOG	Western European and Other Groups
SWMTEP	System Wide Medium Term Environmental Plan	WHO	World Health Organisation
		WMO	World Meteorological Organisation
		WOAD	Welsh Office Agricultural Department
TAG	Technical Assistance Group	WS	Secretary of State for Wales
TC	Technical Cooperation	WWF	World Wildlife Fund
TGWU	Transport and General Workers Union		
TPI	Tropical Products Institute	YHA	Youth Hostels Association
TPRC	Trade Policy Research Centre	YOP	Youth Opportunities Programme
TUC	Trades Union Congress	YTS	Youth Training Scheme